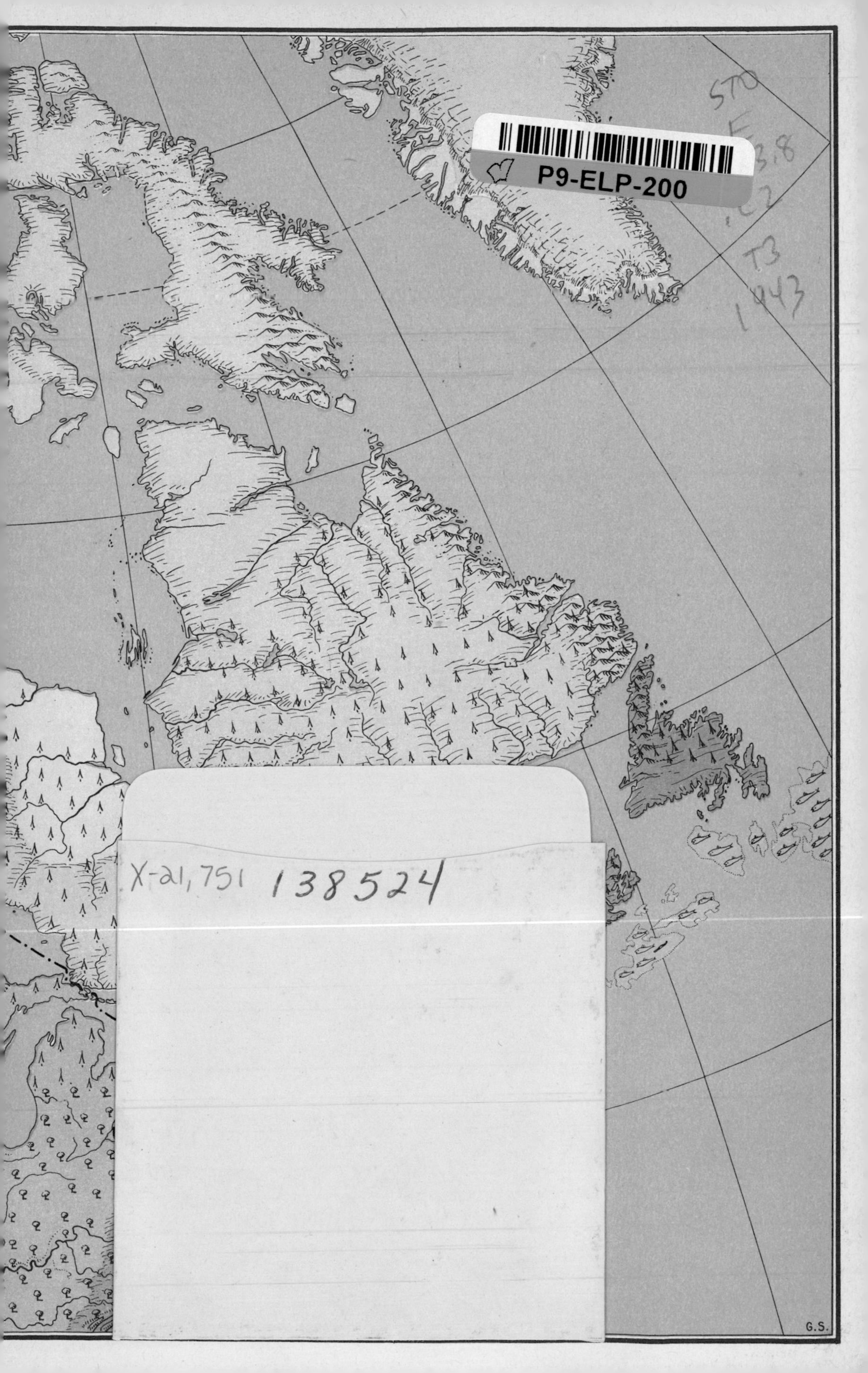
G.S.

CANADIAN-AMERICAN RELATIONS, 1875–1911

THE RELATIONS OF
CANADA AND THE UNITED STATES

A SERIES OF STUDIES
PREPARED UNDER THE DIRECTION OF THE
CARNEGIE ENDOWMENT FOR INTERNATIONAL PEACE
DIVISION OF ECONOMICS AND HISTORY

JAMES T. SHOTWELL, *Director*

CANADIAN-AMERICAN RELATIONS, 1875-1911

BY

CHARLES CALLAN TANSILL
PROFESSOR OF AMERICAN DIPLOMATIC HISTORY
FORDHAM UNIVERSITY

NEW HAVEN : YALE UNIVERSITY PRESS
TORONTO : THE RYERSON PRESS
LONDON: HUMPHREY MILFORD: OXFORD UNIVERSITY PRESS
FOR THE CARNEGIE ENDOWMENT FOR INTERNATIONAL
PEACE : DIVISION OF ECONOMICS AND HISTORY
1943

Printed in the United States of America

TO
HELEN PARKER TANSILL

FOREWORD

THERE are few themes in the history of America, and for that matter in the history of the western world, which present richer and more varied content than that of the relations between Canada and the United States. Earlier volumes in the series dealt with the long, slow processes of exploration and pioneering, in which the wilderness frontier was also that of two divergent European civilizations, the French and the English. The story of that struggle for North American empire has long since been tinged with the colors of romance, but the historian of today, while fully conscious of the lasting appeal of high adventure and solitary daring by which the settlements were planted, has charted the course of the history of that heroic age with more definite outlines drawn from the evidence of documents to which the earlier historians had inadequate access.

It is only now that the full rich harvest of the recent historical renaissance in the history of the American continent has become evident. It was not until some fifty years ago that Canadian history was first introduced into the Canadian schools, and during this half century the history of the United States has been almost as completely reconstituted as that of Canada. In both cases, however, the chief interest has lain in the development of the nation as it forged for itself the instruments of government in the new and great experiment of federalism. The story of external affairs was subordinated to the greater theme of the building of the nation in its own homeland. The extent to which this was true of the United States has recently been stated with great vigor by Mr. Walter Lippmann in his brief for a more realistic American foreign policy coördinated with that of Great Britain, in which he points out the absence of any clear appreciation of the real nature of the history of American foreign policy. In Canada the situation was fundamentally the same, although it differed outwardly from the fact that until twenty-five years ago foreign policy was powerfully influenced in major questions by the Imperial government, to which should be added the relatively greater dependence of Canada upon foreign trade and relatively later unification of local particularisms in a single sense of nationality. Nevertheless the Canadian outlook was primarily continental and domestic in much the same way as that of the neighbor to the south.

Under these circumstances it might seem that the relations between Canada and the United States offered only a subject of minor importance, of the kind that is chiefly of interest to students of history working in undeveloped fields of original research. But, as this series of volumes has shown and as the present one amply proves, the interplay in the history of the two nations is not external or incidental to the fortunes of each of them, but deals with matters which seemed to many at the time to be of vital interest, the kind of questions upon which nations do not readily yield or find satisfactory solution by peaceful means. The hot passions of debates over these issues in dispute have now completely subsided, and it is fortunately impossible for history to revive them. It is equally fortunate that the historians of today are conscious of the fact that a greater theme lies at hand than the mere stirring of the ashes of past controversies. This new theme is the one dictated to the world of today by the tragic lessons of two world wars; it is the study of the way in which statesmanship and common sense have ultimately built up a technique for the settlement of disputes between Canada and the United States which can and should furnish a model to all the world.

The policy of the good neighbor means most where it covers the widest possible area of intercourse between nations rather than where it is given the formal salute of diplomacy with relatively little of actual intercourse involved. Canada and the United States, as has been pointed out repeatedly in this series, have closer economic ties than any other two nations. In the upbuilding of this great North American community it was inevitable that there should be both economic and political disputes, and both nations, bred in the Anglo-Saxon tradition of realism in politics, held stubbornly to what each believed to be its rights, but with equal realism for over a hundred years they refused to allow any dispute to lead to armed conflict. The reason lay in mutual appreciation of the fact that no one issue in dispute was worth endangering a peace which was a fundamental basis of the prosperity and happiness of both nations. It is true that the raucous voice of nationalism could be heard in every dispute and in both countries. The mother country also furnished its quota of jingo politicians, but over against these mischief-makers, some of whom were more blind than evil-intentioned, the pages of history shine with the names of a galaxy of statesmen who never lost sight of the ultimate goal of their endeavor which was the major welfare of their people, furthered and rendered more secure by the welfare of all concerned.

The present volume dealing, as it does, with a series of most difficult controversies, carries us into the heart of this history of hard-pressed statesmen at grips with apparently unsolvable problems, and in its richness of detail, the product of long years of research, it presents the problems as they came before the principal actors on the crowded stage of democratic diplomacy. If at times one has a sense of frustration, this is partly due to the nature of the subjects of dispute themselves; two of them, the cod and the fur-seal fisheries, reaching out to the harvest of the seas, where self-reliance breeds the hardiest of defenders for private rights; another dealing with the last unsettled frontier, that of the Alaska boundary; and finally, the whole vexed question of tariff and commercial arrangements with which the young Dominion was brought face to face in the first decades of its national existence. Difficulties also lay in the tri-partite nature of the negotiations in which the mother country had a share. It was only during the course of the negotiations in the fisheries and boundary disputes that Canadian statesmanship moved out of the colonial background to assume the place which it now so unquestionably occupies, that of an autonomous state within the family of nations.

This development comes to light less in the heat of the debate over either fisheries or boundary, although at the time these issues quickened the sense of Canadian nationality, than in the wider problem of commercial relations. It was in this latter field that a Canadian political party first drafted the platform of what it called a National Policy, and Canadian public opinion was kept aware of this major issue in the debate led by two outstanding figures in Canadian history, Sir John A. Macdonald and Sir Wilfrid Laurier. Unfortunately the problems were never so vital and therefore never so real for the United States as a whole, a fact which added to the difficulty of reaching an international agreement which could frankly get to the heart of the matter.

Students of Professor Tansill's survey of this period of adjustment in Canadian-American relations will be doubly grateful to him for the fact that he has not merely explored the official sources in government records but has drawn heavily upon the private letters and memoranda of the chief actors in the drama, which often reveal what the official documentation purposely or by chance left out of the public record. It was more than a happy coincidence that the author of this volume is also the biographer of Mr. Bayard, the Secretary of State with whom the narrative really begins. The human element, which plays a much larger part in diplomacy than outsiders realize, is never lost sight of in the whole history of these thirty years and more, during which Canadian-American relations finally lost the colonial mold in which they had hitherto been cast. There are figures here of heroic size, Hay, Root and Bryce, and their Canadian peers, Macdonald and Laurier, men with vision and foresight and fundamental integrity of character. But over against such leaders as these in the constructive statesmanship of democratic diplomacy, there were those of narrower outlook and political prejudices to whom local or individual interests in the immediate political scene meant more than the final settlement on the basis of right and justice. The first impression which one gains from a narrative like this is one of discouragement that diplomacy under the representative form of government seems to be frustrated whenever the long-range solutions run counter to immediate interests or traditional habits of thinking. But when one looks back upon the effort as a whole one discovers a reason for confidence in a process which takes account of the inherent limitations of political action at the very time of the action itself. For, after all, a greater instrument for the future settlement of disputes was being forged by the fact that these democracies themselves were reaching maturity in the hard schooling of failure as well as success when dealing with each other.

We must not forget that the very limitations of the procedure of arbitration, to which enlightened opinion in the last quarter of the nineteenth century looked so hopefully as a technique for the settlement of disputes, resulted in the transference of controversies from the area of legalistic procedure to that of increased political understanding and ultimate agreement. It is now a rule of conduct, not only for Canada and the United States but for all the English-speaking nations, unwritten but more firmly established than any formal international covenant, that disputes between them should never be permitted to reach the danger point of apparently irreconcilable conflict of interest. The anxious hours of the Venezuelan controversy or even the bitterness that marked the boundary settlements—for the fishing controversies were also boundary questions—need never be renewed, for all these nations, bred in the tradition of freedom and of justice for the common man, can now take to themselves the fundamental lesson of history of which this volume supplies a part, and help to build for themselves and other nations the practice as well as the institutions of international coöperation. In this broader setting of world affairs Canadian-American relations have much to offer, and the realistic study of their struggles and their failures as well as their successes is a matter to engage the earnest thought of all thoughtful men.

The monograph describes in authentic detail the diplomatic history of a period in which a substantial part of the foundation for cordial relations between the United States and the British Commonwealth of Nations was laid by the settlement of long-standing disputes. The narrative furnishes a comprehensive and scholarly survey based to a very large degree upon hitherto unused manuscript material. The Public Archives of Canada, the National Archives of the United States and the vast collections in the Library of Congress have been carefully explored and worked to great advantage. In the treatment of The North Atlantic Fisheries, that great stumbling block on the path of Anglo-American amity, Dr. Tansill offers a contribution to history in the story of the negotiations themselves, and a picture of the close interrelation between politics and diplomacy. In the decade that preceded the turn of the century, the partisanship in Congress was still tinged with the memories of the Civil War which rendered exceedingly difficult the foreign policy of a democratic President, especially if, as in the case of Cleveland, his chief interest and outlook lay in domestic affairs. The Alaska Boundary controversy had for three-quarters of a century remained a dangerous irritant in the relations between the United States and Britain. In the 'seventies and 'eighties, as the tide of nationalism mounted higher, Canadian and American statesmen earnestly strove to find a formula of settlement. Here again Dr. Tansill reaches into the heart of a problem which, even when settled, left a residuum of Canadian irritation that helped to check the movement toward commercial reciprocity and hastened the development of Dominion status. In his chapter on the fur-seal dispute, Dr. Tansill had access to diplomatic correspondence in the Bayard, the Cleveland and the Foster Papers which had been largely neglected, and also explored fully for the first time the voluminous records in the Canadian Public Archives. His final chapter on commercial union and commercial reciprocity deals with wider issues, analyzing both political and economic trends which profoundly affected the relations between Canada and the United States. His story, in this regard, is a twice-told tale, but here, as elsewhere throughout the volume, the author speaks with the authority which comes from an intimate knowledge of the wide range of pertinent documentary evidence.

Happily alongside the narrative, sometimes almost like a running commentary upon it, there are significant side-lights on the conduct of Canadian-American foreign policy. There are highly interesting vignettes of American statesmen in action, and there are frequent indications of the dangers that attend the obstructive tactics of politicians. But the bonds that bind the Canadian and the American peoples are emphasized, the essentials of their mutual interest furnish a theme that runs throughout the volume.

In the presentation of his material Professor Tansill has wisely chosen the topical rather than the chronological method. Only in a series of monographic studies could sufficient detail be given on each of the major problems with which the volume deals. These studies, however, are closely interrelated and together furnish the warp and woof to be woven into the rich design of North American history. The same method of presentation was found necessary in the preceding volume in this series, which dealt with the history of Canadian-American relations during the third quarter of the nineteenth century. Its especial value lies in the opportunity which it offers to go to the heart of the matter in each case, instead of having to turn from one subject to another in the actual conduct of affairs. On the other hand, it necessarily takes for granted a basic knowledge of the general history of the period upon the part of the reader. For the informed student of public affairs, however, this method of presentation is doubly valuable because, in addition to its narrative, it supplies guidance to the original sources themselves. In respect to all of these services to scholarship, Professor Tansill has offered in this volume contributions of great and lasting value.

JAMES T. SHOTWELL.

PREFACE

The present world conflict has focussed attention upon the important topic of Canadian-American relations. As companions in arms in defence of a way of life that both countries have helped to create, Canadians and Americans have become increasingly aware of a bond that grows stronger as the common sacrifice grows greater. It is a bond as old as the English language and as imperishable as the noble thoughts expressed in that language from the days of Magna Carta to the outbreak of the Second World War. During certain periods of our history the ties that bind together the English-speaking peoples have been sharply strained and political differences have resulted in open warfare; but these family quarrels have always pointed the way to closer co-operation and a deeper understanding. Some serious difficulties in Anglo-American relations can be traced to disputes between Canada and the United States with reference to territorial adjustments or to alleged violations of maritime rights. In this monograph the major issues in Canadian-American relations will be given a comprehensive treatment, and emphasis will be placed upon the manner in which age-old controversies have been settled by peaceful procedures.

The period covered by this volume includes the years from 1875 to 1911. From the beginning of this period until the last years of the nineteenth century, Canada was seriously handicapped by the Great Depression that checked its industrial development and brought hard times to every corner of the Dominion. It is against this dark background of economic maladjustment that we have to view Canadian-American relations during the first two decades covered by this study. The Dominion Government felt constrained to seek closer commercial connections with the United States as a means of escaping impending economic ruin, and repeated rebuffs failed to stop these overtures that were dictated by severe pressures. Political leaders in Canada realized that intimate economic ties with the United States might lead to eventual annexation, but apparently there was no alternative. Even the Macdonald Government that was so loyal to all the traditions of the Empire was compelled to open negotiations for a system of commercial reciprocity that had obvious political implications. In 1896, the new economic revolution in Europe led to an age of steel that demanded a higher degree of industrialization and a larger factory population that was directly dependent upon an increased volume of imports of foodstuffs. Canada's ample supplies of cereals now found the market that had been so eagerly sought in the United States, and Canadian eyes turned towards Europe rather than towards their great neighbor south of the border.

With Canada safely out of the slough of economic despond, there was no need for her statesmen to approach the United States with the same concern that had marked their advances during earlier decades. The wheat boom and the development of rich mineral resources led to the good times that characterized Canadian economy after the turn of the twentieth century. With these good times came Canadian confidence in the future and a feeling of independence with regard to relations with the United States. Canadian nationalism, long developing and deeply rooted, became a factor of increasing importance in the equation of Anglo-American relations.

In the United States prosperity was even more conspicuous than it was in Canada, and German statesmen began to ponder over plans for a middle European customs union that would serve as a barrier against the rising flood of American products. The easy defeat of Spain in the Spanish-American War had indicated to enthusiastic Americans the tremendous military potential of the United States. The thunder of Dewey's guns at Manila Bay had been heard round the world. Their strident tones had announced the fact that American isolation was a mere myth: the political clothes suited to the age of Washington were no longer modish in a century whose fashions required a similar costume both in Europe and in America.

British statesmen were quick to catch the implications of the new situation, and they took immediate steps to create an Anglo-American understanding that would bind the English-speaking peoples into an alliance that needed no formal treaty to confirm its terms. This task involved certain concessions on the part of the British Government. Pressure was exerted upon Canada to consent to sacrifices for the good of the Empire. The controversy concerning the Alaska boundary was settled to the satisfaction of the American Government, and constant efforts were made to remove all the differences that still vexed Canadian-American relations. The present accord that exists between Canada and the United States stems directly back to the endeavors of British statesmen who builded better than they knew.

In my endeavor to tell the story of Canadian-American relations during a period of storm and stress, I have been aided at every turn by the inspiration of Dr. James T. Shotwell, who symbolizes as no one else can, the essential unity of the Canadian and American peoples. Professors J. Bartlet Brebner and Allan Nevins, of Columbia University, have given my manuscript the benefit of a careful reading, and their suggestions have been of great value. Certain chapters have been read by Professors Philip C. Jessup, Thomas A. Bailey, Frank H. Underhill, Chester Martin, and Lionel M. Gelber. Their emendations were gratefully received and duly recorded. I wish also to mention my deep indebtedness to Mr. Arthur E. McFarlane of the literary staff of the Carnegie Endowment who aided me in numerous ways and to Miss Harriet J. Church for the index which affords a key to all the varied material in the volume.

I wish to record my obligations to the Carnegie Endowment for International Peace for assistance along numerous lines. It would be difficult adequately to express my indebtedness to Mrs. W. S. Hilles, who gave me unlimited access to the Bayard Papers.

In Ottawa I was given unusual liberties by Dr. Gustav Lanctot and Dr. James F. Kenney, who have made the Public Archives of Canada a place where American scholars can find the true meaning of the phrase, "Canadian courtesy."

In Washington the staff of the Library of Congress was exceedingly helpful. I owe a deep debt of gratitude to Dr. St. George L. Sioussat, Dr. Thomas P. Martin, Mr. Verner W. Clapp, Mr. David C. Mearns, Mr. Henry S. Parsons, Mr. Archibald B. Evans, Miss Grace G. Griffin, and Mr. Vincent L. Eaton.

My researches in the National Archives were made pleasant and fruitful through the courtesy and assistance of Dr. Philip M. Hamer, Dr. Almon Wright, Dr. Roscoe R. Hill, Mrs. Natalia Summers, Miss Edna Vosper, and particularly, Miss Julia Bland.

There are many personal friends who have been of great assistance to me. Among them are: Miss Hazell Harris, Judge John Bassett Moore, Mrs. B. R. Parker, Mr. Raymond T. Parker, Mr. Samuel E. Collegeman, Miss Amy Holland, Miss Mary W. MacTarnaghan, Mr. John S. Enright, Dr. John S. Brooks, Mr. and Mrs. Alexander Cavan, Dr. Reinhard H. Luthin, and Miss Eleanor Poland. My son, William R. Tansill, has assisted me in some minor research which was of considerable value.

I am happy to record the assistance of the Reverend Robert I. Gannon, S.J., President of Fordham University, whose generosity has helped me in innumerable ways. I owe a special debt of gratitude to the Reverend Gustave Dumas, S.J., Dean of the Graduate School of Arts and Sciences, Fordham University, for many favors that I shall not forget. I cannot overlook the inspiration of my good friend, the Reverend Gerald G. Walsh, S.J., whose numerous suggestions have been of great value.

My mother has shown great interest in this volume, and my wife has accompanied me through every page of composition. Her sage counsel and sunny wisdom have helped to guide me along many tangled paths of scholarship and literary expression. She has been more than the mere term helpmate implies.

CHARLES CALLAN TANSILL

Fordham University.

CONTENTS

ABBREVIATIONS

A.B.T.—*Alaskan Boundary Tribunal.*
C.S.P.—*Canada: Sessional Papers.*
F.R.—*Foreign Relations of the United States.*
F.S.A.—*Fur Seal Arbitration.*
P.A.C.—Public Archives of Canada.
R.R.C.D.P.R.—*Report of the Royal Commission on Dominion Provincial Relations.*

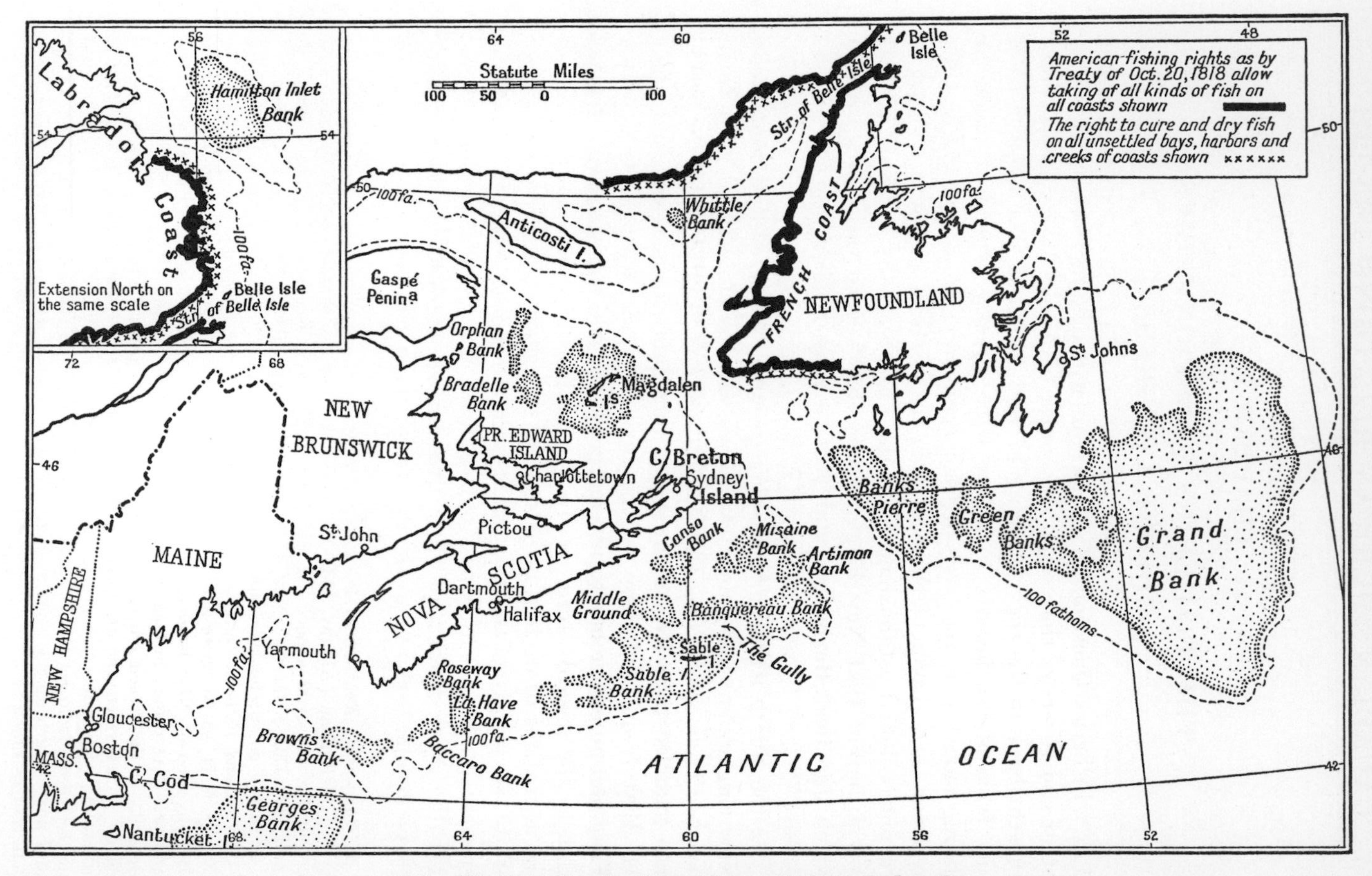

The Fishing Banks from Cape Cod to Labrador

CANADIAN-AMERICAN RELATIONS, 1875–1911

CHAPTER I

THE FISHERIES QUESTION COMES BEFORE CONGRESS

THE "Fisheries Question" had more ancient origins than many of the other controversies that vexed the course of Anglo-American relations. It went back to the very founding of New England. The English colonies from Massachusetts to Maine were directly dependent upon the fishing industry as the basis of their economic structure, and the markets for their product extended from the ports of southern Europe to various colonial establishments in the Caribbean. As early as 1661 it was apparent that New England was the "key to the Indies without which Jamaica, Barbadoes and ye Charibby Islands are not able to subsist."[1]

In the North Atlantic the fishing grounds traversed by these sturdy New Englanders were quite extensive, with Newfoundland as a focal point in their operations. In storms, fogs, and in bitter cold, the fishermen gambled their lives against the uncertain catch of cod and other fish that frequented these waters during certain seasons of the year. They had no choice but to live dangerously, and the casualties were as high as the rewards were low. In the pictures of some painters, and in the narratives of certain novelists, the everyday existence of these men of the sea is given an epic quality that has been summed up in the graphic phrase, "Captains Courageous." But even a hurried glance into the stark realism of their lives dispels most of the glamor that genius has bestowed upon the careers of these fishermen.[2] Long hours of

1. *Documents Relative to the Colonial History of the State of New York,* ed. by E. B. O'Callaghan (Albany, 1856–1887), III, 40. For an interesting and valuable survey of the Imperial aspects of the New England fishing industry, see Harold A. Innis, *The Cod Fisheries* (New Haven, 1940), chaps. ii–vii.

2. In the comprehensive and scholarly monograph by George Brown Goode, *The Fisheries and Fishery Industries of the United States* (Washington, 1887), Section IV, pp. 9, 11, 95–96, there are the following comments upon living conditions among the fishermen of New England: "Prior to 1840 almost all the fishing vessels of New England were owned in large part by the fishermen themselves. . . . At present the majority of the vessels engaged in the Grand Bank and cod fishery . . . are manned chiefly by fishermen who are hired by the trip or paid monthly wages. . . . A capable fisherman, with ordinary success, engaged in fishing at all seasons of the year, should make at least from $300 to $500. It is probable that the fishermen of those New England ports which do not engage in the winter fisheries do not, as a rule, make more than half as much."

hard toil, with grave danger as a constant companion, was the usual lot they might expect. Some merchant owners and some skippers earned tidy fortunes from this perilous calling, but most of those who followed the sea gained only a scanty substance from their efforts.

The American Revolution brought hard times to the fishing industry of New England, and this period of economic distress was extended after the Peace of Paris by Orders in Council that shut the doors of commerce in the British West Indies to American shipping.[3] As a counterpoise to this British action, and as a much-needed means of assisting a struggling industry to recover some measure of its former prosperity, Congress, in 1789, established a bounty system, which was later replaced by other forms of subsidy.[4]

These subsidies and the development of new fishing grounds helped to revive the fallen fortunes of the hard-pressed fishermen of New England. Another factor that served a useful purpose was the successful diplomacy of John Adams in the treaty negotiations of 1782. The third article of the Treaty of Paris provided that Americans still possessed the *right* to "take Fish of every kind on the Grand Bank and on all the other Banks of New-foundland, also in the Gulph of St. Lawrence, and at all other places in the Sea where the Inhabitants of both Countries used at any time heretofore to fish." They would enjoy, however, merely the *liberty*[5] to "take Fish of every Kind on such part of the Coast of New-foundland as British Fishermen shall use, . . . and also on the

3. Herbert C. Bell, "British Commercial Policy in the West Indies, 1783–1793," *English Historical Review,* XXXI (1916), 429–441; G. S. Graham, *British Policy and Canada, 1774–1791* (London, 1930), pp. 64 ff.; Raymond McFarland, *A History of the New England Fisheries* (New York, 1911), chap. viii.

4. There are two monumental studies on the general subject of the North Atlantic fisheries. The first is the classic account by Lorenzo Sabine, *Report on the Principal Fisheries of the American Seas* (Washington, 1853). The other standard work is the co-operative monograph prepared under the direction of the Commissioner of Fisheries and the Superintendent of the Tenth Census: *The Fisheries and Fishery Industries of the United States* (Washington, 1884–1887). This government report fills seven volumes which review every aspect of the fisheries of New England. A briefer survey of value is the volume by McFarland, *op. cit.*

5. It is significant that with reference to fishing on the high seas the word "right" is used, whereas the word "liberty" is used with regard to operations within British waters. The distinction is apparently made that the enjoyment of a *right* is not a grant, whereas a *liberty* is the grant of a privilege to be exercised within the jurisdiction of the country making it. In later years, John Adams described the situation in Paris in 1782. The British negotiators said that the word liberty meant the same thing as right, "for liberty was right and privilege was right; but the word *right* might be more unpleasing to the people of England than *liberty;* and we did not think it necessary to contend for a word." *Works of John Adams,* ed. by C. F. Adams (Boston, 1856), X, 404. It was not long before the British made good use of this distinction which in 1782 they said did not exist.

Coasts Bays & Creeks of all other of his Britannic Majesty's Dominions in America, and that the American Fishermen shall have Liberty to dry and cure Fish in any of the unsettled Bays Harbours and Creeks of Nova Scotia, Magdalen Islands, and Labrador."[6]

Thanks to these generous terms, American fishermen returned to their old haunts off the coasts of Newfoundland and Nova Scotia, and some of the more venturesome began to frequent the Bay of Chaleur and other rich fishing grounds. In 1792 Canadians began to complain that American vessels were taking "unwarrantable liberties" along the Labrador coast. Shortly after the turn of the nineteenth century, New England was sending annually some 300 ships and more than 10,000 fishermen to the Gulf of St. Lawrence. In 1805, there were not less than 900 American vessels engaged in trading and fishing upon Canadian shores "from Davis Streights thro' the streights of Belleisle and up as far as the isle of Anticosti."[7] By 1807 three-quarters of the dried fish exported from Massachusetts came from these newly visited regions, and British observers began to take alarm at these incursions of Yankee fishermen who "swarmed like flies" along Canadian coasts.[8]

The Embargo Act of 1807 and the War of 1812 dealt severe blows to this expanding fishing industry. Further difficulties were added by the failure of the American representatives to secure in the Treaty of Ghent (December 24, 1814) the renewal of inshore fishing privileges that had been granted to Americans in Article III of the Treaty of Paris. In 1815 H.M.S. *Jasseur* began the practice of seizing American vessels in the inshore waters of Canada, and these seizures continued in following years.[9]

In an effort to arrive at some understanding with reference to the use of Canadian fisheries within the three-mile limit, negotiations were initiated, and the Treaty of 1818 was finally signed. During the course of these negotiations, the British Government adhered to the view that the Peace of Paris had been abrogated by the War of 1812. According

6. Treaty between the United States and Great Britain, September 3, 1783. Hunter Miller, *Treaties and Other International Acts of the United States of America* (Washington, 1931), II, 153–154.

7. D. C. Harvey, "Uniacke's Memorandum to Windham, 1806," *Canadian Historical Review,* XVII (1936), 52.

8. John Quincy Adams, *Duplicate Letters, the Fisheries and the Mississippi* (Washington, 1822), pp. 210–213. See also, Samuel E. Morison, *The Maritime History of Massachusetts, 1783–1860* (New York, 1921), chap. x.

9. Innis, *op. cit.,* pp. 219–248. See also, *Niles' Weekly Register,* XII, 299. Despite these seizures, the tonnage employed by American fishermen in their trips to the Gulf of St. Lawrence and the Labrador coast rose from 17,855 tons in 1814 to 64,807 tons in 1817. McFarland, *op. cit.,* p. 156.

to Lord Bathurst, the Treaty of Peace (September 3, 1783) contained provisions of

> different characters—some in their own nature irrevocable, and others of a temporary nature. . . . The nature of the liberty to fish within British limits, or to use British territory, is essentially different from the right to independence. . . . In the third article, Great Britain acknowledges the *right* of the United States to take fish on the Banks of Newfoundland and other places, . . . but they are to have the *liberty* to cure and dry them in certain unsettled places within His Majesty's territories. If these liberties . . . were to be as perpetual and indefeasible as the rights previously recognized, it is difficult to conceive that the plenipotentiaries of the United States would have admitted a variation of language so adapted to produce a different impression.[10]

Lord Bathurst made a sharp distinction between *rights* and *liberties* with reference to fishing in Canadian waters; but John Quincy Adams denied that any such distinction existed. The title by which the United States

> held those fishing rights and liberties was the same. It was not possessory use of the right . . . at any time theretofore, as British subjects, and the acknowledgment by Great Britain of its *continuance* in the people of the United States after the treaty of separation. It was a national right, and . . . the right or liberty to . . . exercise this trade could no more be affected or impaired by a declaration of war than the right to the territory of the nation. . . . The fishery liberties could be lost only by express renunciation of them in the treaty.[11]

The British Government refused to adopt the reasoning of Mr. Adams, so, in the first article of the Treaty of October 20, 1818, a compromise was effected. American fishermen were given the liberty "forever to take" fish along certain portions of the southern, western, and northern coasts of Newfoundland, and along "the coasts, bays, harbours, and creeks from Mount Joly on the southern coast of Labrador, to and through the Streights of Belleisle and thence northwardly indefinitely along the coast." They were also to enjoy the "liberty forever to dry and cure fish in any of the unsettled bays, harbors and creeks of the southern part of the coast of Newfoundland hereabove described, and of the coast of Labrador."

In this same article the American negotiators renounced any liberty heretofore enjoyed to take, dry, or cure fish on, or within three marine

10. Lord Bathurst to John Quincy Adams, October 30, 1815, *American State Papers, Foreign Relations,* IV, 354–356.
11. Adams, *op. cit.,* pp. 96, 184–190.

miles of any of the coasts, bays, creeks, or harbors of His Britannic Majesty's dominions in America "not included within the abovementioned limits."[12] This renunciation of the inshore fisheries along a large portion of the Canadian coast was a significant restriction of the inshore fishing privileges that had long been profitably used by American fishermen. But it was balanced by the Canadian concession with reference to drying and curing fish. In the opinion of Mr. McFarland, the important differences between the Treaties of 1783 and 1818 were first that the "Americans gave up the inshore fishing along certain parts of the coast, and secondly, that facilities for drying and curing fish were enlarged in favor of American fishermen."[13]

It was soon apparent that the Treaty of 1818 would not put an end to the controversy between Great Britain and the United States concerning the North Atlantic fisheries.[14] The treaty had provided that American fishermen would be admitted to the bays and harbors along the restricted portions of the Canadian coasts "for the purpose of shelter and of repairing damages therein, of purchasing wood, and of obtaining water, and for no other purpose whatever." This limitation would prevent the purchase of bait and other supplies in Canadian harbors, and it would also preclude the landing and transshipment of fish from these harbors to other ports. Certain strained interpretations of international law added to the growing confusion. British officials inclined towards the view that American fishermen should be excluded from *all bays* no matter how wide. They claimed the right to draw lines from headland to headland, and to forbid American vessels to come within three miles of this line. This would mean that not only were American ships to be excluded from great arms of the sea like the Bay of Fundy and the Bay of Chaleur, but they would also be forbidden to enter all indentations of the coast, such as the north coast of Prince Edward Island from North Cape to East Cape and the northeast coast of Cape Breton from North Cape to Cow Bay.[15]

12. Miller, *op. cit.,* II, 658–666.

13. McFarland, *op. cit.,* pp. 158–159. There is an excellent map in Innis, *op. cit.,* p. 7, depicting the coasts along which the American fishermen had the liberty of the inshore fisheries and the liberty of curing and drying fish.

14. In 1819 (Act of June 14, 1819, 59 Geo. III, c. 38) the British Parliament enacted a law which condemned to forfeiture vessels of the United States, and of all other nations foreign to Great Britain, for fishing or "preparing to fish" within the territorial waters of the British North American colonies.

15. John Bassett Moore, *A Digest of International Law* (Washington, 1906), I, 783; Sabine, *op. cit.,* pp. 398–476; Charles B. Elliott, *The United States and the Northeastern Fisheries* (Minneapolis, 1887), pp. 106–117; Wallace Graham, "The Fisheries of British North America and the United States Fisherman," *Collections of the Nova Scotia Historical Society,* XIV, 215 ff.

There was an economic basis for the attitude adopted by the officials of Nova Scotia towards American fishermen. After 1830, the fishing industry of Nova Scotia entered into a decline, and this led to the enactment of drastic measures to exclude American fishing vessels. In 1835, the *Java, Independence, Magnolia,* and *Hart* were seized and confiscated, and on March 12, 1836, the Hovering Act (6 Wm. IV, c. 8), was passed. This legislation provided that local officers might seize and bring into port vessels hovering on the coasts of Nova Scotia, and it repeated the penalty of forfeiture for vessels fishing or preparing to fish within the prohibited waters.[16] Armed with this authority, H.M.S. *Champion* was sent to patrol Chaleur Bay, Gaspé, and the North Shore, while H.M.S. *Wanderer* patrolled the Bay of Fundy. After the Council and Assembly of Nova Scotia had filed a complaint against the "habitual violation" by American citizens of the Treaty of 1818, the British Government, in 1838, gave an assurance of a stricter enforcement of the terms of that convention.[17]

In April, 1841, the Government of Nova Scotia submitted to the law officers of the Crown a series of questions dealing with the right of American fishermen to navigate the Strait of Canso, to fish in the bays of Fundy and Chaleur, and to land on the coasts of the Magdalen Islands. The Crown lawyers gave the answers that were expected of them. American fishermen, they asserted, had neither the right to pass through the Strait of Canso nor to land on the shores of the Magdalen Islands. They also expressed the opinion that the authorities of Nova Scotia had a right to keep any Yankee interlopers from fishing in the bays of Fundy and Chaleur. In a labored justification of their opinion that a line of exclusion should be drawn from headland to headland across these Nova Scotian bays, these lawyers referred to the alleged use of the term "headland" in the Treaty of 1818. Inasmuch as this term *does not* appear in this treaty, it is evident that the opinion was hastily prepared and incorrectly phrased.[18]

But the officials of Nova Scotia were quick to give it application. On May 10, 1843, the American fishing schooner *Washington* was seized

16. For the text of this Act see *North Atlantic Coast Fisheries Arbitration* (Washington, 1912–1913), V, 1033–1037.

17. Innis, *op. cit.*, pp. 344–347; *Journals of the Assembly, Nova Scotia, 1837,* Appendix No. 75, and *ibid., 1839,* App. No. 9. During the years 1838–1840, sixteen American vessels "were proceeded against at Halifax and all confiscated except one." *Senate Doc. No. 231,* Pt. 8, 56 Cong., 2 sess., p. 364.

18. Secretary Everett to J. R. Ingersoll, December 4, 1862, *Great Britain. Instructions,* XVI, MS. Dept. of State; Moore, *op. cit.*, I, 785; Charles Isham, *The Fishery Question, its Origin, History and Present Situation* (New York, 1887), pp. 51–53; Sabine, *op. cit., House Ex. Doc. No. 23,* 32 Cong., 2 sess., pp. 398–476.

in the Bay of Fundy when anchored some ten miles from the shore. The vessel was taken to Yarmouth, Nova Scotia, where the judge of the vice-admiralty court decreed that the seizure was in accordance with the terms of the Treaty of 1818. The *Washington* and her stores were ordered to be sold, and restitution was not made until many years later.[19]

Although the British Government insisted upon the relaxation of the punitive regulations as far as the Bay of Fundy was concerned, seizures of American vessels continued in other Canadian waters.[20] On April 15, 1843, Prince Edward Island enacted a law similar to the Hovering Act of Nova Scotia,[21] and on May 3, 1853, New Brunswick followed suit.[22] American fishing vessels were now faced with new hazards.

The questions that gave most difficulty in connection with the fishing operations were (1) whether great bays like those of Chaleur or Fundy were really British territorial waters, and whether (2) the provincial officers could expel American vessels from provincial bays and harbors when in the judgment of these authorities such vessels were not in real need of repairs and shelter.

It was very difficult to answer these questions to the satisfaction of both the provincial officials and the American fishermen, and sharp friction ensued. In order to protect American fishing vessels from illegal seizures, President Fillmore sent Commodore Matthew C. Perry to the North Atlantic fishing grounds,[23] and on July 25, 1852, Daniel Webster, Secretary of State, made a speech in which he gave warning to the British Government that American fishermen would be protected, "hook and line, and bob and sinker."[24] With the British and American Governments differing widely as to the correct interpretation of the provisions of the Treaty of 1818, there was serious danger of open conflict. Anxious to avoid such a contingency, the British and American Governments sought some solution in the form of mutual concessions, and finally on June 5, 1854, the Treaty of Washington was signed.[25]

19. John Bassett Moore, *History and Digest of International Arbitrations to Which the United States Has Been a Party* (Washington, 1896), IV, 4342–4344. In this connection it is significant to observe that the Bay of Fundy is a very large body of water, some 65 to 75 miles wide, and 130 to 140 miles long. Innis, *op. cit.*, pp. 344–351. For pertinent documents see *Journals of the Assembly, Nova Scotia, 1837,* App. No. 75; *ibid., 1839,* App. No. 9; *ibid., 1841,* App. No. 27; *ibid., 1844,* App. No. 68; *ibid., 1848,* App. No. 89; *ibid., 1852,* App. No. 25.

20. *North Atlantic Coast Fisheries Arbitration,* IV, 240–241.

21. *Ibid.,* V, 1040–1044.

22. *Ibid.,* pp. 1052–1055.

23. *House Ex. Doc. No. 120,* 32 Cong., 1 sess., pp. 107 ff.

24. *Senate Ex. Doc. No. 22,* 32 Cong., 2 sess., pp. 444–445.

25. Charles C. Tansill, *The Canadian Reciprocity Treaty of 1854* (Baltimore, 1922),

Under the terms of this treaty, American fishermen recovered the inshore fishing liberties that had been denied to them in the Treaty of 1818. This concession was a valuable one to the fishing industry of New England, and it put an end to the friction that might have been the prelude to war. But this respite from difficulties with Canada was short-lived. The Treaty of Washington went into effect on March 16, 1855; on March 17, 1866 it was terminated upon notice by the American Government.

There were several reasons for this action. The protectionist program in Canada, initiated after the conclusion of the Treaty of Washington, had angered American manufacturers. The fact that a large section of British public opinion had favored the cause of the South during the American Civil War gave further irritation to many Americans, and when the agents of the Southern Confederacy used Canada as a base from which to launch raids against certain states of the Federal Union, indignation against Great Britain reached a high point. It was also true that after the close of the Civil War, protectionist sentiment in the United States became strongly opposed to commercial reciprocity with Canada. Because of these factors, termination of the Treaty of Washington became inevitable.[26]

There was another element in this situation that requires some comment. In the United States there was a strong sentiment in favor of the annexation of Canada. According to Professor J. P. Smith, American political leaders like Stanton, Butler, Chandler and Henry Winter Davis had shown throughout the spring of 1865 "unmistakable signs of a willingness to lead their party into a war with Great Britain for a conquest of Canada. During the next year practically every leading

pp. 39–53. In order to adjust the many claims that had arisen in connection with differences of treaty interpretation, a claims convention was signed on February 8, 1853 by representatives of the United States and of Great Britain. The commission that was provided for in this treaty met in London from September 15, 1853 to January 15, 1855. The awards in favor of American claimants amounted to $329,-734.16, and to British claimants, $277,102.88. W. M. Malloy, *Treaties, Conventions, etc.* (Washington, 1910), I, 664–668. The case of the *Washington,* seized in the Bay of Fundy in 1843, came before this tribunal, and Mr. Joshua Bates, the umpire, awarded $3,000 to the owners. In this regard, Mr. Bates rejected the British claim that the Bay of Fundy was under the exclusive control of British and provincial authorities. He considered that this bay, like the Bay of Biscay, was a large body of water over which no nation could claim the right of sovereignty. *North Atlantic Coast Fisheries Arbitration,* IV, App., 365–366.

26. Wilfrid Bovey, "Confederate Agents in Canada during the American Civil War," *Canadian Historical Review,* II (1921), 46–57; Edward Porritt, *Sixty Years of Protection in Canada* (London, 1908), pp. 119–158; Donald C. Masters, *The Reciprocity Treaty of 1854* (New York, 1936), pp. 113–173; Lester B. Shippee, *Canadian-American Relations, 1849–1874* (New Haven, 1939), pp. 159–179. See also, *Ex. Doc. No. 88,* 39 Cong., 1 sess.

member of the Republican Party . . . had acquiesced in the adoption of a commercial policy avowedly designed to force the British colonials in North America to sue for annexation to the United States."[27]

Under the impact of this threat of annexation to the United States, the provinces of Nova Scotia, New Brunswick, Quebec and Ontario formed, on July 1, 1867, a federation which they called the Dominion of Canada.[28] Although Prince Edward Island and Newfoundland were not members of this union, it was possible for the Dominion to take a firm stand with reference to the fisheries question. The termination of the Treaty of 1854 (March, 1866) had deprived American fishermen of the liberty to fish within the three-mile limit along Canadian coasts. Although this liberty had not been as valuable as many Americans had anticipated, nevertheless there were numerous masters of fishing vessels who found it profitable to frequent these territorial waters at the cost of a small license fee.[29] But suddenly in 1867 this license fee was raised from 50 cents to one dollar, and in 1868 it was advanced to $2 per ton. This was so high that only a small number of American fishermen purchased licenses in 1868–69.[30]

This rapid rise in the cost of fishing licenses was merely one of the means employed by Sir Charles Tupper to compel the American Government to negotiate for a new reciprocity treaty along the lines of the Treaty of 1854.[31] As a further step in this direction he assisted in the

27. *The Republican Expansionists of the Early Reconstruction Era* (Chicago, 1933), p. 97.

28. Reginald Trotter, *Canadian Federation, Its Origins and Achievement* (London, 1924), pp. 84–137.

29. During the year 1866 some 454 American fishing vessels paid a license fee of 50 cents per ton in the waters of Nova Scotia, New Brunswick, Prince Edward Island, and Canada, at a total cost of $13,037.85. In 1867, with the license fee raised to $1 per ton, only 295 American fishing vessels bought licenses to fish in the waters above-mentioned, but the total cost of these fees amounted to $15,714.92. When the fee was advanced in 1868 to $2 per ton, the number of licenses purchased by American fishing vessels was only 61, and the total cost of fees dropped to merely $5,824.75. *Documents and Proceedings of the Halifax Commission, 1877* (Washington, 1878), pp. 197–218. Under the authority of these licenses, American fishermen could fish the Canadian inshore waters, buy bait, ice, and supplies, recruit members for crews, and ship fish in bond from a Canadian port.

30. *Canada: Sessional Papers, 1868,* No. 12, pp. 1–45. Hereafter referred to as *C.S.P.*

31. In a letter to Sir John Macdonald, April 18, 1868, Tupper remarks: "I think I also satisfied his Grace that assent ought to be immediately given to raising the fishing licenses to two dollars. . . . I have presented in the strongest terms the fact that the licensing was only assented to by the colonies for a single year and that the plan proposed is practically to abandon the fisheries altogether, and keep up the existing restrictions on trade and promote continued difficulty with the United States. . . . The policy we proposed would lead to a renewal of reciprocity and settle the whole question permanently." E. M. Saunders, *The Life and Letters of the Right Honourable Sir Charles Tupper* (Toronto, 1916), I, 164–166.

passage of two important Dominion statutes—the Act of May 22, 1868 (31 Vict., c. 61), and May 12, 1870 (33 Vict., c. 15).[32] A final measure of restriction was the abolition of the system of licenses. American fishermen would now be in such sore straits that they would clamor for a return to the situation that had existed between 1855 and 1866.

Under the terms of legislation that was in force, American fishing vessels could be seized and confiscated on the following grounds: (1) fishing within prohibited waters; (2) anchoring or hovering inshore during calm weather without any ostensible cause, having on board ample supplies of wood and water; (3) lying at anchor and remaining within bay to clean and pack fish; (4) purchasing and bartering bait and preparing to fish; (5) selling goods and buying supplies; (6) landing and transshipping cargoes of fish.

The prompt seizure of American vessels for infractions of Canadian fishing regulations aroused the indignation of New England fishermen, and this was soon translated into political pressure upon the Grant Administration. The British Foreign Office, always responsive to American complaints, openly deprecated the haste with which the Dominion Government had acted, and even Sir John Macdonald began to entertain doubts about the wisdom of enforcing the regulations in too rigid a manner.[33] In his annual message to Congress (December 5, 1870), President Grant expressed the opinion that the Dominion Government had acted in an "unfriendly way" in the matter of the fisheries. Inasmuch as this attitude might become a fixed one, he recommended that Congress authorize him to suspend the bonding privilege, and possibly, to refuse permission to Canadian vessels to enter American ports.[34]

It was evident that some solution must speedily be found for the fisheries dispute. In February, 1871, a Joint High Commission was appointed to deal with all the problems that disturbed Anglo-American

32. The Act of May 22, 1868, authorized the officials to require any vessel which was not hovering on the coast, but which had come within a harbor, to depart from such harbor on twenty-four hours' notice, and, on failure of such departure, to bring her into port for that mere cause, without any limitation as to the length of time she might be detained. The burden of proving innocence was placed on the claimant, and no suit could be brought for any illegal conduct of the customs officers until after a month's notice in writing.

Under the terms of the Act of May 12, 1870, an officer could seize any vessel being within any harbor in Canada, or hovering in British waters within 3 miles of the coast, and search her cargo without any previous notice to depart.

For the text of these Acts see *North Atlantic Coast Fisheries Arbitration,* V, 1061–1064.

33. Shippee, *op. cit.,* pp. 279–283.

34. James D. Richardson, *Messages and Papers of the Presidents* (Washington, 1898), VII, 102–103.

relations. After several months of negotiations, during the course of which Sir John Macdonald proved a doughty defender of Canadian interests,[35] the Treaty of Washington was finally signed (May 8, 1871). Article XVIII restored to American fishermen, for a period of ten years, the liberty to use the inshore fisheries of the provinces of Quebec, Nova Scotia, and New Brunswick, and the colony of Prince Edward's Island.[36] On the assumption that the value of this liberty was greater than any privileges extended to British subjects under the terms of Articles XIX and XXI,[37] it was provided (Article XXII) that commissioners should be appointed to determine the amount of compensation which should be paid to the British Government.[38]

The exact sum to be paid for the inshore fishing liberties was left to the determination of a Joint High Commission of three members; one to be nominated by the President of the United States, one by the Queen of England, and the third member to be selected by the President and the Queen acting conjointly. The choice of this third member was a delicate task, and after canvassing many personalities, Secretary Fish submitted a list of names to Sir Edward Thornton, the British Minister. Thornton raised objections to these nominations, and after receiving an intimation from Ottawa, he submitted the name of the Belgian Minister at Washington, Maurice Delfosse. Fish immediately objected that Delfosse had been discourteous to the American Government. Moreover, Belgium was "so completely under the control and protection of Gr. Britain" that the American people would view such an appointment with suspicion. But the British Government held firm, and Fish, after some further delay, agreed that Delfosse should be the third member of the Joint Commission.[39]

35. In the *Diary* of Hamilton Fish, May 8, 1871, there is the following entry which describes the attitude of Sir John Macdonald: "When Sir John Macdonald was about to sign, while having the pen in his hand, he said to me (in a half-whisper), 'Well, here go the fisheries.' To my reply, 'you get a good equivalent for them,' he said, 'No, we give them away—here goes the signature'; and thereupon signed his name, and rising from the table, said, 'They are gone.'" Allan Nevins, *Hamilton Fish, the Inner History of the Grant Administration* (New York, 1937), p. 490.

36. Malloy, *op. cit.*, I, 700–716. See also, *Senate Confidential Ex. Doc. A,* special session, 1871, pp. 1–192.

37. The liberty to use the inshore fisheries applied solely "to the sea fishery." All other fisheries "in the rivers and in the mouths of rivers" were reserved exclusively for British fishermen.

38. Article XIX admitted, for a period of ten years, British subjects to the inshore fisheries of the United States north of the thirty-ninth parallel of north latitude. Article XXI admitted into the United States, free of duty, fish oil and fish of all kinds (except fish taken from the inland waters) which were the produce of the "fisheries of the Dominion of Canada, or of Prince Edward's Island."

39. Nevins, *op. cit.*, pp. 869–870; Secretary Fish to Sir Edward Thornton, August 21, 1873, *British Legation, Notes to,* XVI, MS. Dept. of State.

British insistence upon the appointment of Delfosse bore good financial fruit for the British Government. When the Joint Commission met at Halifax in 1877, it finally decided by a vote of two to one (Alexander T. Galt, the British Commissioner, and Maurice Delfosse, the Belgian Commissioner, against Ensign H. Kellogg, the American Commissioner) that the United States should pay $5,500,000 in gold for the liberty to use the Canadian inshore fisheries.[40]

Many historians have regarded the award of the Halifax Commission with suspicion, and a distinguished Canadian publicist has condemned its "abrupt and arbitrary tone." It was a surprising fact that the reasoning by which the majority had reached its conclusions was not given in the award or in any record. Therefore the "size of the compensation comes as a shock to the reader perusing the available records and if, as is to be presumed, the commission had good grounds for the amount awarded, they should have stated them."[41]

The decision of the Halifax Commission aroused widespread indignation in the United States. Spurred on by this outburst of public sentiment, Congress, on February 26, 1883, adopted a resolution which directed the President to give notice to the British Government of the termination of Articles XVIII to XXV, inclusive, and also of Article XXX of the Treaty of May 8, 1871.[42] The President carried out this

40. In *Documents and Proceedings of the Halifax Commission, 1877,* p. 88, there is an estimate that the number of American fishing vessels annually frequenting British North American waters was "between 700 and 1200." The amount of capital invested in the fishing industry was placed at approximately $7,000,000. See also, Moore, *Digest of International Law,* I, 703–753; *Senate Rept. No. 429,* 45 Cong., 2 sess.

41. P. E. Corbett, *The Settlement of Canadian-American Disputes* (New Haven, 1937), pp. 33–34. See also, the *Record of the Proceedings of the Halifax Fisheries Commission* (London, 1877), and *Foreign Relations, 1878* (hereafter referred to as *F.R.*). During the ten-year period, 1873 to 1882, the total catch of the American fishing fleet within the three-mile limit was only 78,827 barrels of mackerel valued at $598,429. For the twelve years that the treaty provisions were in force the United States "paid about eight times as much for the privilege as our fishermen secured from it, besides remitting the duty, at one cent per pound, on millions of pounds of Canadian fish imported into the country." McFarland, *op. cit.,* pp. 329–330.

42. *Congressional Record,* 47 Cong., 2 sess., pp. 3055–3056. In a pamphlet published by Henry Y. Hind, in 1884, the charge was made that the statistics printed in the British Case before the Halifax Commission were falsified "to an enormous extent in favor of Canada, by the collusion of Canadian officials with the Chief of the United States Bureau of Statistics." Hind had served as the British "scientific witness" before the Halifax Commission, and his charges aroused great interest in the United States. The title of the Hind pamphlet was *Fraudulent Official Records of Government.*

For a criticism of Hind's pamphlet, see Oscar D. Skelton, *The Life and Times of Sir Alexander T. Galt* (Toronto, 1920), p. 513. In this biography of Galt there is some pertinent data on the background of the Halifax award and on the role played by M. Delfosse.

direction, and on July 1, 1885 the liberty granted to American fishermen to use the Canadian inshore fisheries came to an end.

It had long been apparent to British and American statesmen that the lapse of this fishing liberty might lead to serious friction. In order to forestall this trouble, Lord Derby, the Colonial Secretary, in December, 1884, wrote to Lord Lansdowne, the Governor-General of Canada, and requested a definite expression of policy concerning the fisheries question. Lansdowne replied that he did not think that the Canadian Government should take the undignified stand of appearing as a suitor for American favors. Moreover, it was quite likely that negotiations could be conducted to better advantage after March 4, 1885 when the Cleveland Administration would come into power. But some *modus vivendi* would have to be arranged for the approaching fishing season. In this regard the Canadian Government would be willing to agree to "an extension of the operation of the clauses [in the Treaty of Washington] in regard both to 'free fishing' and 'free fish' until the 1st of January, 1886."[43]

Sir Lionel West, the British Minister at Washington, later on popularly known as Sackville-West, discussed with Secretary Frelinghuysen this matter of extending the operation of the "free fishing" and "free fish" clauses of the Treaty of Washington. After consulting with several Senators, Frelinghuysen informed Sir Lionel that such a suggestion was "impracticable," so a Presidential proclamation was issued on January 31, 1885, warning American fishermen of the termination of the privileges they had enjoyed under that treaty.[44] The fisheries question was in this unsettled and unsatisfactory state when on March 6, 1885, Thomas F. Bayard assumed office as Secretary of State.

In all his relations with the British Foreign Office in connection with Canadian affairs, Secretary Bayard shows to good advantage. His long and distinguished service in the Senate (1869–1885) gave him an intimate acquaintance with many important problems in American foreign policy, and his candor and common sense were qualities that served him in good stead in the discussion of Canadian-American difficulties during the years from 1885 to 1889. During his tenure as Secretary of State he insisted upon conducting American foreign policy upon an elevated plane whose atmosphere was far too thin for the robust politicians of his day. Even in his own party he was openly praised by some

43. Lord Lansdowne to the Earl of Derby, December 26, 1884, *Macdonald Papers, Washington Treaty, 1888,* II, 6–11, P.A.C.

44. Secretary Frelinghuysen to Senator Edmunds, January 15, 1885, *Domestic Letters,* CLIII, MS. Dept. of State; Secretary Frelinghuysen to Sir Lionel West, January 20, 1885, *Great Britain, Notes to,* XIX, MS. Dept. of State.

who secretly denounced him. He rejected wholeheartedly the idea that statesmanship is a series of wise compromises. On questions of principle he never entertained any thought of a halfway answer, and this inflexible attitude often made him appear as some Lancelot lost in a strange world of political intrigue. If he had been an adroit politician rather than a rigid moralist, he would have been more successful in his frequent clashes with the Senate. During the first Cleveland Administration the Senate was in Republican hands, and Republican Senators were not, as Whistler once described himself, "delicately contentious." They fell upon Bayard with all the fury that political passions could inspire. Cleveland was the first Democratic President since the Civil War. Republicans had grown accustomed to holding the seats of the mighty, and they looked with sharp disfavor upon the new Chief Executive who diverted party plums into the capacious laps of deserving Democrats. It was soon evident to Bayard that no program of foreign policy formulated by a Democratic Secretary of State had any chance of acceptance by a Republican Senate.

In Canada, the reins of authority rested in the able hands of Lord Lansdowne and Sir John A. Macdonald. Lansdowne was an ideal type of English gentleman. As one reads through his extensive correspondence as Governor-General of Canada it can be readily seen that he had the vision and courage of a real statesman.[45] He developed a deep affection for Canada, but he never forgot that Canada was merely one portion of an empire on the seven seas, and at times he insisted upon lifting the gaze of Sir John Macdonald from Dominion considerations to the distant horizons of imperial goals.

Macdonald was the ablest politician of his generation. He was neither an orator nor a skillful debater, but he had that supreme gift of leadership that made men follow him blindly, with no thought of recompense save a brief word of approval or a hurried glance that bestowed an eagerly-sought accolade upon the shoulders of his ardent henchmen. He was not always scrupulous in his handling of political problems, and his opponents asserted that his conscience was not his guide but his accomplice. But he had that gift of political magic that made the chief items in his program assume the appearance of national imperatives

45. In Lord Newton's biography, *Lord Lansdowne* (London, 1929), there is a very inadequate chapter on Lansdowne as Governor-General of Canada, 1883–1888. One has to read with care the large volume of Lansdowne letters in the *Sir John Macdonald Papers* in the Public Archives of Canada (Ottawa) in order to appreciate the active interest that Lansdowne took in every aspect of Canadian affairs, and his unusual ability to handle with success the many problems that clamored for settlement.

that must be adopted for patriotic reasons. It may be that such a quality is one of the chief tests of true statesmanship.[46]

As soon as the Cleveland Administration came into office, Macdonald wrote to Lord Lansdowne and suggested that the time might be ripe to discuss with Secretary Bayard the troublesome fisheries question. Even if nothing would come of a Canadian overture in this regard, it would be a gesture of "good will," and it might lead to something worth while.[47] As a reflection of this conciliatory spirit, Sir Lionel West left with Bayard (March 12) a memorandum in which an inquiry was made whether it would be possible to extend until January 1, 1886 the operation of the treaty clauses that had dealt with the inshore fisheries and the admission of Canadian fish into American ports.[48]

Bayard turned this memorandum over to Alvey A. Adee, the Second Assistant Secretary of State, who expressed the opinion that the proposed arrangement could not be effected without approval by Congress.[49] Bayard conveyed this information to West during an interview on March 27, and he let drop a hint that, with reference to the fisheries question, it would be "very convenient if a little delay could be had."[50]

From his conversations with Bayard, Sir Lionel gathered the impression that Bayard would favor an arrangement whereby the President would ask Congress to authorize the appointment of a joint high commission to study the fisheries question and to admit, pending this study, Canadian fish and fish oil into American ports. Canada, on her part, would keep open the inshore fisheries to American fishermen.[51] Lansdowne lost no time in acquainting Sir John Macdonald with his opinion that this proposal might well be the basis "for a satisfactory arrangement."[52]

46. T. W. L. MacDermott, "John A. Macdonald—His Biographies and Biographers," *Rept. of the Canadian Historical Association, 1931,* pp. 77–84.

47. Sir John Macdonald to Lord Lansdowne, March 9, 1885, *Macdonald Papers, Macdonald Letter Books,* XXIII, 132, P.A.C.

48. *Memorandum* of Sir Lionel West, March 12, 1885, *British Legation, Notes from,* CXI, MS. Dept. of State. He is usually referred to as Lord Sackville.

49. After discussing the Congressional resolution which had been approved on March 3, 1883, Adee remarked: "It is clear that, when the notified termination takes effect, on a day fixed, to wit, July 1, 1885, the fisheries legislation of the Act of March 1, 1873, stand absolutely repealed, and the laws of the United States are to be enforced as if the treaty had never existed. . . . We could not, in extending . . . the Fishery clauses until January 1, 1886, revive or continue the repealed statutes on which our reciprocal privileges to British products depend." *Memorandum* written by A. A. Adee, March 17, 1885, *Bayard MS.*

50. *Memorandum* written by Bayard after a conversation with Sir Lionel West, March 27, 1885, *ibid.*

51. Sir Lionel West to Lord Lansdowne, April 10, 1885, *Macdonald Papers, Governor-General's Correspondence,* XII, 389–390, P.A.C.

52. Lord Lansdowne to Sir John Macdonald, April 13, 1885, *ibid.,* p. 387.

On April 22, Bayard handed to Sir Lionel West the anticipated memorandum, and it repeated with one important exception the items that West had included in his note to Lord Lansdowne. In the Bayard memorandum there was no mention that the President would ask Congress to admit, temporarily, Canadian fish and fish oil into American ports.[53] Sir Lionel called Lord Lansdowne's attention to this omission, and he stated that Bayard had explained it by saying that any such recommendation would "indispose Congress to adopt measures for the final settlement of the fisheries question, and he wished to avoid any allusion to the Halifax award to which it might give rise."[54]

Lansdowne was not ready to give any final reply to the Bayard proposal, but he requested Sir Lionel to convey to the Secretary of State the assurance that his project would receive the "most careful consideration and that the Government of the Dominion is sincerely desirous of placing its relations with the Government of the United States . . . upon a footing advantageous and satisfactory to both."[55] To Lord Derby, Lansdowne wrote in a similar vein, and he recommended that Sir Lionel be authorized "to continue the negotiations."[56] Derby then inquired if the Dominion Government would concur in the memorandum submitted by Bayard "on the understanding that the arrangement therein proposed is only of a temporary nature and would be assented to strictly on condition that it should not prejudice such equivalents as might be deemed fair to be required in the course of negotiations for a more permanent settlement of the Fisheries question."[57]

Lansdowne's answer was clear and affirmative. The Dominion Government was ready to do "everything in its power" to prevent friction between American fishermen and Canadian officials. It was willing to agree to a temporary arrangement whereby the inshore fisheries would be granted to these American fishermen, but it should be remembered that such a "one-sided" settlement would not be popular in Canada. In connection with this proposed *modus vivendi* it should be indicated that in the Bayard memorandum there was no mention of Canadian fishermen being permitted to fish within the "territorial waters of the United States."[58]

53. *Memorandum* by Bayard, April 22, 1885, *British Legation, Notes to,* XIX, MS. Dept. of State.

54. Sir Lionel West to Lord Lansdowne, April 23, 1885, *Macdonald Papers, Governor-General's Correspondence,* XII, 404–406, P.A.C.

55. Lord Lansdowne to Sir Lionel West, April 28, 1885, *Macdonald Papers, Washington Treaty, 1888,* II, 25–26, P.A.C.

56. Lord Lansdowne to Lord Derby, April 28, 1885, *ibid.,* pp. 34–35.

57. Lord Derby to Lord Lansdowne, May 12, 1885, *ibid.,* p. 37.

58. Lord Lansdowne to Lord Derby, May 18, 1885, *ibid.,* pp. 38–47.

With Canadian and English officials in a conciliatory mood, there seemed to be a good possibility that Bayard would soon be able to arrive at some working agreement in the matter of the fisheries. He quickly discovered, however, that the New England fishing industry was strongly opposed to any remission of the duties on Canadian fish. Charles L. Woodbury sent a warning that "every fisherman along the shore from Block Island to Eastport" would rise in arms against any postponement of the tariff charges on Canadian fish.[59] Other correspondents from New England sent similar warnings.[60]

Lord Lansdowne did not clearly realize the strength of New England opposition to a temporary remission of the tariff duties on Canadian fish, and he continued to hope for an early solution of the fishery dispute. In a letter to Sir Lionel West he discussed the resentment that would be aroused in Canada over a "one-sided" arrangement with the United States. But Canadian criticism would be avoided if assurances were given that any *modus vivendi* would merely be a prelude to a final settlement of the fishery controversy and to the "opening of negotiations for a wider measure of commercial reciprocity."[61]

After receiving this Lansdowne letter, West went to the Department of State and discussed the situation with Bayard, who frankly admitted that the reason his memorandum had not included any permission for Canadians to use American territorial waters was because of the fact that Canadians had never made use of such a privilege. He was entirely in favor of such use. With reference to commercial relations, Bayard stated that he was "by no means unfavourable to a wider measure of reciprocity," but the British Government should not make any "formal proposal in this sense" until the Department of State had made a thorough canvass of the situation.[62]

Lansdowne realized that time was pressing in the matter of the *modus vivendi* concerning the fisheries, and he was willing to postpone formal negotiations relative to a renewal of commercial reciprocity. But he still clung to the hope that it would be possible to make some announcement that these negotiations would take place in the near future.[63]

59. Charles L. Woodbury to William C. Endicott, May 11, 1885, *Bayard MS.* Secretary Endicott sent Woodbury's letter to President Cleveland (May 13, 1885), and it was later turned over to Bayard.

60. George Steele to Secretary Bayard, May 10, 1885, and Charles L. Woodbury to Bayard, June 13, 1885, *ibid.*

61. Lord Lansdowne to Sir Lionel West, May 18, 1885, *Macdonald Papers, Governor-General's Correspondence,* XII, 431–432, P.A.C.

62. Sir Lionel West to Lord Lansdowne, May 22, 1885, *ibid.,* pp. 429–430.

63. Lord Lansdowne to Sir John Macdonald, May 25, 1885, *ibid.,* p. 428.

In England there was a strong feeling in favor of an early adjustment of the fisheries dispute. Edward J. Phelps, the new American Minister, was greatly pleased at the cordial reception accorded him by the second Gladstone Ministry. Lord Granville, the Foreign Secretary, was endowed with a personal charm that made visits to the Foreign Office an exercise in genuine diplomatic courtesies. Even British royalty was unusually conciliatory. The Queen was "very cordial" to Phelps, and the Prince of Wales was courteous to a "marked degree." At a dinner given by the Lord Mayor of London, the American Minister was tendered a "tumultuous" reception. There was no doubt in the mind of Phelps that the Cleveland Administration was "very popular" in England, and he had noticed that there was "much satisfaction" at the selection of Bayard as Secretary of State.[64]

In Washington there was a strong reflection of the Anglo-American amity that was so evident in London, and Secretary Bayard and Sir Lionel West soon reached an agreement that was recorded in an exchange of diplomatic notes. They expressly recognized the fact that the arrangement giving American fishermen access to Canadian inshore waters was "only temporary." Similar privileges were to be extended to British vessels engaged in fishing in the waters of the United States. As a means of arriving at a comprehensive and permanent settlement of Canadian-American difficulties, President Cleveland would recommend to Congress an authorization for the appointment of a joint high commission which would deal not only with the fisheries question but with the whole subject of "good neighborhood and intercourse."[65]

Bayard was delighted with this *modus vivendi* which would "lift a rather difficult question out of the reach of personal irritations and controversies, and save a number of our citizens from loss and annoyance. We can better approach the consideration of the subject next winter in an amiable frame of mind." He was particularly pleased with the prospect of more cordial relations between the United States and Great Britain. It was ardently to be hoped that the Cleveland Administration would "steadily and quietly cement" this Anglo-American connection.[66]

64. E. J. Phelps to Secretary Bayard, *Private,* June 5, 1885, *Bayard MS.* For a general estimate of Lord Granville as a statesman see Lord Edmond Fitzmaurice, *Life of the Second Earl Granville* (London, 1905, 2 vols.).

65. Secretary Bayard to Sir Lionel West, June 19, 20, 22, 1885; West to Secretary Bayard, June 20, 22, 1885, *British Legation, Notes to,* XX; *British Legation, Notes from,* CXII, MS. Dept. of State.

66. Secretary Bayard to Phelps, June 27, 1885, *Personal, Bayard Letter Book,* I, *Bayard MS.*

In many circles in England there was warm satisfaction at the thought that the basis was about to be laid for a settlement of the fisheries question, but in Canada there were many evidences of the discontent that Lansdowne had anticipated. He believed they would disappear in the face of a comprehensive arrangement that would deal not only with the fisheries but also with the subject of commercial reciprocity. On August 24, 1885 he wrote a long letter to Sir John Macdonald in which he made an inquiry as to the objectives that Canada sought in the proposed settlement with the United States.[67] Macdonald's answer was detailed. It would be advisable to ask for a renewal of the abrogated articles of the Treaty of Washington. It was also important to have these treaty provisions extended to "whale and seal-oil" as well as to "free fish and fish-oil." Some effort should be made to get the Canadian Pacific Coast marine products included in the treaty. Arbitration should be asked in order to ascertain the value of the concessions made on each side. As to general commercial relations, Canada would be "satisfied with the terms of the Reciprocity Treaty of 1854," but a treaty "affecting manufactures would not be entertained by the United States nor . . . by England."[68]

There was small chance that American protectionists would be willing to renew the provisions of the Treaty of 1854, but there was a possibility that some compromise arrangement could be effected. If English good-will towards the United States were an important factor in preparing the way for a settlement of difficulties, it was evident that this could be relied upon in full measure. Shortly after the Salisbury Government assumed office, Sir Stafford Northcote (later Lord Iddesleigh) wrote Bayard in a very friendly vein,[69] and on August 4 he sent a second letter in which he commented upon the "strongly-marked kindness of feeling exhibited between English and Americans."[70] Phelps, in London, remarked upon the cordial feelings of most Britishers towards the United States,[71] and Sir Ambrose Shea gave assurances that the Brit-

67. Charles C. Tansill, *The Foreign Policy of Thomas F. Bayard* (New York, 1940), pp. 200–201.

68. Sir John Macdonald to Lord Lansdowne, September 5, 1885, *Macdonald Papers, Macdonald Letter Books,* XXIII, 277–278, P.A.C.

69. Sir Stafford Northcote to Secretary Bayard, June 11, 1885, *Bayard MS.* In a letter to Phelps, June 27, 1885, Bayard remarked that he had first met Northcote in 1871 when he was a member of the Joint High Commission that drew up the Washington Treaty. The Salisbury Ministry assumed office during the second week in June, 1885, and Sir Stafford Northcote (on July 6 he became Lord Iddesleigh) was given the sinecure office of First Lord of the Treasury.

70. Lord Iddesleigh to Secretary Bayard, August 4, 1885, *Bayard MS.*

71. Phelps to Secretary Bayard, August 6, 1885, *ibid.*

ish Government was "much pleased with what has been done as a temporary measure."[72]

It now occurred to David A. Wells, an able American economist, to pay a visit to Newfoundland and study conditions on that island. He found things in a "rather pitiful condition," and felt that American policy towards contiguous countries had been "mean and contemptible."[73]

Bayard had sympathy for these Newfoundlanders whose struggle for bare subsistence was a strenuous one,[74] but his first duty was to American fishermen whose lot was far from easy. Certain Canadian capitalists had been busy in their efforts to cripple the American menhaden[75] fishery, and Francis Wharton, the Solicitor of the Department of State, had looked into the matter for Bayard. After reading the correspondence in the Department of State, Wharton grew so angry that he expressed to Bayard his desire to "give the British lion a slap with one of our best Manhaydens."[76] Wharton also informed Bayard that in the matter of the award of the Halifax Commission the United States had been "scandalously outwitted."[77]

It was apparent that there was a pressing need for a careful and impartial survey of all the varied aspects of the fisheries question, and President Cleveland, in accordance with the promises that Bayard had given to Sir Lionel West, included in his message to Congress (December 8, 1885) a recommendation for the appointment of a commission in which "the Governments of the United States and Great Britain shall be respectively represented, charged with the consideration and settlement, upon a just, equitable, and honorable basis, of the entire question of the fishing rights of the two Governments and their respective citizens on the coasts of the United States and British North America."[78]

Through partisan spite, Congress rejected this recommendation of the President and thus re-opened the fisheries dispute with the resulting friction that had been feared by Bayard. Political sabotage became an established practice on the part of Republicans in Congress, and partisan ends rather than patriotic objectives were the goals of party leaders. In the following chapter this will be dealt with at greater length.

72. Sir Ambrose Shea to Secretary Bayard, August 15, 1885, *ibid.*
73. David A. Wells to Bayard, August 27, 1885, *ibid.*
74. Bayard to David A. Wells, August 29, 1885, *Bayard Letter Book,* I, *Bayard MS.*
75. The name "menhaden" is applied to a species of the herring family.
76. Francis Wharton to Secretary Bayard, October 10, 1885, *Bayard MS.*
77. Francis Wharton to Secretary Bayard, October 10, 1885, *ibid.*
78. Richardson, *op. cit.,* VIII, 332.

CHAPTER II

PRESIDENT CLEVELAND SUBMITS THE FISHERIES QUESTION TO A JOINT HIGH COMMISSION

It was President Cleveland's fond hope that Congress would favor the creation of a joint high commission that would deal with the age-old problem of the North Atlantic fisheries. He had agreed to the *modus vivendi* of June, 1885, because he believed it would temporarily quiet the friction that had arisen in connection with the Canadian inshore fisheries and thus eliminate all serious difficulties during the sessions of the proposed commission. It was evident that the main task of the commission was to provide some economic basis for Canadian-American good will. This could best be done by combining the fisheries settlement with a system of commercial reciprocity along the lines that had been followed under the Treaty of 1854. There had been little doubt in his mind that Canada and the United States would derive mutual advantage from the establishment of more intimate commercial relations. These relations should be in accordance with a plan "based on the free interstate commerce of the [American] Union."[1]

This desire of the President for closer commercial relations between Canada and the United States was to remain unfulfilled, and the temper of Congress soon made it clear that no co-operation could be expected from that body. There was a growing fear in New England that the Administration favored an arrangement whereby the liberty to use the Canadian inshore fisheries would be balanced by the admission of Canadian fish and fish oil into the United States free of duty.[2] In Congress the representatives from Maine, Vermont and Massachusetts played upon this fear in order to create political capital, and they did not hesitate to distort truth if such dubious tactics would lead to some party advantage.

The New England contingent in the Senate was composed of men whose personal lives were above reproach. In politics, however, they had a more flexible code of conduct, and at times they stooped quite low in order that they might conquer. In this regard they remind one of the comment of Josh Billings (Henry Wheeler Shaw): "Christians seem to

1. Sir Lionel West to Lord Salisbury, December 11, 1885, quoted in Tansill, *Bayard,* p. 204.
2. Henry L. Nelson to Secretary Bayard, December 21, 1885, *Bayard MS.*

fite under cover, but the Devil stands boldly out and dares the world to combat."

At the head of the New England delegation in the Senate was George F. Edmunds, of Vermont. He was one of the ablest constitutional lawyers in the United States. He entered the Senate in April, 1866, and at once joined in the assault upon the hard-pressed Andrew Johnson, who was having scant success in carrying out Lincoln's policy of conciliation towards the South. Edmunds could never throw off the Civil War complex that colored all his thoughts. Democrats had wished to destroy the Union, and had waged a bloody war for the purpose of accomplishing that shocking objective. They were always suspect in his mind, and long after Appomattox he continued to be fearful of Democratic statesmen and Democratic policies. The accession of President Cleveland to the Presidency in 1885 was viewed with open distaste by Edmunds, and he was constantly on the alert for some evidence that the new Administration was ready to betray American sovereign rights. He was a powerful debater in the Senate, and his style of expression was so incisive and so unrestrained that he could well have adopted the slogan of Ambrose Bierce: "My trade is abuse."[3]

Another outstanding Republican in the Senate was George F. Hoar, who entered the House of Representatives during the period when the South was being treated like a "conquered province." He quickly succumbed to the contagion of partisan bitterness that prevailed in Republican ranks, and for many years he viewed the South and the Democratic Party with a jaundiced eye. His *Autobiography* is a sort of an *apologia* which does not always carry conviction. In dealing with his career in the Senate, Hoar makes a detailed defence of his attitude towards party questions, but to the objective reader many of his comments betray a certain "fallen archness."[4]

William P. Frye was the third important member of this New England trinity that attempted to save the country from Democratic conspiracies. After serving for a decade in the House of Representatives, he was elevated to the Senate in 1881 and immediately joined with Edmunds and Hoar in a stalwart defence of Republican principles. He was of smaller political stature than his two intimate associates, but he succeeded in building up a nuisance value that was a considerable

3. There is no biography of George F. Edmunds. The brief account in the *Dictionary of American Biography* (hereafter *D.A.B.*), VI, 24–27 (by William A. Robinson) does not give a clear picture of the importance of Edmunds as a political figure.

4. There is no biography of George F. Hoar. There is a brief estimate of his political career by George H. Haynes, *D.A.B.*, IX, 87–88.

factor in the party struggles of the eighties.[5] In order to harass the Cleveland Administration and to interpose difficulties in the way of any adjustment between Canada and the United States, Frye introduced on January 18, 1886 a resolution which expressed the view that in "the opinion of the Senate" there was no need for the appointment of a joint commission to consider and recommend a settlement of the fisheries controversy. He was certain that the fishing industry did not desire any renewal of the provisions of the Treaty of Washington, and he expressed the view that British pressure had been responsible for the President's recommendation to Congress.[6]

Senator Edmunds gave prompt support to the Frye resolution. Secretary Bayard's action in arranging a *modus vivendi* without the previous consent of the Senate he regarded as a "very grave question of the exertion of executive power." Senate prerogatives had been invaded, and the President should be told in no uncertain terms about the limitations upon his powers.[7]

This Senate debate was followed with keen interest by Sir Lionel West. He clearly understood the motives of politicians like Frye and Edmunds, and he complained to Lord Salisbury that they were really opposed to "any amicable agreement whatsoever with Her Majesty's Government."[8] He was certain that many of their statements were untrue, but mendacity was a favorite weapon with politicians. The great danger in the situation lay in the fact that the *modus vivendi* concerning the inshore fisheries expired on January first, and the Canadian Government would enforce the provisions of the Treaty of 1818. This might lead to "serious difficulties."[9]

On February 19, West expressed these fears to Bayard. Bayard

5. Frye was not of sufficient importance to warrant a biography. For a short account of the man and his works see Charles R. Lingley, *D.A.B.*, VII, 51–52.

6. *Congressional Record,* 49 Cong., 1 sess., p. 702.

7. *Ibid.*, p. 702.

8. Sir Lionel West to Lord Salisbury, January 20, 1886, *Macdonald Papers, Washington Treaty,* II, 129–132, P.A.C. When the Gladstone Ministry fell in June, 1885, Lord Salisbury became Prime Minister and held the post of Foreign Secretary until the third Gladstone Ministry came into power in February, 1886.

9. Sir Lionel West to Lord Rosebery, February 2, 1886, *Macdonald Papers, Governor-General's Correspondence,* XIII, 24–25, P.A.C. When the third Gladstone Ministry assumed office on February 1, 1886, Lord Rosebery became Secretary for Foreign Affairs. In a letter to Lord Lansdowne, February 4, 1886, Sir Lionel West repeats the gist of certain remarks of Senator Allison, of Iowa, to the effect that Secretary Bayard had been "outwitted" by British diplomats. *Ibid.*, pp. 16g–16i. Two days previously, Lansdowne had observed to Sir John Macdonald that certain Canadians were abusing the Macdonald Government for "allowing the Americans to get the better of us." *Ibid.*, pp. 16c–16d.

made no attempt to minimize them and he inveighed bitterly against the Republican Senators who were thwarting the President's endeavors to clarify the situation.[10] His helplessness in the face of an adverse Senate was frankly confessed in a letter to Phelps. The attitude of the Senate majority seemed "averse to the consideration of any public measure from a high or patriotic point of view." Blind and obstructive partisanship was their only "rule of action." But these Republican leaders should not shoulder all the blame for the fishery difficulties. In Canada, many officials had placed a strained interpretation upon the terms of the Treaty of 1818. They had read that convention with their prejudices rather than with their eyes. American fishermen really had a right to purchase bait in Canadian ports, and the legislation in Canada which forbade this practice was not a "fair construction" of the provisions of the treaty. The "release by the United States under the Treaty of 1818 was of the right to '*take, dry, and cure fish.*' " The restrictions intended by the treaty referred only to those three items, and they should not be extended to items that had not been released.[11]

To Bayard it seemed obvious that the Canadian Government did not appreciate the political dangers that lurked in the situation. Friction over the seizures of American vessels would give rise to a feeling of sharp resentment in many American circles, and "Blaine and Company" would make use of this ill-feeling to further their political ends. He emphasized this peril in his letters to Phelps, and Phelps, in turn, warned Lord Rosebery of the mischiefs that might result from the "utterly unscrupulous tactics of Mr. Blaine." Rosebery readily agreed that the existing disputes between Canada and the United States should be speedily settled as a means of checking Republican designs,[12] and as a step in this direction he instructed Sir Lionel West to inquire if the American Government intended to "give notice to the United States fishermen that they are now precluded from fishing in British American territorial waters."[13]

Bayard gave an ambiguous answer to this plain inquiry, but it was evident that no warning had been given to American fishermen.[14] The

10. Sir Lionel West to Lord Salisbury, February 19, 1886, *ibid.*, pp. 54–55.

11. Secretary Bayard to Phelps, March 7, 1886, *Bayard Letter Book*, II, *Bayard MS.*

12. Phelps to Secretary Bayard, March 13, 27, 1886, *Bayard MS.*

13. West to Secretary Bayard, March 19, 1886, *British Legation, Notes from*, CXIII, MS. Dept. of State.

14. Secretary Bayard to Sir Lionel West, March 23, 1886, *British Legation, Notes to*, XX, MS. Dept. of State. In a personal memorandum which West sent to Secretary Bayard, March 19, 1886, attention was called to the expiration of the *modus vivendi* and the liability of American fishing boats to seizure if they frequented the

reason for this inaction was that Bayard wished to make a further study of all the implications in the fisheries controversy. He had recently received a letter from George Steele, President of the American Fishery Union, in which the matter of the right to purchase bait was discussed. Bayard turned this letter over to Francis Wharton, who expressed the view that the refusal to permit the purchase of bait would be a discrimination against the United States, and therefore, would constitute a "violation of treaty obligation."[15]

In his reply to George Steele, Bayard contended that inasmuch as American fishing vessels sailed not only under "regularly issued domestic fishing licenses," but also had "permission to touch and trade at any foreign port prescribed in Revised Statutes, sec. 4364," they should be regarded as either fishing vessels or as regularly enrolled trading vessels according to "the circumstances under which they may enter a foreign port or approach within the three-mile limit of the British-American coast." It was quite clear that an

> American fishing vessel, having obtained permission for foreign trade according to sec. 4364, may rightfully enter any British North American port of entry, on compliance with the regular customs formalities, and there purchase any commodity offered for sale which it may be lawful for any foreign vessel to purchase. The assent of this Government could not be given to any claim of the Imperial or Dominion authorities to prohibit the purchase of supplies, such as food, ice, salt or bait, by an American fishing vessel in a British North American port of entry. The rightfulness of any discrimination against them because they are *fishing* vessels cannot be admitted.

American vessels which had not obtained permission for foreign trade, and which were therefore purely fishing vessels, could not purchase bait within the fishing limits that had been renounced by the Treaty of 1818. But along certain coasts [Labrador and parts of the southern, western and northern coasts of Newfoundland] the inshore

Canadian inshore fisheries. He was certain that the British Government had done "their utmost" to provide the means for a satisfactory solution of the fisheries dispute. *Bayard MS.*

15. *Memorandum* by Francis Wharton, March 31, 1886, *ibid.* In an undated memorandum, Wharton develops his views more at length: "I am clear as to the following: (1) The treaty of 1818 does not exclude our fishing vessels, bearing our flag and complying with port laws in the same way as do other trading vessels, from purchasing bait or anything else in ports of entry. (2) By the law of nations, vessels of all kinds may visit foreign shores, whether at ports of entry or otherwise, when necessity requires. (3) The treaty of 1818, in renouncing the right to 'take' fish in Canadian territorial waters, reserves, by force of the rule 'exclusio unius,' the right to *buy* fish. (4) This 'buying' of fish was held unanimously by the Halifax Commissioners not to be a thing for which compensation could be awarded to Great Britain." *Ibid.*

fishing privileges had been guaranteed by the Treaty of 1818, and even these vessels that were devoted exclusively to fishing had a right in such waters to buy bait.[16]

Bayard next wrote to Spencer F. Baird, Director of the United States Commission on Fish and Fisheries, and inquired if bait were needed only for open-sea fishing (outside the three-mile limit).[17] Baird replied that Bayard was entirely right "in supposing that the question of obtaining bait in Provincial ports affects only vessels fishing upon the high seas." Mackerel were sometimes caught within the three-mile limit, but owing to the introduction of the purse seine, bait was no longer required in this type of fishery.[18]

While Bayard was gathering this information concerning fishing bait, the Senate of the United States was debating Mr. Frye's resolution which declared that Congress should not advise the appointment of a joint commission to settle the fisheries question. The President's recommendation in his message of December 8 received little support even from Democratic Senators, and on April 13 the Frye resolution was adopted by the overwhelming vote of 35 yeas to 10 nays.[19]

To Bayard this debate in the Senate was a "mere blowing of fish horns,"[20] but this raucous chorus took on a more strident note when Canadian officials began to seize American fishing vessels for alleged infractions of the Treaty of 1818. On May 7 the American schooner,

16. Secretary Bayard to George Steele, March, 1886, *ibid.* The confusion that existed in Canadian minds with regard to the enforcement of the provisions of the Treaty of 1818 is revealed in the following excerpt from a despatch sent by M. H. Phelan, United States Consul-General at Halifax, to James D. Porter, Assistant Secretary of State, April 9, 1886. Captain P. A. Scott, in command of the Marine Police, had abruptly ordered all American vessels from Canadian ports and coasts. Phelan asked Captain Scott by what authority he was acting. He replied that his authority would be found "in the Statutes of Canada, but an examination of these statutes resulted in a failure to find such authority. . . . He called the next day to say he found his authority in . . . 59 George III, chap. 38 (year 1818). Being informed that this was an Imperial Act and could not be enforced by a local officer unless such officer was commissioned by the Imperial Government, . . . he stated that a mistake had been made by someone and he would do nothing further until the Minister of Marine and Fisheries passed on these questions." *Halifax, Consular Despatches,* XIV, MS. Dept. of State.

17. Secretary Bayard to S. F. Baird, April 9, 1886, *Bayard Letter Book,* II, *Bayard MS.*

18. S. F. Baird to Secretary Bayard, April 9, 1886, *Bayard MS.* It is significant to note that the mackerel fisheries declined in an extraordinary manner after 1885. In 1885 the New England catch of salt mackerel amounted to 329,943 barrels. In 1886 the catch slumped to 79,998 barrels, and in 1889 it fell to 21,918 barrels. In 1885 the New England catch of codfish amounted to 902,455 quintals; in 1889 it declined to 498,989 quintals. McFarland, *op. cit.,* pp. 369–371.

19. *Congressional Record,* 49 Cong., 1 sess., p. 3440.

20. Secretary Bayard to David A. Wells, April 12, 1886, *Bayard Letter Book,* II, *Bayard MS.*

David J. Adams, was seized in Digby Basin and later towed to St. John, New Brunswick.[21]

As soon as the news of this seizure reached London, Phelps sent a note to Lord Rosebery and expressed his great regret that such action should have been taken "at this juncture when it will be immediately availed on by the party desirous of making trouble with England for the sake of the Irish vote."[22]

In the United States the seizure of the *David J. Adams* aroused widespread protest, and William C. P. Breckinridge hurriedly wrote to Bayard to find out the best way to answer the enemies of the Administration who would undoubtedly endeavor to make political capital out of the incident.[23] Bayard showed that he was not worried about the political intrigues of opponents. Everything possible had been done to protect American interests in Canadian waters, and the correspondence in the Department of State would clearly reveal this fact.[24]

The immediate task facing Bayard was to pen a protest to Sir Lionel West with reference to seizures of American fishing vessels in Canadian waters. With the aid of Alvey A. Adee and Francis Wharton, a strong note was hurriedly prepared and sent to the British Minister on May 10. It was long and closely-reasoned. Attention was directed to the fact that the seizures of American vessels had been in land-locked harbors where there had been no intention on the part of American fishermen to engage in fishing.[25] A short summary was then given of the legislation enacted by the British and American Governments with reference to the establishment of commercial contacts between the United States and British colonial possessions. These contacts would be seriously affected if the restrictive measures recently adopted by the colonial authorities

21. The *David J. Adams* was condemned and sold by order of the Vice-Admiralty Court in 1889. The case was brought before the miscellaneous claims tribunal which began its work in 1913 and completed the first schedule submitted to it in 1926. The *Adams* had been seized for purchasing bait, but inasmuch as the Act of 1886 (49 Vict., c. 114) had been passed subsequent to this seizure, and in consideration of the innocence and poverty of the owner, the tribunal urged the British Government, as an act of grace, to compensate him for his loss. Fred K. Nielsen, *American and British Claims Arbitration* (Washington, 1926), pp. 432–435.

22. Phelps to Secretary Bayard, May 8, 1886, *Bayard MS.*

23. W. C. P. Breckinridge to Secretary Bayard, May 9, 1886, *ibid.*

24. Secretary Bayard to W. C. P. Breckinridge, May 10, 1886, *Bayard Letter Book,* II, *Bayard MS.*

25. The viewpoint of the Canadian Government is clearly expressed in a note from Lord Lansdowne to Sir John Macdonald, July 5, 1886: "Our contention is, I take it, simply that the purchase of bait does constitute a preparation to fish; that it is not necessary to establish that the fishing for which preparation is made is illegal fishing; that in the case of the 'Nickerson' the court adopted this view, and that we have taken the first opportunity of testing the law." *Macdonald Papers, Governor-General's Correspondence,* XIII, 396–397, P.A.C.

were permitted to remain in force. The Treaty of 1818 was made by the United States and Great Britain as the high contracting parties, and they alone could deal "responsibly with questions arising thereunder."

The action of Canadian officials would not only seriously interfere with the operations of American fishermen on the high seas but would also "practically destroy" the right of American vessels to visit the inshore waters along the Canadian coast for the objects of "shelter, repair of damages, and purchasing wood and obtaining water." Owing to the extensive use of the purse seine, the purchase of bait had reference only to fishing outside the three-mile limit, and any action taken to prevent such purchases would be equivalent to expanding the terms of the Treaty of 1818 to objects "wholly beyond its purview, scope and intent." In view of the fact that there was no longer any inducement for American fishermen to dry and cure fish on the interdicted coasts of the Canadian Provinces, and as bait was no longer used or needed in order to "take" fish in the inshore waters, the recent seizures of American vessels for exercising the "reasonable rights and privileges of trade" were unwarranted and showed a most unfriendly spirit.

The customary rights and privileges extended to American vessels in Canadian ports should include the "purchase of ship-supplies of every nature, making repairs, the shipment of crews in whole or part, and the purchase of ice and bait for use in deep-sea fishing." These same rights and privileges had long been

> freely extended to and are fully enjoyed by the Canadian merchant marine of all occupations, including fishermen, in the ports of the United States.

The American Government would do anything in its power to cause its citizens to conform to the obligations of the Treaty of 1818, but it was highly important that ordinary commercial intercourse between the United States and Canada be free from "harsh measures and unfriendly administration."[26]

Phelps, in London, was in entire agreement with Bayard's viewpoint. Canadian officials had been too rigorous in their enforcement of the Treaty of 1818. If a technical infraction of the terms of that treaty had been committed by American fishermen, that did not "authorize the seizure and confiscation of the vessel." Neither the provisions of the treaty nor any rule of international law justified such a proceeding. They might as well "hang the crew."[27]

26. Secretary Bayard to Sir Lionel West, May 10, 1886, *British Legation, Notes to*, XX, MS. Dept. of State.

27. Phelps to Secretary Bayard, May 11, 1886, *Bayard MS.*

On May 11, Mr. M. H. Phelan, the United States Consul-General at Halifax, sent a telegram to the Department of State in which he declared that the charge against the *Adams* for "violating the Customs was so trifling that it seems they have abandoned it and gone back to the charge of violating the Fishery laws. The officers don't seem to know what to do."[28]

Impressed with the gravity of the situation, Bayard expressed to Sir Lionel West the opinion that the summary seizure of the *Adams* had not only furnished a cause for "retaliatory action" but had also created serious "new difficulties."[29] The British Minister promised to telegraph to Lord Lansdowne to see what could be done in the matter,[30] and Bayard remarked that he hoped the Governor-General would be able to secure "more circumspect and amicable action upon the part of the Canadian officials."[31]

Lansdowne was entirely willing to advise Canadian officials to be more "circumspect and amicable" in their relations with Americans, but he had no intention of receding from the position that the Canadian Government had taken. He informed Sir Lionel West that the legal proceedings against the *Adams* were based on three counts—violation of the Customs Act of 1883, the Dominion Fishery Act of 1868, and the Treaty of 1818.[32]

Two days later, Lansdowne wrote to Sir John Macdonald with reference to the note that Bayard had sent to Sir Lionel West on May 10. He did not agree with Bayard's statement that the attitude of the Canadian Government in the matter of the seizure of the *Adams* indicated an attempt to impede the "ordinary commercial intercourse of the two countries." He denied that American fishing vessels had a right to trade in Canadian ports. The refusal to sell bait to American fishermen, even though this bait was used exclusively in deep-sea fishing, was not a "destructive expansion" of the Treaty of 1818. The object of that treaty was to protect Canadian fishing interests in the same manner that tariff walls had protected American industries. Bayard's attempt

28. M. H. Phelan to James D. Porter, May 11, 1886, *ibid.* In order to enforce the restrictive fishing laws and regulations, Canadian officials boarded some 700 fishing vessels in 1886, and 1362 in 1887. See *Special Report on the Fisheries Protective Service of Canada, 1886* (Ottawa, 1887); *Correspondence Relative to the Fisheries Question, 1885–1887* (Ottawa, 1887); *Senate Ex. Doc. No. 221,* 49 Cong., 1 sess.; *House Ex. Doc. No. 19,* 49 Cong., 2 sess.; *Senate Rept. No. 1683,* 49 Cong., 2 sess.; *C.S.P., 1887,* No. 16. For a useful summary of the situation, see Isham, *op. cit.*

29. Secretary Bayard to Sir Lionel West, May 11, 1886, *Bayard MS.*

30. West to Secretary Bayard, May 12, 1886, *ibid.*

31. Secretary Bayard to West, May 12, 1886, *Bayard Letter Book,* II, *Bayard MS.*

32. West to Secretary Bayard, May 13, 1886, *ibid.*

to "impugn" the validity of the restrictive legislation was ill-advised. That legislation had been confirmed by the Imperial Government, and it was as "valid as an Imperial Statute."[33]

But Lansdowne was anxious for a "final and complete settlement" of the points at issue between Canada and the United States,[34] so he wrote to Sir John Macdonald to inquire if it would not be possible to "concoct a mollifying despatch to Sir L. West explaining Captain Scott's conduct and expressing an anxiety to act in the spirit of Mr. Bayard's letter."[35] It is evident that Lansdowne's outlook was far broader than that of Macdonald. He kept constantly in mind the interests of the British Empire as a whole, while Macdonald confined his vision largely to Canada.

This contrast in viewpoint is clearly shown in 1886 when Macdonald stood sponsor for a bill in the Dominion Parliament which would broaden the provisions of the Act of 1868. Lansdowne opposed the new legislation as unnecessary and provocative. In the existing dispute with the United States it was important to exclude all feelings of "bitterness." If at the very beginning of the present controversy the Canadian Government should seek to gain an advantage by a "sort of legislative *coup de main*," this action would increase the tension that was already rising. The existing law supplied a remedy against the masters of American vessels guilty of infractions of the Treaty of 1818. The remedy was a "clumsy one," but it was good enough to serve in the present contingency.[36]

On the following day, Lansdowne wrote two more notes to Sir John Macdonald in an attempt to convince him that it was expedient to adopt a more moderate attitude towards the United States. With reference to the threat of American retaliatory legislation, it should be noted that the bills introduced by Senator Frye and Representative Dingley would merely prevent "Canadian *fishing* vessels from trading in United States ports." This type of legislation would not hurt Canadian interests and it could be safely ignored.[37]

In this regard, Lansdowne was quite mistaken. Canadian fishermen had long followed the practice of fitting out their vessels in Gloucester, Massachusetts, where they could purchase supplies more cheaply than

33. Lansdowne to Sir John Macdonald, May 15, 1886, *Macdonald Papers, Governor-General's Correspondence,* XIII, P.A.C.

34. Lansdowne to Lord Granville, May 18, 1886, Lord Newton, *op. cit.,* p. 41.

35. Lansdowne to Sir John Macdonald, May 14, 1886, *Macdonald Papers, Governor-General's Correspondence,* XIII, 160–161, P.A.C.

36. Lansdowne to Sir John Macdonald, May 20, 1886, *ibid.,* pp. 171–174.

37. Lansdowne to Sir John Macdonald, May 21, 1886, *ibid.,* pp. 180–182.

in Canadian ports.[38] These commercial privileges so freely extended to Canadian fishermen who visited American ports, were not only denied to American fishermen who sought to buy bait in Canadian harbors, but to masters of vessels who attempted to purchase herring for export.[39]

Confronted with this situation which constantly grew more serious, Bayard engaged the services of two distinguished lawyers, William L. Putnam of Portland, Maine, and George W. Biddle, of Philadelphia. They were requested to go at once to Halifax, Nova Scotia, and take part in the case of the *David J. Adams* which was being tried in the vice-admiralty court.[40] Bayard then addressed a note to Sir Lionel West in which he reviewed the new evidence with reference to the summary seizure of the *Adams*. There was little doubt that the circumstances surrounding this seizure were of a character that boded ill for continued friendly relations between Canada and the United States.[41]

On May 21 Bayard had a conference with Sir Lionel West, who read a telegram from Lord Rosebery that clearly showed the evident eagerness of the British Government to find some formula that would settle the fisheries controversy. West himself offered three suggestions: he thought it might be expedient to revise the terms of the Treaty of 1818; to suspend all retaliatory legislation; and to initiate negotiations for some sort of commercial reciprocity between the United States and Canada. But Bayard was in no hurry to revise the Treaty of 1818. The

38. Secretary Bayard to W. C. P. Breckinridge, May 15, 1886, *Bayard Letter Book*, II, *Bayard MS.*

39. Secretary Bayard to Sir Lionel West, May 20, 1886, *ibid.* Bayard was specifically referring to the refusal of the authorities at Digby, Nova Scotia, to sell herring for export. Senator W. P. Frye wrote to Bayard on May 20 and protested against such action. In reply, Bayard stated that he regarded the adverse attitude of the Canadian officials as a "gross breach of the commercial rights of a citizen of the United States." He assured the importunate Senator that the "interests and honor" of the United States were not suffering through any neglect on the part of the Democratic Administration. Bayard to Senator W. P. Frye, *ibid.*

40. Secretary Bayard to W. L. Putnam, May 20, 1886, and Bayard to G. W. Biddle, May 20, 1886, *ibid.*

41. Secretary Bayard to Sir Lionel West, May 20, 1886, *British Legation, Notes to*, XX, MS. Dept. of State. The treatment accorded to the captain and crew of the *David J. Adams* was commented upon by Bayard in this note to West: "By the information thus derived it would appear that after four several and distinct visitations by boats' crews from the *Lansdowne,* in Annapolis Basin, Nova Scotia, the *David J. Adams* was summarily taken into custody by the . . . *Lansdowne* and carried out of the Province of Nova Scotia, . . . and into the port of St. John, New Brunswick, and without explanation, . . . taken back again by an armed crew to Digby, in Nova Scotia. . . . In Digby the paper alleged to be the legal precept for the capture and detention of the vessel was nailed to her mast in such manner as to prevent its contents being read. . . . Nor was the United States consul-general able to learn from the commander of the *Lansdowne* the nature of the complaint against the vessel."

main difficulty in that regard was with reference to the strained interpretation that Canadian officials placed upon its terms. After listening to Bayard's remarks, West suggested the advisability of a new *modus vivendi.*[42] Two days later, West sent to Bayard a confidential note containing an outline of the proposed arrangement. In view of all the circumstances in the case, it would seem that the British and American Governments could formally "declare their intention of at once entering into negotiations on the subject, pending which all restrictive and retaliatory actions should be suspended."[43]

Bayard had already indicated in an instruction to Phelps the main points that should be included in any *modus vivendi.* He also inquired whether American vessels that had been seized in Canadian waters would be released without prejudice, and if instructions could be issued that would prevent, pending the negotiations, any further enforcement of the Treaty of 1818 except under Imperial authority.[44]

When Phelps asked Lord Rosebery if the seizures of American vessels could not be discontinued at once, he received the reply that the British Government would "have difficulty in asking the Dominion Government to suspend their legal action if nothing were offered as a *quid pro quo.*" Rosebery then inquired if some indication could be given of American readiness to negotiate upon this fisheries problem. In reply, Phelps stated that President Cleveland could negotiate "without consulting the Senate," and he was certain there would be no difficulty in reaching a satisfactory arrangement.[45]

Rosebery, however, was so noncommittal that Phelps believed the

42. *Memorandum* written by Bayard after a conference with Sir Lionel West, May 21, 1886, *Bayard MS.* The importance to American fishermen of the right to purchase bait in Canadian ports was obvious to Bayard. There were a few shipments of bait from Canada to Gloucester or Boston, but most American fishermen were compelled to visit Canadian ports to secure the necessary bait. See L. Saltonstall to Secretary Bayard, May 24, 25, 1886, and W. A. Wilcox to E. T. Colby, May 24, 1886, *ibid.* The difference in the attitude of the American and the Canadian authorities with reference to the right of fishing vessels to carry on commercial operations was clearly exemplified in a letter that J. B. Richardson wrote to Representative John D. Long, May 16, 1886. Some years previous, a small vessel from Nova Scotia had "put into the port of Gloucester, Massachusetts, where it was learned that the master had on board . . . a few pairs of woolen socks. . . . The whole value of the socks was less than $15 or $20, but they were of Nova Scotia *manufacture* and were *dutiable,* and his . . . vessel was *less than 100 tons burden,* and for this . . . the *cargo* and *vessel* were both liable to forfeiture to the United States, and they were libelled and seized. . . . The Secretary of the Treasury, . . . after a full investigation, stopped the proceedings for forfeiture, and ordered the vessel and cargo restored to the master after his paying the trifling duty and the costs of the proceedings." *Ibid.*

43. Sir Lionel West to Secretary Bayard, May 23, 1886, *Personal, Bayard MS.*

44. Secretary Bayard to Phelps, May 22, 1886, *Great Britain, Instructions,* XXVIII, MS. Dept. of State.

45. Phelps to Secretary Bayard, May 29, 1886, *Personal, Bayard MS.*

American Government might have to take "strong and decided ground" in order to compel some speedy action in the matter of a *modus vivendi*. Before receiving this letter, Bayard had already sent to Phelps an instruction that strongly protested against a bill that was pending in the Canadian Parliament. It was the same bill that had awakened the apprehension of Lord Lansdowne.[46] Phelps was to inform Lord Rosebery that the United States would hold the British Government liable for all losses which might be sustained by American citizens "in the dispossession of their property growing out of the search, seizure, detention or sale of their vessels lawfully within the territorial waters of British North America."[47]

In response to this instruction, Phelps secured an interview with Lord Rosebery, who did not seem "inclined to interfere with Canadian action." Rosebery also complained that the American Government did not seem eager to enter upon negotiations for a settlement of the fisheries dispute. Phelps then pointed out that it was a most unpropitious time to commence negotiations when Canadian cruisers were busily engaged upon the seizure of American fishing vessels.[48]

These strong protests from Bayard awakened a definite alarm in the minds of British officials in the Foreign Office. Sir Lionel West expressed to Lord Lansdowne the opinion that the situation was "serious,"[49] and Lord Rosebery, who at first upheld the Canadian view of the fishery question, began to have serious doubts about the expediency of this stand. This new viewpoint was communicated to Lord Granville, who promptly cabled to Lansdowne to see if it were not possible to have this proposed Canadian legislation set aside.[50]

46. This was House of Commons Bill No. 136. It proposed the "forcible search, seizure, and forfeiture of any foreign vessel within any harbor in Canada, or hovering within three marine miles of any of the coasts, bays, creeks, or harbors in Canada, where such vessel has entered such waters for any purpose not permitted by the laws of nations, or by treaty or convention, or by any law of the United Kingdom, or of Canada now in force."

47. Secretary Bayard to Phelps, May 29, 1886, *Great Britain, Instructions,* XVIII, MS. Dept. of State. In a note of the same day (May 29) to Sir Lionel West, Bayard expressed the views that the proposed Canadian legislation was highly objectionable because it contained the "wholly unwarranted proposition" that Canadian officials could enforce the provisions of the Treaty of 1818 according to their own construction of that convention. Secretary Bayard to Sir Lionel West, May 29, 1886, *British Legation, Notes to,* XX, MS. Dept. of State.

48. Phelps to Secretary Bayard, May 29, 1886, *Great Britain, Despatches,* CLIII, MS. Dept. of State. See also Sir Charles Tupper to Sir John Macdonald, May 27, 1886, Saunders, *op. cit.,* II, 94.

49. Lansdowne to Sir John Macdonald, May 30, 1886, quoted in Tansill, *Bayard,* p. 223.

50. Lord Granville to Lansdowne, June 2, 1886, *Macdonald Papers, Governor-General's Correspondence,* XIII, 201, P.A.C.

After receiving this telegram, Lansdowne thought there was "no course open but to 'reserve' the Bill."[51] Sir John Macdonald disagreed with this viewpoint. It seemed to him that the bill should be "disallowed by Lord Granville, . . . rather than reserved by you." No harm could be done by its enactment by the Dominion Legislature. There could be no conviction for months under the new act, and long before that could take place, Lord Granville would have plenty of time to make up his mind "on the question of disallowance." It would be unwise to give way before Bayard's protests.[52]

But Lansdowne was not convinced by Sir John's reasoning, and he was prepared to "reserve" the bill.[53] But this action was not enough to satisfy Granville who had become thoroughly alarmed at the situation. In a telegram to Lansdowne he complained that he could not "understand" the position taken by the Dominion Government in the matter of continued seizures of American fishing vessels. Such a policy would "necessarily preclude friendly negotiations."[54]

Lansdowne was somewhat piqued at the peremptory tone of Lord Granville's telegram. He was certain that the Colonial Secretary did not fully realize the consequences of an announcement that "no further seizures are to be made, nor does he explain whether his suggestion is that all seizures . . . are to be discontinued, or whether he would like us to make the concession only in reference to vessels attempting to buy bait or to enter our harbours for a purpose not specified as lawful." He hoped, however, that there would not be "many more seizures."[55]

This impatience on the part of Lord Granville is partly explained by the strong pressure that was being exerted by the American Government upon the Foreign Office. On June 2, Phelps sent to Lord Rosebery a long note in which the attitude of the Department of State was given firm and cogent expression. In conclusion, Phelps trenchantly remarked: "In any view, therefore, which it seems to me can be taken of this question, I feel justified in pronouncing the action of the Canadian

51. Lansdowne to Sir John Macdonald, June 2, 1886, *ibid.*, p. 199.

52. Sir John Macdonald to Lansdowne, June 2, 1886, *ibid.*, p. 294.

53. Lansdowne to Sir John Macdonald, June 2, 1886, *ibid.*, p. 203. In a telegram to Lord Granville, June 2, 1886, Lansdowne said: "Please have it clearly explained that bill is reserved solely on the ground mentioned in my telegram of this day. We object altogether to position taken by Bayard in despatch May 29th. Great indignation will be felt here if reservation should be construed as acquiescence by Her Majesty's Government in Bayard's contention as to competence of Canadian Parliament and authorities." *Ibid.*, p. 205. This bill was reserved on June 2, 1886, but was approved on November 26, 1886.

54. Lord Granville to Lansdowne, June 3, 1886, *ibid.*, p. 214.

55. Lansdowne to Sir John Macdonald, June 4, 1886, *ibid.*, pp. 210–212.

authorities in seizing and still retaining the *David J. Adams*, to be not only unfriendly and discourteous, but altogether unwarrantable."[56]

In a personal letter to Bayard, Phelps explained that he had written his note to Lord Rosebery "in some haste and without access to all the documents" in the case, but he thought that it presented the American viewpoint with "sufficient accuracy and distinctness."[57] Bayard assured him that he had read the note with "much satisfaction," and that the "views and arguments" contained therein were "fully in accord" with the instructions that had already been sent to London.[58]

In the meantime, Bayard had warned Sir Lionel West that there was no "possible justification" for the "harsh and harassing actions" of the Canadian authorities against "peaceful commerce."[59] The length to which these Canadian officials would go in their enforcement of treaty provisions is revealed in a note from Alvey A. Adee to Bayard. An American fishing vessel had landed at a Prince Edward Island port and purchased some potatoes. The authorities at that port hastily boarded the vessel and not only seized the potatoes, "but administered an emetic to the Captain and landed the mate's ejections so as to make sure that no insular potato should be taken out of port by an American fisherman."[60]

Lansdowne himself recognized that at times the intemperate zeal of

56. Phelps to Lord Rosebery, June 2, 1886, enclosed in Phelps to Bayard, June 5, 1886, *Great Britain, Despatches,* CLIII, MS. Dept. of State. The argument employed by Phelps in his note to Lord Rosebery was clear and to the point. He did not understand it to be "claimed by the Canadian authorities that the vessel seized has been engaged or was intending to engage in fishing within any limit prohibited by the treaty of 1818. The occupation of the vessel was exclusively deep-sea fishing, a business in which it had a perfect right to be employed. The ground upon which the capture was made was that the master of the vessel had purchased of an inhabitant of Nova Scotia . . . a small quantity of bait to be used in fishing in the deep sea, outside the three-mile limit. The question presented is whether, under the terms of the treaty, . . . that transaction affords a sufficient reason for making such a seizure and for proceeding under it to the confiscation of the vessel and its contents. . . . Such a literal construction [of the Treaty of 1818] is best refuted by considering its preposterous consequences. If a vessel enters a port to post a letter, or send a telegram, or buy a newspaper, . . . it would, upon this construction, be held to violate the treaty stipulations maintained between two enlightened . . . nations. . . . If a vessel is not engaged in fishing she may enter all ports; but if employed in fishing, not denied to be lawful, she is excluded, though on the most innocent errand. . . . At the time of the seizure of the *David J. Adams* and other vessels there was no Act whatever, either of the British or Colonial Parliaments, which made the purchase of bait by those vessels illegal."

57. Phelps to Secretary Bayard, June 5, 1886, *Personal, Bayard MS.*

58. Secretary Bayard to Phelps, June 18, 1886, *Great Britain, Instructions,* XXVIII, MS. Dept. of State.

59. Secretary Bayard to Sir Lionel West, June 1, 1886, *Bayard MS.*

60. A. A. Adee to Secretary Bayard, June 1, 1886, *ibid.*

Canadian customs officers had carried them too far. In a note to Sir John Macdonald he deprecated the action of the authorities in this "potato case." Their attitude had been "needlessly vexatious." If officials pounced upon every American boat which "spends a few cents in our waters, I fear we shall accumulate against ourselves such a volume of irritation as to render a reasonable settlement unattainable."[61]

This irritation was constantly mounting because of the actions of Canadian officials. The special counsel employed by Bayard (W. L. Putnam and George W. Biddle) after a careful examination of all the evidence in connection with the seizures of American vessels, reported that the charges lodged against American skippers were largely inconsequential and could have been overlooked. With reference to the purchase of bait, there was "grave doubt" whether there was any statute covering that question. Research had failed to discover any law which made it an offence "to purchase bait or other supplies in Dominion waters."[62]

This "needlessly vexatious" attitude on the part of Canadian officials aroused open resentment in the United States, and this was reflected in the actions of certain members of the President's Cabinet. Secretary of the Navy Whitney wished to have a squadron of American warships sent to Canadian waters to protect American fishermen. Bayard knew that such an action might lead to serious trouble. A certain American rear-admiral had recently used very explosive language in Central American waters in connection with the defence of American rights, and there was a possibility that these same "violent expressions" might be used by other naval officers in more northerly latitudes. Before taking any action in this regard, Bayard advised Whitney to bring the matter before the President's Cabinet for careful consideration.[63] (As Secre-

61. Lansdowne to Sir John Macdonald, June 5, 1886, *Macdonald Papers, Governor-General's Correspondence,* XIII, 230–232. Sir John Macdonald was not as conciliatory as Lansdowne, and he often growled at the Yankee attitude towards the fishery question. In a letter to Sir Charles Tupper, June 10, 1886, he observed: "The American Government has not behaved well in the Fishery matter. The President, with the best intentions, agreed to recommend a Joint Commission to Congress and to press it; but the Republicans . . . snub him on every occasion and refuse to entertain his recommendation. The Irish in the United States . . . have sided with the Yankee fishermen, and the Republicans are working strongly for the Fenian vote. The President and the Democrats, seeing this, have regularly caved in, and are going one better than Blaine." Saunders, *op. cit.,* II, 95.

62. W. L. Putnam to Secretary Bayard, June 4, 1886, *Bayard MS.*

63. Secretary Bayard to Secretary W. C. Whitney, June 5, 1886, *Personal and Confidential, Bayard MS.* On this same day, June 5, 1886, Mr. George Steele, President of the American Fishery Union, addressed a letter to Bayard in which he suggested that American warships be sent to Canadian waters "to protect our flag, our citizens, and their property." *F.R., 1886,* p. 502.

tary of the Navy, Whitney was also a thorn in Bayard's side in the Samoan difficulties that were mounting each day.)

If British officials had been as belligerent as Secretary Whitney, the friction over the seizures of American vessels might have developed into a dangerous quarrel. But Lord Granville strongly desired to find some formula that would save the situation, and he placed strong pressure upon Lord Lansdowne. Lansdowne was cautious about giving any sweeping promises. He did assure Granville, however, that there would be no further seizures except for "clear and deliberate violations" of the Treaty of 1818 and of the Canadian statutes enforcing it.[64]

Before making this promise to Lord Granville, Lansdowne had conferred with Sir John Macdonald. The Canadian Prime Minister was of the opinion that the Dominion Government could not make any far-reaching concessions for the fishing season of 1886. Canada had met with "nothing but ingratitude and discourtesy for . . . doing so last year."[65] But he was willing to have instructions issued to Captain Scott directing him "not to seize vessels merely for buying bait."[66] He also indicated to Lansdowne that he was in complete agreement with the view that everything should be done to avoid "all causes of irritation and that the undue zeal of our officers should be restrained."[67] In reply to these notes, Lansdowne remarked that he was "glad that we are, for the present, to have no more seizures for trading."[68]

This conciliatory disposition might lead to happy results, but Bayard was fearful that if he should go ahead and initiate negotiations looking towards some settlement of the fisheries controversy, the Republican majority in the Senate would reject any treaty or even *modus vivendi* that would be placed before it. Despite these doubts, he felt it was his duty as Secretary of State to "go straight ahead" and endeavor to "procure a reasonable, equitable and just settlement of this long-vexed question."[69]

In London, Phelps was suspicious of the real attitude of the British

64. Lansdowne to Lord Granville, June 7, 1886, *Macdonald Papers, Governor-General's Correspondence,* XIII, 259, 465–470, P.A.C.

65. Sir John Macdonald to Lansdowne, June 5, 1886, *ibid.,* pp. 300–302.

66. Sir John Macdonald to Lansdowne, June 6, 1886, *ibid.,* p. 306.

67. Sir John Macdonald to Lansdowne, June 7, 1886, *ibid.,* p. 312.

68. Lansdowne to Sir John Macdonald, June 8, 1886, *ibid.,* pp. 260–261.

69. Secretary Bayard to Phelps, June 9, 1886, *Personal, Bayard Letter Book,* II, *Bayard MS.* In a letter to Lord Lansdowne, June 5, 1886, Sir Lionel West remarks: "The Secretary of State is accused of not acting with sufficient vigour, and if Blaine takes the matter up for electioneering purposes, the Senate will refuse to sanction any arrangement simply in order to keep up the irritation." *Macdonald Papers, Governor-General's Correspondence,* XIII, 265, P.A.C.

Government. He was confident that the Foreign Office would be very reluctant to take any action that would be distasteful to Canada. A show of force was the only way to clarify the situation. If Bayard would take some "very decided and sharp ground," the British Government would show a conciliatory spirit.[70]

Bayard was willing to take very decided ground with reference to the question of the right of the Dominion authorities to enforce the provisions of the Treaty of 1818. In a letter to Phelps (June 18) he expressed the view that the "law officers of the Crown should have an opportunity to come to a decision on the proper enforcement to be given to the Treaty of 1818, and of the necessity of Great Britain enforcing upon her provinces a sense of *her* responsibility under it."[71]

In this regard Bayard's stand was distinctly dubious. Canadian authorities were certain that the Dominion Parliament had the right to pass laws enforcing treaties between the United States and Great Britain. In a letter to Lord Granville, Lansdowne gives clear expression to the Canadian viewpoint:

Your Lordship is no doubt aware that legislation of this kind has been frequently resorted to by the Parliament of the Dominion for the purpose of enforcing Treaties. . . . The right of the Dominion Parliament to legislate for these purposes . . . has not been seriously called in question. Such legislation, unless it is disallowed by the Imperial Government, becomes a part of the law of the Empire.[72]

This matter of the competence of the Dominion Parliament to enact legislation for the enforcement of treaties was a subject that gave great uneasiness to Sir Lionel West. He was fearful that "Blaine, Frye & Company" would try to make it appear that the Dominion Government had been disavowed by the British Ministry. There was no doubt

70. Phelps to Secretary Bayard, June 15, 1886, *Personal, Bayard MS.* In London, Sir Charles Tupper was doing his utmost to stiffen British opposition to any concessions to the United States. He had directed his efforts "to convincing the Government and all concerned that the only way to reach a satisfactory solution was by the firm and unflinching maintenance of our rights." Saunders, *op. cit.,* II, 95.

71. Secretary Bayard to Phelps, June 18, 1886, *Personal, Bayard Letter Book,* II, *Bayard MS.*

72. Lansdowne to Lord Granville, June 7, 1886, quoted in Tansill, *Bayard,* p. 231. In a letter from N. H. Meagher to W. L. Putnam, June 16, 1886, the statement is made: "There is a great deal of force in the contention that under the Dominion Act (the British North America Act, 1867) Great Britain has delegated her powers in respect to inland and coast fisheries to the Dominion." Putnam had much the same idea, and he frankly expressed his opinion in a previous letter to Meagher, June 11, 1886, *Bayard MS.*

that Blaine wanted "some foreign question for a 'platform,' and catches at any straw that may be blowing about."[73]

But Blaine was not the only American who was looking for trouble in the summer of 1886. Secretary Whitney still nursed a belligerent feeling towards Canada, and he was making active preparations for a cruise of American warships in Canadian waters. Such a cruise might lead to unpleasant incidents with international complications. In order that the commander of the American naval squadron be prepared to meet any emergency that could possibly develop, Whitney thought it expedient to have Professor J. R. Soley accompany the fleet as an adviser upon questions of international law. He informed Soley that American relations with Great Britain concerning Canada were moving "satisfactorily at present," but we should be "prepared for a change."[74] These were ominous words.

When Bayard inquired as to the precise scope of the duties that had been assigned to Professor Soley,[75] Whitney replied that inasmuch as certain incidents might arise while the American fleet was in Canadian waters, it was important to attach someone to the staff of the commanding officer in order that no "blunders" be committed through "ignorance of the law."[76]

At the same time that Secretary Whitney was making preparations to send a squadron of American warships to Canadian waters, Lord Lansdowne was writing to Lord Granville to request the "support of the Queen's ships on the Halifax Station." There was no doubt in Lansdowne's mind that this support would be very "valuable," and he was at great pains to point out to the Colonial Secretary how "much its absence will be felt if it is withheld."[77]

This request met with little support from Granville, who was striving to remove all friction between Canada and the United States.[78] The

73. Sir Lionel West to Lord Lansdowne, June 25, 1886, *Macdonald Papers, Governor-General's Correspondence,* XIII, 399–401, P.A.C.

74. Secretary W. C. Whitney to Secretary Bayard, June 27, 1886, *Bayard MS.*

75. Secretary Bayard to Secretary Whitney, June 28, 1886, *ibid.*

76. Secretary Whitney to Secretary Bayard, June 28, 1886, *ibid.* On July 5, 1886, Robert Winthrop wrote to Bayard and expressed the view that it would be expedient to have a body of American police "to arrest our Fishermen when they are doing wrong, and to protect them when they are doing right—the arbitrary seizure of American fishermen by British cruisers is apt to stir the blood on a 4th of July." *Ibid.*

77. Lansdowne to Sir John Macdonald, July 1, 1886, quoted in Tansill, *Bayard,* p. 232.

78. Lansdowne to Sir John Macdonald, July 2, 1886, quoted in Tansill, *ibid.,* p. 232. See also, Granville to Lansdowne, June 24, 1886, and Lansdowne to Sir John Macdonald, June 25, 1886, *Macdonald Papers, Governor-General's Correspondence,* XIII, 368–373, P.A.C.

British Ministry was evidently embarrassed by the attitude of Canadian officials, and every effort was made to settle a dispute which might develop into open conflict.[79]

In the United States there was a great deal of tinder that only awaited a spark to start a blaze of anti-British prejudice. Bayard believed that there was a large class that could be "easily kindled into noisy aggression." The situation had such dangerous possibilities that he was amazed that the Foreign Office had not exerted strong pressure upon Canadian officials in favor of a more friendly attitude towards American fishermen.[80] The attitude of these officials was, at times, exceedingly vexatious. The secretive manner in which they administered the fishery regulations was unfair and highly irritating.[81] Their conduct in this regard had grown so unjustifiable that "serious consequences" might easily develop.[82]

To Phelps it was plain that the "dignified, friendly and courteous remonstrances" that the American Government had made to the Foreign Office had been "entirely unavailing." The American Government must "either submit to these outrages, or give the British Government distinctly to understand that they will not be submitted to, and that reprisals will be immediately made unless peaceable redress is given."[83]

Such a bold course would be successful only in the event that Bayard had the united support of Congress and the country at large. From the Republican majority in the Senate he could expect nothing but political sabotage. On July 10 the Senate passed a resolution which requested the President to communicate any information in the possession of the Government "concerning the alleged seizure of the United States fishing vessel *David J. Adams* while engaged in lawful commerce in one of the ports in the Dominion of Canada."[84] The President promptly responded to this Senatorial request,[85] and Bayard had to answer many personal requests for additional information. But these inquiries were made for the purpose of gathering political ammunition and they did not indicate any growing support of a Presidential policy of defiance to Canada. Indeed, it was clear that the attitude of the Senate Com-

79. Phelps to Secretary Bayard, June 26, 1886, *Personal, Bayard MS.*

80. Secretary Bayard to Phelps, July 3, 1886, *Personal, Bayard Letter Book,* III, *Bayard MS.*

81. Secretary Bayard to W. L. Putnam, July 16, 1886, *Personal, Bayard MS.*

82. Secretary Bayard to Phelps, July 17, 1886, *Personal, Bayard Letter Book,* III, *Bayard MS.*

83. Phelps to Secretary Bayard, July 20, 1886, *Personal, Bayard MS.*

84. *House Ex. Doc. No. 19,* 49 Cong., 2 sess., p. 141.

85. *Ibid.,* pp. 140–146.

mittee on Foreign Relations was decidedly partisan. Their "noble ambition" was limited to "obstruction and contradiction."[86]

While he was busily engaged in meeting the attacks of Republicans in the Senate, Bayard became involved in fresh difficulties with Canadian officials. On July 30 he sent a note of protest to Sir Lionel West with reference to the illegal action of the customs officer on the northwestern coast of Newfoundland in driving from the waters of Bonne Bay the American schooner, *Thomas F. Bayard.* Under the terms of the Treaty of 1818 these waters were open to American fishermen, and the expulsion of the schooner was a "flagrant violation" of treaty rights.[87]

In a personal letter to Phelps, Bayard also drew attention to the action of Canadian authorities in denying to American fishermen the right to enter Chaleur Bay. Inasmuch as this bay was "over twenty miles wide at its mouth," it was only upon the "headland pretension" that this alleged right to exclude American vessels could be based. During this time of tension with Canada it was comforting to hear that there was a possibility that Lord Iddesleigh might be made Secretary for Foreign Affairs in the new British Cabinet. Such an appointment would be a good augury for better relations between England and the United States.[88]

But Lord Rosebery showed that he was sincerely desirous of good relations between the United States and Great Britain by instructing Sir Lionel West to inform Bayard that the British Government was prepared to enter upon a "frank and friendly consideration" of the fishery question, with a "most earnest desire" to arrive at a settlement "consonant with the rights and interests of Canada and of the United States."[89] As early as July 1, 1886, Sir John Macdonald had broached

86. Secretary Bayard to Phelps, July 29, 1886, *Personal, Bayard Letter Book,* III.

87. Secretary Bayard to Sir Lionel West, July 30, 1886, *British Legation, Notes to,* XX, MS. Dept. of State.

88. Secretary Bayard to Phelps, July 29, 1886, *Personal, Bayard Letter Book,* III, *Bayard MS.* In a letter to Lord Granville, Lansdowne made the following pertinent remarks about the Canadian attitude towards Chaleur Bay: "It is not necessary upon the present occasion that I should recur to the past history of the 'Headlands Question,' or that I should do more than state that Mr. Bayard's suggestion that the Bay des Chaleurs does not form a part of the waters from which United States fishermen are excluded, is one in which my Government cannot acquiesce. Throughout the negotiations which have at different times taken place in regard to these waters, no such admission has ever been made on the part of the Dominion, or, as far as I am aware, by the Imperial Government." Lansdowne to Lord Granville, August 4, 1886, *Macdonald Papers, Governor-General's Correspondence,* XIII, 521–522, P.A.C.

89. Lord Rosebery to Sir Lionel West, July 23, 1886, enclosed in a note from Charles Hardinge to Bayard, August 2, 1886, *British Legation, Notes from,* CXIII, MS. Dept. of State.

the idea of settling all the points in dispute between Canada and the United States by means of arbitration. A month later, Lansdowne hoped that the interest that the United States Senate was taking in the fisheries question might lose its partisan background and lead to the appointment of "special commissioners" who might suggest some formula that would solve the problems that were now so pressing.[90]

It seemed clear to Bayard that any hope for an early settlement of the fisheries dispute depended in great measure upon the willingness of the British Government to exert pressure upon Canada in favor of a more liberal attitude towards American fishermen. On July 30 he sent an instruction to Phelps protesting against the exclusion of American fishing vessels from Bonne Bay, Newfoundland.[91] In carrying out this instruction, Phelps lodged a strong complaint with Lord Iddesleigh against the idea that nothing could be done in the matter of Canadian seizures of fishing vessels until the legal proceedings in Canadian courts had been brought to a conclusion. The interpretation of a treaty, "when it becomes the subject of discussion between two governments," was not a matter to be settled solely by the courts of either country. That would be "placing its construction in the hands of one of the parties to it." Questions between nations as to national rights secured by treaty must be solved "in another way." The United States Government was "no party to the proceedings instituted by the British authorities in Canada," nor could it consent to "become a party." It would be inconsistent with the dignity of a sovereign power like the United States to seek redress in any way in the courts of another country for what it claimed to be a violation of treaty stipulations by the authorities of that country. The interpretation of the Treaty of 1818 was a matter between Great Britain and the United States, and would have to be settled by some formal agreement.[92]

90. Lansdowne to Sir John Macdonald, August 2, 1886, *Macdonald Papers, Governor-General's Correspondence,* XIII, 498–505, P.A.C.

91. Secretary Bayard to Phelps, July 30, 1886, *Great Britain, Instructions,* XXVIII, MS. Dept. of State.

92. Phelps to Lord Iddesleigh, September 11, 1886, enclosed in a despatch from Phelps to Secretary Bayard, *Great Britain, Despatches,* CLIV, MS. Dept. of State. It was apparent to Phelps and to Bayard that these cases in Canadian courts could drag on for years. This was exactly what Sir John Macdonald and Lansdowne anticipated and wished for. In a note to Lansdowne, July 26, 1886, Sir John Macdonald remarks: "Thompson is of opinion that a masterly inactivity is the true policy (with reference to the *David J. Adams*), and there is much in what he says. . . . Should by any chance the decision be against us now, the American fishermen would flock into our waters in pursuit of mackerel and bait. . . . We can gain nothing by an early judgment." *Macdonald Papers, Governor-General's Correspondence,* XIII, 480–483, P.A.C. In reply, Lansdowne, August 5, 1886, observed: "I quite agree that there is no reason why we should hurry on the decision in the *Adams* case." *Ibid.,* pp. 510–511.

The firm stand taken by Phelps in the fisheries controversy made a deep impression upon the Colonial Office, and it led to new efforts to conciliate the American Government.[93] Lord Lansdowne was in London on a visit, and on August 20 he wrote to Sir John Macdonald to complain that all his efforts to induce Her Majesty's Government to send some warships to the Canadian coasts were in vain. All pressure in this regard had met with a "very determined resistance" on the ground that the "sudden appearance of one of Her Majesty's ships would add to the already existing exasperation."[94]

It is apparent that this conciliatory attitude on the part of the British Government with reference to the fisheries controversy was one of the main reasons why Canadian-American relations did not take on a more serious aspect. The Congressional elections of 1886 would soon be held, and in the face of Republican efforts to discredit his Administration, President Cleveland had to be attentive to all political considerations. On August 14 he had a conversation with Bayard on the question of the fisheries, and he expressed a desire that the American public be informed of the strong stand that had been taken by the Department of State in defence of American rights. Bayard gave assurances that the correspondence with the British Foreign Office would clearly indicate the care that had been taken to protect all American fishing interests, and he promised to send the President a condensed version of this correspondence.[95]

In reply to this note from Bayard, Cleveland expressed his great interest in every aspect of the fisheries dispute. He was of the opinion that the Canadian Government had a right to deny commercial privileges to fishing vessels, but this denial would create in the United States such a feeling of "exasperation" that some retaliatory measures would have to be taken. It would be wise to indicate to the British Foreign Office that a "persistence in the present course" would be equivalent to "furnishing aid and comfort to an element in this Country hostile to everything English and glad of any pretext to fan the flame of hatred and mischief." Blaine was preparing to make a speech that would

93. In the latter part of August, 1886, Phelps had a conversation with Lord Iddesleigh during which he remarked that the American Government was "not now engaged in making a new Treaty, but in the administration of the existing one, and are asking nothing whatever that we are not already entitled to. . . . I expressed to him my grave apprehensions that unless the conduct of Canadian authorities is restrained before Congress meets, a war of retaliation will take place which would be very injurious to both sides and to the friendly relations of the Governments." Phelps to Secretary Bayard, August 28, 1886, *Personal, Bayard MS.*

94. Lansdowne to Sir John Macdonald, August 20, 1886, *Macdonald Papers, Governor-General's Correspondence,* XIII, 523–524, P.A.C.

95. Secretary Bayard to President Cleveland, August 15, 1886, *Cleveland MS.*

assail the Administration on the ground that it had not protected the fishery industry. The American public should know that these criticisms had no foundation in fact.[96]

On August 24, 1886, Blaine made his long-heralded speech which opened the Congressional campaign of 1886.[97] It was not the impressive performance that the President had feared, and he wrote to Bayard to assure him that he had never entertained a doubt that the "Fishery question was in proper shape and had been properly handled." His only fear had been that the American public might be affected by the barrage of misinformation that Republican politicians were directing at all voters.[98]

But despite these attacks upon his conduct of American foreign relations, Bayard still harbored hopes that a *modus vivendi* could be arranged that would quiet the fisheries controversy until a satisfactory solution could be discovered. In his letter of August 28, Phelps had spoken of the warm desire of Lord Iddesleigh to find some means of settling this dangerous dispute,[99] and Bayard had expressed to W. L. Putnam his eagerness to find some way out of existing difficulties.[100]

It was soon apparent to Bayard that he would have to work fast if he were to have a real opportunity to arrange for a *modus vivendi.* Republican leaders in the Senate were determined to discredit the Administration in the matter of the fisheries. On September 6 he received a letter from Senator Edmunds requesting a list of all "the seizures of vessels by the British or Dominion authorities during this season, with the alleged grounds thereof." Edmunds was chairman of a subcommittee of the Committee on Foreign Relations, and he and his colleagues were about to visit certain New England ports to gather data on conditions in the fishery industry.[101] These data, of course, would be useful for partisan purposes.

Bayard realized that something should be done at once to save the situation. On September 6 he sent a telegram to W. L. Putnam directing him to report in Washington on the "earliest day possible."[102]

96. President Cleveland to Secretary Bayard, August 15, 1886, *Bayard MS.*

97. New York *Tribune,* August 25, 1886.

98. President Cleveland to Secretary Bayard, August 26, 1886, *Bayard MS.*

99. Phelps to Secretary Bayard, August 28, 1886, *ibid.*

100. Secretary Bayard to W. L. Putnam, August 30, 1886, *Bayard Letter Book,* III, *Bayard MS.*

101. Senator George F. Edmunds to Secretary Bayard, September 6, 1886, *Bayard MS.*

102. Secretary Bayard to W. L. Putnam, September 6, 1886, *ibid.* See also, *Senate Misc. Doc. No. 146,* 49 Cong., 1 sess.; *Senate Ex. Doc. No. 217,* 49 Cong., 1 sess.; *Senate Ex. Doc. No. 54,* 49 Cong., 2 sess.

After discussing the various aspects of the fishery dispute with Putnam, Bayard drew up the basis of a *modus vivendi* which he decided to send to Phelps.[103] But he soon discovered that Phelps had little faith in the efficacy of this pacific procedure. It seemed to him that the Administration would not secure any favorable response from the British Government until a "vigorous system of retaliation" was put into operation.[104] Undismayed by this advice from Phelps, Bayard continued to work upon the idea of perfecting a temporary arrangement with the British Government in the matter of Canadian fisheries, and by the last week in September he had nearly completed the outline of a *modus vivendi*.[105]

But Bayard's efforts to find a solution for the fisheries dispute were made difficult by the attitude of Canadian officials who continued to seize American fishing vessels on the slightest pretext. Sir John Macdonald had the strange idea that these seizures had not aroused any "real exasperation" in the United States. He believed there was a good deal of what "Lord Westbury called 'simulated indignation' among the professional politicians in Maine and along the New England coast, . . . but this obtains nowhere else in the United States."

Instead of having some appreciation of the pacific policy formulated by the Department of State, Macdonald was of the opinion that Blaine had opened fire upon Canada, and that Bayard was "endeavoring to outjingo Blaine." In the face of this show of American belligerence, the only policy for Canada to follow was to "pursue a steady course of protection to our waters, and condemnation of vessels committing undoubted breaches of the Treaty of 1818." If any weakness were shown "on the part of the British Government or of ours, these waters will be continually invaded and we shall have to submit to a series of diplomatic bullyings . . . which may culminate in a cessation of friendly intercourse. Nothing can be gained by submission."[106]

103. The terms of this *modus vivendi* were: "(1) Release of the *Adams* and the *Doughty*. (2) Remit all fines imposed this season on fishing vessels for alleged violation of Customs Acts. (3) Express a willingness when the above is done to negotiate a treaty pursuant to protocol of Mr. Seward as amended. (4) Pending negotiations—(a) U.S. fishermen to have rights of favored nations in commercial ports. (b) U.S. and G.B. to give concurrent warning as to Canadian customs regulations and U.S. to admonish its fishermen to comply with them. (c) U.S. and G.B. each to keep cruisers in Dominion waters to co-operate. (d) U.S. and G.B. to co-operate in such other matters as may from time to time appear needful to prevent irritation." *Bayard MS.*

104. Phelps to Secretary Bayard, September 13, 1886, *ibid.*

105. Secretary Bayard to Phelps, September 24, 1886, *Bayard Letter Book*, III, *Bayard MS.*

106. Sir John Macdonald to Lansdowne, September 4, 1886, *Macdonald Papers, Letter Book*, XXIV, 20–23, P.A.C.

Under the inspiration of Macdonald, Canadian officials continued to seize American fishing vessels upon shadowy grounds. On October 19 Bayard wrote to Sir Lionel West to protest against the detention of the American vessel *Everett Steele* on the charge that the captain had failed to report at the customhouse when driven by a storm into the harbor of Shelburne, Nova Scotia.[107] On the following day he sent another note to West with reference to the seizure of the *Pearl Nelson* on similar charges.[108] No effort was being made to conciliate the United States, and certain Americans regarded with satisfaction the seizures by American revenue cutters of Canadian sealing vessels in Behring Sea for alleged breaches of American laws.[109]

Bayard breathed a sigh of relief when November arrived and the fishing season was about over. In reviewing the work of the Canadian customs service it was apparent that there had been only one American vessel seized for "actually infringing upon the inshore fisheries of the Dominion." Every other seizure had been "for alleged breach of Customs regulations." In the enforcement of these regulations the Canadian Marine Police had, at times, been unnecessarily rude, one Captain Quigley going so far as to pull down the American flag that was flying at the masthead of the *Marion Grimes*. Such incidents could lead to dangerous consequences, and it was surprising that the Canadian Government was so shortsighted as to employ men of Quigley's caliber to enforce their regulations.[110]

On November 6 Bayard returned to these charges against Canadian officials. The most alarming feature of the whole matter was the "indifference displayed by the British Administration to the insolent provocation and irritating pretensions" of these cantankerous Canadians. Their actions had become "almost intolerable," but no satisfaction could be secured from representations to Sir Lionel West. This state of affairs could not continue. The British Government would have to take some action, or the United States would deal with the Canadians in a very "practical way."[111]

Bayard wished to postpone this action as long as possible, and he still strove to settle the fishery difficulties in a friendly manner. On November 15 he sent to Phelps an instruction to which was appended a

107. Secretary Bayard to Sir Lionel West, October 19, 1886, *Great Britain, Notes to,* XX, MS. Dept. of State.

108. Secretary Bayard to Sir Lionel West, October 20, 1886, *ibid.*

109. Tansill, *Bayard,* chap. xiv.

110. Secretary Bayard to Phelps, November 1, 1886, *Bayard Letter Book,* III, *Bayard MS.*

111. Secretary Bayard to Phelps, November 6, 1886, *ibid.*

modus vivendi. In article one of this proposed arrangement it was suggested that a mixed commission be appointed to deal with all the questions arising out of the fishery dispute.[112] Other articles reflected some of the viewpoints for which Bayard had long contended.

But Phelps did not favor any policy of conciliation. He continued to cling to the opinion that pacific measures were outmoded. It was "idle and beneath the dignity of the United States to waste any more argument or importunity on the subject." The Department of State had been forbearing and courteous in presenting its case, but the Foreign Office had not even extended the scant courtesy of an adequate reply. The time had "now come for decisive action," and the country would sustain the Administration in the adoption of "extreme measures" to settle the fisheries controversy.[113]

Two weeks later, Phelps wrote again to Bayard in the same vein. He thought that the American Government had done everything possible to bring about an adjustment of the fisheries dispute, but he had little hope "of any favourable result until we *compel* it by stringent measures."[114] Bayard was not ready for any belligerent measures, and he gave little heed to this advice from Phelps. He inclined towards the view that the situation might be helped by the publication of some of the correspondence dealing with the fisheries, so on December 8, 1886, President Cleveland sent a special message to Congress in which he enclosed a large number of the more important diplomatic notes dealing with the seizures of American vessels in Canadian waters. In this message the President suggested that Congress authorize the appointment of a commission to take proofs of the losses sustained by the fishermen. He also hinted that it might be necessary for him to make recommendations for "such remedial legislation as may become neces-

112. Secretary Bayard to Phelps, November 15, 1886, *Great Britain, Instructions,* XXVIII, MS. Dept. of State. In this proposed *modus vivendi,* bays and harbors that were ten miles wide or less were to be regarded as territorial waters, and the three-mile limit was to be drawn from a line that was to be drawn across the water in the part nearest the entrance at the first point where the width did not exceed ten miles. American fishing vessels were not to be seized unless they were found within three marine miles of the coasts, bays, creeks, and harbors of Her Majesty's dominions in America, and were fishing, completing fishing operations, or preparing to fish. American fishing vessels were to have in the ports of entry of Her Majesty's dominions in America the same commercial privileges as other vessels of the United States, including the purchase of bait and other supplies. The British Government should release all American fishing vessels that had been seized by Canadian officials for failure to report at customhouses when seeking shelter, repairs, or supplies, and to refund all fines exacted for this failure to report.

113. Phelps to Secretary Bayard, November 20, 1886, *Bayard MS.*

114. Phelps to Secretary Bayard, December 3, 1886, *ibid.*

sary for the protection of the rights of our citizens engaged in the open-sea fisheries of the North Atlantic waters."[115]

The publication of this correspondence evoked a favorable response from a large section of the press and from many persons in close touch with the fisheries industry. This friendly reaction was very heartening to Bayard who wrote to Phelps and expressed his satisfaction that the "spattering retraction of the Blaine School" had been effectively answered and rebuked. Knowing the sincere intentions of the Administration to avoid collisions and to strengthen the "united forces and elements of civilization and liberty which Great Britain and the United States chiefly contain and represent in the world," he was amazed to see the apparent indifference of British Ministers to the importance of a prompt settlement of the fisheries controversy.[116]

To Phelps it appeared obvious that "mere argument" would never settle the fishery question. The British Government should be plainly informed that the United States would not submit to a "renewal of the outrages of last season." This firm stand and the fact that the Canadians themselves had discovered that they had "gone too far" in the matter of the seizures of American fishing vessels, might bring about an eventual settlement of existing difficulties.[117]

There was some truth in the report that the Canadian Government

115. *House Ex. Doc. No. 19,* 49 Cong., 2 sess., p. 1. During the autumn of 1886, Senator Edmunds and other members of a sub-committee of the Senate Committee on Foreign Relations conducted an intensive investigation of many aspects of the fishing industry of New England. On January 19, 1887, as an antidote to the special message of President Cleveland (December 8, 1886), Mr. Edmunds submitted the report of his sub-committee (*Senate Rept. No. 1683,* 49 Cong., 2 sess.). According to this report, it was clear that "the right to fish within 3 miles of the Dominion shores is of no practical advantage whatever to American fishermen. The cod and halibut fishing has been for many years almost entirely carried on at long distances from the shore. . . . As regards the obtaining of bait for this class of fishing, the testimony taken by the committee in its inquiries clearly demonstrates that there is no necessity whatever for American fishermen to resort to Canadian waters for that purpose. . . . In view of all these facts, . . . it must be considered as conclusively established that there would be no material value whatever in the grant by the British Government to American fishermen of absolutely free fishing." After calling attention to the fact that American fishing vessels had no commercial privileges in Canadian ports, the sub-committee recommended that the President be invested with the power, and "that it be made his duty that whenever he shall be satisfied that unjust, unfair, or unfriendly conduct is practiced by the British Government in respect of our citizens and their property within the ports or waters of the British dominions in North America, to deny to the subjects of that Government in British North America . . . such privileges in the waters and ports of the United States as he may think proper to name." *Senate Doc. No. 231,* Pt. 5, 56 Cong., 2 sess., pp. 628–630.

116. Secretary Bayard to Phelps, December 17, 1886, *Bayard Letter Book,* IV, *Bayard MS.*

117. Phelps to Secretary Bayard, January 1, 1887, *Bayard MS.*

was disposed to listen to American proposals for a friendly adjustment of the fishery dispute. In a note to Sir John Macdonald, Lord Lansdowne commented upon the "moderation" of the President's language in his message to Congress. He did not understand, however, the President's statement that negotiations had been initiated for a settlement of the fishery difficulties.[118]

Shortly after he sent this note to Macdonald, Lansdowne was shown the outline of a *modus vivendi* that had been sent to Lord Iddesleigh. He was not favorably impressed with it. From all appearances it was a "one-sided and disingenuous proposal," which decided against Canada "all the debatable points."[119]

Mr. Foster, the Canadian Minister of Marine and Fisheries, was equally dissatisfied with the *modus vivendi* proposed by Bayard. To his mind there was not a "sparkle of a single generous sentiment in it. Mr. Bayard offers nothing, settles most disputed points offhand in his own favour, and sets a machinery in motion by which he hopes to gain the remainder."[120]

With Canadian statesmen in this frame of mind, there was little possibility that the basis for a *modus vivendi* could be quickly reached. This possibility was made even more slender when the news arrived in the United States that Queen Victoria, on November 26, 1886, had given the royal assent to certain Canadian legislation dealing with the fisheries. This Act of the Dominion Parliament had been reserved by Lord Lansdowne on June 2, 1886, for "the signification of the Queen's pleasure thereon." The fact of royal assent was made known in a proclamation issued on December 24, 1886. Thereafter, any American fishing vessel that entered Canadian waters for "any purpose not permitted by treaty," could be immediately seized by Canadian officials, and "such ship, vessel, or boat, and the tackle, rigging, apparel, furniture, stores, and cargo thereof shall be forfeited."[121]

118. Lansdowne to Sir John Macdonald, December 9, 1886, *Macdonald Papers, Governor-General's Correspondence,* XIII, 647, P.A.C.

119. Lansdowne to Sir John Macdonald, December 25, 1886, *ibid.,* pp. 558–559.

120. G. E. Foster to Sir John Macdonald, December 28, 1886, *ibid.,* pp. 573–575; *House Ex. Doc. No. 19,* 49 Cong., 1 sess.

121. *House Rept. No. 4087,* 49 Cong., 2 sess., p. 17. According to the Boston *Journal,* December 30, 1886, the provisions of the Act of 1886 would make it possible "for any petty customs official to bring into port any American vessel found within three miles of the Canadian coast, to search her cargo and to examine her master under oath."

In commenting upon this statute of November 26, 1886, the sub-committee of the Senate Committee on Foreign Relations, January 19, 1887, stated: "It would seem that it is the deliberate purpose of the British Government to leave it to the individual discretion of each one of the numerous subordinate magistrates, fishery offi-

This action on the part of the British Government awakened instant resentment in the United States. Francis Wharton, the Solicitor of the Department of State, wrote a brief note to Bayard inquiring whether it would not be worth while to get in touch with some of the Senators from New England and see "what is their idea of a 'counterpoise' in case the new statute is carried into effect."[122] It was not necessary for Bayard to see these new England legislators with reference to retaliatory legislation. For several weeks, Senator Edmunds had been conducting an intensive examination into every aspect of the fisheries question, and on January 19, 1887, he introduced a bill which provided that whenever the President was satisfied that American rights were being violated in Canadian waters he was authorized, by proclamation, to deny to all "vessels their masters and crews, of the British Dominions of North America, any entrance into the waters, ports, or places of or within the United States."[123]

Two days previously (January 17, 1887), Mr. Belmont had introduced in the House of Representatives a bill authorizing the President to forbid the entrance into the United States of "all merchandise coming by land from the provinces of British North America, and may also forbid the entrance into the United States of the cars, locomotives or other rolling stock of any railroad company chartered under the laws of said provinces."[124]

Phelps was strongly in favor of this proposed retaliatory legislation. He was convinced that the British Government would make no move to solve the fisheries controversy until strong pressure was applied one

cers, and customs officers of the Dominion of Canada to seize and bring into port any American vessels, whether fishing or other, that he finds within any harbor in Canada or hovering within Canadian waters. The statute does not even except those Canadian waters on which, along a large part of the southern coast and the whole of the western coast of Newfoundland, they are entitled to fish, to say nothing of the vast extent of the continental coast of Canada. The committee repeats its expression of the firm opinion that this legislation is in violation of the treaty of 1818, as it respects American fishing vessels, and in violation of the principles of comity and good neighborhood that ought to exist in respect of commercial intercourse or the coming of the vessels of either having any commercial character within the waters of the other." *Senate Doc. No. 231,* Pt. 5, 56 Cong., 2 sess., pp. 624–625.

122. Francis Wharton to Secretary Bayard, January 3, 1887, *Bayard MS.*

123. *Congressional Record,* January 19, 1887, 49 Cong., 2 sess., p. 793. This bill was S. 3173. It was very distasteful to Bayard, who regarded it "without precedent in the history of our Foreign Affairs." Bayard to W. L. Putnam, January 20, 1887, *Bayard Letter Book,* IV, *Bayard MS.* At Bayard's instigation, Senator Arthur P. Gorman introduced several amendments to the Edmunds bill, but they were voted down by a large majority. *Congressional Record,* January 24, 1887, 49 Cong., 2 sess., pp. 947–952. See also, *Senate Ex. Doc. No. 32,* 49 Cong., 2 sess.

124. *Congressional Record,* January 17, 1887, 49 Cong., 2 sess., p. 737.

way or another. The movement towards retaliation had "done more good than all the argument."[125] Three days after he wrote this letter to Bayard, Phelps had an interview with the British Foreign Secretary. The result was not satisfactory because the British Government was "unwilling to coerce Canada." It was clear that the American Government could secure satisfaction only through a program of retaliation aimed directly at Canada.[126]

Despite this continued advice from Phelps in favor of strong measures against Canada, Bayard adhered to his policy of conciliation, and he sent an instruction to London couched in these terms.[127] Phelps had to carry out this instruction, but he let Lord Salisbury know that Congress, "with almost entire unanimity" was pressing the Administration to adopt a more positive policy in this matter of the fisheries.[128]

In recounting to Bayard the attitude of Lord Salisbury towards this warning, Phelps sounded a discouraging note. Salisbury had been very noncommittal. He had remarked that "Great Britain stood as a broker between the United States and Canada, and had great difficulty in managing their Canadian clients." In connection with the question of the purchase of bait, he was "inclined to take the Canadian view." With respect to the proposed *modus vivendi* he hoped to make "some communication ere long."

This reluctance to take a decided stand against Canadian practices aroused Phelps's ready resentment. The British Government was "either afraid or unwilling to attempt to coerce Canada." No amount of argument, no appeal "to the sense of justice, no considerations of friendship or comity will induce them to take any firm ground antagonistic to Canadian views." The United States had no recourse but to bring Canada "to terms" through retaliatory legislation.[129]

Under the impact of this constant drum-fire of belligerent counsel from Phelps, Bayard was finally routed from his stand of conciliation towards Canada, and in a letter to Perry Belmont he expressed the opinion that Congress should pass legislation which should be "unquestionable as to its intent, and clear and positive in its prohibitory results." The British Government was evidently not prepared to "compel Canada to accept her counsels, or modify her action against our fisher-

125. Phelps to Secretary Bayard, January 25, 1887, *Bayard MS.*

126. Phelps to Secretary Bayard, February 4, 1887, *Great Britain, Despatches,* CLV, MS. Dept. of State.

127. Secretary Bayard to Phelps, February 4, 1887, *Great Britain, Instructions,* XXVIII, MS. Dept. of State.

128. Phelps to Lord Salisbury, February 5, 1887, *Bayard MS.*

129. Phelps to Secretary Bayard, February 5, 1887, *ibid.*

men." Some strong measure should be immediately passed by Congress to protect American interests.[130]

With relations between Canada and the United States growing steadily worse, Senator Hoar added difficulties to the situation by introducing February 24, 1887, a resolution which opposed any negotiation with Great Britain "in regard to existing difficulties with her province of Canada which has for its object the reduction, change, or abolition of any of our existing duties on imports."[131] This action was a direct blow at any attempt on the part of the Department of State to settle the fisheries dispute along the lines of the reciprocity treaty of 1854. Such interference with the conduct of foreign relations was indicative of the partisan attitude that the Republican majority in the Senate adopted towards so many public questions, and it infuriated Bayard. To him it was merely another proof of "the reckless, selfish, and mercenary spirit" that for years had been shown by Republican leaders.[132]

But there was no way to counter these political moves, and President Cleveland (March 3, 1887) approved the bill introduced by Senator Edmunds with reference to the establishment of commercial non-intercourse with Canada.[133] The measure was not to the liking of Bayard, but he realized that it might serve as a wedge that would force the British Government to open up the whole question of the fisheries and thereby lead to some satisfactory settlement. On March 2, Henry White wrote Bayard a confidential letter from London to the effect that officials in the British Foreign Office were "amazed" at the way the Canadian Government had acted, and their patience was "well-nigh exhausted." A *modus vivendi* was being prepared, and would soon be submitted to the Department of State.[134] On March 24, Lord Salisbury indicated that he was prepared to accept Bayard's suggestion for the appointment of a mixed commission to study and report upon the fisheries question. He had no doubt that Canadian officials would make every effort to enforce their regulations in such a manner as to "cause

130. Secretary Bayard to Perry Belmont, February 18, 1887, *Bayard Letter Book,* IV, *Bayard MS.; House Repts. Nos. 3648, 4087,* 49 Cong., 2 sess.

131. *Congressional Record,* 49 Cong., 2 sess., p. 2191.

132. Secretary Bayard to Senator J. M. Beck, February 26, 1887, *Bayard Letter Book,* IV, *Bayard MS.*

133. *F.R., 1887,* pp. 466–467. Bayard was strongly opposed to the implications of this legislation. In a letter to Horace White, October 16, 1887, he developed his viewpoint: "It was wholly unprecedented to invest the President with power in his discretion to declare non-intercourse with a country with which we were at peace. Heretofore in our history, . . . embargoes and the like were the acts of Congress, giving to the Executive the power to suspend their operation." *Bayard Letter Book,* VI, *Bayard MS.*

134. Henry White to Secretary Bayard, March 2, 1887, *Confidential, Bayard MS.*

the smallest amount of inconvenience to fishing vessels entering Canadian ports under stress of weather or for any other legitimate purpose." As a gesture of good will, Lord Salisbury announced that the British Government was willing to "revert for the coming season, and, if necessary, for a further term, to the condition of things existing under the Treaty of Washington, without any suggestion of pecuniary indemnity."[135]

Phelps was not pleased with the tone or the contents of this note from Lord Salisbury. He regarded it as "uncordial and unfair in its second-hand defence of conduct that is utterly incapable of defence." He was of the opinion, however, that the idea of a mixed commission was one that should be adopted because it seemed to "afford the only probable means of arriving at an agreement on the points in dispute." This commission should be held in Washington, and he suggested, as the American representatives, the names of George W. Biddle, William L. Putnam, and James B. Angell, President of Michigan University.[136]

To John Bassett Moore, the British offer to revert to the "condition of things existing under the Treaty of Washington, without any suggestion of pecuniary indemnity," was of little consequence. If the American Government had not given "notice of the Treaty of 1871, we certainly would have had Lord Salisbury's boon without paying a dollar for it." He believed that the opposition to Bayard's handling of the fisheries question had been voiced by persons who had wished for an open break between Canada and the United States. This break would have resulted in the exclusion of Canadian fish from American markets, and this was exactly what Senators Frye and Edmunds had devoutly desired.[137]

Bayard had contempt for such a narrow policy, and he anxiously sought for some friendly solution of the fishery difficulties. This might be found in a comprehensive arrangement that would combine the fishery question with that of commercial reciprocity. In Canada there were

135. Lord Salisbury to Henry White, March 24, 1887, enclosed in despatch from White to Secretary Bayard, March 30, 1887, *Great Britain, Despatches,* CLV, MS. Dept. of State. Bayard had outlined the terms of a *modus vivendi* in an instruction to Phelps, November 15, 1886, *Great Britain, Instructions,* XXVIII, MS. Dept. of State.

This formula had been presented to Lord Lansdowne by the Colonial Office on February 24, 1887, and two days later, Lansdowne cabled back that the Canadian Government was "willing to accept your suggestion of reverting temporarily to condition of things existing under the Treaty of Washington without at present raising question of indemnity." *Macdonald Papers, Governor-General's Correspondence,* XIV, 50–51, P.A.C.

136. Phelps to Secretary Bayard, March 27, 1887, *Bayard MS.*

137. John Bassett Moore to Secretary Bayard, April 25, 1887, *ibid.*

many publicists who were in favor of such a formula, and support was promptly given to it by the Toronto *Globe*.[138] Advocates of commercial union between Canada and the United States were certain that closer commercial ties would pave the way for a permanent settlement of all outstanding issues between the two countries. Erastus Wiman was an enthusiastic member of this group, and he wrote to Sir Charles Tupper and suggested that he visit Washington and see what could be done. Tupper thought that something might be accomplished by *informal* conversations with Bayard, so in May, 1887, he paid a visit to Washington.[139]

It was high time that something was done by Canadian officials to conciliate American opinion. On April 22, Bayard wrote a confidential note to the American Consul-General at Halifax to complain of the recent refusal of "the Canadian Government to allow American fishing vessels, driven by storm into their ports, to repair damages to their supplies as well as to their . . . rigging, etc. . . . The situation is seriously strained by this action of the Canadian Government."[140] To Phelps, Bayard sent a personal letter in which he frankly stated that it was "essential that such action on the part of Canada . . . be stopped."[141]

Phelps was fearful that the "hostile state of mind" that was "rapidly growing up in both countries" might lead to an early explosion,[142] and he was greatly relieved when Sir Ambrose Shea wrote to him and suggested that Newfoundland and the United States open negotiations for a "separate arrangement for fisheries and trade."[143] This proposal was a "most important step toward the solution of existing difficulties," and Phelps could not see why the American Government should hesitate to accept such a fruitful suggestion.[144]

While Sir Ambrose Shea was making this friendly overture to Phelps, Sir Charles Tupper was holding out an olive branch to Bayard. On May 21, 1887, he arrived in Washington, and lost no time in calling at

138. Toronto *Globe,* April 20, 1887. See also letter of William McDougall in Montreal *Herald,* April 18, 1887.

139. Erastus Wiman to Secretary Bayard, April 18, 22, 30, 1887, and Secretary Bayard to Wiman, April 23, 1887, *Bayard MS.*

140. Secretary Bayard to M. H. Phelan, April 22, 1887, *ibid.*

141. Secretary Bayard to Phelps, April 23, 1887, *ibid.* To William L. Putnam, the course of the British Foreign Office was a "puzzle." He thought that its policy might be to "turn its back on the whole question until Canada has got herself thoroughly into a scrape and herself calls out for conciliation, thus enabling the British Government to avoid all responsibility so far as Canada is concerned." *Ibid.*

142. Phelps to Secretary Bayard, April 23, 1887, *Private and Confidential, Bayard MS.*

143. Sir Ambrose Shea to Phelps, May 10, 1887, *ibid.*

144. Phelps to Secretary Bayard, May 11, 1887, *ibid.*

the Department of State. Apparently, Bayard greeted Sir Charles with the frank declaration: "The confederation of Canada and the construction of the Canadian Pacific Railway have brought us face to face with a nation, and we may as well discuss public questions from that point of view."[145]

After discussing the matter of commercial reciprocity, Bayard and Tupper turned to the question of the fisheries. Of one thing Bayard was certain—it would not be possible to grant to Canadian fishermen free entry for their catch until Congress authorized such action. The best way to handle this whole situation was through the appointment of a joint high commission that could study and report upon the important questions that were clamoring for early settlement. Tupper was not opposed to this suggestion, and he left Washington with a conviction that definite progress had been made towards an accommodation of differences.[146]

On May 31, Bayard wrote to Tupper and assured him that he was prepared to meet the authorized agents of Great Britain at Washington "at the earliest day, and enter upon negotiations for a settlement of all differences."[147] The main question that worried Bayard was the attitude of Congress towards the appointment of a joint high commission. In the previous year, Congress had advised against the creation of such a commission. What action should be taken in the face of such opposition?

Senator Morgan immediately expressed the view that there was no need for the President to request any authorization from Congress in the matter of the appointment of a joint high commission. Under the treaty-making power the President had ample authority to appoint representatives to negotiate for the settlement of all questions that dealt with American foreign policy. There was no necessity to consult Congress![148]

Armed with this Senatorial opinion concerning the extent of the President's appointing powers, Bayard instructed Phelps to propose to

145. Sir Charles Tupper, *Recollections of Sixty Years* (New York, 1914), p. 176.

146. *Memorandum* written by Bayard after a conversation with Sir Charles Tupper, May 21, 1887, *Bayard MS.*

147. Secretary Bayard to Sir Charles Tupper, May 31, 1887, Tupper, *op. cit.*, pp. 177–180. On this same day, May 31, Bayard wrote to Phelps and explained that the time was not ripe to enter upon separate negotiations with Newfoundland. All outstanding questions between Canada and the United States should first be settled through the recommendations of a joint commission that would soon be appointed. *Bayard Letter Book,* V, *Bayard MS.*

148. Henry M. Wriston, *Executive Agents in American Foreign Relations* (Baltimore, 1929), p. 283; *Congressional Record,* 49 Cong., 1 sess., pp. 3434–3435. See also Phelps to Bayard, June 1, 1887, *Bayard MS.*

Lord Salisbury the appointment of an Envoy Extraordinary and Minister Plenipotentiary to meet in Washington with a Minister Plenipotentiary of the United States, "both of whom shall be duly authorized to treat of and discuss the mode of settling all questions which have arisen out of the fisheries on the Coasts of British North America." Bayard enclosed in this instruction a long document arranged in three columns. The first column contained the *modus vivendi* which had been presented to the British Government on November 15, 1886. The second column was devoted to the observations of the British Foreign Office upon this *modus vivendi*, and the third column presented Bayard's reply to the British observations.[149]

While Bayard was waiting for a reply to this instruction, he began to give some thought to the personnel of the Joint High Commission. He was of the opinion that it would be expedient to appoint a "moderate Republican" as a member of this body, and he finally chose James B. Angell.[150] William L. Putnam was selected as the second American representative, and Bayard then decided that for a few weeks he would turn over the affairs of the Department of State to his able assistants, and would sit as the third member of the American delegation.[151]

The British Government chose as its representatives on the Joint High Commission, Joseph Chamberlain, Sir Charles Tupper, and Sir Lionel West. Chamberlain's appointment aroused both criticism and praise in certain American circles.[152] In Canada, Lord Lansdowne expressed the opinion that Chamberlain was an "excellent man of business."[153]

There was no doubt about the accuracy of this characterization, but business men are often too blunt to be good diplomats, and at times their eyes are fixed upon definite dividends rather than upon the in-

149. Secretary Bayard to Phelps, July 12, 1887, *Great Britain, Instructions*, XXIX, MS. Dept. of State.

150. Phelps suggested the name of Angell in a letter to Bayard, August 2, 1887, *Bayard MS.* Bayard offered Edward D. White, of Louisiana, a place on the commission, but White declined to serve. White to Secretary Bayard, September 28, 1887, *ibid.*

151. Secretary Bayard to President Cleveland, July 30, 1887, *Bayard Letter Book*, V, *Bayard MS.* The American press was very friendly to the appointments of Angell and Putnam, and even the New York *Tribune*, September 30, 1887, admitted that the "fitness" of both men for a position on the joint commission would be recognized by "the country."

152. The Boston *Post*, September 1, 1887, thought that Chamberlain's appointment would be "favorably received" in the United States; the New York *World*, August 30, 1887, expressed the view that the appointment would be "received with satisfaction by the people on this side of the Atlantic," and the New York *Evening Post*, August 31, 1887, had some complimentary things to say about Chamberlain.

153. Lansdowne to Sir John Macdonald, August 31, 1887, *Macdonald Papers, Governor-General's Correspondence*, XIV, 236–243, P.A.C.

tangible items that bulk large in the ledgers of international good will. Before the Joint High Commission opened its sessions, Chamberlain assumed the pose of honest broker. After he had been in Washington a few days he threw aside all pretence of neutrality and gave full support to the arguments that had been drawn up by Canadian statesmen. Bayard was not greatly surprised at this sudden change of position, but he deeply resented the "Birmingham tone" which Chamberlain adopted in his conversations with the American Commissioners. It seemed as though this representative of British "big business" was trying to put price tags upon all the things that draw nations together.

Sir Charles Tupper was even worse. Bayard had been pleased with Tupper's appointment as a member of the Joint High Commission,[154] and he had anticipated no difficulty with the Canadian representative. But Tupper was inclined to haggle over every point under discussion. He was a Nova Scotian who clearly realized the importance of the fishing industry. For two decades he had advocated a policy of restricting American fishing liberties to such an extent that American statesmen would be glad to give sweeping tariff reductions on certain Canadian products in return for concessions to Yankee fishermen. At Washington he never lifted his eyes from the close scrutiny of tariff schedules to the more restful vista of Canadian-American co-operation in a program conceived in friendly interest and dedicated to the proposition that neighboring countries in the New World have a natural affinity which draws them close together. For Tupper, the pull of political gravitation was to the east and not to the south, and in his dealings with the American Commissioners he would have them pay a pound of interest on a shilling concession. He was an aggressive man who dominated not only the timid Sir Lionel West but also the self-sufficient Joseph Chamberlain.[155] With such a man in such a position, it was inevitable that friction would develop during the sessions of the Joint High Commission, and both Bayard and Tupper speak of "stormy meetings" that ended abruptly.

The American delegation was composed of less explosive elements.

154. Bayard wrote to W. L. Putnam, October 15, 1887, and remarked that he regarded Tupper's appointment as a member of the joint commission with "much favor." *Bayard Letter Book,* VI, *Bayard MS.* Putnam thought that Tupper's selection was the "wisest one which could have been made." Putnam to Secretary Bayard, October 14, 1887, *Bayard MS.*

155. Sir Charles Tupper had a conference with Chamberlain in Birmingham in September, 1887, with reference to Canadian-American relations. Tupper was certain that he had succeeded in impressing Chamberlain with "the vital importance of the United States understanding clearly that England was at one with us in supporting our rights. . . . I think he takes a broad view of the whole question, and . . . you will find him prepared to sustain our position." Tupper to Sir John Macdonald, September 15, 1887, Saunders, *op. cit.,* II, 99.

Bayard was quietly tenacious but never belligerent. Putnam and Angell were not public officials who had to put on a bold front to please their constituents, and they were not unduly contentious. Putnam and Bayard had made an exhaustive study of the fisheries question, while Angell had an alert mind that enabled him quickly to grasp the main points under discussion. They were men who would readily concede minor points in order to focus attention upon the major items in the agenda. Although they were anxious to find some formula that would remove the chief causes of Canadian-American misunderstanding, they would not incline towards any compromise that would seriously affect important American interests. They were, however, entirely willing to meet the British delegation halfway along the road to a friendly settlement of long-existing differences, and they hoped the terms of reference were broad enough to meet all emergencies.

These terms of reference, or the items which were to be given consideration, were as vague and as ambiguous as any diplomat could desire. They were expressed in the following formula:

To consider and adjust all or any questions relating to rights of fishery in the seas adjacent to British North America and Newfoundland which are in dispute between the Governments of Her Britannic Majesty and that of the United States of America, and any other questions which may arise, and which they may be authorized by their respective Governments to consider and adjust.[156]

Lord Lansdowne had been anxious to have the Behring Sea or Fur-Seal dispute specifically included in the terms of reference, and he was in favor of making them wide enough to embrace "every outstanding dispute between Great Britain and the United States, including even such questions as that of the Nicaraguan isthmus."[157] Later, he complained of the "vagueness" of the terms,[158] and when they were not clarified, he expressed his doubts about the "result of the negotiations."[159] In reply to these misgivings, Sir John Macdonald sounded a note of frank pessimism. He was afraid that "no fair dealing" could be expected of any American Government, and therefore, how could one expect to arrive at any satisfactory arrangement with them?[160]

156. Secretary Bayard to Sir Lionel West, September 14, 21, and October 19, 1887; Sir Lionel West to Secretary Bayard, September 20, and October 24, 1887, *Bayard MS.*

157. Lansdowne to Sir John Macdonald, August 31, 1887, *Macdonald Papers, Governor-General's Correspondence,* XIV, 236–243, P.A.C.

158. Lansdowne to Sir John Macdonald, September 18, 1887, *ibid.,* pp. 267–271.

159. Lansdowne to Sir John Macdonald, September 26, 1887, *ibid.,* pp. 290–291.

160. Sir John Macdonald to Lord Lansdowne, October 3, 1887, *Macdonald Letter Books,* XXV, 243.

On the American side there was more hope that a far-reaching settlement could be effected through the labor of a Joint High Commission. Bayard had been serving in the Senate during the meetings of the Joint High Commission that had negotiated the Treaty of Washington, and he firmly believed that there was no real obstacle in the path of a complete understanding between the British and American Governments with reference to every Canadian complication. He was familiar with the resolutions that the Senate and the House of Representatives[161] had agreed to in favor of the adoption of international arbitration as a "practical method for the determination of international differences," and he had followed with great interest the English reaction to these gestures of good will. In August, 1887, a tide of pacific sentiment towards the United States reached a high point in England. In that month, Randal Cremer had secured the signatures of 234 members of the House of Commons to a memorial urging the American Government to compose all differences between the British Empire and the United States by resort to arbitration. Accompanied by a delegation of peace advocates, Cremer visited the United States, and on October 31, 1887, he presented the memorial to President Cleveland.[162] In reply to remarks by Mr. Cremer, the President gave assurances that he and the American people would "gladly hail the advent of peaceful methods in the settlement of national disputes."[163] Against such a background it seemed obvious that every effort would be made by the Joint High Commission to eliminate all points of serious friction between the two governments, and although these efforts were frustrated by a partisan Senate, it should be remembered that within the next three decades every question that clamored for settlement in 1887 was settled by peaceful procedures. Time was on the side of Anglo-American understanding.

161. On June 23, 1874 the Senate agreed to a resolution in favor of international arbitration (*Congressional Globe,* 43 Cong., 1 sess., p. 5407). On June 17, 1874, the House of Representatives took similar action (*Congressional Globe,* 43 Cong., 1 sess., p. 5114). In December, 1882, Senator G. F. Hoar sponsored a resolution in favor of international arbitration (*Congressional Record,* 47 Cong., 2 sess., p. 457), and in December, 1885 several bills of like character were introduced in Congress (*Congressional Record,* 49 Cong., 1 sess., pp. 154, 475, 732).

162. Charles C. Tansill, "The United States and International Arbitration, 1872–1914," *Thought,* XVI, 701.

163. London *Times,* November 2, 1887. It is interesting to note that Mr. E. J. Phelps, the American Minister in London, was strongly opposed to the conclusion of any important arbitration treaty with England, and he tried to belittle the Cremer mission to the United States. See Phelps to President Cleveland, November 5, 1887, *Cleveland MS.,* Library of Congress.

CHAPTER III

THE SENATE REJECTS THE BAYARD-CHAMBERLAIN TREATY

ENCOURAGED by the many gestures of good will made by British peace advocates like Randal Cremer, Bayard ardently hoped that the hour had arrived when a British-American accord could be reached by the settlement of all questions at issue between the two countries. He was confident that there was no valid reason why a friendly understanding could not be reached, but he was distinctly fearful that a Republican Senate might attempt to block his efforts merely in order to gain some dubious political advantage. In order to forestall any moves along this line, Bayard decided to take early action to mobilize American public opinion in favor of a policy that would employ international conciliation as a means of advancing American interests. He would endeavor to make American voters see that friendly relations and expanding commerce are far more profitable than constant friction and commercial non-intercourse. As a first step in this direction he wrote a letter to a friend, Samuel L. Barlow, who was acquainted with every aspect of "big business" in New York City. Bayard believed that Barlow could clearly indicate to the business world the dangers of the attitude assumed by the Republican leaders in the Senate. Perhaps some servitor of the vested interests like Chauncey M. Depew could be enlisted as a leader in this fight to promote business by conciliating Canada![1]

Bayard next wrote to Horace White, who was familiar with certain members of the New York Chamber of Commerce.[2] As the financial editor of the New York *Evening Post*, White could present to a wide circle of influential business men the importance of giving support to the program of the Cleveland Administration. It was even possible that the two Senators from New York might be brought into line.[3]

White lost no time in carrying out these suggestions. After a talk with Gustav Schwab, White was inclined to believe that the Chamber of Commerce would favor a treaty along the lines that Bayard was

1. Secretary Bayard to Samuel L. Barlow, October 12, 1887, *Bayard Letter Book*, VI, *Bayard MS.*

2. White was strongly favorable to the Bayard program, and his letters in the Bayard manuscripts indicate his many efforts to be of service.

3. Secretary Bayard to Horace White, October 16, 21, 1887, *ibid.*

working, and there was no doubt that the Senators from New York would give some heed to the wishes of the Chamber.[4]

On November 3, 1887, the Chamber of Commerce held its regular monthly meeting and unanimously adopted a resolution in favor of an "early adjustment of the fishery question."[5] After this action had been taken, White was certain that it would be possible to secure the endorsement of the Chamber for any program that Bayard saw fit to lay before it. If this were done, the New York Senators would be "obliged to give it the most respectful attention."[6]

After an approach had been made to Jay Gould, the railroad magnate who had a wide influence in financial circles,[7] Bayard then wrote a long letter to G. B. Roberts, President of the Pennsylvania Railroad. Bayard referred to the relations between Roberts and the two Pennsylvania Senators, and expressed the hope that these legislators could be made to see the importance of supporting an arrangement with Canada that would solve the present difficulties.[8] When both Gould and Roberts responded in a friendly fashion to these overtures, Bayard grew more optimistic about the action of the Republican majority in the Senate.[9] The pressure that could be exerted by "big business" upon Republican Senators was a factor of great importance in the political equation.

But Bayard was soon assailed by new doubts. In the Boston *Post* of November 7, a statement had appeared by a "New England Senator" to the effect that the President would have to send to the Senate for confirmation the nominations of W. L. Putnam, James B. Angell, and Secretary Bayard as the American members of the Joint High Commission that was soon to open its sessions in Washington. These nominations would be rejected by the Senate, and the Commission could not legally be organized. But if the Administration went ahead with its plans and the Commission did meet and finally produced some scheme or treaty dealing with the fishery question, the Senate would reject this treaty.[10]

This declaration of war against the program of the Cleveland Administration aroused the deep indignation of Bayard. The President had undoubted power to nominate American representatives on a joint

4. Horace White to Secretary Bayard, October 21, 1887, *ibid.*
5. New York *Herald,* November 4, 1887.
6. Horace White to Secretary Bayard, November 3, 1887, *Bayard MS.*
7. Jay Gould to G. L. Miller, October 19, 1887, *Cleveland MS.*
8. Secretary Bayard to G. B. Roberts, November 21, 1887, *Bayard MS.*
9. G. B. Roberts to Secretary Bayard, January 13, 1888, *ibid.*
10. Boston *Post,* November 7, 1887.

commission without consulting the Senate, and this advance notice that the Republicans in the Senate would defeat any fishery treaty sent to it by the President, was an impressive illustration of the partisan spite of Republican leaders.[11]

This political picture was none too bright, but there were other aspects of the situation that were more encouraging. Joseph Chamberlain was showing a friendly disposition, and there was a possibility that the work of the Commission would be so free from legitimate criticism that even a Republican Senate would have to be satisfied with its labors. On August 31, Chamberlain had written to Phelps in warm advocacy of a plan to bring into closer intimacy the "English-speaking nations."[12] Bayard was in such close accord with this sentiment that he began to base many of his hopes for a far-reaching settlement of Canadian-American difficulties upon the "breadth and comprehensive justice" of the mind and character of Chamberlain.[13]

Chamberlain landed in New York City on November 7, and as a speaker at a dinner given in his honor by the Chamber of Commerce, he made a very favorable impression.[14] Visiting Canadians were likewise impressed, and John S. Thompson, the Canadian Minister of Justice, thought that Chamberlain was "quite ready for Mr. Bayard."[15] When the Joint High Commission opened its sessions, this bustling representative of British "big business" tried hard to live up to these predictions. He was anything but the calm "arbitrator" that Phelps had so enthusiastically described.[16]

In Washington, Chamberlain discovered that Sir Charles Tupper was flanked by several "advisers." Besides John S. Thompson, there was Mr. James Winter, who represented the Government of Newfoundland. The British Foreign Office had been opposed to the appointment of a Newfoundlander upon the Commission because it could not be certain that he "would always vote straight."[17] But under pressure, consent was finally given to the selection of Mr. Winter, Attorney-General of Newfoundland, as the Agent of the Governor, and a promise was made

11. Secretary Bayard to Horace White, November 8, 1887, *Bayard Letter Book,* VI, *Bayard MS.*

12. Joseph Chamberlain to Phelps, August 31, 1887, *Bayard MS.*

13. Secretary Bayard to Phelps, October 20, 1887, *Bayard Letter Book,* VI, *Bayard MS.*

14. J. S. Moore to Secretary Bayard, November 17, 1887, *ibid.*

15. John S. D. Thompson to Sir John Macdonald, November 18, 1887, *Macdonald Papers, Washington Treaty, 1888,* III, 5–7, P.A.C.

16. Phelps to Secretary Bayard, October 29, 1887, *Bayard MS.*

17. H. J. Holland to Sir Charles Tupper, August 9, 1887, Saunders, *op. cit.* (London, 1916), II, 97; Sir Charles Tupper to Sir John Macdonald, November 21, 1887, *Macdonald Papers, Washington Treaty, 1888,* III, 64–76, P.A.C.

that no treaty would go into effect until it had been submitted for the approval of the island government.

The first meeting of the Joint High Commission was of an informal character, and it was held on November 21. Powers were exchanged, and Chamberlain paid Bayard the graceful compliment of proposing his name as the presiding officer of the conference. Bayard did not believe it was necessary to have an officer direct the course of the proceedings along strictly formal channels, but it was agreed that protocolists be appointed in order that some record could be kept of motions and votes.[18] Twenty-nine meetings of the Commission were held, and they extended from November 22, 1887 to February 15, 1888.

The first question that came up for discussion on November 22 was with regard to the extent of the terms of reference that had been agreed upon by the British and American Governments. These terms had emphasized the importance of the North Atlantic fisheries, but they had also made provision for discussion of "any other questions which may arise," or which the Commissioners might be authorized by their respective Governments to "consider and adjust." The instructions that Lord Salisbury gave to the British Commissioners were in keeping with these terms of reference.[19] There was, however, a "vagueness" of definition that disturbed Lord Lansdowne, and he anticipated difficulties between the American and British delegations.

Bayard had realized that the Senate would reject any treaty that contained the slightest provision looking towards the establishment of commercial reciprocity with Canada. For that reason he was determined to restrict the discussions of the Joint High Commission to the sole question of the North Atlantic fisheries, and he flatly refused to authorize the American Commissioners to discuss the other issues that had long been outstanding between Canada and the United States. But he was willing to give an intimation to the effect that Congress might feel disposed to make tariff concessions to Canadian products in exchange for favors to the American fishing industry.[20]

18. Sir Charles Tupper to Sir John Macdonald, November 21, 1887, *ibid.*, pp. 64–75.

19. Tupper, *op. cit.*, pp. 186–190. The protocols of the meetings of the Joint High Commission are given in *Senate Ex. Doc. No. 176*, 50 Cong., 1 sess., but they are very brief and unsatisfactory.

20. In a letter to Phelps, December 6, 1887, Bayard told of his struggle with the British delegation in connection with the terms of reference: "Mr. Chamberlain and Sir Charles Tupper verbally gave strong expression to the misapprehension with which they had come hither, and affected to say that an arrangement of more liberal commercial relations between Canada and the United States was the only method by which harmony could be expected to be obtained, or be lost sight of. The 'personal and unofficial' letter from me to Sir Charles Tupper written in June, 1887, . . . was quoted to give meaning to the terms of reference so carefully prepared and amended

With reference to the fisheries question, Bayard stated that the privilege of "taking, drying and curing fish within three miles of the coasts" was not the "subject of this conference." The American Government had no complaint concerning the exclusion of fishermen "from that belt nor of the confiscation when apprehended there for fishing." American fishermen had certain liberties under the Treaty of 1818 (shelter, repairs, wood and water), and it was with reference to these liberties and to commercial privileges like the purchase of bait, that the United States was principally concerned. Canada had imposed so many burdens upon the use of these liberties that our fishermen had found them "injuries and not benefits." If American fishermen could exercise their treaty rights of repairs, shelter, wood and water "only in established ports of entry, and not frequent for such purposes the unfrequented parts of the coast, would not additional security accrue to Nova Scotia and opportunity for illicit trade be taken away?" In these ports, under close supervision, what greater injury could be apprehended from a fishing vessel than from a trading vessel? Therefore, why could not commercial privileges be extended to these fishing vessels unless "the *open sea fishing* is to be impeded [by refusal to sell bait], and that is a distinct act of unfriendliness and is not warranted by any Treaty or international law."[21]

It was evident to Bayard that the inshore fisheries along the Canadian coasts were not as important as they had been before the introduction of the purse seine. Moreover, the use of larger ships with extensive refrigeration facilities had diminished the importance of the liberty to take, dry and cure fish within the three-mile limit. What American fishermen most needed was the liberty to buy bait in Canadian ports for deep-sea fishing, and for this commercial concession Bayard thought that Congress might reduce or remove the duties on certain Canadian products.[22]

by Lord Salisbury, and recited in the powers given to the Plenipotentiaries. Sir Charles even went so far as to seek to control the terms of the conference by what he said verbally to me when he made his unofficial visit to Washington in May last. . . . I need not say that such an attempt at unauthorized substitution was at once stated to be wholly inadmissible." *Bayard MS.*

21. *Memorandum* written by Bayard, November 22, 1887, *ibid.*

22. In his letter to Sir John Macdonald, November 24, 1887, Sir Charles Tupper makes the following comments: "I wish you and your colleagues carefully to consider the questions that I have reason to think may arise—the extension of the right of purchasing supplies, transshipment *etc.,* to deep-sea fishing vessels in certain defined Ports and with restrictions that would prevent fishing or smuggling in our waters, in exchange for the abandonment of all Territorial rights in Canada and Newfoundland, and the assurance that the duties on a large class of our natural products would be taken off by the independent action of Congress." *Macdonald Papers, Washington Treaty, 1888,* III, 93–100, P.A.C.

To the members of the Commission it was soon evident that agreement upon the questions at issue would be possible only after many long and arduous sessions. The second session was to be held on November 28, but before that date arrived, something occurred that had a profound influence upon the life of Joseph Chamberlain. A widower nearing his fifty-second birthday, with a large family of children and many political and business interests, was hardly the person to open the door of his heart to a belated knock by romance. But love draws its own designs for living, and Chamberlain, who professed to like all Americans, suddenly found his chief interest in life centered in Mary Endicott, the attractive daughter of the Secretary of War in President Cleveland's Cabinet.

On November 26, 1887, Sir Lionel West gave a reception in honor of Chamberlain, and the *élite* of Washington society crowded into the spacious chambers of the British Legation. Mary Endicott accompanied her father to the reception. As soon as Chamberlain met her, he forgot his duties to the other guests in the Legation, and assumed one of the principal roles in that most ancient of mysteries—the way of a man with a maid.[23]

But this romantic interlude did not soften Chamberlain's heart towards American claims, and he proved a difficult person to deal with during the sessions of the Joint High Commission. It may be that a man in a courting mood takes on the air of a conqueror and is more belligerent than usual. If Chamberlain had remained an uninspired widower with a heavy load of family cares, he might have turned out to be the impartial arbiter about whom Phelps had written so glowingly. With the tonic of love to give him new assurance, Chamberlain took great interest in the proceedings of the Commission, and he strongly supported the contentions of Canadian statesmen. On November 24, Tupper reported to Sir John Macdonald that "nothing could be more satisfactory than the manner in which Mr. Chamberlain sustained our position in the discussion on Tuesday."[24]

When Macdonald showed to Lansdowne the report made by Tupper of the refusal of the American Commissioners to expand the terms of reference, Lansdowne thought it was difficult to "acquit Bayard of

23. James L. Garvin, *The Life of Joseph Chamberlain* (London, 1933), II, 335–341; Sir Willoughby Maycock, *With Mr. Chamberlain in the United States and Canada, 1887–1888* (London, 1914), pp. 50–55. In order to avoid all political difficulties, Chamberlain's marriage to Miss Endicott was postponed until after the Presidential election of 1888.

24. Sir Charles Tupper to Sir John Macdonald, November 24, 1887, *Macdonald Papers, Washington Treaty, 1888,* III, 93–100, P.A.C.

duplicity." On October 3, 1887, Sir John had warned Lansdowne against "the faithlessness of the American Government." There was "no fair dealing to be expected from them."[25] This warning now came back to Lansdowne, and he inclined towards the belief that one should always be suspicious of American promises. But it was apparent that the present situation was not to be determined by "hard logic." Each side had made up its mind, and unless the Commission could put a stop to a "mere dialectical controversy," no progress could be expected. The Canadian Commissioners should be wary, however, of placing any reliance upon American assurances that Congress would reduce the duties upon Canadian products as a *quid pro quo* for Canadian concessions. American assurances were not always carried out.[26]

Bayard was just as suspicious of the Canadians as they were of him. In a letter to Phelps he complained that at the meetings of the Commission, Sir Charles Tupper would do nothing but "talk shop," and Chamberlain's "object seems mainly to satisfy Canada." There was no chance for Canada to secure a reciprocity treaty, and the best they could hope for was some tariff concession that Congress might be disposed to offer.[27]

At the second meeting of the Joint High Commission on November 28, Bayard recited a list of American complaints against the actions of the Canadian Government and ended his indictment with a condemnation of the Treaty of 1818 as a *damnosa hereditas*. "Good," interjected Chamberlain, "now replace it by another."[28] At the third session of the Commission, Bayard referred Chamberlain to the American memorandum which had been turned over to the British delegation, but this was denounced as "utterly unacceptable." Angell then remarked that these British demands for equivalent concessions would make it "useless to go on." Tupper grew angry at this comment and condemned the American memorandum as "an invitation to a complete surrender." Putnam could keep quiet no longer, and he burst out with a criticism of the Canadian contentions, and stated that the British Foreign Office had never supported them.[29]

25. Sir John Macdonald to Lansdowne, October 3, 1887, *Macdonald Letter Books*, XXV, 243, P.A.C.

26. Lansdowne to Sir John Macdonald, November 30, 1887, *Macdonald Papers, Governor-General's Correspondence*, XIV, 365–367, P.A.C.

27. Secretary Bayard to Phelps, December 6, 1887, *Bayard Letter Book*, VI, *Bayard MS.*

28. *Protocol* of the second meeting of the Commission, November 28, 1887, *Macdonald Papers, Washington Treaty*, V, 36–62, P.A.C.

29. *Protocol* of the third meeting of the Commission, November 30, 1887, *ibid.*, pp. 64–94.

At the fourth session of the Commission, Chamberlain denied that the Foreign Office had refused to support Canadian contentions, and Tupper then took up the battle. At the close of the meeting, the British delegation submitted a proposal that favored a return to the condition of affairs existing under the Treaty of Washington, together with some arrangement "providing for greater freedom of commercial intercourse between the United States and Canada."[30] This proposal was rejected by the American Commissioners, and a deadlock was in sight. In a memorandum written on December 8, Bayard summed up the situation:

The United States believes the *main question* to be good neighborhood, and that friendly relations and kind feelings should not be imperilled or impaired without sufficient cause. Canada has pressed forward a commercial arrangement in which an equivalent for her relaxation of a strict and offensive interpretation . . . of the Treaty of 1818 is made a condition precedent. . . . From Canada not a word or act calculated to support the friendly attitude and action of the British.[31]

On December 7, the American Commissioners sent a formal note to the British members of the Commission in which they rejected all thought of commercial reciprocity between the United States and Canada. Such a system would require "an adjustment of the present tariff of the United States by Congressional action." This adjustment would be "manifestly impracticable of accomplishment through the medium of a treaty," and it was impossible to forecast what action Congress would take. The best course for the Commission to pursue was to abandon any plans for commercial reciprocity and concentrate upon settling the fisheries controversy by "agreeing to an interpretation or modification of the treaty of 1818, which will be honourable to both parties and remove the present causes of complaint."[32]

It was apparent to Chamberlain that the negotiations had reached a "critical position." At the suggestion of Sir Charles Tupper, Chamberlain paid a visit to Bayard's residence for a confidential canvass of the situation. He opened the conversation by suggesting a treaty based upon four conditions: (1) a system of Canadian licenses for American fishermen, the licenses to be paid for as long as Canadian fish were taxed under the American tariff; (2) free fishing for Americans and a

30. *Protocol* of the fourth meeting of the Commission, December, 1887, *ibid.*, pp. 96–123; Sir Charles Tupper to Sir John Macdonald, December 3, 1887, *ibid.*, III, 148–161.
31. *Memorandum* written by Bayard, December 8, 1887, *Bayard MS.*
32. Saunders, *op. cit.*, II, 103–104.

base for supplies, with full commercial privileges; (3) a release by the United States of their rights under the Treaty of 1818 along the coasts of Newfoundland, the Magdalen Islands, and Labrador; (4) free fish in American markets.[33]

Bayard re-phrased these conditions to read: (1) the appointment of a mixed commission which would be empowered to settle the difficult question of territorial waters; (2) full commercial privileges to American fishing vessels in the territorial waters of Canada and Newfoundland, the American Government, at the same time, renouncing the privileges granted under the Treaty of 1818 with reference to the taking, drying and curing of fish in the exclusive territorial waters of Canada and Newfoundland; (3) the free importation of fish and fish oil into the United States. Bayard was also ready to discuss further American concessions in connection with the exclusion of fishermen from certain bays like Chaleur Bay.[34]

Throughout this conversation with Chamberlain, Bayard had stressed the importance of establishing between the United States and Canada an "entente cordiale." A close understanding between the two countries was of paramount importance, and it could serve as the basis for the wider commercial relations so ardently desired by many Canadians.[35]

Chamberlain professed to be strongly desirous of helping to establish this era of good feelings between Canada and the United States, and in order to promote such a worthy objective he decided to visit Canada and discuss the situation with Lord Lansdowne and Sir John Macdonald. But first of all he wished to have a talk with President Cleveland. Bayard arranged for this meeting (December 14), and after the conference had been concluded, Chamberlain paid another call upon Bayard. He stated that the President had given his approval to the

33. Sir Charles Tupper to Sir John Macdonald, December 9, 1887; Tupper to Macdonald, December 10, 1887, Saunders, *ibid.*, pp. 104–106.

34. See Chamberlain's memoranda of his conversation with Secretary Bayard, December 10, 1887, *Macdonald Papers, Washington Treaty, 1888,* III, 391–416, P.A.C. In a letter to Sir John Macdonald, December 10, 1887, Sir Charles Tupper observed: "Mr. Bayard said that he would agree to give up the Bay Chaleurs and fix the others at ten miles width, and was anxious to have a more prompt and less expensive tribunal, that the United States Senate would not renounce the territorial rights as suggested, but he did not object to the licensing, but thought he could carry a Treaty in the Senate providing for free fish, oil, etc., in exchange for supplies and transshipment. This will not only suit us, but will, in consequence of the removal of the irritation, lead to almost all the articles in the Treaty of 1854 being made free by legislation at an early day." Saunders, *op. cit.,* II, 105.

35. *Memorandum* written by Bayard after a conversation with Chamberlain, December 10, 1887, *Bayard MS.* See also, Chamberlain to Secretary Bayard, December 10, 1887, *ibid.*

items that Bayard had enumerated on December 10.[36] Additional comments upon the President's position were then made by Chamberlain, who was deeply interested in the influence that could be exerted by the American Chief Executive upon the Senate.

At the close of his conversation with Bayard, Chamberlain brought forth a list of concessions he expected the American Government to make. One of the most important of these dealt with the exclusion of American fishing vessels from Chaleur Bay. Bayard had already accepted this item, and he now expressed his conviction that it would be highly regarded in Canada as a counterpoise to Canadian concessions. In conclusion, Bayard indicated the advantages that the Canadian fishing industry enjoyed under the present American tariff. They were more considerable than most Canadians realized.[37]

Chamberlain set out on his Canadian trip on December 19,[38] and was soon in conference with Canadian officials. He found Lord Lansdowne in none too friendly a mood towards American statesmen. In a letter to Sir John Macdonald, Lansdowne had discussed the dispute between the American and British Commissioners concerning the scope of the terms of reference. In criticism of Bayard's stand he remarked: "How Bayard can without blushing, after all that took place between himself and Sir Charles Tupper, state gravely that he cannot discuss commercial relations without . . . an extension of his own instructions, passes my comprehension. There is a disingenuousness throughout his argument which lowers him in one's estimation."[39]

36. *Memorandum* written by Chamberlain, December 14, 1887, *Macdonald Papers, Washington Treaty, 1888,* III, 391–416, P.A.C. President Cleveland had clearly expressed to Chamberlain his belief that Canada should give commercial privileges to American fishing vessels in return for tariff concessions by Congress.

37. *Memorandum* written by Bayard after a conversation with Chamberlain, December 14, 1887, *Bayard MS.* During this conversation, Bayard referred to the American concessions extended to Canadian fish in American markets. Canadian cured fish paid a duty of 20 per cent; fresh fish no duty. For the year 1886 the duty collected on Canadian cured fish amounted to $191,540. During this same year, Canadian fresh fish to the amount of $1,065,416 had been admitted free of duty. On December 15, Bayard had a conversation with President Cleveland, and he noted that their minds were "in agreement generally." *Memorandum* by Bayard, December 15, 1887, *ibid.*

38. In a letter to W. L. Putnam, December 19, 1887, Bayard referred to Chamberlain's visit to Canada and observed: "I hope he may infuse into the minds of the rulers of that Country a wiser view than they seem yet to have taken of their relations to the United States. Cases come dropping in of last year which indicate but too plainly the intent to destroy the few poor privileges secured to our Fishermen under the Treaty of 1818." *Bayard Letter Book,* VI, *Bayard MS.*

39. Lansdowne to Sir John Macdonald, December 10, 1887, *Macdonald Papers, Governor-General's Correspondence,* XIV, 383–385, P.A.C.

Chamberlain had a difficult time in Canada trying to convince Lansdowne and Macdonald that the American concessions formed a real basis for agreement. On January 3, 1888, he was back in Washington and at once addressed a short note to Bayard in which he remarked that he had experienced "some difficulty with the good people on the other side of the border," but he had succeeded in securing their consent to Bayard's proposals, and "to a plan for giving them effect."[40]

Bayard was glad that Chamberlain had been able to secure the consent of "our Cousins in Canada" to the proposals that had been agreed upon during the conversations at Bayard's residence on December 10 and 14. He then suggested that another private conversation be held on January 5.[41] When Chamberlain arrived he commented upon the trouble he had experienced in bringing Sir Charles Tupper around to meet his view, but in the main he had succeeded. He had been pleased to discover that Sir John Macdonald was a man of "breadth and ability." Sir John was willing to have a commission pass upon the headlands question and the delimitation of the three-mile line with regard to bays ten miles in width or less. He was also willing to make other concessions. The penalties provided for American vessels fishing or preparing to fish in Canadian territorial waters would not be rigorously carried out, and "minor penalties" could be fixed by the proposed commission. Commercial privileges for American fishing vessels in Canadian ports[42] could be balanced by tariff concessions by Congress. In the event that the Senate would not agree to any settlement on the terms proposed by the Commission, then a system of fishing licenses could be established. The fees for such licenses would "not be collected whenever free admission

40. Chamberlain to Bayard, January 3, 1888, *Bayard MS.*

41. Secretary Bayard to Chamberlain, January 4, 1888, *ibid.*

42. Bayard was very insistent upon the extension of commercial privileges to American fishing vessels. The arguments he presented to Chamberlain were set forth in detail in his memoranda of conversations. The following comments are typical: "At the period in question, 1818, there were no commercial rights or privileges for *any* American vessels in Canada because commerce was interdicted by law between the two countries. American fishing vessels alone had rights to enter Canadian waters, and these secured and regulated by treaty and therefore not to be diminished without mutual consent. Not until after 1830 could any distinction between the rights of trading vessels and fishing vessels have existed or been considered, because the *latter alone* could enter the jurisdictional waters for the four purposes named in the proviso to the renunciation. Can it be supposed that these rights of American fishermen were to diminish and be subjected to increased restrictions as the wealth and commerce of Canada increased? . . . Since 1818 telegraphic communication has been brought into use, . . . yet under the words 'for no other purpose whatever,' an American fisherman seeking shelter in a Canadian port is not allowed by the laws there in force to announce to the widow of the man lost overboard in a storm at sea the fact of her husband's death."

of Canadian fish should be provided by United States Laws." As an additional concession, the Canadian Government was willing to abolish "all pilotage charges for fishery vessels."[43]

Bayard accepted these proposals *ad referendum*, and it was agreed that the next meeting of the Joint High Commission should be held on January 9, 1888. Bayard realized that all the points in the outline proposed by Chamberlain would have to be discussed with great care by the American members of the Commission. Republican opposition could be counted upon with certainty as far as any treaty was concerned, and already Henry Cabot Lodge had opened an assault upon the policy of the Administration.[44] But Republicans were not the only ones who were sharply critical of Canada. To Phelps, in London, the situation had dangerous possibilities: "The Canadian demand that we should purchase exemption from manifest outrage by modifying our tariff, and be coerced into a new treaty by plain violation of the old one, is what in my judgment neither Congress nor the country will tolerate."[45]

Bayard had to take note of this strong opposition to any unbalanced bargain with Canada, and at the meeting of the Commission on January 14 he filed a sharp indictment against Canadian practices. While he believed that the paramount end in view in holding the meetings of the Commission was the "establishment of good feeling and friendly relations between the two countries," he was opposed to carrying this spirit of good will too far. The American plenipotentiaries must not only consider "their own judgments and their willingness to accept any proposal which may be made," but they must also "look beyond and contemplate what would be the result should they fail to obtain two-thirds of the Senate *as now constituted*." In conclusion it was well to remember that any far-reaching change in tariffs on Canadian goods must be made by Congress, and not by the President through the negotiation of a treaty. It was necessary, therefore, for the British Commissioners to keep in mind the fact that the program adopted by the Joint High Commission should be drawn up with a definite view of conciliating Congress and thereby securing Congressional approval.[46]

It had been plain to Bayard that "the sole point upon which the negotiation has been hung by the British Plenipotentiaries has been

43. *Memorandum* written by Bayard after a conversation with Chamberlain, January 5, 1888, *ibid.* See also, *memorandum* written by Chamberlain after his conversation with Bayard, January 5, 1888, *Macdonald Papers, Washington Treaty, 1888,* III, 391–416, P.A.C.

44. W. L. Putnam to Secretary Bayard, December 16, 1887, *Bayard MS.*

45. Phelps to Secretary Bayard, December 20, 1887, *ibid.*

46. *Memorandum* written by Bayard, January 14, 1888, *ibid.*

an alteration in the United States tariff so as to admit *all* fish free of duty. This has been with them from the first a *sine qua non*, and every proposition submitted by them has contained this feature and made to depend upon its acceptance."[47]

When Bayard frankly stated that the President was not able, by means of a treaty, to satisfy these Canadian demands for "free fish," Chamberlain and Tupper grew very angry and the meeting was so "stormy" that it was agreed that no record of it should be kept.[48] A serious crisis had been reached in the work of the Commission, and Chamberlain, realizing that something would have to be done at once, wrote Bayard a long letter in which he reviewed the whole situation and complained that the American Commissioners were guilty of bad faith. He had taken the trouble to submit to Bayard a series of proposals which he had been led to believe were acceptable. After receiving this assurance he had made the long trip to Ottawa to discuss the situation with Lord Lansdowne and Sir John Macdonald. He had banished their suspicions of American policy and had finally won their approval of the program he had outlined. Upon returning to Washington he had been astounded to learn that the American Commissioners were now raising objections to proposals they had formerly favored.[49]

Bayard saw at once that Chamberlain was endeavoring to pin a charge of broken promises upon the American delegation, and thus, if the negotiations ended in a deadlock, he could side-step any responsibility for the failure. It was an old diplomatic trick but it was clumsily handled. Bayard's reaction to Chamberlain's letter is indicated in some comments he jotted down on an old piece of State Department stationery:

Two admitted facts control this question of settling an intricate treaty by conversations and unsigned memos. (1) Mr. Chamberlain's visit to Canada was to *prepare to make proposals,* and was announced to be for that purpose. (2) Mr. C. sought me individually and . . . agreed that everything . . . that passed at these interviews was in all cases *ad referendum*. How then is it possible to treat such discussions as proposals agreed upon and to express suspicion when they are not promptly carried in our meeting.[50]

In his reply to Chamberlain's letter, Bayard stated that "with full recollection of all that has passed," he was not able to agree that

47. Undated *memorandum* written by Bayard, *ibid.*

48. Sir Charles Tupper to Sir John Macdonald, January 19, 1888, *Macdonald Papers, Washington Treaty, 1888,* III, 358–363, P.A.C.

49. Joseph Chamberlain to Secretary Bayard, January 15, 1888, *Bayard MS.*

50. *Memorandum* written by Bayard, January 15, 1888, *ibid.*

Chamberlain had "'reasons for some little surprise' and anxiety in finding that the proposals of the British Plenipotentiaries were not 'promptly and completely accepted.'" He had made it clear in his conversations concerning Canadian-American relations, that all proposals made by either party were merely *ad referendum.* They could not be accepted until they had been approved by the President and by the three American Commissioners. This had been clearly stated, and Chamberlain should have understood this fact.[51]

In a letter to W. L. Putnam, Bayard expressed the opinion that Chamberlain was "disingenuous, at least in the matter of papers passed in the conferences and distinctly agreed to on both sides as part of the record. He has been uncandid and unsatisfactory. What with my notes and Mr. Moore's, however, I believe we can establish the true proceedings. Mr. Bergne's memory too was slippery, but he took refuge behind Chamberlain's orders and remembered only when it was convenient."[52]

According to Sir Charles Tupper, Chamberlain regarded the American Commissioners as a "lot of dishonest tricksters." He did not believe that anything could be accomplished by the Joint High Commission, and was ready to return to England and "fight our battle in and out of Parliament against the United States as the most . . . unfair people in the world."[53]

While Chamberlain was still in this disturbed state of mind, he sent to Bayard an outline of a *modus vivendi* which could be adopted in the

51. Secretary Bayard to Chamberlain, January 15, 1888, *ibid.*

52. Secretary Bayard to W. L. Putnam, March 3, 1888, *Bayard Letter Book,* VII, *Bayard MS.* Bergne was Chamberlain's clerk.

53. Sir Charles Tupper to Sir John Macdonald, January 19, 1888, *Macdonald Papers, Washington Treaty, 1888,* III, 358–363, P.A.C. In this same letter, Tupper further remarked: "Even if we break up without any solution, I believe much good will have been done in England, Canada and here, and that our position will be improved in every way. . . . Her Majesty's Government and the people of England will better understand our position and support us with more enthusiasm and I am sure our intercourse with Senators, Representatives and influential people here has dispelled a great deal of prejudice and will bear fruit at no distant day."

Maycock, *op. cit.,* pp. 200–201, gives a highly colored but dubious account of this disagreement between Bayard and Chamberlain: "It was at this crisis, early in January, that Mr. Chamberlain and I took a walk one morning towards the Washington Memorial. He then told me of his intention to make an announcement in the Plenary Conference that afternoon, that further parley being apparently useless, he had resolved to break off negotiations and return home. I suggested as an alternative that we might utilize Sir Lionel West: 'Get him to go and see Mr. Bayard at once, with the gloomiest countenance he can assume. Let him tell Mr. Bayard that your patience is exhausted.' . . . Mr. Chamberlain thought this a good idea and adopted it. West went and saw Bayard, with the result that when the Conference met that afternoon a change had come o'er the spirit of the dream."

event that the Commission could not agree upon a treaty. This *modus* provided that American fishing vessels could enter the bays and harbors of Canada and Newfoundland to purchase bait and fishing supplies upon the payment of an annual license fee. In the event that the American tariff duties on Canadian fish and fish oil, whale oil, seal oil, and other fish products should be removed, the licenses to American fishermen would be granted without charge.[54]

On January 18, Chamberlain thought that the negotiations looked "less promising than at any previous time,"[55] but three days later Bayard assured President Cleveland that the conference had not "broken up."[56] He then went to the White House and had a talk with the President, who apparently felt that the best way of meeting Chamberlain's display of temperament was to read the riot act to him. Cleveland reminded Bayard that Congress had empowered him, under the terms of the Retaliation Act, to strike a severe blow at Canadian commerce. If the sessions of the Commission ended in a stalemate, he would not consent to the appointment of another commission. In view of the possibility that Congress might feel disposed to grant certain tariff concessions to Canada, it might be well to adjourn the sessions of the Commission and "await results."[57]

Bayard himself began to grow weary of the way that Chamberlain and Tupper were acting, and on the last day of January he put some thoughts down on paper. For some unexplained reason, Chamberlain had "yielded the control of the negotiations over to Sir Charles Tupper," who subjected all questions to "the demands of Canadian politics." Again and again the question of tariff concessions to Canada had come before the Commission, and everything had been placed upon a "mercenary basis." The important matter of establishing good relations between Canada and the United States was beyond the comprehension of Tupper, who thought only in terms of "dollars and cents."

54. Chamberlain to Secretary Bayard, January 16, 1888, *Bayard MS.*

55. Garvin, *op. cit.,* II, 332.

56. Secretary Bayard to President Cleveland, January 21, 1888, *Bayard Letter Book,* VII, *Bayard MS.*

57. *Memorandum* written by Bayard after a conversation with President Cleveland, January 21, 1888, *Bayard MS.* One of the topics that disturbed the even tenor of the sessions dealt with the matter of damages to be paid by the British Government because of Canadian seizures of American fishing vessels. The British delegation refused to agree to any payment unless the liability of the American Government for the Behring Sea seizures was admitted. On February 3, 1888, Tupper offered to resign his office as Canadian High Commissioner and act merely as an officer of the Imperial Government if this action would be of any service to Sir John Macdonald in the fight concerning the treaty. Tupper to Sir John Macdonald, February 3, 1888, *Macdonald Papers, Tupper Correspondence,* IV, 74–75.

In this "contest of the counter, the ordinary terms of international amity" were overlooked, and "the commonest rights of food and needed supplies are refused to American fishing vessels *because* they are fishing vessels."

It was a singular circumstance that the relations between the United States and Great Britain had been placed in the hands of "such a trio as Chamberlain, Sir Charles Tupper, and Sir Lionel West." At times, Mr. Chamberlain had been "disposed to take an English and liberal view of the whole question," but he had yielded "point after point to the steady shop-keeping insistence of his Canadian colleague who sees but the items of his fish bills." Tupper had never for an instant "wandered from his track." He was a "mere bargainer, and wants to know and see what he is to get for every point conceded." He wants "pay for kindness."

Chamberlain had exhibited no "touch of a wider wisdom," and sometimes one could hear "the true *Birmingham tone*" in his commercial discourse. His habit and manner were distinctly "commercial, and unmoved by anything higher." As for Sir Lionel West, he had not "opened his mouth since the conference opened except once to *equivocate* about a message he had delivered to me from his Colleagues. The point was not of essential importance, but had it been so, Her Britannic Majesty's Minister would have said whatever the apparent exigency required of him."[58]

These diplomatic bickerings and disputes continued until February 15, when the members of the Commission finally signed a treaty covering most of the points under discussion. Provision was made for the appointment of a mixed commission that would delimit the waters along the coasts of Canada and Newfoundland in which the United States had, by the Treaty of 1818, renounced forever any liberty to take, dry and cure fish. The three-mile limit was to be measured seaward from the low water mark, but at every bay, creek or harbor not otherwise specially provided for in the treaty, the three-mile line was to be drawn from a straight line drawn across the bay, creek or harbor in the part nearest the entrance at the first point where the width did not exceed ten marine miles. Specific stipulations were made as to the lines that were to be drawn in certain bodies of water like Chaleur Bay and

58. *Memorandum* written by Bayard, January 31, 1888, *Bayard MS*. It is interesting to note the impact of Tupper's letters upon Lord Lansdowne. On January 19 he wrote to Sir John Macdonald: "I am beginning to form a poor opinion of Mr. Bayard, but I suppose we can form no opinion of the undercurrents which run beneath the surface of Washington politics." *Macdonald Papers, Governor-General's Correspondence,* XV, 25–26, P.A.C.

the Bay of Miramichi, but it was expressly provided that nothing in the treaty would affect the free navigation of the Strait of Canso by the fishing vessels of the United States. American fishing vessels were to conform to harbor regulations, but they need not report, enter, or clear when putting into such bays or harbors for shelter or repairing damages, nor when putting in outside the limits of established ports of entry for the purpose of purchasing wood or of obtaining water, unless they remained in port more than twenty-four hours, or communicated with the shore. They would not be liable in such bays or harbors for compulsory pilotage, nor would they be liable for harbor dues, tonnage dues, buoy dues, light dues, or similar dues when they put into port for the purpose of shelter, repairing of damages, obtaining water, or purchasing wood. They could, when entering under stress of weather, unload, reload, transship, or sell all fish on board when necessary as incidental to repairs, and might replenish outfits, provisions and supplies lost or damaged by storm. Licenses to purchase, for the homeward voyage, such provisions and supplies as were ordinarily sold to trading vessels, would be granted to fishing vessels promptly and without charge. Fishing vessels of Canada and Newfoundland would have on the Atlantic coast of the United States all the privileges secured by the treaty to American fishing vessels in Canada and Newfoundland. The penalty for "unlawfully fishing" in prohibited waters might extend to forfeiture of the vessel and cargo. The penalty for "preparing to fish in such waters" would be fixed by the court. Whenever Congress removed the duties from fish oil, whale oil, seal oil, and fish of all kinds coming from Canada and Newfoundland, the fishing vessels from the United States would be permitted to purchase (by procuring annual licenses, free of charge) provisions, bait, ice, seines, lines and all other supplies and outfits.[59]

Chamberlain professed to be pleased with the treaty. In a letter to Sir Charles Tupper he stated that he regarded it as a "fair and hon-

59. *Senate Ex. Doc. No. 113,* 50 Cong., 1 sess., pp. 132–138. Accompanying this treaty was a *modus vivendi* which provided that, for a period of two years, American fishing vessels would be granted annual licenses, at a fee of $1.50 per ton, for the purchase of bait, ice, seines, lines, and all other supplies and outfits. The privileges of transshipping their catch and of shipping crews were also accorded to American fishing vessels. In the event that the American Government removed the duties on fish, fish oil, whale and seal oil, these licenses would be issued free of charge. American fishing vessels entering Canadian and Newfoundland harbors for the four purposes specified in the Treaty of 1818, would not be required to enter or clear at the custom houses if they did not remain in port more than twenty-four hours. The penalty of forfeiture would be exacted only for the offences of fishing or preparing to fish in territorial waters.

ourable settlement of the controversy."[60] Bayard was glad that the long labors of the Joint High Commission were ended, and he thought it was evident that the American representatives had "maintained our position and procured such a practical and decent interpretation of the Treaty of 1818 as, if observed honorably and honestly, will prevent future friction and allow wholesome and amicable intercourse to progress between the two populations."[61]

President Cleveland sent the treaty to the Senate on February 20, with an indication of what he considered to be the more important features of that instrument. The delimitation of the lines of the exclusive fisheries from the common fisheries would give certainty and security "to the area of their legitimate field." The "headlands theory" of imaginary lines was abandoned by Great Britain, and the uninterrupted navigation of the Strait of Canso was expressly affirmed. The enforcement of penalties for unlawfully fishing, or preparing to fish, in Canadian territorial waters would no longer be carried out in an arbitrary manner. The old and irritating regulation compelling fishing vessels to make formal entry on every occasion of temporarily seeking shelter in Canadian ports was at last wiped out.[62]

Bayard was fearful that the partisan spirit of the Republican majority in the Senate would lead to a rejection of the treaty,[63] and Phelps shared this pessimistic view.[64] The Republican press, led by the New York *Tribune*, began a barrage of criticism that spared no feature of the treaty. The *Tribune* regarded it as marking the "lowest point of degradation which American diplomacy has ever reached."[65] Other Republican papers were equally defamatory, but Democratic and Independent journals were loud in their praise of the treaty.[66]

60. Chamberlain to Sir Charles Tupper, February 15, 1888, *Macdonald Papers, Washington Treaty, 1888,* IV, 235–240, P.A.C.

61. Secretary Bayard to Phelps, February 20, 1888, *Confidential, Bayard Letter Book,* VII, *Bayard MS.*

62. Message of February 20, 1888, *Senate Ex. Doc. No. 113,* 50 Cong., 1 sess., pp. 127–131. See also, *Senate Ex. Doc. No. 127,* 50 Cong., 1 sess.

63. Secretary Bayard to Phelps, February 20, 1888, *Bayard Letter Book,* VII, *Bayard MS.*

64. Phelps to Secretary Bayard, February 11, 1888, *Bayard MS.*

65. New York *Tribune,* February 23, 1888.

66. For favorable comments on the treaty see the New York *Evening Post,* February 22, 1888; the New York *Times,* February 23, 1888; the New York *Herald,* February 22, 1888; the Barnstable *Journal,* March 3, 1888; and the Boston *Post,* February 23, 1888. Hamilton Fish expressed the opinion that Bayard had concluded a "very successful treaty." New York *Herald,* February 17, 1888. The Toronto *Mail,* the Montreal *Herald,* and the Ottawa *Free Press* were outspoken in their critical comments upon the treaty. See New York *Times,* February 23, 1888.

On February 28, Chamberlain paid a farewell visit to Bayard. During the course of the conversation he alluded to certain comments he had heard respecting the treaty. A distinguished Republican, who was "one of the candidates for the Presidential nomination," had remarked to Chamberlain: "The fact is that just now we cannot afford to let this Administration do anything."[67]

It was soon apparent that a large number of Republicans shared this sentiment. After making a careful canvass of the political situation, Mr. Angell confessed to Bayard that he felt "depressed."[68] W. L. Putnam was certain that the "active opponents" of the treaty were determined to "kill it";[69] Carl Schurz was apprehensive lest an "unscrupulous party spirit" cry the treaty down;[70] and Samuel L. Barlow was dubious

67. *Memorandum* written by Bayard after a conversation with Joseph Chamberlain, February 28, 1888, *Bayard MS.*

68. J. B. Angell to Secretary Bayard, March 4, 1888, *ibid.*

69. W. L. Putnam to Secretary Bayard, March 6, 1888, *ibid.*

70. Carl Schurz to Secretary Bayard, March 7, 1888, *ibid.* In Canada this same party spirit prevailed. On March 7, Sir Charles Tupper introduced the treaty in the Canadian House of Commons by reading the message from Lord Lansdowne. On April 10, the debate began and lasted through the 16th. The division was strictly along party lines; the Conservatives supporting it and the Liberals voicing their opposition. It was significant that the majority of the members from the Maritime Provinces opposed the treaty. Sir Charles Tupper led the fight for it, and was supported by George E. Foster, Minister of Marine and Fisheries, General Laurie, of Shelburne, and several other Conservative members. The opposition forces were led by Louis H. Davies, of Queens, Prince Edward Island, but they proved to be obstructionist rather than defeatist. Their attitude was well expressed by Laurier who stated that while the "treaty is a surrender of most valuable rights that belong to Canada, still it is the duty of Canadians to adopt the treaty because it will put an end to a most dangerous state of things." *Canada: House of Commons, Debates, 1888,* I, 851 ff. See *ibid.,* pp. 86, 673, 693, 704, 779, 788, 793, 813, 861.

The Canadian newspapers adopted the same party lines that were followed by the legislators; the Conservatives supporting and the Liberals opposing the treaty. The Toronto *Mail* (February 17–20, 1888) was sharply critical of British diplomacy concerning Canada. It had been one long story of failure with the exception of the Halifax award. The Toronto *Globe* was also critical. The Toronto *Empire* (Conservative) and the Toronto *World* (Independent) were in favor of the treaty.

In Ottawa, the *Citizen* (Conservative) was favorable, the *Evening Journal* (Independent) was noncommittal, while the *Free Press* (Liberal) was abusive. It regarded the treaty as a betrayal of Canadian interests.

In Montreal, *La Patrie* (Liberal) and *L'Etendard* (Independent) were in the opposition, but the *Gazette* (Conservative), the *Shareholder* (Independent), and *La Minerve* (Conservative) supported the treaty.

In Quebec, the *Daily Telegraph* (Independent) and *L'Electeur* (Liberal) were anti-treaty, while the *Mercury* (Conservative), the *Chronicle* (Conservative), *Le Journal* (Conservative), and *Le Canadien* (Conservative) were pro-treaty. In Halifax, the *Herald* (Conservative) was objective, and the *Chronicle* was opposed.

With reference to the Bayard-Chamberlain Treaty see Charles E. Cayley, "The North Atlantic Fisheries in United States–Canadian Relations," MS. Ph.D. dissertation (University of Chicago, 1931), pp. 289–295.

In England the *Times* was strongly in favor of the treaty, and a large number of

about its fate because of the opposition of the Anglophobes and the "wild Irish."[71]

The first Republican attack in the Senate against the treaty came in the form of a resolution introduced by Senator Frye on March 15, 1888. It requested the President to transmit to the Senate copies of the minutes and the daily protocols of the meetings of the Commissioners who negotiated the treaty. This resolution did not include the usual formula which made this request contingent upon the fact that the transmission of these data would not be detrimental to the "public service."[72]

Bayard regarded Frye's resolution as "without precedent in form and in substance,"[73] and it seemed to him that the deterioration "in tone and moral grade of the Senate" was both "mystifying and exasperating."[74] With regard to the treaty he was inclined to believe that it would be voted upon in the "light of partisanship and not patriotism."[75]

A serious blow to his hopes for a speedy ratification of the treaty came in the form of a resolution adopted by the Chamber of Commerce of the City of New York (March 1, 1888), advising rejection because the "same full reciprocity to the United States fishing vessels was not accorded in Canada as was permitted at present under United States laws to Canadian fishermen here." After all the serious efforts that Bayard had made to secure the support of "big business" on behalf of the treaty, this action was extremely discouraging.[76]

As soon as the Republicans in the Senate saw that important business interests in New York City were opposed to the fisheries treaty, they lost no time in attempting to give direction to this opposition. Their chief spokesmen were soon attacking the terms of the treaty as a base surrender to Great Britain, and they accused the President of

other newspapers were friendly because it appeared as an indication that the United States was leaning towards more liberal tariff views. This British reaction was noted by United States Senators who were opposed to the treaty, and it helped to mobilize opposition to it. *Congressional Record,* 50 Cong., 1 sess., p. 7476; New York *Tribune,* February 24, 1888.

71. Samuel L. Barlow to Secretary Bayard, March 8, 1888, *Bayard MS.*

72. *Congressional Record,* 50 Cong., 1 sess., p. 2093. On March 19, 1888, the New York *Tribune* printed a long letter from Walker Blaine in which the treaty was vehemently attacked, and on March 23, a critical commentary by William H. Trescot was published. Bayard replied to these criticisms in a letter published in the New York *Times,* March 26, 1888.

73. Secretary Bayard to Senator George Gray, March 15, 1888, *Bayard Letter Book,* VII, *Bayard MS.*

74. Secretary Bayard to Phelps, March 16, 1888, *ibid.*

75. Secretary Bayard to W. L. Putnam, March 21, 1888, *ibid.*

76. Secretary Bayard to Gustave Schwab, March 10, 1888, *ibid.; House Misc. Doc. No. 133,* 50 Cong., 1 sess.; *Senate Ex. Doc. No. 113,* 50 Cong., 1 sess.

violating the Constitution by neglecting to send to the Senate for confirmation the names of the three American members of the Commission.[77] Once more the Senate was to be the scene of a fight in which many politicians were to rehearse the old argument that the President did not have undivided responsibility in the actual negotiation of treaties.[78]

On May 7, the Senate Committee on Foreign Relations submitted two reports on the fisheries treaty. The majority report, signed by John Sherman, George F. Edmunds, William P. Frye, William M. Evarts, and J. N. Dolph, was sharply critical. Special emphasis was laid upon the fact that President Cleveland had appointed the American members of the Commission in open defiance of Senate opposition to any negotiations on the fisheries question. It was quite possible that this Presidential procedure might constitute a dangerous precedent that in future years would tend to undermine the foundations of the American Republic: "In evil times, when the President of the United States may be under the influence of foreign adverse interests, such a course of procedure might result in great disaster to the interests and even the safety of our Government and people."[79]

The report of the minority of the Senate Committee on Foreign Relations had been prepared in close concert with Secretary Bayard.[80] The data taken from the files of the Department of State made it unmistakably clear that since 1815 many Presidents had disregarded the Senate in the matter of seeking confirmation for the nominations of

77. Senator John T. Morgan to Secretary Bayard, March 23, 1888, *Bayard MS.*

78. It is apparent that the fisheries treaty had strong support in many circles. On March 9, E. L. Pierce, of Boston, sent to Bayard a cordial invitation signed by "a number of representative men of Eastern New England," to visit Boston and present an objective version of the fishery settlement. On March 17, W. L. Putnam wrote to Bayard and expressed the opinion that he had "not met a business man . . . who has not expressed himself privately with great warmth in its favor." *Ibid.*

79. *Senate Doc. No. 231,* Pt. 8, 56 Cong., 2 sess., p. 271. The majority report also emphasized the fact that Bayard had abandoned his fight for the extension of commercial privileges to fishing vessels without the purchase of licenses: "The treaty is a complete surrender of any claim of a right . . . for vessels of the United States engaged in fishing . . . to enter any port of British North America for any commercial purpose whatever." It also called attention to the fact that under the terms of the treaty Bayard had made certain concessions to the British headlands theory with reference to large bays being territorial waters. The treaty frankly recognized that important bodies of water like Chaleur Bay, the Bay of Miramichi, Egmont Bay, St. Ann's Bay, Fortune Bay, Sir Charles Hamilton Sound, Barrington Bay, Chedabucto Bay, Mira Bay, Placentia Bay, and St. Mary's Bay could be legally closed to American fishermen.

80. Secretary Bayard to Senator John T. Morgan, April 7, 1888, *Bayard Letter Book,* VII, *Bayard MS.*

treaty negotiators. President Cleveland's action in refusing to send to the Senate the nominations of the three American members of the Joint High Commission, was in accord with a long list of precedents. The criticisms contained in the majority report were merely partisan slander.[81]

But partisan slander can be an effective political weapon if it is incessantly repeated to a large audience that is unfamiliar with the facts in the case. Republican Senators were well aware of the truth of this fundamental axiom in the dissemination of propaganda, and they decided to give their accusation nation-wide publicity by having the debates upon the fisheries treaty in open instead of in executive session. They would use the Senate Chamber as a great sounding board which would throw the noise of their criticisms into every corner of the United States, and it was quite possible that the average American would be so impressed by this din and shouting that he would vote the Republican ticket.

Bayard had no objections to open sessions of the Senate in connection with the debates on the treaty, and he nursed the hope that the American public would take such an interest in the fisheries treaty that Republican Senators would not dare to reject it despite their loud cries of objection. Such hopes were ill-founded.

The debate in the Senate opened on May 29, 1888, with Senator Frye in the vanguard of Republican critics. To him the treaty was the "most disgraceful, humiliating and cowardly surrender the American Republic has ever been called upon to submit to."[82] Senator Chandler then took up the fight and denounced the treaty because it had been nego-

81. *Senate Doc. No. 231,* Pt. 8, 56 Cong., 2 sess., pp. 286–333. See also, *Senate Misc. Doc. No. 109,* 50 Cong., 1 sess., pp. 17, 38, 103–105. Bayard was impressed with the fact that the majority report frankly stated that "it does not seem to the Committee that the existing matters of difficulty are subjects for treaty negotiations." Later on the Committee report remarked that no attempt would be made to offer amendments that would make the treaty acceptable to the majority. These statements seemed to Bayard to "place the United States outside the pale of civilization, and dismiss reason and argument as standards of justice and right. Retaliatory measures are alone to be relied on, and the United States are to decline at whatever cost to enter into any amendatory stipulations or engagements." Bayard to Horace White, May 12, 1888, *Bayard Letter Book,* VII, *Bayard MS.* To White the position taken by the Republican majority in the Senate was "immoral, dangerous and degrading," and he intended to "Show it up in that light in a series of articles beginning today." White to Bayard, May 15, 1888, *Bayard MS.* After Bayard had studied the report of the majority of the Senate Committee on Foreign Relations, he wrote to W. L. Putnam, May 24, 1888, and denounced it as the "most discreditable paper that ever emanated from a body of public men in the United States." *Bayard Letter Book,* VII, *Bayard MS.*

82. *Congressional Record,* 50 Cong., 1 sess., pp. 4695–4708.

tiated by "so-called plenipotentiaries" whose nominations had not been confirmed by the Senate. President Cleveland's action in ignoring the Senate in this regard was a "gross violation of the Constitution, wilfully, recklessly and defiantly perpetrated."[83]

Senator Chandler's statements were challenged by Senator Morgan, and even so stalwart a Republican as Senator Sherman had to admit that the President had complete control over the choice of treaty negotiators. He could choose any kind of a man, "a dumb man, a blind man, or a deaf man."[84]

After this rebuff, Republican Senators sought other points of attack. Riddleberger took the ground that the sixth and twelfth articles of the treaty admitted Canadians into the coastwise fisheries of the United States. After dilating upon these alleged dangers, he concluded his remarks by giving the British lion's tail one of the twists that were popular in that day. He was certain that the United States would never have a truly national government until it had administered another whipping to England. He then asked why the American Government wished "to make a treaty with such a government anyhow?"[85]

Senator Teller was equally belligerent. There was no doubt in his mind that the United States would have to whip England "a third time." The British were the "most aggressive, the most bloodthirsty," and the "most destructive of the human race." It would be a grievous mistake to conclude any more treaties with such faithless people.[86]

Senator Blair was more concerned with the intrigues of devious Democrats than with the wickedness of base Britons. The special object of his wrath was President Cleveland, whom he denounced as a "pigheaded Executive" who refused to follow the safe light of Republican counsel.[87]

In striking contrast with this partisan bluster and empty challenge, was the speech of Senator George Gray, of Delaware. Combining common sense with scholarship, he easily disposed of the fears of Senator Riddleberger that the sixth and twelfth articles of the fisheries treaty

83. *Ibid.*, pp. 6345–6358.

84. *Ibid.*, p. 7287. Even before this debate was opened in the Senate, Bayard had anticipated the result and was feeling discouraged. In a letter to D. A. Wells, April 23, 1888, he remarked: "I wish I was in better spirits, but being knocked down in every round becomes monotonous, and my earnest work is defeated by the Senate so systematically that I am discouraged. But I am not the less determined, because I am discouraged, and shall go on to make the record just, and 'keep my rudder true.'" *Bayard Letter Book*, VII, *Bayard MS.*

85. *Congressional Record*, 50 Cong., 1 sess., pp. 7155–7157.

86. *Ibid.*, p. 7220.

87. *Ibid.*, p. 7392.

were a surrender of the inshore fisheries of the United States. He was certain that it was not within the "competence of the Government of the United States under its treaty-making power to confer upon any foreign government . . . the right to participate in the fisheries of the territorial waters of the States that compose this Union." The language of Article XII said that the "fishing vessels of Canada and Newfoundland" should have certain privileges along the American coasts. What were these privileges? They were merely the same ones that American vessels enjoyed in Canadian waters—the right of refuge from storm, the right to obtain wood, water, and fuel, and commercial privileges to buy on all occasions needful supplies. There was nothing fearsome about these rights or privileges.[88]

Bayard was very glad to have the assistance of Senators like Gray and Morgan, but he knew that his Republican opponents would defeat the treaty unless the business interests were able to exert strong pressure upon them.[89] Neither Jay Gould nor G. B. Roberts had been able to enlist Senatorial support in favor of the Bayard program, and the Chamber of Commerce of the City of New York had adopted an adverse stand. It was true that the Baltimore Board of Trade (June 4, 1888) had come out in strong support of the treaty, but this action would affect few Senate votes.[90] A strong and insistent public demand for ratification was the only means of saving the treaty, and this demand could not be easily created. Bayard hurriedly wrote to Benoni Lockwood and Daniel Magone about the possibility of securing strong support from the "commercial circles of New York,"[91] but these last-minute efforts were in vain. On August 21, 1888, the Senate took final action on the fisheries treaty, and it was rejected by a vote of Yeas—27, Nays—30, Absent—19.[92]

This vote was not surprising. In the early months of 1888, Joseph Chamberlain had informed Bayard that a distinguished Republican was openly stating that his party could not "afford" to let the Cleveland Administration have the credit for a treaty that settled the age-old fisheries controversy.[93] These intimations came so clearly to the

88. *Ibid.*, p. 7477.

89. Secretary Bayard to W. L. Putnam, June 20, 1888, *Bayard Letter Book,* VIII, *Bayard MS.*

90. New York *Evening Post,* June 5, 1888.

91. Secretary Bayard to Benoni Lockwood, June 16, 1888; Secretary Bayard to Daniel Magone, June 15, 1888, *Bayard Letter Book,* VIII, *Bayard MS.*

92. *Congressional Record,* 50 Cong., 1 sess., p. 7768.

93. *Memorandum* written by Bayard, February 28, 1888, *Bayard MS.* It is significant that "not one Democrat voted against" the treaty, "nor did one Republican vote

British Legation that Cecil Spring Rice, as early as April 27, was certain that the "Fisheries treaty is practically dished."[94]

Many Democrats had early foreseen the defeat of the treaty, and W. L. Putnam advised Bayard to place the responsibility squarely upon the Republican Senate. He believed the President should "send a message throwing the whole responsibility on the Senate, distinctly intimating that, in his view, the necessity for the President's exercising a discretion under the Act of March, 1887, had gone by, . . . and that it remained for the Senate to inaugurate such measures in the way of legislation as the case requires."[95]

Cleveland accepted this counsel, and on August 23 the Republicans in the Senate were surprised by a special message on the fisheries question. Taken unawares by the President's tactics, Senator Edmunds secured an immediate adjournment of the Senate in order that his party colleagues could discuss the situation before taking any action.[96] On the following day (August 24) the Senate listened to the reading of the President's message which called for retaliatory legislation against Canada.[97] This action was necessary because of the Senate's apparent determination to defeat any treaty negotiated by a Democratic Administration: "It is of importance to note that this treaty has been rejected without any apparent disposition on the part of the Senate to alter or amend its provisions, and with the evident intention . . . that no negotiation should at present be concluded touching the matter at issue." This partisan attitude had left the Chief Executive with no alternative but to "turn to the contemplation of a plan of retaliation as a mode which still remains of treating the situation."

When Senator Edmunds heard this sharp indictment of Republican practice, he broke into loud complaints that the President had made no attempt to carry out the retaliatory legislation on March 3, 1887. Why had he waited so long? Why had he "been silent for eighteen months, with the whole power of the law in his hands and the easy means of exerting all the functions that the law imputed to him in such a case"?[98]

Senator Morgan replied that Republican members of the Senate

for ratification." Royden J. Dangerfield, *In Defense of the Senate* (Norman, 1933), pp. 243–244.

94. Stephen Gwynn, *The Letters and Friendships of Sir Cecil Spring Rice* (London, 1929), I, 85, 90, 93.

95. W. L. Putnam to Secretary Bayard, August 8, 1888, *Bayard MS.*

96. *Congressional Record,* 50 Cong., 1 sess., p. 7882.

97. Richardson, *op. cit.,* VIII, 620–621.

98. *Congressional Record,* 50 Cong., 1 sess., pp. 7903–7904.

knew only too well that "in the progress of this whole affair the purpose of all this opposition to the President in respect to his dealing with these fisheries has not been to get the interests of the people of the United States into a better shape, but it has been to entrap the Executive in a political strait-jacket." The only reason that the President now reluctantly turned to retaliatory legislation was on account of partisan spite that would not permit the Administration to use a more friendly method of settling the fisheries dispute.[99]

On August 23 a bill was introduced in the House of Representatives authorizing the President to carry out the provisions of the Act of March 3, 1887, and empowering him to protect American interests against unjust discrimination in the use of canals in the British dominions of North America.[100] On September 8, a substitute bill of similar character was passed by the House of Representatives,[101] but it was not acted upon by the Senate, which, controlled by Republicans, was careful not to embark upon a program of retaliation against Canada. Such a course would mean a severe economic loss to the business interests of the northern states from Maine to Minnesota, and this might prove a serious handicap to Republican prospects in the Presidential campaign that was already under way.

After the defeat of the fisheries treaty in the Senate, Bayard was careful to see that the *modus vivendi* of February 15, 1888 went into operation. Under the terms of this agreement, American fishing vessels could, after the purchase of an annual license at the rate of $1.50 per ton, enter the bays and harbors of the Atlantic coasts of Canada and Newfoundland and buy bait, ice, seines, lines, and all other supplies and outfits. They could also transship their catch and could ship crews if it were necessary. If the American Government should remove the duties on fish, fish oil, whale and seal oil, the said licenses would be issued free of charge. American vessels entering the bays and harbors of Canada and Newfoundland for any of the purposes mentioned in Article I of the Treaty of 1818, and not remaining for more than twenty-four hours, would not be required to enter or clear at the custom-house, providing they did not communicate with the shore. Forfeiture was to be exacted only for the offences of fishing or preparing to fish in territorial waters.[102]

Thanks to the good sense and moderation of both the American and

99. *Ibid.*, pp. 7908–7909.
100. *Congressional Record,* 50 Cong., 1 sess., p. 7901 (H.R. 11309).
101. *Ibid.*, pp. 8439–8440 (H.R. 11309).
102. Malloy, *Treaties, Conventions, etc.,* I, 738–739.

the Canadian Governments, this *modus vivendi* provided a satisfactory settlement of the fisheries question until after the turn of the century. The difficulties that arose in 1905 between the United States and Newfoundland were settled by an arbitration that brought to a pacific conclusion the oldest of the many disputes that had vexed the long course of Anglo-American relations.

CHAPTER IV

THE NORTH ATLANTIC FISHERIES CONTROVERSY IS SETTLED BY ARBITRATION

THE *modus vivendi* of 1888 temporarily eliminated the chief difficulties with which American fishermen had been faced in the waters of Newfoundland and the Dominion of Canada. For a while it seemed as though it would be the prelude to a treaty that would deal with commercial reciprocity as well as with liberties granted to American fishermen. In August, 1889, the British *chargé d'affaires* in Washington reported that Secretary Blaine, who had been placed in charge of the Department of State by President Harrison, had expressed his "very sincere desire" to settle the fisheries controversy,[1] and in February, 1890, Charles H. Tupper informed Sir John Macdonald that Blaine had spoken to him in similar fashion and had given assurances of his warm desire to "remove all difficulties between England and the United States."[2] Two weeks later, Blaine began to toy with the idea of offering to the British Government a treaty that would "follow the lines of the rejected Bayard-Chamberlain treaty of 1888 with some arrangements that will secure the privileges of the *modus vivendi* without a reduction of the duties on fish." Tupper told Sir Julian Pauncefote that Sir John Macdonald would never agree to such a proposition,[3] so Blaine dropped all thoughts of fishery negotiations concerning access to Dominion waters.

He next turned to the Government of Newfoundland for discussions on the subjects of reciprocity and fisheries. In October, 1890, Robert Bond, the colonial secretary of Newfoundland, paid a visit to Washington, and after several conferences with Secretary Blaine, a reciprocity treaty was drafted.[4] Owing to strong Canadian opposition, this treaty was not consummated, and the *modus vivendi* remained in operation.[5]

1. Lord Knutsford to Lord Stanley, August 31, 1889, *Macdonald Papers, Behring Sea,* III, 28, P.A.C.
2. C. H. Tupper to Sir John Macdonald, February 27, 1890, *Macdonald Papers, Behring Sea, Correspondence of C. H. Tupper,* I, 23–60, P.A.C.
3. C. H. Tupper to Sir John Macdonald, March 10, 1890, *ibid.,* pp. 152–169.
4. Alice F. Tyler, *The Foreign Policy of James G. Blaine* (Minneapolis, 1927), pp. 349–350.
5. *C.S.P., 1892,* No. 23, pp. 1–175; *ibid., 1893,* Nos. 20d–20f, pp. 1–62; *Newfoundland: Journal of the Assembly, 1891,* pp. 490 ff. The *modus vivendi* expired on February 15, 1890, but the Canadian Parliament continued the license system, and in

In 1893, Newfoundland had a bad fishery season which ushered in a period of hard times.[6] One of the results of this economic distress was the passage of an anti-bait Act (May 24, 1893) which provided that any "foreign fishing vessel within any port on the coasts of this Island, or hovering in British waters within 3 marine miles of any of the coasts . . . in this island," could be boarded and searched. If it was discovered that the master of this foreign fishing vessel had bought bait within the territorial waters of Newfoundland or had shipped a crew there, he was liable to a penalty that might extend to forfeiture of the vessel and cargo.[7]

Under the first clause of this Act, provision was made for the issuance of licenses ($1.50 per ton) that would extend to foreign fishing vessels the privileges of buying bait and other supplies, and would also permit them to ship crews in Newfoundland waters. The masters of American fishing vessels purchased these licenses, and no difficulties were experienced. But the very fact that fishing liberties depended upon a mere *modus vivendi* caused deep concern to the Department of State. It was important to arrange for a permanent settlement of the fisheries dispute and all the other questions at issue between Canada and the United States. In order to prepare the way for such an arrangement, another Joint High Commission was appointed and held sessions in Quebec from August 23 to October 10, 1898, and in Washington from November 9, 1898 to February 20, 1899.[8]

1892 (55–56 Vict., c. 3, May 10, 1892) enacted legislation authorizing the Governor in Council to keep this system in operation without the necessity for additional action by the Parliament. By the terms of this Act, the license system was continued by Canada until December 31, 1923. *Canadian Annual Review, 1923,* pp. 54–55. Under this system the number of licenses issued each year by the Canadian Government varied greatly. In 1892 the number was 108, and the amount of fees collected reached a total of $13,410.00, but in 1895 this had dropped to 47 licenses with an income of only $5,571.00. A decade later (1905), the number of licenses issued had risen to 107, with an income of $12,550.00. In 1904 the license system was officially considered to apply only to sailing vessels, and after 1906, the number of licenses issued began to decline.

Although the license system was in some way injurious to Canadian fishing interests, it was administered in a very judicious manner, and there were few seizures of American vessels. See annual *Reports of the Department of Marine and Fisheries, 1888–1923.*

6. Innis, *The Cod Fisheries,* p. 454.

7. The text of the anti-bait Act of May 24, 1893, is given in *F.R., 1906,* Pt. 1, pp. 757–758. See also, J. D. Rogers, *A Historical Geography of the British Colonies, Newfoundland* (London, 1931), pp. 232–233.

8. The American Commissioners were Charles W. Fairbanks, chairman; Nelson Dingley, Judge George Gray, John W. Foster, John A. Kasson, T. Jefferson Coolidge, and Charles J. Faulkner (appointed to fill the vacancy created by the resignation of Judge Gray). The British Commissioners were Baron Herschell, Sir Wilfrid Laurier, Sir Richard Cartwright, Sir Louis Davies, John Charlton, and Hon. James Winter.

In the instructions that were given to the American Commissioners it was pointed out that the *modus vivendi* had really expired on February 15, 1890, and was merely being kept in force by the courtesy of the Canadian and Newfoundland Governments. At any moment, "trivial violations of the treaty rights, not as they actually are, but as they are construed by Great Britain, may result in the seizure and forfeiture of vessels, and involve the country in a repetition of the diplomatic complications of 1886 and 1887." Although the fishing industry was not of as much importance economically as it had been in earlier years, the rights of American fishermen "to pursue their vocation and to be protected as citizens of this country" were just as "paramount and binding on the General Government today as they ever were when the great wooden codfish hung in the Massachusetts State House as a constant reminder of the sources from which so great a part of the wealth of the Union was derived."[9]

When this Joint High Commission opened its sessions in Quebec on August 23, 1898, the British Commissioners expressed the hope that the fisheries question might be settled "on the basis of the arrangement agreed to by the two Governments in 1888, or at all events by a provision for 'free fish' in return for a renunciation by Great Britain of the rights of restriction which she claimed under the Treaty of 1818." When the sessions of the Commission were shifted from Quebec to Washington, the British representatives were informed that the "arrangement" they had hoped for was impossible "owing to the strong local feeling opposed to it." When they asked for some suggestions as to a possible settlement of the fisheries dispute, the American Commissioners remained silent. Finally, Lord Herschell proposed arbitration, at the same time expressing the disappointment of the British Commissioners at the failure of the American representatives to signify their assent to a treaty similar to the Chamberlain-Bayard Treaty.[10]

In defence of the stand taken by the American Commissioners, Senator Fairbanks expressed the opinion that the decisive vote in the Senate on the Chamberlain-Bayard Treaty had unmistakably indicated that no convention of a like character could command a two-thirds vote of approval. It was exceedingly doubtful whether Congress would favor any reduction of tariff duties on Canadian fish, so there was hardly any use in negotiating a treaty that included this important item.[11]

9. "The Fisheries Off the Atlantic Coast," *Pamphlets Printed for the Use of the Joint High Commission, 1898,* pp. 23–25, Dept. of State.

10. Lord Herschell to Senator Fairbanks, December 21, 1898, *Alaska Boundary Papers,* MS. Dept. of State.

11. Senator Fairbanks to Lord Herschell, December 24, 1898, *ibid.*

The American Commissioners then accepted the proposal to arbitrate the fisheries dispute. An outline for an arbitral convention was drawn up, and articles were prepared which specifically defined the terms of the submission and its conditions. Two questions concerning the construction of the Treaty of 1818 were to be placed before the arbitrators: (1) What was meant by the terms "bays" and "harbors"? This question would necessarily involve a consideration of the "headlands theory." (2) Did British legislation subsequent to 1830, with special reference to the navigation acts of 1839 and 1849, confer upon the fishing vessels of the United States full commercial privileges when they had a license designating a particular port in the British colonies or when they merely had a general fishing license?

After an extended canvass of these questions, the British Commissioners suddenly came to the conclusion that it was not necessary to submit such matters to arbitration: the Joint High Commission had the authority and the capacity to find the proper answers. The American Commissioners acquiesced in this decision, and a long discussion ensued. The British representatives agreed to accept the American contention concerning the meaning of the term "bay," but they requested the insertion of an article in the proposed treaty which would name certain bays from which American fishermen could be excluded. In exchange for this concession, American fishing vessels should have "all commercial privileges in the ports of the Dominion of Canada and Newfoundland enjoyed by other vessels of the United States, with certain provisions in addition guarding and protecting American fishing vessels from petty annoyances."[12]

David Mills, the Canadian Minister of Justice, was present at Washington during the sessions of the Joint Commission, and when he heard of these proposals he wrote to Sir Wilfrid Laurier in prompt protest. He thought that the Canadian Government should be glad to consent to "the transshipment of fish in bond by the United States," and he believed that if American fishermen were admitted to Canadian ports for the "purpose of buying the supplies which they may need, other than bait, it certainly would be to the advantage of the people of the Maritime Provinces." It would be a great mistake, however, to enumerate in any treaty the bays from which American fishermen could be excluded. The sovereignty "over bays in all countries is regarded as territorial beyond all controversy." Therefore, to consent to "name a certain number of bays as belonging to us, and permitting the larger bays to be treated as parts of the High Seas, . . . would be to put

12. Senator Fairbanks to Secretary Hay, March 25, 1899, *ibid.*

Canada in a position distinctly inferior to every other State in Christendom that has a Maritime Coast."[13]

But notwithstanding this protest from Mr. Mills, the British Commissioners were still anxious to secure the item concerning bays. They showed a conciliatory disposition with reference to other items on the agenda, and Senator Fairbanks was hopeful that some general settlement could soon be effected. The only serious obstacle in the way of this agreement, as we shall see in the next section, was the Alaska boundary dispute which was also up before the Commission and it, rather than the fisheries dispute, finally led to the adjournment of this Joint High Commission.[14]

During the sessions of the Commission, Lord Herschell made a special point of having luncheon with Senator Lodge. Although Lodge found that Herschell was a "most agreeable man personally," he also discovered that the British jurist was somewhat fixed in his ideas concerning the fisheries. In this regard, Lodge frankly informed Herschell that it was

> utterly out of the question to expect that we should give Canada free fish. That notion may as well be abandoned first as last. It is not a question of the value of the Gloucester fisheries, although the value is considerable and the industry large. It is the fact that they are a nursery of seamen. . . . In the late war, Gloucester alone sent over 400 men, first-class seamen, into the regular Navy of the United States. . . . The trouble is, as I told Lord Herschell and as he admitted, that Canada has nothing to give, and that is the obstacle to making a bargain. He said if we failed to settle the fisheries . . . Canada would then proceed to enforce the laws with great strictness, but two can play at that game, and the President now has authority under law to prohibit absolutely the entrance of Canadian fish into this market. . . . I said to Lord Herschell that it seemed to me that if we could not come to an agreement on the fisheries we might easily settle up the other questions,

13. David Mills to Sir Wilfrid Laurier, January 25, 1899, *Laurier Papers,* P.A.C.

14. Senator Fairbanks to Secretary Hay, March 25, 1899, *Alaska Boundary Papers,* MS. Dept. of State. In a letter to Secretary Hay, March 20, 1899, Mr. T. Jefferson Coolidge, one of the American representatives on the Joint High Commission, remarked: "I think we should have but little trouble with the New England fisheries because the fish no longer frequent the bays and coasts of Nova Scotia and New Brunswick, and our fishermen seem entirely indifferent to the trade." *Ibid.* In another letter to Mr. Kasson, March 21, 1899, Mr. Coolidge comments adversely upon the tactics of the Canadian Commissioners. According to this account, the Canadians "offered to let our fishermen have the same rights as other merchant vessels, . . . but they tacked on exceptions which made the clause worthless. They forbade the purchase of bait and the transshipping of crews, and excluded our fishermen from fishing in some twenty bays over six miles wide. This was worse than the Chamberlain Treaty." *Kasson Papers,* MS. Dept. of State.

to which he made the extraordinary reply that he did not see any use in closing four holes and leaving one open. Now this position seems to be absurd.[15]

Lodge and Joseph Chamberlain were of the opinion that it would be highly unfortunate if the Joint High Commission failed to reach some definite agreement on the main points at issue between Great Britain and the United States with special reference to Canada, but the failure to make headway with the Alaska boundary controversy led to the adjournment of the commission on February 20, 1899. Nothing further was done about reciprocity or fisheries until 1902 when Secretary Hay revived the Blaine-Bond negotiations of 1890–1891. Sir Robert Bond, the Prime Minister of Newfoundland, arrived in the United States in August, 1902, and initiated conversations with Mr. Adee, the Acting Secretary of State. He showed a disposition to ignore the British Embassy as much as possible, but this tendency was checked by an intimation from Adee that direct negotiations between Newfoundland and the United States would not be countenanced by the Department of State.[16]

Secretary Hay was distinctly dubious about the attitude of the Senate towards any treaty that contained provisions for reciprocal trade, and he expressed to Adee the opinion that it might be "a waste of time" to go ahead and conclude a treaty with the Government of Newfoundland.[17] In order to remove these doubts he sent telegrams to Senators Lodge and Frye and inquired about their attitude towards a renewal of the Blaine-Bond negotiations. Encouraged by their replies, Hay continued his conversations with Bond, but he was careful to keep in close touch with Senator Lodge. He thought that the "political advantages" of the treaty outweighed "the slight objections which may be raised on the part of some of our citizens interested in fishing." This statement drew from Lodge a warning that the treaty had better be signed after the fall elections. He also suggested that Hay talk with the

15. Senator Lodge to Henry White, January 7, 1899, *White MS.* With reference to this claim that the Gloucester fishing industry was a nursery of seamen for the American Navy, Sir Robert Bond, in his speech in the Newfoundland Parliament, April 7, 1905, remarks: "It would amuse the House if I were to lay before them the special paper which was forwarded by the fishing interests of New England to the United States Senate on this point. . . . Out of 8,000 fishermen who man the fishing fleets of New England, some 4,000 are Newfoundlanders, about 1,500 are of American birth, and the balance consists of Nova Scotians, New Brunswickers, Portuguese, and Scandinavians. . . . During the recent war with Spain the United States Government sent two man-of-war ships to Gloucester for recruiting purposes, and although they remained there the whole summer there was only an enlistment of about 300 men, the majority of whom were not American born. At the same time the commercial city of Boston enlisted from its workshops and factories more than 1,700 men for the same purpose." *F.R., 1906,* Pt. 1, p. 764.

16. Tyler Dennett, *John Hay* (New York, 1933), p. 423.

17. *Ibid.,* p. 423.

Collector of the Port of Gloucester concerning the fisheries situation. Hay did not take kindly to this suggestion about consulting Collector Jordan before taking any further action. If the matter were submitted to the men of Gloucester they would merely "think up some further demands which Newfoundland cannot grant."[18] But Lodge was insistent upon this consultation, and he wrote to President Roosevelt that the Senators from Massachusetts could not support the treaty "unless it was reasonably satisfactory to the Gloucester people." The mere knowledge that the treaty had been signed might "turn Gloucester against us and cost us the Congressional district."[19]

Hay realized that political considerations bulked larger in Lodge's mind than national interests, and he also knew of Lodge's solicitude for the re-election of his son-in-law (Augustus P. Gardner) from the Congressional district that included Gloucester. On October 17, Hay had expressed to the President the view that Gloucester was safe for Gardner by a "large majority." To Lodge himself, Hay wrote a long letter in which he reviewed the whole situation. He adverted to the fact that he had inquired about the expediency of reviving the Blaine-Bond negotiations, and had received an affirmative answer with one condition attached to it—Gloucester would have to be satisfied. This was an impossible condition and could not be taken seriously. After discussing the matter with John W. Foster and John A. Kasson, the President's viewpoint had been sought. Having secured White House approval for the proposed treaty, the formality of signature would be postponed until after the elections.

Because of the fact that Senatorial wishes had been consulted in advance, Hay expressed the hope that the treaty would receive the support of the Republican majority in the Senate. He was certain that there was nothing in its provisions that would injure the fishing industry in New England, and the articles that opened Newfoundland markets to American manufactures free of duty, would be a boon to "big business." The treaty would serve as a breach in the "whole Imperial system of preference between Great Britain and her other colonies." Imperial economic unity would be shattered. This fact would compel Canada to be more conciliatory towards the United States, and would make it easier to settle the controversies that still vexed the course of Canadian-American relations.[20]

Lodge was not convinced by this letter, so after a few days, he wrote

18. *Ibid.*, pp. 424–425.

19. Senator Lodge to President Roosevelt, October 20, 1902, *Selections from the Correspondence of Theodore Roosevelt and Henry Cabot Lodge, 1884–1918* (New York, 1925), I, 543.

20. Secretary Hay to Senator Lodge, October 21, 1902, Dennett, *Hay*, pp. 426–427.

to the President that he would like to "save the treaty" but the Gloucester fishermen were "very sensitive and suspicious," and their approval should be secured before the treaty was signed.[21] Hay did not carry out this injunction, but he did wait until the elections were over and Lodge's son-in-law (Mr. Gardner) had secured his seat in the House of Representatives.

On November 8, 1902 the Hay-Bond Convention was formally concluded. It greatly resembled the treaty that Blaine and Bond had negotiated in January, 1891.[22] American fishing vessels entering the waters of Newfoundland would have the privilege of purchasing bait and other supplies. They would also have the privilege of "touching and trading, buying and selling fish and oil." In return for these privileges, cod oil, seal oil, whale oil, unmanufactured whalebone, ores of metals from Newfoundland mines, untrimmed slates from quarries, salted codfish, sealskins, herrings and other fish would be admitted into the United States free of duty. When the treaty became effective, a long list of American manufactures and some raw materials would be admitted into Newfoundland ports without the imposition of tariff duties.[23]

On December 3, 1902, President Roosevelt sent the treaty to the Senate, and Lodge immediately evinced his opposition. Written protests poured into the Senate, where they were promptly assembled and printed as Government documents.[24] But in some quarters in Massachusetts there was open support for the treaty, and the Boston *Transcript* expressed the hope that Gloucester would not be too unreasonable in its attitude.[25]

In the Senate the treaty was referred to the Senate Committee on Foreign Relations where it was securely pigeonholed. On April 2, 1903, in a talk before the Home Markets Club, Senator Lodge referred to the Hay-Bond Convention. To his mind there was only one test that could be applied to such a treaty: would the United States receive proper equivalents for the concessions it made? In this case the equivalents were not enough to justify support of the treaty. Moreover, the admission of cured or salted codfish from Newfoundland, free of duty, would mean that the factories in Massachusetts where this salting was now done would be forced to migrate to Newfoundland. Even the

21. Senator Lodge to President Roosevelt, October 27, 1902, *Selections, etc.*, I, 544.
22. *North Atlantic Coast Fisheries Arbitration,* IV, 77–79.
23. *Ibid.,* IV, 79–82.
24. *Senate Docs. Nos. 14, 50, 78, 94,* 57 Cong., 2 sess.
25. December 11, 1902. See also, *Senate Doc. No. 65,* 57 Cong., 2 sess.; P. T. McGrath, "The Atlantic Fisheries Question," *Atlantic Monthly,* XC (December, 1902); and *ibid.,* "The Hay-Bond Treaty," *Nineteenth Century,* LIII (1903), 924–936.

Gloucester fishermen would be tempted to leave their old homes in Massachusetts and move to this British island.[26]

Because of this alleged danger to the fishing industry of Massachusetts, Lodge continued his opposition to the Hay-Bond Convention. As the months passed he seemed to grow suspicious of British policy in general, and Sir Mortimer Durand, the new British Ambassador,[27] discovered that Lodge was something of an Anglophobe.[28] In November, 1904, the President made a half-hearted attempt to secure some action on the Hay-Bond Treaty. In a letter to Lodge he expressed the opinion that Republican leaders should get together and agree upon any amendments that were needed. The treaty should then be reported from the Senate Committee on Foreign Relations, and discussed and voted upon.[29]

Lodge was in no hurry to carry out this suggestion of the President, and it was not until February, 1905 that the Hay-Bond Treaty was acted upon by the Senate. Far-reaching amendments were then attached to it, and the concessions to Newfoundland were so reduced that the Boston *Transcript* remarked: "No American would have the effrontery to ask Sir Robert Bond to accept it."[30]

Secretary Hay was furious at the way Lodge had handled the matter of the Hay-Bond Treaty, and he poured forth his feelings in a letter to Ambassador Choate: "As to the treatment by Mr. Lodge of the Newfoundland treaty, from which is eliminated absolutely everything the Newfoundlanders wanted and our demands largely increased, it seems to me as stupid a piece of bad manners as any country has ever been guilty of. But as the old darkey preacher once observed: 'Bredren, we are all in the hands of an unscrupulous Providence,' and we must make the best of it."[31]

Some weeks later he again referred to the fate of the Hay-Bond Treaty. He had just heard that Lodge had remarked that

> a conciliatory spirit in Sir Robert Bond might do much to save the Newfoundland Treaty. This is of a piece with the contemptible hypocrisy which has characterized the whole of the opposition to that Treaty. They (I mean

26. Boston *Transcript,* April 3, 1903.

27. Durand arrived in the United States in November, 1903.

28. Sir Percy Sykes, *The Right Honourable Sir Mortimer Durand* (London, 1926), pp. 271–274.

29. President Roosevelt to Senator Lodge, November 12, 1904, *Selections, etc.,* II, 110.

30. February 9, 1905. See also, the *Nation,* LXXX, 238–239, and the *Outlook,* LXXIX, 408–409.

31. Secretary Hay to Joseph H. Choate, February 10, 1905, *Choate MS.*

Hale and Lodge) are determined to kill the treaty, but they have not the courage of their selfish malice, and cannot help lying about it. The Treaty is dead, and no amount of generous concession from Sir Robert Bond could save it, so long as Lodge is a Senator and his son-in-law represents Gloucester in the House. But bless my soul! this is lèse-majesté.[32]

Hay expressed his distrust of Lodge without reserve or qualification. In April, 1914, ex-President Taft, in a letter to Philander C. Knox, repeats some of Hay's remarks at the time of the defeat of the Hay-Bond Treaty: "I [Taft] don't know how Lodge regards his own action as to arbitration treaties. He poses now as the great admirer of Hay, and yet Hay told me that Lodge had given him more trouble and was a liar and everything that was detestable. He had promised to support a Newfoundland treaty and then had pigeonholed it on account of Gloucester."[33]

Lodge himself admitted that he bore some responsibility in the Newfoundland affair because he had not discouraged Bond and Hay with reference to the initiation of negotiations. But Hay was also to blame "for refusing to consult anyone who knew anything of the subject, despite my prayer that he would, and so making a treaty that any fishery man would have told him in a minute was impossible."[34]

Hay would have replied that the Gloucester fishing interests would not have been satisfied with any treaty that did not give them special privileges at the cost of the rest of the country. Hay was opposed to coddling these fishermen because they happened to control the political fortunes of Lodge's son-in-law. Worn out with this latest struggle with the Senate, Hay vainly sought new vigor in a trip to Europe. But the sands of his life were fast running out, and on July 1, 1905, he died at his summer home in New Hampshire.

Long after the death of Hay, the echoes of the Hay-Lodge fight continued to disturb political circles in Massachusetts. In October, 1905, Osborne Howes charged that Secretary Hay had been hurried to a premature death by the questionable tactics of Senator Lodge in connection with the Hay-Bond Treaty. Lodge replied that Hay had been one of his "dearest friends," and that no shadow had ever come over their friendship.[35] But the fact remains that as one reads the intimate correspondence of Hay, it is obvious that he did not look upon Lodge

32. Secretary Hay to Choate, April 17, 1905, *ibid.*
33. Ex-President Taft to Philander C. Knox, April 12, 1914, *Knox MS.*
34. Senator Lodge to President Roosevelt, June 3, 1905, *Selections, etc.*, II, 128.
35. Boston *Herald,* October 28, 29, 1905; Boston *Transcript,* November 1, 1905. Secretary Root was inclined to take the side of Lodge in this controversy concerning

as a real friend. Other prominent Republicans were equally suspicious of Lodge, and his career brings to mind Oscar Wilde's comment upon Ernest Harrowden: "He was a man who had no enemies, but was thoroughly disliked by his friends."

The action of the Senate in amending the Hay-Bond Treaty, led the Parliament of Newfoundland to pass a law (June 15, 1905) which terminated the *modus vivendi* under whose terms American fishermen had been able to purchase in Newfoundland ports the bait, ice, seines, and other supplies needed for the fishery. They had also enjoyed the right to ship Newfoundlanders as members of their crews. These privileges were now abolished, and far-reaching punitive measures were authorized. Newfoundland officials could board any foreign fishing vessel within "any port on the coasts of this Island, or hovering in British waters within three marine miles of any of the coasts," and bring it into port for an extended examination of her cargo. If the vessel had on board any herring, caplin, squid, or other bait fishes, ice, lines, seines, or other outfits purchased within any port of the Island, or if the master had engaged or attempted to engage any person to form part of the crew of his vessel, such vessel and cargo would be liable to forfeiture.[36]

It was apparent to Secretary Root that this fisheries controversy with Newfoundland had many implications that could be understood only by those who had an intimate acquaintance with local conditions.[37] For this reason he made arrangements for a trip to Newfoundland in the summer of 1905. After an extensive trip along the Newfoundland coasts, Root had "a new appreciation of the whole controversy." He thought it was inevitable that disputes should break out between the local fishermen and the fishermen who came from distant lands. When the Newfoundlanders were "finally given the authority to make the regulations for the fishing industry," they naturally made them "in the interest of their own people." When they prohibited fishing on Sunday they did little damage to local interests, but to the New Englanders who came to Newfoundland "with ships and crews costing money

the alleged breach of faith on the part of the Senator. In a letter to Lodge, January 6, 1906, Root remarked: "I have in my possession the original letters from you to Mr. Hay regarding the Newfoundland treaty. They sustain without the possibility of a misunderstanding or doubt that, before the terms of the Hay-Bond treaty were determined upon, you gave fair notice that you could not agree to any treaty which would not satisfy the Gloucester fishing interests, and that, after the terms of the treaty had been agreed upon, you refused to assent to it because it would sacrifice the interests of the Gloucester fishermen." *Root MS.*

36. *North Atlantic Coast Fisheries Arbitration,* V, 1284–1286.

37. Root assumed the duties of Secretary of State on July 7, 1905.

by the day, dependent upon the weather, the necessity of ceasing from fishing on Sunday was almost ruinous."[38]

While Root was on this trip in which he successfully mixed business with pleasure, Lodge wrote to the President about the attempt of the Newfoundland Government to interfere with American fishermen along the west coast of that Island. Sir Robert Bond had attempted to draw an "absurd distinction" between "coasts and inlets and harbors." Inlets and harbors were as much a part of the coast as headlands or projections. No question had been raised about it hitherto "for nearly ninety years." It might be a good idea to send a "small cruiser" to Newfoundland in order to give adequate protection to American treaty rights.[39]

To the President it was evident that the case concerning the Newfoundland fisheries was not a "simple one," and there was no use in "hiding from ourselves the fact that the course followed in connection with the unfortunate effort to negotiate the treaty has given deep offense to Newfoundland, and most naturally." Nothing was to be gained by trying to apportion the responsibility for the mistakes in the negotiation of the treaty or in its treatment by the Senate. The essential fact was that the fishery interests in Gloucester would oppose any treaty with Newfoundland, and it would have been far better if the negotiations had never been started. Under the circumstances it would be expedient for the United States to show as much patience and forbearance as possible until the exasperation of the Government of Newfoundland had "worn off." The despatch of a warship to Newfoundland would be a "provocative to trouble," and it would be condemned by many Americans who were not pleased "with the showing made by Gloucester." The best policy was one of watchful waiting with no appearance "of bullying or of inviting trouble."[40]

Impressed with the importance of delaying any retaliatory action in connection with the recent Newfoundland legislation, the President invited Secretary Root to Oyster Bay to talk matters over with Choate and Lodge.[41] This meeting helped to clarify the situation for Secretary

38. Elihu Root to Philip C. Jessup, March 19, 1934, *Jessup MS.* I am deeply indebted to Professor Philip C. Jessup for permission to use his file of manuscript letters and memoranda collected for the purpose of completing his biography of Elihu Root. This collection will hereafter be referred to as the *Jessup File,* and will be indicated by the initials *JF.*

39. Senator Lodge to President Roosevelt, August 16, 1905, *Selections, etc.,* II, 173–174.

40. President Roosevelt to Senator Lodge, August 19, 1905, *ibid.,* pp. 175–176.

41. President Roosevelt to Senator Lodge, September 6, 15, 1905; Senator Lodge to President Roosevelt, September 17, 1905, *ibid.,* pp. 190, 194, 202.

Root, who was determined not to commit Hay's mistake in not consulting Lodge with reference to the fisheries matters. A few days after this important conference, Lodge wrote to the President and expressed the hope that the Government of Newfoundland would take the "very sensible course of allowing our fishermen to catch herring, as has been done in the past."[42] He then returned to the idea of sending some Government vessel to the coast of Newfoundland to protect the rights of American fishermen. It was quite possible that the fishermen of Newfoundland would cut American nets and otherwise interfere with fishing operations. Even a mere revenue cutter would be of some service.[43]

Lodge wrote to Root in the same vein, and received a cogent reply. It seemed to Root that the main difficulty about sending a Government vessel to Newfoundland was the assumption that there was "going to be trouble." Such an assumption might bring on serious trouble. He doubted whether Newfoundland fishermen would endeavor seriously to interfere with American fishing rights along their coasts. They had been acknowledged for ninety years, and were too well established to be challenged. It would be a mistake to act as though the British Government was about to "interfere or permit its people to interfere with the peaceful exercise by our fishermen of the rights as we understand them." The best course for American fishermen to follow was to continue their fishing operations with no apprehension of interference. If they were given any express assurances that their rights would be protected, they would assume that these assurances were a promise of protection by force. Such a promise could be given only by Congress.[44]

It was apparent to Senator Lodge that Root was putting a very strict construction upon the powers of the President. In previous administrations warships had been sent to distant coasts in order to protect American interests, and Lodge referred to certain recent instances where revenue cutters had been sent to Canadian waters. He wished to have this practice repeated in order to prevent serious trouble. He feared that Newfoundland fishermen would cut American nets and this would result in a "row." Prime Minister Bond was talking in a very "threatening" manner about excluding American vessels from bays and inlets and thus enforcing the obnoxious "headlands theory." If these threats were carried out, the New England fishermen would find their means of existence seriously menaced: it was too much to expect them to suffer in silence. It was well and good for Root to have extended

42. Senator Lodge to President Roosevelt, September 22, 1905, *ibid.*, pp. 202–203.
43. Senator Lodge to President Roosevelt, September 26, 1905, *ibid.*, p. 203.
44. Secretary Root to Senator Lodge, September 27, 1905, *Root MS.*

conversations with the British Ambassador about the situation, but he would probably discover that these talks would not result in any "rapid action" on the part of the British Government.[45]

In the second week in October, 1905, the apprehensions of Lodge appeared fulfilled. News came to the Department of State that the Government of Newfoundland had forbidden American fishing vessels "already on the treaty coast to take fish within the treaty limits prescribed in Article I of the treaty of 1818." Secretary Root immediately sent an instruction to Ambassador Reid, in London, directing him to represent to the British Foreign Office, in an urgent manner, that all questions of treaty interpretation should be settled through diplomatic channels and not left to the discretion of Newfoundland officials. The American Government would insist upon the recognition of the rights that American fishermen "have always enjoyed under the treaty of 1818."[46]

Although Ambassador Reid informed Root that the Foreign Office had received word from Newfoundland that no attempt had been made to interfere with the rights of American fishermen,[47] Root, nevertheless, sent a strong note to the British Ambassador in Washington. He had learned from Representative Gardner that American vessels had been forbidden to fish on the treaty coast of Newfoundland. He had also been informed of certain Newfoundland legislation that violated the rights of American fishermen. Under the terms of the Act of June 15, 1905, Newfoundland officials were authorized to "stop an American vessel while fishing upon the treaty coast and compel it to leave the fishing grounds, to prevent it from going to the places where the fish may be, to prevent it from departing with the fish which it may have taken, and to detain it for an indefinite period during a search of the cargo." This law did not require that the fishing vessel shall have been charged with any violation of the laws of Newfoundland or even that she shall have been suspected of having violated these laws. When it was considered that these Newfoundland officials were members of fishing communities that were in active competition with American fishermen, it was plain that the enforcement of this law might lead to serious complications. This was particularly true in view of the fact that the Act further provided that the presence on board an American vessel of fishing gear

45. Senator Lodge to Secretary Root, September 29, 1905, *ibid.*

46. Secretary Root to Ambassador Reid, October 13, 1905, *F.R., 1905,* p. 489. Whitelaw Reid assumed his duties as Ambassador in June, 1905.

47. Ambassador Reid to Secretary Root, October 16, 1905, *ibid.,* p. 489.

was *prima facie* evidence of "a criminal offense against the laws of Newfoundland." The same was true of the presence on board of "the fish which the vessel has a right to take under the treaty."

It should be apparent that this Newfoundland legislation was "inconsistent with the rights of the United States under the treaty of 1818 and ought to be repealed." In the meantime, the British Government should request the Governor in Council, on the island, to suspend the operation of the Act.[48]

On October 20, the British Ambassador, Sir Mortimer Durand, acknowledged the receipt of this strong note, and gave assurances that he would do all he could to prevent any violations of the Treaty of 1818 by officials of the Newfoundland Government.[49] Two days later, the Ambassador informed Secretary Root that he had received word from the Governor of Newfoundland that no action was being taken to prevent "American vessels from fishing on the treaty coast, and that no distinction is being drawn between registered vessels and licensed vessels."[50]

In reply to these notes, Secretary Root expressed his "high appreciation" of the manner and spirit in which the British Ambassador had handled the situation. Nothing could more promote the "patience and good temper which we agree to be so important on the part of every

48. Secretary Root to the British Ambassador, October 19, 1905, *F.R., 1905,* pp. 490–494. In this note, Root made the following list of propositions that he regarded as correct: "(1) Any American vessel is entitled to go into the waters of the treaty coast and take fish of any kind. She derives this right from the treaty . . . and not from any permission or authority proceeding from the government of Newfoundland; (2) an American vessel seeking to exercise the treaty right is not bound to obtain a license from the government of Newfoundland, and, if she does not purpose to trade as well as fish, she is not bound to enter at any Newfoundland custom-house; (3) the only concern of the government of Newfoundland with such a vessel is to call for proper evidence that she is an American vessel and therefore entitled to exercise the treaty right, and to have her refrain from violating the laws of Newfoundland not inconsistent with the treaty; (4) the proper evidence that a vessel is an American vessel and entitled to exercise the treaty right is the production of the ship's papers of the kind generally recognized in the maritime world as evidence of a vessel's national character; (5) when a vessel has produced papers showing that she is an American vessel, the officials of Newfoundland have no concern with the character or extent of the privileges accorded to such a vessel by the Government of the United States. No question as between a registry and license is a proper subject for their consideration . . .; (6) if any such matter were a proper subject for the consideration of the officials of Newfoundland, the statement of this Department that vessels bearing an American registry are entitled to exercise the treaty right should be taken by such officials as conclusive."

49. The British Ambassador to the Secretary of State, October 20, 1905, *ibid.,* pp. 494–495.

50. The British Ambassador to the Secretary of State, October 22, 1905, *ibid.,* p. 496.

one on the treaty coast than a knowledge of the spirit in which the subject is being dealt with by both governments."[51]

Root's friendly attitude, and the rapid subsidence of the excitement caused by the news from Newfoundland, must have been a great relief to Sir Mortimer Durand. It was not only the Newfoundland legislation of June 15, 1905 that disturbed Durand, but it was also the belligerent speech of Sir Robert Bond on April 7, 1905 that awakened his apprehensions. Bond had gone out of his way to fling a challenge at the United States. He flatly stated that his purpose in sponsoring legislation adverse to American fishing interests, was to make Newfoundland the mistress of the seas and to bring the United States to terms. American objections were eloquent evidence "as to the value of the position we occupy as mistress of the northern seas so far as the fisheries are concerned." They also indicated "that it is within the power of the legislature of this colony to make or mar our competitors to the North Atlantic fisheries."[52]

These belligerent words, together with the rumors of interference with the rights of American fishermen in Newfoundland waters, stirred the ready ire of President Roosevelt, who blurted out to Sir Mortimer Durand: "My people cannot be expected to take it lying down."[53] Assurances that Newfoundland officials were not taking any action against American fishermen had the effect of quieting the explosive temper of the President, and the fisheries controversy moved along more pacific channels.

But Secretary Root knew there was plenty of tinder ready for a big blaze with regard to the fisheries matter, and he was determined to prevent any diplomatic sparks from flying in that direction. Unlike Secretary Hay, he invited Representative Gardner to the Department

51. The Secretary of State to the British Ambassador, October 25, 1905, *ibid.*, p. 497.

52. *United States Counter Case*, App., pp. 446–448. In this same speech, Sir Robert Bond also announced a new theory regarding the interpretation of the Treaty of 1818. In Article I of this treaty the inhabitants of the United States were given the privilege of taking fish on the southern, western and northern coasts of Newfoundland. In addition they were given the privilege of taking fish on the "Coasts, Bays, Harbours, and Creeks from Mount Joly on the Southern Coast of Labrador, to and through the Straights of Belleisle, and thence Northwardly indefinitely along the Coast." In this description there is no specific mention of fishing liberties along the *coasts, bays, harbours, and creeks of Newfoundland.* In view of this language, Sir Robert Bond held that American fishermen possessed liberties in the coasts, bays, harbors and creeks of Labrador and *not* of *Newfoundland.* The American view was that the larger word included the smaller—the word *coast* included the smaller designations of bays, harbors and creeks. They were merely a legal repetition with the same meaning. For the speech of Sir Robert Bond, April 7, 1905, see *ibid.*, p. 414.

53. Sykes, *op. cit.*, p. 295.

of State for a conference, and the Gloucester fishermen felt that something was being done in their interest.[54] It was evident to Root, however, that the fishing interests of Gloucester were not of paramount importance, and he received many suggestions about merging the fisheries question in a comprehensive arrangement for commercial reciprocity with Newfoundland. Senator Proctor, of Vermont, was an ardent advocate of this solution, and he thought that Root could push the matter through to a successful conclusion: "You trample relentlessly on all law and precedent, and nobody calls you to account or denounces you for the tyrant you are, for you maintain such a childlike and bland demeanor."[55]

There was no real chance that this reciprocal arrangement could be consummated in the autumn of 1905, and Root had all he could do to prevent serious friction between American fishermen and Newfoundland officials over such a minor question as the exercise of fishing liberties on the west coast of Newfoundland. The British Foreign Office protested that platforms were being constructed by American fishermen for freezing herring on the shore of the Bay of Islands on the west coast of Newfoundland. This area was not included in the grant of liberties contained in Article I of the Treaty of 1818, and therefore, American fishermen had no right to frequent this coast.[56]

Secretary Root gave assurances that these activities would not be continued, but he called attention to complaints that American nets were being cut in Newfoundland waters.[57] Sir Edward Grey lost no time in investigating these charges. On December 28 he informed the American *chargé d'affaires*, in London, that the rumors of net cutting were unfounded. Nets had been destroyed, but this damage was due to inclement weather.[58]

As this game of charge and counter-charge was being played, Secretary Root called attention to the ambiguous language of the British Foreign Office memorandum of December 16, 1905. In this memorandum the impression was given that American fishermen had the liberty of taking fish merely on the southern coast of Newfoundland, whereas, in Article I of the Treaty of 1818, this liberty also applied to certain areas on the western and northern coasts of that island.[59]

54. Secretary Root to Senator Lodge, October 23, 1905, *Root MS.* For a brief account of the difficulties leading up to the North Atlantic Fisheries Arbitration, see chap. xxx, of Professor Jessup's excellent biography of Elihu Root.

55. Senator Redfield Proctor to Secretary Root, October 23, 1905, *ibid.*

56. Mr. Carter to the Secretary of State, December 16, 1905, *F.R., 1905,* p. 500.

57. Secretary Root to Mr. Carter, December 16, 1905, *ibid.,* p. 500.

58. Mr. Carter to Secretary Root, December 29, 1905, *ibid.,* p. 502.

59. Secretary Root to Mr. Carter, January 3, 1906, *F.R., 1906,* p. 663.

Sir Edward Grey was in no great hurry to answer this latest note from Secretary Root. He was at work upon a comprehensive document that would serve as a complete reply to many points that had been raised by the American Secretary of State in his long complaint of October 19, 1905. The first point involved in the American contention was the claim that "any American vessel is entitled to go into the waters of the treaty coast and take fish of any kind." This claim was denied by Sir Edward Grey. The privilege of fishing in Canadian waters was conceded to the inhabitants of the United States and not to American vessels. Therefore, fishing operations should be conducted in these waters by American vessels with American crews. Secretary Root had next contended that "an American vessel seeking to exercise the treaty right is not bound to obtain a license from the government of Newfoundland, and if she does not purpose to trade as well as fish, she is not bound to enter at any Newfoundland custom-house." The British Government did not maintain that a license should be required of American vessels seeking to "exercise the treaty right." Secretary Root's third proposition was that the only concern of the government of Newfoundland with an American vessel was with regard to the evidence of American registry which would prove that it was entitled to exercise the treaty right. In answer to this proposition, Sir Edward Grey held that American fishermen could not exercise their right of fishery under the Treaty of 1818 on a footing of greater freedom than British subjects. The American fishery under that treaty was "not a free but a regulated fishery," and American fishermen were bound to "comply with all colonial regulations" as long as these were "not in their nature unreasonable," and are applicable "to all fishermen alike." His Majesty's Government was prepared to admit that no law of Newfoundland should be enforced "on American fishing vessels which would unreasonably interfere with the exercise by the American fishermen on board of their rights under the convention." The Newfoundland law required that fishing vessels entering the inner waters of the Bay of Islands should report at a custom-house. The British Government did not regard this requirement as unreasonable even when applied to fishing as well as to trading vessels.

It was also indicated that His Majesty's Government did not regard the mere production of American registry as sufficient evidence to establish a vessel as one engaged only in fishing. Further evidence was necessary in order to prevent the possibility of smuggling operations being carried on.

Sir Edward Grey then complained that American fishing vessels had lately refused to pay light dues. This action was probably the result of the denial by the Newfoundland Government of the trading privileges that had been allowed in recent years. But this denial did not entitle American vessels to any "exemption from light dues in the ports in which they fish," and the exaction of these dues could not be regarded as an "unreasonable interference with the exercise of treaty rights."

The British note concluded with a discussion of the implications of the Newfoundland "foreign fishing-vessels act" of June 15, 1905. This Act was quite similar to the previous Act of May 24, 1893.[60] In that Act provision had been made for the issuance of licenses to foreign fishing vessels authorizing them to enter Newfoundland ports and purchase bait, ice, seines and other fishing supplies, and to ship crews. The Act of June 15, 1905 contained no provision for the issuance of such licenses.[61] The license system had been abolished, and it was within the power of the Parliament of Newfoundland to do this. With reference to the punitive provisions in this law of June 15, 1905, it should be remembered that under section 7 of that Act provision was made that "nothing in this act shall affect the rights and privileges granted by treaty to the subjects of any state in amity with His Majesty." This section was a guarantee against any violations of the liberties granted in the Treaty of 1818.[62]

Secretary Root waited many months before sending a specific answer to this note from Sir Edward Grey. On May 3, 1906 he addressed a long letter to the British Ambassador in which he reviewed the many questions at issue between the United States and Canada. With reference to the fisheries situation he called attention to the "very strong and, at times, almost bitter feeling in the United States that the legislation of the British Colonies to the north of us, and the administration by them of the laws and regulations which they conceive to be applicable to American fishermen, have been actuated by a settled purpose to hinder and embarrass American fishermen in the exercise of their rights to such an extent as to make those rights practically worthless." Because of the existence of this feeling, it was hardly worth while to attempt to settle the fisheries question by a "reciprocal grant of new and additional rights." The only wise course was to endeavor to "ascertain and determine what the existing rights really are, and then to secure

60. For this Act of May 24, 1893, see *North Atlantic Coast Fisheries Arbitration,* V, 1234–1236.

61. The provisions of the Act of June 15, 1905 are given in *ibid.,* pp. 1284–1286.

62. Secretary of State for Foreign Affairs to Ambassador Reid, February 2, 1906, *F.R., 1906,* pp. 669–674.

the same fair and liberal treatment of the persons seeking to exercise them as is accorded in all the other multitude of cases in which the citizens of our respective countries are exercising rights dependent upon fair treatment by the government of the other country."[63]

In order to clarify the situation with reference to the rights and liberties of American fishermen in Canadian waters, Root sent a lengthy instruction to Ambassador Reid in which he took issue with many of the statements in Sir Edward Grey's note and memorandum of February 2, 1906. He agreed with the British contention that, under the Treaty of 1818, fishing liberties were conferred upon the "inhabitants" of the United States and not upon American fishing vessels. This was a distinction of no great importance unless the Foreign Office was endeavoring, in this indirect way, to assert that whenever an American skipper frequents the treaty coast for fishing, or enters the harbors for the purpose of shelter, or in order to secure wood or water, he must furnish evidence that "all the members of his crew are inhabitants of the United States." The American Government could not "for a moment admit the existence of any such limitation upon our treaty rights." No right to control the means which Americans use in fishing could be admitted unless it were "provided in the terms of the treaty, and no right to question the nationality of the crews employed is contained in the terms of the treaty." Since 1818 it had been customary for masters of fishing vessels to employ crews of various nationalities, and during all this period no suggestion had ever been made by the British Government of a right to "scrutinize the nationality of the crews employed in the vessels through which the treaty right has been exercised."

Root then went to the heart of the question at issue between Newfoundland and the United States. According to the British contention, American fishermen could carry on their operations only at the times and "in the manner prescribed by the regulations of Newfoundland." The only basis for American objections to these regulations would be with reference to their alleged "unreasonable" character.

This British contention was strongly challenged by Root. The American Government failed to find in the Treaty of 1818 "any grant of right to the makers of colonial law to interfere at all, whether reasonably or unreasonably, with the exercise of the American rights of fishery, or any right to determine what would be a reasonable interference with the exercise of that American right if there could be any interference." In the British memorandum it was argued that the right

63. Secretary Root to Sir Mortimer Durand, May 3, 1906, *MS.*, JF.

of American fishermen to fish upon the treaty coast was based upon the fact that this right was possessed by them "in common with the subjects of His Britannic Majesty," and also upon the proposition that "the inhabitants of the United States would not now be entitled to fish in British North American waters but for the fact that they were entitled to do so when they were British subjects." These arguments were distinctly weak. The real meaning of the above-quoted provision in the Treaty of 1818 was that "the liberty to take fish shall be held in common, not that the exercise of that liberty by one people shall be the limit of the exercise of that liberty by the other." It was a matter of "no concern to the American fishermen whether the people of Newfoundland choose to exercise their right or not, or to what extent they choose to exercise it." British statutes limiting the exercise of the British right were mere voluntary ordinances which might be repealed at any time; in no sense were they any measure of American rights.

The British memorandum had stated that "the American fishermen can not rightly claim to exercise their right of fishery under the convention of 1818 on a footing different than if they had never ceased to be British subjects." If this were true, "what was the meaning of independence? What was it that continued the power of the British Crown over this particular right of Americans formerly exercised by them as British subjects, although the power of the British Crown over all other rights formerly exercised by them as British subjects was ended?"

Another contention advanced by the Foreign Office was the claim of a right "to regulate the action of American fishermen in the treaty waters, upon the ground that those waters are within the territorial jurisdiction of the colony of Newfoundland." Such a claim was without any foundation in fact. The Treaty of 1818 granted "a perpetual right to the inhabitants of the United States which is beyond the sovereign power of England to destroy or change. . . . The existence of this right is a qualification of British sovereignty within that territory. . . . An appeal to the general jurisdiction of Great Britain over the territory is, therefore, a complete begging of the question."

The American Government deeply regretted that the Foreign Office was taking a "much more extreme position than that taken in the last active correspondence upon the same question arising under the provisions of the treaty of Washington." The claim recently asserted that the colony of Newfoundland was entitled "at will to regulate the exercise of the American treaty right, is equivalent to a claim of power to completely destroy that right." The American Government was willing to agree to reasonable regulations for the "due control of the fishermen of both countries in the exercise of their rights, but this Government can not permit the exercise of these rights to be subject to the will of the colony of Newfoundland."[64]

This note was so cogently argued and so forcefully expressed that it contained a covert threat that American rights would be protected no matter what the cost might be. Root was an Anglophile, and he was also a fervent advocate of international peace. But he was first of all an ardent American who was exceedingly tenacious in his defence of American rights against every other nation. He was in no mood to make concessions that would seriously affect American fishermen in Newfoundland waters, and his correspondence with President Roosevelt shows how seriously he viewed the situation. In a note of July 3, he referred to his recent instruction to Ambassador Reid, and remarked: "You will see that it suggests, without threatening, the sending of our cruisers to protect our own fishermen. . . . We may have to make this plainer as matters proceed."[65]

Secretary Root next wrote to Congressman Gardner, who represented the Gloucester fishermen, and informed him that the Department of State was of the opinion that the Newfoundland regulation against the use of purse seines by American fishermen was unreasonable. If American fishermen continued the use of purse seines, the Department of State would "do everything in its power to help them, and if vessels should be seized or their fishing interfered with, to secure adequate compensation."[66]

Root's letter to Congressman Gardner was published in the Boston newspapers, and it was received with "many manifestations of pleasure." This situation gave increasing concern to the British Ambassador, at Washington, who placed the matter before the Foreign Office.[67] Sir Edward Grey turned copies of this correspondence over to the Colonial Office, and in due time, the Governor of Newfoundland was apprised of the American attitude. It was evident to the Colonial Office that there was such a "wide divergence of view between the two Governments" that no "immediate settlement of questions involved is possible." But any attempt to put into force the regulations adopted by the Newfoundland Government might give rise to "a highly undesirable and even dangerous situation." It was important, therefore, to

64. Secretary Root to Ambassador Reid, June 30, 1906, *F.R., 1906,* Pt. 1, pp. 685–692.

65. Secretary Root to President Roosevelt, July 3, 1906, *Root MS.*

66. Representative A. P. Gardner to the Gloucester Board of Trade, July 7, *F.R., 1906,* Pt. 1, pp. 716–717.

67. Sir Mortimer Durand to Sir Edward Grey, July 18, 1906, *ibid.,* pp. 716–718.

agree upon some *modus vivendi* in the hope that an eventual settlement of the fisheries controversy could be effected. As a temporary measure, would the Government of Newfoundland be willing to permit the use of purse seines in return for a prohibition of Sunday fishing?[68]

Before the answer of the Newfoundland Government could reach London, Sir Edward Grey assured Ambassador Reid that the Foreign Office was prepared "to confer with the United States Government with a view to some arrangement which will secure the peaceable and orderly conduct of the forthcoming fishery."[69] The Colonial Office then cabled to Governor MacGregor, of Newfoundland, and strongly urged the importance of agreeing to a *modus vivendi* for the fishing season.[70] There seemed to be little doubt in the minds of English officials that the Government of Newfoundland would promptly fall in line with regard to these suggestions. But it was soon discovered that Newfoundland officials could be unexpectedly stubborn, and Governor MacGregor reported on August 19 that his ministers felt that the contentions of the United States were so unreasonable that they could not be accepted. The regulations adopted by the Government of Newfoundland were necessary for the protection of the fishing industry, and they were not unreasonable. It was strongly urged that the interests of the British Empire and "not those of colony alone, require that rightful sovereignty within its own dominions should be maintained inviolate," and the Newfoundland Government could not "accept the view that any foreign power has a statutory claim in matter of framing, adoption, or carrying out of laws for government any portion of this colony."[71]

This telegram from Governor MacGregor was most unsatisfactory to the Colonial Office which promptly replied that the Government of Newfoundland had failed to appreciate the "serious difficulty in which their policy has placed both them and His Majesty's Government." For the sake of Imperial interests, the Foreign Office was proposing to the Department of State a *modus vivendi* that would settle the controversy during the present fishing season. It was hoped that this arrangement would obviate the "grave difficulties and dangers" which were facing His Majesty's Government.[72]

68. The Earl of Elgin to Governor Sir W. MacGregor, August 8, 1906, *ibid.*, pp. 718–719.
69. Sir Edward Grey to Ambassador Reid, August 14, 1906, *ibid.*, p. 720.
70. The Earl of Elgin to Governor MacGregor, August 19, 1906, *ibid.*, p. 721.
71. Governor Sir W. MacGregor to the Earl of Elgin, August 19, 1906, *ibid.*, pp. 721–724.
72. The Earl of Elgin to Governor Sir W. MacGregor, September 3, 1906, *ibid.*, pp. 730–731.

On September 3, 1906, Sir Edward Grey proposed to Ambassador Reid a *modus vivendi* in which the British Government would promise that the punitive sections of the Newfoundland Acts of June 15, 1905, and May 10, 1906,[73] would not be enforced. As a further concession, the payment of light dues would not be required. In return the United States should direct their fishermen "to comply with the colonial fishery regulations . . . with the exception of certain breaches of the prohibition of Sunday fishing." One of these important regulations dealt with the use of purse seines, which were regarded with strong disfavor by Newfoundland authorities. In connection with the prohibition of Sunday fishing it should be kept in mind that this regulation was in force not only in Newfoundland but also in Canada. In view of the widespread feeling against Sunday fishing, the disregard of it was fraught with "possibilities of serious disorder." It was also hoped that the American Government would direct the masters of fishing vessels to comply with the provisions of the colonial customs law as to reporting at a custom-house upon arrival and departure from colonial waters.[74]

Secretary Root was glad to show a conciliatory disposition in this matter of arranging for a *modus vivendi*, and the Foreign Office was informed that the American Government was ready to concede that American fishermen should pay light dues and report, when possible, at Newfoundland custom-houses. Even Sunday fishing would be given up temporarily, but the use of purse seines could not be abandoned by American fishermen.[75]

After presenting this memorandum to the Foreign Office, Ambassador Reid wrote to President Roosevelt to express the hope that he would be able to

> bring the slow-moving Colonial Office around to an early agreement on a *modus vivendi*. The only point between us is as to the use of purse nets. I have tried to convince the Foreign Office that they have forced this upon us by their efforts to embarrass our fishermen, and that while we agree to everything else they propose, they ought not to ask us to agree to this. Sir Charles Hardinge, the permanent Undersecretary, with whom I had a long talk on

73. The Act of May 10, 1906, prohibited "residents" of Newfoundland from shipping as members of the crews of "foreign fishing vessels." This struck at the practice of American masters of fishing vessels of hiring Newfoundlanders for their crews. The Act also prohibited the hiring or selling of boats, nets, or fishing gear to the masters of "foreign fishing vessels." This action would probably seriously affect the operations of American fishermen in Newfoundland waters. The text of the Act of May 10, 1906, is given in *ibid.*, pp. 782–784.

74. Sir Edward Grey to Ambassador Reid, September 3, 1906, *ibid.*, pp. 731–733.

75. *Memorandum* presented by Ambassador Reid to the Foreign Office, September 12, 1906, *ibid.*, p. 703.

the subject day before yesterday, seemed to accept our views, and his disposition to reach a speedy conclusion was certainly all that could be desired. He said frankly (and of course unofficially): "You know, of course, your difficulty is not with us, but that our Colonials are sometimes pretty hard to manage. In fact you probably know them quite as well as we do!"[76]

This trouble with British "colonials" was well exemplified when on September 15, the Colonial Office received a telegram from Governor MacGregor vehemently protesting against any *modus vivendi* that would suspend the operation of the punitive sections of Newfoundland legislation. Such action would interfere with the "internal affairs" of the colony, and was in violation of the pledge furnished by Lord Salisbury on May 5, 1891.[77]

In reply to this importunate telegram, the Colonial Office pointed out that Lord Salisbury's pledge of May, 1891, drew a clear distinction between the internal affairs of Newfoundland and matters of international interest, and "insisted strongly on right of Imperial Government to intervene in matters coming within the latter category." As to the Newfoundland legislation of 1905 and 1906, the Colonial Office had never approved the policy embodied in those Acts.[78]

After sending this reproof to the Governor of Newfoundland, the Foreign Office indicated to Ambassador Reid its consent to the use of purse seines by American fishermen during the current fishing season. The hope was then expressed that the masters of American fishing vessels would be restrained from the practice of "engaging Newfoundland fishermen just outside the 3-mile limit."[79]

Despite further spirited protests from the Government of Newfoundland, the Foreign Office went ahead and arranged, through an exchange of notes, a *modus vivendi* that would temporarily prevent serious friction in Newfoundland waters. The American Government promised that the shipment of Newfoundlanders by American fishermen outside the 3-mile limit would be done by the masters of American vessels only when "necessary," and these shipments would be made "far enough from the exact 3-mile limit to avoid any reasonable doubt." A pledge was then given that American fishermen would not fish on Sunday, and it was agreed that light dues would be paid if the fishermen were not deprived of their rights to fish. In return for these concessions,

76. Ambassador Reid to President Roosevelt, September 14, 1906, *Roosevelt MS.*

77. Governor MacGregor to the Earl of Elgin, Received, September 15, 1906, *F.R., 1906,* Pt. 1, pp. 734–735.

78. The Earl of Elgin to Governor MacGregor, September 19, 1906, *ibid.,* p. 736.

79. *Memorandum* communicated to Ambassador Reid, September 25, 1906, *ibid.,* p. 744.

the British Government agreed to permit the use, by American fishermen, of purse seines. They also promised not to bring into force certain punitive sections of the Newfoundland laws of June 15, 1905, and May 10, 1906.[80]

The negotiation of this *modus vivendi* by the Foreign Office is convincing testimony of the strong desire of Sir Edward Grey to be on friendly terms with the United States. He knew that there would be many politicians who would try to make an issue of the manner in which the interests of Newfoundland were pushed aside in order to pave the way for Anglo-American amity. In November, 1906, there was considerable excitement in the House of Commons concerning this Newfoundland situation, and Ambassador Reid gave his version of the affair in a personal note to President Roosevelt:

To my surprise, the hubbub over our Newfoundland *modus vivendi* has increased. This is due, no doubt to the excessively bumptious conduct of the authorities in the irresponsible little colony, and to the keen desire of the Conservatives here to impress the British public with the idea that they are the only people who can manage foreign policy. Some even of our good friends are lending themselves to this kind of nagging at the Ministry. They have already had two questions in the House of Commons on the subject, and the Foreign Office tells me they are sure to have a debate in the House on it. . . . The moral of the whole row is to show how extremely dangerous it is to leave these old questions outstanding. I sincerely hope before another season comes around, a permanent settlement may be reached, even if we should have to make some unimportant concession to get it.[81]

80. Ambassador Reid to Sir Edward Grey, October 6, 1906; Sir Edward Grey to Ambassador Reid, October 8, 1906, *ibid.*, pp. 748–750.

81. Ambassador Reid to President Roosevelt, November 6, 1906, *Personal, Roosevelt MS.* In a letter to Ambassador Reid, October 24, 1906, Secretary Root gave his opinion of the situation in Newfoundland: "I congratulate you on concluding the Newfoundland *modus vivendi.* It was done in good shape and is very satisfactory. Or course, the Newfoundlanders, like the Canadians, are unreasonable because they have no responsibility whatever, either for keeping the peace or defending themselves if peace is broken, and they insist, and always will insist, upon having everything absolutely their own way. The curious thing about the Newfoundland situation, however, is that it is not really the people of Newfoundland who feel this way. The fishermen, who make up the majority of the people, are really on our side of the controversy. They wish to ship on our vessels and they are now crossing the line in hundreds to do so. They wish to sell herring and bait to our vessels. All these restrictive Newfoundland laws are designed to prevent the fishermen of Newfoundland from doing what they wish to do. The laws are made in the interest of the big mercantile concerns who wish to prevent the Americans from competing with them for the labor and the product of the fishermen. . . . If the Newfoundlanders who have a voice continue their present unreasonable attitude, would not Great Britain agree that it would be a useful thing for us to send a couple of cruisers up to the coast, as France has been in the habit of doing?" *Specially Confidential, Root MS.*

Secretary Root was entirely willing to make unimportant concessions for the sake of settling the fisheries controversy, and in order to get a closer view of the situation, he paid a visit to Canada in January, 1907. He had many talks with Earl Grey, Lord Strathcona, Sir Wilfrid Laurier, and other statesmen of importance. In Ottawa and in Montreal he was able to get many side-lights on the Newfoundland fisheries dispute, and they helped him to chart his diplomatic course with judicious insight of realities.[82]

Root knew that the British Foreign Office and not the Newfoundland Government would be the decisive factor in this fisheries equation. For this reason he was greatly pleased when James Bryce supplanted Sir Mortimer Durand as the British Ambassador. When Bryce made his first appearance at the Department of State in the spring of 1907, he intended to discuss this tangled question of the North Atlantic fisheries, but before he could read his prepared statement, Secretary Root held up his hand and quietly remarked: "Just one moment, Mr. Ambassador." He then began pacing back and forth across his office, and his footsteps punctuated the cogent argument he delivered to Mr. Bryce. The Ambassador was so impressed with Root's discourse that he decided not to read his instruction from the Foreign Office.[83] Long formal statements would have little effect upon the situation. In the course of frank and friendly conversations he and Secretary Root could drop the mask of diplomacy and discuss the realities of world politics. It was not long before they were fast friends, and Bryce became not only an ambassador of good will but also a symbol of closer concert between England and the United States.

In his note of June 20, 1907, Sir Edward Grey expressed his appreciation of the "fairness with which Mr. Root has stated the American side of the question." But the Foreign Office did not permit this growing accord to alter its convictions with regard to the more important questions that were involved in the Newfoundland fisheries dispute. The British Government claimed that the Treaty of 1818 "gave no fishing rights to American vessels as such, but only to inhabitants of the United States and that the latter are bound to conform to such Newfoundland laws and regulations as are reasonable and not inconsistent with the exercise of their Treaty rights." The United States Government, on the other hand, asserted that

American rights may be exercised irrespectively of any laws or regulations

82. P. C. Jessup, *Elihu Root* (New York, 1938), II, 88–90.
83. Esme Howard, *Theatre of Life, 1905–1936* (London, 1936) p. 139.

which the Newfoundland Government may impose, and agree that as ships strictly speaking can have no rights or duties, whenever the term is used, it is but a convenient or customary form of describing the owners' or masters' rights. . . . They consider that it is probably quite unimportant which form of expression is used.

His Majesty's Government could not accept any interpretation of the Treaty of 1818 which would "withdraw Newfoundlanders from the jurisdiction of their own Government so as to entitle them to fish in the employment of Americans in violation of Newfoundland laws." The main question at issue was "that of the application of the Newfoundland regulations to American fishermen." On this vital point of principle there did not seem to be "any immediate prospect of agreement with the United States views." Therefore, it seemed expedient to "endeavour to find some temporary solution of the difficulty as to the regulations under which the Americans are to fish." This solution lay in the form of a proposed *modus vivendi.* Under the terms of this working agreement, as outlined by Sir Edward Grey, the American Government would concede every important point for which the Foreign Office had contended. American vessels should enter and clear at Newfoundland custom-houses; the use of the purse seine should be prohibited; no Sunday fishing should be permitted, and American vessels should pay light dues upon entering Newfoundland ports.[84]

Root regarded this proposed *modus vivendi* as the "coolest piece of cheek" he had ever seen.[85] Sir Edward Grey was asking sweeping concessions from the United States and was extending none in return. At times, the game of diplomacy might require a big bluff with low cards, but Grey should have known that Root could not be easily hoodwinked, and the very fact that he resorted to bluff is an indication that he was

84. Sir Edward Grey to Ambassador Reid, June 20, 1907, *North Atlantic Coast Fisheries Arbitration,* IV, 843–847. In a personal letter to President Roosevelt, June 7, 1907, Ambassador Reid discusses certain parallels between the situations in California and in Newfoundland: "The parallel you draw between our situation over California outrages on the Japanese and the British situation over Newfoundland's head-strong course as to our treaty rights, is a striking one and our English friends have not failed to notice it. In fact, Sir Edward Grey has spoken to me about it more than once, when I have remarked that it was grotesque for this little Newfoundland colony to imagine that it would be permitted by Great Britain to force it into the position of denying to us the treaty rights it had guaranteed. But shouldn't we be in a weak position if we attempted to use this argument against them? They might retort on us that they at least overruled their insubordinate colony to the extent of suspending its laws for the purpose of the *modus vivendi* which we secured here last autumn." *Roosevelt MS.*

85. Secretary Root to President Roosevelt, July 8, 1907, *Root MS.*

an amateur diplomat. Root soon learned that Grey did not expect the Department of State to accept his proposals,[86] and that he had "talked big" merely to prepare the way for a compromise.

Root and Bryce would never have conducted negotiations in such a manner. They never felt it necessary to give even lip service to the old ritual followed by European diplomats; they walked straight towards their objectives and not around them.[87]

In the note written by Ambassador Reid to Sir Edward Grey, July 12, 1907, Root's viewpoint was presented with no thought of evasion. The Department of State believed that any "surrender of the right to hire local fishermen, . . . and the surrender at the same time of the use of purse seines and of fishing on Sunday, would . . . render the Treaty stipulation worthless to us." It was a hopeless task to attempt to reconcile the views of the British and the American Governments. Perhaps the matter could best be settled by referring the fisheries dispute to arbitration before The Hague Tribunal. Pending this reference to arbitration, the present *modus vivendi* could be renewed, and it should be clearly understood by the British Government that American fishermen could never abandon the use of purse seines unless it was frankly admitted that they had the privilege of shipping Newfoundlanders as members of their crews.[88]

The first American offer of arbitration had been made by Ambassador Reid to Sir Edward Grey during a conversation on July 10, and it had now been renewed in the note of July 12.[89] On July 24, Grey informed Reid that the Foreign Office had decided to accept the proposal "in principle, and were now consulting with the Newfoundland authorities about that and the question of a temporary *modus vivendi*."[90] Two weeks later, Reid wrote to the President to inform him that the proposal for arbitration had been orally accepted, and "Sir Robert Bond, in

86. Ambassador Reid to Secretary Root, July 10, 1907, *ibid.*

87. On February 1, 1909, Ambassador Bryce wrote a letter to Root with reference to the termination of Root's tenure as Secretary of State. He conveyed, first of all, a message from Sir Edward Grey, who wished to record his recognition of "the impartial and friendly manner" in which Root had disposed of "so many questions of difficulty" that had caused deep concern to England and the United States. Bryce then spoke of his own feeling towards Root: "It has been a real pleasure to me through these two years to discuss the relations of our countries with you who have dealt with everything in so direct and friendly a manner and in so large and candid a spirit." *Root MS.*

88. *North Atlantic Coast Fisheries Arbitration,* III, 1007–1008.

89. Ambassador Reid to Secretary Root, July 16, 1907, *MS.* JF.

90. Ambassador Reid to Secretary Root, July 24, 1907, *ibid.*

spite of his opposition to it in the early summer, has made no difficulty."[91]

This *modus vivendi* was effected by an exchange of notes between Ambassador Reid and Sir Edward Grey, September 4–6, 1907. Its terms were similar to those agreed to in October, 1906, but in 1907 Secretary Root made the additional concession of abandoning the use of purse seines by American fishermen.[92] Sir Robert Bond had striven for a harder bargain, but his efforts had been in vain.[93]

Secretary Root's next move was to sign, on April 4, 1908, a general arbitration treaty with Great Britain.[94] This convention provided that "differences which may arise of a legal nature or relating to the interpretation of treaties existing between the two Contracting Parties and which it may not have been possible to settle by diplomacy, shall be referred to the Permanent Court of Arbitration established at the Hague by the Convention of 29th of July, 1899." A month later, Root sent to Bryce a projet which dealt with the questions that should be submitted to the arbitral tribunal.[95] Canada and Newfoundland were requested to draft similar proposals. Sir Robert Bond and J. S. Ewart complied with this request and thus prepared the way for the signature of the special agreement of January 27, 1909.[96]

Secretary Root was anxious that this special agreement should secure not only a judicial interpretation of the Treaty of 1818, but should also provide the machinery for an arbitral determination of all future controversies between the two nations concerning the fisheries. In Article IV provision was made for the Tribunal to recommend rules and a method of procedure under which "all questions which may arise in the future regarding the exercise of the liberties above referred to may be determined in accordance with the principles laid down in the award." If the High Contracting Parties should not adopt these rules, any differences which might arise relating to the interpretation of the Treaty of 1818 should then be referred to the Permanent Court at The Hague for a decision.

The first article of this special agreement of January 27, 1909, enumerated the questions which Great Britain and the United States

91. Ambassador Reid to President Roosevelt, August 9, 1907, *Roosevelt MS.*

92. Ambassador Reid to the British Foreign Office, September 4, 1907; British Foreign Office to the American Ambassador, September 6, 1907, Malloy, *op. cit.*, I, 847–848.

93. Ambassador Reid to President Roosevelt, August 11, 1907, *Roosevelt MS.*

94. Malloy, *op. cit.*, pp. 814–815.

95. Chas. E. Cayley, "The North Atlantic Fisheries in United States-Canadian Relations," *MS.* Ph.D. dissertation (Chicago, 1931), p. 357.

96. Malloy, *op. cit.*, I, 835–841.

agreed to arbitrate. They were seven in number, and they included all the important controversies that had arisen in connection with the interpretation of the Treaty of 1818.[97]

The Tribunal assembled on June 1, 1910, and delivered its award on September 7, 1910.[98] Root's argument began on August 2, and lasted for six days. It is one of America's great legal classics, and it securely

97. (1) Can Great Britain regulate (a) without the consent of the United States the hours, days, or seasons when fish may be taken on the treaty coasts, such regulations being of a "reasonable" character; (b) the methods, means and implements to be used in taking fish or in carrying on fishing operations upon such coast; and (c) any other matters of a similar nature relating to fishing? (2) Can the inhabitants of the United States in the prosecution of the fisheries rightly employ as members of the fishing crews of their vessels persons not inhabitants of the United States? (3) Can the exercise of the fishing liberties referred to in the Convention of 1818 be subjected, without the consent of the United States, to the requirements of entry, or report at custom houses or the payment of light and harbor or other dues or any other similar requirement or condition or exaction? (4) Can the right of American fishermen to enter certain bays or harbors for shelter, repairs, wood or water, and for no other purposes whatever, be made conditional upon the payment of light or harbor or other dues, or upon entering and reporting at custom houses? (5) From where must be measured the three marine miles of any of the coasts, bays, creeks or harbors referred to in the Treaty of 1818? (6) Have the inhabitants of the United States, under the Treaty of 1818 or otherwise, the liberty to take fish in the bays, harbors and creeks on that part of the southern coast of Newfoundland which extends from Cape Ray to Rameau Islands, or on the western and northern coasts of Newfoundland from Cape Ray to Quirpon Islands, or on the Magdalen Islands? (7) Are the inhabitants of the United States whose vessels resort to the treaty coasts for the purpose of exercising the liberties referred to in Article I of the Treaty of 1818 entitled to have for those vessels, when duly authorized by the United States in that behalf, the commercial privileges on the treaty coasts accorded by agreement or otherwise to United States trading vessels generally?

98. The members of the Tribunal were the Honorable George Gray, Judge of the United States Circuit Court of Appeals; the Right Honorable Sir Charles Fitzpatrick, Chief Justice of the Dominion of Canada; Dr. Heinrich Lammasch, Professor of International Law at the University of Vienna; His Excellency Jonkheer A. F. de Savornin Lohman, Minister of State of the Netherlands; and the Honorable Luis M. Drago, formerly Minister of Foreign Affairs of the Argentine Republic. Professor Lammasch had served as a judge in the arbitration at The Hague between Venezuela and the Allied Powers in the Venezuelan Preferential Cases in 1904, and had been President of the Tribunal of Arbitration in the Maskat controversy between France and Great Britain in 1905. Dr. Lohman had served as arbitrator in the Pious Fund Case in 1902, and in the Maskat controversy.

The Agent for the United States was Chandler P. Anderson. The Counsel were: Elihu Root; George Turner; Samuel J. Elder; Charles B. Warren; James Brown Scott; and Robert Lansing.

The Agent for Great Britain was the Honorable Allen B. Aylesworth, K.C., Minister of Justice for Canada. The Counsel were: The Right Honorable Sir William S. Robson, K.C., M.P., His Majesty's Attorney General; the Right Honorable Robert B. Finlay, K.C., M.P.; the Honorable Sir Edward P. Morris, LL.D., K.C., Prime Minister of Newfoundland; the Honorable Donald Morison, K.C., Minister of Justice of Newfoundland; Sir James S. Winter, K.C.; Mr. John S. Ewart, K.C.; Mr. W. N. Tilley; Mr. Raymond Asquith; Mr. Geoffrey Lawrence; Mr. Hamar Greenwood; Messrs. Blake and Redden, Solicitors.

establishes Root's fame as an outstanding jurist. It was not delivered in a dramatic manner, and there were no verbal pyrotechnics. It was soon apparent, however, that Root, by a miracle of organization, had placed in cogent sequence a colossal mass of data dealing with the fisheries question.[99] In a small, thin voice hardly heard by the members of the Tribunal, he began his presentation of the American case. There was no need for the arguments of the other American counsel; Root's brief went to the heart of the questions at issue, and his knowledge of all the points involved in the fisheries dispute seemed inexhaustible.[100]

But his impressive performance was largely in vain. As he remarked in a letter to Joseph Choate in September, 1910: "There were several difficulties in the case. One was that the judges had decided it against us before the argument began."[101] In this regard, Root had particular reference to Professor Lammasch. Lammasch felt a certain inclination towards the side of Great Britain because of the friendly attitude of the British Government towards Austria during the Balkan crisis of 1908. Root believed that the eminent Austrian jurist had permitted his pro-British sentiment to affect his judgment with regard to the award of the Tribunal.

This award was delivered on September 7, 1910. Professor Callahan has expressed the opinion that the decision of the Tribunal was a diplomatic defeat for the United States,[102] but Root regarded it as a "great and substantial victory" for the American contention.[103] The truth lies somewhere between these two opinions. There is no doubt that the award

99. *North Atlantic Coast Fisheries Arbitration,* XI, 1927–2231.

100. In a letter to Root from Secretary Knox, September 19, 1910, high tribute was paid to Root's argument before the Tribunal: "I have . . . before me for the first time our reports of the Fisheries Arbitration, and so am able to arrive at some appreciation of the monumental task so brilliantly carried to a successful conclusion. I quite agree with the remark of the London *Times* that the case of the United States might well have rested upon your speech alone." *Root MS.*

101. Jessup, *op. cit.,* II, 95.

102. J. M. Callahan, *American Foreign Policy in Canadian Relations* (New York, 1937), p. 522.

103. Jessup, *op. cit.,* II, 96. See also, E. M. Borchard, "The North Atlantic Coast Fisheries Arbitration," *Columbia Law Review,* XI (1911), 1–23; and Robert Lansing, "The North Atlantic Coast Fisheries Arbitration," *American Journal of International Law,* V (1911), 1–31.

The British and Canadians were well pleased with the verdict which they ascribed to the justice of their case and the expert way they handled the assembling of pertinent data. In a letter to Sir Wilfrid Laurier, September 7, 1910, Nelson R. Butcher, British Official Reporter at the North Atlantic Coast Fisheries Arbitration, remarked: "The very satisfactory result in this case is an example of the old story that 'what is worth doing is worth doing well.' If ever a case was well-prepared and diplomatically handled, it was the British side of the Fisheries case." *Laurier MS.,* P.A.C.

was in the nature of a compromise, and in order to attain this balance the members of the Tribunal closed their eyes to certain facts and indulged in extended exercises in confused thinking. But after all criticisms have been expressed, it must be remembered that the award brought to a close an ancient controversy that at times had led Great Britain and the United States to the very verge of war. It was an important landmark along the road to Anglo-American understanding. Through his efforts, Root had laid the basis for a more intimate association between Great Britain and the United States, and he had given real substance to the phrase, "Hands across the sea." Since November, 1794, articles had been inserted into Anglo-American treaties calling for the submission of disputes to international arbitration. It was the unique contribution of Elihu Root to translate these treaty provisions from the distant realm of aspiration to the everyday world of actual accomplishment.[104] No other American statesman had been able to do as much.

104. It is important at this point to give a brief version of the main points laid down in the award of the Tribunal. Question I had dealt with the time and manner during which and by which American fishermen might take fish off the treaty coasts of Newfoundland. The American counsel had contended that in so far as the common fishery was concerned, there should be common regulation. The British counsel had argued that the British Government should have sole power to determine the reasonableness of regulations affecting the fisheries. In its award the Tribunal held that Great Britain could "make regulations without the consent of the United States whenever these regulations were necessary for the preservation of public order and good morals, or whenever they were fair as between local fishermen and fishermen coming from the United States." But if the reasonableness of the regulations was contested by the United States, then the matter would be settled by an "impartial authority in accordance with the principles hereinabove laid down." This meant that before the objectionable regulations could go into force they would have to be passed upon by a Mixed Fishery Commission that would render a disinterested verdict.

Question II was concerned with the right of the masters of American fishing vessels to employ as members of their crews "persons not inhabitants of the United States." The Tribunal supported the American contention that the masters of these American vessels had a right to employ aliens as members of their crews while fishing in Newfoundland waters, but their decision did not touch upon the important question of the right of the Newfoundland legislature to pass a law forbidding British subjects to fish in British waters as members of the crews of American vessels.

Question III pertained to the enforced payment of light and harbor dues by American fishing vessels, and the requirement of entry and clearance from British custom houses. In the award of the Tribunal it was decided that this requirement to report at a custom house was not unreasonable as applied to fishing vessels "if proper conveniences for doing so are at hand." But these fishing vessels should not be subjected "to the purely commercial formalities of report, entry and clearance at a custom-house." Furthermore, they should pay only the light, harbor and other dues that were imposed upon Newfoundland fishermen.

Question IV dealt with the treaty rights enjoyed by fishing vessels in nontreaty waters. It was decided that these vessels should have the enumerated rights of shelter, repair of damages, the purchase of wood and the obtaining of water, but if they remained longer than forty-eight hours they would have to inform local authorities if it could be done without unreasonable inconvenience.

Question V was concerned with the British "headlands theory" as applied to bays. The British Government had long maintained that American fishermen could be excluded from all bays no matter what size. A line should be drawn from headland to headland and American fishermen should not approach within three miles of this line. The United States had insisted that some large bays are a part of the high seas and should not be shut off from fishermen. If bays were more than six miles across, American fishermen could enter them and take fish. In this case the Tribunal held that "the three marine miles are to be measured from a straight line drawn across the body of water at the place where it ceases to have the configuration and characteristics of a bay." But this ruling was so ambiguous that it would be difficult to follow, so the Tribunal recommended the acceptance of the ten-mile rule as laid down in the North Sea convention of 1882 and in the Bayard-Chamberlain treaty of February 15, 1888. This rule was to the effect that the three-mile line should be drawn across the part of the bay nearest the entrance, at the first point where the width does not exceed ten miles.

Question VI involved the right of the inhabitants of the United States to take fish in the bays, harbors and creeks along the southern, northern and western coasts of Newfoundland. Sir Robert Bond had discovered that the language of Article I of the Treaty of 1818 did not include in its enumeration of fishing liberties granted to American fishermen, any specific mention of the privilege to fish within the harbors, creeks or coves of Newfoundland. The American Government had contended that the general word "coast" included the smaller terms of description, and this contention was upheld by the Tribunal.

Question VII dealt with the question of whether American fishing vessels had the commercial privileges on the treaty coasts accorded by agreement or otherwise to American trading vessels. This question had been vehemently argued for many years, the American Government expressly holding that fishing vessels, duly licensed under the Revised Statutes as commercial vessels, had full commercial privileges. This point was very important to the fishing industry of New England. The Tribunal held that an American vessel cannot at one and the same time enjoy the liberty of fishing and of commercial privileges, "because treaty rights and commercial privileges are submitted to different regulations and restraints."

See *North Atlantic Coast Fisheries Arbitration,* I, 64–101.

CHAPTER V

THE ALASKAN BOUNDARY DISPUTE: HISTORICAL BACKGROUND, 1825–1877

THE Alaskan Boundary Dispute has a long background of territorial claims made by Russia, Great Britain and the United States with reference to certain lands along the Northwest Coast of our continent. As early as 1639, adventurous Cossacks had crossed the mountains that formed the eastern border of Siberia, and had reached the shores of the Pacific Ocean.[1] In 1727, Vitus Behring, a Dane in Russian employ, discovered the strait that bears his name, and fourteen years later he explored the Aleutian Islands and sailed along the coast of Alaska.[2] Russian traders eager to secure furs for the Chinese market at Kiakta made repeated visits to the Aleutian Islands, and in 1778 Captain Cook found them firmly established in that vicinity.[3]

As a result of the friction between these Russian traders, the Czar issued on July 8, 1799, a ukase which provided for the organization of the Russian American Company. To this company he granted for a term of twenty years a monopoly of the trade and the exclusive occupation of that part of the American coast north of the 55th degree of north latitude. The company was also empowered to "make new discoveries not only north of the fifty-fifth degree of north latitude, but farther to the south, and to occupy the new lands discovered . . . if they have not been previously occupied by . . . any other nation."[4]

This imperial ukase quieted the friction between Russian traders along the Northwest Coast but it did not put a stop to the visits of American vessels to points within the Russian jurisdiction. After the close of the American Revolution, Yankee merchants opened a lucrative trade with the Chinese port of Canton, and it was soon discovered that wealthy Chinese were willing to pay high prices for good furs. In order to secure these valuable pelts, American traders sailed along the Alaskan coast in open disregard of the restrictions contained in the imperial ukase. Shipments of furs to Canton increased rapidly in vol-

1. F. A. Golder, *Russian Expansion on the Pacific, 1641–1850* (Cleveland, 1914); Hubert H. Bancroft, *History of Alaska, 1730–1885* (San Francisco, 1886).
2. F. A. Golder, *Bering's Voyages* (New York, 1922).
3. Captain James Cook, *A Voyage to the Pacific Ocean* (London, 1784), III, 359–383.
4. *Proceedings of the Alaskan Boundary Tribunal* (Washington, 1904), II, 23–25.

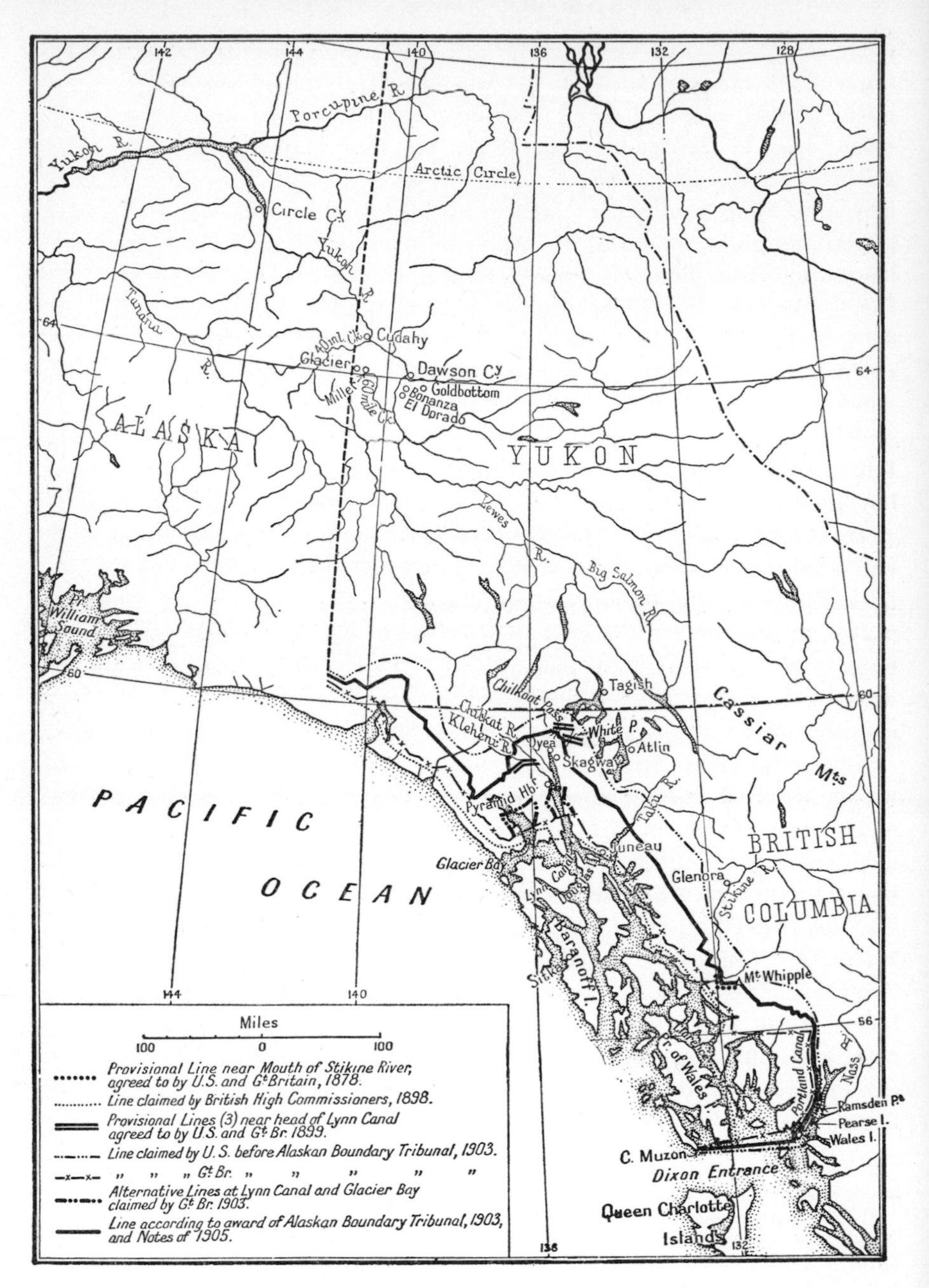

The Alaskan Boundary and the Klondike

ume, and the wrath of the Russian American Company rose accordingly. Protests were filed by the Russian Minister at Washington, but nothing was accomplished.[5] Perhaps another ukase would settle the situation. On September 16, 1821, the Czar issued an edict which granted to Russian subjects a monopoly over the "pursuits of commerce, whaling, and fishery, and of all other industry on all the islands, posts, and gulfs, including the whole of the northwest coast of America, beginning from Behring Straits to the 51° of northern latitude." All foreign vessels were forbidden not only to land on these coasts but "to approach them within less than 100 Italian miles." Nine days later (September 25, 1821) a second charter was issued to the Russian American Company. Under its terms the monopoly of the fur trade and fisheries was renewed, commencing "from the northern point of the Island of Vancouver, under 51° north latitude, to Behring Straits and beyond them."[6]

In a note to Lord Castlereagh, the Russian Minister at London indicated that the purpose of the ukase was to prevent any further trading operations by "vagabonds" who not only carried on an illegal traffic in furs with the natives along the Northwest Coast but who also furnished them with firearms and ammunition.[7] These "vagabonds" were, of course, American traders engaged in collecting furs for the Canton market.

The claim of the Russian Government to sovereignty over the waters within 100 miles of the Alaskan coast was regarded by the law officers of the British Crown as directly in conflict with the principles of international law.[8] Fortified with these opinions, Lord Castlereagh registered a cautiously worded protest against this Russian pretension and also questioned the territorial claims of Russia on the American continent.[9]

The American Government did not receive official notification of the terms of the imperial ukase until February 11, 1822. In his reply, Secretary Adams expressed surprise that the Russian Government had extended its territorial claims along the Northwest Coast from fifty-five to fifty-one degrees of north latitude. The pretension to authority

5. Tyler Dennett, *Americans in Eastern Asia* (New York, 1922), pp. 34–43; Morison, *Maritime History of Massachusetts*, pp. 41–78; Hildt, *op. cit.*, pp. 158 ff.

6. *Alaskan Boundary Tribunal*, II, 25–28. Hereafter referred to by initials *A.B.T.*

7. Baron de Nicolay to the Marquis of Londonderry, November 12, 1821, *ibid.*, pp. 95–97. See also Count Nesselrode to Count Lieven, October 7, 1821, and Sir Charles Bagot to the Marquis of Londonderry, November 17, 1821, *ibid.*, pp. 99–102.

8. Lord Stowell to Lord Melville, December 26, 1821, and Christopher Robinson to the Marquis of Londonderry, November 20, 1821, *ibid.*, pp. 102–103.

9. Marquis of Londonderry to Count Lieven, January 18, 1822, *ibid.*, pp. 104–105.

to exclude American vessels from approaching within 100 Italian miles from the shores of this coast was challenged and the Russian Minister at Washington was called upon to "give explanations of the grounds of right, upon principles generally recognized by the laws and usages of nations, which can warrant the claims." These "explanations" were promptly furnished by the Chevalier de Poletica in a long note that failed to carry conviction to Secretary Adams, and the controversy continued until the conclusion of the treaty between Russia and the United States, April 17, 1824.[10]

In the meantime, the British Government had flatly refused to accept the Russian pretensions as outlined in the ukase of September 16, 1821. In adopting this attitude Canning, then Foreign Secretary, had been influenced by representations made to him by the fur-trading interests in the Northwest. In March, 1821, the North West Company was merged into the Hudson's Bay Company, and in the following July Parliament authorized the Crown to grant to this enlarged corporation the exclusive privilege of trading with "the Indians in all such parts of North America" as "did not form part of the company's previous possessions, the royal provinces, or the territory of the United States."[11] Some two months later, J. H. Pelly, the deputy governor of the Hudson's Bay Company, wrote to the Foreign Office and sounded a warning that the British fur trade would be greatly injured if "the claims of Russia be admitted by the British Government." He then outlined the scope of the operations of the Hudson's Bay Company, and gave the impression that they extended between the Rocky Mountains and the Pacific Ocean, and on the coast from the Fraser River to 60° north latitude.[12]

Canning accepted Pelly's statements at face value, and they were repeated in a memorandum which Wellington handed to Count Nesselrode during the sessions of the Congress of Verona.[13] Bagot carried out

10. Chevalier de Poletica to Secretary Adams, February 28, April 2, 1822; Secretary Adams to Chevalier de Poletica, February 25, March 30, 1822, *ibid.*, pp. 32–38. Under the terms of the Russo-American treaty of April 17, 1824, the Russian Government abandoned its right to exclude American citizens from approaching closer than 100 Italian miles from the Northwest Coast above the 51st parallel of north latitude. The treaty also fixed the southern boundary of Russian possessions at fifty-four degrees and forty minutes of north latitude. Miller, *op. cit.,* III (Washington, 1933), 151–162.

11. *A.B.T.,* I, 17.

12. J. H. Pelly to Canning, September 25, 1822, *ibid.,* II, 109–110.

13. Wellington to Mr. G. Canning, November 28, 1822, *ibid.,* pp. 113–114. In his memorandum of October 17, 1822, Wellington asserted that "the much more easily proved, more conclusive, and more certain title of occupation and use ought to decide the claim of sovereignty."

these instructions by suggesting to Poletica a boundary line that would be drawn "through Chatham strait to the head of Lynn canal, thence northwest to the 140° of longitude."[14] When this line was rejected by the Russian Government, Bagot made three other proposals that were not acceptable to Count Nesselrode. His purpose in making these proposals was to "secure the posts upon the continent belonging to the Hudson Bay Company," and the "embouchures of such rivers as might afford an outlet for our fur trade into the Pacific." He was particularly anxious to secure access to the Pacific Ocean, and to fix the "fifty-sixth degree of north latitude as the British boundary upon the coast."[15]

From the Russian point of view it was essential to establish a barrier "at which would be stopped, once and for all, . . . the encroachments of the English agents of the amalgamated Hudson Bay and Northwest English Company."[16] In order to accomplish this objective the Russian Government had proposed the line 54° 40′ as the southern frontier of Russian possessions, and had suggested that "upon the continent and towards the east, this frontier could run along the mountains which follow the sinuosities of the coast as far as Mount Elias." This proposal would assure to Russia a narrow strip (*lisière*) along the coast of the mainland, and would leave to the English settlements all the "needful space for increase and extension." To Count Nesselrode it seemed apparent that the key-note of the negotiations was the fact that Russia wished merely "to keep" while the "English companies wish to obtain."[17]

But the British Foreign Secretary was really quite conciliatory in his attitude towards Russia, and on July 12, 1824 he instructed Sir Charles Bagot to accept a line "drawn from the southernmost point of Prince of Wales Island . . . through Portland Channel till it strikes the mainland in latitude 56; thence following the sinuosities of the coast along the base of the mountains nearest the sea to Mount Elias." Realizing only too well the imperfections in contemporary maps, Canning was suspicious about the location of the range of mountains that was supposed to run parallel to the coast. In any event, the British

14. The Chevalier de Poletica to Count Nesselrode, November 3, 1823, *ibid.,* pp. 137–142; Secretary Canning to Sir Charles Bagot, January 15, 1824, *ibid.,* pp. 144–149; Sir C. Bagot to Secretary Canning, March 29, 1824, *ibid.,* pp. 153–157.

15. Sir Charles Bagot to Canning, March 29, 1824, *ibid.,* pp. 153–157. The four proposals of Sir Charles Bagot are clearly outlined on Map No. 3, in the Atlas accompanying the "American Case."

16. Poletica to Count Nesselrode, November 3, 1823, *A.B.T.,* II, 137–142.

17. Count Nesselrode to Count Lieven, April 17, 1824, *ibid.,* pp. 172–175.

Government would not be willing to have the boundary line of the Russian possessions on the mainland exceed "a distance of 10 leagues" from the coast.[18]

Armed with these instructions and the draft of a treaty, Sir Charles Bagot resumed the negotiations, but he was too inflexible to be successful. He insisted upon securing the "liberty" for British subjects "to navigate and trade *forever* along the coast of the *lisière* which it is proposed to cede to Russia from the Portland Channel to the sixtieth degree of north latitude." He also strongly contended that British subjects should enjoy the perpetual right of trade with the Russian port of Sitka. Denied these concessions, he terminated the negotiations.[19] But the British Government was anxious to conclude a treaty with Russia that would settle all the difficulties that were threatened by the ukase of September, 1821, and Stratford Canning was sent to St. Petersburg to resume the discussions broken off by Bagot. In the instructions that were given to the new British Minister to Russia, it was clearly indicated that the Foreign Office was particularly concerned with the pretensions of the Russian Government to prohibit trade along the Northwest Coast within one hundred miles of the shore. The settlement of the limits of the respective possessions was proposed by the British Government only

> as a mode of facilitating the adjustment of the difference arising from the ukase. It is comparatively indifferent to us whether we hasten or postpone all questions respecting the limits of territorial possession, . . . but the pretensions of the Russian ukase of 1821 to exclusive dominion over the Pacific could not continue longer unrepealed. . . . It is *not* on our part essentially a negotiation about limits. It is a demand of the repeal of an offensive and unjustifiable arrogation of exclusive jurisdiction over an ocean of unmeasured extent.

Secretary Canning was willing to recede from Bagot's extreme position, and he expressed his willingness to accept a Russian proposal to open the port of Sitka merely for a period of ten years. He was also ready to accept a similar limitation with reference to the right "to frequent . . . the interior seas, the gulfs, havens and creeks" in the Russian *lisière* or strip along the Northwest Coast.[20] This conciliatory disposition on the part of the British Government removed all difficulties that might check the conclusion of the negotiations, and finally, on

18. Canning to Sir Charles Bagot, July 12, 1824, *ibid.,* pp. 181–185.
19. Sir Charles Bagot to Canning, August 12, 1824, *ibid.,* pp. 190–192.
20. Canning to Stratford Canning, December 8, 1824, *ibid.,* pp. 208–212.

February 28, 1825, a treaty was signed in St. Petersburg. Under its terms the Russian Government withdrew from its pretensions to control navigation 100 miles from the shores of its possessions along the Northwest Coast. This was a signal diplomatic victory for Great Britain, and the British Foreign Office was glad to make concessions in other articles of the treaty. Trade with the port of Sitka and with the natives in the *lisière* along the coast was limited to a term of ten years, and traffic in firearms or ammunition was expressly forbidden. The limits of the *lisière* or strip of land along the Northwest Coast were fixed as follows:

Commencing from the southernmost point of the island called *Prince of Wales* Island, which point lies in the parallel of 54 degrees 40 minutes, north latitude, . . . the said line shall ascend to the north along the channel called *Portland Channel,* as far as the point of the continent where it strikes the 56th degree of north latitude; from this last-mentioned point, the line of demarcation shall follow the summit of the mountains situated parallel to the coast, as far as the point of intersection of the 141st degree of west longitude, . . . and finally, from the said point of intersection, the said meridian line of the 141st degree, in its prolongation as far as the Frozen Ocean. . . . Whenever the summit of the mountains which extend in a direction parallel to the coast . . . shall prove to be at the distance of more than 10 marine leagues from the ocean, the limit between the British possessions and the strip of coast which is to belong to Russia, . . . shall be formed by a line parallel to the sinuosities of the coast, and which shall never exceed the distance of 10 marine leagues therefrom.[21]

It is apparent from the terms of this treaty that the negotiators, relying upon contemporary maps, believed that a mountain range ran along the coast not far from the sea. This mountain range is clearly indicated upon Captain George Vancouver's chart of the Northwest Coast,[22] and upon a map published in St. Petersburg in 1802 by the Russian quartermaster-general's department.[23] A line following the crest of these mountains would exclude the British from the coast line above fifty-four degrees forty minutes of north latitude.

A cartographical expression of what the Russian Government thought it had secured by the treaty with Great Britain is shown by the Russian Admiralty chart number 1266, published in St. Petersburg in 1826. On it the boundary line is depicted as running from the head

21. *Ibid.*, pp. 14–16.

22. Vancouver's chart "showing part of the coast of N. W. America," Map No. 4, *United States Atlas, A.B.T., Maps and Charts Accompanying the Case and Counter Case of the United States* (Washington, 1904).

23. Map No. 6, *United States Atlas, A.B.T.*

of Portland Channel around the heads of all the inlets to the 141° of longitude, and thence northward along that meridian. This unbroken *lisière* gave to the Russian Government the unquestioned control over all the fiords along the coast north of 54° 40′.[24] Three years later there was published in St. Petersburg another map which closely followed the preceding admiralty chart.[25] These maps indicated exactly what the Russian representatives thought they had agreed upon in the negotiations of 1824–26, and it is significant that the British Foreign Office filed no protest concerning this boundary line. On the contrary, British officials and cartographers accepted the Russian maps as authentic. In 1831, Joseph Bouchette, deputy surveyor-general of the province of Lower Canada, published in London a map which resembled the Russian charts.[26] The Arrowsmith map, revised to 1833, is along similar lines,[27] and so is the map drawn by Thomas Devine by order of Joseph Cauchon, Canadian Commissioner of Crown Lands, in 1857.[28] The British-Russian boundary as drawn on all these maps clearly shows an unbroken *lisière* extending from the head of Portland Channel to Mount St. Elias, and this line is reproduced on subsequent British maps.

There was no dispute about the lines on contemporary maps, but there was a serious difficulty about the interpretation of the terms of the treaty of 1825. This controversy arose in June, 1834, when a vessel of the Hudson's Bay Company, the *Dryad,* attempted to ascend the Stikine River for the purpose of establishing a British post above the ten league line. It was stopped by Russian officials and had to return to Naas, a new post of the Hudson's Bay Company on Observatory Inlet.[29]

This action was in contravention of articles six and seven of the treaty of 1825, and prompt protest was made to the Russian Government along with a bill for damages amounting to £22,150.[30] Although Count Nesselrode deprecated the unfriendly attitude of the Russian

24. Map No. 11, *ibid.*

25. Map entitled "Carte Générale . . . de la Côte N. W. de L'Amérique," published in St. Petersburg in 1892. See Thomas W. Balch, *The Alaska Frontier* (Philadelphia, 1903), Map No. 7.

26. Map No. 14, *British Atlas, A.B.T.*

27. Map No. 12, *United States Atlas, A.B.T.*

28. Map No. 19, *ibid.*

29. *Report* of Chief Trader Peter S. Ogden, 1834, *A.B.T.,* II, 267–270. See also, Ogden to John McLoughlin, December 20, 1834, *ibid.,* pp. 271–272.

30. John McLoughlin to the Governor of the Hudson's Bay Company, March 17, 1835, *ibid.,* pp. 272–273; Baron Wrangell to Board of Directors of the Russian American Company, April 30, 1835, *ibid.,* pp. 274–278; Lord Durham to Count Nesselrode, December 11, 1835, *ibid.,* pp. 285–287.

officials in connection with the stopping of the *Dryad*,[31] he claimed that the British ship should have disregarded the slight opposition that was offered to this passage up the Stikine River. The responsibility for turning back should be laid upon the master of the *Dryad* and not upon the Russian authorities.[32] The British Government was not satisfied with these explanations, and the dispute was finally settled on February 6, 1839 by an agreement whereby the Russian American Company leased to the Hudson's Bay Company, for a period of ten years, all of the *lisière* from Cross Bay down to fifty-four degrees and forty minutes.[33]

The importance of this *Dryad* incident lies in the fact that both the British and the Russian officials agreed that the boundary line of the *lisière* crossed the Stikine River at a point ten marine leagues (30 miles) from its mouth.[34] Other British officials were to make similar admissions a few years later. In 1849 the lease of the *lisière* by the Hudson's Bay Company was renewed, and subsequent renewals made the lease effective until the Russian Government sold Alaska to the United States in 1867. During the Crimean War the possessions of Russia and of Great Britain along the Northwest Coast were neutralized under an agreement between the Russian American Company and the Hudson's Bay Company. This agreement was approved by both governments and was faithfully carried out.[35] In 1857, in his testimony before a select committee of the British House of Commons, Sir George Simpson, Governor of the Hudson's Bay Company, discussed the meaning of this neutrality agreement and remarked as follows: "The British territory runs along inland from the coast about 30 miles; the Russian territory runs along the coast; we have the rights of navigation through the rivers to hunt the interior country."[36]

31. Count Nesselrode to the British Ambassador, December 21, 1835, *ibid.*, pp. 287–289.

32. Count Nesselrode to the British Ambassador, March 10, 1837, *ibid.*, pp. 292–293.

33. The correspondence relative to the *Dryad* affair is quite voluminous and may be found in *ibid.*, pp. 271–312. The date of the beginning of the lease was June 1, 1840. D. C. Davidson, "Relations of the Hudson's Bay Company with the Russian American Company on the Northwest Coast, 1829–1867," *British Columbia Historical Quarterly*, V (1941), 33–66.

34. Baron Wrangell to Board of Directors of Russian American Company, April 30, 1835, *A.B.T.*, II, 274–278; Deputy Governor J. H. Pelly to ———, October 24, 1835, *ibid.*, pp. 278–279.

35. F. A. Golder, "The Purchase of Alaska," *American Historical Review*, XXV, 411–425; Bancroft, *op. cit.*, pp. 570–571.

36. *Great Britain: Parliamentary Papers, 1857. Rept. of Select Committee on the Hudson's Bay Company, Repts. from Committees*, XV, 59.

The questions of the chairman of this Parliamentary committee, and the answers of Sir George Simpson, are significant:

1732. Chairman. I think you made an arrangement with the Russian Company by which you hold under lease a portion of their territory?—Yes.

1733. I believe that arrangement is that you hold that strip of country which intervenes between your territory and the sea, and that you give them £1500 a year for it?—Yes.

1734. What were your objects in making that arrangement?—To prevent difficulties existing between the Russians and ourselves; as a peace offering.

1735. What was the nature of those difficulties?—We were desirous of passing through their territory, which is inland from the coast about 30 miles. There is a margin of 30 miles of coast belonging to the Russians. We had the right of navigating the rivers falling into the ocean, and of settling the interior country. Difficulties arose between us in regard to the trade of the country.[37]

As a means of illustrating the testimony of Sir George Simpson, the select committee published two maps at the end of their report which clearly indicated the extent of the *lisière* that had been leased from the Russian American Company.[38] These maps were convincing evidence that this *lisière* completely shut off the Hudson's Bay Company from all access to the fiords that deeply indented the Alaskan coast. It was this very fact that made certain Canadians express a wish that the *lisière* could be purchased from Russia. In 1863 the newspaper *The Colonist*, published at Victoria, British Columbia, made the following pertinent observation:

It is not desirable that the business of such a highway [the Stikine] should reach the interior through a Russian door of 30 miles. . . . The strip of land which stretches along from Portland Canal to Mount St. Elias, with a breadth of 30 miles, and which according to the Treaty of 1825 forms a part of Russian America, must eventually become the property of Great Britain.[39]

Thanks to the imperialistic views of Secretary William H. Seward, the United States was able to anticipate any move by the British Government to purchase Alaska or even the *lisière* which ran from Mount St. Elias to 54° 40′. On March 30, 1867 Baron Stoeckl signed at Washington a treaty which ceded Alaska to the United States for the

37. *Ibid.*, p. 91.

38. One of the maps was entitled "Map of North West Part of Canada, Hudson's Bay and Indian Territories." The other map was entitled "Aboriginal Map of North America."

39. *A.B.T.*, II, 321–323.

sum of $7,200,000.[40] The eastern boundary of Alaska was described as the "line of demarcation between the Russian and the British possessions in North America, as established by the convention between Russia and Great Britain in February 28–16, 1825."

The ratifications of the treaty were exchanged on June 20, 1867, and the formal transfer of the territory was effected at Sitka on October 18, 1867. In order to indicate clearly the limits of Alaska, Secretary Seward had a map published. This map depicted the boundary line as it had already appeared on the previous maps of Krusenstern, Bouchette, and Arrowsmith, and the British Government did not present a protest with regard to it. British cartographers had no qualms about accepting the boundary line as laid down on the Seward map, and in *Black's General Atlas of the World*, published in Edinburgh in 1870, there is a map which conforms to the Seward version.[41] This is also true of the map of "North America" included in Alexander K. Johnston's *Royal Atlas of Modern Geography*, published in Edinburgh in 1885.[42]

But this British acquiescence in the matter of the Alaskan boundary line was not to continue indefinitely. About the time of the cession of Alaska to the United States, gold was discovered in the Cassiar region of British Columbia. Access to these gold deposits could best be effected through travel up the Stikine River, and this fact brought to the front the question of a survey which would determine exactly the location of the boundary line between British and American possessions.[43] On July 11, 1872, Joseph W. Trutch, Lieutenant Governor of British Columbia, wrote to Joseph Howe, Secretary of State for the Dominion, and referred to the importance of an early settlement of this boundary line. He was of the opinion that the line as described in the treaty of 1825 could not "in practice be determined," and he suggested that some other boundary be fixed.[44]

This matter was promptly taken up with the British Foreign Office, which in turn instructed the British Minister at Washington to discuss the situation with Secretary Fish. Fish remarked that he was perfectly satisfied as to "the expediency of such a measure," but he feared that Congress "might not be willing to grant the necessary funds." He

40. Benjamin P. Thomas, *Russo-American Relations, 1815–1867* (Baltimore, 1930), pp. 143–166; Golder, *op. cit.,* XXV, 411–425. For the text of the treaty see Malloy, *op. cit.,* II, 1521–1524.

41. Map No. 39.

42. Map No. 43.

43. John W. Foster, "The Alaskan Boundary," *National Geographic Magazine,* X, No. 11 (November, 1899), 450.

44. J. W. Trutch to Joseph Howe, July 11, 1872, *A.B.T.,* III, 224.

promised, however, that President Grant would recommend in his next message to Congress the appointment of a commission to determine the Alaskan boundary.[45] This promise was duly carried out by the President in his message of December 2, 1872,[46] and a bill was introduced into Congress for the purpose of "surveying and marking the line of boundary."[47] But this matter of marking the boundary line was a complicated task which might cost about a million and a half dollars for the United States alone, and it might stretch over a period of ten years. Under existing circumstances the American Government thought it would be sufficient to decide upon particular points to be surveyed such as the head of Portland Canal, and also where the boundary line crosses "the Rivers Shoot, Stakeen, Taku, Iselcat, and Chelkaht, Mount St. Elias, and the points where the 141st degree of west longitude crosses the Rivers Yuken and Porcupine." But even this limited task would consume about four years and would cost $500,000. Because of the magnitude of the work to be done and the high attendant cost, Secretary Fish doubted "whether Congress would ever be induced to vote so large a sum as was deemed necessary to lay down the boundary completely."[48]

The Canadian Government was not discouraged by this opinion of Secretary Fish, and some months later Captain D. R. Cameron was requested to submit an approximate estimate of the cost of determining the Alaskan boundary.[49] This action was followed by a resolution of the House of Assembly, of British Columbia, to Lieutenant Governor Trutch, calling his attention to the recent "discovery of rich and extensive gold mines in the Northern portion of the Province." This discovery had greatly increased the "importance and urgency" of having the exact line between British Columbia and Alaska properly defined. It was clear that the "boundary of the 30 mile belt of American territory running along a part of the seaboard" seriously affected "vital questions bearing upon navigation and commerce." In view of these facts the Lieutenant Governor was requested "to urge upon the Federal Government the necessity of taking immediate steps for having the said boundary established."[50]

45. Sir Edward Thornton to Earl Granville, November 18, 1872, *ibid.*, pp. 226–227.

46. Richardson, *Messages and Papers of the Presidents,* VII, 187.

47. *House Misc. Doc. No. 20,* 42 Cong., 3 sess. (H.R. 3254).

48. Sir Edward Thornton to Earl Granville, February 15, 1873, *A.B.T.,* III, 230–231; Shippee, *op. cit.,* p. 475.

49. David Christie to Capt. D. R. Cameron, November 27, 1873, *A.B.T.,* III, 236–237. Cameron, as will be seen, became in course of time, Major, Colonel and General.

50. J. Roland Hett, Clerk of the Assembly, to the Hon. Joseph W. Trutch, January 8, 1874, *A.B.T.,* IV, 50.

The Dominion Government, at Ottawa, looked into this situation at once, and on February 17, 1874, J. S. Dennis, Surveyor-General of Canada, made a report to the Minister of the Interior on the subject of the Alaskan boundary. In this report Mr. Dennis significantly remarked: "The United States surveys of the coast could be advantageously used to locate the coast line in deciding the mouths of the rivers in question, as points from whence the necessary triangulation surveys should commence, in order to determine the ten marine leagues back."

As a means of illustrating his report, Mr. Dennis published a map which shows the boundary line running ten leagues back from the mouths of the Stikine and the Taku Rivers. In both the report and the map, Mr. Dennis reveals that he accepted the view that the American Government controlled a continuous *lisière*, approximately ten leagues wide, from Cross Sound to the head of Portland Channel.[51]

In the report submitted by Major D. R. Cameron on February 18, 1875, additional support is given to the American contention. The cost of determining the boundary line between British Columbia and Alaska would not be "less than $425,000 nor more than $2,230,000, and the time for its completion will be from two to seven years from the commencement of operations." With reference to the technical work of the boundary commissioners, Major Cameron remarks:

> The Treaty describes a line which, in its course northerly from Portland Channel to its intersection with the meridian of 141 west longitude, traverses a very mountainous and heavily wooded country, and defines it as follows: "The summit of the mountains situated parallel to the coast," or, where mountains are not within ten marine leagues of the sea, then "parallel to the windings of the coast" at no greater distance than ten leagues.
>
> To carry out these terms it would be necessary to complete a survey of the belt of country between the coast line and mountain summits, about 900 miles in length, and occasionally, perhaps, ten marine leagues in breadth. The coast line might furnish an exceptionally advantageous base for supplies; but notwithstanding this advantage the difficulties with which the surveying parties would have to contend in their progress inland, the necessarily circuitous course of their movements, and the extreme irregularity of the line to be marked—at times passing from mountain top to mountain top, at others repeating the meandering of a coast, broken by numerous bays, long, narrow inlets and river mouths—would be of the most serious description. . . . Principal depots should be established at . . . the mouth of Portland Channel, . . . at Fort Yukon, [and] . . . at the head of navigation up Linn Channel.[52]

51. *Report* of J. S. Dennis to the Minister of the Interior, February 17, 1874, *ibid.*, pp. 242–243. For a copy of the map see *C.S.P., 1878,* XI, No. 125, facing p. 28.

52. *Report* of Major D. R. Cameron to the Secretary of State, Dominion of Canada, February 18, 1875, *A.B.T.,* III, 244–247.

It seems clear that Major Cameron's references to the "coast" and the "coast line" have direct relation to the coasts of the bays and inlets that indent the *lisière*. His reference to the establishment of a depot at the head of Lynn Channel is particularly significant in this regard.

Major Cameron's viewpoint may have been influenced by the fact that in 1868 Professor Leach was employed by the Hudson's Bay Company to survey thirty miles inland from the coast, at the mouth of the Stikine River, in order to fix a location for the establishment of a trading post on British soil. This location was estimated to be "thirty-one miles from salt water, on air-line—sixty miles by the meanders of the river."[53] Major Cameron may also have known that in 1874 a British Customs House was established at Buck's Bar, on the upper reaches of the Stikine River.[54]

On September 23, 1875 Secretary Fish had a conversation with the British Minister in which he drew attention to reports that certain British subjects were preparing to make a settlement on the Stikine River within American territory.[55] These reports also indicated that even the newly established British Customs House on the Stikine River was supposed to be within United States territory, "that is, within the ten marine leagues from the coast at which the boundary should be in accordance with the provisions of the 4th Article of the convention of February 28, 1825, between Great Britain and Russia." When Secretary Fish inquired as to the best course to pursue in this matter, the British Minister suggested that officers should be sent, on behalf of each country, to take observations and determine on whose territory the new settlers had established themselves. Fish was somewhat fearful that the funds for even this partial survey would be difficult to secure from Congress, and he advanced the view that inasmuch as the weight of evidence seemed to be in favor of the "point in question being in United States territory, the settlers should be called upon to suspend operations . . . until the question of territory could be decided."[56]

In Canada, a committee of the Privy Council reported that it was "undoubtedly in the interests of both nations to encourage the settlement and development of the country in the vicinity of the Stikine," and the hope was expressed that something could soon be done about a survey of the boundary line. In this report the committee remarked

53. Statement of George Collins, March 3, 1876, *ibid.*, IV, 73.

54. Printed *notice* of Canadian Collector of Customs, Victoria, March 14, 1874, *ibid.*, p. 61.

55. Fish had assumed the duties of Secretary of State on March 11, 1869.

56. Sir Edward Thornton to the Earl of Derby, September 27, 1875, *A.B.T.*, IV, 68.

that the "Stikine River intersects the international boundary in the vicinity of the 57th degree of north latitude." Such a designation is in accordance with air-line of ten marine leagues from the mouth of the Stikine River.[57]

The Privy Council was unquestionably right in its belief that it would be "in the interests of both nations" to determine the boundary line in the "vicinity of the Stikine River." Incidents were bound to arise in this twilight zone of jurisdiction that would seriously embarrass relations between the United States and Canada. In 1876 the Secretary of the Treasury was informed that a Canadian trader named Choquette had settled within American territory along the Stikine River. He immediately instructed the Collector of Customs at Sitka, Alaska, to tell Choquette that his trading post was within the "recognized limits of the Territory of Alaska," and therefore he should pay "duties on his goods or to remove them within a definite time without the Territory."[58] Choquette protested that his post was located in British territory, and further action was suspended until after Canadian officials had made a survey.

While preparations were being made to conduct this survey, another incident arose that gave additional emphasis to the importance of determining the boundary between British Columbia and Alaska. In September 6, 1876 a naturalized American citizen, Peter Martin, was tried before the Court of Assizes at Laketon, in British Columbia, for assault upon an officer. He was found guilty and sentenced to fifteen months' imprisonment in the jail at Victoria. While en route to jail the prisoner and constables camped a "few miles" from the mouth of the Stikine River. While there, Martin attacked one of the constables and endeavored to escape. He was finally overpowered and lodged in the jail in Victoria.

On November 2, 1876 Secretary Fish wrote a note to the British Minister at Washington and, after reviewing the facts in the case, remarked: "It is suggested that the person in question should not be tried for the offense with which he is charged, it having been committed . . . within the jurisdiction of the United States, and that such being the case he should be set at liberty."[59] Some two weeks earlier, Judge John H. Gray, of the Supreme Court of British Columbia, had written a letter to Prime Minister Mackenzie in which he referred to the diffi-

57. *Report* of a committee of the Honorable the Privy Council, November 23, 1875, *ibid.*, pp. 68–69.

58. Secretary Morrill to M. P. Berry, July 14, 1876, *ibid.*, pp. 69–70.

59. Secretary Fish to Sir Edward Thornton, November 2, 1876, *ibid.*, III, 251–252.

culty of transporting prisoners from the Cassiar district to the jail at Victoria without passing through American territory. He then alluded to the order of the Secretary of the Treasury which directed Mr. Choquette to pay duties or to remove his post within British territory. Judge Gray thought that the purpose behind this order was to ruin Choquette's business and to compel the Indians to deal with the American posts at Wrangel and Sitka. The difficulty in transportation and the dispute about the location of Choquette's post could best be settled by looking into the matter of the Alaskan boundary line. According to the treaty of 1825, the line should run along the summit of the range of mountains that bordered the Northwest Coast. From personal examination of the terrain in question, Gray was certain that this coast range rose "immediately from tide waters, and the summit of that range is within fifteen miles of the sea." Recognition of this fact would reduce very considerably the width of the *lisière* claimed by the Americans, and it would give to British subjects a larger claim to the mineral wealth of the region in question.[60]

In view of the Choquette and the Peter Martin incidents, the Canadian Privy Council and the Prime Minister were increasingly anxious that some steps be taken immediately to determine the Alaskan boundary,[61] but the American Government was not ready to take this step. Instead, Secretary Fish sent a note to the British Minister in which he flatly stated that Canadian constables had transported Peter Martin through what was "unquestionable territory of the United States," and they had thereby committed a "violation of the sovereignty of the United States." His recapture on American soil was an "illegal, violent and forcible act," for which there was no justification, and therefore, he should at once "be set at liberty."[62]

The British Minister replied by adverting to the "extreme expediency" of taking some measures for defining the boundary between Alaska and British Columbia. He then referred to the Choquette incident and made a suggestion with regard to the proper interpretation of the treaty of 1825. It is apparent that he had been advised as to the contents of the letter from Justice Gray to Prime Minister Mackenzie on October 16, 1876. In his note to Secretary Fish he repeats with only the insertion of the word "appears," the following statement of Justice

60. Justice J. H. Gray to Prime Minister Alexander Mackenzie, October 16, 1876, *ibid.*, III, 256–258.

61. Earl of Dufferin to the Earl of Carnarvon, November 25, 1876, *ibid.*, pp. 253–256.

62. Secretary Fish to Sir Edward Thornton, January 10, 1877, *ibid.*, pp. 264–266.

Gray: "The coast range rises immediately from tide waters, and the summit of that range appears to be within fifteen miles of the sea."[63]

The Canadian Minister of Justice was also influenced by Justice Gray's contention that the summit of the coast range of mountains was within fifteen miles of the coast, and after a résumé of the evidence in the case he came to the conclusion that in the Peter Martin case it did not appear "that the landing took place on the territory of the United States or that the sovereignty of that country has been violated." Therefore, there was no ground for discharging Martin from the imprisonment decreed at Laketon.[64]

Owing to this confusion about the exact location of the Alaskan boundary line, it became evident to Canadian officials that some provisional survey would have to be made at once, so on March 3, 1877, instructions were given to Joseph Hunter to proceed to the vicinity of the Stikine River and commence operations.[65] Mr. Hunter submitted his report in June, 1877, and he contended that he had found the point where the mountain range, described in the treaty of 1825 as "parallel to the coast," touched the Stikine River. He fixed this point at a distance of 24.74 miles from the mouth of the river, and from the coast in a direct line, 19.13.[66] In a supplemental report, Hunter stated that the Canadian constables had taken Peter Martin within American territory en route to the jail at Victoria,[67] and upon being advised of this fact, the Dominion Government finally agreed to his release.[68]

It is apparent that the boundary fixed by Mr. Hunter in the Stikine River region was a compromise line. Justice Gray had contended for a line drawn along the crests of the mountains that were located "within fifteen miles from the sea." Mr. Hunter's line was along the crest of mountains that ran about twenty miles from the coast. In reality it was practically impossible to select a real range of mountains that ran parallel to the coast. In January, 1877 H. Clay Wood, Assistant Adjutant General, made a report to General O. O. Howard with reference to the difficulties in surveying the Alaskan boundary near the Stikine River. He stated that there was "no well defined range of mountains

63. Sir Edward Thornton to Secretary Fish, January 15, 1877, *ibid.*, pp. 270–271.

64. *Report* of the Minister of Justice, Edward Blake, February 5, 1877, *ibid.*, pp. 272–283.

65. J. S. Dennis to Joseph Hunter, March 3, 1877, *ibid.*, pp. 296–298.

66. *Report* of Joseph Hunter, respecting his survey of the Stikine River, June, 1877, *ibid.*, pp. 299–305.

67. *Report* of Joseph Hunter as to place where assault by Peter Martin was committed, June, 1877, *ibid.*, p. 305.

68. Earl of Carnarvon to the Earl of Dufferin, August 16, 1877, *ibid.*, pp. 305–306; W. B. Richards to the Earl of Carnarvon, September 20, 1877, *ibid.*, p. 308.

extending in direction parallel to the coast. A rugged, broken region extends back from salt water a considerable distance; the mountain peaks visible seeming to stand in groups or clusters; a confused mass of hills of varying altitudes."[69] Captain S. P. Jocelyn, located at Fort Wrangel, had a similar view of the situation. He had personally examined the country around the basin of the Stikine River and was impressed with "the difficulty that would arise in determining a continuous summit of the Coast mountains. There is no range or chain, but rather for the entire distance of over one hundred miles, . . . a confused mass of mountain peaks."[70]

Because of this uncertainty regarding the boundary between Alaska and British Columbia, both the British and Canadian Governments continued to press for the appointment of a commission to survey and determine the exact line.[71] Finally, the British Minister at Washington suggested to Secretary Evarts that the survey recently made by Mr. Hunter along the Stikine River be accepted as a provisional boundary for that region.[72] Secretary Evarts accepted this suggestion on the understanding that it would not be construed "as affecting in any manner the rights under the treaty to be determined whenever a joint survey shall be made."[73]

The importance of this provisional line across the Stikine River lies in the fact that the British Government was ready to accept a compromise line which was located inland twenty miles from the coast. There was no insistence upon a line that ran close to the mouth of the Stikine River. In fact, the line of the Hunter survey was a disappointment to certain Canadian statesmen like Edward Blake who had strongly contended that the Peter Martin incident had probably happened on Canadian soil, and therefore, there was no necessity for releasing that individual to American officers. American acceptance of this Hunter line as the provisional boundary in the Stikine River region terminated the first chapter in the Alaskan boundary dispute on a note of conciliation. Succeeding chapters were not so peaceful.

69. H. Clay Wood to General O. O. Howard, January 15, 1877, *ibid.,* IV, 78–79.

70. Capt. S. P. Jocelyn to Assistant Adjutant General H. Clay Wood, October 1, 1876, *ibid.,* pp. 79–80.

71. Mr. Plunkett to Secretary Evarts, October 1, 1877, *ibid.,* III, 310–311.

72. Sir Edward Thornton to Secretary Evarts, January 19, 1878, *ibid.,* pp. 316–317.

73. Secretary Evarts to Sir Edward Thornton, February 20, 1878, *ibid.,* p. 317.

CHAPTER VI

IN SEARCH OF A COMPROMISE BOUNDARY LINE

WHEN Secretary Evarts accepted the Hunter survey along the Stikine River as the provisional boundary line in that region, he took a long step along the road that would lead to further American concessions. Congress had been too penurious to appropriate funds for the creation of a commission that would make a complete survey of the boundary between British Columbia and Alaska, and the Department of State felt that it was expedient to adopt some compromise that would temporarily settle a frontier difficulty that had dangerous implications. Evarts must have realized that his action would probably influence the decisions of the commission that would eventually be chosen to fix a permanent boundary. Along the diplomatic front, one surrender usually paves the way for another.

It is to Judge John H. Gray, of British Columbia, that the credit should go for this British diplomatic victory. In his letter to Prime Minister Mackenzie in October, 1876, he had strongly contended that in the region along the Stikine River there was a coast range that closely bordered tide water. The summit of this range he estimated to be within fifteen miles of the sea. American acceptance of such a contention would reduce to a very considerable extent the width of the *lisière* that had been claimed in this watershed by the Department of State. Realizing this fact, certain Canadian statesmen supported the viewpoint of Judge Gray, and the British Minister at Washington echoed the same sentiments.

Encouraged by the success of his bold move, Judge Gray began to enlarge the limits of his claims, and in the early summer of 1884 he wrote a report, officially adopted by the Executive Council of British Columbia, which indicated how far he was prepared to go in support of his viewpoint. After emphasizing the importance of the mineral deposits that lay along the Alaskan boundary, the Judge then stressed the necessity of safeguarding them for Canada's benefit. As an additional factor that should enlist Canadian attention, he pointed to the rich fur trade that was developing in British Columbia, and he advocated an interpretation of the treaty of 1825 that would reduce the *lisière* to a tiny strip north of latitude 56°. The starting point in marking this boundary should be "Cape de Chacon." From there the line would "ascend northerly along the channel [Clarence Strait] until it strikes the continent at 56° N." Thence "turn northerly from that point, ascend the channel, and strike the continent at 56° on the N.W. point of Burrough's Bay. Thence the summit of the mountains parallel to the coast, at or within ten marine leagues from the coast, as far as the intersection with 141° W. L."

This line, he believed, was the only one that could be drawn in accordance with the phraseology of the treaty of 1825. In Hertslet's *Collection of Treaties* and in Henry Wheaton's treatise on *International Law*, the articles of the treaty of 1825 were reproduced, and Article IV spoke of the boundary line as starting from the southernmost point of the island called Prince of Wales Island and ascending "to the north along the channel called Portland Channel as far as the point of the continent where it strikes the 56th degree of north latitude." But Judge Gray was certain that the term "Portland Channel," as printed in Hertslet and Wheaton was an "interpolation" that was not in the official treaty. If these words "be admitted into the language of the Treaty, it is impossible to reconcile a line drawn from the initial point, as indicated by the latitude and longitude and local definition specified in the Treaty, to and up the Portland Channel, with a single one of the topographical features pointed out as guides to govern the line." The "assumed line laid down on some of the modern maps and charts as passing through Portland Channel, was not laid down, acquiesced in, or sanctioned, as far as can be ascertained in British Columbia, by any competent authority before the transfer of Alaska to the United States."[1]

In a note to Prime Minister Sir John Macdonald, August 6, 1886, Judge Gray remarks: "It must be borne in mind *throughout*, that in the original convention of 1824 the term 'Portland Channel' was not used at all—it was a *subsequent interpolation*, and followed afterwards by Wheaton with the necessary *other interpolations* to make it stick."[2]

It is apparent that Judge Gray was badly mistaken in believing that the words "Portland Channel," as given by Hertslet in Article IV of the treaty of 1825, were an "interpolation." They were in the official version of the treaty, and were not inserted by Hertslet or anyone else.[3] It is important to note, however, that once more a suggestion of Judge Gray bore fruit. In 1898 the British members of the Joint High Com-

1. *Report of a Committee of the Honourable the Executive Council of British Columbia on the Question of the Boundary between Canada and Alaska*, July, 1884, pp. 1–11, Public Archives of Canada, hereafter referred to as P.A.C.

2. This note from Judge Gray to Sir John Macdonald was written on the frontispiece of the above-quoted pamphlet.

3. *A.B.T.*, II, 15.

mission advanced a claim that was very similar to the line proposed by Judge Gray. The line was to ascend the Duke of Clarence Strait to the 56° of north latitude, and thence along the summit of the mountains parallel to the coast as far as the 141° W.L. It was a claim too bold to be allowed.

While Judge Gray was engaged upon the task of drawing up a report which was later to be adopted by the Executive Council of British Columbia, Mr. William H. Dall, of the United States Coast and Geodetic Survey, attempted to open up a correspondence with Dr. G. M. Dawson, of the Geological Survey of Canada. It seemed to Mr. Dall that the matter of the Alaskan boundary line should "be stirred up." The language of the treaty of 1825 was so indefinite that if any "serious international question were to arise regarding jurisdiction, there would be no means of settling it by the Treaty." There was really no "natural boundary and the continuous range of mountains parallel to the coast shown on Vancouver's charts, . . . having no existence as such, the United States would undoubtedly wish to fall back on the 'line parallel to the windings of the coast!' " It would, however, be "impracticable to trace any such winding line over that 'sea of mountains.' " The whole question should be referred to a committee of geographers, a survey should be made, and a new treaty concluded with "determinable boundaries."[4]

Dr. Dawson apparently believed that he could not with advantage "stir up" the matter of the Alaskan boundary, and he did not take the trouble to answer Mr. Dall's letter. But the question of the boundary was of such real importance to Great Britain and the United States that the incoming Cleveland Administration was anxious to find some solution for it. On November 20, 1885 Secretary Bayard sent a long instruction to E. J. Phelps, the American Minister in London, in which he canvassed the situation. It was apparent to the President that there was an "urgent necessity" for a "speedy and certain establishment of the boundary line between Alaska and British Columbia." This was particularly true because the line indicated in the treaty of 1825 was found to be "of uncertain if not impossible location for a great part of its length." The boundary from the southernmost point of Prince of Wales Island to the 56th parallel of north latitude was usually shown as following the central line of the main channel known as Portland Inlet, but on some British charts this line was deflected so as to make "British territory of Pearse and Wales Islands." There was some ground in the text of Vancouver's writings to support the theory that

4. William H. Dall to Dr. G. M. Dawson, April 24, 1884, *ibid.*, III, 323–324.

he might have regarded Pearse Canal as the lower part of Portland Canal, but there were "very evident reasons for believing that this was not the construction intended by the authors of the Anglo-Russian treaty of 1825."

One of the first difficulties that would challenge the surveyors of the boundary was the fact that the Portland Channel does not strike the 56th parallel of north latitude. It was probably the intention of the negotiators of the treaty of 1825 to have the boundary line follow Portland Channel, midway between its shores, to its head and thence inland until the range of mountains should be reached near the 56th parallel as shown on Vancouver's map. The line was then to run along the crest of these mountains to the 141st meridian of west longitude. Unfortunately, Vancouver's map was incorrect, and there was "no such range of mountains" as was shown on this chart.

The delimitation of this boundary would not be of great importance were it not for the fact that there was a mineral-bearing region close to the provisional line. It was evident that the time had arrived when the American and British Governments should "agree upon some boundary line capable of survey at a reasonable cost, yet so precisely and practically described that in case of need any given point thereon may be readily determined."[5]

The Administration's desire for a speedy settlement of this boundary difficulty was frankly indicated in a paragraph in President Cleveland's first annual message to Congress, December 8, 1885. Modern exploration had disclosed the fact that the boundary as outlined in the treaty of 1825 was "impracticable." It was expedient, therefore, to have some provision made for a "preliminary reconnoissance by officers of the United States, to the end of acquiring more precise information on the subject." An invitation had already been extended to the British Gov-

5. Secretary Bayard to E. J. Phelps, November 20, 1885, *Senate Ex. Doc. No. 143*, 49 Cong., 1 sess., pp. 2–8. In this instruction to Phelps, Secretary Bayard quoted some pertinent excerpts from a recent letter he had received from William H. Dall with reference to drawing the boundary line in accordance with the treaty of 1825: "The single continuous range being non-existent, if we attempt to decide on the 'summit' of the mountains we are at once plunged into a sea of uncertainty. Shall we take the ridge of the hills nearest the beaches? This would give us in many places a mere strip of territory not more than three miles wide meandering in every direction. Shall we take the highest summit of the general mass of the coast ranges? Then we must determine the height of many thousands of scattered peaks, after which the question will arise between every pair of equal height and those nearest to them. . . . In short, the 'summit of the mountains' is wholly impracticable. We may then fall back on the line parallel with the windings of the coast. Let any one with a pair of drawing compasses having one leg, a pencil point, draw this line on the United States Coast Survey map of Alaska (No. 960 of 1884). The result is sufficient to condemn it. Such a line could not be surveyed: it crosses itself in many places."

ernment to consider the "adoption of a more convenient line."[6] The situation was thus placed squarely before Congress which, as usual, showed little interest in the Alaskan boundary.

In London, Phelps found out that there was a great deal of "uncertainty" with respect to the administration of the British Government. This was chiefly due to the "nearly equal divisions of political parties in the new Parliament," and he feared that this political conflict would make it difficult to focus attention upon the matter of the Alaskan boundary.[7] But Lord Salisbury always took an active interest in questions affecting Anglo-American relations, and on January 12 he had a long conversation with Phelps. He quickly indicated his favorable reaction to Bayard's suggestion about a joint high commission to determine the boundary line between Alaska and British Columbia, but before taking any action in that regard he wished first to ascertain the views of the Canadian Government.[8]

Encouraged by Lord Salisbury's receptive attitude, Phelps sent to the Foreign Office on January 19 a note which expressed the substance of Bayard's instruction. The description of the boundary line in the Anglo-Russian treaty of 1825 was based upon Vancouver's charts which had indicated a "range of mountains apparently continuous and sharply defined, running parallel with the coast about 10 marine leagues inland, from the 56th degree of north latitude to their intersection with the 141st degree of west longitude." Recent explorations had shown that these charts were incorrect. Instead of a continuous range of mountains along the summit of which a tangible and reasonably direct line could be run, the whole region was a "sea of mountains, with spurs running in various directions." By no criterion, whether of height, direction or continuity, could a line be laid down that followed the summits of a definite range of mountains running parallel to the coast. Because of this difficulty it might be suggested that the boundary should run ten marine leagues inland, following the sinuosities of the interior bays and inlets. But the coast was so irregular that it was not possible, except at immense expense of time and money, to run a line that would be parallel to it. In view of this situation, it would be expedient to appoint a joint high commission to determine a conventional boundary.[9]

6. Richardson, *op. cit.,* VIII, 332–333.

7. Phelps to Secretary Bayard, December 8, 1885, *Senate Ex. Doc. No. 143,* 49 Cong., 1 sess., p. 12. *Great Britain, Despatches,* CLIII, MS. Dept. of State.

8. Phelps to Secretary Bayard, January 13, 1886, *Senate Ex. Doc. No. 143,* 49 Cong., 1 sess., p. 12.

9. Phelps to Lord Salisbury, January 19, 1886, *ibid.,* pp. 13–15.

Lord Salisbury promptly replied that the suggestion concerning the appointment of a joint high commission with reference to the Alaskan boundary would receive "the immediate attention of Her Majesty's Government,"[10] and Secretary Bayard waited anxiously for further news from Phelps.[11] In the meantime, Lord Salisbury had placed the matter squarely before Lord Lansdowne, the Governor General of Canada. Lansdowne lost no time in writing to Sir John Macdonald about the situation. The American Government had, as has been said above, in Chapter II, suggested the appointment of a joint high commission, which would, for one thing, determine the Alaskan boundary. The instructions to be given to the British members of this commission would require very careful phrasing because of the ambiguity of the terms of the treaty of 1825. It would probably be inexpedient to allow "such a commission to actually determine the international frontier." It was possible that the American commissioners would "encourage pretensions on the part of their Government to territory the cession of which can scarcely have been contemplated by the framers of the treaty." It would seem wiser, therefore, to limit the work of the proposed commission to the "exploration of the debatable territory and to the recommendation of a new line."[12]

In a second letter to Sir John Macdonald, Lansdowne again expressed the opinion that a joint high commission should soon be appointed to look into the matter of the Alaskan boundary, but he had some misgivings concerning the work of this body. He had been carefully studying the documents with regard to the boundary, and had been surprised to discover "how shifty the Americans had been over the question when we were ready to have it dealt with between 1872 and 1878."[13]

Sir John Macdonald shared Lord Lansdowne's views concerning the expediency of taking some action with regard to the Alaskan boundary, and he was in favor of informing the British Colonial Office by telegram that the Dominion Government was ready to agree, "in principle," to a "preliminary survey by commission." He believed that the line should run from the "northern extremity of the Portland Channel until the 141° of west longitude" was reached, and this line should in no case "exceed 10 marine leagues from the ocean." This limitation being accepted by both sides, the line could "easily be obtained at any

10. Lord Salisbury to Phelps, January 26, 1886, *ibid.,* p. 15.

11. Secretary Bayard to Phelps, February 18, 1886, *ibid.,* p. 15.

12. Lord Lansdowne to Sir John Macdonald, February 23, 1886, *John Macdonald Papers, Alaska Boundary, 1886–1888,* pp. 82–84, P.A.C.

13. Lord Lansdowne to Sir John Macdonald, February 26, 1886, *ibid.,* pp. 86–89.

point by a measurement with a surveyor's chain from the ocean." Even though the coast was very irregular, a "conventional line correcting some of the greater irregularities might be reported by a Commission and submitted to Parliament."[14]

In accordance with these views, Lord Lansdowne sent to the Colonial Office a telegram agreeing in principle to the appointment of a commission of inquiry with reference to the Alaskan boundary.[15] He was of the opinion, however, that in the "absence of fuller knowledge of the configuration of those regions," it would not be wise to make any far-reaching commitments.[16]

The British *chargé d'affaires* at Washington informed Bayard of the willingness of Lord Lansdowne to agree to the appointment of a commission that would be empowered to make a "preliminary survey" of the Alaskan boundary,[17] and Bayard immediately expressed to Phelps, in London, the hope that negotiations for a convention in relation to this matter could be brought to an "early and favorable conclusion."[18] On March 19 the British representative called at the Department of State and left a memorandum which emphasized the fact that the Canadian Government was favorable to the appointment of a commission of inquiry that would make merely a *preliminary* survey of the Alaskan boundary. After this survey had been made, further steps could then be taken for the determination of the boundary line.[19]

After receiving this memorandum from the British Legation, Secretary Bayard wrote to Phelps and modified the instruction of November 20, 1885 which had in mind the appointment of a joint high commission that would fix a conventional boundary line between Alaska and British Columbia. It was apparent that the Canadian Government was not willing to go that far at present, and the negotiations at London should be limited to the "formulation of an agreement . . . for a preliminary survey of the Alaska boundary, with a view to the discovery of such natural outlines and objects as may be made the basis for a future formal convention."[20]

14. Sir John Macdonald to Lord Lansdowne, March 9, 1886, *Macdonald Letter Books,* XXIII, 416–417, P.A.C.

15. Lord Lansdowne to Sir John Macdonald, March 9, 1886, *Macdonald Papers, Governor-General's Correspondence,* XIII, 69–70, P.A.C.

16. Lord Lansdowne to Sir John Macdonald, March 14, 1886, *ibid.*, pp. 81–83.

17. H. O. Helyar to Secretary Bayard, March 12, 1886, *Senate Ex. Doc. No. 143,* 49 Cong., 1 sess., p. 16.

18. Secretary Bayard to Phelps, March 16, 1886, *ibid.,* p. 16.

19. *Memorandum* dated March 19, 1886, *Great Britain, Notes from,* Vol. CXIII, Dept. of State. See also, Sir Lionel West to Lord Lansdowne, March 19, 1886, *Macdonald Papers, Alaska Boundary, 1886–1888,* pp. 94–95, P.A.C.

20. Secretary Bayard to Phelps, March 19, 1886, *Senate Ex. Doc. No. 143,* 49 Cong., 1 sess., p. 17.

On April 3 Sir Lionel West informed Secretary Bayard that the British Government accepted the Canadian view that the first step in the Alaskan matter was a "preliminary investigation of the boundary." This investigation might well be conducted without the services of a joint high commission.[21] Bayard had no quarrel with this British viewpoint. It was evident to him that a "preliminary reconnaissance" could be carried on separately by Great Britain and the United States, but he was of the opinion that a "final boundary line" could not be laid down "without some form of joint determination."[22]

This fact was doubtless quite obvious to Lord Rosebery, who was not interested in conducting further negotiations until he found out what steps the Cleveland Administration would take with "regard to applying to Congress for an appropriation."[23] In the meantime, the British and Canadian Governments could acquire additional information concerning the Alaskan boundary. With this end in view, the Canadian Government secured the appointment of Colonel D. R. Cameron, R.A., C.M.G., as an expert upon this matter of the boundary.[24] In his report to the Colonial Office he stated that the

> passage from the ocean, by Tongas Island, through Pearse's Channel, is part of the Portland Channel, of which the medial line is, in accordance with the Anglo-Russian Convention of 1825, a portion of the International boundary. The United States Government, however, assumes that the passage from the ocean through Observatory Inlet entrance, is the line indicated by the Treaty, and Mr. Secretary Bayard records his opinion that this can never be called in question.

Because of this difference of opinion, Colonel Cameron was in favor of settling the matter in a spirit of mutual concession. It was of the utmost importance to British Columbia to command the ocean entrance to Observatory Inlet. This inlet provided the nearest ocean communica-

21. Sir Lionel West to Secretary Bayard, April 3, 1886, *ibid.*

22. Secretary Bayard to Phelps, April 8, 1886, *ibid.*, pp. 17–18.

23. Lord Rosebery to Phelps, April 15, 1886, *ibid.*, p. 19. In commenting upon the development of the negotiations relative to the Alaskan boundary, Phelps, in a private letter to Secretary Bayard, May 8, 1886, remarks as follows: "Mr. West's proposal to you in regard to the Alaskan boundary commission differs from my understanding with Lord Rosebery which was for a *joint* commission not to settle the question, but to make the survey and examination necessary to settle it. From your instruction (No. 270) I do not understand that you attach importance to the survey being a *joint* one. I shall see Lord Rosebery shortly, and will ascertain precisely the views of the Government." *Bayard MS.*

24. Sir Charles Tupper to Sir Robert Herbert, February 10, 1886, *Macdonald Papers, Alaska Boundary, 1886–1888*, p. 22; R. G. W. Herbert to War Office, March 6, 1886, *ibid.*, p. 25.

tion for a vast British area of about 480,000 square miles. The defence of this large inland waterway would be easy if both shores of it were in the possession of British Columbia. On the other hand, the possession by an enemy of the islands between Pearse's Channel and Portland Inlet would "make the position useless if not quite untenable." Canadian control over Observatory Inlet could best be effected by securing from the United States a cession of the whole *lisière* or strip of land from Pearse's Channel to the meridian of 141° west longitude. This strip of territory would be of little real value to the United States from an economic point of view, and the survey of the boundary line would cost the American Government at least £300,000.[25] If the United States should be

> prepared to consider the question of the cession of the coast strip, the peculiar circumstances of the case are such that mutually advantageous terms might possibly be arrived at. The United States paid for the whole of the vast territory ceded to them by Russia about £1,500,000. . . . The coast strip from Pearse's Channel to 141° W. long., formed but a small and unimportant fraction of the ceded territory. . . . Consequently, regarded as a mere financial transaction, the cession of this strip by the United States to the British, only with the object of avoiding the further expenditure of £250,000 upon the demarcation of its boundary, could not be regarded as imprudent. But if in addition the United States received from £50,000 to £100,000, . . . the financial transaction would be a remunerative one to both powers.[26]

As soon as Judge Gray learned of the suggestions contained in Colonel Cameron's report, he wrote at once to Sir John Macdonald and strongly protested against their acceptance. Any offer to purchase the *lisière* or strip from Pearse's Channel to the 141° of west longitude was

> the maddest proposition that could possibly be suggested. It would be a clear admission that we had no right. . . . The British Government would not pay, and I do not believe the Canadian Parliament in the face of our clear legal right could ever be induced to pay. . . . I can see pretty plainly—Canada has got to look after herself or be plucked of course. . . . My own personal feeling is that the sooner the Americans understand that Canada is not a mere pasture field for them to ride over, simply because Great Britain won't have a row, the better.[27]

25. The cost of the American survey from Pearse's Channel to the 141° of west longitude was estimated by Colonel Cameron at £250,000. The survey along the meridian line of the 141st degree of west longitude would cost but £50,000.

26. Colonel D. R. Cameron to the Under-Secretary of State for the Colonies, October 29, 1886, *Macdonald Papers, Alaska Boundary, 1886–1888,* pp. 40–42, P.A.C.

27. Judge John H. Gray to Sir John Macdonald, May 4, 1887, *ibid.,* pp. 13–16.

Despite his vehement language to Sir John Macdonald, Judge Gray believed that in the conduct of relations with the United States both "tact" and "judgment" should be used. Negotiations carried on in this manner would probably result in a compromise line, and the future of Canada on the Pacific coast depended more on this conventional boundary than the people of eastern Canada could ever "dream of."[28]

Judge Gray knew that the Canadian Government was in favor of the appointment of a commission of inquiry which would make a preliminary report on the Alaskan boundary, and he modestly intimated to Sir John Macdonald that his special knowledge of the region around the Stikine River would admirably fit him to serve as one of the British representatives.[29] But Sir John was not to be stampeded into any premature appointments. In May he sent Sir Charles Tupper to Washington to see Secretary Bayard. Again, as told in another connection, in Chapter II, Bayard immediately indicated his support of the idea of a joint commission which would sit in Washington, and which would be empowered to settle *all* questions at issue between the United States and Canada.[30]

Lord Salisbury was delighted with Bayard's conciliatory attitude, and he instructed the British Minister at Washington to inform the Secretary of State that Her Majesty's Government was ready to agree to the appointment of a joint commission.[31] In August, 1887, the British Foreign Secretary informed Phelps that Joseph Chamberlain would be one of the British commissioners,[32] and shortly afterwards it was announced that the other members of the British delegation would be Sir Charles Tupper and the British Minister at Washington, Sackville-West. Bayard was tired of waiting for Congress to take some action with reference to the appointment of a joint commission to discuss Canadian-American relations, so without any further reference to that body he induced President Cleveland to appoint W. L. Putnam and James B. Angell as members of the American delegation. Bayard himself would serve as the third American representative.

The terms of reference authorized the commissioners to

consider and adjust all or any questions relating to rights of fishery in the

28. Judge J. H. Gray to Sir John Macdonald, March 1, April 19, 1887, *ibid.,* pp. 13–16.

29. Judge John H. Gray to Sir John Macdonald, March 1, 1887, *ibid.,* pp. 5–6.

30. *Memorandum* written by Bayard after a conversation with Sir Charles Tupper, May 21, 1887, *Bayard MS.* See also, Bayard to Sir Charles Tupper, May 31, 1887, in Tupper's *Recollections of Sixty Years,* pp. 177–180. See Chapter II, above.

31. Lord Salisbury to Sackville-West, July 11, 1887, *Bayard MS.*

32. Phelps to Secretary Bayard, August 30, 1887, *ibid.*

seas adjacent to British North America and Newfoundland which are in dispute between the Governments of Her Britannic Majesty and that of the United States of America, and any other questions which may arise and which they may be authorized by their respective Governments to consider and adjust.[33]

These terms of reference could be easily expanded to cover all questions at issue between the United States and Canada, but in view of the bitter partisan opposition to the foreign policy of the Cleveland Administration, Bayard believed it would be best to limit the work of the Joint High Commission to the question of the North Atlantic fisheries. This did not prevent, of course, informal conversations between Bayard and some of the members of the British delegation with reference to the Alaskan boundary. On December 14, 1887, Joseph Chamberlain called at the residence of Secretary Bayard, and after some reference had been made to the North Atlantic fisheries and the fur seal fisheries, the question of the Alaskan boundary came up for discussion. Chamberlain expressed the view that the boundary line should be fixed "in advance of settlement." Bayard agreed with this opinion and remarked that he knew "nothing of the country—only the Treaty which was evidently obscure in its descriptions." Chamberlain then suggested a division "upon new lines" and proposed certain "new boundaries." Bayard cautiously replied that he "knew nothing of the value of the Coast line, but could plainly see that it kept British Columbia in the background." Nothing more was said "except that both agreed upon the expediency of a settlement."[34]

Several days later, Chamberlain wrote Bayard a short note concern-

33. Secretary Bayard to Sackville-West, September 14, 21, and October 19, 1887; Sackville-West to Secretary Bayard, October 24, 1887, *ibid.*

34. *Memorandum* written by Bayard after a conversation with Joseph Chamberlain, December 14, 1887, *ibid.* At this point it is probably pertinent to refer to the Schwatka incident. In 1883 Lieutenant Schwatka was sent by General Miles to Alaska Territory to report upon conditions especially as they affected the relations between the settlers and the Indians. In his report he drew attention to the fact that the "country beyond Perrier Pass in the Kotusk mountains lies in British territory." This being true, it would lessen "the interest of this trail beyond the pass to the military authorities of our government." *A.B.T.*, IV, 89. On August 20, 1887 Lord Salisbury wrote to the British Minister at Washington and remarked that Lieutenant Schwatka's report showed that he had extended his reconnaissance into British territory. He had also indicated two points, "Perrier's Pass and 140th degree west longitude, which he has determined as defining the international boundary." Although the British Government had agreed in principle to a preliminary investigation of the Alaska boundary, they were not prepared "to admit that the points referred to by Lieut. Schwatka in any way fix where the lines should be drawn." *Ibid.*, III, 334. There was nothing in this note to indicate that the British Government was ready to assert control over the inlets into the *lisière* or strip of coast claimed by the United States.

ing the Alaskan boundary. He understood that the British delegation had

> full proof that the entrance to Portland Channel is really Pearse's Channel, and that which is sometimes called the entrance is really the entrance or continuation of Observatory Inlet. However this may be, it is clear that any demarcation of the boundary [in accordance with] the terms of the old treaty will be a very difficult and expensive business, and I sincerely hope that we may agree on some easier and more reasonable method. . . . General Cameron . . . appears to know the country well, and he tells me that there are placer gold deposits in the territory which I suggested should go to the United States in return for the ship and Coast lines in part of British Columbia.[35]

It is apparent that Chamberlain had accepted without question the views of General Cameron regarding the importance of British control over Observatory Inlet. He had also been influenced by Cameron's opinion that some compromise line should be drawn that would involve concessions on the part of both countries.

This idea of a compromise line was also supported in a letter from Mr. Dall, of the United States Coast and Geodetic Survey, to John Bassett Moore, the Third Assistant Secretary of State. Mr. Dall would not make a precise stand on the wording of the treaty of 1825 but would draw the line as follows:

> Let a point be determined on each of the four passage ways into the interior —Chilkoot, Taku, Stikine, and Observatory (or Portland) Inlet Rivers—at ten marine leagues (or any other mutually satisfactory) distance from the coast. Then let the territory drained by branches coming into these rivers seaward of this point (which should be shown by a permanent monument) belong to the United States; that drained by streams coming in eastward of the monument be British. The boundary would follow the water parting between the two. At Portland Inlet and at the head of Lynn Canal the divide between the interior and coast water-sheds should form the line. This would be easy of definition as the pass is narrow and the ridge sharp and distinct.[36]

Bayard had probably read this letter of Mr. Dall before Chamberlain called at the Bayard residence on January 5, 1888 to discuss some settlement of the outstanding questions at issue between Canada and the United States. With reference to the Alaskan boundary, Chamberlain expressed the opinion that "arbitration seemed the best resort," but he proposed a compromise line which "would give British Columbia

35. Joseph Chamberlain to Secretary Bayard, December 17, 1887, *Bayard MS.*
36. William H. Dall to John Bassett Moore, January 3, 1888, *A.B.T.*, III, 336–337.

the whole seaport and island south of it, and give the United States some country in the rear." In area the United States "would receive 48,000 square miles, and cede about 22,000 square miles." Bayard made no reply except to indicate "*very* different views."[37]

At this conference with Secretary Bayard, Chamberlain suggested the advisability of bringing Dr. George Dawson to Washington to have some conferences with Mr. Dall with regard to the Alaskan boundary. Bayard fell in with this idea, and Dr. Dawson arrived in Washington on February 1, 1888.[38] But before he had put in an appearance in Washington, Chamberlain had already brought the matter of the Alaskan boundary before the Joint High Commission. He did this at the first meeting of the commission after the Christmas recess, but he had not informed Sir Charles Tupper of this decision. Because of his lack of preparation on this point, Sir Charles made no attempt to discuss the various aspects of the boundary question, and it was the opinion of John S. Thompson, one of the Canadian delegates then in Washington, that Chamberlain had made a mistake

> in treating the boundary as a subject of dispute until we had at least presented our view of what the boundary should be. If either the interpretation of the British Columbian Government, or that of General Cameron can be accepted by the United States, . . . we shall be in a much better position to negotiate for an improved boundary than when Mr. Bayard fancies that the right to push the line thirty miles inland is incontrovertible.[39]

When Dr. Dawson arrived in Washington on February 1, 1888, he lost no time in conferring with certain members of the Canadian delegation like John S. Thompson, George E. Foster, and General Cameron on the matter of the Alaskan boundary. Mr. Thompson believed that there was no basis for the contention of the British Columbian Government that the boundary line should run "north through part of the Duke of Clarence Straits and then branch off either through Behm's Canal or Ernest Sound to the continental coast at latitude 56°N." Mr. Foster, on the other hand, thought that the British Columbian contention was an "arguable one" that might be advanced with "possible advantageous results." Dr. Dawson was of the opinion that it was the intention of the negotiators of the treaty of 1825 to "run the line from

37. *Memorandum* written by Bayard after a conversation with Chamberlain, January 5, 1888, *Bayard MS.*

38. Sir Charles Tupper to Sir John Macdonald, February 1, 1888, *Macdonald Papers, Washington Treaty, 1888,* IV, 2–3, P.A.C. See also *memorandum* written by Bayard, January 30, 1888, *Bayard MS.*

39. J. S. Thompson to Sir John Macdonald, January 12, 1888, *Macdonald Papers, Treaty of Washington, 1888,* III, 30–32, P.A.C.

Prince of Wales island to and through Portland Canal," and he sided with Mr. Thompson in opposing the British Columbian contention. Sir Charles Tupper himself thought it was "unwise to attempt to maintain the British Columbian view." The strength of the British Case in negotiations with the United States had hitherto depended upon "the circumstance that we have advanced nothing which we could not substantiate." In the event that the British Columbian contention was abandoned, it would be possible to compensate that province by some "readjustment of the inter-provincial boundaries."[40]

After receiving this letter from Sir Charles Tupper, Sir John Macdonald telegraphed to the Provincial Government in British Columbia and placed the situation before it. He warned Sir Charles, however, that any cession of territory in the region of British Columbia would have to be sanctioned by the Parliament. He was determined that there should be "no repetition" of the Webster-Ashburton Treaty.[41]

Because of the deep interest of the officials of British Columbia in any treaty negotiations respecting the Alaskan boundary, the Canadian delegation in Washington thought it was advisable to send for Judge Gray. While awaiting his arrival, several informal conferences were held between Mr. Dall and Dr. Dawson. In presenting the Canadian Case to Mr. Dall, Dr. Dawson made use of the arguments advanced by General Cameron and Judge Gray. It seemed apparent to Dr. Dawson that the "only line of mountains which is practically identical on the various charts" of Vancouver's detailed description, is that which is "represented as everywhere rising immediately from the coast and which borders upon the sea. It is therefore to the summits of these mountains immediately bordering on the coast that the words of the convention must be understood to refer." In reply, Mr. Dall remarked that there is "not in Vancouver's Atlas any continuous line of mountains represented as everywhere arising immediately from the coast and which borders upon the sea. The sea-shore forms the edge of an area conventionally indicated as mountainous, which is a different thing." Dr. Dawson then quoted General Cameron to the effect that "in the second clause of the fourth article provision is made for the case of the mountains being found at more than 10 marine leagues inland, and it is there laid down that the measurements shall be made not from inlets, but from the ocean." As quoted by General Cameron, the pertinent words in the fourth article read as follows: "Que partout où la crête des montagnes, qui s'étendent dans une direction parallèle à la côte . . . se trouverait à la distance de plus de dix lieues marines de

40. Sir Charles Tupper to Sir John Macdonald, February 2, 1888, *ibid.,* IV, 42–52.
41. Sir John Macdonald to Sir Charles Tupper, February 6, 1888, *ibid.,* p. 87.

l'océan . . . la limite . . . sera formée par une ligne parallèle à la côte, et qui ne pourra jamais en être éloignée que de dix lieues marines."

It is significant that this quotation used by General Cameron is not an accurate reproduction of the wording of the treaty of 1825. He omits the key word in this quotation—"sinuosités," as applied to the coast.[42] A line following the sinuosities of the coast is very different from a line that merely follows the general trend of the coast.

After using this inexact quotation, Dr. Dawson advanced General Cameron's contention that the word "ocean" is "wholly inapplicable to inlets." Therefore, the line, "whether marked by mountains or only by a survey line, has to be drawn without reference to inlets." None of the inlets between Portland Channel and the meridian of 141 degrees west longitude is six miles in width, excepting, perhaps, a short part of Lynn Canal; "consequently, with that possible exception, the width of territory on the coast . . . may not be measured from any point within the mouths of the inlets."[43] Mr. Dall replied by referring to the historical background of the treaty of 1825 and the interpretation of its limits from 1825 to 1867. From this survey he concluded that Russia had needed, asked, and obtained "the possession of the entire undivided coast margin, subject only to a hypothetical right of navigation through the rivers heading in the interior, which was never exercised."

42. The exact wording of article IV reads as follows: "Que partout où la crête des montagnes qui s'étendent dans une direction parallèle à la côte . . . se trouverait à la distance de plus de dix lieues marines de l'Océan, la limite . . . sera formée par une ligne parallèle *aux sinuosités* de la côte, et qui ne pourra jamais en être éloignée que de dix lieues marines."

43. In this regard Dr. Dawson was relying upon the contention of General Cameron. See undated *memorandum* of General Cameron, enclosed in letter from Lord Lansdowne to Mr. Raikes, August 18, 1902, *A.B.T.*, IV, 161–162. In this memorandum General Cameron remarks: "From the ocean entrance to Lynn Canal, the head of boat navigation up the Chilkoot is about 80 miles; from this point to Perrier Pass is somewhat in excess of 30 miles, or 10 marine leagues. Lynn Canal has water-ways of less than 6 miles in breadth at no great distance from its entrance. It is contended on the Canadian side that the 10 marine leagues given as the maximum breadth of the United States' coast territory in the second subsection of Article IV, Russo-British Convention of 1825, may not be measured from any point within an inlet not exceeding 6 miles in breadth, and that, consequently, it is not, under any circumstances, possible that the international boundary can be anywhere so far inland as Perrier Pass. To avoid the inconvenience of the ascent to the Perrier Portage, a diverging route called White Pass . . . has recently been explored. . . . The greater part, if not all, of this divergent line is . . . within British territory."

It is interesting to note in this connection that General Cameron in his report of February 18, 1875, *ibid.*, III, 245–266, expressed very different views as to the coast line and its measurement from the inlets. In order to complete a survey of the boundary, the "coast line might furnish an exceptionally advantageous base for supplies; but notwithstanding this advantage the difficulties with which the surveying parties would have to contend in their progress inland, the necessarily circuitous course of their movements, and the extreme irregularity of the line to be marked—at times passing from mountain top to mountain top, at others repeating the meandering of a

Dr. Dawson, following General Cameron, then remarked that "if the sovereignty over inlets does not pass in accordance with the doctrine that they are part and parcel of the surrounding territory, there was no occasion for the reciprocal concession made in the seventh article for right to navigate these inlets." In answer to this argument it was easy for Mr. Dall to state that if "the heads of all the inlets were British territory there was no need of any concession by Russia for her to reach them." Great Britain would have had "the right of access, without any treaty, to her own ports," and any such concession as that of Russia would have operated to diminish those rights rather than increase them. Moreover, it was nothing less than

> preposterous to suppose that Russia would have accepted a treaty which cut her "strip" of mainland into several portions, or that Great Britain, having the right to occupy with trading posts the richest fur region of the archipelago, and represented by the Hudson's Bay Company, . . . should nevertheless not only not assert and use these rights, but on the other hand pay money and otter skins for these very privileges to a foreign and competing corporation.

In concluding his remarks relative to the Alaskan boundary, Dr. Dawson presented the contention of Judge Gray that the line should ascend Clarence Strait instead of Portland Channel.[44] This contention had been rejected by J. S. Thompson, Sir Charles Tupper, and by Dr. Dawson himself, and it was elaborately refuted by General Cameron in two letters to Sir John Macdonald.[45] Needless to say, Mr. Dall was in vigorous opposition to the viewpoint of Judge Gray, and there seemed little chance of Dr. Dawson and Mr. Dall agreeing upon anything im-

coast, broken by numerous bays, long narrow inlets and river mouths—would be of the most serious description. . . . Principal depots should be established at Fort Simpson . . . and at Fort Yukon, . . . to meet the requirements of the expedition if the proposed alteration in the Treaty stipulation be not adopted. Should the alteration be approved, no principal depot would be needed at Fort Simpson, but instead, one would have to be established at the head of navigation up Linn Channel." It is obvious that there would have been no need for the establishment of a depot at the head of Lynn Canal for the purpose of marking a line parallel to a coast line crossing Lynn Canal more than fifty miles seaward of the head.

44. This résumé of the viewpoints of Dr. Dawson and Mr. Dall is based upon the following letters: Mr. Dall to Secretary Bayard, February 13, and December 18, 1888, with accompanying memoranda, *ibid.*, IV, 94–113. Also, Dr. Dawson to Sir Charles Tupper, February 7, 11, 1888, *ibid.*, III, 338–343.

45. General D. R. Cameron to Sir John Macdonald, January 3, 1888, *Macdonald Papers, Alaska Boundary, 1886–1888,* pp. 130–139, P.A.C. See also, General Cameron to Sir John Macdonald, February 15, 1888, *ibid.*, pp. 143–145. In his letters to Secretary Bayard, Mr. Dall assumed that General Cameron was in favor of running the boundary line up the Clarence Strait instead of Portland Channel. In this case he was entirely mistaken. That contention was Judge Gray's and not General Cameron's.

portant with reference to the Alaskan boundary. On February 7 Joseph Chamberlain reported to the Joint High Commission that Mr. Dall and Dr. Dawson had "not made any progress,"[46] and three days later, at a meeting of the Commission, Secretary Bayard announced that the American delegation had come to the conclusion that they could "not entertain any proposal for an exchange of territory in connection with the Alaskan Boundary." It was then agreed that both countries should conduct an "exploratory survey" that would furnish the data for a conventional boundary.[47]

What Dr. Dawson regarded as a fair conventional boundary is indicated on a map prepared by Mr. Johnston, chief draftsman of the Canadian Department of the Interior. On this Johnston map, Dr. Dawson drew three boundary lines: (1) the line claimed by the American Government, (2) the line which Dr. Dawson thought followed the summits of the mountains parallel to the coast, and (3) one of the conventional lines discussed during the conferences held with Mr. Dall.[48] Needless to say, this conventional line drawn by Dr. Dawson would give British Columbia access to the headwaters of the Stikine and Taku Rivers, and establish control over the upper waters of the Lynn Canal.[49]

In subsequent years, Lord Lansdowne appeared to take the Dall-Dawson conferences and map quite seriously, and he contended that Dr. Dawson's views had been those of the British Government.[50] The inaccuracy of such a contention is obvious when one examines the language of the letter Mr. Dall wrote to Secretary Bayard on February 13, 1888:

I have the honor to report that the suggested informal conference between Dr. George M. Dawson, of Ottawa, Canada, and the writer has been held. Dr. Dawson and myself conferred on several occasions (February 4–11) and discussed matters connected with the Alaska boundary question freely and informally. It was mutually announced and agreed that the meeting was entirely informal; that neither party had any delegated powers whatever, and that its object was simply the arrival at a consensus of opinion as to

46. Lord Lansdowne to Mr. Raikes, August 18, 1902, *A.B.T.*, IV, 159–160. In a *memorandum* written by Secretary Bayard, February 7, 1888, with reference to the meeting of the Joint High Commission on that day, there is the following statement: "As a result of the discussion it is understood the Alaskan Boundary question will not be considered by this Conference." *Bayard MS.*

47. Sir Charles Tupper to Sir John Macdonald, February 10, 1888, *Macdonald Papers, Washington Treaty, 1888,* IV, 144–145.

48. For a description of the circumstances surrounding the drawing of these lines, see letter of Lord Lansdowne to Mr. Raikes, August 18, 1902, *A.B.T.*, IV, 159.

49. See *British Atlas,* Map No. 34.

50. Lord Lansdowne to Mr. Raikes, August 18, 1902, *A.B.T.*, IV, 159.

some reasonable and business-like way of settling upon a line satisfactory to both countries.[51]

Many of the maps published under British auspices after 1887 clearly demonstrate the fact that during the informal conferences held in Washington in February, 1888, Dr. Dawson did not represent the British Government. This is particularly true of the maps contained in the different editions of the *British Colonial Office List* from 1887 to 1902, and in the ninth edition of the *Encyclopedia Britannica.* Attention should also be called to the *British Admiralty Charts* from March, 1889 to August, 1901.[52]

But this British indifference to Canadian claims along the Alaskan boundary was repeatedly challenged in the latter decades of the nineteenth century, and in the summer of 1888 the Canadian Government brought the matter to the attention of the Colonial Office. On June 19, 1888 A. M. Burgess, Deputy Minister of the Interior, in Canada, wrote to Sir John Macdonald and informed him of a rumor that "certain persons" were about to receive a charter from "the Alaskan authorities to construct a trail from Lynn Canal by way of White Pass to the interior of Alaska." If the Canadian claims were well-founded, "the entire route of this trail, as well as the trail by the Chilkoot Pass, is in Canadian territory." In view of the

well-based contention on our part, that the heads of the larger inlets which penetrate that portion of Alaska which consists of the coast line from Mount St. Elias to Portland Channel, and more particularly the head of Lynn Canal, are within our territory, it would appear to be important to protest against the granting of any rights by the United States or Alaskan Governments at the heads of these inlets.[53]

On August 1, 1888 Sir Charles Tupper brought this letter to the attention of the Colonial Office, and he enclosed for their instruction a memorandum of the views that General Cameron had pressed during the Dall-Dawson conferences to the effect that the headwaters of the important inlets running into the *lisière* really belonged to British Columbia.[54] After the lapse of nearly a month, Lord Salisbury wrote to the British Minister at Washington about this rumor of a charter being granted "by the Alaskan authorities of the United States for certain

51. Mr. Dall to Secretary Bayard, February 13, 1888, *ibid.,* p. 94.
52. "Maps and Charts," *ibid.,* pp. 245–250.
53. A. M. Burgess to Sir John Macdonald, June 19, 1888, *ibid.,* III, 344–345.
54. Sir Charles Tupper to Colonial Office, August 1, 1888, *ibid.,* pp. 344–346.

privileges in that part of Alaska which is claimed by this country." Salisbury believed that such a rumor must be unfounded because "the territory in question is part of Her Majesty's dominions."[55]

This note from Salisbury to Sackville-West is very brief and does not go into detail concerning the limits of British territory in western Canada. He makes no attempt to file a claim for British control over the headwaters of the inlets that cut deeply into the *lisière* from Portland Channel to Mt. St. Elias, and the British Minister's note to Secretary Bayard was equally vague.[56] Bayard replied by merely denying any knowledge of the request for such a charter, and he refrained from discussing the boundaries of Alaska.[57] Neither nation was ready to enter into any further negotiations concerning the Alaskan situation, and the matter was postponed until a preliminary survey had been completed.

This survey had been made possible by an appropriation by Congress, and on November 26, 1888, B. A. Colonna, of the United States Coast and Geodetic Survey, wrote to Dr. Dawson to acquaint him with this fact. The equipment for the American surveying party would soon be ready, and Mr. Colonna made a polite inquiry about the intentions of the Canadian Government with reference to a joint survey.[58] Dr. Dawson referred Colonna to Mr. Dewdney, the Canadian Minister of the Interior,[59] and American inquiries were now directed to this official,[60] who replied that the matter was "under consideration."[61]

Canadian consideration of this matter of a joint survey lasted for many months, and finally, on December 22, 1890, the British Minister at Washington called at the Department of State and left a memorandum which suggested the appointment of a Joint High Commission to deal with seven important questions at issue between the United States

55. Lord Salisbury to Sir Lionel West, August 31, 1888, *ibid.,* p. 346.

56. Sackville-West to Secretary Bayard, September 10, 1888, *ibid.,* p. 347.

57. Secretary Bayard to Sackville-West, September 15, 1888, *ibid.,* p. 347.

58. B. A. Colonna to Dr. G. M. Dawson, November 26, 1888, *ibid.,* IV, 174–175. The appropriations made by Congress for the work of surveying the Alaskan boundary, are listed as follows in a memorandum of Henry L. Bryan in the *Olney Papers:* "The first appropriation by Congress for a survey of the Alaskan boundary was made in the sundry civil appropriation act of October 2, 1888, based upon the message of the President of May 17, 1886 (*Senate Ex. Doc. No. 143,* 1 sess., 49th Cong.) and an annual appropriation was made thereafter until and including the sundry civil act of March 3, 1893."

59. Dr. Dawson to Mr. Colonna, December 1, 1888, *A.B.T.,* IV, 175.

60. Mr. F. M. Thorn, Supt. of the Coast and Geodetic Survey, to Hon. G. Dewdney, December 14, 1888, *ibid.,* pp. 176–177.

61. G. Dewdney to F. M. Thorn, December 27, 1888, *ibid.,* p. 177.

and Canada. The seventh item on this list dealt with the boundary between Alaska and British Columbia.[62]

In a memorandum of reply, Secretary Blaine stated that it would be "utterly idle" to attempt to secure the appointment of a Joint High Commission to deal with the questions at issue between Canada and the United States, but the Department of State was ready to have a "full but private conference with the British Minister and one or more Agents from Canada and will go over every point of difference and consider every subject upon which a mutual interest could be founded."[63] Owing to repeated postponements by Secretary Blaine, this informal conference at Washington was not held until February, 1892.[64]

In the meantime, on June 5, 1891, the British Minister wrote a note to Secretary Blaine in which he quoted the following paragraph from the annual report of the Director of the United States Coast and Geodetic Survey:

By recent Congressional enactments a preliminary survey of the frontier line between Alaska and British Columbia, in accordance with plans of projects approved by the Secretary of State, has been placed in charge of this Bureau. Such a preliminary survey, involving the determination of a number of points in geographical position and their complete marking by permanent monuments, will have to be carried from Cape Muzon *through the Portland Canal* to the 50th degree of north latitude, thence northwestwardly, following as nearly as practicable, *the general trend of the coast,* at a distance of *about 35 miles from it,* to the 141st degree of west longitude, and thence due north to the Arctic Ocean, a total distance of about 1400 miles.

Sir Julian Pauncefote then reminded the Department of State of the fact that "the question of the boundary at this point is, at the present time, the subject of some difference of opinion and of considerable correspondence, and that the actual boundary line can only be properly determined by an International Commission."[65]

Secretary Blaine paid little attention to this letter, and the question of the determination of the Alaskan boundary had to wait until February 10, 1892, when Blaine and John W. Foster had a conference with Sir Julian Pauncefote and three Canadian representatives, John S. Thompson, the Minister of Justice, George E. Foster, the Minister of Finance, and MacKenzie Bowell, the Minister of Customs. On February 12, the Canadian representatives submitted a proposal to refer the

62. *Memorandum* left with the Secretary of State by the British Minister, December 22, 1890, *ibid.,* p. 115.

63. *Memorandum* given to Sir Julian Pauncefote, December 22, 1890, *ibid.,* p. 115.

64. Sir Julian Pauncefote to Secretary Blaine, April 4, 8, 18, 1891, January 14, 27, 1892; Secretary Blaine to Sir Julian Pauncefote, February 1, 1892, *ibid.,* pp. 118–121.

65. Sir Julian Pauncefote to Secretary Blaine, June 5, 1891, *ibid.,* III, 349–350.

question of the Alaskan boundary to "some impartial authority" for decision.[66] Objection was made on the part of the United States to this proposal, and it was pointed out that the "existing difference of views was not of such a character as to call for more than a joint survey and report which would enable the two Governments to agree upon the fixation of the boundary." On February 15, 1892 the following proposal was agreed to by both parties:

It is agreed that a joint survey be made of the territory adjacent to the boundary line of the United States of America and the Dominion of Canada between the Territory of Alaska and the Province of British Columbia and the Northwest Territory of Canada, from the latitude of 54 degrees, 40 minutes north, to the point where said boundary line encounters the 141st degree of West longitude, with a view to the ascertainment of the facts and data necessary to the permanent delimitation of said boundary line in accordance with the spirit and intent of the existing treaties in regard to it between Great Britain and Russia and between the United States and Russia. . . . The two Governments agree that, as soon as practicable after the report or reports of the Commission shall have been received, they will proceed to consider and permanently establish the boundary line in question.[67]

After agreeing to this joint survey of the Alaskan boundary line, the conference adjourned. Several months later (July 22, 1892), a convention was signed in Washington by Secretary Foster and the British *chargé d'affaires* which gave formal sanction to the idea of a joint survey which would lay the basis for a permanent delimitation of the Alaskan boundary line.[68]

The ratifications of this treaty were exchanged on August 23, and on September 8, 1892, Secretary Foster wrote to Dr. Mendenhall,

66. The protocols of these conferences are contained in the *Kasson Papers, Reciprocity Treaties, 1898–1907*, MS. Dept. of State.

67. *Ibid.* See also, John W. Foster to Secretary Hay, November 7, 1899, *A.B.T.*, IV, 122–123. It was significant that at these conferences the Canadian representatives made no claim to control the headwaters of the inlets along the Alaskan boundary line such as the Lynn Canal. *C.S.P.* 1893, No. 52, pp. 1 ff.

68. Convention of July 22, 1892, *A.B.T.*, III, 350–351. In the British Case presented to the Alaskan Boundary Tribunal it was claimed that the United States, by agreeing to the treaty of July 22, 1892, had abandoned all of its rights that might be based upon the interpretation put upon the Treaty of 1825 by "maps published or acts done with the acquiescence of Great Britain," and had thus relegated the whole matter to an interpretation *de novo* of the treaties themselves without regard to what had transpired for a period of 67 years. This position was not a strong one, and it was really rendered untenable by the wording of the Convention of 1892 which provided for a survey "with a view to the ascertainment of the facts and data necessary to the permanent delimitation of said boundary line in accordance with the spirit and intent of the existing treaties in regard to it between Great Britain and Russia and between the United States and Russia." This convention merely made provision for the collection of data that would assist in fixing the permanent boundary line.

Superintendent of the Coast and Geodetic Survey, to inform him that he had received the appointment as Commissioner of the United States to carry out the survey of the Alaskan boundary. The Act of May 13, 1892 had appropriated $25,000 for this preliminary survey. Under the terms of the convention of July 22, the American Commissioner was directed to go to Ottawa and meet the Canadian Commissioner. As soon as practicable thereafter, the two Commissioners should undertake the "active discharge of their duties," and as far as they were able to agree, should make a joint report to each of the two governments.[69] The British Government was more dilatory carrying out the terms of the convention of July 22, 1892, and it was not until March 8, 1893 that Lord Rosebery informed Mr. W. F. King of his appointment as the Canadian Commissioner.[70]

In his instructions to Mr. O. H. Tittmann, Dr. Mendenhall directed him first to establish an astronomical station at "some convenient point at or near the mouth" of the Stikine River. He was then to carry on his survey to a "point on the Stikine River distant not less than thirty nautical miles from the coast of the mainland in a direction at right angles to its general trend."[71] On March 18 Dr. Mendenhall gave similar instructions to John E. McGrath with respect to Taku Inlet,[72] and the phraseology he employed could be interpreted to mean that in surveying thirty miles from the coast the distance might be reached while yet on Taku Inlet. In the British Case this very interpretation is arrived at, and it was claimed that it was "evident that Dr. Mendenhall did not consider the shore line of an inlet as being part of the 'coast.' "[73] If the boundary line should be measured from the coast and not along the inlet, this would mean that the headwaters of these inlets would be British.

But any ambiguity in this matter of surveying the boundary was removed by Dr. Mendenhall's instructions to J. F. Pratt in March, 1894.[74] He was directed to go to Lynn Canal and execute "the triangulation and topographical reconnaissance of the Chilkat and Taiya

69. Secretary Foster to Dr. Thomas C. Mendenhall, September 8, 1892, *ibid.,* IV, 268–269.

70. Lord Rosebery to W. F. King, March 8, 1893, *ibid.,* III, 353–354.

71. Dr. T. C. Mendenhall to O. H. Tittmann, March 16, 1893, *ibid.,* pp. 355–357.

72. Dr. T. C. Mendenhall to John E. McGrath, March 18, 1893, *ibid.,* pp. 357–359.

73. "Case of Great Britain," *ibid.,* p. 75.

74. The time allowed by the Treaty of July 22, 1892 for the completion of the preliminary survey was to expire on November 28, 1894. Realizing that this period was too short, Secretary Gresham and the British Minister at Washington signed on February 3, 1894 a new treaty which extended the time to December 31, 1895, *ibid.,* pp. 351–352.

Inlets to the ten marine league limit."[75] The Chilkat and Taiya Inlets were at the very head of Lynn Canal, and these instructions clearly indicate that the boundary line was to be measured from the headwaters and not from the mouth of this important canal. In his instructions to J. A. Flemer, in April, 1894, Dr. Mendenhall spoke of a reconnaissance "of the country to the northward and eastward of Taiya Inlet and River to the 10 marine league limit."[76] This language unmistakably implies that the measurement was to be taken from the head of Taiya Inlet and not from the mouth of the Lynn Canal.

On June 25, 1895 Secretary Olney informed the British representative at Washington that Mr. W. W. Duffield, Superintendent of the United States Coast and Geodetic Survey, had been designated as the boundary commissioner in place of Dr. Mendenhall.[77] This appointment was approved by the Canadian Privy Council,[78] and on August 10 Mr. Duffield met the Canadian Commissioner at Rochester, New York. Mr. King lost no time in stating that he had "determined the latitude of Cape Chacon, the most southern point of Prince of Wales Island, Cape Muzon, the most southern point of Dall Island, and Point Nunez, the most southern point of Bean Island." He also declared that the "initial point of the boundary line between Alaska and British Columbia was not clearly defined, and that either of these three points might be so regarded." Mr. Duffield insisted that the terms of the Treaty of 1825 clearly defined the initial point as the "most southern point of Prince of Wales Island, . . . and therefore the question was not open for discussion." Mr. Duffield could account for this statement of Mr. King's only upon the theory that the Canadian Commissioner realized that if the initial point was thrown westward to Cape Muzon, the next step would be to "claim Clarence Straits as the arm of the sea up which the boundary line should run instead of Portland Channel, . . . and then limit the territory of the United States to the Coast Islands alone and deprive them of all right to any portion of the mainland coast south of the parallel of fifty-six degrees north."[79]

In transmitting Mr. Duffield's letter to Secretary Olney, Mr. Adee, the Second Assistant Secretary of State, wrote a brief note which contained the following remark: "The treaty language is 'the southern-

75. Dr. T. C. Mendenhall to J. F. Pratt, March 21, 1894, *ibid.*, IV, 276–277.

76. Dr. T. C. Mendenhall to J. A. Flemer, April 9, 1894, *ibid.*, pp. 280–281.

77. Secretary Olney to Viscount Gough, June 25, 1895, *ibid.*, III, p. 365.

78. Report of the Committee of the Honourable the Privy Council, approved by His Excellency on the 30th July, 1895, *ibid.*, p. 364.

79. Mr. Duffield to Secretary Olney, August 12, 1895, *Olney MS.*, Library of Congress.

most point of the island called Prince of Wales Island,' which seems clear enough for any but an Englishman playing the grab game."[80]

Mr. Duffield knew only too well that neither he nor Mr. King could determine what the boundary line should be. Their task was limited to the gathering of pertinent data concerning this boundary in accordance with the terms of the treaties of July 22, 1892 and February 3, 1894. On December 31, 1895 Mr. Duffield and Mr. King submitted a joint report, accompanied by maps and photographs, on the topography of the region along the Alaskan boundary. These data, it was believed, could serve as the basis for a permanent delimitation of the line between Alaska and British Columbia.[81]

It was soon apparent that it would be expedient for both nations to fix this permanent boundary line as soon as possible. In his letter to Secretary Olney, August 12, 1895, Mr. Duffield had expressed the view that the British Boundary Commissioner was endeavoring to lay the basis for a claim that the boundary line, on the south, should ascend the Duke of Clarence Strait instead of Portland Channel. In this same

80. Alvey A. Adee to Secretary Olney, August 19, 1895, *ibid.*

81. *Joint Report of the United States and British Commissioners on the Alaskan-Canadian Boundary,* December 31, 1895 (Washington, 1898). See also, Map. No. 37 in *British Atlas* accompanying the Case of Great Britain. On August 20, 1895 Viscount Gough, the British representative at Washington, sent a note to Secretary Olney in which he referred to the "recent development of the mineral resources of the country drained by the Yukon River and the growing importance of the administration of that region." In view of these facts it was "highly desirable that the precise limits of the jurisdiction of the United States and the Dominion, respectively, should be more exactly determined." The treaties between the United States and Great Britain of July 22, 1892 and February 3, 1894 dealt with the survey of the Alaskan boundary from latitude 54° 40′ to the point where it encounters the 141° of west longitude. Viscount Gough was interested in having a preliminary survey made of the boundary along the 141st meridian "as far as the Frozen Ocean." In the event that the American Government did not wish to incur any expense in this regard, it could recognize as a provisional line the one about to be surveyed by Mr. William Ogilvie. (See Viscount Gough to Secretary Olney, August 20, 1895, *Olney MS.*) Viscount Gough's letter was turned over to Henry L. Bryan, of the Department of State, for study, and he reported that there was no "urgent necessity" for a survey along the 141st meridian of west longitude, but if it should be deemed convenient to have the point of demarcation visibly marked at certain localities, a "conditional acceptance of the Canadian survey, reserving all rights under the treaty, might serve temporarily." (See Bryan's undated *memorandum* in *ibid.*) Alvey A. Adee, the Acting Secretary of State, after reading the Bryan memorandum wrote to Viscount Gough and suggested that the question of the survey along the 141st meridian be delayed until after application had been made to Congress for funds. (A. A. Adee to Viscount Gough, September 6, 1895, *ibid.*) On December 2, 1895 President Cleveland sent his annual message to Congress, and in a long paragraph he made special reference to the importance of granting an appropriation that would make possible a joint survey of the boundary along the 141st meridian. (Richardson, *op. cit.,* IX, 631–632.) On January 30, 1897 a treaty was signed in Washington providing for this survey. (*A.B.T.,* III, 371–373.)

year (1895) an official map of British Columbia was published by the Canadian Government, and the boundary line was shown exactly as Mr. Duffield had anticipated.[82]

On March 6, 1896 a reporter for the New York *Times* brought this map to the attention of Mr. Duffield and inquired if there was "any authority for the line which the Canadian officials have designated on their map?" Mr. Duffield replied: "Not at all. The only map of that country in existence at the time the Russo-British treaty was executed was that of Captain Vancouver of the British Royal Navy, and that shows the boundary line to have been located in Portland Canal. The water there known by that name was identically the same as that now called Portland Canal, in and along which the boundary line must run."[83]

This Canadian claim was pushed forward more and more despite Mr. Duffield's denial of its validity, and the necessity for some settlement of the Alaskan boundary became painfully obvious to the Department of State. John Hay had just been installed as American Ambassador in London, and he reported to President McKinley that the British Government was manifesting a very friendly spirit towards him.[84] But Canadian disinclination to meet America halfway in the settlement of questions at issue was a serious problem that had to be faced, and Hay deprecated the apparent dependence of the British Government upon the whims of Canadian statesmen. In a letter to John W. Foster, Hay distilled the essence of the situation in the alembic of the following pungent paragraph:

> It is far more to Canada's advantage than ours to be on good terms with us. Lord Salisbury, in a private conversation the other day, compared her to a coquettish girl with two suitors, playing off one against the other. I should think a closer analogy would be to call her a married flirt, ready to betray John Bull on any occasion, but holding him responsible for all her follies.[85]

Some weeks later, Hay was still fearful that Canadian opposition would defeat any worth while arrangement between the United States and Great Britain. In another letter to Foster he remarked: "It is as you have known from the beginning. They cannot act here [London] independently of Canada, and Canada will do nothing unless she is bought off. We are on the right track in acting on our own responsibility inside of our own rights."[86]

82. *British Atlas,* Map No. 28 (e). 83. New York *Times,* March 7, 1896.
84. John Hay to President McKinley, May 9, 1897, *McKinley Papers,* Library of Congress.
85. John Hay to John W. Foster, December 27, 1897, *Confidential, John W. Foster Papers,* Library of Congress.
86. John Hay to John W. Foster, January 17, 1898, *ibid.*

Joseph Chamberlain had hopes that he could effect some arrangement that would be satisfactory to England, the United States and Canada, but Hay thought that the task was too titanic even for the political genius of the statesman from Birmingham. Moreover, any settlement that could be arrived at would "have desperate odds against it in the Senate on the eve of a Presidential campaign."[87]

Balfour was another British statesman who wished to smooth the uneven path of Canadian-American relations, and he confided to Henry White his great desire to do "anything to show friendship for the United States."[88] But White was as pessimistic as John Hay with regard to any prompt settlement of the chief questions at issue between Canada and the United States. White frankly informed Balfour that the attitude of Canada towards the United States was the "chief obstacle" to the establishment of harmonious Anglo-American relations. In the event that the Canadian Government could be persuaded to be more "conciliatory" with respect to American desires, the "chances of cordial and hearty co-operation between our Governments would seem to me much more probable." But White complained to Senator Lodge that Canada would probably not change her views except under compulsion, and any such type of "control over Canada is beyond the power of any British Government."[89]

But something would soon have to be done about settling the Alaskan boundary or serious difficulties would arise. Representative Lewis wrote to Secretary John Sherman and expressed the fear that border clashes might occur between American farmers and Canadian collectors of customs over the matter of the exact location of the boundary line.[90] Lyman J. Gage, Secretary of the Treasury, was equally concerned over the friction that might be aroused over the activities of Canadian collectors of customs who had suddenly moved their post from "Lake Bennett to the summits of the White and Chilkoot Passes and are collecting duties at those points upon American goods passing over those routes."[91] Such action was particularly regrettable in view of the fact that the American Government had established ports of entry at Dyea and Skagway where British vessels could land their cargoes and passengers. This favor had been greatly appreciated by some Canadian

87. John Hay to Henry White, November 25, 1897, *White Papers,* Library of Congress.

88. Henry White to Horace Porter, March 12, 1898, *ibid.*

89. Henry White to Senator Henry Cabot Lodge, March 5, 1898, *ibid.*

90. Representative James Hamilton Lewis to Secretary Sherman, March 17, 1898, *Miscellaneous Letters,* March, 1898, Pt. 2, MS. Dept. of State.

91. Secretary Gage to Secretary John Sherman, March 8, 1898, *ibid.,* Pt. 3. See also, W. P. McBride to Secretary Gage, Port Sitka, Alaska, March 10, 1898, and Howard Griffith to Joseph R. Stonebraker, Dyea, Alaska, February 28, 1898, *ibid.*

officials, but apparently it did not prevent certain actions that stirred deep resentment in American circles in Alaska.[92]

The friendly disposition of the American Secretary of the Treasury in establishing ports of entry at Dyea and Skagway for British vessels was commented upon in the Canadian House of Commons with warm approbation. Clifford Sifton, Minister of the Interior, in referring to this action, remarked as follows:

So far as the Government of the United States is concerned, . . . we have met with every courtesy at their hands, and although they have difficulties, . . . I would venture to say that the common sense of honorable members . . . will agree with me when I say that it was an act of the greatest possible friendliness on the part of the Secretary of the Treasury of the United States to amend their regulations and provide such regulations at Dyea and Skagway as are calculated to facilitate and promote Canadian trade. . . . If honorable gentlemen will refer to the map, they will see that Dyea and Skagway, at the entrance to this Yukon district, are nearly a thousand miles from Vancouver. And we could not send in an officer, we could not send a rifle or a revolver or a single charge of ammunition or a pound of provisions without the leave of the United States. . . . We were in the position of having to provide for a vast territory a thousand miles from the nearest of our cities, and we could not get into it without going through the waters or the territories of the United States. And our honorable friend who leads the party with the instinct of government would have had us wave the bloody shirt and say we would have nothing to do with these grasping Yankees.[93]

On February 11, 1898 Clifford Sifton proved equally friendly to the American contentions concerning ownership of the territory at the head of Lynn Canal, but he supported the Canadian claim that the summits of White and Chilkat Passes were in British territory. In discussing this situation, Sifton remarked:

Difficulties arose in the White Pass [in 1876–1877], behind the village of Skagway, and at Chilkat Pass behind Dyea. I believe our contention is that Skagway and Dyea are really in Canadian territory, but as the United States have had undisputed possession of them for some time past, we are precluded from attempting to take possession of that territory.

Sir Charles Hibbert Tupper: May I be excused for saying that I do not think the Honorable Minister meant to say "undisputed possession."

The Minister of the Interior: There has been no protest made. It must be taken as undisputed when there has been no protest made against the occupation of that territory by the United States. . . . There is nothing in the records to show that any protest has been made—an unfortunate thing for

92. Secretary Gage to Secretary Sherman, March 21, 1898, *Miscellaneous Letters*, Pt. 2, MS., Dept. of State.

93. *Canada: House of Commons, Debates, 1898,* February 15, 1898, I, 588.

us, but it is a fact. . . . We have taken the position that there can be no doubt raised as to the Canadian territory beginning at the summit; we have taken the position that the claim of Canada to occupy the territory inside of the summit from the boundary at White Pass and Chilkat Pass is not deniable, and we cannot admit it is debatable.[94]

On February 16, 1898 Mr. Prior, a Canadian Member of Parliament, asked Sir Wilfrid Laurier whether his attention had been called to certain paragraphs in the press to the effect that the American Government was about to send two companies of troops to be permanently stationed at Dyea and Skagway, at the head of the Lynn Canal. Inasmuch as this was in "disputed territory," Mr. Prior inquired whether any protest had been lodged at Washington with regard to the sending of these troops. In reply, Sir Wilfrid remarked:

My honorable friend is aware that, although this is disputed territory, it has been in the possession of the United States ever since they acquired this country from the Russian Government in 1867, and, so far as my information goes, I am not aware that any protest has ever been raised by any Government against the occupation of Dyea and Skagway by the United States. It is only in recent years that the attention of the public has been drawn to it.[95]

Because of the growing danger of serious friction along the Alaskan boundary, the British Government made further efforts to find some solution of this difficulty, and on February 23, 1898, Sir Julian Pauncefote addressed a brief note to Secretary Sherman in which he emphasized the fact that the recent discovery of gold in the Yukon district had made the question of the boundary one of particular importance. The British Government, therefore, proposed that the "determination of the coast line of the boundary south of Mount St. Elias should at once be referred to three Commissioners (who should be jurists of high standing), one to be appointed by each Government, and a third by an independent Power." It was further suggested that this Commission should proceed at once to "fix the frontier at the head of the inlets through which the traffic for the Yukon valley enters, continuing subsequently with the remaining strip or line of coast."[96]

On April 18, Sir Julian Pauncefote called at the Department of State and left a memorandum which suggested that the boundary at the head of Lynn Canal be fixed provisionally "at the Watershed at the first summit north of Dyea, such a provisional boundary would be at a

94. *Ibid.,* February 11, 1898, I, 407. 95. *Ibid.,* February 16, 1898, I, 619.

96. Sir Julian Pauncefote to Secretary Sherman, February 23, 1898, *A.B.T.,* III, 375–376.

distance from the coast of considerably more than ten leagues."[97] In reply, Secretary Day agreed that the provisional boundary line should follow "the summit of the watershed surrounding the head of Lynn Canal." In accordance with this arrangement, suitable monuments would be placed at the summit of White, Chilkoot and Chilkat Passes. It was understood, however, that this boundary was merely a temporary one, and the *modus vivendi* was not to be construed "as affecting in any manner rights under existing treaties for the ultimate . . . establishment of the boundary line in question."[98]

It is quite significant that Sir Julian Pauncefote was entirely willing to agree to a provisional line that would be fixed at the watershed of the first summit north of Dyea, such line being "at a distance from the coast of considerably more than ten leagues." He had offered this compromise upon the suggestion of the Canadian Government, and it is clear that at this time the leading members of that government must have inclined towards the view that the headwaters of the Lynn Canal belonged to the United States, and that the coast referred to in Pauncefote's memorandum was the coast at the head of this inlet.

This conciliatory spirit was bound to produce results, and on May 25, 1898, a conference was held at the Department of State between Sir Julian Pauncefote, John W. Foster and John A. Kasson. They quickly agreed that it was desirable that all controversies between the United States and Canada should be "amicably settled," and that a spirit of cordial friendship should exist between the two governments. The chief questions at issue were arranged under eleven headings, and provision was made for the establishment of a Joint High Commission to deal with these problems. On May 30, 1898 a protocol, setting forth the results of five conferences, was signed by John W. Foster, John A. Kasson, Sir Julian Pauncefote and Sir Louis Davies. In order to implement this protocol, the American Government appointed six commissioners.[99] The British Government took similar action,[100] and on

97. *Memorandum* on the Alaska Boundary, April 18, 1898, *ibid.*, p. 376.

98. Secretary Day to Sir Julian Pauncefote, May 9, 1898, *ibid.*, p. 377.

99. The American commissioners were Senator Charles W. Fairbanks, chairman, Representative Nelson Dingley, Judge George W. Gray, John W. Foster, John A. Kasson, T. Jefferson Coolidge, and Charles J. Faulkner (appointed to fill the vacancy created by the resignation of Judge Gray). Mr. Dingley died during the session of the Commission, and his place was taken by Sereno Payne.

100. The British commissioners were Sir Wilfrid Laurier, Sir Richard Cartwright, Sir Louis Davies, John Charlton, the Hon. James Winter, and Baron Herschell, the English Lord High Chancellor. It was significant that the first four members of this delegation were Canadians, the fifth was from Newfoundland, and the sixth was from England. In 1871 and in 1888 the British delegations on the Joint High Commissions were weighted in favor of England. In 1898 the British delegation was dominated by Canadians, and this may be one of the reasons why nothing was accomplished.

August 23, 1898, at Quebec, the first meeting of the Joint High Commission was held.[101] The inconclusive results of the labors of this commission are discussed in the following chapter.

101. The protocol of the conferences held in Washington, May 25–30, 1898, is printed in Malloy, *op. cit.,* I, 770–773.

In a memorandum written by Alvey A. Adee, Second Assistant Secretary of State, August 3, 1898, and given to the members of the Joint High Commission for their guidance, a careful canvass is made of the negotiation leading up to the Russo-British Treaty of 1825 concerning Alaska. In summing up his conclusions with regard to this treaty, Mr. Adee remarks: "The whole course of the negotiation shows that the British plenipotentiaries, and Mr. George Canning as well, had a perfectly clear conception of the *lisière,* upon which Russia insisted so strenuously. It was to be Russia's impenetrable barrier to any alien access to the inner region of the mainland, a strip of territory between the water's edge and the interior possessions of Great Britain, beginning at 54° 40′ at the northern lip of the mouth of Portland Channel and running thence to the one hundred and forty-first meridian, near Mount St. Elias. . . . It constituted a definite expanse of territory, over which and over the tide water and islands beyond it, Russia possessed an exclusive jurisdiction which has been ceded in its entirety to the United States. . . .

"The interior of this strip formed the line of demarcation between the Russian and British North American possessions. It is expressly located upon the mainland, indifferently styled *terre ferme* and *le continent* and sometimes *le côte,* in contradistinction to the outlying islands. Its absolute continuity as an effective defense against foreign lodgment on the shore of the mainland north of the mouth of Portland Channel was of the essence of the persistent Russian contention.

"That the character, location, and effect of the required *lisière* were fully comprehended by Great Britain is shown by the repeated efforts made by the English negotiators between 1823 and 1825 to shift its southern extremity farther northward or to minimize its effectiveness as a barrier to a mainland lodgment on the tide water north of 54° 40′ . . .

"There is no room to doubt that *'les sinuosités de la côte'* were intended by Russia and understood by the British negotiators to comprise all indentations, curves, hollows, inlets, arms, and small shallow bays (anses) of the mainland shore, and that *'la côte'* ended wherever tide water began. It is impossible to imagine that Great Britain, . . . could soberly assert, in face of the testimony furnished by the records of the tedious negotiation which preceded its signature, that the sinuosities of the coast can be the general contour of the territorial mass formed by the continent and its adjacent islands. That would involve the tracing of a parallel contour line, now on the mainland, now cutting straits, bays and inlets, now leaping from island to island, dividing each in its passage into conflicting territorial jurisdictions. Such a plan . . . would be utterly incompatible with the successful Russian demand for a continuous *lisière* . . . serving forever to separate north of 54° 40′ the British interior territory . . . from the tide waters of the sea." *Alaska Boundary Papers,* MS. Dept. of State. See also the *Memorandum* prepared by Henry S. Pritchett, Superintendent of the Coast and Geodetic Survey, July 30, 1898, which is along the lines of the Adee statement.

CHAPTER VII

THE JOINT HIGH COMMISSION FAILS TO SETTLE THE ALASKAN BOUNDARY DISPUTE

THE first meeting of these sessions of the Joint High Commission was held in Quebec on August 23, 1898.[1] After a session of two weeks, a recess was called, and then another session of two weeks was held in that city. During these meetings an attempt was made to discuss all the items in the lengthy agenda,[2] but difficulties were quickly encountered in the matter of the Alaskan boundary, and this question proved to be such a thorny one that the Quebec conferences came to a close on October 10 without achieving the settlement of a single one of the important issues between the two countries. The sessions were resumed in Washington on November 9, 1898, and were brought to a fruitless conclusion on February 20, 1899.

Sir Wilfrid Laurier had anticipated this unsuccessful outcome of

1. In the survey of the background of the Alaskan boundary controversy that was prepared by the Department of State and sent to the American representatives on the Joint High Commission, an outline was given of the arguments that would probably be presented by the British representatives: "Lord Salisbury's instructions to the British commissioners indicate that an effort will be made on the part of Great Britain, to so delimit this line that 'sinuosités de la côte' will be disregarded and an attempt will be made to parallel not the 'sinuosités' but the general trend, so that by drawing imaginary lines across the headlands of the bays and inlets, especially in the Lynn Canal, the 30-mile limit can be brought west of the upper navigable waters of the inlet, so as to locate one or more inland seaports in British territory, and, as already intimated by Dr. Dawson, a theory will probably also be advanced that 'la côte' should be considered as being the ocean shore of the islands, and not the shore line of the mainland." *Alaska Boundary Papers,* MS., Dept. of State.

2. These items were listed as follows: (1) The questions in respect to the fur seals in Bering Sea and the waters of the North Pacific Ocean. (2) The Fisheries off the Atlantic Coast—Fisheries in waters contiguous to the United States and Canada. (3) Delimitation of the Boundary between Alaska and British Columbia. (4) Transit of merchandise to and from either country and (5) across intermediate territory. (6) The Alien Labor Laws applicable to the citizens and subjects of the United States and Canada. (7) Mining rights of the citizens or subjects of each country within the territory of the other. (8) Such readjustment and concession as many be deemed mutually advantageous of customs duties applicable in each country to the products of the soil or industry of the other, upon the basis of reciprocal equivalents. (9) A revision of the Agreement of 1817 respecting naval vessels on the Lakes. (10) Arrangements for the more complete definition and marking of any part of the frontier line, by land or water, where the same is now so insufficiently defined or marked as to be liable to dispute. (11) Provisions for the conveyance for trial or punishment of persons in the lawful custody of the officers of one country through the territory of the other. (12) Relating to wreckage and salvage.

the sessions of the Joint High Commission,[3] but he was keen enough to realize that there were certain factors that were preparing the way for an Anglo-American accord. This new international alignment would compel Canadians to be more responsive to English pressure in favor of compromises that would settle the more persistent problems in Canadian-American relations in a manner that would not wound Canadian pride. Laurier could discern the shadows that foretold coming events of prime importance to the Dominion, and he was wise enough to know that Canada would have to pay the price of certain Imperial bargains. America had become a world power whose good will was essential to the success of policies that were being formulated in the British Foreign Office. Canada might delay the execution of these plans, but acquiescence was inevitable no matter how bitter the pill.

This surrender was made particularly galling by the fact that in 1896 Canada entered upon a new era of prosperity that greatly lessened her former dependence upon the United States for economic favors. The wheat boom brought rich returns to the farmers of "Canada West," and the discovery of gold in Yukon Territory seemed to indicate mineral wealth far beyond the dreams of the most optimistic prospectors. The "Klondike rush" brought thousands of miners into the Yukon Territory, and it advertised in a most dramatic manner the boundless possibilities that awaited the advent of Canadian pioneers. No other event or combination of events occurring outside the area of the battlefield had, during the nineteenth century, so "profoundly affected the English-speaking people and generally had so wide an influence in so short a space of time."[4]

In order to reach this new Eldorado, prospective miners had to follow certain trails. Three of these trails started in American territory. On the Chilkoot Inlet which formed a part of the headwaters of the Lynn Canal, there were two important trails: (1) the Dyea Trail over the Chilkoot Pass; and (2) the Skagway and White Pass Trail. On Chilkat Inlet, which also branched off the headwaters of the Lynn Canal, was located Pyramid Harbor. From this harbor, over the Chilkat Pass, the way was open along the Dalton Trail to Fort Selkirk.[5]

3. Oscar D. Skelton, *Life and Letters of Sir Wilfrid Laurier* (Toronto, 1921), II, 126.

4. Harold A. Innis, "Settlement and the Mining Frontier," *Canadian Frontiers of Settlement* (Toronto, 1936), IX, 178–183; J. B. Tyrrell, "The Gold of the Klondike," *Transactions of the Royal Society of Canada* (1912), Sec. IV, 25–29; R. A. Bankson, *The Klondike Nugget* (Caldwell, 1935).

5. Innis, *op. cit.*, p. 184; William Ogilvie, *The Klondike Official Guide* (Toronto, 1898).

Over these and other trails in 1897 and 1898, thousands of miners poured into Yukon Territory. On May 29, 1898, Major Steele estimated that "more than 30,000 persons . . . had passed down the Yukon."[6] By midsummer of that year, some 18,000 persons were encamped at Dawson, and multitudes were working in the mines.[7] In 1897, more than $2,500,000 in gold was mined in the Yukon country, and this reached the peak of $22,275,000 three years later.[8] In 1898, William Ogilvie stated in London that in the Klondike region there were at least "one hundred million dollars in sight," and "another hundred millions, probably two of them, to be discovered."[9]

It is with reference to this background of good times in Canada and the discovery of gold in the Yukon Territory that one has to view the actions of the British members of the Joint High Commission in 1898–99. The Commission held its first meeting in Quebec on August 23, 1898. In accordance with instructions from Lord Salisbury, they were to give careful consideration to the Alaskan boundary dispute. In connection with the southern section of the boundary there was wide divergence between the views of the two governments. Her Majesty's Government, however, was content to leave it to the "discretion and judgment of the Commissioners," to devise "some machinery" for the settlement of existing difficulties.[10]

In their response to these instructions the British members of the Joint High Commission failed to reveal any great discretion. In 1884, Judge Gray had secured the approval of the Executive Council of British Columbia with reference to the claim that the southern end of the Alaskan boundary line should start at Cape Chacon and ascend

6. S. B. Steele, *Forty Years in Canada* (London, 1915), pp. 310–312.

7. Tappan Adney, *The Klondike Stampede* (New York, 1900), pp. 385–386.

8. Innis, *op. cit.*, p. 219; *Annual Report of the Mineral Production of Canada, 1926* (Ottawa, 1926), p. 117.

9. *Early Days on the Yukon* (London, 1913), pp. 105–136, 205–224. In Lord Salisbury's instructions to the British members of the Joint High Commission, July 19, 1898, special reference is made to the Klondike gold fields: "There are two special reasons for an early delimitation of this part of the boundary. In the first place, owing to the discovery of the Klondyke gold-fields, there has already been a large influx of miners and others into the territory to which access lies mainly through the strip. The necessity of establishing a Customs frontier on the inlets on the coast is therefore obvious. In addition to this consideration, there is the fact that the whole of the strip of Alaska bordering on the Pacific is believed to be auriferous. . . . If gold should be found in large quantities at points in disputed territory, serious difficulties may ensue, and Her Majesty's Government therefore consider that steps should be taken as early as possible for arriving at an agreement as to the intention of the Parties to the Treaty of 1825 as to how the boundary-line along the strip from Portland Canal to Mount St. Elias should be drawn." Pauncefote to W. R. Day, *Great Britain, Notes from,* CXXX, MS. Dept. of State.

10. Lord Salisbury to the High Commissioners, July 19, 1898, *A.B.T.*, III, 384–386.

Clarence Strait until it struck the continent at 56° north latitude.[11] In March, 1886, Sir John Macdonald had disagreed with this viewpoint and had expressed the view that the line should run from the "northern extremity of Portland Channel" to the "141° of west longitude." The limitation of ten marine leagues from the ocean could "easily be obtained at any point by a measurement with a surveyor's chain from the ocean."[12]

In February, 1888, the matter of the boundary had been discussed by the British members of the Joint High Commission, and John S. Thompson had expressed the opinion that there was no basis for the contention of British Columbian officials that the line should run "north through part of the Duke of Clarence Straits and then branch off either through Behm's Canal or Ernest Sound to the Continental coast at latitude 56° N." Dr. Dawson had agreed with Mr. Thompson's viewpoint, and Sir Charles Tupper had expressed the belief that it was "unwise to attempt to maintain the British Columbian view."[13]

In his discussion with Mr. Dall at this time, Dr. Dawson suddenly adopted, for the sake of argument, the contentions of the British Columbian officials and also the arguments that had been advanced by General Cameron with regard to the Alaskan boundary. He then produced a map that had drawn upon it a line that would give British Columbia access to the headwaters of the Stikine and Taku Rivers. This line was also extended so as to establish Canadian control over the headwaters of the Lynn Canal.[14] Needless to say, Mr. Dall immediately rejected these ambitious claims, and the conferences adjourned with no agreement in sight.

In February, 1898, both Clifford Sifton, the Canadian Minister of the Interior, and Sir Wilfrid Laurier, the Prime Minister, admitted the strength of the American claim to ownership over both Dyea and Skagway.[15] But despite these admissions by Canadian leaders, the meetings of the Commission were soon made stormy by a revival of all the old claims that had been advanced by Dr. Dawson in February, 1888. Indeed, the claims advanced by the British members of the Joint High Commission in 1898 went beyond the contentions of British representatives in the previous decade. As one compares the official British Columbia maps of 1893 and 1895, it is evident that British claims are in an ascending scale.[16] This is particularly true of the map from the *Year Book of British Columbia, 1897*.[17] The map presented by the

11. See *ante*, pp. 139–140.
12. See *ante*, pp. 144–145.
13. See *ante*, pp. 151–152.
14. See *ante*, pp. 152–155.
15. See *ante*, pp. 165–166.
16. *A.B.T., United States Atlas*, Map No. 28 (d) and (e).
17. *Ibid.*, Map f.

British members of the Joint High Commission in August, 1898, was merely a copy of this latest British Columbia chart.[18] At the southern end of the boundary there were two alternatives. The line could either run from Cape Chacon through Clarence Strait and Ernest Sound to the continental coast at 56° north latitude, or it could run from Cape Chacon along Pearse Canal to the head of Portland Canal, thence directly to the coast where it should follow the nearest mountains to the coast, crossing all the inlets of the sea, up to Mount St. Elias. Either one of these lines from 56° northwards, would "give the United States a strip of an average width of less than five miles, broken at short intervals by the arms of the sea, and would transfer the greater portion of all the inlets to British territory."[19]

John W. Foster, as one of the American members of the Commission, filed an immediate protest against these British claims which would give them control over all the inlets in the *lisière*. He also stated, "distinctly and emphatically," that "no claim to any portion of the Lynn Canal had been made previous to 1898."[20]

This battle of claim and counter-claim was carried on for several weeks until it became apparent that no accord could be reached at these Quebec conferences. On October 10 an adjournment was voted, and meetings were resumed in Washington on November 9, 1898. The atmosphere in Washington seemed conducive to a real understanding of the situation, and Sir Wilfrid Laurier thought that a new spirit of "general good-will" was clearly in evidence.[21]

But fresh difficulties soon appeared, and they were of a personal nature. The Canadian members of the Joint High Commission appeared agreeable to an understanding that could soon be reached, but Lord Herschell, direct from England, was less favorable to compromise. Complaints about his unreasonable attitude began to pass current in American circles, and Senator Lodge presented the following indictment in a letter to Henry White:

> Mr. Chamberlain gave me clearly to understand that Lord Herschell was sent out to mollify and . . . bring to reasonable terms the Canadians who are difficult to deal with. . . . But Lord Herschell goes far beyond them. He is making most of the trouble in the Commission; he is sharp, often violent, . . . and if it had not been for him we might have done something ere

18. *Ibid.*, Map No. 27

19. John W. Foster, "The Alaskan Boundary," *National Geographic Magazine*, X (November, 1899), 455.

20. John W. Foster to Secretary Hay, September 10, 1899, *Alaskan Boundary, 1899–1903, Miscellaneous Archives*, MS. Dept. of State.

21. Skelton, *Laurier*, II, 127.

this with the Canadians. . . . I want the Commission to make a treaty. I want a treaty that we can ratify in the Senate. I want to avoid a fight there. If things go on as now there will be no agreement. . . . If the Government does not want to wreck the negotiations either in the Commission or the Senate, they had better give Lord Herschell a pretty broad, strong and speedy hint.[22]

Secretary Hay wrote in the same vein to White. He had heard from several members of the Commission that

by far the worst member of the Commission to deal with is Lord Herschell, who is more cantankerous than any of the Canadians, raises more petty points, and is harder than any of the Canadians to get along with. In fact he is the principal obstacle to a favorable settlement. If you could . . . in conversation with Balfour or Villiers, or even Lord Salisbury, . . . intimate this state of things so that they might speak a word which would moderate his excessive lawyer-like zeal to make a case, it might be a good thing.[23]

White carried out these instructions from Secretary Hay,[24] but he received little satisfaction for his pains, and Joseph Chamberlain replied in a letter that defended Herschell and attacked John W. Foster. Herschell continued his strong advocacy of Canadian interests and made a special point about the importance of British control over Pyramid Harbor. The headwaters of Lynn Canal branched off into two bodies of water called Chilkoot Inlet and Chilkat Inlet. On Chilkoot Inlet were located the two towns of Dyea and Skagway,[25] and beyond Skagway was the important White Pass leading into the interior. Pyramid Harbor was located on Chilkat Inlet, and access to the Yukon Territory could be gained by passing through Chilkat Pass and along the Dalton Trail to Fort Selkirk.[26]

Shortly after the opening of the Quebec conferences, Herschell made the proposal that the American Government cede to Canada, Pyramid Harbor with a strip of land connecting it with Canadian territory to the northwest. This proposal was rejected by the American Commissioners who countered on December 14, 1898, with the suggestion that the Canadian Government abandon all claim to territory in the neighborhood of the Lynn Canal and receive in return permission for the

22. Senator Lodge to Henry White, December 3, 1898, *White MS.*

23. Secretary Hay to Henry White, December 3, 1898, *ibid.* Hay took up the duties of Secretary of State in the summer of 1898.

24. Henry White to Joseph Chamberlain, December 26, 1898, *Personal and Confidential, ibid.*

25. The continuation of Chilkoot Inlet was called Taiya Inlet.

26. Allan Nevins, *Henry White* (New York, 1930), pp. 188–189.

commercial vessels of the Dominion to "use all ports and harbors on the Lynn Canal as freely, and subject only to the same conditions and restrictions as those of the United States." The Dominion Government would also have the right to establish an office on the Lynn Canal for the "collection of customs and superintendence of transit." Two days later, the British Commissioners rejected this suggestion because it implied that the American contention as to the boundary line was correct. In conclusion they renewed their proposal that "Pyramid Harbor and a strip behind it should belong to Great Britain." If this were not acceptable, there seemed "no alternative but to leave the question of boundary to the determination of legal experts."[27]

In explanation of the British stand, Lord Herschell wrote to Senator Fairbanks and reviewed the whole situation. He had clung to the hope that the Joint High Commission could settle the boundary question "by compromise." It had seemed to him that "between the two nations whose disposition to one another was friendly and who neither of them desired to take undue advantage of the other, such a settlement ought not to be impossible." The only part of the boundary where it was of any

great importance whether your contention or ours be well founded is in the neighborhood of the Lynn Canal. If this part of the question could be settled by agreement I do not think the rest of it would present substantial difficulty. Our view is that on the true construction of the Treaty the line ought to be so drawn as to leave all the land surrounding the upper part of the Lynn Canal in British Territory, and that nothing has been done or happened since the date of the Treaty to vary the rights which on its true construction we are entitled to. . . . I have suggested by way of compromise that the boundary line should leave all the land bordering on the Lynn Canal within the United States territory except Pyramid Harbor and a strip of land behind it giving access to Canadian territory. This proposal concedes almost the whole of the territory in dispute to the United States. Even if their claim be much stronger than the British, this would, I submit, be a fair compromise. . . . I named Pyramid Harbor but should be quite prepared to entertain the suggestion that it should be some harbor other than that. . . . Surely under these circumstances, such a compromise as that suggested would, as between nations negotiating in a friendly spirit, be a very reasonable one.[28]

Senator Fairbanks promptly replied that the American Commissioners were "heartily in favor of an amicable settlement" of the questions

27. Lord Herschell to Senator Fairbanks, February 13, 1899, *Alaska Boundary Papers,* MS. Dept. of State. Fairbanks was later on destined to serve as Vice-President during the Theodore Roosevelt Administration.

28. Lord Herschell to Senator Fairbanks, December 21, 1898, *ibid.*

at issue between Canada and the United States, and they desired no settlement which would not be "absolutely as just and equitable to British as to American interests." With regard to the Alaskan boundary, the American representatives had been disposed to treat the whole question with "all possible liberality." They had offered the "fullest and freest possible use of Pyramid Harbor" at the head of Lynn Canal for customs purposes. This offer had embraced all "but the sovereignty of the soil," and it granted everything that could be of any commercial or practical value—port, customs and transit privileges.

Senator Fairbanks thought that it was significant that the British Government, previous to the sessions of the Joint High Commission, had never voiced a claim to the headwaters of the Lynn Canal. British officials might have been inclined to the view that these waters really belonged to Canada, but this viewpoint had never been formally presented to the American Government.[29]

In a State Department memorandum preserved by Secretary Hay, the chief points at issue that had arisen during the meetings of the Joint High Commission were clearly outlined:

First—the British Commissioners asked for a perpetual lease [of Pyramid Harbor]; the Americans refused this, but offered a lease for fifty years. Second—The British designed to make it exclusively a British port; this would prevent American vessels from carrying goods from British ports, such as

29. Senator Fairbanks to Lord Herschell, December 24, 1898, *ibid.* Accompanying this letter of Senator Fairbanks is a memorandum entitled "American Proposition as to Grant of Port and Strip of Territory." Article 2 of this proposal reads as follows: "There shall be granted for a period of fifty years to the British Government the occupation, use and control of the port or harbor in the Territory of Alaska known as Pyramid Harbor, on Chilkat Inlet of Lynn Canal, occupying a shore frontage of not exceeding two statute miles; and the occupation, use and control of a strip of territory not exceeding two statute miles in width, extending from said port or harbor in a northwesterly direction along the Chilkat River and Pass to the boundary line fixed between the territory of the United States and the Dominion of Canada. The said port and strip of territory . . . shall be subject to the exclusive jurisdiction of the civil and criminal laws and authorities of the British and Canadian Governments. 3. The rights of individuals and corporations heretofore acquired in the said port and strip of territory shall be respected during said occupation; and citizens and vessels of the United States shall have equal treatment therein with British subjects and vessels. 4. It is to be stipulated that no part of said port or strip of territory shall be fortified, or used for military or naval purposes."

In the British counter draft the American proposal for a grant of Pyramid Harbor for fifty years was changed to a grant without limit as to time. The British counter draft also left out the clause whereby citizens and vessels of the United States should have equal treatment with British subjects and vessels, and it omitted the restrictions as to fortifications and military and naval uses. It added that "vessels of the United States, and of British or Canadian register, shall have equal treatment in the harbors of Pyramid, Skagway and Dyea."

Victoria and Vancouver, to the leased port; and would permit British vessels to carry goods from San Francisco, Seattle and other American ports to the leased port. The Americans insisted that the lease should not change the existing conditions of the carrying trade to and from the Lynn Canal.[30]

But despite these difficulties it had seemed for a while that some compromise might be reached. Joseph Chamberlain indicated to Henry White his readiness to be of service,[31] but White believed there was little prospect "of either side's being willing to give way on important points."[32] Secretary Hay himself was none too optimistic, and he found it hard to

treat with patience the claim set up by Lord Herschell that virtually the whole coast belongs to England, leaving us only a few jutting promontories without communication with each other. Without going into the historical or legal argument, as a mere matter of common sense it is impossible that any nation should ever have conceded, or any nation have accepted, the cession of such a ridiculous . . . boundary line. We are absolutely driven to the conclusion that Lord Herschell put forward a claim that he had no belief or confidence in for the mere purpose of trading it off for something substantial. And yet, the slightest suggestion that his claim is unfounded throws him into a fury.[33]

It is very likely that Chamberlain exerted some pressure upon Lord Herschell, who suddenly began to cultivate Senator Lodge. These tactics were quite successful, and we find Lodge writing to Henry White that Herschell was a "most agreeable man personally." But Lodge was opposed to any far-reaching surrender of what he regarded as American rights. He thought the American Government was ready to "compromise the boundary by giving them [the Canadians] access to the sea and a free port with places for their buildings, etc., but no territorial sovereignty." He would not consent to the establishment of another Halifax or Esquimault. After a study of the terms of the treaty of 1825 he was convinced that the Canadians did not have "a leg to stand on." Their "whole case is manufactured."[34]

But this compromise suggested by Senator Lodge was regarded by

30. Undated *memorandum* in the Department of State.

31. White to Secretary Hay, December 30, 1898, telegram, *White MS.*

32. White to Secretary Hay, December 30, 1898, *ibid.* In this letter White expressed the opinion that Chamberlain was "anxious for a thorough understanding between the two countries and willing to make a good many sacrifices towards that end personally." See also, Chamberlain's letter to White, December 27, 1898, *ibid.*

33. Secretary Hay to Henry White, January 3, 1898, *Personal and Confidential, White MS.*

34. Senator Lodge to Henry White, January 7, 1899, *White MS.*

many Canadians as insufficient, and David Mills, Minister of Justice, expressed to Sir Wilfrid Laurier the view that it would be

> little short of a calamity to accept a mere easement which would give us admission to a harbour on the Lynn Inlet. A concession which falls short of sovereignty is not worth taking. It would simply cripple us for active work elsewhere within our own limits, and would make us helots to the Republic, in building up a town, and investing money which they must ultimately control. . . . I am sure that in Ontario the public will be much better satisfied if you stand for your rights, than if you make what they regard as undue concessions for the sake of obtaining a treaty. . . . It will be a terrible blow to the strong Imperial feeling which has grown up during the past few years, if a treaty is concluded in which large concessions are made to the United States. . . . It will be said . . . that the Government of the United Kingdom are always ready to sacrifice this country at the demand of the United States.[35]

The British Government was well aware of Canadian uneasiness with reference to possible concessions to the United States, and this fact made the conduct of Anglo-American relations a very complicated and difficult matter. Even in connection with questions totally unrelated to the Alaskan boundary, these Canadian susceptibilities had to be considered. This was especially true of negotiations relating to the abrogation of the Clayton-Bulwer Treaty. It had long been apparent to American Secretaries of State that this treaty of April 19, 1850 was hopelessly out of date as far as American desires were concerned, and Mr. Blaine carried on a futile correspondence with Lord Granville in this regard. Blaine looked upon the Clayton-Bulwer Treaty as an old-fashioned garment that no longer deserved a place in the Anglo-American diplomatic wardrobe, but Lord Granville thought that its lines were still quite modish and he refused to agree to its destruction.[36] The Spanish-American War had furnished the American Government with an impressive lesson in the importance of sea-power, and the long voyage of the battleship *Oregon* round Cape Horn had indicated the necessity of an inter-oceanic canal through which American warships could rapidly pass in case of emergency.[37] The chief item in every program for American national defence was the construction and control over an isthmian canal, and this fact loomed large in the vision of Secretary Hay.

35. David Mills to Sir Wilfrid Laurier, January 25, 1899, *Laurier MS.* P.A.C.
36. Tansill, *Bayard,* pp. 674–677; J. Fred Rippy, *The Caribbean Danger Zone* (New York, 1940), pp. 105–112.
37. Harold and Margaret Sprout, *The Rise of American Naval Power, 1776–1918* (Princeton, 1939), pp. 223–249.

On December 7, 1898 he had instructed Henry White to sound out Lord Salisbury with reference to a revision of the Clayton-Bulwer Treaty.[38] During a week-end stay at Hatfield the matter was completely canvassed. Salisbury expressed the view that British control over the Suez Canal had lessened British interest in an inter-oceanic canal in the Western Hemisphere. He thought that such a canal could be built only as a great national enterprise by some strong Power that could protect it. This Power was, of course, the United States. In conclusion, he confided to White that he did not regard the existing treaty rights of Great Britain under the terms of the Clayton-Bulwer Treaty as a matter of "serious importance."[39]

Encouraged by these assurances, Secretary Hay and Sir Julian Pauncefote, the British Ambassador in Washington, started to discuss the terms of a new treaty that would supersede the Clayton-Bulwer convention, but White sent a warning that certain Canadian statesmen would like to have some share in the settlement of this question.[40] This desire was not unusual when one considers the fact that an isthmian canal could be a factor of great importance in the equation of expanding Canadian commerce. If this canal were to be under exclusive American control, would this mean that American shipping would receive favors denied to vessels under British registry? Could Canada afford to permit the United States to have additional advantages in the contest for commercial supremacy in the Pacific? These were questions that clamored for answers, and some British and Canadian statesmen thought that concessions to the United States in the matter of the isthmian canal should be balanced by concessions to Canada in the matter of the Alaskan boundary.

But Secretary Hay endeavored to carry on separate negotiations with England in connection with a revision of the Clayton-Bulwer Treaty, and he sent a draft convention to London for examination and comment. His only object was to make it possible for the United States "to take charge and build the canal without in any way violating our international obligations to England."[41]

White lost no time in discussing with Lord Salisbury the terms of this draft convention and he urged "prompt action." He discovered, however, that the convention would have to be submitted to the British Cabinet and to various Government Departments before an answer would be forthcoming. He was very apprehensive of a delay in this

38. Secretary Hay to Henry White, December 7, 1898, *White MS.*
39. Henry White to Secretary Hay, December 23, 1898, *ibid.*
40. Allan Nevins, *Henry White,* p. 145.
41. Secretary Hay to Henry White, January 13, 1899, *White MS.*

matter unless the Joint High Commission would soon arrive at some understanding on the questions before it. It was apparent that the British Government was "fearful of being unable to justify before Parliament and country prompt acceptance of arrangement likely to be considered chiefly . . . beneficial to us, while they cannot obtain concessions from us on Canadian matters."[42]

Secretary Hay, however, was well aware of the fact that any far-reaching concessions to Canada would arouse bitter opposition in many parts of the United States. This was especially true of the Pacific Coast region. On February 2, 1899 the ship-owners on the Pacific Coast sent a telegram to Senator George C. Perkins in which they indicated that the states of Washington, Oregon and California were "very much exercised over a report that the Joint High Commission has conceded to Canada a waiving of the boundary line between Alaska and British Columbia which gives Canada a Port on Lynn Canal." Such action would be regarded as "highly detrimental" to American shipping.[43] Senator Perkins sent a copy of this telegram to the Department of State, and Secretary Hay had no difficulty in recognizing its implications.[44]

It was becoming increasingly difficult to find some formula that would solve Canadian-American problems, and Secretary Hay strongly deprecated the fact that the British Government insisted on making an arrangement in the

42. White to Secretary Hay, January 26, 1899, *Personal and Confidential, ibid.*

43. American Ship-owners to Senator George C. Perkins, February 2, 1899, *Alaska Boundary Papers,* MS. Dept. of State.

44. Secretary Hay had already, on April 26, 1898, received a letter from Erastus Brainerd, a prominent business man of Seattle, with reference to the importance of the Alaskan boundary issue to the business interests of the Pacific Northwest. In this letter Mr. Brainerd remarked: "So long as the territory in dispute between Alaska and Canada was thinly populated, no serious detriment or injury was incurred by leaving the question unsettled. . . . The past nine months have wrought an extraordinary change in conditions, which, to those near their scene and familiar with their causes, seems to call for greater activity in determining the disputed issue. According to carefully collected figures gathered from the clearances from the Port of Seattle, and from the statements of responsible agents of transportation companies, 14,566 persons had left the City of Seattle alone, between January 1st, 1898 and March 20th, bound for Alaska ports, chiefly for the ports of Skagway and Dyea. From other Pacific Coast ports it is estimated that perhaps 7,500 persons have left in the same time for the same ports. . . . It is estimated that about 8,000 persons left Puget Sound for the same destinations in the latter months of 1897. . . . It is known that a great part are still within the territory in dispute, making a total approximately of 20,000 to 30,000 persons, chiefly citizens of the United States. These citizens have . . . established considerable settlements, and in two places large, well built towns. . . . On behalf of many of these citizens I would respectfully urge that an examination and report may be made . . . into this statement of facts." *Ibid.*

Clayton-Bulwer matter depend on the successful issue of the Canadian negotiations. The two questions have nothing to do with each other. Every intelligent Englishman is ready to admit that the Canal ought to be built, that the United States alone will build it, . . . that when built it will be to the advantage of the entire civilized world, and this being the case, it is hard to see why the settlement of the matter ought to depend on the lumber duty or the Alaska boundary.[45]

To the British members of the Joint High Commission it appeared obvious that all the questions affecting Canadian-American relations should be lumped together and settled *en bloc*. If the American Government would not adopt the usual rule of give and take that governed so many diplomatic arrangements,[46] the only way out was to settle the points at issue by a reference to arbitration. On December 16, 1898, they had proposed to refer the Alaskan boundary dispute to arbitration, and during the first week in February, 1899, they repeated this proposal.[47]

When this offer was made to the American members of the Joint High Commission, it was rejected because it took "no note of the rights and equities which in other treaties of arbitration have been recognized as necessary." The American Commissioners then suggested that, pending further action on the Alaskan boundary dispute, it would be expedient to "proceed with the remaining questions in the Protocol. They are well advanced; in fact nothing but formal assent is necessary to dispose of several of them. The differences with respect to others have been reduced to a very small number, and in the main do not seem insuperable."[48]

Lord Herschell's reply to this American statement is very frank and much to the point. As early as December 16, 1898, the British Commissioners had suggested the arbitration of the entire boundary line. This offer had been rejected. In a note from Mr. Fairbanks, February 11, 1899, a complaint had been made that the recent British proposal

45. Secretary Hay to Henry White, February 14, 1899, *White MS.;* William R. Thayer, *The Life and Letters of John Hay* (New York, 1916), pp. 217–218.

46. Chamberlain confided to Henry White that "it would be really a great advantage to the Government if we could in return for their assent to 'waive their rights' under the Clayton-Bulwer Treaty come to a settlement on other matters; that there is a certain feeling here that of late we have usually got the best of any arrangement between the United States and this country, and that he feared that this feeling might be aggravated if so large a concession without any *quid pro quo* were to be announced." *Memorandum,* February 4, 1899, *White MS.*

47. *Memorandum,* February 4, 1899, A. L. P. Dennis, *Adventures in American Diplomacy, 1896–1906* (New York, 1928), pp. 136, 146.

48. Charles W. Fairbanks to Lord Herschell, February 11, 1899, *Alaska Boundary Papers.* MS. Dept. of State.

to arbitrate the questions at issue took "no notice of the rights and equities which in other treaties of arbitration have been regarded as necessary." In answer to this charge, Lord Herschell observed:

> We must recall to your recollection the circumstances under which our proposal of arbitration was submitted on Wednesday . . . last. When an agreement to settle the boundary seemed impossible, we repeated our proposal of arbitration and asked whether you were willing to assent to it. To this we were unable to obtain a distinct reply, either in the affirmative or negative. You asked us to submit a proposition on the subject in writing. I pointed out that it was scarcely fair to expect me to draw out an arbitration agreement until I had learnt whether arbitration was accepted in principle. As however, you proposed the matter, I said I would draw a sketch of an agreement on the subject which would be sufficient to ascertain whether the proposal of arbitration was to be agreed to. It never occurred to me under the circumstances that I was expected to insert any detailed provisions or more than the barest outline. . . . It was quite open to you . . . to add to our proposal such provisions relating to "rights and equities" as you refer to in your letter. If an arbitration covering the entire boundary in dispute is assented to in principle, we are prepared at once to discuss all the details of such an arbitration and to assent on our part to any reasonable provisions which have been recognized as necessary in treaties of this description. In considering all the details, we shall be prepared to act in the most conciliatory spirit.[49]

The reply of Senator Fairbanks was immediate and negative. The American Commissioners appreciated the conciliatory spirit shown by Lord Herschell but they would not arbitrate the matter of the boundary line in the vicinity of the Lynn Canal. During the long period from 1825 to 1898 no claim had ever been made by the British Government to territory around Dyea, Skagway and Pyramid Harbor. Since 1867 American sovereignty had been exercised in this region, and it would be unfair to have the title to such territory passed upon by any arbitral body. It had long been recognized that there was some difference of views with reference to where the boundary line crossed "certain rivers and mountain passes," and the American proposal provided for the submission to arbitration of "all questions and of all points which have been the subject of correspondence between the two Governments up to the time of the assembling of the Joint High Commission." Beyond this point the American Commissioners would not go. They were anxious, however, to resume consideration of "the several other questions committed to us and confessedly of great importance."[50]

49. Lord Herschell to Senator Fairbanks, February 13, 1899, *ibid.*
50. Senator Fairbanks to Lord Herschell, February 14, 1899, *ibid.*

In his reply Lord Herschell denied that the American Commissioners had received their first intimation of British claim to the headwaters of Lynn Canal when the Joint High Commission opened its meetings in Quebec in August, 1898. In the instructions that Lord Salisbury had given to the British members of the Joint High Commission, July 18, 1898, there was a statement that Her Majesty's Government had a very definite claim to territory around Skagway or Pyramid Harbor. A copy of these instructions had been sent to Secretary Hay on August 1, 1898, and he had acknowledged their receipt in a reply written four days later. On August 30, at the meeting of the Joint High Commission, the matter of the Alaskan boundary had been discussed in detail and

no suggestion was then made that the claim to the upper part of the Lynn Canal . . . was a matter which by the terms of the Protocol was not submitted to us for determination. The matter was referred to a sub-committee, and this particular part of the question was again argued for many hours without any such point being raised. After that the negotiation proceeded on the basis of an endeavor to arrive at an agreement as to the course of the boundary line, and those negotiations related mainly to the boundary in the neighborhood of the Lynn Canal. We maintained that in respect of our territorial claim in that region we ought to possess a port on the Canal, and suggested that if this were not agreed to there should be an arbitration as to the boundary line. The American Commissioners offered us certain rights in ports on the Lynn Canal in consideration of our giving up our territorial claims around a portion of it, which however seemed to be insufficient. . . . In your letter of December 24, 1898, . . . you proposed that we should have Pyramid Harbor with everything but the sovereignty of the soil, all being granted that was "of any commercial or practical value, to wit: port, customs, and transit privileges." Not a suggestion at that time that our claim to a part of the Lynn Canal was not a matter for determination under the terms of the Protocol. The negotiations proceeded for weeks after our return in January, and indeed until Wednesday last, on the same basis. When on that day an agreement seemed impossible and we asked for an arbitration, we were not even then told that a part of our claim was not within the terms of the Protocol; and as late as last Friday . . . the first clause of that proposal contained a formal admission that the territorial line dividing the possessions of the respective Governments was to be ascertained and established as nearly as possible in accordance with . . . the Convention between Russia and Great Britain of 1825. And now, after months of negotiation, chiefly with reference to the part of the boundary line near the Lynn Canal, we are told that this is a matter not within the purview of our negotiations and with which you are therefore not competent to deal with by way of arbitration.

We cannot but feel seriously aggrieved by the course which has been taken. . . . We think we ought in common justice to have been informed at the very outset that this view was to be insisted on, if it is now to be maintained, and not allowed to waste our time in advancing arguments upon a question which after six months we are told was not before the Commission. . . . We are quite unable to concur in your construction of the Protocol. The words are "provisions for the delimitation and establishment of the Alaska-Canadian Boundary." The natural meaning of this is the entire boundary. You seek to limit it to those parts of the boundary as to which there had been actual controversy prior to the Protocol. This seems to be an impossible construction and one which could not have been in the contemplation of the parties, and which we have conclusively shown was not on the 5th of August regarded by the United States Government as having been in their contemplation. So far as we are aware, there had been no controversy in terms between the two Governments as to any specific parts of the boundary, except on the Stikine in 1878 and recently at the top of the pass above Dyea. If your view of the Protocol be correct, it would exclude from treatment the whole of the boundary except at these two points. . . . Great Britain has never placed before the Government of the United States in detail its contention as to the line which the boundary should take, . . . nor has the United States ever submitted to the British Government any complete statement of her claim. . . . We have had no evidence brought before us that since the Treaty of 1825 Russia and the United States have . . . exercised undisputed sovereignty over and possession of the territory now under discussion. . . . The only evidence adduced appears to us to prove the contrary.

. . . What then is to be done when two friendly nations differ as to the construction of a Treaty or as to matter of fact? . . . We know of nothing except to obtain the opinion of a capable tribunal both independent and impartial.[51]

This cogent letter to Senator Fairbanks clearly indicated that Lord Herschell, while anxious to find some compromise that would settle the Alaskan boundary dispute, was not disposed to sacrifice what he considered to be the legitimate claims of Great Britain. In anticipation of an adverse American reply to his suggestions, he had cabled to London to request permission to break off negotiations unless the American Commissioners would agree to submit to arbitration the whole question of the Alaskan boundary. This matter was promptly laid before the British Cabinet, and Lord Herschell's position was sustained. In the event that the American Commissioners accepted arbitration according to the British formula, the British Government was ready to give its assent to Secretary Hay's revision of the Clayton-Bulwer Treaty.[52]

51. Lord Herschell to Senator Fairbanks, February 15, 1899, *ibid.*

52. Henry White to Secretary Hay, February 15, 1899, telegram in cipher, *Great Britain, Despatches,* vol. CXCVI, MS. Dept. of State. See also, Henry White to Secretary Hay, February 17, 1899, *White MS.*

Senator Fairbanks was well aware of the fact that Lord Herschell's letter of February 15 was in the nature of an ultimatum. There would be no talk of further compromise unless the American Commissioners agreed to submit to arbitration the entire boundary line including the question of the possession of the headwaters of Lynn Canal. After talking the matter over with the other American Commissioners, Senator Fairbanks sent to Lord Herschell a letter which he knew would break off further negotiations. He informed the British Commissioners that the American members of the Joint High Commission had not seen Lord Salisbury's instructions until the Commission had met at Quebec. According to their interpretation of the instructions from Secretary Hay, they were to "construe and determine the disagreements of our respective Governments which had engaged their attention prior to the signature of the Protocol of May 30, 1898." British claims to the headwaters of Lynn Canal "had not been presented to the United States prior to the signature of the Protocol," and therefore could not be considered by the Joint High Commission. It was still possible, of course, to "devise a method, or agree upon a Tribunal of Arbitration by which the rights of both Parties may be fairly secured and settled."[53]

In accordance with this suggestion of Senator Fairbanks, the British Commissioners on February 18, 1899, proposed that the question of the Alaskan boundary be submitted to the arbitration of three jurists of repute, one to be chosen by the United States, one by Great Britain, and the third by the two jurists just selected. These judges should be governed by certain prescribed rules.[54] The American Commissioners were willing to accept rules "a" and "b" that had been suggested by the British members of the Joint High Commission, but they insisted upon amending rule "c."[55] This amendment was rejected by the British

53. Senator Fairbanks to Lord Herschell, February 16, 1899, *Alaska Boundary Papers,* MS. Dept. of State.

54. *C.S.P., 1899,* Vol. XXXIII, No. 99. The following rules were proposed by the British Commissioners: "(a) Adverse holding or prescription during a period of fifty years shall make a good title. The arbitrators may deem exclusive political control of a district, as well as actual settlement thereof, sufficient to constitute adverse holding or to make title by prescription. (b) The arbitrators may recognize and give effect to rights and claims resting on any other ground . . . according to international law, and on any principles of international law which the arbitrators may deem to be applicable to the case, and which are not in contravention of the foregoing rule. (c) In determining the boundary line, if territory of one party shall be found by the tribunal to have been at the date of this treaty in the occupation of the subjects or citizens of the other party, such effect shall be given to such occupation as reason, justice, the principles of international law, and the equities of the case shall, in the opinion of the tribunal, require."

55. The American Commissioners wished to have rule "c" amended as follows: "In considering the 'coast' referred to in said treaties, mentioned in Article III, it is understood that the coast of the continent is intended. In determining the boundary

Commissioners, who also went on record as being unalterably opposed to the selection of an umpire from one of the states in the Western Hemisphere. The American Commissioners then proposed an arbitral body consisting of "three jurists on each side, a majority to determine." An arbitral court so organized would eliminate any necessity for a "foreign umpire" who would act in case of a tie vote. Secretary Hay realized the dangers that might attend the employment of an impartial umpire, and he was determined that no such formula should be used in the settlement of the Alaskan boundary dispute. An arbitral body composed of three British members and three American members was more to his liking because he realized that in such an arrangement the United States could not lose. In the fluid condition of existing world politics there was an excellent chance that Canada might be called upon to pay the price of Anglo-American friendship.[56]

On February 20, when it was apparent that no compromise could be reached, the Joint High Commission adjourned until August 2. Three days earlier, Henry White had written to Secretary Hay about the close connection between the decisions of the Commission and the willingness of the British Government to consent to the abrogation of the Clayton-Bulwer Treaty. If the American Commissioners would make any real concessions in order to arrive at an agreement on Canadian questions, Her Majesty's Government would "readily assent" to such modifications of the Clayton-Bulwer Treaty as "shall enable the Nicaragua Canal to be constructed under the auspices of the Government of the United States, either directly at its own cost or otherwise; its regulation and management after construction to be in our hands."[57]

The American Government was not ready to make these concessions even to secure the abrogation of a canal treaty that had long been distasteful to it. The Department of State had high hopes that time was on the side of the United States, and it was willing to postpone the definitive settlement of the Alaskan boundary dispute. In commenting upon the situation, the London *Times* remarked that it was not neces-

line, if territory of one party shall be found by the tribunal to have been at the date of this treaty in the occupation of the subjects or citizens of the other party, such effect shall be given to such occupation as reason, justice, the principles of international law and the equities of the case shall, in the opinion of the tribunal, require; and all towns and settlements on tide water, settled under the authority of the United States and under the jurisdiction of the United States at the date of this treaty, shall remain within the territory and jurisdiction of the United States."

56. Secretary Hay to Henry White, February 18, 1899, cipher telegram, *Great Britain, Despatches,* Vol. CXCVI, MS. Dept. of State. See also, Lionel M. Gelber, *The Rise of Anglo-American Friendship* (London, 1938), pp. 44–45.

57. Henry White to Secretary Hay, February 17, 1899, *Great Britain, Despatches,* Vol. CXCVI, MS. Dept. of State.

sary to assume "that two kindred nations will be in any degree drawn apart because it has been found impossible, for the time being to come to an understanding on a technical and local dispute. . . . Good will and sympathy go far to diminish friction between great peoples, and we are sure that neither here nor in the United States is there any wish to allow a quarrel to arise out of contested rights on the Alaskan border."[58]

Secretary Hay had a surplus of good will for the British Government, but he had scant sympathy for the stand taken by the British members of the Commission. It was his opinion that the American Commissioners had gone to "the very verge of concessions to induce the Canadians to make a treaty." His only explanation of the obstinacy of the Canadian Commissioners was their desire to stand alone "before the Canadian Parliament in the attitude of stout defenders of Canadian rights and interests."[59]

Lord Salisbury's reaction to the failure of the Joint High Commission to arrive at a compromise, is given in the following excerpt from a letter of Henry White to Secretary Hay:

Lord Salisbury seemed hopeful that we might arrange matters by diplomacy before the Commission meets again. Evidently he personally takes no special interest in the points insisted on by the Canadians about the Alaska boundary but is very much interested in our coming to an agreement on all the questions at issue. He said he did not quite understand our aversion to a European umpire, as he could hardly imagine that you would prefer a South American, and if Americans and Canadians were barred as they would be, the former would be the only alternative save a Mexican or a European jurist. I said that no Continental jurist or statesman understood our laws and system of Government, . . . and I thought your hope was to do without an umpire altogether, feeling that the six jurists would settle it, to which he said, "But supposing they don't—and one must provide for that possibility—there must be an umpire unless we toss up and surely neither of us would wish to place ourselves in the hands of a South American." Confidentially

58. February 23, 1899. On February 27, 1899, the London *Times* makes further comments upon the implications of the Alaskan boundary dispute. It regretted that Sir Charles Tupper would go so far as "to advocate a general adoption of measures for the exclusion of aliens the working of which, under the lately passed Act of the British Columbian Legislature has, we are informed, operated to prevent an influx of no less than 10,000 American miners to the Atlin Lake gold-fields this spring. That such a condition of affairs should prevail between two Anglo-Saxon peoples of the North American continent is from every point of view deplorable. . . . To exclude 10,000 Americans with their varied energies . . . from helping to develop a British Columbian goldfield, is a policy . . . which will be viewed with little sympathy in this country. . . . We can comprehend the extremely difficult position in which the representatives of American interests are placed."

59. Secretary Hay to Henry White, February 21, 1899, *White MS.*

(indeed it was all confidential) he added that tossing up would in his opinion be preferable to the latter alternative.[60]

In summing up the situation resulting from the adjournment of the Commission, T. Jefferson Coolidge, one of the American Commissioners, expressed the view that it would be unwise to have the meetings resumed in August. During the seven months that the Commission had lasted, there was not a "single thing in which the Canadians yielded. . . . We have got along under the present conditions for many years, and can probably get along for some years longer until the Canadians realize that a diplomatic compromise means yielding on both sides."[61]

The tragic death of Lord Herschell on March 1, 1899, gave a somber tone to the diplomatic scene in Washington. The Senate of the United States promptly passed a resolution of sympathy which was forwarded to Queen Victoria,[62] but in many American minds there lingered the impression that Herschell's uncompromising spirit had been one of the chief causes for the failure of the Joint High Commission to arrive at some general agreement. The appointment of Chief Justice Sir Charles Russell to succeed Herschell as one of the British Commissioners was not reassuring to some Americans in public life. Russell was known as one of the "sharpest lawyers" that Ireland had ever contributed to the English bar, and it was feared that the sessions of the Joint High Commission would be stormy and fruitless.[63] Sharing this feeling to some extent, Secretary Hay made no attempt to revive the Commission. He was ready to make further efforts to settle the Alaskan boundary dispute by the usual methods of diplomacy. His failure to accomplish this purpose is told in the following chapter.[64]

60. Henry White to Secretary Hay, *Confidential,* February 27, 1899, *ibid.*

61. T. Jefferson Coolidge to Secretary Hay, March 20, 1899, *Alaska Boundary Papers,* MS. Dept. of State.

62. Joseph H. Choate to Secretary Hay, March 23, 1899, *Great Britain, Despatches,* Vol. CXCVI, MS. Dept. of State. In 1899 Choate succeeded John Hay as American Ambassador at London. He remained in that office until the summer of 1905.

63. T. J. Coolidge to Secretary Hay, March 20, 1899, *Alaska Boundary Papers,* MS. Dept. of State.

64. In recounting the failure of the Joint High Commission to arrive at any settlement of the questions at issue between Canada and the United States, Senator Fairbanks made the following remarks to Secretary Hay concerning the Alaskan boundary dispute: "The real and substantial difference is with respect to a harbor at the head of Lynn Canal. There would be no difficulty in agreeing upon a boundary line at all points if a harbor were ceded to the British Government at the head of Lynn Canal. Early recognizing this, the American Commissioners proposed to give the Canadian Government the use of Pyramid Harbor and a strip of territory back of it to the frontier. The criminal and civil laws of Great Britain were to be extended over the territory, and the territory was not to be fortified or made the basis of military

or naval operations. British occupancy was to be limited to fifty years. The present condition of the coast-wise trade on the Pacific Coast was not to be disturbed.

"The British Commissioners demanded practically the perpetual occupancy of the harbor and territory mentioned. They were willing that conditions in the nature of conditions of defeasance, however, should be inserted in the treaty, that is to say, if they failed to maintain peace and order, or ceased to use the territory for the purpose indicated, or should attempt to fortify or use it as a basis of military operations, it would revert to the United States.

"They were unwilling to put any restrictions upon the coast-wise trade, and insisted that the port should, for all purposes of commerce, be an English port. To this we could not agree.

"Failing in an adjustment upon the above basis, some method of determining the boundary by arbitration was attempted. The British Commissioners were willing to adopt the Venezuelan form of arbitration. The American Commissioners felt unable to accept this plan, without amendment or qualification, holding that the two cases were dissimilar, and feeling that if they should so agree, the treaty would be rejected by the Senate. In the Venezuelan case, the Venezuelan Government had protested against British encroachments from the very first, and had repeated its protest at frequent intervals subsequently, while the territory in dispute in Alaska occupied by the United States, was occupied without objection or protest from Great Britain, prior at least to the signature of the Protocol of May 1898. I speak more especially with reference to the territory occupied about the head of Lynn Canal.

"The American Commissioners were willing to submit the boundary in dispute to an arbitral board composed of three eminent jurists upon each side, the decision of four arbitrators to be final. With this exception, and one or two others of form rather than substance, they were willing to adopt the plan of the Venezuelan arbitration. They felt that paragraph 'c' of the rules should be enlarged so that all towns and settlements at tide-water settled under the authority and jurisdiction of the United States should remain within its territory and jurisdiction. Skagway and Dyea had been built by American citizens without a word of objection from the British Government, and it was deemed by us unwise to leave their citizens uncertain as to their fate for two years, or during the period of arbitration, although they would doubtless finally be set over to the United States under the rules of the Venezuelan plan of arbitration.

"The British Commissioners would consent to no modification of the Venezuelan form of arbitration. Being unable to modify our respective views, the British Commissioners deemed it necessary to refer the question to their Government." Senator Fairbanks to Secretary Hay, March 25, 1899, *ibid.*

CHAPTER VIII

PRESIDENT ROOSEVELT RELUCTANTLY AGREES TO A JUDICIAL SETTLEMENT OF THE BOUNDARY DISPUTE

It was the opinion of John W. Foster that the "impartial world" would not justify the "British-Canadian Commissioners in their persistency in breaking off negotiations on account of a failure to agree upon a single question, the Alaskan boundary."[1] To some extent, Secretary Hay and President McKinley shared this same view. In an instruction to Ambassador Choate, Hay remarked that the failure to arrive at an agreement in the matter of the Alaskan boundary was a "source of disappointment and deep regret to the President," who thought it was "most unfortunate that the months of labor and careful study of the various important questions submitted to the Commission should become fruitless because of the determination of the British Commissioners to make the negotiations on all the questions depend upon an adjustment satisfactory to them of a single one." The instruction then concluded with an expression of hope that some arrangement could soon be agreed upon. As an indication of what the State Department desired, Secretary Hay enclosed the draft of a treaty which largely embodied the proposals of the American members of the Joint High Commission.[2]

In a second instruction to Ambassador Choate, Secretary Hay once

1. John W. Foster, *Diplomatic Memoirs* (Boston, 1909), II, 188–189. The members of the Opposition in the Canadian House of Commons were sharply critical of the Laurier Government for not breaking off negotiations with the American Commissioners at the very moment when it was apparent that the Canadian contentions would not be seriously considered by the Joint High Commission. On March 20, 1899, Sir Charles Tupper discussed the adjournment of the sessions of the Joint High Commission, and after referring to the friendly attitude shown by the British Government towards the United States during the Spanish-American War, he remarked: "I felt that if there was anything in the shape of gratitude in the heart of man, it was simply impossible that the United States of America could fail to recognize the deep obligation under which they stood to Great Britain. . . . In my judgment, Her Majesty's Government could have made no happier appointment to the position of leader of the British delegation than that of the late lamented Lord Herschell. . . . So far as we can judge from the statements in the press, . . . the people in Canada have been placed in the most unfortunate position of being humble suppliants at the feet of the people of the United States. . . . The United States . . . must be brought to recognize the fact that they are dealing with a country as great and powerful as they." *Canada: House of Commons, Debates,* 1899, March 20, 1899, I, 40–42, 60.

2. Secretary Hay to Ambassador Choate, April 19, 1899, *Great Britain, Instructions,* XXXIII, MS. Dept. of State.

more referred to the difficulties surrounding any settlement of the Alaskan boundary dispute. The draft treaty which he had enclosed in the instruction of April 19 was founded upon the general arbitration convention of 1897 agreed upon by Secretary Olney and Sir Julian Pauncefote, but it was even more favorable to Great Britain than that treaty which had provided for a court of three judges from each nation, with the proviso that no decision should be final unless agreed to by five arbitrators. In the draft treaty that Hay submitted, the decision could be made by agreement merely between four arbitrators.

In his recital of the efforts he had made to settle the boundary dispute, Hay spoke of the *modus vivendi* he had attempted to arrange with Ambassador Pauncefote. Lord Minto, Governor-General of Canada, had rejected this proposal "on the ground that it gave us more territory than we had a right to claim."[3] This action was deeply regretted by Hay, who was disturbed by the report that the Canadian Mounted Police were encroaching upon American territory "everywhere along the boundary." He was also worried by rumors that many miners who had taken up claims in the disputed territory were in "great anxiety lest they should be ousted from their holdings by the operation of the British Columbia alien acts."

It was quite possible that the situation along the Alaskan boundary might grow worse every hour:

> I do not believe we are asking anything unreasonable, and I am sure if the matter depended on direct negotiations between the United States and England, it would be very speedily and satisfactorily settled, but we were driven to the conclusion before the Conference closed that the Canadians did not wish any settlement; that they preferred the present risky and unsettled state of things to any decision which would leave them open to attack from the Opposition. . . . I do not see that anything is to be gained by calling the Conference together again. . . . Especially . . . should we deprecate the filling of Lord Herschell's place on the Commission by another lawyer, who would come with the intention of making the utmost of his case as an advocate instead of with the purpose of settling the matter in a spirit of mutual fairness and moderation. . . . The Dominion politicians care little for English interests. Their minds are completely occupied with their own party and factional disputes. . . . I hope it may be possible for you in your

3. On March 20, 1899, Secretary Hay had written a note to Sir Julian Pauncefote suggesting that the boundary line at the headwaters of the Lynn Canal be temporarily fixed at "the watershed on the summit of White and Chilkoot passes, and at a point 30 marine miles from Pyramid Harbor on the Chilkat Pass and otherwise known as the Dalton Trail." This suggestion was sent to the Canadian Government and was rejected March 30, 1899, on the ground that the line should be fixed "at the crest of the mountains nearest to the coast." *F. R. 1899,* pp. 321–323.

conversations with Lord Salisbury to cause him to feel the desirability of finding . . . some arrangement of these troubles which . . . are likely at any moment to embitter the relations between our two countries, solely in the interest of warring factions in Canada.[4]

These instructions from Hay moved Ambassador Choate to fresh exertions in the matter of the boundary dispute, and on May 12 he sent a cablegram to the Department of State in which he inquired if the Secretary would agree that the arbitral tribunal should consist of "seven jurists of repute, three on the part of Great Britain, . . . three on the part of the United States, . . . and of a seventh jurist, nominated by the high contracting parties."[5]

In a letter to Secretary Hay in explanation of his telegrams, Ambassador Choate expressed the view that the British contention in favor of a tribunal of five or seven members, was "not unreasonable." There was always a possibility that in a commission composed of an equal number of delegates from each nation, a deadlock would ensue and prevent a decision. In the event that Hay would agree to this new British proposal, Lord Salisbury and Joseph Chamberlain would "do their best to secure the consent of Canada."[6]

As soon as Hay received the cablegrams from Ambassador Choate, he wrote a letter to President McKinley and placed the matter before him. It seemed to Hay that the British proposal was "about as good a one as we can get," and he thought the suggestion of appointing two jurists on a side instead of three was "good." It was to be expected that the Senate would be deeply exercised over the matter of the appointment of the "odd Arbitrator," but as "there are only three ways of settling such questions, by agreement, by arbitration, or by war," there was nothing to do "but to arbitrate it."

With the possibility of an early compromise in mind, Hay thought it would be expedient to postpone the despatch of any American soldiers to Pyramid Harbor. An announcement of this military action had appeared in the press, and had led to a "very strongly worded note of remonstrance" from the British *chargé d'affaires*.[7]

President McKinley was inclined to agree with Secretary Hay with regard to this British proposal, but he suggested the advisability of

4. Secretary Hay to Ambassador Choate, April 28, 1899, *Confidential and Personal, Choate MS.*

5. Ambassador Choate to Secretary Hay, May 12, 1899, *McKinley Papers,* Library of Congress. In second telegram, May 12, 1899, Choate inquired if Hay would agree to a tribunal of five instead of seven members.

6. Ambassador Choate to Secretary Hay, May 12, 1899, *Choate MS.*

7. Secretary Hay to President McKinley, May 13, 1899, *McKinley MS.*

consulting with Secretary Gage and Senator Fairbanks before any action should be taken. If an agreement were reached with reference to the British proposal there would be "no necessity for the soldiers."[8]

In the meantime, on May 13, F. H. Villiers, of the Foreign Office, had informed Ambassador Choate that the British Government had secured Canadian consent to separate the Alaskan boundary dispute from other questions at issue between the two countries. The Canadian Government was willing to have this dispute submitted to arbitration, and it was hoped that the procedure would follow the lines agreed to in the controversy over the boundary of British Guiana.[9] In a letter several days later from Lord Salisbury, Mr. Choate discovered that Canadian consent to arbitration was based upon the condition that if, as a result of an arbitral award, "Pyramid Harbour is found to be within the territory of the United States, it will be and remain within the territory, and under the jurisdiction of Great Britain."[10]

Mr. Choate rejected this condition concerning Pyramid Harbor and was at a "loss to understand" how such a proposal could be advanced by the British Government. It set at naught the whole negotiation with respect to the boundary dispute, and put "an entirely new aspect upon the situation.[11] In his despatch to Secretary Hay, Choate commented upon this "astounding and unreasonable" proposal of Lord Salisbury which he regarded as "utterly inadmissable." He believed that the Canadian Government hoped to capitalize upon the friendly feelings existing between the United States and Great Britain and thus secure a much-coveted port "to which they have no right."[12]

Secretary Hay was in full accord with the spirit of Ambassador Choate's indictment of the British proposal concerning Pyramid Harbor, and he clearly expressed his disapproval of any such bargain.[13] There was no chance for any agreement along those lines.

In a personal letter to Sir Julian Pauncefote, Mr. Choate characterized Lord Salisbury's proposal as an "utterly impossible proposition." He deeply regretted this action on the part of the Foreign Office because Secretary Hay was on the point of accepting the arbitral proposal of May 12.[14] In his letter of reply, Sir Julian indicated his distress at the "failure of our efforts in the matter of the Alaskan Boundary. It only shows how difficult it is to satisfy politicians whose tenure of

8. President McKinley to Secretary Hay, May 14, 1899, *ibid.*
9. F. H. Villiers to Ambassador Choate, May 13, 1899, *A.B.T.*, IV, 124–125.
10. Lord Salisbury to Ambassador Choate, May 17, 1899, *ibid.*, p. 125.
11. Ambassador Choate to Lord Salisbury, May 19, 1899, *ibid.*, pp. 127–128.
12. Ambassador Choate to Secretary Hay, May 19, 1899, *Choate MS.*
13. Ambassador Choate to Lord Salisbury, May 20, 1899, *ibid.*
14. Ambassador Choate to Sir Julian Pauncefote, May 20, 1899, *ibid.*

office is at stake." The Canadians knew "quite well that under the terms of the Rules laid down in the Anglo-Venezuelan Treaty, it is quite certain that Dyea and Skagway must be and remain American territory; but they dare not put it in the Treaty in so many words as it looks as a concession granted without an equivalent." Sir Julian then suggested a new version of rules of procedure which treated "both Parties exactly alike and at the same time secures beyond any doubt that Dyea and Skagway will in any case be confirmed to the U. S."[15]

Before Secretary Hay received this letter from Sir Julian Pauncefote, he wrote a long personal letter to Ambassador Choate which reflected his chagrin and annoyance at the stand taken by Lord Salisbury. To insist upon a cession of Pyramid Harbor as a

> condition to arbitration seemed merely derisory. . . . Dyea and Skagway are American Towns, in territory occupied and developed by Americans, never claimed or thought of as British territory until last year, while Pyramid Harbor is more than thirty miles within the frontier which we have always claimed and has never been occupied by the Canadians. The simple fact is that the whole Canadian claim was invented about a year ago for the purpose of getting a foothold on the ocean, the result of which would be to cut off southeastern Alaska from the rest of the Territory.
>
> . . . A regrettable consequence of this failure of our negotiations as to Canada is the fact that it carries with it a failure of our convention as to the Clayton-Bulwer treaty. Of course it is absurdly illogical to make the one depend upon the other. Both our Governments are agreed that the modification of the treaty is demanded not only for our advantage but the advantage of all commercial nations and of England especially, . . . and yet Lord Salisbury informed Mr. White . . . that . . . he would not care to go before Parliament with a convention modifying the Clayton-Bulwer treaty unless at the same time he was able to announce the settlement of all matters in which Canada was concerned.
>
> The attitude of Canada as to such matters makes the whole affair hopeless. After a careful observation of two years I am convinced that the Canadians prefer that nothing shall be settled between the two countries. Sir Wilfrid Laurier and the Liberals . . . found it easier to sustain themselves as stalwart defenders of Canadian rights and interests against Yankee encroachments than it would be to have the job of justifying a reasonable treaty. . . . I cannot at this moment look forward in any hopeful spirit to a renewal of our negotiations.[16]

Five days later, Secretary Hay sent a cablegram to Ambassador Choate which stated that American officials in Alaska were making

15. Sir Julian Pauncefote to Ambassador Choate, May 22, 1899, *ibid.*

16. Secretary Hay to Ambassador Choate, May 22, 1899, *Private and Confidential, Choate MS.*

"constant complaints" about Canadian encroachments on American soil. He was of the opinion that some *modus vivendi* was "imperatively required." As a provisional boundary he suggested the summits of White and Chilkoot Passes, and on the Dalton Trail a line passing north of the Indian village of Klukwan.[17] In commenting upon the situation, Hay informed Henry White, in London, that he was having "considerable trouble" in the negotiations concerning the Alaskan boundary. Mr. Choate's management of affairs was "admirable," but the Canadian "spoiled child" was upsetting the American apple cart.[18]

On June 6, Choate sent a cablegram to Secretary Hay to the effect that the British Foreign Office was willing to agree to a provisional boundary line along the summits of the White and Chilkoot Passes and on the Dalton Trail at a line north of the village of Klukwan. In addition, however, the Foreign Office wished this line to run "south of the junction of the Tlehini with the Chilcat." Hay accepted this arrangement with certain reservations.[19]

When Ambassador Choate presented this instruction to Lord Salisbury he was assured that "there could be little doubt" of its acceptance. The British Colonial Secretary had cabled to the Canadian Government for its assent to the *modus vivendi*, and it appeared as though the matter would soon be satisfactorily arranged. But this reference of even the "minutest details" to the Canadian Government was bound to produce some delay in the negotiations. In order to expedite matters as much as possible, Joseph Chamberlain had cabled to Ottawa and suggested that some expert be sent to London as a consultant with regard to the Alaskan boundary.

As a result of these conversations with Lord Salisbury, Mr. Choate had received a

strong impression that the British Government do not have much faith in the Canadian claim, and think that we should be so safe under any form of arbitration that they rather wonder at our being unwilling to accept the Venezuelan form. I told him, however, that he was mistaken if he thought that was open for consideration—that it had been so emphatically rejected that it was of no use to discuss it. . . . I told him most emphatically that under no circumstances would that form be accepted by us. I then reiterated the grounds of our objection to that form of treaty as applicable to this case—its subject-

17. Secretary Hay to Ambassador Choate, May 27, 1899, *Great Britain, Instructions*, XXXIII, MS. Dept. of State.

18. Secretary Hay to Henry White, May 29, 1899, *White MS.*

19. Secretary Hay to Ambassador Choate, June 9, 1899, *Great Britain, Instructions*, XXXIII, MS. Dept. of State. It is worth while to note that Hay often refers to the *Tlehini* River, whereas the proper name was the *Klehini* River.

ing Skagway and Dyea to peril, and the wide and absolute difference between the two cases.[20]

To John Hay the Canadian contention was much like that of a kidnapper who stole one of your children and then remarked that "his conduct was more than fair, it was even generous, because he left you two." If the British Foreign Office continued to support the Canadian proposal as to Pyramid Harbor, there was "little room for negotiation or for argument."[21]

On June 23 Ambassador Choate sent a cablegram to the Department of State which conveyed Canadian objections to a line on the Dalton Trail passing north of the Indian village of Klukwan. The Canadian Government wished the boundary to run *south* of Klukwan.[22] Upon the receipt of this cablegram, Secretary Hay wrote a note to John W. Foster and expressed the view that the Canadian Government could not make up its mind with regard to the boundary along the Dalton Trail. The Department of State had decided that it would be unwise to give the Canadians

> another inch of concession on the Dalton Trail. Our proposition was a perfectly fair one—the South line of the Tlehini from its junction with the Chilkat to where it crossed the Dalton Trail. The only reason they rejected it and proposed another line was their desire to get the miners in the Porcupine district south of the Tlehini under their control, but it seems to me that their policy is as stupid as it is uncandid. It would be no advantage to them whatever to have an opportunity to harry and persecute those American miners, and it would cost them a great deal more than it would come to.[23]

As the excitement among the miners in the Porcupine district continued to increase, Hay sent a terse telegram to Choate: "I do not wish you to assume tone of ultimatum, but British Government should understand that we cannot recede from line of Tlehini as proposed."[24]

20. Ambassador Choate to Secretary Hay, June 16, 1899, *Choate MS.* On June 14, 1899, Secretary Hay wrote to John W. Foster: "There is a great mystery about the state of the *modus.* We were within a few inches of an agreement a week ago. I made a suggestion for a very slight modification . . . to which I thought no possible objection could be made, but a week has passed by, and . . . not a word has yet come from Mr. Choate." *Foster MS.*

21. Secretary Hay to Ambassador Choate, June 15, 1899, Thayer, *op. cit.,* II, 206-207; Dennett, *Hay,* p. 232.

22. Ambassador Choate to Secretary Hay, June 23, 1899, *Alaskan Boundary, Miscellaneous Archives,* MS. Dept. of State.

23. Secretary Hay to John W. Foster, July 5, 1899, *John W. Foster Papers,* Library of Congress.

24. Secretary Hay to Ambassador Choate, July 6, 1899, *McKinley MS.*

Choate replied that Sir Julian Pauncefote believed the Canadian Government would have to yield "in respect to the *modus vivendi*, making the Tlehini River the provisional line." Lord Salisbury was somewhat optimistic and expressed the view that there was no danger of an "outbreak" in the Porcupine district, and that the Canadians "did not intend to interfere with American miners." Choate himself, looked upon the situation as "not discouraging."[25]

In the face of continuing unrest in the Porcupine district with resulting friction between the United States and Canada, the British Government proposed to Ambassador Choate that the United States grant to Canada a perpetual lease of territory consisting of half a square mile at a suitable spot on the Lynn Canal on conditions similar to those on which territory was held by the British Government on the right bank of the Chinde River in the Portuguese province of Mozambique, Africa.[26] When Mr. Choate raised a question about the use of the word "perpetual" in connection with the proposed lease, Lord Salisbury indicated that the Chinde concession was for ninety-nine years. The British also wished to have the right to construct and have exclusive control over a railway line that should be connected with the concession, and this line should "not be interfered with by the United States."[27]

In a cablegram of July 20 Choate inquired whether some scheme similar to the Chinde concession could "afford basis for settlement of boundary question."[28] Secretary Hay referred this matter to Alvey A. Adee for consideration, and Mr. Adee wrote an undated memorandum

25. Ambassador Choate to Secretary Hay, July 15, 1899, *Choate MS.* On July 7, Secretary Hay wrote to Mr. Foster to inform him that no word had been received from Lord Salisbury. When it came a copy would be sent to Mr. Foster who could take such action as he thought proper. The British Government was "so much in the habit of taking their time about such matters that we need not be in any particular hurry in answering this communication." *Foster MS.*

26. Ambassador Choate to Secretary Hay, July 18, 1899, *McKinley MS.*

27. Ambassador Choate to Secretary Hay, July 19, 1899, *Alaska Boundary Papers,* MS. Dept. of State. In his letter of July 19 Choate enclosed a copy of the Chinde concession. The land so leased was to be "used exclusively for the purposes of landing, storage, and transshipment of goods, and for such purposes as may be considered subsidiary thereto; and that the only permanent residents shall be, besides British Consular officials, their families and servants, or the persons employed in the charge, and for the security of such goods." It is important to note that in this despatch of July 19, 1899, Mr. Choate makes a mistake and inadvertently stated that the British Government wished a "block on Lynn Canal half a mile square." What the British Government desired, and what Mr. Choate himself said in his telegram of July 18, was that the British Government wished an area of "half a square mile" on the Lynn Canal. It is obvious that "half a square mile" is twice the area of "half a mile square." Needless to say, the British Government wished to lease the larger area.

28. Ambassador Choate to Secretary Hay, July 20, 1899, *ibid.*

which contained a warning against giving to Canada any concessions that would "change the state of the commerce of Alaska to the great injury of the Pacific States."[29]

While the matter of the Chinde concession was under consideration, Secretary Hay once more outlined his objections to referring the Alaskan boundary dispute to arbitration in accordance with the procedure established by the Venezuelan boundary arbitration. He endeavored to make it very clear that the two boundary controversies were so "radically dissimilar" that it was unwise to push any comparison too far. The Alaskan boundary dispute was a "new question" raised for the first time after the organization of the Joint High Commission. In the case of the Venezuelan boundary controversy the line had been the subject of discussion for more than fifty years. The Government of the United States could easily assert that "Great Britain was estopped at this late day . . . from setting up any claim whatever to the territory or waters in question," but the President might be disposed to consider a submission of the claim of Great Britain to arbitration if the towns, settlements and industries established before this new British claim was made should be "expressly excepted from the arbitration."[30]

Four days later, Hay sent an instruction to Ambassador Choate in which he outlined a temporary boundary line at the headwaters of the

29. This memorandum reads in part as follows: "The subject of the lease of a port on the Lynn Canal was discussed at great length in the sessions of the Joint High Commission. The points of difference of most importance were two in number—First: The British Commissioners asked for a perpetual lease; the Americans refused this, but offered a lease for fifty years. Second: The British designed to make it exclusively a British port; this would prevent American vessels from carrying goods from British ports, such as Victoria and Vancouver, to the leased port; and would permit British vessels to carry goods from San Francisco, Seattle and other American ports to the leased port. The Americans insisted that the lease should not change the existing conditions of the carrying trade to and from the Lynn Canal. . . . If the Portuguese lease is correctly epitomized in Mr. Choate's cablegram, it would be safe to apply its terms to the half a square mile now asked for in the British proposition, coupled with the right to construct and operate a railroad through American territory from the leased land to British territory in the Yukon district. . . . But it is believed it will be found that in addition to asking for a perpetual lease, the Canadians will insist upon making the land an exclusively British port, ruled only by British laws and authority; and in place of a right to construct a railway over American territory, they will ask for a perpetual lease of a strip of territory leading from the leased port to the Yukon district, thus separating the territory of Alaska into two parts. . . . The United States should go to great lengths to maintain peace and friendship with Great Britain and bring about a better understanding with Canada, but it should not do it by a surrender under such conditions of its territory as a perpetual lease would virtually be; nor should a lease be made upon such conditions as will change the state of the commerce of Alaska to the great injury of the Pacific States." *Alaskan Boundary, Miscellaneous Archives, 1899–1903,* MS. Dept. of State.

30. Secretary Hay to Ambassador Choate, July 20, 1899, *Great Britain, Instructions,* XXXIII, MS. Dept. of State.

Lynn Canal.[31] Although this line would give the United States a "little more ground" than had previously been asked, it appeared to be the "best settlement possible from the point of view of equity and topography."[32]

Shortly after Hay had sent this instruction to Choate, he received a letter from John W. Foster concerning the Chinde concession. Foster thought this matter required "very serious consideration," and was "preferable to arbitration," but the American Government should limit the lease to a period of 99 years and insist upon protecting our "coastline trade."[33]

Hay shared Foster's apprehensions concerning arbitration. In a letter to Whitelaw Reid he expressed the view that if the Alaskan boundary dispute were submitted to an arbitral body, even though "our claim is as clear as the sun in Heaven, we know enough of arbitrations to foresee the fatal tendency of all arbitrators to compromise."[34]

With these fears in mind Hay wrote to President McKinley and suggested the acceptance of some arrangement along the lines of the Chinde concession. He realized that a "great many people will object to any arrangement we can possibly make with England," but Hay thought that this was a "chance not to be thrown away."[35]

In a letter to Secretary Gage, Hay expressed the same thought,[36]

31. This suggested line started "from the Peak number 6500, runs in a northeasterly direction across the Tlehini River and to Peak numbered 5025; thence to the junction of the Tlehini and Chilkat, and thence across the valley to 5490." See Sheets 17–18, *A.B.T., Atlas of Award.*

32. Secretary Hay to Ambassador Choate, July 24, 1899, *Great Britain, Instructions,* XXXIII, MS. Dept. of State. In a *memorandum* preserved in the archives of the Department of State, there is the following illustrative comment upon Hay's proposal: "The Secretary of State proposed the junction of the Chilkat and Klehini rivers as a convenient point for a temporary dividing line between the American and British jurisdictions, . . . and as the thoroughfare through that region is the Dalton trail, he thought it expedient to mark the point on that trail where it crosses the river. The British Government has shown with great force that this latter point is too vague. . . . They therefore proposed a line across the valley from certain mountains lying to the southwest through the junction of the Chilkat and the Klehini to the mountains on the northeast; but this threw under British jurisdiction a large number of Americans who are at work along the banks of Porcupine Creek. . . . There is no line to the south Klehini but will violate the very intention of the entire negotiation by placing a large number of Americans under Canadian jurisdiction. . . . There is, therefore, no other alternative than to take the most convenient series of hills on the north of the Klehini and draw the line through them, and through the junction of the Chilkat and Klehini, and thence to the range on the east." MS. Dept. of State.

33. John W. Foster to Secretary Hay, July 25, 1899, *Alaskan Boundary, Miscellaneous Archives,* MS. Dept. of State.

34. Secretary Hay to Whitelaw Reid, July 27, 1899, Thayer, *op. cit.,* II, 207.

35. Secretary Hay to President McKinley, July 29, 1899, *McKinley MS.*

36. Secretary Hay to Secretary Lyman J. Gage, July 29, 1899, *Alaska Boundary Papers,* MS. Dept. of State.

but Gage believed it was important to include in the proposed lease an express stipulation to the effect that

> the citizens of the United States, during the existence of the lease, should have the right of ingress and egress to and from the Northwest Territory in the province of British Columbia under the same terms, conditions, and restrictions as are or may be enjoyed by the subjects of Her Britannic Majesty; that, subject to the lease relating thereto, citizens of the United States may enter mining claims, acquire titles to the same or any other form of landed or personal property, and may be allowed to prosecute generally any kind of business lawful to British subjects in the territory and province above named.[37]

Senator Cushman K. Davis, chairman of the Senate Committee on Foreign Relations, was even more solicitous about inserting protective clauses in any lease agreement with the British Government. As a proposition *de novo*, he would be extremely

> reluctant to make the concessions indicated. I have pored over the description of the line of demarcation in the treaty with Russia many times and I feel perfectly clear that none of the various constructions which have been given to it by England, or rather by Canada, have the slightest foundation. . . . I greatly fear that if we open the door just little enough to let the foot of England into this territory and coast we shall have trouble in keeping her whole body out hereafter. . . . Any treaty with such concessions will be opposed in the Senate by the same political influences which resisted the ratification of the treaty for the annexation of Hawaii and the treaty of peace with Spain. . . . It might be advised and consented to by the Senate, but not this year or the next year. . . . Sir W. Laurier's declaration for arbitration or war was very ill-timed and unfortunate. It is regarded here as a threat to compel arbitration.[38]

In his answer to Senator Davis, Hay spoke of the "utter baselessness of the Canadian claim to Alaska." He was certain that no impartial court would entertain it, but where could one find an "impartial court"? The American Government was so "sure" of its case that it was not "willing to put it in jeopardy before some chance arbitration." There was no course left, therefore, but to make "a lease arrangement."[39]

A long draft of this proposed lease arrangement was sent to Secre-

37. Secretary Gage to Secretary Hay, August 1, 1899, *ibid.* Gage served as Secretary of the Treasury from 1897 to 1902.

38. Senator C. K. Davis to Secretary Hay, July 31, 1899, *Choate MS.*

39. Secretary Hay to Senator C. K. Davis, August 4, 1899, Dennett, *op. cit.*, pp. 235–236.

tary Hay by John A. Kasson. Kasson would have the lease made out to a person rather than to a Government, and he would have an express provision to take care of American coastwise shipping. It should also be provided that the railway projected by the British Government should transport the goods and merchandise of American citizens "on equal terms" and "at the same rates with those granted to the most favored subjects of Her Britannic Majesty." But before this lease should be executed the British Government should offer some fair settlement of the Alaskan boundary dispute.[40]

Before receiving this letter from Mr. Kasson, Secretary Hay had written to the President in a pessimistic vein concerning the feasibility of the lease arrangement. He had just heard from Whitelaw Reid, of the New York *Tribune*, who threatened opposition to any such measure. Reid had just heard of Root's appointment as Secretary of War, and his jealousy had made him "simply frantic." There was no way of estimating the importance of Reid's opposition.[41]

Choate, in London, still hoped that the lease would meet with favor in the United States, and he believed that such an arrangement "would be mutually satisfactory to both countries."[42] While waiting for definite news from the Department of State, he wrote a long letter to Lord Salisbury in which he reviewed many aspects of the Alaskan boundary dispute and frankly stated that President McKinley was of the opinion that the procedure followed in the Venezuelan boundary arbitration was "wholly inapplicable to the present subject of controversy."[43]

Hay, in the meantime, was growing increasingly worried over the situation. He had fled from the heat of Washington to his summer home in Newbury, New Hampshire, but he became fearful of the consequences of inaction and decided to pay a hurried visit to the White House and talk things over with the President.[44] After his return to Newbury, he wrote a long letter to Ambassador Choate. Although he was absolutely

40. John A. Kasson to Secretary Hay, August 4, 1899, *Alaska Boundary Papers*, MS. Dept. of State. Article I of the Kasson project provides that "the use of said leased land and wharves at Pyramid Harbor is limited to the landing, storage and transshipment of goods, wares and merchandise destined to or arriving from the territory of Canada." Article II—"An annual rent of one thousand dollars shall be paid by the Lessee to the Collector of Customs of the United States for the district embracing Pyramid Harbor." VII—"The sovereignty of the United States and the jurisdiction of its laws are continued over said leased property." VIII—"This Lease is not to be construed as in any way modifying or affecting any provisions of law or treaty regulating the coasting trade of the respective countries as hitherto existing."

41. Secretary Hay to President McKinley, August 4, 1899, *McKinley MS.*

42. Ambassador Choate to Secretary Hay, August 4, 1899, *Choate MS.*

43. Ambassador Choate to Lord Salisbury, August 9, 1899, *A.B.T.*, IV, 129–132.

44. Secretary Hay to President McKinley, August 10, 1899, *McKinley MS.*

certain of the justice of American claims in Alaska, he knew that an arbitral body has a strong tendency to compromise the issues before it. If the question of the control over the headwaters of the Lynn Canal was submitted to arbitration he was very much afraid that the Canadians would secure a "foothold on the coast." It was for this reason that he had received with much pleasure the "suggestion of the lease of a bit of ground and a right-of-way for a railroad" which Lord Salisbury had made. The President and Cabinet had agreed that if the details could be satisfactorily arranged it would be a "reasonable solution" of the matter. But Senator Davis, of the Senate Committee on Foreign Relations, had expressed disapproval of some features of the lease arrangement and had voiced the belief that it could not pass the Senate. A defeat in the Senate with regard to the lease might have an adverse effect upon the elections of 1900 and pave the way for Bryan's accession to the Presidency. Such a contingency was so fearful to contemplate that caution became a necessity and watchful waiting a line of policy to be followed.[45]

45. Secretary Hay to Ambassador Choate, August 18, 1899, *Choate MS*. This letter was printed in Dennett's *Hay* (pp. 236–237) in such a garbled form that it is probably worth while to reproduce certain paragraphs of it. After adverting to the lease arrangement, Hay said: "I thought it prudent to invite some expression of opinion from the leading members of the Committee on Foreign Relations of the Senate as to the probability of such an arrangement passing the Senate. To my great chagrin I received the enclosed letter from Senator Davis. . . . The Democratic Press evidently thinks there is some political capital to be made by denouncing any arrangement with England and they, in common with a large number of German newspapers, are ready to attack any treaty with England, no matter how advantageous to us, as a hostile act towards Ireland and Germany. The Democratic Convention of Iowa has adopted . . . resolutions in this sense, which seem too ridiculous to treat seriously; but all these senseless charges indicate the intention of the opposition to make a party matter of our relations with England, and to oppose any treaty we may make with that country. . . .

"It is for these reasons that I have sent you the instruction you will receive by the same mail as this letter. I think it may be as well if you do not accelerate the progress of your negotiation for a few weeks. You can do little or nothing, in any case, during the summer and early autumn. By that time we shall get fuller and more accurate information in regard to the possibilities in the Senate. . . . In regard to the *modus vivendi,* I do not feel the situation is now critical. The season is drawing to a close, and the danger of collisions is growing constantly less. I do not think we can afford to recede an inch south of the Klehini River. The British have shown . . . that the river forms a most unsatisfactory boundary. This we admit, and propose a simple and satisfactory one which brings us . . . a little north of the River, but still on ground clearly our own, and occupied exclusively by our people. If they reject this reasonable and definite line, we are ready to adopt the inconvenient line of the River, provided always that the valley of Porcupine Creek shall remain in our jurisdiction. If they do not accept this, our consciences are at rest, and we shall go on as we are, on the Dalton Trail, and if the Canadian police come too far south, we will do what we can with the case when it comes up."

In a letter to President McKinley, Hay makes similar comments. The Chief Executive, the Cabinet, Ambassador Choate, John W. Foster, John A. Kasson, Senator Fairbanks and Senator Morgan were all agreed that the lease agreement at Pyramid Harbor was "preferable to the probable result of any arbitration." But Senator Davis said that it could not pass the Senate; the German press would be sharply hostile, and even a stanch Republican like Whitelaw Reid had threatened open opposition. It was difficult to determine whether to go ahead with the lease arrangement and defy opposition, or "drop the negotiations and resume our old relations of simmering hostility with England, with all this implies in Canada, Nicaragua, China and elsewhere." It was a "painful and humiliating state of things," but there was no escape from it "since the Fathers in their wisdom chose to assume that one third of the Senate in opposition would always be right, and the President and the Majority generally wrong."[46]

Under directions from Secretary Hay, Mr. Adee sent an instruction to Ambassador Choate informing him that the lease arrangement was receiving from the President "the serious consideration which its importance requires." In this connection it was essential to know whether the acceptance of this arrangement would "bring about the permanent settlement of the Alaskan boundary according to the American interpretation of the Treaty of 1825."[47]

While this instruction was on its way to England, efforts were being made by Joseph Chamberlain to effect some provisional settlement of the boundary at the headwaters of the Lynn Canal. On August 3 Secretary Hay had proposed to the British Government alternative proposals concerning this provisional boundary: "(1) The line to be drawn from the peak west of Porcupine Creek marked 6500, across the Klehini River to the peak 5025, and thence to the junction of the Chilkat and Klehini rivers. (2) The line to be drawn from 6500 in the direction of 5025, but to stop at the Klehini and follow its course to its junction with the Chilkat; thence to the summit of the peak 5490."

On August 9 Mr. Chamberlain cabled to Lord Minto, in Ottawa, and expressed the opinion that Secretary Hay's second proposal should be "accepted."[48] When this matter was turned over to Mr. W. F. King, the Canadian Chief Astronomer, he remarked that this second proposal would give Canada "a little more territory than the first, but is open to

46. Secretary Hay to President McKinley, August 19, 1899, *McKinley MS.*
47. Acting Secretary A. A. Adee to Ambassador Choate, August 21, 1899, *Great Britain, Instructions,* XXXIII, MS. Dept. of State.
48. Joseph Chamberlain to Lord Minto, August 9, 1899, *Laurier MS.* P.A.C.

the objection of the undefinable river boundary. By either proposition the United States would get more territory than they asked for last time. Evidently they want the south bank of the Klehini, and apparently no settlement will be made unless they get it."[49]

In reply to Mr. Chamberlain's cablegram, Lord Minto said that the Canadian Government would agree to this second proposal subject to a slight modification.[50] Although willing to agree to this provisional line, the Prime Minister and his Cabinet were anxious for "immediate reference to arbitration of permanent boundary."[51]

This decision of the Canadian Government was conveyed to Secretary Hay in a note from the British *chargé d'affaires* on August 27, 1899.[52] After carefully considering this Canadian modification, Secretary Hay indicated his acceptance of it in a note to the British *chargé*. In this communication Hay set forth in express terms the new provisional boundary.[53] On the following day the British *chargé d'affaires* acknowledged receipt of this note from Secretary Hay and assured him that he would convey this "gratifying intelligence" to Lord Salisbury.[54]

News of Secretary Hay's conciliatory note was immediately broadcasted in the American press. In the New York *Times* the statement was made that

49. *Memorandum* of W. F. King, August 11, 1899, *ibid.*

50. This proposed modification was that the boundary line, instead of following the course of the Klehini should follow "high bank of same," because the course of the river shifted from year to year "on account of gravelly bottom."

51. Lord Minto to Mr. Chamberlain, August 16, 1899, *ibid.*

52. Reginald Tower, British *chargé d'affaires,* to Secretary Hay, August 27, 1899, *F. R., 1899,* pp. 324–325.

53. Secretary Hay to Reginald Tower, September 6, 1899, *ibid.,* pp. 325–326. The formula proposed by Secretary Hay reads as follows: "It shall be agreed between the Governments of the United States and Great Britain that the boundary line between Canada and Territory of Alaska in the region about the head of Lynn Canal shall be provisionally fixed without prejudice to the claims of either party in the permanent adjustment of the international boundary. In the region of the Dalton trail, a line beginning at the peak west of Porcupine Creek, marked . . . with the number 6500; thence running to the Klehini River in the direction of the peak north of that river marked 5020; . . . thence following the high bank of the Klehini River to the junction thereof with the Chilkat River, a mile and a half, more or less, north of Klukwan, provided that this line shall be so drawn as to permit the free ingress and egress of American citizens to and from the valley of the Porcupine Creek; and from said junction to the summit of the peak east of the Chilkat River marked on the aforesaid maps 5490. On the Dyea and Skagway trails, the summits of the Chilkoot and White passes. . . . The Government of the United States will at once appoint commissioners, in conjunction with commissioners to be named by the Government of her Britannic Majesty, to mark the temporary line thus agreed upon by the erection of appropriate monuments." In fixing this line Secretary Hay had constant reference to map No. 10, of the United States Commission, December 31, 1895, and map No. 5, Department of the Interior, Ottawa, March 1898.

54. Reginald Tower to Secretary Hay, September 7, 1899, *F. R., 1899,* p. 326.

the Washington and British Governments have about reached a practical agreement upon a basis of settlement, for a time, of the boundary between Alaska and the British possessions. The *modus vivendi* expected to be adopted . . . contemplates the abandonment by Great Britain of the demand for a free port on the Lynn Canal, pending final adjustment of the controversy. . . . Klukwan, which has acquired unexpected importance in the eyes of Canada and the United States since Canada manifested a determination to include it in British territory, will remain under the flag and jurisdiction of the United States. . . . The reassembling of the joint commission will not, it is intimated, be hastened, and will not be suggested for a definite date until it has been informally agreed that its next meeting will be held to permanently adjust the boundary question. The temptation offered or to be offered to Great Britain is a free port on the Lynn Canal under conditions entirely satisfactory to the United States![55]

After this news had circulated in the American press, Secretary Hay wrote to Henry White and gave him a brief résumé of the situation:[56]

So far as Tower and I are concerned the *modus vivendi* on the Alaskan boundary is settled. . . . I shall be savagely attacked on the Pacific Coast, . . . but the fact remains we have done very well indeed. Naturally we have not yet got the line so far north as we claim we own, but on the other hand we have pushed the Canadians back fifteen miles from tide water, and by drawing the line north of Klukwan we have got them even away from canoe navigation. A few of our miners will be found outside of the line, but we insist on equitable treatment for them, and they ought all to be very grateful —though they won't be.

I can see no immediate prospect of our agreeing on the permanent boundary. There is a dull malignant feeling of opposition in the Senate to any arrangement, which I am afraid would be sure to carry one third of the votes.[57]

If Secretary Hay had known of the sentiments of certain important Canadians relative to the Alaskan boundary he would have been even more pessimistic concerning any early settlement of the issue. In a report to the Governor-General of Canada, David Mills, Minister of Justice, took the following uncompromising stand:

The Government of Canada have, on more than one occasion, sought to have a delimitation of this boundary, in accordance with the provisions of the Treaty, but to this the United States were not ready to assent, and they can

55. New York *Times,* September 7, 1899.

56. A badly garbled edition of this letter was published in A. L. P. Dennis, *Adventures in American Diplomacy,* pp. 151–152.

57. Secretary Hay to Henry White, September 9, 1899, *White MS.;* Nevins, *White,* p. 49.

hardly now set up a claim to territories that belong to Canada, because they have for a time occupied them after having refused a quarter of a century ago to join in the work, declaring because the territory was unoccupied . . . the survey of the boundary was unnecessary. . . . It is stated . . . that the coast line including the inlets had been under Russian control down to 1867, and since then under the control of the United States. The accuracy of this statement is not admitted by Canada. In 1825 the boundary was agreed upon between the Governments of Great Britain and Russia. The entire coast was unoccupied. . . . The Canadian Government deny that the Government of Russia . . . maintained its claim to a strip of land 30 miles in width on the mainland of the continent. . . . The Treaty gave to Russia no portion of the mainland south of the 56th degree of north latitude. It gave to the Russian Government nothing . . . behind the crest of the mountains which are nearest to the coast.[58]

Even the relatively unimportant matter of the provisional boundary north of Klukwan seemed to be difficult to settle because of the great amount of time that the Prime Minister and the British Cabinet had to expend on the numberless details arising out of the conduct of the war against the Boers. Owing to this situation, Ambassador Choate thought that the American Government must be prepared for "some further delays" in arriving at any adjustment of the Alaskan boundary dispute.[59] Two days later, however, Lord Salisbury asked Choate a point-blank question as to the "exact definition of boundary according to American interpretation of the treaty, especially about Lynn Canal."[60]

Secretary Hay took no immediate action with reference to this in-

58. David Mills to the Governor-General, September 18, 1899, *Laurier MS.*, P.A.C. On August 14, 1899, Mills had expressed much the same view in an interview with a correspondent of the Chicago *Tribune*. On that occasion he had remarked as follows: "It is too clear to require argument that the limitary line was to follow the coast range and the summit of that coast range, whether high or low was to be the boundary, when it was not more than ten leagues from the coast. In many places inlets extend through canyons through the mountains, and so much of each of those inlets as would be cut off, by a line drawn from the summit of the mountain upon the one side, to the summit of the mountain upon the other, is Canadian territory. The line cannot be removed further inland, because there may be a gap in the mountains into which an arm of the sea extends. The coast range approaches these inlets on each side, in most cases, near the waters of the ocean. When you pass the Lynn Inlet, it will be found that the coast range embraces peaks from 10,000 to 18,000 feet high, and it does seem to me preposterous to contend that the provisions of the treaty can be applied by drawing a line in the rear of those mountains, as certainly would be done, if the boundary passed around the head of Lynn Inlet. It is, I think, manifest that the framers of the treaty assumed, that harbours, inlets, and arms of the sea, would be found, when the boundary was drawn, within British territory, and certain provisions of the treaty were entered into upon this assumption." *A.B.T.*, IV, 206.

59. Ambassador Choate to Secretary Hay, September 20, 1899, *Choate MS.*

60. Alvey A. Adee, Acting Secretary of State, to President McKinley, September 23, 1899, *McKinley MS.*

quiry. He had been busy with political matters. The Democrats of Ohio had made a charge that Secretary Hay had negotiated a secret treaty between England and the United States, and an effective answer to this canard had to be written. With regard to the proposed *modus vivendi* with Great Britain concerning the territory around the Lynn Canal it must have been apparent to White that Canada had

> squabbled for every inch they could beat out of us, . . . but if it goes through with my conditions I am sure we have done very well. . . . We shall be savagely attacked by the Bryanites, . . . but that is all in the day's work. I am not perfectly sure the thing is settled. Canada may object to my claiming access to Porcupine Creek and still more to my insisting on fair treatment of our miners who may find themselves on the wrong side of the provisional line. If they do, the *modus* fails. I shall not yield either of these points. Laurier has just been making a most injudicious speech.[61]

Hay still retained some hope that the lease arrangement at Pyramid Harbor might be perfected and pushed through the Senate if Senator Davis would throw his influence behind such a move. With this idea in mind, Hay wrote to John W. Foster and asked him to talk things over with Davis and try to win his support of such a project.[62] Apparently, Senator Davis was none too responsive to the arguments of Mr. Foster, and Secretary Hay discovered that he could not rely upon strong support from that quarter.

As a matter of fact he could not rely upon the Canadian Government for support of the lease arrangement unless he was willing to make further concessions. In a conversation with F. H. Villiers, at the British Foreign Office, Henry White found out that the Canadian Government had sent Sir Louis Davies to London to serve as an expert upon Canadian matters. When the Foreign Office had talked the situation over with this Canadian representative it was suddenly made clear that

> the proposed lease as suggested by Lord Salisbury did not quite meet their requirements. I [Henry White] inquired what they want now and he [Villiers] replied "more than they will get," but at the same time he thought it might be possible for us to accede in part to what they want. He did not vouchsafe further particulars, and in view of our present situation I did not press him, thinking it better to let the matter come out in the form of a note to Mr. Choate and in that way we can throw the blame in not completing the agreement upon the refusal of the Canadians to agree to what the British Government had proposed in their behalf.[63]

61. Secretary Hay to Henry White, September 24, 1899, *Most Confidential, White MS.*
62. Secretary Hay to John W. Foster, September 26, 1899, *Foster MS.*
63. Henry White to Secretary Hay, October 4, 1899, *White MS.*

On October 7 David J. Hill, Acting Secretary of State, informed Ambassador Choate that the American Government was anxious to have the question of the *modus vivendi* settled as soon as possible. When this question had been settled, the related questions of the lease at Pyramid Harbor and the permanent boundary could be given further consideration.[64] A few days later the British *chargé d'affaires* sent to Secretary Hay a note which contained an amended version of the *modus vivendi* proposed by the American Government on September 6. It was the opinion of Lord Salisbury that the American proposal with regard to freedom of access to the valley of the Porcupine Creek would render it impossible to draw the provisional boundary line without transferring both banks of the Klehini River to the American side. In order to obviate this difficulty, Lord Salisbury had suggested several amendments to the American proposal.[65] Secretary Hay added certain verbal corrections to this British draft which was then accepted by both governments as a *modus vivendi* for the provisional boundary in the region of the headwaters of the Lynn Canal.[66]

64. David J. Hill, Acting Secretary of State, to Ambassador Choate, October 7, 1899, *Great Britain, Instructions,* XXXIII, MS. Dept. of State. The Department of State was fully aware of the importance of arriving at some understanding with Great Britain concerning a lease of territory at Pyramid Harbor. It was apparent to Secretary Hay that any lease of territory would evoke bitter opposition along the Pacific Coast and in Alaska. On October 13, 1899, Mr. S. G. Kaufman, Secretary of the Skagway Chamber of Commerce, sent to President McKinley a copy of a resolution adopted by the chamber protesting against the lease or cession of any territory on Lynn Canal. The resolution was in part as follows: "Whereas, as citizens of the United States we are unalterably opposed to the concession of one foot of territory over which the sovereignty of the United States can be rightfully maintained: and whereas, we realize the disastrous results to ourselves as citizens of the United States, of the District of Alaska, in the town of Skagway, which would result from such a concession to the British, because of the almost total destruction of the transportation business, and the great and growing commerce of this place . . . Resolved, that we do this publicly and most earnestly protest against a settlement of the boundary dispute . . . upon any such terms, . . . believing . . . that it will virtually destroy property values which now amount to millions of dollars." *Alaska Boundary Papers,* MS. Dept. of State.

65. Mr. Tower to Secretary Hay, October 13, 1899, *F. R., 1899,* pp. 327–328.

66. Secretary Hay to Mr. Tower, October 20, 1899, Mr. Tower to Secretary Hay, October 20, 1899, *ibid.,* pp. 329–330. The text of the *modus vivendi* reads as follows: "It is hereby agreed between the Governments of the United States and of Great Britain that the boundary line between Canada and the Territory of Alaska in the region about the head of Lynn Canal shall be provisionally fixed as follows, without prejudice to the claims of either party in the permanent adjustment of the international boundary: In the region of the Dalton Trail a line beginning at the peak west of Porcupine Creek, marked on the map No. 10 of the United States commission, December 31, 1895, and on sheet No. 19 of the British Commission, December 31, 1895, with the No. 6500; thence running to the Klehini (or Klaheela) River in the direction of the peak north of that river, marked 5020 on the aforesaid United States map and 5025 on the aforesaid British map; thence following the high or right bank of the said

Ambassador Choate was promptly advised of the formal acceptance of the *modus vivendi* by both Governments,[67] and the press announced to the world the erection of another important milestone on the pathway to an intimate Anglo-American understanding.[68] But this understanding needed to be strengthened and confirmed, and this could be accomplished only through a permanent settlement of the issues outstanding between Great Britain and the United States. This fact was clearly seen by the statesmen of both countries, and they continued their search to find some formula of arbitration that was acceptable.

Klehini River to the junction thereof with the Chilkat River, a mile and a half more or less, north of Klukwan—provided that persons proceeding to or from Porcupine Creek shall be freely permitted to follow the trail between the said creek and the said junction of the rivers, into and across the territory on the Canadian side of the temporary line wherever the trail crosses to such side, and subject to such reasonable regulations for the protection of the revenue as the Canadian Government may prescribe, to carry with them over such part or parts of the trail between the said points as may lie on the Canadian side of the temporary line such goods and articles as they desire, without being required to pay any customs duties on such goods and articles; and from said junction to the summit of the peak east of the Chilkat River, marked on the aforesaid map No. 10 of the United States commission with the number 5410 and on the map No. 17 of the aforesaid British commission with the number 5490.

"On the Dyea and Skagway trails, the summits of the Chilkoot and White passes.

"It is understood, as formerly set forth in communications of the Department of State of the United States, that the citizens or subjects of either power, found by this arrangement within the temporary jurisdiction of the other, shall suffer no diminution of the rights and privileges which they now enjoy.

"The Government of the United States will at once appoint an officer or officers, in conjunction with an officer or officers to be named by the Government of Her Britannic Majesty, to mark the temporary line agreed upon by the erection of posts, stakes, or other appropriate marks." *Ibid.*, pp. 330–331. See *ibid.*, p. 330, for map of the territory affected by this provisional arrangement.

67. Secretary Hay to Ambassador Choate, October 20, 21, and 26, 1899, *Great Britain, Instructions*, XXXIII, MS. Dept. of State.

68. In the New York *Times*, October 21, 1899, the following statement was made concerning the acceptance of the *modus vivendi:* "The State Department is confident that it has conserved every American interest in the arrangement without unjustly treating Canada. . . . The Canadians are not allowed to reach any point on the Lynn Canal. Moreover, there is no permission given for a free port, or even for the free transfer across American territory of Canadian goods, except of miners' belongings. . . . Some of the more important advantages that accrue to the American side through today's settlement would escape observation save through a study of the map which is attached to the notes. Thus it appears that, instead of placing the line directly at the town of Klukwan, which marks the head of canoe navigation, as the British sought to do, it has been located several miles above that town directly at the junction with the Chilkat River of the important tributary, Klehini. This maintains the Indians at Klukwan under American jurisdiction without question, and also provides a natural and unmistakable boundary line such as is always sought by topographers in the shape of a considerable river. Then, when it comes to the point of departure from this river, the Klehini, the line has been prolonged towards its source so as to include in American territory the mining town of Porcupine, the head of mining operations in the Porcupine section."

On August 9, 1899, Choate had addressed to Lord Salisbury a long note which contained a strong defence of the American viewpoint concerning the arbitral procedure that should be followed. In concluding his note he frankly stated the opinion, which, as we have seen, he had written Hay a few weeks earlier, that the procedure that had been followed in the Venezuelan boundary settlement was "wholly inapplicable" to the Alaskan situation. He also repeated one of Hay's statements to the effect that it was not until after the creation of the Joint High Commission that either Great Britain or Canada had advanced a "claim to any portion of territory lying adjacent to the inlets of the ocean" or to the "waters thereof."[69]

The British Foreign Office waited for many weeks before an answer was given to Mr. Choate's note. The fact that some attention was being paid to the matter was disclosed by an inspired article in the London *Times* on July 31, 1899. In this article the Alaskan boundary dispute was treated at length, and with reference to the territory about the headwaters of the Lynn Canal the statement was made that "for twenty years, from 1872 to 1892, the occasional steps taken by the American officials were met by periodic protests on the British side." In support of this statement the article contained references to a military reconnaissance in Alaska by Lieutenant Schwatka in 1883; to certain American claims of jurisdiction over White Pass in 1888, and to conflicting claims brought before the Joint High Commission of 1887–1888.

In an instruction to Ambassador Choate, October 2, 1899, Secretary Hay strongly contested the statements in the article in the *Times*. That article had mistakenly asserted that Schwatka had been sent on his trip by the American Government, and that during his reconnaissance he had fixed "some points for the international boundary, includ-

69. Ambassador Choate to Lord Salisbury, August 9, 1899, *A.B.T.*, IV, 129–132. In this letter to Lord Salisbury, Choate had remarked as follows: "The coast line of the main-land (the *lisière* of the Treaty), including the inlets, had been in the possession or under the control of Russia and the United States since the Treaty between Russia and Great Britain in 1825—and the settlements on the inlets, especially those about the head of the Lynn Canal, have been made with the authority and under the jurisdiction of the United States, without any protest or claim of territorial ownership on the part of Great Britain—whereas, in the Venezuela case, the British occupation and settlements involved were upon the territory claimed by Venezuela, and against the constant protest of Venezuela; thus constituting, as Venezuela alleges, a series of advancing encroachments upon what that country claimed to be her territory. . . . It appears clearly that not until after the Joint High Commission was created, 30th May, 1898, did either Great Britain or Canada ever advance the claim to any portion of territory lying adjacent to the inlets of the ocean, nor to the waters thereof; nor have they objected to the occupation of the same by the Government of the United States or its citizens—and at no time has any part of the territory so lately put in dispute, been held or occupied by Canadian or British Authorities."

ing one at Chilcoot Pass at the head of Lynn Canal." As a matter of fact, Schwatka had been sent by his superior military officer merely to visit certain Indian tribes, and his instructions did not authorize him to "make any survey or fix any points for the international boundary." The *Times* article stated that in 1888 the British Government pointed out that White Pass was in territory claimed by Canada. By a reference to the diplomatic correspondence of that year, Secretary Hay showed that the note of the British Minister at Washington, September 10, 1888, made no mention whatever of White Pass. The third point brought out in the *Times* article was the alleged fact that in the meetings of the Commission of 1887–1888 "the Canadian claim for a boundary which should cross the Lynn Canal at ten marine leagues from the ocean was put forward." Secretary Hay indicated that this Canadian claim was brought forward not during the sessions of the Commission but in an informal meeting between Professor W. H. Dall and Dr. G. M. Dawson where "neither party had any delegated powers whatever."[70]

Secretary Hay's reason for sending this instruction of October 2 was to put Ambassador Choate on his guard against any official British claims along the lines of the *Times* article of July 31. His foresight in this regard was fully justified on October 14 when Lord Salisbury sent an instruction to Mr. Tower, the British *chargé d'affaires* in Washington, which reproduced in part the statements that had appeared in the press. Salisbury at once challenged the American view that the British claim to territory around the headwaters of Lynn Canal was one that had first been put forward after the creation of the Joint High Commission in May, 1898, and reviewed the history of the case as follows: On August 27, 1886 the Earl of Iddesleigh, in a note to Mr. Phelps, had stated his refusal to recognize the boundary line as indicated on a certain map of that day. In the following year (September 14, 1887) the British Minister at Washington had gone on record as not recognizing any points fixed by Lieutenant Schwatka along the Alaskan boundary, and during an informal session between Professor Dall and Dr. Dawson the Canadian claim that the boundary line should be drawn along the summits of the coast range had been clearly stated. The treaty of July 22, 1892 had provided for a joint survey of the boundary "with a view to the ascertainment of facts and data necessary to the permanent delimitation of said boundary line." From this outline of history, Salisbury drew the conclusion that the question of the interpretation of the Treaty of 1825 was left over for discussion after the

70. Secretary Hay to Ambassador Choate, October 2, 1899, *Great Britain, Instructions,* XXXIII, MS. Dept. of State.

completion of the preliminary survey. In 1892 "neither Government claimed to have any rights in the disputed territory arising out of possession, occupation, or political control. Nor does it appear that any such claims were preferred on the part of the United States until the meetings of the Joint High Commission." There was, therefore, no fundamental difference between the Venezuela boundary dispute and the Alaskan dispute, and the same form of arbitration could be safely followed.[71]

In his reply to this note of Lord Salisbury, Secretary Hay referred to the fact that in his instruction of October 2 he had anticipated some of the points contained in it. With reference to certain other points, he was in sharp disagreement. In support of the assertion that the Alaskan boundary was regarded by the two Governments as an entirely open question, Lord Salisbury had cited Secretary Bayard's instruction to Mr. Phelps, November 20, 1885. It was true,

as noted in Lord Salisbury's despatch, that Mr. Bayard stated that no question concerning the true location of the line stipulated in the treaty had ever arisen between Great Britain and Russia prior to the cession of Alaska to the United States. But in the same paper and in the same connection he [Bayard] had said: "It is certain that no question has arisen since 1867 between the Governments of the United States and Great Britain in regard to this boundary." In the face of these declarations, I cannot understand how Secretary Bayard could be held to support the view that in 1885 the boundary was an open question. Mr. Bayard did refer to a "doubt in certain quarters" as to a portion of the boundary, which was an allusion to a map which had just been published in British Columbia, based upon the views of General Cameron afterwards advanced by Dr. Dawson, mentioned in my No. 222, of October 2nd last to you.

If the views of Her Majesty's Government as to the boundary were fully stated at the conference held in Washington in February 1892 with members of the Canadian Cabinet and the British Minister, and a proposition was submitted for a reference of the question to arbitration, it does not appear of record in this Department. . . . So far as the records of this Department disclose, the first proposition submitted by the British Government for an arbitration of the Alaska boundary was contained in the note of February 23, 1898, of the British Ambassador . . . to Secretary Sherman. . . . This was the last statement of the views of the British Government before the creation of the Joint High Commission, and it developed the fact that up to that time the "divergence" now so much emphasized was more apparent than real, as it recognized that the line in dispute about the head of Lynn Canal was in the vicinity of the passes.[72]

71. Lord Salisbury to Mr. Tower, October 14, 1899, *A.B.T.*, IV, 132–138.

72. Secretary Hay to Ambassador Choate, November 10, 1899, *Great Britain, Instructions,* XXXIII, MS. Dept. of State.

Before receiving this instruction from Secretary Hay, Ambassador Choate had written a brief letter in which he stated that Lord Salisbury had sent to the Canadian Government the draft of a new arbitration agreement relative to the Alaskan boundary. It had been intimated to Mr. Choate that the new draft would "have the effect to secure actual American settlements to us in any event, without expressly naming them." In the meantime it might be worth while for the Department of State to ascertain from General Benjamin Harrison his views as to the expediency of arbitrating the Alaskan boundary dispute. The General's recent experiences in Paris had led him to adopt a very emphatic opinion that any arbitration agreement similar to the Venezuelan treaty would result in a "compromise instead of an actual judicial determination of the Treaty line."[73]

It was evident to Secretary Hay that the negotiations concerning the Alaskan boundary had reached an *impasse*. Lord Pauncefote had remarked that this dispute could be settled in an hour's discussion between himself and Secretary Hay, but this statement was unduly optimistic. The Canadian Government was difficult to deal with, and the "narrowness and prejudice" of the members of the American Senate from the Northwest was beyond belief. The way to balance this puzzling international equation was to introduce new political factors into it.[74] Before Hay could turn to this task, Choate sent a long and cogently-argued note to Lord Salisbury in answer to the communication of October 14.

He first showed that the Venezuelan boundary convention afforded no real precedent for a settlement of the Alaskan boundary dispute. After developing this point in some detail, he reviewed the history of the controversy and took sharp issue with the viewpoints of Lord Salisbury. The British Foreign Secretary had maintained that Bayard's instruction to Mr. Phelps, November 20, 1885, had admitted that the Alaskan boundary was an "open question." According to Choate, the real contention of Secretary Bayard in 1885 was merely that "the demarkation of the line was undetermined and was full of difficulties in the then state of topographical knowledge." When the Earl of Iddesleigh sent the Canadian map to Mr. Phelps with his note of August 27, 1886, and felt called upon to disavow the correctness of the boundary line depicted upon it, he raised no question about the interpretation of the treaty of 1825—certainly none as to whether the *lisière* ran around the inlets. In

73. Ambassador Choate to Secretary Hay, November 1, 1899, *Private and Unofficial, Choate MS.*

74. Secretary Hay to Ambassador Choate, November 13, 1899, *Personal and Confidential, Choate MS.*

the Dawson letter of February, 1888, no real claim was made that the boundary should cross all narrow waters that were of such width as to be within territorial jurisdiction. The statements in the Dawson letter relative to the territory around the headwaters of the Lynn Canal were simply the reflection of the views of General Cameron, and they were not in any sense a claim on the part of Her Majesty's Government. Later, during the sessions of the Joint High Commission in 1898, the British delegates asserted that the boundary line should give them the control over the headwaters of the Lynn Canal, and this was the first time that such a claim was advanced. The American delegation promptly rejected this British pretension, and the question was still open for arbitration.[75]

It was apparent to Secretary Hay that any final settlement of the Alaskan boundary dispute would largely depend upon certain political factors. In October, 1899, war broke out between Great Britain and the Boer republics in South Africa. This conflict lasted two years and eight months, and it brought serious embarrassments to the British Government which directly affected its foreign policy. Secretary Hay strongly espoused the cause of England in these difficulties with the Boers. Even before the outbreak of hostilities, he had written to Henry White and expressed the hope that England would "make quick work of Uncle Paul. Sooner or later, her influence must be dominant there, and the sooner the better."[76] Later expressions were equally friendly.[77]

Along with this friendly feeling for Great Britain during the Boer War, Hay also drew close to the British Government in the matter of checking the partition of China by certain European Powers in 1899. Although American policy in the Far East had long been in favor of the Open Door and the preservation of Chinese territorial integrity, it would not have been possible to make effective public announcement of these principles without British support. Secretary Hay's famous notes of September 6, 1899, and July 3, 1900 were a clear indication of an Anglo-American understanding with reference to the situation in the Orient.[78]

These exercises in Anglo-American co-operation were bound to have

75. Ambassador Choate to Lord Salisbury, January 22, 1900, *A.B.T.*, IV, 138–155. It is interesting to note that Lord Salisbury informed Mr. Choate that he regarded this letter of January 22 as a "powerful document." Choate to Hay, February 2, 1900, *Choate MS.*

76. Secretary Hay to Henry White, September 24, 1899, *White MS.*

77. John H. Ferguson, *American Diplomacy and the Boer War* (Philadelphia, 1939), pp. 122–129, 162–167, 200–221.

78. A. Whitney Griswold, *The Far Eastern Policy of the United States* (New York, 1938), chap. ii.

an important influence upon the settlement of questions that had long been at issue between the two countries. Lord Salisbury had hesitated to take any action with regard to the Alaskan boundary until the American Government made some show of concession. With the signing of the *modus vivendi* of October 20, 1899, the British Foreign Office felt that the Alaskan boundary dispute had been temporarily settled and that other Anglo-American questions could now be given further consideration. The question that pressed for immediate settlement was with reference to the abrogation of the Clayton-Bulwer Treaty. A bill had been introduced into the House of Representatives providing for the construction of an isthmian canal. Secretary Hay was apprehensive as to the effects of this bill because it "absolutely ignored" the Clayton-Bulwer Treaty and was, in many features, an "absolute violation of it." There was little doubt, he believed, that an isthmian canal would eventually be constructed under American auspices. Nothing in the Clayton-Bulwer Treaty could prevent this procedure. That treaty was simply out of date as far as Anglo-American relations were concerned and it should be superseded by some convention that was more in keeping with current realities in world politics. It would be deplorable if the British Government, "by persisting in postponing the consideration of this matter until all the Canadian questions are closed up, . . . should be made to appear in the attitude of attempting to veto a work of such world-wide importance; and the worst of all for international relations is that the veto would not be effective." If Lord Salisbury would consent to the negotiation of a new treaty, this instrument could be sent to the Senate in advance of any legislation that would invalidate the Clayton-Bulwer Treaty.[79]

Choate lost no time in discussing this matter with Lord Salisbury, who said very emphatically that he would "have to bring it before the Cabinet so as to give Mr. Chamberlain a chance to be heard for Canada." Choate protested that

> Canada had nothing to do with it, but he recalled their former claims and said that they were so angry at our position in regard to the Alaska boundary that they must be heard now. I reminded him of what had passed between him and me about it, and more emphatically between Mr. White and himself before I came, to which he replied that the war and Canada's participation therein had changed the situation which must be considered as it now stands.[80]

79. Secretary Hay to Ambassador Choate, January 15, 1900, *Private and Confidential, Choate MS*. See also, Lord Pauncefote to Lord Salisbury, January 21, 1900, R. B. Mowat, *The Life of Lord Pauncefote* (London, 1929), pp. 276–277.

80. Ambassador Choate to Secretary Hay, January 27, 1900, *Private and Confidential, Choate MS.*

On January 30 Joseph Chamberlain sent a note to Lord Minto, in Ottawa, and strongly urged that Canadian consent be given to the negotiation of a new isthmian canal treaty. Refusal to do so would be regarded by the United States as "an affront." In view of the dangerous situation in which the British Empire was placed because of the Boer War, it was extremely important to conciliate America.[81]

Sir Wilfrid Laurier and his Cabinet promptly responded to this pressure from Mr. Chamberlain and gave their consent to the signature of a new canal treaty.[82] Lord Salisbury told Ambassador Choate that Canada had been "very considerate and surrendered her special scruples." Choate himself thought that the Canadian Government should be given a "long credit mark for this, considering the great heed paid to her wishes by the Imperial Government in these days of ardent loyalty."[83]

Delighted with this mark of Canadian conciliation, Hay hurriedly signed with Lord Pauncefote the new canal treaty (February 5, 1900). It provided for the construction of an isthmian canal under American auspices, but it recognized the general principle of neutralization along the lines of the Suez Canal Convention of 1888. The fact that this treaty did not abrogate but merely amended the Clayton-Bulwer Treaty, stirred up strong disapproval in many quarters. Theodore Roosevelt quickly pointed out that unless the United States controlled the canal, its construction would be a serious menace to our national safety.[84] Other Americans were equally sharp in their criticism of the treaty, and it was evident that the Senate would insist upon amendments.

Immediately after the Hay-Pauncefote Treaty had been sent to the Senate, Hay seemed hopeful that it would meet with the approval of that body, and he asked Choate to convey to Lord Salisbury his deep appreciation of the "generosity and perfect magnanimity" that had been shown by the British Foreign Secretary.[85] But as the months

81. Joseph Chamberlain to Lord Minto, January 30, 1900, Mowat, *op. cit.,* pp. 279–280.

82. Skelton, *Laurier,* II, 139–140.

83. Ambassador Choate to Secretary Hay, February 7, 1900, *Private and Unofficial, Choate MS.*

84. Theodore Roosevelt to Secretary Hay, February 18, 1900, Thayer, *op. cit.,* II, 339–341. Hay wrote a reproachful letter to Roosevelt on February 12, 1900 and asked why he could not "leave a few things to the President and the Senate." *Roosevelt MS.* On the other hand, Albert Shaw praised Roosevelt for the "prompt and unhesitating courage you showed in making that statement. . . . I think you were wise and statesmanlike." Shaw to Roosevelt, February 16, 1900, *Roosevelt MS.*

85. Secretary Hay to Ambassador Choate, February 6, 1900, *Choate MS.*

quickly passed, this optimism faded. On February 27, he confided to Henry White that it had never entered his mind that "anyone out of a madhouse could have objected to the Canal Convention."[86] A few days later he denounced some of the opposing Senators as "howling lunatics,"[87] and on March 13 he sent his resignation to President McKinley.[88] McKinley refused to accept it, and Hay continued to serve as Secretary of State. But he regarded the Senate with an increasing contempt that made it difficult for him to formulate and conduct American foreign policy.[89]

In order to bring the Alaskan boundary dispute to a successful conclusion it was necessary to have friendly relations with the British Government. The Anglophobia so prevalent in certain American circles proved very embarrassing to Hay during the summer of 1900. The New York *Sun*, supposedly a McKinley organ, was particularly severe in its attacks upon the State Department. In a letter to Choate, Hay complained of the tactics of his opponents:

> Just now they are having all colors of fits over our *modus vivendi* in Alaska. That was, as you know, one of the best bargains for us ever made. I cannot even defend myself by saying how good the bargain was. I do not want to publish to the world the details of an arrangement some of whose features are as yet incomplete, and it is abominable form for a Government to brag of its diplomatic success. So I must let the tempest of dust and foul air blow itself out. Any form of regular diplomatic work is rendered impossible by the conditions of our political life. Other countries can negotiate with us, and when an agreement is reached the work for them is done. For us it is only begun. It takes ten times the energy, the labor, the care, the wear and tear of nerves involved in negotiation with other countries to convince our Committee on Foreign Relations and a majority of our own people that we have not betrayed the country.[90]

One of the Senators about whom Secretary Hay bitterly complained, was Senator Henry Cabot Lodge. Lodge was not an Anglophile like Hay, and in September, 1900 he wrote to Henry White in sharp criticism of British policy. It seemed to him that the British Ministry had

> completely lost its wits and utterly failed to understand the situation in China. . . . They keep nagging about the Alaska Boundary when they ought

86. Secretary Hay to Henry White, February 27, 1900, Nevins, *op. cit.*, pp. 150–151.
87. Secretary Hay to Joseph H. Choate, March 7, 1900, *Choate MS.*
88. Secretary Hay to President McKinley, March 13, 1900, Thayer, *op. cit.*, II, 226–227.
89. See for example Hay's letter to Henry White, March 18, 1900, *White MS.*
90. Secretary Hay to Ambassador Choate, August 22, 1900, *Choate MS.*

to drop the whole controversy, and the result is that instead of drawing toward us they are drawing away and leaving us to unite with others, for we know exactly what we are about and propose to put it through if it can possibly be done. It looks as if England's political capacity has gone with her military capacity.[91]

Some weeks later, Lodge wrote again to Henry White and told him that it was generally understood in Washington that the Alaskan boundary dispute would soon be the subject of conversations between Lord Pauncefote and Secretary Hay. Lodge hoped that both of them would "have the sense to let it alone." It was no time for the British Government to "press their claims" in Alaska, "especially as they have no claims except those of their own manufacture."[92]

In Canada, Sir Wilfrid Laurier was reluctant to make any more concessions to the United States. In October, 1900, John W. Foster sent to the Canadian Prime Minister a copy of a book that he had written on American diplomacy. In his reply, Sir Wilfrid assured Foster that he would read the book with great interest, but "at the same time with some regret, for I will see therein the many instances where American diplomacy has had the better of British diplomacy."[93]

In England, the sentiment towards the United States was distinctly friendly. James Bryce expressed to Foster his deep satisfaction that the relations between the two countries "should be so cordial,"[94] and Choate found that Lord Lansdowne, who had just been made Foreign Secretary, was the embodiment of courtesy.[95]

It was fortunate that these cordial relations rested upon a secure basis. They were soon tested by the action of the Senate (December 20, 1900)[96] in amending the Hay-Pauncefote Treaty.[97] To Secretary Hay these amendments seemed entirely unnecessary and were merely the reflection of partisan opposition in its lowest form.[98] He believed, how-

91. Senator Lodge to Henry White, September 3, 1900, *White MS.*

92. Senator Lodge to Henry White, October 8, 1900, *ibid.*

93. Sir Wilfrid Laurier to John W. Foster, October 15, 1900, *Foster MS.*

94. James Bryce to John W. Foster, November 7, 1900, *ibid.*

95. Ambassador Choate to Secretary Hay, November 21, 24, 1900, *Choate MS.*

96. In a letter to Henry White, December 24, 1900, Senator Lodge discussed the basis of the Senate's objection to the treaty: "The opposition to the treaty, as it stood, was genuine and uniform. The Senate did not think that the treaty without amendment was safe for the United States, and there was no hostility to England in putting on the amendments and no desire to have the treaty fail." *White MS.*

97. *Sen. Ex. Jour.*, XXXII, 598–599, 609, 620–624. See also, W. S. Holt, *Treaties Defeated by the Senate* (Baltimore, 1933), pp. 184–193.

98. In a letter to Ambassador Choate, December 21, 1900, Hay frankly unburdened his soul. The Hay-Pauncefote Treaty had been prepared entirely by the State Depart-

ever, that the "bad manners and the ill-will involved in the action of the Senate" were directed more at himself and the President than at England. Indeed, taking into consideration the spirit of the Senate, it was "rather to be wondered at" that the treaty came through that body "so nearly intact as it did." He had talked the matter over with Lord Pauncefote who was "altogether in favor of an acceptance of the amendments *en bloc* as a choice of evils."[99]

In his discussion with Lord Lansdowne concerning the Senate amendments to the Hay-Pauncefote Treaty, Mr. Choate expressed the hope that the British Government would take no action that would "disturb the cordial relations and feelings now existing between the two countries." Lord Lansdowne assured him that he need not fear "any harsh treatment of the matter," although the Senate action had been a "little abrupt."[100]

In the meantime, Secretary Hay was awaiting with "deep anxiety" the result of these discussions between Mr. Choate and Lord Lansdowne. Although the Senate amendments were "futile, impertinent and altogether improper," it was extremely important to have them ac-

ment "without solicitation on the part of Great Britain. It was altogether to our advantage, and was accepted by Lord Salisbury in a spirit of generous good will, without the change of a word. . . . In negotiating the Convention we did not lose sight of the fact that it would require a two-thirds vote of the Senate for its ratification. I was well aware of the difficulty of securing the vote of the Senate to any proposition which gave an opportunity of discussion. . . . But the arrangement in this case was so clearly to our advantage . . . that I could not regard its rejection as possible, and I even hoped it might pass unanimously. But . . . from the first moment the first opposition developed itself, I had no hope of the treaty going through intact. As soon as the Senate assembled it was evident that a combination of two or three groups of recalcitrants could command more than a third of that body. . . . Yesterday the Senate voted. They adopted . . . besides the Davis Amendment, two others. . . . I deeply regret the adoption of these amendments. They deform and disfigure the Treaty; they take much from the grace and value of the concession which Great Britain had made us; but beyond the matter of taste and good manners, I consider them of little moment. . . . The Davis Amendment is a mere *brutum fulmen;* it leaves intact the provision against the fortification of the Canal; it reserves to us in vague terms a right which can never be exercised. . . . The British Government . . . have a perfect right to reject the amended Treaty. . . . They generously gave us our release from the Clayton-Bulwer Convention, in terms we ourselves suggested. *We* have suffered a rebuff at the hands of the Senate. . . . If Great Britain should now reject the Treaty the general opinion of mankind would justify her in it." *Choate MS.*

99. Secretary Hay to Ambassador Choate, January 11, 1901, *Personal, Choate MS.*

100. Ambassador Choate to Secretary Hay, January 15, 1901, *Personal and Confidential, Choate MS.* In a confidential letter to Henry White, December 18, 1900, Senator Lodge made the following comments: The American people will never consent to building a canal at their own expense, which they shall guard and protect for the benefit of the world's commerce, unless they have virtually complete control. There is no use arguing about the wisdom of this attitude. This is what the American people . . . demand." *White MS.*

cepted by the British Government. It would be almost "impossible to get the Senate to accept anything else."[101]

But despite Hay's anxious hopes that the Senate amendments would be accepted by the British Government, Lord Lansdowne, on February 22, 1901, sent to Lord Pauncefote a long note rejecting the amended treaty.[102] Hay received this communication on March 11, and was surprised to find that the British Foreign Secretary had stated that the American Government had really "acquiesced in the rejection of the amendments." This statement was not in accord with the facts in the case, and Hay could not acknowledge the receipt of the British note until "this matter is settled."[103]

After the British Government replied according to the State Department formula, Hay once more began to think of a Canal treaty that would be acceptable to the Senate. Senator Lodge informed him that the Senate would consent to a treaty that

> abrogated and superseded the Treaty of 1850, and which agreed that the United States could maintain and defend the canal, keep it open for the commerce of all nations, at the same rates of toll which were imposed on vessels of the United States, and which further agreed that the United States would maintain the neutrality of the canal as between belligerents when the United States itself was not engaged in war.[104]

With this assurance in mind, Hay began new conversations with Lord Pauncefote, and in London, Ambassador Choate secured Lord Salisbury's consent to further negotiations.[105] In the summer of 1901, Senator Lodge visited England and talked with Lord Lansdowne and certain cabinet ministers.[106] These conversations were supplemented by a week-end visit of Henry White to Hatfield, the country estate of Lord Salisbury. When White referred to the need for a new canal treaty, Salisbury once more mentioned the need for compensations with reference to the Alaskan boundary. When White vigorously protested against joining these two questions, Salisbury remarked that there would be an advantage in dealing with the canal question alone, for

101. Secretary Hay to Ambassador Choate, January 22, 1901, *Confidential, Choate MS.* See also, Hay to Choate, January 25, 1901, and February 5, 1901, *ibid.*

102. Marquis of Lansdowne to Lord Pauncefote, February 22, 1901, *Diplomatic History of the Panama Canal, Senate Doc. No. 474,* 63 Cong., 2 sess., pp. 11–18.

103. Secretary Hay to Ambassador Choate, March 13, 1901, *Personal and Confidential, Choate MS.*

104. Senator Lodge to Secretary Hay, March 28, 1901, Thayer, *op. cit.*, II, 259–260.

105. Mowat, *op. cit.*, pp. 284–285; Dennis, *op. cit.*, pp. 162–163.

106. "Memoir of Henry Cabot Lodge," *Proceedings of the Massachusetts Historical Society,* April, 1925, LVIII, 336–337.

then "we should have only one antagonist, whereas in respect of Alaska there would be two—yourselves and Canada."[107]

Secretary Hay helped matters along by conferring with important Senators on the terms of the proposed treaty. In a letter to Choate he remarked that he had gone over the treaty project "word by word" with Senator Foraker, and had discussed its general terms with Senators Cullom, Frye, Lodge, Fairbanks, Spooner, and "other leading senators." They had assured him that if this new convention were accepted by the British Government it would be accepted by the Senate.[108]

It seemed to Hay that the British Government had shown "a most friendly and reasonable disposition" to meet American desires in the negotiation of this new canal treaty,[109] and President McKinley had indicated his approval of the project.[110] The assassination of McKinley in September, 1901, had no effect upon these negotiations. Secretary Hay continued in office as Secretary of State, and President Roosevelt was in complete harmony with Hay's desire to settle this canal issue as soon as possible.[111]

After the projected canal treaty had reached the final stage of negotiations, Lord Lansdowne spoke to Mr. Choate about the Alaskan boundary dispute. He inquired unofficially why the American Government had wished to have

a Tribunal of Six, three from each side without an umpire. I said I believed the idea was that a purely legal question might safely be left to six judges, half English and half American. He asked me why we objected to arbitrate. I said there was really nothing to arbitrate—our right was so perfectly clear there was really nothing to arbitrate—had been so recognized for 70 years. "Well, if so clear why not arbitrate?" "Well, you know what arbitrators generally try to do, is to divide, but don't let us bring up anything about

107. Henry White to Secretary Hay, July 24, 1901, *White MS.;* Nevins, *op. cit.,* p. 158.

108. Secretary Hay to Ambassador Choate, August 5, 1901, *Choate MS.*

109. Secretary Hay to Ambassador Choate, August 26, 1901, *ibid.*

110. Secretary Hay to Ambassador Choate, September 2, 1901, *ibid.*

111. In a letter to President Roosevelt, September 28, 1901, Mr. Choate remarks as follows: "I wish I could convey to you some idea of the interest and sympathy for you personally which your accession to office has excited among the English people, but it is simply impossible. . . . Your first utterances that have been reported here have satisfied them that the relations between the United States and Great Britain will be practically the same as they would have been if President McKinley had lived, and . . . that you will reciprocate the friendly and conciliatory spirit with which the British Government is now disposed to meet us on all controverted questions. I was very much rejoiced to hear from the Secretary of State that you are in perfect accord with him in regard to this Isthmian Canal Treaty which seems now approaching a very happy adjustment." *Ibid.*

Canada or Alaska until this Canal business is out of the way. Let's get the treaty ratified first before we take up anything else," and he agreed that that was the only way.[112]

There was no further obstacle in the way of arriving at an agreement on the question of the isthmian canal, and the second Hay-Pauncefote Treaty was signed on November 18, 1901. Under its terms the Clayton-Bulwer Treaty was abrogated, and the American Government was authorized to construct and manage the canal. In keeping with the spirit of the Monroe Doctrine, no nations were invited to join with the United States in guaranteeing the neutralization of the canal, and the absence of any provision prohibiting the fortification of the waterway might be understood by the American Government as giving tacit consent to defence works.

This second Hay-Pauncefote Treaty was quickly propelled through the Senate by Senator Lodge, and was proclaimed in February, 1902.[113] The Alaskan boundary dispute could now be taken up and negotiations resumed. In November, 1901, Lord Minto wrote to Joseph Chamberlain concerning the best method of arbitrating this question. The Canadian Government was opposed to Secretary Hay's proposal to submit the dispute to an arbitral commission of six jurists, three on each side. Such an arrangement would not "afford security in the event of differences of opinion." Prime Minister Laurier was willing, however, to agree upon a tribunal of six jurists providing "that at least one of the American arbitrators shall not be a citizen of the United States, . . . and that at least one of the British arbitrators shall not be a British subject."[114]

Such a proposal was not calculated to awaken the interest of the President who preferred to let the matter rest for a while. When the British Ambassador sent to Secretary Hay a long memorandum which discussed the possibility of submitting the Alaskan boundary dispute to arbitration, the Department of State took no immediate notice of it.[115] In a letter to Ambassador Choate, Hay observed: "I am afraid

112. Ambassador Choate to Secretary Hay, October 2, 1901, *Private and Confidential, Choate MS.*

113. Secretary Hay to Henry White, December 26, 1901, *ibid.* On October 7, 1901, Albert Shaw wrote to President Roosevelt and stated: "I take it myself that you will scrupulously avoid friction with England and yet will not mortally wound Western sentiment by making any concessions on the Alaskan Boundary question." *Roosevelt MS.*

114. Lord Minto to Joseph Chamberlain, November, 1901, *Laurier MS.*

115. *Memorandum,* February 28, 1902, *Alaskan Boundary, 1899–1903, Miscellaneous Archives,* MS. Dept. of State. This memorandum was largely a repetition of the memorandum prepared by Lord Minto in November, 1901.

we shall not have any definite program to put forward in regard to Canadian matters at this time. The President seems to think that sufficient to the day is the evil thereof."[116]

The reason for this Presidential inactivity was the fact that Great Britain was still engaged in the Boer War. In the United States a strong pro-Boer sentiment had become manifest, and the President preferred to postpone the consideration of the Alaskan boundary dispute until the British Government had brought the Boer War to a successful conclusion. Otherwise, it was quite likely that this American pro-Boer sentiment might influence the settlement of Canadian questions. This fact was very clear to George W. Smalley who wrote to the Duchess of Sutherland and gave her some insight into the situation: "I spent two hours one morning with the President. . . . We discussed the opening of a certain question. He said, 'I don't want it reopened because I am friendly to England, and while the South African War is unfinished I don't want to give the American pro-Boers a chance.' "[117]

Pauncefote saw the situation with equal clarity. After presenting to Secretary Hay the long memorandum of February 28, he was puzzled for a time at the lack of response on the part of the Department of State. He then learned "from a private but reliable source" that the President was "anxious to postpone the question until after the termination of the war in South Africa." He could not but suspect that "this sudden desire to postpone the question is due to political considerations of a domestic character, such as pressure from the Western States and the agitation raised against England at the present time by the pro-Boer and Irish parties."[118]

Apparently, Senator Lodge had no real appreciation of the situation. He did not realize that it was President Roosevelt and not Lord Lansdowne who was postponing the settlement of the Alaskan boundary controversy. Being naturally querulous, he became impatient at this diplomatic inactivity, and he complained to Henry White that he did not

like the looks of things in Alaska. The Canadians are anxious to settle and yield to us, as I know directly from their leading men. They want to get the matter out of the way and would abandon their claims if we would make the road easy for them, but England stands out now and again just where Herschell did. I cannot go into details on this matter, . . . but let me assure

116. Secretary Hay to Ambassador Choate, January 7, 1902, *Choate MS.*

117. George W. Smalley to the Duchess of Sutherland, February 18, 1902, *Smalley MS.*, Library of Congress.

118. Lord Pauncefote to the Marquess of Lansdowne, March 28, 1902, *Laurier MS.*, P.A.C.

you that this course is most unwise and that the sooner England comes to terms with us on that boundary the better for all concerned.[119]

The President himself did not like the way things were shaping up in Alaska, so on March 27, 1902 he instructed the Secretary of War to send "as quietly and unostentatiously as possible," some additional troops to southern Alaska so as to be able "promptly to prevent any possible disturbance along the disputed boundary line."[120] These instructions were immediately executed by Secretary Root, and the situation grew more precarious.[121]

In May, 1902, the President informed one of the staff of the British Embassy that he was "going to be ugly" over the question of the Alaskan boundary.[122] With this information at hand, the British Government knew that something would have to be done at once to settle this dangerous situation, so Lord Lansdowne requested Ambassador Choate to talk things over with Sir Wilfrid Laurier and Lord Minto. When Choate referred this matter back to Washington he was instructed to have the interview with the Canadian officials, but he was advised that President Roosevelt was of the opinion that "the Canadian claim has not a leg to stand on and that compromise is impossible."[123]

Before Choate could have his interview with Sir Wilfrid Laurier, Henry White sought out the Canadian Prime Minister and had a frank discussion with him concerning the Alaskan boundary. Sir Wilfrid was very frank and informed White that he realized that it would be impossible to turn the Americans out of the Skagway district even though some Canadians seemed to think this possible. As for himself, he was anxious for some sort of arbitral arrangement

in order to "save his face" so to speak, vis-à-vis his people; his idea being that if the arbitrators were to decide that our view of the boundary is correct, there would be an end to the whole business, . . . and he could say that he had done his best for them. If on the other hand the arbitrators should decide that our view was not the correct interpretation of the treaty, Canada would be entitled to compensation elsewhere, either in land or in *money,* for the Skagway district.[124]

119. Senator Lodge to Henry White, March 26, 1902, *White MS.*

120. George B. Cortelyou to Secretary Elihu Root, March 27, 1902, *Root MS.*

121. Secretary Root to Mr. Cortelyou, March 29, 1902, enclosing orders to Brigadier-General G. M. Randall, *Roosevelt MS.*

122. John W. Dafoe, *Clifford Sifton in Relation to His Times* (Toronto, 1931), pp. 214–215.

123. David Jayne Hill to Ambassador Choate, June 30, 1902, *Great Britain, Instructions,* XXXIV, MS. Dept. of State.

124. Henry White to Secretary Hay, June 28, 1902, *White MS.*

After receiving this letter, Secretary Hay wrote to the President and expressed the view that Prime Minister Laurier had arrived at the conclusion that there was no longer any hope of Canada securing any part of the Lynn Canal. The controversy had dragged on for so many years that Laurier was anxious for some speedy settlement of it. Lord Lansdowne was also desirous for some early adjustment of the dispute, and was doubtless convinced that if anything were to be accomplished it would have to be done along the lines indicated by the American Government.[125]

When Hay submitted this letter to the President, the latter replied by rejecting the Canadian claim in a characteristically Rooseveltian survey of the history of the case.[126] Hay seems to have been somewhat nettled at its tone. He promptly indicated that he also considered the Canadian case to be extremely weak, but that he was, nevertheless, reluctant to submit the case to arbitration, "the besetting sin of which is to split the difference. My suggestion was a submission of the question of the interpretation of the treaty of 1825 to a tribunal of six, three on a side, a majority to decide. In this case it is impossible that we should lose, and not at all impossible that a majority should give a verdict in our favour."[127] He then asked the President for instructions as to whether Ambassador Choate should "drop the matter at once" or talk the situation over with Lord Lansdowne. Roosevelt replied that he was perfectly willing to have Choate discuss the boundary dispute with

125. Secretary Hay to President Roosevelt, July 7, 1902, *Roosevelt MS.*

126. President Roosevelt to Secretary Hay, July 10, 1902, *ibid.* In this letter to Hay, the President commented on the fact that "in the Cabinet room there stands a globe made in London by the map-makers for the Admiralty. On this the boundary in question is given as it is on the British admiralty charts of the same period, this boundary being precisely that now claimed by us, which was also the boundary claimed or conceded by both the British and Canadian authorities until the last few years. The terms of the original treaty seem to me to be well-nigh impossible of any construction other than that which the Russians and we ourselves have always put upon them, save only as regards the southernmost portion of the boundary. As regards this portion of the boundary there is an evident ambiguity, one well-known channel being *named* while the rest of the *description,* including the fixing of the latitude and longitude and an allusion to a certain island, being seemingly incompatible with this same well-known channel being the one actually meant. If the treaty were now to be construed for the first time, . . . there would be room for an honest difference of opinion about this southernmost portion. But even this doubt must necessarily vanish in view of the construction put upon the terms . . . by the British and Canadians alike until within the last few years. The Russian maps and our own maps have always presented the boundary according to our present contention. Almost without exception the English maps, official and unofficial, have adopted the same construction, and until some fifteen years ago, this was likewise true of the Canadian maps. . . . The Canadian view of the boundary was precisely the view we now take."

127. Secretary Hay to President Roosevelt, July 14, 1902, *ibid.*

Lord Lansdowne, but it was difficult to come to any decision with reference to submitting the matter to arbitration. He would be willing to

appoint three commissioners to meet three of their commissioners, if they so desire, but I think I shall instruct our three commissioners when appointed that they are in no case to yield any of our claim. I appreciate the bother of the matter and even the possibility of trouble, although I think if we put a sufficient number of troops up there the miners will be kept in check. As you know, Root has been quietly strengthening the garrisons, although I think we should still have some additional men. It seems to me that the Canadians have no right to make a claim based upon the possible effect of their own wrong doing. In a spirit of bumptious truculence which for years England has resisted, but to which she has now come at bottom with much reluctance, the Canadians put in this wholly false claim. They now say that as they have got the false claim in, trouble may come if it is not acted on. I feel a great deal like telling them that if trouble comes it will be purely because of their own fault, and although it would not be pleasant for us it would be death for them.[128]

Senator Lodge was in complete agreement with the President with reference to the weakness of the Canadian case in connection with the Alaskan boundary. It appeared to him that the British statesmen were "utterly unable to grasp the situation," and he was certain that serious trouble would arise if they continued to support such a "preposterous claim." It would be difficult to imagine "a greater folly than their doing so," especially when it was "so important to them to have good relations with us."[129]

In the meantime, Ambassador Choate had an interview with Sir Wilfrid Laurier on the Alaskan boundary dispute. After a review of the chief points involved in the controversy, Laurier conceded that "if the

128. President Roosevelt to Secretary Hay, July 16, 1902, *ibid.* In a letter to J. St. Loe Strachey, July 18, 1902, Roosevelt made further comments on the Alaskan boundary situation: "At this moment in my relations with Great Britain I am suffering from anxiety from an entirely different reason. I do not think the Canadians have a leg to stand on in the Alaska boundary business; and this being the case I do not see how I can assent to any compromise. And yet I thoroughly understand how the English, in this moment of victory, when the Canadians as well as the citizens of the other colonial commonwealths have stood by them so loyally, feel that they must stand by the Canadians in return." *Ibid.*

Professor Philip C. Jessup, in his authoritative biography, *Elihu Root,* I, 390–392, discounts any real danger of serious friction along the Alaskan boundary because of the concentration of American troops. The sending of American troops to Alaska did not constitute "secret preparations for war"; it was merely making "rather reasonable precautions to prevent the international negotiation of the Alaskan boundary question from being complicated by local disturbances."

129. Senator Lodge to Henry White, July 11, 1902, *White MS.*

question to be arbitrated could be satisfactorily arranged, he would not be disposed to hold out against your way of constituting the Court, that it was so important to get the matter settled that, other things being satisfactory, they would not stand out on that." He also stated that he was willing to agree to an arbitration which would provide that "if the Court found Skagway and Dyea to be in British Territory, they should remain American—they didn't want them and wouldn't take them."

In spite of the friendly tone of this long interview, Laurier remarked that he was "very much disappointed" at the course the conversation had taken, and was not "at all hopeful" of arriving at a satisfactory settlement of the dispute. Several days later, the conversation was renewed and Laurier repeated his statement about being willing to leave Dyea and Skagway in American hands if some adequate pecuniary compensation could be arranged as a substitute. But he concluded his remarks with the complaint that the American attitude towards Canadian claims in this matter of the boundary dispute was so uncompromising that it was practically "impossible" to come to an agreement. Choate, however, was certain that the Canadian Government was "more anxious than heretofore to settle, and will yield more in the arrangement of the terms of Arbitration than they have been willing to contemplate before."[130]

Hay assured Choate that he "cordially approved" of the stand the Ambassador had taken in his conversations with Laurier, but he thought it would be difficult to "arrange a tribunal for Alaska boundary which would have any chance in the Senate."[131] Choate was more hopeful about the possibility of an early settlement of this issue, and he suspected that Laurier was feeling some pressure from Canada in favor of an amicable arrangement. During an interview with Lord Lansdowne, this matter of the boundary dispute came up for consideration, and Choate remarked that his chief desire in his conversation with Laurier was to make clear the President's "disinclination to anything like a compromise, or to an arbitration in any form that would necessarily involve a compromise." Lansdowne assured him that the British Government was well acquainted with the views of the President on this point, and Choate left the interview with the impression that while Lord Lansdowne was friendly, it was not likely that any settlement could be arranged until the new Balfour Ministry was ready to look

130. Ambassador Choate to Secretary Hay, July 5, 1902, *Choate MS.*
131. Secretary Hay to Ambassador Choate, July 18, 1902, *ibid.*

into the matter. He believed that Balfour's "sympathies with us will be more *active* than Lord Salisbury's were."[132]

After reading this letter, Hay thought there was "nothing more to be done in the matter" until the British Government made some definite move.[133] Lord Lansdowne made this move on August 18 when he finally answered Mr. Choate's note of January 22, 1900.[134] This British note added nothing of importance to the literature on the dispute and Choate regarded it as a "singularly feeble document."[135]

The scene now shifts to Ottawa where Laurier had to explain to his Cabinet the exact situation with reference to the Alaska boundary. Before leaving for London he had promised to uphold "without flinching," the Canadian contention concerning the boundary. Upon his return to Canada in October, 1902, he informed his colleagues that he had accepted the idea of a reference of the dispute to an "even-numbered commission." Although this was in direct contravention to Canadian desires, he had discovered in London "that he had no option but to yield the point." The Canadian Cabinet gave reluctant support to this arrangement by the Prime Minister, and the wheels of diplomacy once more began to move.[136]

On October 17 Secretary Hay, during a conversation with the British Ambassador, renewed the proposal made to Lord Pauncefote in the preceding March, to the effect that "a Tribunal should be appointed, the members of which should merely place their reasoned opinions on record."[137] Joseph Chamberlain immediately communicated this proposition to the Earl of Minto, in Ottawa,[138] and received the reply that the Canadian Government was willing to accede to this proposal with the proviso that "the reference to the Tribunal should include all aspects of the question."[139] Lord Lansdowne accepted this Canadian amendment and forwarded it to Washington.[140] Secretary Hay stated that he would be "willing that the decision of the Judicial Tribunal should be final, in the event of an agreement being arrived at by it," but he would have to consult the President about this matter.[141]

132. Ambassador Choate to Secretary Hay, July 19, 1902, *Private and Confidential, Choate MS.*

133. Secretary Hay to Ambassador Choate, August 2, 1902, *ibid.*

134. Lord Lansdowne to Mr. Raikes, August 18, 1902, *A.B.T.,* IV, 156–162.

135. Ambassador Choate to Secretary Hay, August 28, 1902, *Choate MS.*

136. Dafoe, *op. cit.,* pp. 216–218.

137. Sir Michael Herbert to the Marquess of Lansdowne, October 17, 1902, *A.B.T.,* V, 11.

138. Joseph Chamberlain to the Earl of Minto, October 31, 1902, *ibid.,* p. 11.

139. Earl of Minto to Mr. Chamberlain, November 18, 1902, *ibid.,* p. 12.

140. Marquess of Lansdowne to Sir M. Herbert, December 6, 1902, *ibid.,* p. 12.

141. Sir M. Herbert to Marquess of Lansdowne, December 8, 1902, *ibid.,* p. 12.

When this statement of Secretary Hay was referred to the Canadian Government for comment,[142] the Earl of Minto replied that his Ministers could not give "proper consideration to question submitted till exact text of proposed reference or the composition of Tribunal is before them."[143] At this point, President Roosevelt stepped upon the diplomatic stage. After informing Senator Lodge that he was willing to make one more effort to settle the Alaskan boundary dispute by offering to refer it to a "judicial commission" rather than to an "ordinary arbitration tribunal with an umpire," he gave the Senator a draft of a convention which would be submitted to the British Government. Lodge went over the draft with great care and deleted all reference to an "arbitration tribunal." He was of the opinion that "the word 'arbitration' should go out and that it should be clearly a tribunal of a different kind."[144]

On December 18, 1902 Secretary Hay submitted this draft treaty to Sir Michael Herbert who objected that Article IV merely gave prominence to the American contention that the Treaty of 1825 was intended to give Russia a strip of coast of at least ten marine leagues on the mainland. The Canadian claim that the line should follow the crest of the mountains parallel to the coast, including bays, ports and inlets, was not mentioned.[145] Hay consented to the amendments suggested by Herbert, and the draft was sent to Lord Lansdowne.[146]

Under pressure from the American Government for a speedy settlement of the Alaska boundary dispute, the Earl of Onslow (Colonial Secretary) cabled to Lord Minto to the effect that Sir Michael Herbert strongly advocated that the judicial tribunal be composed of three justices of the United States Supreme Court, together with the Lord Chief Justice of England, the Chief Justice of Canada, and a justice of the High Court of Great Britain.[147] Lord Minto replied at once that his Ministers were satisfied with "the questions to be submitted to the Tribunal," but they still objected to the composition of the proposed tribunal and ardently hoped that its personnel might in part, at least, be chosen from independent jurists who were "not subjects of either State."[148] When these suggestions were brought to the attention of

142. Earl of Onslow to Earl of Minto, December 11, 1902, *ibid.*, p. 13.

143. Earl of Minto to Earl of Onslow, December 15, 1902, *ibid.*, p. 13.

144. "Memoir of H. C. Lodge," *Proceedings of the Massachusetts Historical Society*, LVIII, 339.

145. Sir Michael Herbert to Secretary Hay, December 18, 1902, *A.B.T.*, V, 16.

146. Sir Michael Herbert to the Marquess of Lansdowne, December 19, 1903, *ibid.*, pp. 15–16.

147. Earl of Onslow to Earl of Minto, January 12, 1903, *ibid.*, p. 17.

148. Earl of Minto to Colonial Office, January 13, 1903, *ibid.*

Secretary Hay he expressed his regret that the Canadian Government still entertained objections to the composition of the tribunal, but he could only repeat that the President was unable to accept any form of arbitration other than that proposed in the draft treaty.[149]

In the face of this determined stand on the part of President Roosevelt with reference to the composition of the boundary tribunal, Lord Lansdowne gave way, and on January 23 he instructed Sir Michael Herbert to sign the convention submitted by Secretary Hay.[150] The treaty was finally signed on January 24, 1903, and the Senate consented to ratification on February 11.[151] According to its terms, the tribunal was to consist of "six impartial jurists of repute who shall consider judicially the questions submitted to them." Three members of the tribunal were to be appointed by the President of the United States, and three by His Britannic Majesty. All questions were to be decided by a "majority of all the members" of the tribunal.[152]

Sir Michael Herbert was delighted with the signature of the treaty, and he expressed the hope that it would be a "step in advance for the betterment of the relations between the two countries."[153] Sir Wilfrid Laurier was equally pleased with the treaty, and he indulged the hope that "a strong body of jurists will forever dispose of that question."[154] He could not bring himself to think that President Roosevelt would disappoint these ardent desires for a friendly settlement of the Alaskan boundary dispute by appointing two American representatives who could not under any stretch of the imagination be considered as "impartial jurists of repute." He was soon to discover that the American Chief Executive was more interested in gaining a favorable verdict than in conciliating Canada by even a pretence of impartiality.

149. Sir Michael Herbert to the Marquess of Lansdowne, January 18, 1903, *ibid.*

150. Marquess of Lansdowne to Sir Michael Herbert, January 23, 1903, *ibid.*, pp. 19–20.

151. Sir Michael Herbert to the Marquess of Lansdowne, February 11, 1903, *ibid.*, p. 21.

152. The text of the treaty (January 24, 1903) may be conveniently found in *ibid.*, II, 1–6.

153. Sir Michael Herbert to John W. Foster February 2, 1903, *Foster MS.*

154. Sir Wilfrid Laurier to John W. Foster, February 4, 1903, *ibid.*

CHAPTER IX

SIR WILFRID LAURIER POINTS THE WAY TO THE BRITISH COMMONWEALTH OF NATIONS

ALTHOUGH President Roosevelt consented to the signature of the treaty of January 24, 1903, he did not regard this convention as an arbitral arrangement. His definition of an arbitration was where "some outside body decides the question at issue between the two parties." He considered it a "foolish misuse of words" to call the Alaska treaty "an arbitration." He frankly confided to one of his friends that he would never have given his approval to any proposal for a judicial settlement of the Alaskan boundary controversy, and to attach the term "arbitration" to the arrangement of January 24 was as "absurd as to speak of the correspondence that has gone on between the foreign office and the State Department for the last year and a half on the subject by the same name."[1]

This Presidential disinclination to consider the treaty of January 24 as an arbitration convention was partly responsible for the type of American representatives that Roosevelt chose to sit on the boundary tribunal. It would appear that he approached, in turn, *all* the members of the Supreme Court with reference to service on the tribunal, but had met with refusal in every case.[2] After going through this ritual in none too serious a spirit, he then felt free to give a distinctly political complexion to his selections. He had received from Senator Lodge some intimations that the Alaska treaty would be viewed with suspicion by the Pacific Coast Senators unless they received some reassurances as to the character of the men who would be chosen to represent the United States on the tribunal. These suspicions would be banished by the appointment of Senators Lodge and Turner, whose views on the boundary

1. President Roosevelt to Frederick W. Holls, February 3, 1903, *Roosevelt MS.* Five days after the treaty had been sent to the Senate, the President withdrew it for an important correction. In the preamble the commission had been referred to as an "arbitral tribunal." This descriptive adjective was deleted, and the treaty was then returned to the Senate. Dennett, *op. cit.*, pp. 355–356.

2. Secretary Hay informed Sir Michael Herbert that *all* of the members of the Supreme Court had refused to serve on the boundary tribunal. *A.B.T.*, V, Pt. 4, 21. Professor Thomas A. Bailey, "Theodore Roosevelt and the Alaska Boundary Settlement," *Canadian Historical Review*, XVIII, 125, expresses the opinion that Justices Holmes and White were offered places on the tribunal. It is more than likely that they were NOT *the only Justices* who were offered appointments.

question were already a matter of common knowledge. Roosevelt felt the force of these suggestions, and he regarded Root as an admirable choice. He was certain that these "Three Musketeers" would carry out his orders, and neither Laurier nor Lansdowne had the guile or the cunning of a Richelieu. Impressed with the wisdom of these selections, the Senate, on February 11, 1903, approved the Alaska treaty without amendment.[3]

On February 14 Secretary Hay informed Sir Michael Herbert that the President had chosen Root, Turner and Lodge as the American representatives on the boundary tribunal. When Herbert expressed his disappointment at the absence of any member of the Supreme Court, he was assured that the "President had wished to appoint Justices of the Supreme Court but had been met with a refusal from all of them."[4]

Four days later, the Colonial Office inquired of Lord Minto as to the Canadian reaction in regard to the appointments of Root, Turner and Lodge.[5] Minto replied that his Ministers were strongly of the opinion that Mr. Root, as a member of the President's Cabinet, was disqualified from acting in any objective manner, and it should be apparent to the Roosevelt Administration that Senators Turner and Lodge could not be looked upon as "impartial jurists."[6] In a later communication, Minto once more stressed Canadian dissatisfaction with the Roosevelt appointments, and expressed the fear that the "whole situation" might have to be reconsidered.[7]

In an effort to allay Canadian discontent, Sir Michael Herbert sent the following confidential telegram to Lord Minto:

I am informed by Secretary of State that the judges of the Supreme Court all refused to sit on the Commission. Mr. Root is a man of integrity and a very able lawyer. Secretary of State denies stories in newspapers as to Turner, who was a member of the Supreme Court of his state. Lodge's appointment is due entirely to the President, who appears to have insisted upon it after the judges had refused. I need hardly say how sore I am about the unfortunate selections made by the President, which is not what I had

3. "Memoir of Henry Cabot Lodge," *Proceedings of the Massachusetts Historical Society*, LVIII, 340. On December 19, 1902, Sir Michael Herbert wrote to Lord Lansdowne to inform him that Secretary Hay had consulted "upwards of 30 Senators" in regard to the Alaska treaty, and as far as he was able to judge the situation, the treaty "would receive the approval of the Senate." *Laurier MS.* P.A.C.

4. Sir Michael Herbert to the Marquess of Lansdowne, February 14, 1903, *A.B.T.*, V, Pt. 4, 21.

5. Earl of Onslow to the Earl of Minto, February 18, 1903, *ibid.*, p. 22.

6. Earl of Minto to Earl of Onslow, February 19, 1903, *Laurier MS.*, P.A.C.

7. Earl of Minto to Earl of Onslow, February 21, 1903, *A.B.T.*, V, Pt. 4, 22.

been led to expect, but . . . I fear that it will be inadvisable and useless to protest.[8]

It appeared to Herbert that it would be politic to assume that President Roosevelt had "acted in good faith" in this matter of appointments, and the British Government should go ahead and appoint the "very best men" it could find.[9]

It was impossible for Sir Wilfrid Laurier to accept the situation as calmly as the British Ambassador in Washington advised. His pent-up feelings required some outlet, so he wrote a letter to Secretary Hay in which he filed a protest against the selection of Lodge and Turner as American representatives on the boundary tribunal. He thought it was evident that neither of these men could approach the questions at issue with an "open mind." If these appointments were insisted upon by President Roosevelt, it would be difficult to secure the assent of the Canadian Parliament "to the reference of our case to the tribunal of 'impartial jurists' as it would be constituted."[10]

8. Sir Michael Herbert to Lord Minto, February 20, 1903, *Laurier MS.*, P.A.C.

9. Sir Michael Herbert to the Marquess of Lansdowne, February 21, 1903, Lord Newton, *Lord Lansdowne* (London, 1929), pp. 262–263. In this interesting communication to Lord Lansdowne, Sir Michael Herbert remarked: "The President's Alaska appointments, with the exception of that of Root, are more than unfortunate, and I am naturally disgusted and disheartened. Moreover, all my illusions are gone in regard to men in whom I believed. Everything in this country is subservient to politics, and really an Ambassador in Washington needs more than an ordinary stock of patience. Hay had no defence to make when I reproached him privately beyond: 'Lodge is a friend of the President's,' and I understand that he disapproved of the appointments, but is powerless.

"The President, who has got his back up, takes the line that the Justices having refused, he had to appoint prominent public men, and that no statesman of importance in this country can be found who has not pronounced himself strongly on the Alaska question. In his opinion, the men appointed fulfil the conditions of the treaty. He also states that the U. S. case is so good that he only consented to the Commission because it afforded a means for England to get out of the difficult position in which she has been placed by Canada. In short, he is obstinate and unreasonable. . . .

"The question is: what is to be done? I realise the impossible position in which the Laurier Government has been placed in Canada, . . . but in spite of this, it would be useless and inadvisable for them to protest, and folly to break off as Laurier suggests, for the consequences would be too grave to contemplate."

Sir Michael Herbert died just before the close of the oral arguments before the Alaska boundary tribunal. For a sympathetic appreciation of his services to the cause of Anglo-American amity, see London *Times*, October 2, 1903.

10. Sir Wilfrid Laurier to Secretary Hay, February 24, 1903, Dennett, *op. cit.*, pp. 357–358. On February 27 the Earl of Onslow wrote to the Earl of Minto and laid the situation squarely before him. It would be useless to "press the United States Government to withdraw names put forward," and arguments relative to the fitness of the three American representatives could have "no practical results." *Laurier MS.*, P.A.C.

In Canada there was strong dissatisfaction voiced in the press with reference to President Roosevelt's selection of the American members of the Alaskan boundary

This protest was followed by one from Lord Minto to the Colonial Office. The Canadian Cabinet was deeply disturbed over the situation. Their assent to the Treaty of January 24, 1903 had been obtained on the stipulation "that the members of the Court would be impartial jurists of repute, this stipulation being supplemented by the representations of the British Ambassador at Washington . . . that the impartial jurists of repute would be selected from the higher courts." The appointments announced by President Roosevelt had changed "the whole situation." If the question were "now open to be dealt with entirely from the point of view of Canadian interests," the Cabinet would "hesitate to advise any further participation in proceedings in which there has been such a serious departure from good faith." But the Canadian Government had just been informed that the Alaska treaty had already been "confirmed" by his Majesty's Government, and this fact precluded any further discussion about carrying out its terms. However, in order to show British good faith in every respect, the men selected by His Majesty's Government to sit on the tribunal should be, "in the best sense of the word," impartial jurists of repute.[11]

Tribunal. On February 23, 1903, the Ottawa *Citizen* said: "To Mr. Root there would appear to be no serious objection beyond this, that as a member of the Washington administration he is really one of the parties to the controversy. . . . But in the case of Senators Lodge and Turner, their pronounced views upon the Alaskan boundary question certainly incapacitate them for the exercise of judicial functions in connection therewith." The Victoria *Daily Colonist,* February 24, 1903, expressed the following opinion: "The tone of the English press towards the Boundary Commission foreshadows a surrender to the United States just as certainly as growing twilight foreshadows the setting of the sun. . . . Canadian public opinion is as yet very far from imputing what would be nothing short of treachery on the part of Great Britain to Canada. The thing is so unbearable that the very mention of it strikes us with a nameless fear as to the future of the Empire." See also the Toronto *Globe* February 24, 25, 1903.

11. Earl of Minto to the Earl of Onslow, March 6, 1903, *Laurier MS.,* P.A.C. In a private letter to Ambassador Choate, February 17, 1903, Secretary Hay gave the following account of the background of Roosevelt's appointments of Root, Turner and Lodge. The reasons which had dictated these selections were obvious: "Root is one of the ablest men in public life today, equally distinguished as a lawyer and statesman. Lodge is the President's most intimate friend in the Senate, and has been of very great use to us in getting the treaty ratified. Turner is one of the most prominent lawyers west of the Rocky Mountains, and represents a great body of opinion there which has always been more or less hostile to England, and his influence and standing will be most valuable in influencing the opinion of the northwestern States in favor of a just and amicable settlement with Canada." *Choate MS.*

The Canadian reaction to these Roosevelt appointments, and to the celerity with which the British Government accepted the situation, is well expressed in the following excerpts from a letter addressed to John W. Dafoe by one of his Canadian friends: "As you have no doubt already sized the matter up, the British Government deliberately decided about a year ago to sacrifice our interests at any cost, for the sake of pleasing the United States. All their proceedings since that time were for the

In accordance with this ideal, the Canadian Government chose as its two representatives on the boundary tribunal, Sir Louis A. Jetté, Lieutenant-Governor of the Province of Quebec, and Mr. Justice George Armour, Puisne Judge of the Supreme Court of Canada. When Justice Armour died some months later, his vacancy was filled by the appointment of Mr. Allen B. Aylesworth, K.C., a distinguished Toronto barrister who had declined promotion to the Supreme Court of Canada.[12] The British Government chose as its representative, Lord Alverstone, the Lord Chief Justice of England, and by these appointments a strong and well-merited rebuke was given to President Roosevelt. It is hardly likely, however, that the American Chief Executive gave much thought to such indirect criticism. He was gaining his ends, one by one, and he was not particularly worried if Canada had to pay the bill for his successful excursions into the field of diplomacy. The British Government resented these Rooseveltian tactics, but the changing scene on the stage of world politics made Lord Lansdowne give the President the leading role in this drama of Anglo-American relations even though the harsh recitation of the lines made him wince at certain American accents.

The British Government had been so unwise as to join with Germany in a blockade of the coast of Venezuela during December, 1902 and the early months of 1903.[13] This action had caused deep dissatisfaction in many American circles, and the British Government felt so concerned about the necessity for conciliating American public opinion that it hastened to grant concessions which, in other circumstances, it would never have thought of doing.[14] It was this fact that explained why the British Foreign Office ratified the treaty of January 24, 1903 before giving the Canadian Government any chance to make an effective protest. Once more the claims of Canada would have to be subordinated to long-range British Empire policies.

Senator Lodge had been seriously concerned over the effects of this Venezuelan imbroglio, and in February, 1903 he feared that it might have an adverse influence upon Senatorial opinion of the Alaska treaty.

sake of inveigling us into a position from which we could not retire. . . . It is . . . the most cold-blooded case of absolutely giving away our interests, without even giving us the excuse of saying we have had a fight for it, which I know of." Dafoe, *op. cit.,* pp. 221–222.

12. Earl of Minto to Mr. Chamberlain, March 17, and July 23, 1903, *A.B.T.,* V, Pt. 4, 26.

13. For the Venezuelan imbroglio see J. F. Rippy, *Latin America in World Politics* (New York, 1931), pp. 182–199; Howard C. Hill, *Roosevelt and the Caribbean* (Chicago, 1927), chap. v; Dennett, *op. cit.,* pp. 388–394.

14. Lord Newton, *op. cit.,* pp. 259–261; Gelber, *op. cit.,* pp. 142–147; Dexter Perkins, *The Monroe Doctrine, 1867–1907* (Baltimore, 1937), pp. 319–395.

American public opinion had been anti-German but not anti-British. However, in certain American circles there was a great deal of doubt about the British Government's real intentions in the Venezuelan matter, and suspicions were rife. Lodge had learned upon what he considered good authority, that "the English *Government* appears to be no more friendly than that of Germany. Why the Government should run contrary to the feelings in their own country and take the very great risk of arousing bitter feelings here is something hard to understand."[15]

Although Lord Lansdowne was really very friendly to the United States, the fact that Lodge had suspicions of the policy pursued by the Foreign Office was a factor that might seriously disturb the equation of Anglo-American friendship. But Secretary Hay and Ambassador Choate were conciliatory in their attitude towards the British Government, and they helped to soften any asperities that might creep into correspondence. Because of Choate's excellent standing in England, and also in view of his eminence as a lawyer, Secretary Hay hoped that he would serve as the Counsel for the United States and would present the American case to the boundary tribunal.[16] But Choate thought there was an obvious incompatibility between his position as Ambassador and the proposed appointment as American Counsel. He had discussed many of the points involved in the Alaskan boundary controversy in confidential conversations with Lord Lansdowne, and he did not wish to be placed in the position of appearing to profit by these intimate relationships.[17]

But Choate's refusal to serve as the American Counsel before the boundary tribunal did not mean that he would not assist in the preparation of the American Case. In a series of letters to Mr. J. W. Foster, who was charged with the duty of preparing this case, Choate made many pertinent suggestions and indicated different lines of procedure.[18] In order to save unnecessary trips to England on the part of the American representatives on the boundary tribunal and the legal counsel who were preparing the necessary legal data, it was decided that the British Case could be handed in at the American Embassy in London on May 2, and the American Case could be presented at the Foreign Office on the same day.[19]

15. Senator Lodge to Henry White, February 3, 1903, *White MS.*

16. Secretary Hay to Ambassador Choate, February 17, 1903, *Choate MS.*

17. Ambassador Choate to Secretary Hay, March 6, 1903, *ibid.*

18. Ambassador Choate to John W. Foster, March 6, 10, 11, and 12, 1903, Foster to Choate, March 23, 1903, *ibid.*

19. Secretary Hay to Sir Michael Herbert, March 24, April 11, 17, 1903; Sir Michael Herbert to Secretary Hay, April 15, 16, 1903, *A.B.T.*, V, Pt. 3, 7–10.

While these details were being attended to in a friendly and business-like manner, President Roosevelt suddenly became convinced that Sir Wilfrid Laurier was not conciliatory enough in his attitude towards the settlement of the Alaska boundary dispute. Therefore, he sent a letter of instructions to the American representatives on the boundary tribunal that was written in a most uncompromising spirit.[20] He denounced the Canadian claims as generally "untenable," and expressed the view that there was no basis for the contention that Pyramid Harbor belonged to Canada. There was room for discussion with reference to whether the boundary line should follow the crests of the mountains along the coast or whether it should be "pushed back ten marine leagues," but with regard to "the principle involved, there will, of course, be no compromise." The main question was not one in which it was possible "to consider a reconciling of conflicting claims by mutual concessions." The task before tribunal was to

> determine whether the theory upon which Russia uniformly treated the boundary during her entire period of possession; upon which the United States has uniformly treated it ever since it acquired the territory, and upon which England uniformly treated it for over sixty years after the treaty was adopted, and according to which all the English, as distinguished from the Canadian cartographers, have since continued to treat it, is right in its entirety or wrong in its entirety.[21]

It was apparent to the American representatives on the boundary tribunal that President Roosevelt expected them to bring in a verdict favorable to the United States. The task before them was to have the tribunal convene as quickly as possible and get the matter settled. But the time allotted for preparing the Cases and the Counter-Cases was very short, and Lord Alverstone informed Ambassador Choate that a longer period was necessary.[22] Secretary Hay refused to accept this viewpoint. He thought it was of the "utmost consequence" to the United States, from a political point of view, "that the decision be reached at the earliest possible day." He was anxious, however, to retain Lord Alverstone's good will, for the decision really rested in his hands. He was hopeful that Alverstone's well-balanced mind would incline towards the American Case if Choate would personally handle the situation. If

20. F. W. Howay, W. N. Sage and H. F. Angus, *British Columbia and the United States: the North Pacific Slope from Fur Trade to Aviation* (Toronto, 1942), pp. 371–372.
21. President Roosevelt to Messrs. Elihu Root, Henry Cabot Lodge and George Turner, March 25, 1903, *Roosevelt MS.*
22. Ambassador Choate to Secretary Hay, March 25, 1903, *Choate MS.*

the American arguments were "properly presented" to Alverstone, the result would be "absolutely certain."[23]

But Choate was running into certain difficulties in the matter of securing the documents which he hoped would strengthen the American Case. He was denied access to the "rich store of papers in the Public Record Office bearing on the Alaskan Question." These papers were being used by the lawyers who were preparing the British Case, and they were not available for study by the American Ambassador.[24] Choate had been able to read the English edition of Vancouver's *Voyages*, and he regarded portions of the text as a strong support for the American claim to control over the Lynn Canal. There was no doubt in his mind that Russia was as "much in actual possession of the sites of Skagway and Dyea as of any other part of her vast dominions."[25]

While Choate was gathering data to help strengthen the American Case, Henry White was listening to complaints about the character of the American representatives. Joseph Chamberlain was quite disturbed over the situation, and he confided to White that he greatly feared that "the whole scheme will prove abortive."[26] Secretary Hay could sympathize with these objections as far as they centered upon Senator Lodge. Lodge was never very tactful, and he had recently made a speech in which he had attacked both the Canadians and the Department of State. He was a clever man, but "the infirmity of his mind and character is that he never sees but one subject at a time, and just at present it is the acceptability of his son-in-law to the voters of Gloucester." In his effort to get competent counsel to present the American Case before the boundary tribunal, the President had "consulted the Judges of the Supreme Court," and they had recommended Jacob M. Dickinson and David T. Watson. These men were able lawyers, but were not in the same class with Ambassador Choate, who could present an argument faultless in tone, temper, skill and knowledge of human nature. The British objections to Turner were unreasonable. There was "not a man in the United States out of an idiot asylum, who has not an opinion on the subject." Hay believed in his heart of hearts that there was not "an intelligent Englishman who does not know they have no case." Sir Wil-

23. Secretary Hay to Ambassador Choate, April 3, 1903, *ibid.*

24. Ambassador Choate to J. W. Foster, April 4, 1903, *ibid.* In a letter to Foster, April 7, 1903, Choate states that the Canadian delegation had arrived in London, had taken a "great suite of rooms at the Hotel Cecil, and are working like beavers. . . . Of course they have the full run of all the archives of the Foreign Office and of the Public Record Office."

25. Ambassador Choate to Foster, March 31, 1903, *ibid.*

26. Henry White to Secretary Hay, April 1, 1903, *White MS.*

frid Laurier had despatched to Washington a private messenger to protest against the appointments of Lodge and Turner, and during the course of a conversation this messenger had remarked: "Sir Wilfrid knows, and all of us know, that we have no case."[27]

It seems almost incredible that Sir Wilfrid's messenger would make such an admission, but Sir Wilfrid himself had spoken in a similar vein to Henry White in the summer of 1902 while in London. There is a certain compelling charm in such candor, but it is not usually listed as a favorable item in the catalogue of diplomacy. Perhaps it was a consciousness of the weakness of their case that led the British representatives on the boundary tribunal to seek for an extension of the time that had been allotted for the presentation of the Counter-Case. On April 24 Lord Alverstone expressed to Mr. Choate the opinion that the oral arguments before the tribunal should be held in October and not in September.[28] But Mr. Foster, the Agent for the United States, objected to any postponement, and Secretary Hay instructed Choate to talk with Lord Lansdowne and see whether it would not be possible "to expedite the oral argument."[29]

When Senator Lodge heard of this British desire to postpone the oral arguments until October, he was deeply disturbed and wrote at once to Henry White to file a vigorous protest. The American Government had been very indulgent in fixing the time for these arguments. Under the terms of the treaty the printed argument could be filed any time after the presentation of the Counter-Case, that is, any time after July 3d. The oral arguments, therefore, could have been held in July, but the United States had been willing to postpone matters until September. The boundary tribunal had the authority to fix the time when the proceedings should begin, and the British representatives could deadlock the situation and compel postponement. But this would lead to unnecessary friction, and the members of the tribunal were anxious to avoid needless difficulties. The time had arrived for the British members to show a conciliatory spirit in this regard. It was

absolutely essential that Mr. Root should be back in this country as early as possible in October, for he has to prepare his report to Congress, which meets in regular sessions at the beginning of December. There is to be an extra session of Congress, which will meet at the beginning of November, in order to pass the resolutions approving the Cuban Treaty, a matter of very

27. Secretary Hay to Henry White, April 10, 1903, *Absolutely Confidential, White MS.;* cf. Nevins, *op. cit.*, p. 195 for much of this frank letter.
28. Ambassador Choate to Secretary Hay, April 25, 1903, *Choate MS.*
29. Secretary Hay to Ambassador Choate, May 5, 1903, *ibid.*

great importance. I must be back for the meeting of the Senate. . . . I *must* sail in any event in October. We assented without objection to having the Tribunal meet in London. We might easily have demanded Washington. . . . To oblige us to postpone the hearing for the entire month of September . . . seems to me most unreasonable, and I cannot imagine that the English Government will be so discourteous. . . . I hope you will make every effort to have the Tribunal hear the oral arguments on the first of September, in fact, though I dislike the word, we *must* have it then.[30]

The matter of fixing the time for hearing the oral arguments proved more difficult than had been anticipated, and was only settled after some weeks of discussion. In the meantime the United States Agent was busily engaged upon the preparation of the American Case. There was little doubt that Mr. Foster was doing an excellent job in this regard, but the fact that Mr. Choate would not serve as one of the American Counsel made Henry White a little pessimistic about the outcome of the proceedings before the boundary tribunal. In a letter to Secretary Hay he expressed these misgivings:

I very much fear that even Mr. Choate himself could not have made Lord Alverstone take upon himself the responsibility of being alone in differing from the views of the other British Commissioners and siding with us against them. I am hoping for an opportunity of letting him know privately our view of the situation which is practically that we have consented to the arbitration in order to afford this country a loophole to escape from an untenable position (which Laurier as good as admitted it to be to me in private conversation last year), but no such opportunity has yet presented itself. . . . I shall have a good talk with Arthur Balfour, however, on the subject before the Tribunal meets—a talk of a most confidential character.[31]

With Balfour holding the important position of Prime Minister of England, there was little doubt that his opinion would have tremendous influence upon the mind of Lord Alverstone. This would not mean that Balfour would prejudice Alverstone's mind in favor of the American contention: he would merely impress upon him the importance of viewing the American Case with an open mind. To Secretary Hay this fact was all important, and he thought that everything depended upon "whether Lord Alverstone goes on the Bench with an imperative mandate or not. If he goes there with an open mind, we consider our case as won."[32]

Secretary Hay, with remarkable prevision of the final settlement,

30. Senator Lodge to Henry White, May 8, 1903, *White MS.*
31. Henry White to Secretary Hay, May 13, 1903, *ibid.*
32. Secretary Hay to Henry White, May 22, 1903, *ibid.*

regarded the Canadian contentions as fairly convincing with respect to "the little Islands in Portland Channel," but they were not sound with regard to the "great questions of the *lisière* and of occupation."[33] President Roosevelt, sharing these views of Secretary Hay, cherished no ill-will towards Canada. He assured A. Lawrence Lowell that as far as he could "influence affairs," he would endeavor to have the American Government "adopt an entirely friendly position towards Canada in every way."[34] But this did not mean that he would make concessions that he thought unwise. In the matter of postponing the presentation of the oral arguments before the boundary tribunal, he was adamant in his refusal to consider such a request. On May 15, Mr. Sifton, the British Agent, informed Mr. Foster that it would be "impossible" for him to prepare the Counter-Case for presentation in July. He therefore suggested an extension of two months.[35] Mr. Foster, after consulting with Secretary Hay, replied that such an extension could not be accepted by the American Government.[36] But the British Government was not ready to abandon its hope for an extension of time that would enable its representatives to present their Counter-Case later than July. Sir Michael Herbert stressed the need for an examination of certain original documents in the Department of State. This procedure would require some time, and would make it impossible for the British Counter-Case to be filed within the time stipulated by the American Government.[37]

Secretary Hay, acting as the mouthpiece of President Roosevelt, refused to agree to any extension of time. The American Counter-Case would be ready for presentation on July 3, and the Department of State expected that the Foreign Office would have the British Counter-Case completed by that date.[38] But despite the decisive tone of Secretary Hay's note, the British Ambassador in Washington continued to argue the point,[39] and Mr. Choate expressed the opinion that the British were so "staggered" by the strength of the American Case that they would keep on striving to "get all the delay they can."[40]

On June 19 Mr. Choate endeavored to impress upon Sir Robert Finlay the importance of acceding to the American request concerning the

33. Secretary Hay to President Roosevelt, May 16, 1903, *Roosevelt MS.*
34. President Roosevelt to A. Lawrence Lowell, June 13, 1903, *ibid.*
35. Clifford Sifton to John W. Foster, May 15, 1903, *A.B.T.,* V, Pt. 3, 12.
36. John W. Foster to Clifford Sifton, May 25, 1903, *ibid.,* p. 14.
37. Sir Michael Herbert to Secretary Hay, June 12, 1903, *ibid.,* p. 26.
38. Secretary Hay to Sir Michael Herbert, June 16, 1903, *ibid.,* pp. 27–30.
39. Sir Michael Herbert to Secretary Hay, June 18, 1903, *ibid.,* p. 38.
40. Ambassador Choate to Secretary Hay, June 17, 1903, *Choate MS.*

presentation of the British Counter-Case,[41] and he received assurances that the British Agent would carry out the terms of the treaty. It was quite possible, however, that the Agent would file a statement to the effect that the British Counter-Case was incomplete and would "have to be supplemented in some form."[42]

The British Attorney-General suggested that it might expedite matters if all communications relative to the extension of time for the presentation of the Counter-Case were directed to the British Agent, Clifford Sifton, who was *en route* to Ottawa. Such a suggestion did not please the President or his intimate friend, Senator Lodge. It appeared as though the British Government was merely sparring for more time. On June 23, 1903 Lodge wrote to the President and urged that he "take a stiff tone" with the British Foreign Office. It seemed to Lodge that the British attitude was "in the highest degree disobliging"; the "English brother will always push you as far as you will let him."[43] Roosevelt replied with an assurance that he would not permit the British Government to "do any shuffling now." They would be "kept right up to the mark," and if the Foreign Office would not listen to reason he would "declare the negotiations off, recite our case in the message to Congress, and ask for an appropriation to run the boundary as we deem it should be run."[44]

In this masterful mood, the President wrote at once to Secretary Hay and demanded that the British Government be made to toe the mark. In reply, Hay pleaded for a little patience with the Foreign Office. The British were not acting in "bad faith." Their case was "deplorably weak," and they were merely trying to secure all the time they could in a desperate endeavor to patch it up. There was no need for threats, but nevertheless, he would be as hard upon the Foreign Office "as is decent—perhaps rather more so."[45]

With the President constantly urging him to be firm with Great

41. Ambassador Choate to Sir Robert Finlay, *ibid.,* p. 40.

42. Sir Robert Finlay to Ambassador Choate, June 19, 1903, *ibid.,* p. 40.

43. Senator Lodge to President Roosevelt, June 23, 1903, *Selections from the Correspondence of Theodore Roosevelt and Henry Cabot Lodge,* 1884–1918, II, 32–33.

44. President Roosevelt to Senator Lodge, June 29, 1903, *ibid.,* pp. 36–37.

45. Secretary Hay to President Roosevelt, July 2, 1903, Dennett, *op. cit.,* pp. 359–360. In a letter to John W. Foster, July 2, 1903, Hay made some further comments upon the Alaskan situation: "I have a vehement letter from the President, started by one from Lodge, protesting against any delay in the Alaska Tribunal. I have answered that we are making all haste possible and resisting to the utmost any move for delay. It is of great importance that the matter come to oral argument at the earliest possible day, and Lodge—when I think of his being put to personal inconvenience, I am moved almost to tears." *Foster MS.*

Britain, Hay had no easy time as Secretary of State. On July 1 the British Embassy sent another long note arguing in favor of extending the time for the presentation of the oral arguments.[46] Hay turned a copy of this note over to Mr. Root, upon whom it made a "very disagreeable impression." Root forwarded the letter to Senator Lodge with the comment that it looked to him "like a row and delay."[47] It had the same appearance to Lodge, who wrote at once to the President and inquired whether negotiations were to be broken off.[48] Roosevelt replied that there was no justification for breaking off negotiations. If the British Foreign Office merely wanted "ten or fifteen days extra, or even a month," such a request could "under no conceivable circumstances be taken as an evidence of bad faith."[49] Root also wrote to Lodge and expressed the view that "we should go right along and have meeting in accordance with treaty."[50] But Roosevelt was careful to indicate to Senator Lodge that he was not weakening in his resolve to have the Alaska dispute settled promptly and decisively. If the tribunal could not reach any agreement during their meetings in London, he would ask "Congress at its next meeting to make an appropriation to enable me to run the line on our own theory."[51]

On July 25 Roosevelt wrote a letter to Mr. Justice Holmes, who was on vacation in England, and he expressed himself much as he did in the note to Senator Lodge. If the boundary tribunal could not reach an agreement in London, he would ask Congress to give him authority "to run the line as we claim it, by our own people, without any further regard to the attitude of England and Canada."[52] Holmes was at liberty

46. Mr. Arthur S. Raikes to Secretary Hay, July 1, 1903, *A.B.T.*, V, Pt. 3, 50–52.
47. Elihu Root to Senator Lodge, July 3, 1903, *Root MS.*
48. Senator Lodge to President Roosevelt, July 5, 1903, *Selections etc.*, II, 38.
49. President Roosevelt to Senator Lodge, July 8, 1903, *ibid.*, 38–39.
50. Elihu Root to Senator Lodge, July 7, 1903, *Root MS.*
51. President Roosevelt to Senator Lodge, July 16, 1903, *Selections, etc.*, II, 39.
52. President Roosevelt to Justice Holmes, July 25, 1903, *Roosevelt MS.* This letter to Justice Holmes was published in full in Joseph B. Bishop's *Theodore Roosevelt and His Time* (London, 1920), I, 259–261. In view of this fact it is somewhat surprising to read a letter from Mark Sullivan to Henry White, October 6, 1925 in which it is stated that the complete letter had never been published. According to Sullivan, "portions of this Roosevelt letter are published in some of the volumes of Roosevelt's correspondence. They always omit, however, the closing part of the letter which Roosevelt, on three occasions, described to me. . . . The closing part of the letter, as Roosevelt told me about it, was to the effect that unless the disputed territory should be awarded to the United States, Roosevelt would have no recourse except to reduce it to possession by force of arms. . . . I feel doubtful about the matter of taste and wisdom involved in looking up this letter and printing the portion of it which is deleted in Roosevelt's letters as so far published. I take it no useful service would be performed." *White MS.*

to show this letter to Joseph Chamberlain or to other British statesmen. In this way indirect pressure could be exerted upon Lord Alverstone, who really controlled the decision of the boundary tribunal.

But it was dangerous to count very much upon manipulating the mind of Lord Alverstone so that he could see the American side of the boundary dispute. After reaching London, Senator Lodge was none too sanguine about the outcome of the proceedings before the tribunal, and he expressed serious doubt whether Alverstone would "part from the Canadians and decide the case on the evidence."[53] Several days later, he was still pessimistic about the situation. He had talked matters over with Joseph Chamberlain and Prime Minister Balfour, and it was apparent that both of these statesmen were willing to "do all they can to help things along." The whole difficulty came from the Canadians. The British Government was still fearful of offending Canadian sensibilities, and the Canadians themselves were so "perfectly stupid" that they failed utterly to see that "a disagreement deprives them of their only chance to get out of the matter creditably."[54]

In the meantime, Secretary Hay was having his troubles with the President. He believed that the American Government should be "as liberal as possible in letting the other side get their Counter-Case in. We can perfectly afford to be easy with them and not insist on the letter of the agreement."[55] But the President, under constant pressure from Senator Lodge, was not inclined to grant any favors to the British Government, and he informed Hay that if the boundary tribunal did not reach an agreement, the United States would have to act "in a way which will necessarily wound British pride."[56] Hay countered by offering his resignation, which was not accepted. But even though he had won this gesture of confidence from the President, Hay realized that it would be impossible always to restrain the Chief Executive when he was in one of his impetuous moods. It was extremely important, however, to continue in office until the most outstanding irritants in Anglo-American relations were removed.[57] But these irritants were many, and they required all of Hay's patience to deal with them.

On July 29 Clifford Sifton wrote to John W. Foster and inquired if October 15 would not be a suitable time for a preliminary meeting of the boundary tribunal. At this meeting it would be possible to fix the date for hearing the oral arguments.[58] Mr. Foster at once informed

53. Senator Lodge to President Roosevelt, July 25, 1903, *Selections, etc.*, II, 40–41.
54. Senator Lodge to President Roosevelt, July 30, 1903, *ibid.*, pp. 41–43.
55. Secretary Hay to John W. Foster, July 23, 1903, *Foster MS.*
56. A. L. P. Dennis, *op. cit.*, p. 145. 57. Dennett, *op. cit.*, p. 360.
58. Clifford Sifton to John W. Foster, July 29, 1903, *A.B.T.*, V, Pt. 3, 63.

Mr. Sifton that the American Government had been counting upon the presentation of these oral arguments before the boundary tribunal in September.[59]

President Roosevelt wrote immediately to Foster to compliment him upon the tone of the letter that had been sent to Sifton. It was impossible to determine just what Sifton had meant by such a document.[60] Hay also wrote to Foster to express his amazement at the Sifton letter and yet counselled restraint. But Choate discovered that the whole question of postponement had arisen through a muddle in the Foreign Office, and was assured by Lord Alverstone that the Tribunal would meet, after all, on September 3.[61]

This reassurance given Choate does not seem, however, to have been successful in calming ruffled tempers. On August 8 the President exploded in a letter to Root. The British Government had long been anxious for some sort of settlement of the Alaskan boundary dispute, and

59. John W. Foster to Clifford Sifton, August 4, 1903, *ibid.*, pp. 63–65.

60. President Roosevelt to John W. Foster, August 5, 1903, *Foster MS.*

61. Secretary Hay to John W. Foster, August 5, 1903, *ibid.* On August 5, 1903 Ambassador Choate sent a note to the Foreign Office with reference to the Sifton letter. He had thought his note was quite mild, but it seemed to create "a great flutter in the dove-cote at the Foreign Office. There came a telephone message asking if Mr. Villiers could see Mr. Carter at once, and a few minutes later he appeared bringing my note with him. He stated that he came to make an explanation in regard thereto, which was to the effect that Lord Lansdowne 'had no record to show' that he had ever been informed that the printed argument would be delivered by us in London by September 3d, he being under the impression that the same procedure would obtain in regard to the printed argument as that pursued in regard to the cases and counter-cases, and that therefore, the printed arguments would be delivered simultaneously at the British Embassy in Washington and at our Embassy here respectively on the 3d of September, that he thus reckoned that our printed argument would not reach London before the 13th and that a month would elapse after the delivery before the oral argument was begun, and thus the 15th of October was suggested for the opening of the *oral argument,* and not as I supposed for the mere meeting of the Tribunal.

"This was so utterly inconsistent with everything that had passed between Lord Lansdowne and myself, and so directly contrary to Mr. Sifton's explicit proposal of October 15th for the preliminary meeting to 'fix the date of the oral argument' that I venture to think that it was all Villiers and not Lansdowne at all, especially as Mr. Villiers has always manifested a strong disposition to put the thing off, and repeatedly protested against our crowding them so. . . . However, on the same day, Mr. Villiers saw Lord Lansdowne and the Lord Chief Justice, and got a great light, for at four o'clock he asked Mr. Carter to come to the Foreign Office and suggested that the Tribunal should meet on September 3d. But the best of the story came three or four days after, when I met Lord Alverstone in the lobby of the House of Lords, and said to him that I was glad it was now definitely fixed that they were to meet on the third, and again inveighed against Sifton's letter. 'Oh,' said he, 'You mustn't blame poor Sifton, it wasn't he at all. What he wrote was dictated from here. . . . But . . . we are not only going to accommodate you in that, we shall accommodate your people in subsequent proceedings.' " Ambassador Choate to Secretary Hay, August 14, 1903, *Personal and Confidential, Choate MS.*

had exerted pressure in favor of arbitration. He had taken the trouble to explain

> to Pauncefote and to Colonel Kitson, and Hay explained to Herbert, just what the situation was. When Pauncefote and Kitson pressed for the commission it was because the Canadians had sent their contingent to South Africa and were demanding a *quid pro quo* which the English were anxious to give. I then told both Pauncefote and Kitson that if they were wise they would let the thing rest until the South African business was through, for their own sakes, not for ours, and that in my judgment they had better let sleeping dogs lie. . . . I also repeated this to Herbert last winter. To all of them I explained that if they persisted in taking the thing up it would make it necessary for us to finish it. For instance, with my present feeling, I am inclined to think that if on the main issue the British hold out and refuse to agree with us, I shall at once establish posts on the islands and sufficiently far up the main streams to reduce all the essential points of our claim to actual occupancy, and shall then ask Congress to appropriate money for at least a partial survey of the territory between the posts. This will not be pleasant to do and it will be still less pleasant for the English; but as things appear now, it will be the only alternative.[62]

It is apparent that the President was in no mood to listen to requests for an extension of the time for the presentation of the oral arguments, and his viewpoint in this regard was colored by the opinions of Lodge and Root. On August 19 Root wrote to the President to express his agreement with the stand taken by Lodge. Sifton's letter to Foster had been a "good deal of a shock" to the American representatives, and he was afraid that the Canadians would seek by "dilatory applications, long-winded arguments and frequent adjournments" to delay things as long as they could.[63]

Lodge still harbored suspicions of Canadian tactics, but he thought that the British Government was friendly and would not support the "absurd contentions" of the Canadian representatives.[64] There was,

62. President Roosevelt to Secretary Root, August 8, 1903, *Roosevelt MS.* It is quite true that, at times during the Boer War, Roosevelt expressed himself as strongly on the side of England. In a letter to John R. Proctor, Civil Service Commissioner, December 23, 1899, Roosevelt stated that he thought that "real liberty and real progress are bound up with the prosperity of the English speaking peoples." If some of the European Powers would attempt to intervene in the war and thus attempt to destroy the British Empire, Roosevelt believed that the United States should promptly take sides with England. See also, Roosevelt's letters to Captain R. Wainwright, December 16, 1899, and to Colonel Arthur Lee, January 30, and December 19, 1900, *ibid.*

63. Elihu Root to President Roosevelt, August 19, 1903, *Root MS.*

64. Senator Lodge to John W. Foster, August 20, 1903, *Foster MS.*

however, some doubt about how far British statesmen would go in exerting pressure upon Canada. It was very possible that Lord Alverstone would see eye to eye with the American representatives on most points, but the British were "in such mortal terror of Canada" that there was no telling how they would act. Lodge was certain, however, that they would not go to the extent of war with the United States over the Alaskan boundary.[65] Roosevelt, although harboring some lingering doubts about the attitude of the British Government, could only hope that their statesmen would "act with sanity and propriety in the Alaska business. It will be a great misfortune if they do not—a misfortune for us and a much greater one for England and Canada."[66]

With this background of uncertainty and suspicion, the boundary tribunal finally met in London on September 3, 1903.[67] Lord Alverstone was chosen as President of the Tribunal, and arrangements were made with reference to the procedure that would be followed. It was agreed that three Counsel should be heard on each side. Great Britain should begin the oral arguments, the United States should reply, and then the other Counsel should be heard alternately. After these formalities were completed, the hearings were adjourned until September 15.

At the very beginning of his oral argument, Sir Robert Finlay stated that for more than thirty years the question of the boundary had been in dispute, and he contended that at no time during this period had there "been anything like acquiescence or consent as between the United States of America and Great Britain, as to what is the proper frontier to be drawn of the region now in dispute." After thus

65. Senator Lodge to President Roosevelt, August 30, 1903, *Selections, etc.,* II, 48–49. The anxiety of the Balfour Ministry to be on excellent terms with the United States is clearly revealed in the letters to Andrew Carnegie. See Burton J. Hendrick, *The Life of Andrew Carnegie* (New York, 1932), II, 190–194.

66. President Roosevelt to Secretary Hay, August 21, 1903, *Roosevelt MS.*

67. Jacob M. Dickinson, David T. Watson, Hannis Taylor, and Chandler P. Anderson appeared as Counsel for the United States. Robert Lansing served as Solicitor of the United States' Agency, and O. H. Tittman, W. C. Hodgkins, Otis T. Cartwright, T. John Newton and F. R. Hanna were members of the United States' Agent's staff.

The Attorney-General (Sir Robert Finlay); the Solicitor-General (Sir Edward Carson); Christopher Robinson, F. C. Wade, L. P. Duff, A. Geoffrion, S. A. T. Rowlatt, and J. A. Simon appeared as Counsel for Great Britain. W. F. King and A. P. Collier served as members of the British Agent's staff.

In the London *Times,* Sept. 3, 1903, there is a long account of the background of the Alaskan boundary dispute. It stressed the importance of the gold fields in the Yukon district. The stampede of 1897 and 1898 to the Yukon, led to the development of the towns of Skagway and Dyea, which were at the base of the mountain passes leading to the gold country. Their situation was very strategic, and prospective miners and mining supplies had to go through these towns. The Yukon district had produced $100,000,000 in gold in less than four years.

anticipating the main points in the American argument,[68] Sir Robert then claimed that the only authority reposed in the Tribunal was to "answer the specific questions which are put to it."[69]

After discussing the limitations upon the Tribunal's authority, Sir Robert then presented a lengthy argument of some 340 closely printed pages. This exhaustive presentation of the British Case was cogent and impressive, and it was followed with great attention by the American

68. In preparing the Case and Counter-Case for the United States, John W. Foster decided to have the Case "embrace only the negotiations of the treaties of 1824 and 1825, their history and results, the acts of occupation by Russia on the *lisière,* the cession and transfer to the United States, the American occupation, and the maps up to 1867. We will show our title to the territory and indisputed occupation. It devolves upon Great Britain to show the basis of its claim to title and its right to possession. We shall, then, in the Counter Case show the admissions of Great Britain, embracing all facts as between the two countries since 1867, . . . and shall assert that such admissions on her part and failure to protest at the time of the cession have created an estoppel to her now questioning the title of the United States. The Counter Case will also set forth the British admissions during Russian occupation, as the lease of the Hudson's Bay Company, the Canadian and British maps, etc." Foster to Ambassador Choate, April 13, 1903, *Choate MS.* Choate read the Case and Counter-Case with close attention, and congratulated Foster on "its very satisfactory character." Choate to Foster, May 20, 1903, *ibid.*

69. The questions before the Tribunal were: No. 1. "What is intended as the point of commencement of the line?" No. 2. "What channel is the Portland Channel?" No. 3. "What course should the line take from the point of commencement to the entrance to Portland Channel?" No. 4. "To what point on the 56th parallel is the line to be drawn from the head of the Portland Channel, and what course should it follow between these points?" No. 5. "In extending the line of demarcation northward from said point on the parallel of the 56th degree of north latitude, following the crest of the mountains situated parallel to the coast until its intersection with the 141st degree of longitude west of Greenwich, subject to the condition that if such line should anywhere exceed the distance of ten marine leagues from the ocean, then the boundary between the British and the Russian territory should be formed by a line parallel to the sinuosities of the coast and distant therefrom not more than ten marine leagues, was it the intention and meaning of said convention of 1825 that there should remain in the exclusive possession of Russia a continuous fringe or strip of coast on the mainland, not exceeding ten marine leagues in width, separating the British Possessions from the bays, ports, inlets, havens, and waters of the ocean, and extending from the said point on the 56th degree of latitude north to a point where such line of demarcation should intersect the 141st degree of longitude west of the meridian of Greenwich?" No. 6. "If the foregoing question should be answered in the negative, and in the event of the summit of such mountains proving to be in places more than ten marine leagues from the coast, should the width of the *lisière* which was to belong to Russia be measured (1) from the mainland coast of the ocean, strictly so-called, along a line perpendicular thereto, or (2) was it the intention and meaning of the said convention that where the mainland coast is indented by deep inlets forming part of the territorial waters of Russia, the width of the *lisière* was to be measured (a) from the line of the general direction of the mainland coast, or (b) from the line separating the waters of the ocean from the territorial waters of Russia, or (c) from the heads of the aforesaid inlets?" No. 7. "What, if any exist, are the mountains referred to as situated parallel to the coast, which mountains, when within ten marine leagues from the coast, are declared to form the eastern boundary?"

representatives.[70] But they continued to regard their case as unbeatable. As a reflection of this optimism, Henry White wrote to President Roosevelt, expressing the belief that the decision of the Tribunal would be in favor of the American contention. Lord Alverstone was "daily getting into closer personal touch with Cabot and Root," and had talked quite "freely to them." At first Lodge was of the opinion that "no decision would be possible." A longer residence in London had changed this viewpoint, and his hopes had risen as the oral arguments had proceeded. The American representatives could not help nursing the belief that Lord Alverstone's experience in politics would influence him to take a "sensible and practical view of the situation."[71]

Secretary Hay was of the same opinion. A man of Lord Alverstone's undoubted clarity of vision could not help but incline towards the American side. In order to influence his decision, the Canadians were

70. "Argument of Sir Robert Finlay," September 15–23, 1903, *A.B.T.*, VI, 10–350. In the oral arguments and in the printed Case of the United States the following points were strongly held: 1. It was the intention of the high contracting parties to the convention of February 28, 1825 to confirm in full sovereignty to Russia by that instrument a continuous strip or *lisière* of territory along the continental shores of the Northwest Coast of America, extending from Portland Canal to the 141st meridian of longitude west of Greenwich. 2. It was the intention of the high contracting parties that the width of such *lisière* was to be 10 marine leagues measured from the heads of all gulfs, bays, inlets, and arms of the sea—that is, from tide water—unless within that distance from tide water there was wholly or in part a continuous range of mountains lying parallel to the sinuosities of the coast and extending from Portland Canal to the 141st meridian of longitude west of Greenwich, in which latter case the summit of such range was to form the boundary. 3. The acts of Great Britain and Russia subsequent to the signature of the treaty, and the universal interpretation given to its delimiting articles by governments, geographers, cartographers, and historians of those and other civilized nations, agree with and confirm the intention and meaning as above stated. 4. The United States purchased the territory from Russia, relying upon such interpretation of the treaty. 5. During a period of 30 years after the purchase of Alaska the British Government did not claim any portion of the territory that had been transferred to the United States. 6. The American Government entered into possession of and occupied the *lisière* above described without any protest or objection from the British Government. 7. The United States, from the time of the cession from Russia, has remained in continuous and undisturbed possession of the *lisière*. 8. There is not any point within 10 marine leagues of tide water, between the head of Portland Canal and the 141st degree of longitude, the whole or any part of a continuous range of mountains parallel to the sinuosities of the coast. Therefore the width of the *lisière* is not limited by a boundary line along the summit of such range, but solely by the agreed distance of 10 marine leagues from tide water. 9. Portland Channel was the body of water now commonly known and described as Portland Canal. 10. The boundary line under the treaty of 1825 began at Cape Muzon and ran thence in an easterly direction to the entrance to Portland Canal between Wales and Compton Islands; thence northeasterly along the center of Portland Canal to a point equidistant from Pearse Island and Ramsden Point; thence northerly along the center of Portland Canal until the line touched the mainland at the head of Portland Canal; thence upon the same course to the 56th parallel of north latitude.

71. Henry White to President Roosevelt, September 19, 1903, *White MS.*

stressing the importance of Imperial interests. But it seemed obvious to Hay that these interests would be seriously imperilled if Alverstone voted with the Canadians and thus forced the President to take the action he had threatened. The Canadian Cabinet must be aware of the dangers that lurked in this situation, and they were none too certain of the justice of their claims. Even Laurier had intimated that his Government realized that it had no case.[72]

President Roosevelt was in complete agreement with Secretary Hay in this matter of the Alaskan boundary, and he grew quite angry when he heard that pressure was being exerted upon Lord Alverstone in order to bring him into line with his Canadian colleagues. He wondered if those "jacks" realized that "while it may be unpleasant to us, it will be far more unpleasant to them if they force the alternative upon us; if we simply announce that the country is ours and will remain so, and that so far as it has not been reduced to possession it will be reduced to possession, and that no further negotiations in the matter will be entertained."[73]

Roosevelt's rising anger was partly produced by successive letters from Senator Lodge with reference to the meetings of the Tribunal. Although Henry White, Ambassador Choate and John W. Foster entertained high hopes that everything would turn out favorably for the United States, Lodge, along with Root and Turner, did not feel hopeful and looked "for a disagreement."[74] On September 13 Lodge was still pessimistic about the outcome of the whole affair. The Canadians were "filling the newspapers with articles of the most violent kind, threatening England with all sorts of things if the decision should go against Canada." England was "so afraid of Canada" that Lodge greatly feared the effect of this pressure.[75]

Sir Robert Finlay finished his long oral argument on September 23, and David T. Watson began his formal presentation of the American Case. On the following day, Senator Lodge wrote a long letter to the President and described the situation. He thought that Watson's opening statement was "pretty ragged," and he was afraid that his voice and manner would jar "on English ears." He was hopeful, however, that things would improve. He had talked with Lord Alverstone who felt that he was bound by the law and the facts to

72. Secretary Hay to Henry White, September 20, 1903, *ibid.*

73. President Roosevelt to Secretary Hay, September 21, 1903, *Roosevelt MS.*

74. Senator Lodge to President Roosevelt, September 5, 1903, *Selections, etc.*, II, 53–55.

75. Senator Lodge to President Roosevelt, September 13, 1903, *ibid.*, pp. 55–57.

hold that the line goes round the heads of the inlets, which is, of course, the main contention.[76] He takes very decisively the British view on the Portland Canal. He wants to answer question 7, however, by picking out a series of mountains which will reduce the strip running around the heads of all the inlets to as narrow bounds as possible, his idea being, I presume, to try to let the Canadians down as easily as possible in this way, after having decided against them on the main point. We went over after the session yesterday and had a long talk with Choate on the situation. We all agreed that if Alverstone decided in our favour on the main contention, namely, the heads of the inlets, that we could afford, with a slight modification, to accept their Portland Channel.[77] . . . Root and I after talk today do not see yet how we can accept the mountain theory of Ld. A. But time will show.[78]

In the last week of September, Lodge wrote another letter to President Roosevelt, and once more he expressed his disappointment over the showing made by David T. Watson, who had just concluded (September 28) his oral argument. But Lodge realized that Watson's argument would have very little effect "on the decision of the Tribunal." That decision would "be reached by the Commissioners and it does not depend on the arguments."[79]

Lodge was a practical politician and not a theoretical lawyer, and he knew very well that the American representatives would vote as a

76. On September 18, Sir Robert Finlay had argued at great length that it would be impossible to draw the boundary line "parallel to the sinuosities of the inlets." The treaty referred to the line being parallel to the sinuosities of the coast, and Sir Robert was positive that an inlet "is not a sinuosity." The expression, "sinuosities of the coast," was an expression that was "not applicable to an inlet," and "never would have been used with regard to it." *A.B.T.*, VI, 203. According to Sir Robert, the terms of the treaty meant a line should be drawn "following the sinuosities of the coast parallel to which you could draw another line. It is impossible if you include in sinuosities of the coast a long, deep inlet like the Taku Inlet or Lynn Canal. . . . It is impossible for you to include such inlets as these under the term 'sinuosities of the coast' to get your parallel line." *Ibid.*, p. 218.

It is important to observe that in presenting its case to the Tribunal, the British Government abandoned the claim that the boundary line should run from Cape Chacon through Clarence Strait and Ernest Sound to the continental coast at 56° north latitude. This claim had been pushed by the Government of British Columbia, and had been supported by the British representatives during the sessions of the Joint High Commission in 1898–1899.

77. On September 15 Roosevelt had written to Secretary Hay to the effect that he was not deeply interested in the islands at the mouth of the Portland Channel. He stated that he would "be glad to use them as a make-weight in the Alaska boundary matter." *Roosevelt MS.* On September 19, Henry White wrote to Roosevelt and expressed the opinion that "the Canadians have no doubt an excellent case on the Portland Canal question." *White MS.*

78. Senator Lodge to President Roosevelt, September 24, 1903, *Selections, etc.*, II, 57–59.

79. Senator Lodge to President Roosevelt, September 29, 1903, *ibid.*, pp. 59–62.

unit despite any arguments before the Tribunal. He also suspected that the British Government would respond to pressure and would arrange for a decision favorable to the American contentions. President Roosevelt had this same idea, and with this end in view he wrote a letter to Henry White which he expected would be shown to British statesmen. He adverted to the dangers of a deadlock in the vote of the Tribunal. Such an outcome would be a "bad thing" for the United States, "but it would be a very much worse thing for the Canadians and English, because it would leave me no alternative but to declare as courteously, but as strongly as possible, that the effort to reach an agreement having failed, I should be obliged to treat the territory as ours, . . . and to declare . . . that no additional negotiations of any kind would be entered into."[80]

To reinforce this open threat, Secretary Hay wrote to White much in the same vein. He ardently hoped that Lord Alverstone would favor the American contention, and thus settle a dangerous question. It was not his intention to write in a menacing manner, but the British should be "clever enough" to see what a deadlock in the vote of the Tribunal would lead to. The President would "regard our case as proved—and act accordingly."[81]

It was apparent that American statesmen were relying far more upon political pressure than upon the strength of their arguments in this matter of securing a boundary to their liking. Their Case had undoubted strength, and if one took into consideration the series of maps that supported their viewpoint and the fact of occupation together with British acquiescence in this occupation, it would be difficult to bring in an adverse decision. But the British were pushing for Lord Alverstone to make a judicial decision that would rest largely upon a strict interpretation of the words of the Treaty of 1825 without consideration being given to the fact of American occupation.[82] The wisdom of such a line of procedure was apparent to Ambassador Choate as early as March, 1903, and he gave the following warning to Mr. Foster: "It is quite clear that they will lay great stress upon the verbal construc-

80. President Roosevelt to Henry White, September 26, 1903, *Roosevelt MS.*

81. Secretary Hay to Henry White, September 30, 1903, *White MS.*

82. In commenting upon this fact, Mr. Dafoe, in his biography of Clifford Sifton, remarks: "The argument which was perhaps most strongly stressed by the United States counsel—the alleged acquiescence of Great Britain in the United States occupation of the disputed territory—was one only applicable to arbitration proceedings, as Lord Alverstone said during the argument." In the proceedings before the Tribunal, "in which nothing could be considered except the legal rights conferred by treaty, there was nothing valid in arguments about estoppel and time limitations." *Clifford Sifton in Relation to His Times,* p. 226.

tion of the Treaty, upon which they could make quite an argument if they could separate it from all that went before and after."[83]

On October 1 Sir Edward Carson presented an oral argument before the Tribunal in which he made a strong and sustained attack upon the American Case. It was a fact that there was an evident inconsistency between Vancouver's narrative and his maps, and Sir Edward attempted to show that the negotiators of the Treaty of 1825 did not place much reliance upon those maps. It was his belief that the chain of mountains along whose crest the boundary line was to run was a range that was quite close to the coast. Such a line would give the British control over the headwaters of all the important inlets including the Lynn Canal.[84]

During the course of Sir Edward Carson's oral argument, Lord Alverstone seemed greatly interested in some of the points that were developed. This fact was distinctly alarming to the American representatives on the Tribunal, and Senator Lodge wrote a hurried letter to Henry White requesting him to see Prime Minister Balfour and acquaint him with the seriousness of the situation in the event of a deadlock. He believed that Lord Alverstone's attitude had not undergone

83. Ambassador Choate to John W. Foster, March 24, 1903, *Choate MS.* In his opening argument, Sir Robert Finlay denied that the United States had acquired sovereignty in the territory around the inlets by a prescription consisting in the actual holding, policing, and administering of that land, first by Russia and then by the United States, without any protest from Great Britain for more than seventy years after the Anglo-Russian boundary treaty of 1825. It was the view of Sir Robert that the only purpose in presenting data to the Tribunal was to enable its members to discover "what was the understanding of the parties—that is of both parties—in respect to the limits of their several territorial jurisdictions under the Treaties. . . . A large portion of the Case and Argument submitted on behalf of the United States of America deals with this matter as if it were a question of showing a title by prescription or by occupation." *A.B.T.*, VI, 12–13. Later, Sir Robert again stated: "I should not dispute for a moment that long possession would be an element which any arbitrator would most properly take into account in determining a dispute which was open as between two Powers as to the ownership of a territory, but what I do submit is that all such considerations have been excluded . . . by the terms of the Treaty of Arbitration in the present case." *Ibid.*, pp. 345–346.

Lord Alverstone apparently agreed with this reasoning of Sir Robert Finlay, even though the Privy Council, in the case of *Direct United States Cable Co.* v. *Anglo-American Telegraph Co.*, had recognized the rule of prescription in international law. In order to meet this situation, the American counsel shifted their argument from the right of prescription to the "safer ground that Great Britain's acquiescence was a contemporary and long-continued admission that it was the intention of the treaty of 1825 to run the boundary so as to include the heads of the inlets in Russian territory. They employed unprotested possession . . . as evidence of the correctness of their interpretation of the treaty, not as creating title not previously owned." Corbett, *The Settlement of Canadian-American Disputes*, pp. 103–105.

84. *A.B.T.*, VII, 635–690.

any perceptible change, but one could not be too certain. Alverstone had confided to Lodge that he was

> nearer than ever to our view of question 7, while he is as firm as ever on his main contention of the line going round the head of the inlets which is involved in the reply to question 5. Nonetheless I think it very important that you should speak to Mr. Balfour in the sense you suggest, and my reason is this. Lord A. said to me day before yesterday, that he was in a very trying and disagreeable position; that the Canadians were putting every sort of pressure and making every kind of appeal to him, alleging that Root and Turner and I were trying to lead him on to a decision on the main question, and having got that, would break off on the others. He, of course, knows that this is not true and that we shall be absolutely fair and above board which ever way the thing goes, but nevertheless, their appeals trouble him. Therefore I think that a knowledge of the position of his Government, and that they would stand behind him, would be of great value. If, for example, this could be said or written to him by the Prime Minister: "We know you are going to decide this question impartially on the law and facts. We, of course, should not think of seeking to influence your opinions on any point. But it seems right that you should know that a failure to reach a decision would be most unfortunate. If there is no decision, there will be no arbitration subsequently. The United States will remain in possession of all the disputed territory, and will take possession of any points not occupied. They can only be displaced by war which we all know is impossible." . . .
>
> If something of this sort could be said I am sure it would be a good thing for it would make Lord A. feel that his Government was behind him in the decision he undoubtedly means to make. I strongly advise that you lay the exact facts before Mr. Balfour.[85]

On this same day (October 2) Lodge wrote a second letter to White in which he expressed the fear that Lord Alverstone was beginning to favor the British idea of reducing the *lisière* to "the narrowest limits." The American representatives could not "assent to a whittling down of the strip because that would involve giving over land occupied by Americans."[86]

Elihu Root was also disturbed by the impression which Sir Edward Carson's argument apparently had made upon Lord Alverstone, and he lost no time in writing to Henry White along the same lines as the Lodge letter. He thought it was important for White to avoid saying anything to Balfour that

> might be misconstrued as being in the nature of a threat, yet it seems to me

85. Senator Lodge to Henry White, October 2, 1903, *Confidential, White MS.*
86. Senator Lodge to Henry White, October 2, 1903, *ibid.;* cf. Nevins, *op. cit.,* 200.

that the highest considerations of friendship between the two countries require that the Foreign Office should know how serious the consequences of disagreement must necessarily be, and how impossible it is to expect acquiescence in a surrender of . . . a very considerable part of the territory which they supposed themselves to have bought and to have held so long. National or popular judgments proceed not on close arguments but on broad obvious facts, and no settlement far out of accord with the maps on which the Americans base their judgment can be contemplated by anyone who wishes real friendship between the two peoples, and universal public sentiment in America would demand strong adherence to the line of right as America understands it. The course of the American Government in case of disagreement is inevitable. No administration can avoid it.[87]

Under the impact of these strong letters, White paid a visit to Balfour's country estate, and had a long talk with him concerning the Alaskan boundary situation. Balfour frankly admitted that he attached "far more importance to the agreement of the Tribunal than to any of the Cabinet questions and complications with which he was then bothered." Although Balfour would not indicate what steps he would take in the matter of getting in touch with Lord Alverstone, he clearly showed that he viewed the possibility of a deadlock with deep concern.[88]

It was not difficult, in the highly charged atmosphere of London, for the Canadian representatives on the Tribunal to feel some of the sparks that were flying from the anvil on which President Roosevelt and Prime Minister Balfour were trying to forge a stronger chain between the English-speaking countries. On October 7 Clifford Sifton, sensing the situation, sent a cablegram to Sir Wilfrid Laurier in which he charged that Lord Alverstone was ready to support the American contentions. Mr. Aylesworth and Sir Louis Jetté were exasperated at the stand taken by Alverstone, and were anxious to know whether they should withdraw from the Tribunal. Laurier, who was a statesman and not a mere politician, knew the dangers of such a move, and he instructed the Canadian representatives to remain on the Tribunal and continue to fight for the British contention relative to Portland Channel. That point would have to be decided "in Canada's favour."[89]

The oral arguments before the Tribunal terminated on October 8 when Jacob M. Dickinson concluded his able presentation of the American Case. Senator Lodge was impressed with the manner in which Dickinson handled a vast amount of data which he was able to control and

87. Elihu Root to Henry White, October 2, 1903, *White MS.*
88. Nevins, *op. cit.*, p. 200.
89. Dafoe, *op. cit.*, pp. 228–229; Skelton, *Laurier,* II, 149.

use to evident advantage.[90] Sir Edward Carson had given the impression that the negotiators (particularly the British) had relied on the Vancouver narrative and had not paid much attention to the Vancouver maps. Dickinson challenged this viewpoint and contended that it was quite likely the Vancouver maps were used and not the narrative.[91] In dealing with the question of the mountain range along whose crest the boundary line was supposed to run, Dickinson asserted that this range was clearly depicted on the Vancouver maps, and whether it actually existed or not, the negotiators had bound their respective nations to this bargain.[92] With reference to the British claim to jurisdiction over the headwaters of the inlets, Dickinson pointed out that the British Government had never "sent a ship into any of these interior waters, or even sought in any way, shape, or form . . . to exercise any sort of sovereignty over them. . . . Could there be any more significant fact than that in regard to the interpretation of this Treaty?"[93]

After the oral arguments had been concluded, Choate wrote to Secretary Hay and expressed the opinion that Lord Alverstone was "satisfied that by the true construction of the Treaty, the *lisière* goes round the Inlets and not across them, which, if he will stick to it, wins the Case for us on the main point."[94] Choate was correct in his general statement of Lord Alverstone's views, but he did not indicate that the English jurist wished to restrict the width of the *lisière* that went around the inlets. When this fact was made clear to the American

90. Senator Lodge to President Roosevelt, October 12, 1903, *Selections, etc.,* II, 69.

91. *A.B.T.,* VIII, 741ff.

92. During the course of his argument on this matter of the use of the Vancouver maps, Dickinson remarked: "If you look to the coast and look to the mountains, there is a clear demonstration of what the controlling idea was. If you look to the mountains, . . . the mountains would indicate what they had in view; but when you look to the coast and what was said in regard to that, and then look to the mountains and what was said in regard to them, and put the two side by side, they supplement each other, and make out . . . an irrefragable case for the United States. . . . The way in which it presents itself to my mind is that those mountains on the map were just as effectual as they would be if they actually existed. Those mountains had a relative situation in regard to certain things that were individualised and known, and known just as well at that day as they are at this day. I refer to the inlets. If, knowing these inlets and their situation, they referred to mountains which appeared upon the maps to run around them, and said, 'There we will put the line,' . . . the line is fixed by the mountains just as much as if they were there today. . . . If the mountains appeared to run around the inlets, and leave them clearly on the Russian side, if they made a contract with reference to these mountains and Russia went into possession and sold to America, and America remained in possession, and maps were published showing the interpretation put by the different parties upon this Treaty, I say . . . it does not make any difference whether these mountains walked off or not." *Ibid.,* VII, 848–849.

93. *Ibid.,* pp. 872–873.

94. Ambassador Choate to Secretary Hay, October 9, 1903, *Choate MS.*

representatives on the boundary tribunal, they offered a strong protest, and Senator Lodge flatly told Alverstone that there could be no agreement on that point.[95]

But Senator Lodge did not realize how stubborn Alverstone could be with reference to his opinion on the width of the *lisière*. When he failed to soften under pressure, Ambassador Choate sent a cipher telegram to Secretary Hay asking for instructions.[96] Hay immediately replied that if it could be announced

> that the Tribunal has decided question five favorably to the American contention, and if there is no prospect of a satisfactory decision at present on question seven, the President would not object to an adjournment of the Tribunal for the purposes and for the time you mention: that is to allow

95. Senator Lodge to President Roosevelt, October 12, 1903, *Selections, etc.,* II, 69.

96. This telegram was a clear presentation of the situation in London with reference to the opinions of the members of the boundary tribunal. It read as follows: "No vote yet on any question. Informal expression on third and fifth shows equal division on Portland Canal but with feeling that while preponderance of evidence is in favor of Southern Channel, yet it furnishes reasonable ground to concede passage north of Pearse and Wales Island if final decision of whole matter could be secured thereby but not otherwise. On fifth question English member has read an opinion in favor of affirmative answer, from which it would be difficult although not absolutely impossible for him to retire. On seventh question he stands stiffly for line following mountains nearest the shore around heads of inlets, and giving us a strip only a few miles wide along the shore. He claims that this follows necessarily from the grounds on which he holds with us on fifth question, and that any other view would require a decision of the fifth question in negative. To stand on the ten marine leagues line throughout would in all probability involve a disagreement on all but fifth question and possibly on that question. The survey under Convention of 1892 is incomplete and leaves strip for ten to twenty miles inside of ten marine leagues line wholly unknown. It is therefore impossible except perhaps on St. Elias Alps and along watershed above Lynn Canal to lay out any line by identification of mountains or otherwise which involves any concession whatever from ten marine leagues line or to establish with certainty the fact that there is no mountain crest within meaning of Treaty or to show by comparison the fact that proposed line near the coast cannot be the true line.

"What do you think of suggestion that Tribunal employ experts under Article One to complete survey up to ten marine leagues line, thus giving full material for judicial decision under Question 7, and adjourn long enough to allow next summer and fall for their work, the time for decision being extended under Article 5 of Treaty to some time after November, 1904. It is proper to add it seems improbable from present expression that any additional information concerning topography of country can change view of English Member since he insists on the principle of running line along summits of mountains nearest sea, although does not insist on direct contiguity to water. Even if he should accede to a line which our Commissioners could accept as a compromise, they do not now see, without additional surveys, any tenable theory on which they could sustain such line. Additional survey might or might not give material to sustain a compromise line or might or might not show mountain boundary to be in immediate neighborhood of ten marine leagues line. In view of these facts would an adjournment as suggested be preferable to an immediate vote which would result in a disagreement on all but fifth question and possibly on that?" Ambassador Choate to Secretary Hay, October 15, 1903, *Choate MS.*

experts chosen under Article one of the treaty to complete survey up to ten marine leagues line during next summer and fall, the Commission meeting in November following to decide the question, in view of the authoritative additional information, as to the topography of the region. Most confidential. If it is necessary in order to secure above announcement and if American Commissioners deem it proper, the third question can be decided in favor of English contention as to North Channel of Portland Canal.[97]

It was very apparent that a crisis had arrived in the proceedings of the Tribunal. Some decision would have to be taken at once or the whole matter would be delayed for at least a year, or perhaps forever. Serious friction with England might well result from this postponement of a question that should have been settled years before. Ambassador Choate realized the gravity of the situation, and he placed the matter squarely before Lord Lansdowne, with the hope that the Foreign Secretary would rise to the occasion. As a result of their conversations it was agreed that Lord Alverstone and the American representatives must agree upon some boundary line that was mutually satisfactory. If they had difficulty in reaching such a compromise, then Choate and Lansdowne would agree upon a line and advise the members of the Tribunal of their decision. The Tribunal could not be allowed to adjourn without arriving at a settlement of this long-standing controversy.[98]

97. Secretary Hay to Ambassador Choate, October 16, 1903, *ibid.*

98. Ambassador Choate to Secretary Hay, October 20, 1903, *Private and Confidential, Choate MS.* This letter from Choate to Hay is of such prime importance that a large portion of it deserves quotation: "On Wednesday last, when there seemed to be a tendency to a deadlock between the Commissioners, I had an interview with Lord Lansdowne in which I pressed upon him very urgently the views of the President as expressed by him in our interview in June. He professed not to know what was going on in the Commission, and said that it had always been their rule when any case had once been committed to a judicial Tribunal not to interfere with it in any way. 'But,' said he, 'you have said before that after the oral arguments were concluded you might want to talk with me unofficially.' 'Yes,' said I, 'and the time has come now, and now or never is the time to save the situation. But I wish to talk with you confidentially and unofficially, not to be recorded or reported or put in your blue print or sent round to the Cabinet.' He said that it should be so, only reserving the right to communicate to Mr. Balfour what might pass between us, to which I assented and said that I should be very glad to have him do so. I told him that there was a supreme necessity for this boundary question to be settled by this Commission, and that there never would be another opportunity, that the President in signing this Treaty had gone as far as he could possibly go; that he would never in the event of this Commission failing, consent to an arbitration for the settlement of this boundary, and that if he were inclined to do so, as he certainly was not and never would be, the Senate could by no possibility be induced to consent to any such thing. I told him that in the event of a failure of this Commission to agree, the duty and the responsibility of the President were perfectly clear. The disputed territory had been in the undisturbed possession of the United States and Russia since the Treaty of 1825. He seemed to think this might not be so, but I referred him to the admissions of Canada to this effect, and

There is no doubt that either Lansdowne or Balfour saw Lord Alverstone and acquainted him with the serious consequences that would follow a deadlock in the Tribunal. But Alverstone would not budge from his determination to reduce the width of the *lisière* that ran around the heads of the important inlets. It was in effect a compromise line, although he was supposed to assume the role of judge and not that of arbitrator. The American representatives held that there was no real basis for the Alverstone decision in this regard. Either he should have decided according to the American contention which gave a wide *lisière* not exceeding ten marine leagues, or he should have accepted the British line which followed the crests of certain mountains that ran nearest the coast and cut across the mouths of the inlets. The Alverstone award with regard to the *lisière* was a distinctly dubious performance, but it was even more so in connection with question 3 which dealt with the course of the boundary line from the point of commencement to the entrance to Portland Channel. Did the line run north or south of the Pearse, Wales, Sitklan and Kannaghunut Islands? The Americans claimed that it ran south of these islands which were thus a part of Alaskan territory, but on October 15 Ambassador Choate ad-

that this was even without any protest on its part. That in this situation the people of the United States had regarded it always as a part of their territory, that it would not be a matter of volition of the President, but that after having given this opportunity to the Canadians to establish their claim and they having failed to do so, he would have to send to Congress the fact of failure, and the separate report of our three Commissioners, which would of course be a statement of the United States case which would be absolutely convincing to the American people, and at the same time he could not hesitate to assume the full responsibility of government over the disputed territory, and must continue to treat it all, as it always had been treated, as United States property, and this he must do openly and emphatically; that now was the last chance to settle the question, that only by the decision of this tribunal, which would be final without any action of the Senate, could Canada get anything whatever of what she claimed.

"I told him that I thought Lord Alverstone was entitled to the support of his own government; that I believed he was hard beset by the Canadians; that the Canadian papers were abusing him soundly, and his Colleagues in the Commission were making the performance of his duty very hard. 'Well,' he said, 'what is your idea? What do you think can be done?' and then he went on in a way that indicated to my mind that he knew the exact situation. . . . He even suggested that the only thing that might be agreed on was that the line went around the inlets, and that we might get that important thing decided in our favor and the Canadians nothing. He said the Canadians attached great importance to the ownership of Pearse and Wales Islands. The upshot of our conversation was the Commissioners, or four of them, must agree on the drawing of the line, and that, if necessary, we might ourselves agree on what would be a satisfactory line, and perhaps, if necessary advise the Commissioners what we thought. . . . I left satisfied that he and Mr. Balfour would, if they had not already done so, tell Lord Alverstone what they thought as to the necessity of agreeing upon that line, and that the present chance of settling the controversy ought not to be lost." *Choate MS.*

mitted that there was "reasonable ground to concede passage north of Pearse and Wales Islands."

On October 12 Lord Alverstone was in favor of the British contention that the line ran north of all four of these islands, and he gave to the two Canadian Commissioners a written opinion to this effect. But he quickly responded to pressure from Lansdowne and Balfour, and instead of receding on the question of the width of the *lisière* he decided to reverse his opinion in connection with the ownership of the islands.[99] When this reversal was made known to the Canadian Commissioners they were furious, and Clifford Sifton sent a telegram to Sir Wilfrid Laurier expressing his indignation at this breach of faith. Laurier replied that the concession to the United States of the islands of Kannaghunut and Sitklan could not be justified "on any consideration of treaty." It was one of those performances that had made British diplomacy "odious to Canadian people," and it should be protested against in the most vigorous terms.[100] But scant heed was given to this protest.

On October 20, 1903 the Tribunal met in final session, and the awards were formally pronounced. The Alverstone line around the heads of the inlets was accepted by the American Commissioners, and their bargain with the English jurist concerning American ownership of the islands of Kannaghunut and Sitklan was ratified. These decisions were made by a vote of four to two, both Canadian Commissioners being strongly in the negative, and finally refusing to affix their signatures to the award of the Tribunal.[101]

In commenting upon the outcome of the proceedings of the Tribunal,

99. John S. Ewart, "The Alaska Boundary," in *The Kingdom of Canada and Other Essays* (Toronto, 1908), pp. 318 ff. On October 12, 1903, the London *Times* commented upon the serious aspects of the Alaskan boundary dispute and remarked: "Again, fair as the skies are, the edge of a cloud shows on the far horizon. Suppose the Alaska Tribunal should adjourn without reaching a conclusion. There will remain to be dealt with . . . the most delicate and difficult dispute known this many a day as between these two friendly Powers."

100. Dafoe, *op. cit.*, p. 233.

101. *A.B.T.*, I, 12. In a statement justifying their refusal to sign the award of the Tribunal, the Canadian Commissioners, Sir Louis A. Jetté and Allen B. Aylesworth, remarked: "There is, in our opinion, no process of reasoning whereby the line thus decided upon by the Tribunal can be justified. . . . We do not consider the finding of the Tribunal as to the islands at the entrance to Portland Channel, or as to the mountain line, a judicial one, and we have, therefore, declined to be parties to the award. Our position during the conferences of the Tribunal has been an unfortunate one. . . . We have been compelled to witness the sacrifice of the interest of Canada, powerless to prevent it, though satisfied that the course the majority determined to pursue in respect to the matters above specially referred to ignored the just rights of Canada." *Ibid.*, pp. 12–13, 65–97. The decision of the Tribunal, October 20, 1903, is contained in *ibid.*, pp. 29–32. For opinions of Lord Alverstone and the American members of the Tribunal, see *ibid.*, pp. 33–64.

Henry White assured Secretary Hay that he had never entertained the "slightest doubt" that the result would be satisfactory to most Americans. Although at times a deadlock had appeared to be possible, he knew very well the force of the "undercurrents of diplomacy" that were carrying the British Government and Lord Alverstone to the decision that had been reached. What had surprised Mr. White was the ability shown by Senator Lodge in conducting those little side-shows that mean so much to the real drama of diplomacy. Whenever it became necessary to convey some delicate intimations to Lord Alverstone about the stand he should take, "it was always Cabot who was deputed to do it. He has shown great tact and considerable diplomacy throughout."[102]

As one reads the proceedings of the Tribunal it is apparent that Senator Turner was far more competent than is usually supposed, and Senator Lodge earned some of the praise that was bestowed upon him by Henry White. But Elihu Root failed to employ the outstanding qualities that are usually attributed to him. It is apparent that he largely followed the lead of Senator Lodge. He had reluctantly accepted the appointment as a member of the Tribunal, and he was very "glad to get out of the Alaskan Boundary business alive and without discredit."[103]

Although Root had emerged from this controversy without discredit, the same could not be said for Lord Alverstone. A distinguished Canadian publicist has accused him of "treachery," and has justified this accusation by showing how Alverstone discussed with the American Commissioners, in private, certain concessions he was ready to make without, at the same time, informing his Canadian colleagues of his intentions. In the matter of his decision concerning the ownership of the four islands at the entrance to Portland Channel, it seems very clear that Alverstone's conduct was far from commendable.[104]

Stung by the sharp criticism that the Canadian Commissioners levelled against his opinions, Lord Alverstone prepared a statement for the British Foreign Office (October 24, 1903) in which he defended his stand. Elihu Root thought the statement was an able one, and he regarded the criticism of Sir Louis Jetté and Mr. Aylesworth as "wholly unjustifiable."[105] In a letter to Senator Turner, Root referred to the attacks upon Lord Alverstone, and he expressed the view that these

102. Henry White to Secretary Hay, October 20, 1903, *White MS.*

103. Elihu Root to Willard Bartlett, November 12, 1903, *Root MS.*

104. Ewart, *op. cit.,* pp. 344–347. See also, James White, *op. cit., Canada and Its Provinces* (Toronto, 1914), VIII, 940–941.

105. Elihu Root to Lord Alverstone, November 20, 1903, *Root MS.*

Canadian critics had acted "very badly" towards the English member of the Tribunal.[106]

Not content with his statement to the Foreign Office, Lord Alverstone endeavored to convince Sir Wilfrid Laurier that his decisions in the matter of the Alaskan boundary were "judicial and founded on no other considerations." But Sir Wilfrid remained skeptical, and he frankly informed the Lord Chief Justice that "the reasons you have given in support of your conclusions cannot be reconciled with such a judicial interpretation of the Treaty of 1825 as was imposed upon and expected from the Commission."[107] He did not, however, cherish any personal hostility towards Lord Alverstone. On October 23, 1903, in a speech in the Canadian Parliament, he stated that the chief difficulty that Canada had encountered in this matter of the Alaskan boundary was not Lord Alverstone. It was a political and not a mere personal factor that was involved. He had often regretted that Canada did not have in its hands

> the treaty-making power which would enable us to dispose of our own affairs. . . . Our hands are tied to a large extent, owing to the extent of our connection—which has its benefits but which has also its disadvantages—the fact of our connection with the mother country making us not free agents and obliging us to deal with questions affecting ourselves through the instrumentality of British ambassadors. . . . It is important that we should ask the British parliament for more extensive powers so that if ever we have to deal with matters of a similar nature again, we shall deal with them in our own way, in our own fashion, according to the best light we have.[108]

It was apparent to Lord Alverstone that he had not convinced his Canadian critics of the purely judicial spirit in which his decision in the Alaskan boundary controversy had been written. In a speech in London he again defended his stand: "If when any kind of arbitration is set up they don't want a decision based on the law and the evidence, they must not put a British Judge on the commission."[109] Some years later, in his *Recollections of Bar and Bench*, he refers to his service upon the Alaska Tribunal and assures his readers that nothing but "a sense of duty" influenced his decision. It is a pity that his memory was not as keen as his sense of duty. In commenting upon the personnel of the Tribunal he mentions Mr. Elihu Root, Senator Turner, and Sena-

106. Elihu Root to Senator Turner, November 20, 1903, *ibid.*

107. Skelton, *Laurier,* II, 157.

108. *Canada: House of Commons, Debates, 1903,* October 23, 1903, *Hansard,* VI, 14814.

109. Jessup, *Root,* p. 400.

tor *Oliver* Lodge![110] If he could not distinguish between the great British physicist and the American politician with the same surname, it might seem evident that the Case of Canada had a distinctly poor chance of being understood. President Roosevelt, however, felt a definite sympathy for Alverstone, and he thought the Canadian Commissioners were inexcusable in attacking him so vehemently. The maps submitted to the Tribunal clearly indicated that "there was literally no Canadian case at all on their main points," and Alverstone was bound to recognize this fact.[111]

Secretary Hay was also of the opinion that the Canadians had no case at all on the main points of the controversy. He had long held that view. He was equally certain that he had taken every advantage of the weakness of the Canadian case and had so directed the course of American foreign policy as to insure a diplomatic victory. In a letter to his wife shortly after the award of the Tribunal, he expressed his delight at the way all his ideas "in this great transaction have been carried out. Kasson and I arranged the treaty four years ago. . . . The completeness of the victory is something amazing." All that "poor Canada" got by the decision was the title to two small islands in Portland Channel.[112] There was no doubt in Roosevelt's mind, however, where the credit for success should go. Years later, he remarked to Mark Sullivan: "While John Hay was a fine Secretary of State, he was much too gentle a person to handle the kind of a big stick that was necessary in this particular connection."[113]

It should not be supposed, however, that fear of the Presidential Big Stick compelled Canadian public opinion to register a favorable verdict with reference to the award of the Tribunal. A study of Canadian newspapers in 1903 quickly discloses the fact that a strong flame of resentment burned in Canadian breasts after the award was announced. As early as February, 1903, certain Canadian suspicions began to make their appearance. When the American Government made public the

110. (London, 1914), pp. 240–241.

111. President Roosevelt to Cecil Spring Rice, November 9, 1903, *Roosevelt MS.*

112. Dennett, *op. cit.,* p. 362.

113. Mark Sullivan to Henry White, October 6, 1925, *White MS.* In a pungent letter to Philander C. Knox, former Secretary of State, April 12, 1914, ex-President Taft makes the following remarks concerning the Alaska boundary tribunal: "The truth is that the interests of the United States on certain issues between us and England ought not to be trusted to a man saturated with the atmosphere of London society. Hay was such a one. Choate was and Root and Lodge were affected by their stay in London on that Alaska Boundary Commission. White obtained just such a hold on them as he did on Hay and Choate, and White is much more of an Englishman of the Tory class than he is an American in social view and affiliation." *Philander C. Knox Papers,* Library of Congress.

names of the American members of the arbitral tribunal, the Toronto *World* made the following bitter comment:

President Roosevelt has degraded the honourable title of "impartial jurists of repute" by appointing three of the most pronounced and hostile political partisans to hear the arguments of counsel and to ajudicate upon the legal interpretation of the Anglo-Russian treaty of 1825. . . . Will Great Britain compel Canada to go through the farce of submitting evidence in support of her claim, and retaining eminent counsel to argue it, when it is publicly known that the whole proceeding will be a farce?[114]

As the months passed, Canadian suspicions grew stronger, but some newspapers expressed the view that the "verdict must be accepted, and accepted frankly, without murmuring or recrimination."[115] This was a counsel of perfection that was not followed by the very newspaper that voiced it. After the tribunal made its award, the Toronto *News* said: "Nothing is surer than that Canada has suffered incalculable loss and despoilment through the dealings of British diplomatists with Canadian interests and Canadian territory. . . . The Alaskan treaty, like the Treaty of Washington, seems to be a sacrifice of Canadian interests to the paramount desire of Great Britain to cultivate the good opinion of the United States."[116]

The Manitoba *Free Press* regarded the award as an "unmitigated misfortune" that was "certain to affect prejudicially the relations between Canada and Great Britain. . . . The Alaskan boundary award will take its place with the Ashburton treaty as damning evidence of Great Britain's subserviency to the United States where the latter's interests conflict with those of Canada."[117] To the editor of the Victoria *Daily Colonist* the news of the verdict awakened a feeling of

ungovernable rage that the commission should have come to a decision in which . . . the rights of the contending parties have been entirely overlooked, and the diplomatic relations between Great Britain and the United States alone regarded. . . . This unfortunate commission, unfortunate in its inception, unfortunate in its constitution and doubly unfortunate in its result, has raised questions of the gravest and deepest import which Canada will meet filled to overflowing with loyalty to Canada.[118]

The Ottawa *Citizen* was indignant because the boundary line had been "diverted without apparent reason or justice so as to give to the

114. Toronto *World,* February 23, 1903. See also, Toronto *News,* February 24, 1903.
115. Toronto *News,* October 12, 1903.
116. *Ibid.,* October 21, 1903.
117. October 21, 1903.
118. October 21, 1903.

United States two small islands, utterly unimportant to that country as territory but of immense importance strategically."[119] It seemed apparent to the Montreal *Gazette* that the award was merely "one of those concessions due to a desire to have the good will of Washington, which many English public men seem to think are always in order."[120] The Toronto *Globe* was certain that the award would arouse "strong and lasting indignation all over the Dominion,"[121] while the Toronto *World* regarded the outcome as a clear indication that Sir Wilfrid Laurier wished to have the boundary dispute settled "on the principle of give and take. It has turned out that way—the United States giving and Canada taking it in the neck."[122] The Hamilton *Herald* believed that the sharp protest of the Canadian members of the arbitral tribunal against the verdict would be "endorsed by every patriotic Canadian," and the Brantford *Expositor* sadly reflected that there was "nothing in the whole business which reflects credit on the Americans."[123]

In 1911 this indignation still remained in Canadian minds, and it was partly responsible for the defeat of the reciprocity treaty in that year. But there was also a constructive side to this resentment. It clearly indicated to the British Government the necessity of binding the scattered fragments of the Empire into a more intimate union. In the future, London would give closer heed not only to the voice of Ottawa but to the chorus that came from the capitals of the other far-flung British possessions. Canada pointed the way to the British Commonwealth of Nations, and Sir Wilfrid Laurier was the herald of this new Imperial order.[124]

119. October 21, 1903.
120. October 21, 1903.
121. October 21, 1903.
122. October 22, 1903.
123. Quoted in Toronto *Globe,* October 21, 1903.
124. In the Root manuscripts in the Library of Congress there is an interesting letter to Root from Earl Grey, Governor-General of Canada. The following comments in this letter of January 30, 1908, are pertinent: "Much as I desire to meet any request coming from you I fear I cannot do what you suggest with regard to Lord Alverstone. Unfortunately there is a very strong feeling in Canada against Lord Alverstone, who is supposed to have deliberately and intentionally sacrificed the interests of Canada for the sake of cultivating the goodwill of your Republic. I agree with you that it would be improper for Lord Alverstone to be feted in the United States without also coming to Canada, but owing to the present feeling which exists against him in the Dominion, I have no hesitation in saying that a visit from him to Canada during the present year would be premature."

For further references to Canadian sentiment with reference to the award of the tribunal, see Skelton, *Laurier,* II, 153–159; Gelber, *op. cit.,* pp. 162–166; D. A. MacArthur, "The Alaska Boundary Award," *University Magazine,* VI (1907), 412–426.

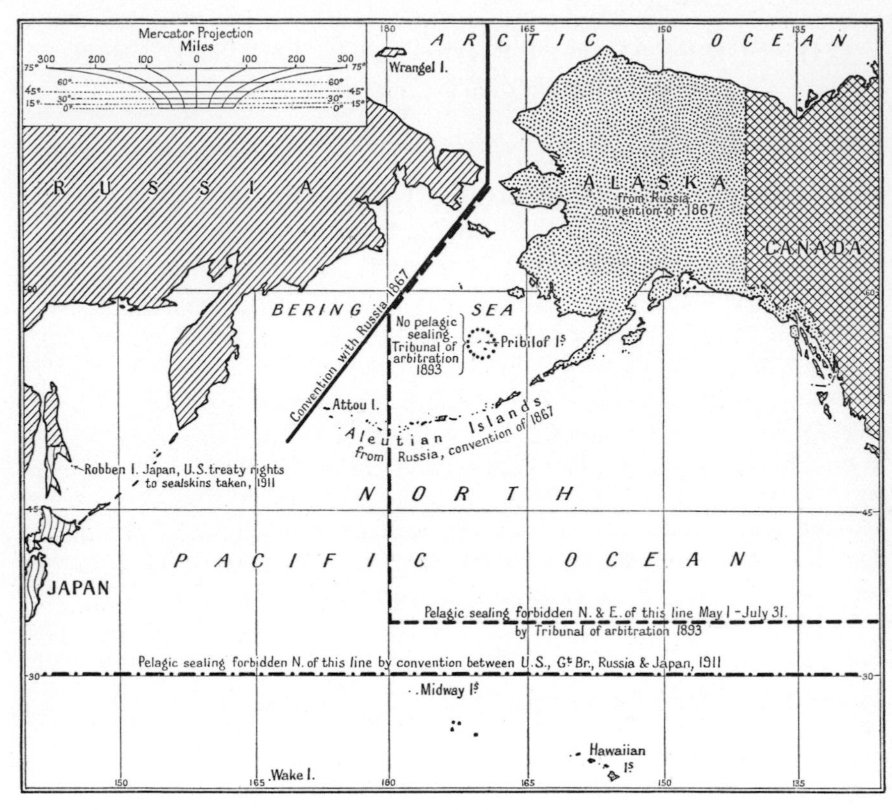

Sealing Restrictions Established by the Paris Award, 1893, and the Treaty of 1911

CHAPTER X

THE FUR-SEAL FISHERIES AND THE DOCTRINE OF THE FREEDOM OF THE SEAS

THE controversy between the United States and Great Britain concerning the fur-seal fisheries was one that directly involved the principle of the freedom of the seas. Through many decades of our early history the American Government had waged an unremitting fight for a free sea. Sometimes it was a mere battle of diplomatic notes in which American Secretaries of State made ample use of strong paragraphs from the works of important publicists from Grotius to Vattel, but this barrage had not greatly disturbed the stronghold of the British Admiralty. In 1812 the United States had finally resorted to open warfare in an effort to convince British statesmen that American vessels had a right to sail unmolested across the seven seas, but at the close of the conflict British men-of-war still controlled the sea lanes. Apparently, American warships had been as impotent as American diplomatic despatches in the matter of changing British maritime practices.

In this fur-seal fisheries dispute it is ironic to note that the American and the British Governments exchanged their historic positions, and we find Lord Salisbury as the doughty defender of the doctrine of the freedom of the seas. It is a little surprising to find President Cleveland engaged in a covert attack upon a principle that previous American statesmen had supported even at the cost of war.

In a previous chapter mention has been made of the voyages of Vitus Behring and the establishment of Russian trading posts along the Northwest Coast of the American continent.[1] American fur-traders followed hard upon the heels of these Russian pioneers, and open friction was the inevitable result.[2] In order to clarify the Russian position, Czar Paul issued on July 8, 1799, a ukase which organized the Russian American Company and conferred upon it a monopoly of the trade along that part of the Northwest Coast which lay above the 55th degree of north latitude. The company was also empowered to make new dis-

1. Golder, *Bering's Voyages.* See also Captain James Cook, *A Voyage to the Pacific Ocean* (London, 1784), III, 359–383; Robert J. Kerner, *The Urge to the Sea* (Berkeley, 1942); and Adele Ogden, *The California Sea Otter Trade, 1784–1848* (Berkeley, 1942).

2. Dennett, *Americans in Eastern Asia,* pp. 34–43; Hildt, *Early Diplomatic Negotiations of the United States with Russia,* pp. 158–159.

coveries "farther to the south," and to occupy these lands if they had not been previously occupied by some other nation.[3]

American traders were not inclined to take these Russian pretensions very seriously, and they continued their visits to the Northwest Coast in search for furs for the Canton market. This scant regard for Russian restrictions led to the filing of diplomatic protests at Washington, but the polite phrases of diplomatic correspondence were no effective check upon the activities of these Yankee interlopers.[4] Somewhat taken aback by this American indifference to alleged Russian rights, Czar Alexander I issued a ukase which forbade all foreign vessels from approaching within 100 Italian miles of the Northwest Coast of America from Behring Straits to the 51° of north latitude.[5] John Quincy Adams (the American Secretary of State) had no intention of recognizing this Russian claim to vast stretches of the Northwest Coast, and after an extended diplomatic duel a treaty was signed on April 17, 1824 in which the southern boundary of Russian America was fixed at the fateful parallel of fifty-four degrees and forty minutes of north latitude.[6] Of special significance to the fur-seal controversy was the fact that in this treaty the Russian Government advanced no claim to sovereignty over the high seas within 100 Italian miles of the Northwest Coast. This Russian renunciation was a very important precedent in the fur-seal controversy that disturbed Anglo-American relations in the last decades of the nineteenth century.

The British Foreign Office had been just as vehement in its protests against Russian pretensions as had been the American Department of State,[7] and on February 28, 1825 a Russo-British treaty had been signed along the same general lines as that concluded between Russia and the United States.[8] It was apparent that the Russian Government had abandoned all attempts to regard Behring Sea as a *mare clausum*.[9] But these extravagant claims were not forgotten by American statesmen, and President Cleveland, in the summer of 1886, suddenly revived them in an effort to prevent pelagic sealing in the North Pacific area. To his dismay he soon discovered that in order to win the game of diplomacy one must have more than bad cards and empty bluff.[10]

On March 30, 1867 the representatives of Russia and the United

3. *Proceedings of the Alaskan Boundary Tribunal* (Washington, 1904), II, 23–25.
4. Benjamin P. Thomas, *Russo-American Relations, 1815–1867* (Baltimore, 1930), pp. 40–46.
5. *Proceedings of the Alaskan Boundary Tribunal*, II, 25–28.
6. Miller, *op. cit.*, III, 151–162.
7. *Proceedings of the Alaskan Boundary Tribunal*, II, 104–105.
8. *Ibid.*, pp. 12–16.
9. Thomas, *op. cit.*, pp. 41–46.
10. With reference to the general topic of the fur-seal fisheries see Moore, *History*

States signed a treaty which ceded to the United States "all the territory and dominion" which the Czar of Russia possessed on the "continent of America and in the adjacent islands."[11] Three years later the Acting Secretary of the Treasury leased to the Alaska Commercial Company the right to take seals on the islands of St. Paul and St. George.[12] Under American auspices the fur-seal industry seemed to have a rosy future, and American officials were anxious to give it every possible protection. In March, 1872, Mr. T. G. Phelps wrote to the Secretary of the Treasury and called his attention to reports of various expeditions being fitted out in Australia and in other Pacific lands for the purpose of conducting sealing operations in the North Pacific. In view of the damage these sealers might inflict upon a valuable American industry, was it not possible, through the employment of revenue cutters, to take some action against them?[13] In his reply, Mr. Boutwell frankly stated that he did not see how the United States "would have the jurisdiction or power to drive off parties up there for that purpose unless they made such attempts within a marine league of the shore."[14]

Nine years later the Treasury Department took a much stronger stand. In March, 1881, Mr. H. F. French, Acting Secretary of the Treasury, informed Mr. D. A. d'Ancona, of San Francisco, that the treaty with Russia contained definite maritime boundaries which included a large part of Behring Sea and the North Pacific. The limits of the cession extended from

> a line starting from the Arctic Ocean and running through Behring Strait to the north of St. Lawrence Islands. . . . Thence in a southwesterly direc-

and Digest of International Arbitrations, I, 755–961; Joseph B. Lockey, "James Gillespie Blaine," in *American Secretaries of State and Their Diplomacy,* VIII, 128–145; William R. Castle, Jr., "John W. Foster," *ibid.,* pp. 193–202; Foster, *Diplomatic Memoirs,* II, 20–50; Tyler, *Blaine,* pp. 302–345; John B. Henderson, *American Diplomatic Questions* (New York, 1901), pp. 3–62; John W. Foster, "The Results of the Bering Sea Arbitration," *North American Review,* December, 1895, Vol. CLXI, 693–702; *Fur Seal Arbitration, Proceedings of the Tribunal of Arbitration* (Washington, 1895, 16 vols.), *Senate Ex. Doc. No. 177,* 53 Cong., 2 sess.

11. Malloy, *op. cit.,* II, 1521–1524.

12. *Fur-Seal Arbitration,* IV, 80. Hereafter referred to as *F.S.A.* In the *Daily Morning Chronicle* (Washington, D. C.), April 15, 1870, attention is directed to a petition submitted to the Senate Committee on Commerce by James Otis, President of the Chamber of Commerce of San Francisco, and by the officers of 56 mercantile firms of that city, protesting against the "fur-seal monopolies" and the leasing "of the islands off Alaska."

13. T. G. Phelps to Secretary Boutwell, March 25, 1872, *F.S.A.,* IV, 82.

14. Secretary Boutwell to T. G. Phelps, April 19, 1872, *ibid.,* p. 83. It should be kept in mind that this letter of Secretary Boutwell does not explicitly refer to the waters of Behring Sea. In a letter to W. W. Eaton, January 18, 1888, Mr. Boutwell stated that his letter of April 19, 1872, had reference "solely to the waters of the Pacific Ocean south of the Aleutian Islands." Moore, *Digest of International Arbitrations,* I, 767–768.

tion so as to pass midway between the island of Attoo and Copper Island . . . to meridian of 193 degrees of west longitude. All the waters within that boundary to the western end of the Aleutian Archipelago and chain of islands, are considered as comprised within the waters of Alaska Territory.

The penalties prescribed by law against the killing of fur-bearing animals would therefore attach against any violation of law within these limits.[15]

But despite this bold assertion of jurisdiction over the waters of the North Pacific, the Treasury Department did not attempt to protect the sealing industry by seizing the ships of other nations found cruising in the area specified. It was not until the first Cleveland Administration that any action was taken in this regard, and in this case the Treasury Department did not bother to consult with the Department of State before sending instructions to the officers in charge of the revenue cutters. Daniel Manning, the Secretary of the Treasury, had left the post of President of the National Commercial Bank of Albany, New York, to assume the burden of chief fiscal officer of the United States, and his mind appeared to be more fixed upon questions of revenue than upon diplomatic difficulties that might arise from seizures of foreign shipping. The sealing industry brought certain revenues into the Treasury, and Mr. Manning would conserve this income even at the cost of serious friction with Great Britain. Pelagic sealing by British vessels must cease at once, and in August, 1886, American revenue cutters began to seize ships conducting sealing operations in the North Pacific.[16]

As soon as the then Governor-General of Canada, Lord Lansdowne,

15. H. F. French to Mr. D. A. d'Ancona, March 12, 1881, *F.S.A.*, IV, 85–86. In a memorandum prepared by Henry W. Elliott for Senator John C. Spooner, January 20, 1905, the following statement is made: "The assertion of our Government that it claimed dominion over the open waters of Behring Sea with reference to the interpretation of 'the waters thereof' of Alaska, as stated in Section 1956 of the Revised Statutes, was first made . . . by Acting Secretary H. F. French . . . in the D'Ancona Case: in this ruling the Treasury Department declared that it considered its jurisdiction as ordered by Section 1956 to be *over all the waters of Behring Sea east of the pelagic boundary in that sea, between Siberia and Alaska, as defined by the terms of the treaty of cession from Russia:* this definition is quoted in full in the 'Sherman Orders' of April 20, 1877, which forbids the clearance of all American vessels into Behring Sea for pelagic fur-sealing." *John C. Spooner Papers,* Library of Congress.

16. On March 6, 1886 Secretary Manning sent to the Collector of Customs at San Francisco a copy of the letter that Acting Secretary H. F. French had addressed to Mr. d'Ancona, with instructions to see that it received adequate publicity. In this way a warning was conveyed to all persons who contemplated fitting out expeditions to kill fur-seals. *F.S.A.*, IV, 92.

It seemed obvious to the officials in the Treasury Department that the herds of fur-seals would soon be destroyed unless pelagic sealing were prohibited. According to

heard of these seizures he wrote to Sir John Macdonald and expressed the opinion that this action by American officials was "far more open to criticism than anything we have done."[17] In London the Foreign Secretary, the Earl of Iddesleigh, was deeply concerned over this situation. Canadian vessels had been seized when they were more than sixty miles from the nearest land, and such action was in open defiance of the principles of international law. Lengthy instructions were sent to the British Minister at Washington, directing him to protest against these infractions of the law of nations.[18] Attention was directed to the fact that the American Government had always made it a point to proclaim in loud tones its adherence to the doctrine of the freedom of the seas. Was it now about to reject one of the most important articles in the faith of the American founding fathers?

At Washington, Sir Lionel West made careful preparations for his diplomatic duel with Secretary Bayard. He was a man who had walked through life along the easy levels of instinct. Intellectually he was not impressive, and Bayard often referred to him as a "mere postage stamp." In the summer of 1886 he made daily calls at the Department of State. He was the ideal ambulatory ambassador, and he furnishes a perfect illustration of Hugh Gibson's dictum that "diplomacy is not hard on the brain, but it is hell on the feet." Clad in the armor of a righteous cause, Sir Lionel strongly pressed the claims of Great Britain.[19] Bayard was impressed with the strength of the British case, and

testimony of C. A. Williams before a Congressional committee, the fur-seal hunters were destroying "hundreds of thousands of fur-seals by shooting them in the water, and securing as many of the carcasses for their skins as they were able to take on board. . . . Of the number of seals killed in the water, not more than one in seven . . . is secured, for the reason that a wounded seal will sink in the sea; so that for every thousand sealskins secured in this manner there is a diminution of seal life at these rookeries of at least 7,000." *House Ex. Doc. No. 450,* 51 Cong., 1 sess., p. 17.

British and Canadian authorities were not convinced by these figures, and they soon produced some of their own which differed materially from the American estimates. See report of George E. Foster, Canadian Minister of Marine and Fisheries, September 21, 1886, *C.S.P., 1887, No. 48,* pp. 2–3; Sir Julian Pauncefote to Secretary Blaine, March 9, 1890, *House Ex. Doc. No. 450,* 51 Cong., 1 sess., pp. 26–51.

17. Lansdowne to Sir John Macdonald, September 20, 1886, *Macdonald Papers, Governor-General's Correspondence,* XIII, pp. 535–541, P.A.C.

18. Earl of Iddesleigh to Sir Lionel West, October 30, 1886, *F.S.A.,* II, 153–155.

19. Sir Lionel West to Secretary Bayard, September 27, 1886, *Senate Ex. Doc. No. 106,* 50 Cong., 2 sess., pp. 1–7; Sir Lionel West to Secretary Bayard, October 21, 1886, *F.S.A.,* II, 153. In a personal letter to Phelps, July 14, 1887, Bayard made the following comments about Sir Lionel West: "On the Canadian questions, . . . I have not exchanged five words, nor received the slightest expression of interest from the present British envoy. I mention this condition of affairs because I consider it a real misfortune that the United States cannot have the benefit of the presence here of a straight-forward sensible man, with whom so much could be quietly conducted in personal intercourse in relation to Canadian matters." *Bayard MS.*

he informed Sir Lionel that he was giving careful study to all the precedents that had any bearing on the matter. It had appeared to him, however, that previous to the treaty of March 30, 1867, Russia had always contended that Behring Sea was a *mare clausum* or closed sea. At this point Sir Lionel adverted to the fact that the American Government had hitherto strongly protested against such a contention. "Yes," replied Bayard, "at that time."[20]

But despite this Delphic utterance on the part of Bayard, Sir Lionel had high hopes for an early adjustment of difficulties. On November 19 he had another conversation with Bayard, who again informed him that copies of the judicial proceedings at Sitka had not reached the Department of State,[21] and some weeks later this same formula was again invoked.[22] It was apparent, said Bayard, that the question of jurisdiction over Behring Sea was a "complicated one," but West could rest assured that the American Government would look into the matter in a spirit of "fairness." The islands of St. Paul and St. George, "although situated . . . more than 200 miles from the mainland, were, he conceived, comprised in the jurisdiction ceded by Russia, but he did not wish to pronounce upon this point at present."[23]

Bayard now turned to Justice Field of the United States Supreme Court for advice,[24] and Field promised to call at the Department of State and discuss the whole matter of American jurisdiction over Behring Sea.[25] Some weeks earlier Bayard had already written to George V. N. Lothrop, the American Minister at St. Petersburg, with regard to the Behring Sea situation. He was particularly interested in

> the nature and extent of marine jurisdiction actually assumed and enforced by Russia in the Behring Sea. . . . I would like to ascertain whether . . . Russia was limited to the distance of three miles from the shore of her islands

20. Sir Lionel West to the Earl of Iddesleigh, November 12, 14, 1886, *C.S.P., 1887,* No. 48, pp. 32–34. See also Secretary Bayard to Sir Lionel West, November 12, 1886, *F.S.A.*, II, 155. During this conversation between West and Bayard on November 12, Bayard remarked that an apology was due because no reply had been sent to the British Minister's first note. The reason for this delay was the failure of the report of the judicial proceedings at Sitka to reach the Department of State. *Memorandum* written by Bayard after a conversation with Sir Lionel West, November 12, 1886, *Bayard MS.*

21. *Memorandum* written by Bayard after a conversation with Sir Lionel West, November 19, 1886, *Bayard MS.*

22. *Ibid.,* December 9, 1886. On this occasion Bayard remarked that Alaska was "very remote," and it would take a long time to "learn all about the matter."

23. Sir Lionel West to the Earl of Iddesleigh, December 10, 1886, *C.S.P., 1887,* No. 48, p. 40. See also West to Bayard, Dec. 7, 1886, *F.S.A.*, II, 156.

24. Bayard to Justice Stephen Field, December 16, 1886, *Bayard Letter Book,* IV.

25. Justice Field to Bayard, December 20, 1886, *Bayard MS.*

or mainland. . . . As the United States succeeded to all the rights and powers of Russia in the waters in question, it becomes important to know what jurisdiction was claimed and practically exercised by Russia prior to the transfer. . . . The value permanently of the seal fisheries depends chiefly upon the power to regulate their capture [of seals], and this can only be done on land. If they be shot at sea without discrimination, extermination will follow.[26]

After making extended inquiries, Lothrop could not discover any "case of seizure and adjudication under the Ukase of 1821."[27]

Bayard now turned to Francis Wharton, the Solicitor of the Department of State, and requested his advice. In reply, Wharton sent him the following memorandum:

I am clear as to three things. (1) Unless under concessions from Great Britain to Russia (passing to us under Alaska treaty), we cannot seize and search (*a fortiori,* we cannot confiscate), British vessels on the high seas of the Northwest Pacific. (2) Round the sea islands, however, we might establish a limited police jurisdiction so as to repel intruders say within eight or ten miles. (3) We ought at once to advise the Alaska Seal company, so that we can understand their case, and not expose ourselves to liability to them on the ground that we gave away their rights. (4) We ought to take a month & consider the matter. I am talking it over with Mr. Moore, and I am about to begin a search into the records of the British correspondence with Russia on this topic. These records are very voluminous. Then we will drive a daring team in which J. Q. Adams and Prince Potemkin will draw double under your whip. But it will take a month to harness and team such steeds.[28]

In the next few days Wharton sent to Secretary Bayard two other memoranda which clearly demonstrated the fact that American revenue cutters had no right whatever to seize British sealing schooners on the high seas.[29] It was the Solicitor's opinion that the Attorney General

26. Bayard to George V. N. Lothrop, October 29, 1886, *Bayard Letter Book,* III, *Bayard MS.*

27. Lothrop to Secretary Bayard, December 3, 1886, *Bayard MS.*

28. Wharton to Secretary Bayard, January 11, 1887, *ibid.*

29. On January 17, 1887, Wharton sent to Bayard the following memorandum: "I find on examination that there were no concessions whatever by G. Britain to Russia by which we as assignees of Russia, can claim any right to seize British sailing vessels on the high seas outside of the three mile band. . . . If it should turn out that the seizures . . . were on the high seas, I concur in the belief that honor and policy require that we should take the earliest opportunity to disclaim the arrests, and to frankly and fully express our regret at their having been made. As soon as you are satisfied that the seizure is on the high seas, should not the Attorney General direct discontinuance?" Two days later (January 19, 1887), Wharton sent another memorandum in which he expressed the view that it was "far better to abandon even the seal fishery than to surrender the doctrine of inviolability of national merchant ships on

should be promptly advised to direct a discontinuance of legal proceedings against the Canadian vessels that had been seized.

While Bayard was gathering this data on the matter of American jurisdiction over Behring Sea, the British Minister was busily engaged in sending notes of protest to the Department of State. On January 8, 1887, Lord Iddesleigh drew Sir Lionel West's attention to the fact that nearly four months had elapsed since the British Government had complained of the seizures of British ships in Behring Sea. No reply had been received from the Department of State, and West was instructed to "urge with all the force which the gravity of the case requires, the immediate attention of the United States Government to the action of the American authorities."[30] West carried out these instructions at once,[31] and Bayard explained that the delay had been occasioned by the absence of "requisite information as to the facts" in the case. He would, however, endeavor to procure the best evidence possible "of the matters inquired of, and will make due response thereupon when the opportunity of decision is afforded to me."[32]

It was apparent to the Cleveland Administration that the Behring Sea situation had dangerous possibilities. After the matter had been discussed at a Cabinet meeting, the Attorney General sent a copy of the legal proceedings to Bayard, with a fervent wish that an early solution could be found.[33] Impressed with the importance of early action, Bayard wrote a long letter to President Cleveland in which he carefully reviewed all that had occurred in this matter of exercising jurisdiction over vast stretches of Behring Sea. Things had come to such a pass that it was necessary for the President to decide as soon as possible

> whether exclusive jurisdiction, and right of search and police control, extends over the whole area of Behring Sea, or is restricted within that marine league from shore, which in the history of this Government, heretofore, has,

the high seas. I think, however, that for *police purposes* we may repel intruders who come within the range of cannon shot of our shores. As to the seals, I think the only remedy is that which you suggest—a joint agreement of maritime powers to protect the rookeries." *Ibid.*

30. Earl of Iddesleigh to Sir Lionel West, January 8, 1887, *C.S.P., 1887, No. 48,* p. 38. The viewpoint of the Foreign Office was undoubtedly influenced by communications from Canada such as Lord Lansdowne's letter to Mr. Stanhope, Nov. 27, 1886, *F.S.A.,* V, 45–46. For detailed data concerning the seizures of Canadian sealing vessels, see *ibid.,* pp. 62–66.

31. Sir Lionel West to Secretary Bayard, January 9, 1877, *Senate Ex. Doc. No. 106,* 50 Cong., 2 sess., p. 7.

32. Secretary Bayard to West, January 12, 1887, *ibid.,* 11.

33. A. H. Garland to Secretary Bayard, January 21, 1887, *Bayard MS.*

in all other localities, been so frequently proclaimed by us as the limit of our territorial control. This Government has never asserted, but has invariably disclaimed, any pretension to authorize the search by officers of the United States, in time of peace, of foreign vessels on the high seas and outside our jurisdiction, and we have repelled successfully, search of our own vessels, even in the most qualified way, by foreign powers under similar circumstances. . . . Having had correspondence on the subject with our Minister at St. Petersburg, and made examination of the archives of this Department, I am unable to find satisfactory grounds to warrant me in advising you that the search and seizure of the vessels referred to, and the proceedings against the masters and crews were justified. . . . This Government is one of law, and yields the same voluntary and self-imposed submission to the rules of public international regulation in the use and navigation of the high seas which it requires from other members of the family of nations.

If the conclusion should be reached that the vessels in question were seized outside of the proper marine jurisdiction of the United States, . . . I believe that the honor of the Government . . . requires that the Attorney General should be requested immediately to direct . . . the District Attorney of the United States, having the cases in charge, to discontinue the prosecutions and discharge the vessels from arrest.[34]

The President yielded to Bayard's importunities and authorized assurances to the British Minister that the pending proceedings against British vessels would be discontinued, and that all persons under arrest in connection with the seizures would be released.[35] This was the limit of concessions, and Sir Lionel West was not able to secure assurances that no further seizures would be made.[36]

Bayard realized that President Cleveland was not fully convinced that the seizures in Behring Sea were in contravention of international law. In order to give the Chief Executive more light upon this question, Bayard prepared a memorandum which discussed this matter of maritime jurisdiction. He was strongly of the opinion that Behring Sea was a "part of the high seas of the world, and equally open to the navigation of all nations." This being true, American jurisdiction in that area did not extend "to a greater distance from the land than is claimed and exercised by the United States . . . over the waters adjacent to its territories on the Atlantic coast."[37]

34. Secretary Bayard to President Cleveland, January 22, 1887, *Bayard MS.*

35. Secretary Bayard to Sir Lionel West, February 3, 1887, *Senate Ex. Doc. No. 106,* 50 Cong., 2 sess., p. 12.

36. Sir Lionel West to Secretary Bayard, April 4, 1887; Secretary Bayard to Sir Lionel West, April 12, 1887, *ibid.,* pp. 12–13.

37. *Memorandum* prepared by Secretary Bayard for President Cleveland, April 28, 1887, *Bayard MS.*

In his memorandum for the guidance of the President, Bayard had stressed the expediency of settling, by international arrangement, all the questions arising out of seal hunting in Behring Sea. In a personal letter to Phelps, in London, he expressed the opinion that it might be well to discuss with Lord Salisbury "the necessity for co-operative action of the two governments over their respective citizens, to prevent the annihilation of the fur seals. I do not see how we can maintain Behring's Sea to be a *mare clausum*, or claim an exclusive jurisdiction beyond the three mile limit."[38]

From Russia the word came that the Government of the Czar would be glad to co-operate with the "United States in any measures for the protection of the legitimate fisheries." If the American Government would take the initiative with reference to a multi-lateral convention dealing with the fur-seal fisheries, such a move would meet with a "favorable response" from Russia.[39]

While Bayard was pondering over plans for an international agreement restricting the killing of seals in the North Pacific, the British Minister showed that the question was not a mere academic one by presenting another protest against new seizures of British vessels in Behring Sea. Lord Salisbury had assumed that Bayard's note of February 3 was an assurance that no further action would be taken by United States revenue cutters.[40] Bayard corrected His Lordship in this regard by indicating that the note of February 3 had merely stated that "all pending proceedings" would be discontinued. It had no relation to future seizures.[41]

It seemed to Bayard that the British Government was in a "marvellous hurry to have our decisive action in Alaska, and yet, after eighteen months, withholds a decision in the two cases of seizure in the Spring of 1886 in Nova Scotia." He felt certain, however, that "an examination of the history of Behring Sea will not sustain our right to exclude other nations from the common right of navigation, fishing, etc., in those

38. Secretary Bayard to Phelps, May 6, 1887, *Bayard Letter Book,* V, *Bayard MS.* In another letter to Phelps, May 30, 1887, Bayard remarked: "I am unable to see how we can withdraw from our traditional refusal to admit the right of search and visitation on the high seas, and our insistence upon the restriction of territorial jurisdiction to a marine league from shore. We have compelled Russia in the Sea of Okhotsk and in Behring Sea to abandon a more extensive claim. We did the same thing with Spain in her Cuban waters and with Great Britain . . . in the Northern Atlantic." *Ibid.*

39. Lothrop to Secretary Bayard, May 28, 1887, *Bayard MS.*

40. Sir Lionel West to Secretary Bayard, August 11, 1887, *Senate Ex. Doc. No. 106,* 50 Cong., 2 sess., pp. 47–48.

41. Secretary Bayard to Sir Lionel West, August 13, 1887, *ibid.,* p. 49.

waters outside the three mile line from shore. This announcement has not yet been made by us, but it must be sooner or later."[42]

This matter of American jurisdiction over Behring Sea came to the front with increased importance in July, 1887, when United States revenue cutters began once more to seize British vessels conducting sealing operations in Behring Sea in violation of American statutes. On July 2 the *Anna Beck*, of Victoria, British Columbia, was seized by the cutter *Rush*, and was turned over to the United States Deputy Marshal at Unalaska.[43] Other seizures followed, and the British Government entered prompt protest.[44]

Bayard promised Sir Lionel West that he would send him copies of the documents relative to these seizures,[45] and at a Cabinet meeting he indicated his attitude towards the whole matter.[46] The President responded by directing the Acting Attorney General to issue an order "for the release of the officers and other persons employed in the vessels lately seized by the Revenue Cutter *Rush* in Behring Sea." It was significant, however, that this direction to the Acting Attorney General began with a reservation to the effect that this order of release would have no effect on the "other questions connected with the alleged violation of the laws of the United States relating to the fur-seal fisheries."[47] This meant that the British ships were not released at this time, and in a brief memorandum attached to the President's letter, Bayard remarked: "The reasons for this release arise from the regard for the personal liberty of the individuals. . . . As to the detention of property, compensation can always be awarded."[48]

President Cleveland was still clinging to the belief that the United States had some control over Behring Sea with special reference to the preservation of the herds of seal that were threatened with destruction by pelagic killing. After a conference with the Chief Executive and the Acting Attorney General, Bayard noted in a memorandum that the

42. Secretary Bayard to Phelps, August 16, 1887, *Bayard Letter Book,* V, *Bayard MS.* To Bayard it appeared obvious that Great Britain had a large financial interest in preserving the fur seal fisheries since some 12,000 persons were "engaged in London in preparing the skins for use."

43. Secretary C. S. Fairchild to Secretary Bayard, August 19, 1887, enclosing letters from Captain Shepard of the revenue cutter *Rush,* July 4, 11, and 18, 1887, *Bayard MS.*

44. Marquis of Salisbury to Sir Lionel West, August 10, 1887, *C.S.P., 1888, 65a,* pp. 21–22; Sir Lionel West to Secretary Bayard, August 19, 1887, *Bayard MS.*

45. Secretary Bayard to Sir Lionel West, August 20, 1887, *Bayard MS.*

46. Secretary Bayard to Secretary Fairchild, August 16, 1887, *ibid.*

47. President Cleveland to George A. Jenks, August 23, 1887, *ibid.*

48. *Memorandum* written by Bayard, August, 1887, *ibid.*

"President seemed disposed to delay giving any order that would indicate the restriction of our jurisdiction *to three miles*."[49]

The New York *Times* construed the President's attitude as a clear indication that the Administration had not "abandoned any of its claims over the waters of Behring Sea far beyond the marine league, and that it still treats this as a 'closed sea.' "[50] This was true as far as the President was concerned, but it was certainly not true of Bayard's viewpoint. In a personal letter to a friend in Philadelphia, Bayard frankly stated that he would not make any claim that was untenable or which would place the American Government in a position "of actual inconsistency." With special reference to the Alaska Commercial Company, Bayard was determined "not to allow the interests of any association of Commercial or trading interests to lead us into a position not based upon law, justice, and consequent National dignity and self-respect."[51]

But Bayard soon realized that the Acting Attorney General was firmly of the opinion that the United States had jurisdiction over vast stretches of Behring Sea. The three-mile limit was scornfully rejected by this lawyer who would not permit his far-ranging vision to be cramped by accepted legal limitations. In a long letter to Bayard, he discussed with legal loquacity the many points involved in the question of preserving the fur seals in Behring Sea, and came to the conclusion that "the United States, as sovereign, has the right to protect the fur seals whose habitat is upon the shores and islands of Alaska, whether within or without the marine belt."[52]

49. *Memorandum* written by Bayard, August 25, 1887, *ibid.*

50. New York *Times,* August 22, 1887.

51. Bayard to Thomas Wright, August 27, 1887, *Bayard MS.*

52. George A. Jenks to Secretary Bayard, August 31, 1887, *ibid.* In this memorandum, Jenks makes the following points: "FACTS: (1) The fur seals within the treaty limits are chiefly begotten and brought forth on the domain of the United States. (2) When they leave the land of their birth they have *animum revertendi.* This is known by their usual custom. (3) They are exhaustible, and of commercial value. (4) They are, by nature, impotent for self-protection, either by defense or escape. (5) When they leave the place of their birth, and are killed in the open sea, it is a cruel waste and destruction. . . . In the open sea their sex and age cannot be determined; so the females, with young, are killed, and male breeders over the age of five years, which are of no commercial value, are uselessly destroyed. (6) They are *ferae naturae.* LEGAL PROPOSITIONS. (1) Animals *ferae naturae,* by prerogative, belong to the sovereign, unless granted out to a subject directly, or as an incident to a grant of land. (2) A qualified property may subsist, in a subject, in animals *ferae naturae,* either *per industriam, propter impotentia,* or *propter privilegium.* (3) Animals *ferae naturae,* are no longer the property of a man than while they are in his keeping or actual possession; but if at any time they regain their natural liberty, his property instantly ceases, *unless they have animum revertendi, which is only to be known by*

After receiving this jolt from the Acting Attorney General, Bayard soon felt the impact of a learned memorandum from Francis Wharton, the Solicitor of the Department of State. In his earlier memoranda Wharton had insisted that the American Government could not claim any jurisdiction in Behring Sea outside the three-mile limit. Now, possibly taking his cue from the President or from Mr. Jenks, Wharton suddenly abandoned his former ground and moved to the position that the "three-mile zone was not an arbitrary cosmopolitan rule, but a rule adopted by compromise and custom for certain specific coasts." Applying this idea to the situation in Behring Sea, Wharton came to the conclusion that "wherever a sovereign has property, there he is to have sufficient police control over the waters adjacent to such property as to enable him to protect it. This is the rule of the law of nations. . . . As far as I recollect, the three-mile rule has never applied to the North Pacific. . . . I do not think the three-mile rule binds the seal fisheries."[53]

While Bayard was trying to digest this legal advice that looked towards the adoption of a policy that was certain to lead to increasing difficulties with England, Phelps, in London, was sounding a note that was distinctly belligerent. Unlike many other American representatives at the Court of St. James's Phelps was never converted into an Anglophile with deep sympathies for the English point of view. He retained his Yankee suspicions of things British, and was sharply critical of the failure of the Foreign Office to court American favor by turning a cold

their usual custom of returning. (4) A qualified property may also subsist in relation to animals *ferae naturae, rationa impotentia,* on account of their own inability. (5) Property in the sea which is local and exhaustible is subject to the right of domain. (6) The prerogative right of the sovereign is founded upon the necessity of protection of the several species of those animals which would soon be exhausted by general liberty. CONCLUSIONS: (1) The United States, as sovereign, has the right to protect the fur seals whose habitat is upon the shores and islands of Alaska, whether within or without the marine belt. (2) Except so far as is necessary to protect such seals, the right to control or forbid the free navigation of the open seas outside of the marine belt, in the pursuit of lawful commerce, is not claimed. (3) The limits to which the United States claims the right of protection referred to in section 1 of Conclusions, are the boundaries set forth in the treaty between the United States and Russia on the twentieth day of June, 1867, for, within those boundaries the seals found therein have no other habitat than upon the public domain of the United States." *Ibid.*

53. Wharton to Secretary Bayard, September 4, 1887, *ibid.* In another letter to Secretary Bayard, September 11, 1887, Wharton remarks: "As to the seal treaty or convention—would it be advisable to extend its operations further than the capture of vessels *engaged* in *seal fishing* within say 20 or 30 miles from shore? Can we, without sacrificing a great deal now—vastly more—than we would gain, authorize the search of vessels in the North Pacific to see whether they are on sealing adventures? We agreed to such search within certain zones for slavers, but even this, as to these narrow waters, has been a matter of great doubt, and only justified by the horror of the slave trade." *Ibid.*

shoulder to Canadian demands. In a letter to Bayard during the last week of August, 1887, Phelps complained of British weakness wherever Canada was concerned. Lord Salisbury had assured him that "he had done what he could to induce moderation in the conduct of the Canadians, but again intimated that the Imperial Government stands much in the situation of *a broker*." This being the case, Phelps advised Bayard to hold on to the Canadian vessels that had been seized in Behring Sea. Such action might induce the Foreign Office to be more conciliatory.[54]

Ill-feeling concerning the Behring Sea seizures was fast rising both in the United States and in Canada, and the American Consul at Halifax reported that one of the newspapers in that city had become "very abusive towards the United States," and had demanded that the "outrages be stopped."[55] In response to these Canadian complaints, Sir Lionel West called at the Department of State and inquired why the Canadian vessels seized in the summer of 1886 had not been released in accordance with the President's order. Bayard replied that if these vessels "had not been taken away by those who owned them it probably was from the insignificant value of the vessels."[56]

It is very likely that the pleasure-loving Sir Lionel West did not relish making these many visits to the Department of State for the purpose of conveying to Secretary Bayard the innumerable protests from the Foreign Office concerning American practices in Behring Sea, but he was given no rest. On September 10, Lord Salisbury returned to the attack in a long instruction which pointed out American infractions of the law of nations. The seizures in Behring Sea had been "effected at a distance from land far in excess of the limit of maritime jurisdiction which any nation can claim by international law." It was hardly necessary to add that such a limit could not "be enlarged by any municipal law." The British Government was inclined to believe that Secretary Bayard would admit the illegality of these seizures, and would take steps to settle this controversy.[57]

On September 23 Sir Lionel West made one of his routine trips to the Department of State to present this protest from the Foreign Office.

54. Phelps to Secretary Bayard, August 27, 1887, *ibid.*

55. M. H. Phelan to Secretary Bayard, September 8, 1887, *ibid.*

56. *Memorandum* written by Bayard after a conversation with Sir Lionel West, September 19, 1887, *ibid.* Bayard tried to make it clear to the British Minister that the State Department had no control over the actions of officers of revenue cutters. The Treasury Department was responsible for the conduct of those officers, and that department was merely executing Federal laws.

57. Marquis of Salisbury to Sir Lionel West, September 10, 1887, *F.S.A.,* II, 162–165.

He knew that the British and American Governments had agreed upon the appointment of a Joint High Commission to deal with many of the problems affecting Canadian-American relations, and he suggested to Bayard the inclusion of the Behring Sea difficulty in the agenda of the commission. But Bayard feared that the bitterness that had already been engendered in Canada concerning these seizures, would make it difficult to adjust this matter except through protracted negotiations. It would be better to limit the agenda of the Joint High Commission to questions dealing with the North Atlantic fisheries, and after a solution for these problems had been found it would then be time to turn to the fur-seal controversy.[58]

When Sir Lionel West realized the strength of Bayard's feeling in this regard, he ceased to press this point and once more presented a request for the release of the Canadian ships still held in custody at Sitka.[59] When Bayard made inquiry at the Department of Justice with reference to the status of these ships, the Attorney General informed him that the United States marshal in Alaska had doubted the genuine character of the order of January 26, 1887 directing him to release the vessels, and had not acted upon it. A new order had been telegraphed to him, and no further difficulty was expected.[60]

58. *Memorandum* written by Bayard after a conversation with Sir Lionel West, September 23, 1887, *Bayard MS.* Certain members of the Canadian Government hoped that the fur-seal dispute could be handled by the Joint High Commission. On September 1, 1887, Sir John Macdonald wrote to Lord Lansdowne about the agenda before the Joint High Commission, and remarked: "As to Behring's straits, the question is a 'burning one,' and should be included, but if the Americans insist on their exclusive claims it may break up the whole arrangement. Surely England would never agree to this monstrous claim." *Macdonald Papers, Macdonald Letter Books,* XXIII, 214–215, P.A.C. See also a statement in the New York *Herald,* August 27, 1887.

Bayard had been strongly advised by some of the officials in the Department of State against including the Behring Sea question in the agenda of the Joint High Commission. In a letter from M. H. Phelan, Consul at Halifax, September 8, 1887, the following comment is made: "The government organ in this city has been very abusive towards the United States, and quite warlike in tone on account of the Behring Strait seizures; demanding that the outrages be stopped and the question settled at once by the coming commission. The object of this is, no doubt, to divert attention from the real question to one new and little understood. The policy of the Dominion Government is to insist on submitting the Behring Straits fisheries, together with those of the Atlantic, to the coming convention, so as to confuse matters, hoping that the outrages of the last two years will be overlooked, and some advantage gained for the maritime provinces." *Bayard MS.*

59. Sir Lionel West to Secretary Bayard, September 29, 1887, *Senate Ex. Doc. No. 106,* 50 Cong., 2 sess., p. 55.

60. Attorney General A. H. Garland to Secretary Bayard, October 12, 1887, *Senate Ex. Doc. No. 106,* 50 Cong., 2 sess., p. 56. In a personal letter to Garland, October 20, 1887, Bayard remarked: "It would be a greater labor than even Hercules essayed, to keep the tattlers, mischief makers, and fools of the newspapers press, from publishing half truths and whole lies. I told one of these people last night that there was not

In the meantime, on August 19, Bayard had addressed to the ministers of the United States to France, Germany, Great Britain, Japan, Russia, Norway, and Sweden, an instruction directing them to request the governments to which they were accredited to co-operate with the United States "for the better protection of the fur-seal fisheries in Behring Sea." Bayard had refrained from raising any questions as to the

exceptional measures which the peculiar character of the property in question might justify this government in taking, and without reference to any exceptional marine jurisdiction that might properly be claimed for that end. It is deemed advisable, and I am instructed by the President so to inform you, to attain the desired ends by international co-operation.[61]

The French Government was willing to consider a draft treaty in connection with the seal fisheries,[62] and the Russian Foreign Office had no hesitation in indicating its readiness to co-operate with the United States and other powers in the matter of preserving the seals in the North Pacific.[63] The Government of Japan was interested in such a treaty, but it expressed the hope that the proposed convention would include a provision for the protection of the sea-otter as well as for the seal.[64]

a particle of foundation for the statement that the Secretary of State and the Attorney General had any differences in opinion concerning the jurisdiction of the United States in Behring Sea, or anywhere else." *Bayard Letter Book,* VI, *Bayard MS.* Bayard's statement is a little ambiguous, for there had been a significant difference of opinion between Bayard and the Acting Attorney General, G. A. Jenks, concerning American jurisdiction in Behring Sea.

61. *Senate Ex. Doc. No. 106,* 50 Cong., 2 sess., p. 84.

62. *Ibid.,* p. 85. See also, *F.S.A.,* II, 168–171.

63. *Ibid.,* p. 116. In a conversation with Bayard, January 6, 1888, the Russian M. de Struve said that the Russian Government "cordially accepted the American suggestion because their interest is precisely the same as our own, but they thought that it should go even beyond the commercial question . . . and be extended so as to assist the claims of humanity of those poor inhabitants of Northeastern Russia who had nothing to live upon but what they caught from the sea. . . . Therefore, this prohibition against killing seals should extend not only to fur seals but to the common seals and to sea lions and all animals of that class." Bayard said that he had no objections to these extensions except that such a move would mean a much more extended description "of the offences." *Bayard MS.*

64. *Senate Ex. Doc. No. 106,* p. 107. On October 14, 1887, the Japanese *chargé d'affaires* had a conversation with Bayard and inquired if the proposed convention could also cover other fur-bearing animals. Bayard replied that he could see no "reason why it should not be so extended." He thought there had been "some misapprehension on the part of Count Ito, as to the proposition of Mr. Hubbard; it was not limited to Behring Sea, but to the protection of fur seals all over the world, and I thought it was only by international agreement that they could be protected elsewhere." *Memorandum* written by Bayard after a conversation with Shiro Akabane, *Bayard MS.*

The British Government was slow to take any action in this regard, and Bayard, in a personal letter to Phelps, stressed the importance of arriving at an early settlement of this troublesome question.[65] Weeks passed by and nothing was heard from London. On December 14 Joseph Chamberlain had a long talk with Bayard and remarked that "Lord Salisbury had not yet received any formal application from Mr. Phelps, but that Sweden and another government (Austria) had applied to Great Britain to learn what she would do." Bayard said there "was evidently some mistake" because his circular note of August 19 had been addressed to the American envoys accredited to France, Germany, Great Britain, Japan, Russia, Norway and Sweden. The question was one "for concerted legislation" to prevent "the extermination of an animal useful to all." Chamberlain agreed with this viewpoint and stated that some "10,000 people in London were employed in seal fur dressing." Bayard closed the discussion by remarking that the Behring Sea difficulties should be kept separate from all discussion of the North Atlantic fisheries. If it was discovered that the American officials "had broken any law we would respond voluntarily, but that the seal fishery, like the Pearl Fishery, was peculiar and needed more than a 3 mile belt."[66]

On January 21, 1888, the Russian Minister called at the Department of State with reference to progress of negotiations looking towards a multi-lateral convention for the preservation of the seals in the North Pacific. Bayard gave assurances that the American Government was proceeding as rapidly as possible in this regard. It should be clear to the Russian Minister that "the interests of Russia and the United States were identical." If they would "pull together in this matter . . . there would be no difficulty in attaining the desired end."[67]

Encouraged by this conversation with the Russian Minister, Bayard sent to Phelps a proposal that the interested powers should "take concerted action to prevent their citizens or subjects from killing fur-seals with firearms, or other destructive weapons, north of 50 degrees of north latitude, and between 160 degrees of longitude west and 170 degrees of longitude east from Greenwich, during the period intervening between April 15 and November 1."[68]

65. Secretary Bayard to Phelps, October 20, 1887, *Bayard MS.*

66. *Memorandum* written by Bayard after a conversation with Joseph Chamberlain, December 14, 1887, *ibid.*

67. *Memorandum* written by Bayard after a conversation with M. de Struve, January 21, 1888, *ibid.*

68. Secretary Bayard to Phelps, February 7, 1888, *Senate Ex. Doc. No. 106,* 50 Cong., 2 sess., p. 88.

Phelps presented to Lord Salisbury a copy of this instruction, and on February 25 he reported that the British Government was willing not only to accede to the arrangement proposed by Bayard, but was inclined "to join the United States Government in any preventive measures it may be thought best to adopt."[69] As soon as Bayard received this letter he wrote to Phelps and expressed the hope that an arrangement could be concluded whereby American revenue cutters could arrest British sealing vessels and turn them over to

> their own courts for punishment. I do not want to be obliged to define our claim of jurisdiction, nor on the other hand to claim that sea to be *mare clausum,* because frankly I think such a claim would be not only highly impolitic, but incapable of being sustained. . . . I wish you would impress Lord Salisbury with the importance . . . of not allowing clearance in British Columbia for vessels proposing to shoot seal in Behring's Sea. I shall advise that secret instructions be given to our Revenue cruisers not to molest British vessels at a distance from the shore in Behring's Sea, on the ground that negotiations are now pending for the concerted exercise of jurisdiction over their citizens by the respective governments, for the protection of seal life in certain months and between certain longitudinal lines.[70]

Before Lord Salisbury could take action upon these Bayard proposals, word was received in London that orders had been issued by the American Government to the commanders of revenue cutters in Behring Sea to continue their seizures of British vessels engaged in sealing operations.[71] When the British Minister talked with Bayard on April 3 he was informed that "no orders had been issued by the Treasury Department on the subject of sealing in Behring Sea."[72] This assurance from Bayard disposed of the rumors that had circulated in London, but it was not enough to satisfy Lord Lansdowne. The Governor-General of Canada wanted a specific answer to the following question: "May we understand that our sealers will not be molested except within the marine league from shore?" Bayard refused to give an affirmative answer to this question when it was placed before him by the British Minister. It was possible that the preservation of seal life in Behring Sea might not require American jurisdiction outside the three-mile limit, but the Department of State would not go on record to that

69. Phelps to Secretary Bayard, February 25, 1888, *F.S.A.*, II, 175.

70. Secretary Bayard to Phelps, March 16, 1888, *Bayard Letter Book,* VII, *Bayard MS.* See also, Bayard to Phelps, March 2, 1888, *F.S.A.,* II, 175–176.

71. Sir Lionel West to Secretary Bayard, April 2, 1888, *Bayard MS.*

72. *Memorandum* written by Bayard after a conversation with Sir Lionel West, April 3, 1888, *ibid.*

effect. The American Government wished merely to protect the herds of seal in Behring Sea from destruction, and there was no wish to encroach on British rights. It was not a "narrow technical point of a three-mile limit"; it was the question of the preservation of an industry that brought lucrative returns to a large number of British as well as American citizens.[73]

The British Colonial Office regarded Bayard's assurances of April 3 as "strictly confidential," and Lord Knutsford expressed to Lord Lansdowne the hope that they would not be made public because such action might lead to the "destruction of the seals." It would be desirable, if possible, to refuse clearances to "vessels about to leave British Columbia for the purpose of shooting seals during the close season . . . from the 15th of April till the first of November."[74]

Lansdowne thought that it was unfair to suppress "the information which has been obtained as to the intentions of the United States Government," and he doubted whether there was any power to refuse clearances to "sealers leaving British Columbia at a particular season of year." He was of the opinion that it was unlikely that the Canadian Government would be able "to prevent" sealers from "fishing as usual during the present season." If the American Government were wise it would leave the sealing schooners alone and would "endeavor to come to some arrangement" with Canada for the "establishment of a close time for the future."[75]

Lord Salisbury was more conciliatory than Lord Lansdowne, and instructions were sent to the Governor-General of Canada to prevent the clearance of vessels from British Columbia intending to shoot seals in Behring Sea during the summer of 1888. It was difficult, however, to hasten negotiations providing for an arrangement that would preserve seal life in the North Pacific. The Russian Government was anxious to have the close season apply to the Sea of Okhotsk as well as to Behring

73. *Memorandum* written by Bayard after a conversation with Sir Lionel West, April 6, 1888, *ibid.* See also Lord Lansdowne to Sir John Macdonald, April 4, 1888, *Governor-General's Correspondence,* XV, 123, *Macdonald Papers,* P.A.C.

On March 21, 1888, Lieutenant Commander W. H. Emory wrote to Secretary Whitney and enclosed a list of vessels that would probably sail from Victoria, British Columbia, for the purpose of conducting sealing operations in Behring Sea. During these operations the sealers would kill "or maim ten or twelve seals before capturing one. The most experienced hunters would not recover more than one seal out of every four or five killed or wounded. In the competition between vessels, the wanton destruction of seal life is even greater than this." *Bayard MS.*

74. Lord Knutsford to Lord Lansdowne, April 6, 1888, *Governor-General's Correspondence,* XV, 127, *Macdonald Papers,* P.A.C.

75. Lansdowne to Sir John Macdonald, April 7, 1888, *ibid.,* p. 125.

Sea,"[76] and it wished to have in the convention an express prohibition against the sale of alcoholic drinks, firearms, gunpowder and dynamite to the natives of those regions. Bayard had no objection to the inclusion of the Sea of Okhotsk in the proposed convention dealing with fur-seals.[77] Lord Salisbury expressed himself in similar vein, and proposed "the inclusion of everything north of north latitude 47 degrees (in order to include Robbin Island) without defining the longitude."[78]

On April 22 Henry White had a long discussion with Lord Salisbury concerning the scope of the proposed treaty for the protection of seal life in Behring Sea. In a previous conversation White had remarked that "all the sea north of 47°" would be an immense area to protect. Salisbury now seized the opportunity to say that "upon consulting the map he had observed that on the East his proposal would include a considerable portion of British Columbian coasts for which he saw no necessity" to patrol. He was inclined, therefore, to "limit the eastern area of the seal protection to Behring Sea, . . . and let the Russians include as much of their coast and Seas as they want."[79]

Salisbury was evidently in a conciliatory mood, and it appeared as though it would not be difficult to arrive at an amicable Anglo-American understanding with reference to seal protection. Bayard was always willing to concede a great deal in order to settle diplomatic disputes, and on May 1 he instructed Henry White to inform the British Foreign Secretary that he would not object to the inclusion of the Sea of Okhotsk in the convention then under discussion. Moreover, he was not insistent that the close season extend from April 15 to November first. As a compromise he suggested April 15 to October 15. With regard to the prohibition of the sale of firearms and liquor to the natives along the shores of Behring Sea, he believed that these matters could best be treated in a separate treaty.[80]

But before the British Government could take any definitive action in connection with a convention preserving seal life in the North Pacific, it would be necessary to consult the wishes of the Canadian Government.[81] Henry White was certain that in Canada there was a real fear that the American Government was

76. Henry White to Secretary Bayard, April 7, 1888, *F.S.A.*, II, 177–178.

77. Secretary Bayard to Henry White, April 9, 1888, *ibid.*, pp. 178–179.

78. Henry White to Secretary Bayard, April 18, 1888, *Bayard MS.* Salisbury also intimated that the close season suggested by Bayard (April 15 to November 1) might be too long. Perhaps October 1 would do. Henry White to Secretary Bayard, April 20, 1888, *F.S.A.*, II, 179–180.

79. Henry White to Secretary Bayard, April 22, 1888, *Bayard MS.*

80. Secretary Bayard to Henry White, May 1, 1888, *F.S.A.*, II, 180.

81. Eric Barrington to Henry White, April 27, 1888; Henry White to Secretary Bayard, April 28, 1888, *Bayard MS.*

trying to "do" them out of something. I have seen Lord Salisbury twice in society since writing to you on the 28th, and he implied that Canada is the source of delay. . . . Lord Salisbury, to whom I communicated verbally your assent to the inclusion of the Sea of Okhotsk, said he thought, since examining the map more thoroughly, your original proposal as to latitude 50° much the best. . . . Lord Salisbury inquired whether I had any instructions as to the *duration* of the proposed Seal Convention. Evidently the Canadians are anxious to cut it as short as possible. I said, "as long a time as possible," but no special time had been mentioned in your instructions. He thought (I fancy, inspired by Canada) about three or five years.[82]

There is little doubt that the necessity of consulting Canadian desires was the main reason for British delay in coming to an agreement with the United States concerning the protection of seal life in Behring Sea. In seeking to effect an arrangement as to the close season, Lord Knutsford proposed that this season operate with reference merely to pelagic sealing. Such a proposal did not please Lord Lansdowne, who wished to have American sealers on the islands in Behring Sea restricted as well as sealers on the high seas.[83] But this arrangement might be difficult to put through, and Lord Knutsford was exceedingly anxious that negotiations relative to sealing in Behring Sea reach a successful conclusion. If they did not, it was likely that the American Government would continue to regard Behring Sea "as part of United States territory," and enforcement of existing regulations might lead to serious friction.[84]

In order to prevent this friction, Bayard prepared for President Cleveland a draft of amended regulations that would not bear so hard upon Canadian sealing schooners in Behring Sea.[85] But Bayard's conciliatory course encountered many obstacles, and one of them that now gave him deep concern was the reluctant attitude of British Columbia to respond to pressure from the British Foreign Office in the matter of refusing clearances for vessels engaged in sealing. To Bayard this attitude seemed unpardonable, and he thought it was difficult "to see why Great Britain should permit one of her colonies to thwart a plan intended to preserve the race of seals from extermination."[86] He was soon to discover, however, that Lord Salisbury was extremely solicitous about catering to Canadian desires. In a letter from Henry White he learned that the Foreign Office would take no further action

82. Henry White to Secretary Bayard, May 2, 1888, *ibid.*
83. Lord Lansdowne to Sir John Macdonald, May 5, 1888, *Governor-General's Correspondence,* XV, 177–178, *Macdonald Papers,* P.A.C.
84. Lord Knutsford to Lord Lansdowne, May 9, 1888, *ibid.,* p. 179.
85. Secretary Bayard to President Cleveland, May 9, 1888, *Bayard MS.*
86. *Memorandum* written by Bayard, May 17, 1888, *ibid.*

concerning a convention for the preservation of seals until a full report had been received from the Canadian Government. Canadian interests seemed to bulk very large in the eyes of Lord Salisbury, who paid increasing attention to the protests that came from Ottawa.[87]

While Bayard was waiting for some news from the British Foreign Office, Sir Lionel West called at the Department of State to discuss what course should be followed with reference to British vessels that had been seized by United States revenue cutters. In a note to the Department of State, April 30, 1888, the British Minister had spoken of the "skippers" of these vessels as being in jail. Bayard referred to this statement and remarked that he was "not aware that there was any personal imprisonment in the Behring Sea cases." With reference to the possibility that appeals could be taken from the decisions of Judge Dawson, of the United States District Court in Alaska, Bayard believed that the owners of the vessels had permitted too much time to elapse before filing the necessary papers. He could not see how the President could "change the time fixed by law for the taking of the appeal in these cases."[88]

87. In a long personal letter to Bayard, Henry White, May 17, 1888, gave the following account of the attitude of Lord Salisbury: "A few evenings ago I met Lord Salisbury at dinner at the Russian Embassy, and finding that he had still nothing from Canada on the seal question, I asked him whether he could not proceed without waiting any longer, in view of the approach of the seal shooting season and of the great importance of protecting them this year if possible. He seemed to think this course might be feasible and a meeting between Lord Salisbury, the Russian Ambassador and myself was arranged for yesterday afternoon, which took place. Unfortunately, however, Lord Salisbury had just received previously a communication from the Canadian Government stating that a memorandum was in course of preparation on the subject and would be shortly forwarded to London; and pending its arrival Canada begged that nothing would be settled. Under these circumstances Lord Salisbury felt that he could only await this memorandum, of the contents of which he said he was not aware. . . .

"I succeeded in obtaining an intimation that the probable ground of Canada's objection will be that the proposed Convention would break up an important British Columbian and Canadian trade; as, while we and the Russians have our own islands from which to obtain these animal skins, the former can only get them in the open sea. I was careful at once to reply that the admission of any such plea as that would imply absolute and very speedy extermination of the seals from both Sea and Islands, which must be prevented, and to this Lord Salisbury seemed quite to agree. I have no idea that the British Government will allow objections on the part of Canada to interfere with the Convention; but they feel bound to hear what that Province has to say. Lord Salisbury appeared to regret the delay as much as I did. . . .

"I may add that the Canadians proposed . . . that the Convention should be for two years; but Lord Salisbury at once saw that this period would be ridiculously short. He thinks, however, that five years will be the longest period to which he can get Canada to consent." *Ibid.*

88. *Memorandum* written by Bayard after a conversation with Sir Lionel West, May 28, 1888, *ibid.*

After dealing with this legal interlude, Bayard looked to London for further news in connection with the proposed fur-seal convention. Phelps reported on June 23 that Lord Salisbury was still awaiting some action on the part of Canada, and it was understood that he was growing "impatient" at the delay occasioned by Canadian tactics.[89] But this impatience did not seem seriously to worry the Canadian Government, and negotiations continued their leisurely course. On July 13 Phelps informed Bayard that there was no progress

> in the seal fishery convention owing solely to the opposition of Canada. England and Russia agree with us. I shall continue to press it, and unless soon disposed of, shall recommend a course in which Russia will join, and to which England will not, I am sure, take much exception—the seizure of all vessels found engaged in the exterminating cruelty which it is sought to put an end to. I do not doubt that such a course may be supported.[90]

Bayard read at a Cabinet meeting (July 5) some of the correspondence from Phelps in which repeated reference had been made to the difficulties of arriving at some arrangement concerning the preservation of the fur-seals. Bayard was growing increasingly impatient with the British Government because of its reluctance to put pressure upon Canada, and he was strong in his conviction that the "Behring Sea questions" should not "be impeded by Canadian views." In the North Pacific there was "no question of territorial waters in which Canada has any pretext of interest," and action in conjunction with Russia might become "necessary." It might be well to acquaint Lord Salisbury of the "serious danger and unwisdom of Canadian Rulers playing into the hands of Republicans" in the United States through a policy of needless obstruction.[91]

But Phelps found that the British Foreign Office continued to defer to Canadian desires, and was slow to take any action looking towards

89. Phelps to Secretary Bayard, June 23, 1888, *ibid.* See also White to Secretary Bayard, June 20, 1888, *F.S.A.*, II, 181.

90. Phelps to Secretary Bayard, July 13, 1888, *Bayard MS.*

91. Secretary Bayard to Phelps, July 26, 1888, *Bayard Letter Book*, VIII, *Bayard MS.* On August 3, 1888, Baron Rosen had a conversation with Bayard at the Department of State, during the course of which Rosen inquired about the progress of the fur-seal negotiations. Bayard informed him that there "was evidently a hitch caused by Canadian matters; that it was not a Canadian question at all, but a British question, and it was very awkward having Canadian interposition paralyzing the action of the responsible Government. As long as they were in Canadian waters they were Canadian vessels, but were British vessels when outside Canadian jurisdiction. I said we were pressing . . . the matter, but could not tell what would be the result of it." *Memorandum* written by Bayard after a conversation with Baron Rosen, August 3, 1888, *Bayard MS.*

an effective control over the fur-seal fisheries in the North Pacific. The situation called for firm action on the part of the United States. America

> must show Canada that she cannot outrage us with impunity. And the moment we take a firm stand all the trouble will cease. That is the surest way to avoid difficulty. *And you may be sure it will be satisfactory to the present British Government, which is embarrassed by Canadian conduct which she can not control, and can not justify, and can not afford to fight for.*[92]

This belligerent advice was given to Bayard in a personal letter from Phelps in the second week in September, 1888. In an official despatch of the same date, Phelps writes in the same aggressive spirit. There were merely two alternatives for the American Government to take. It would either have to "submit" to Canadian practices which were destroying the seals, or it must take preventive measures by seizing the offending sealers. Between these two alternatives there should not be the slightest hesitation. The question of a *mare clausum* was really not involved in this dispute. The real issue was whether the citizens of British Columbia should be permitted to ruin a thriving American industry by sealing operations which were against the "common dictates of humanity." The three-mile limit had been invoked by the British Government as a prohibition against the seizure of Canadian vessels on the high seas, but this limit had no universal application in international law. It should also be kept in mind that international law is not a collection of dusty precedents that statesmen keep in national archives against the day when they may be used to advantage. International law is something that is constantly expanding and taking on new aspects: it had "arisen from precedents that have been established when the just occasion for them arose, undeterred by the discussion of abstract and inadequate rules."[93]

92. Phelps to Secretary Bayard, September 12, 1888, *ibid.* In this same letter to Bayard, Phelps further remarks: "We shall not get a Convention on the subject from Great Britain, much as she desires it, because Canada objects. Our only course is the resolute one, of self defense, by seizing vessels engaged in this nefarious business, and holding on to those already captured. This course will save the seal from extermination by the Canadians, and nothing else will. I have no manner of doubt of our right to it. Russia and probably all nations interested will join us. You may be sure that England will not back up Canada in this business, because she admits it to be wrong, has in vain requested Canada to desist from it, and her large interests in the business are affected by it very injuriously. I have no doubt it would be satisfactory to the British Government to have us put a stop to it."

93. Phelps to Secretary Bayard, September 12, 1888, *F.S.A.,* II, 181–183. Some months later, December 14, 1888, Bayard, during a conversation with Baron Rosen, discussed the matter of the fur-seal fisheries. In a *memorandum* of that date, he

But Bayard was not ready to adopt such a belligerent course of action.[94] He was familiar with the fact that one nation cannot make international law, no matter how pressing the exigency. He continued to adhere to the position that the best way to settle the seal fisheries dispute was through an "international arrangement which would enable the nations to co-operate for the purpose of preventing the destruction of the seal."[95] This international arrangement must have a background of friendly understanding rather than a prelude of sharp friction that might lead to war.

Although Bayard constantly clung to this policy of conciliation, there were many officials in the Cleveland Administration who thought that the only way to bring the British Government to terms was through the adoption of a policy of defiance. In Congress this was a common viewpoint, and on February 18, 1889, Poindexter Dunn, Chairman of the Committee on Merchant Marine and Fisheries of the House of Representatives, reported back from his committee a bill (H.R. 12432) to provide for the better protection of the fur-seal and

makes the following statement: "He [Baron Rosen] asked about the Behring Sea matter. I told him I had not heard anything further, but I was disappointed that the English Government had not made a better agreement; that I understood they had been stopped by a Canadian suggestion. I said, of course I understood that the Russian Government was most anxious to co-operate with us, and that they wished to include a little Island called Robin Island within the operation of the Treaty. I remarked that I thought any region frequented by seal ought to be included within the regulations." *Bayard MS.*

94. Bayard would probably have been impressed with the cogency of the following *Memorandum,* prepared by George E. Foster, Acting Minister of Marine and Fishery in Canada:

"It is a well-known fact that seals do not begin to enter the Behring's Sea until the middle or end of May; they have practically all left those waters by the end of October. The establishment of the proposed close season, therefore, prohibits the taking of seals during the whole year. . . .

"But the United States Government propose to allow seals to be killed by their own citizens on the rookeries, the only places where they haul out in Alaska, during June, July, September and October. . . .

"It is to be noted that the area proposed by Mr. Bayard to be affected by the close season virtually covers the whole portion of the Behring's Sea in which the exclusive right of sealing has, during 1886 and 1887, been practically maintained by the United States Government. To this is added a part of the North Pacific Ocean, north of 50° of north latitude, and which commands the approach of the seals to the passes leading into Behring's Sea. By the adoption of this area and close season the United States would gain, by consent, what she has for two years held in defiance of international law and the protests of Great Britain and Canada.

"The device, if successful, would feed and perpetuate the rookeries on St. Paul and St. George Islands, and add immensely to their value, while it cuts off at one blow the most valuable portion of the high seas from all participation by the sealers of all other nations."

95. *Memorandum* written by Bayard after a conversation with Baron Rosen, March 1, 1889, *Bayard MS.*

salmon fisheries of Alaska. One paragraph in this bill amended Section 1956 of the *Revised Statutes of the United States* so that its terms included "all the waters of Behring Sea" embraced within the boundaries as described in the treaty of March 30, 1867. Provision was also made for the President, at a timely season in each year, to issue a proclamation warning all persons against entering these waters for the "purpose of violating the provisions of said section."[96]

In his speech in support of this bill, Mr. Dunn remarked:

> Our Government took by that treaty all the rights, powers, interests, jurisdiction and dominion of Russia in that Territory and over those waters. . . . The Territory was purchased chiefly because of the great value of the marine products of Behring Sea. . . . Chief amongst these interests was the fur-seal rookery on the Pribylov Islands. . . . The herd of seals have been protected and taken care of reasonably well, although the Committee have ascertained that there has been laxness in the protection of the herd in the open seas during the last three years, and that is provided for in the amendatory law now proposed. . . . The next provision is to tighten up and make certain the protection of seal life in these waters. The law prohibits any person from killing any fur-bearing animal in the Territory of Alaska, or any fur-seals in the waters of Behring Sea except under the authority of the United States Government, and the regulations of the Secretary of the Treasury in pursuance of the same. . . .
>
> The contention made by those who have heretofore been arrested and whose vessels have been seized, is that this Government had no jurisdiction over that sea. That authority was exercised by Russia strictly, and without relinquishing that power we bought the country.[97]

When Mr. Dunn was questioned about the vessels that had been seized in Behring Sea and then released from custody, he replied:

> Some have been condemned and some have been released. The courts of the United States have sustained the jurisdiction of this Government over the sea and the right of the Government to protect the fisheries. . . . I do not understand that in any case the rights of the United States were waived or relinquished. . . . There has been no decision by the State Department that in any way has made the concession that it is an open sea. If there has been any leniency on the part of any Department of the Government, it has merely been a conciliatory step but one which did not relinquish in any way the rights of this Government or any interest of this Government.[98]

Mr. Dingley, in response to certain questions concerning American jurisdiction over Behring Sea, flatly stated that

96. *Congressional Record,* 50 Cong., 2 sess., XX, Pt. 3, February 18, 1889, 2021–2022.
97. *Ibid.,* pp. 2022–2027.
98. *Congressional Record,* 50 Cong., 2 sess., XX, Pt. 3, 2024.

the State Department has steadily maintained the position that Behring Sea is a closed sea, and is under the exclusive jurisdiction of the United States for the purposes referred to. It is known to the House that the Secretary has been engaged in negotiations with the leading European powers to bring about an international arrangement for a close time for seals in all these waters, but I am advised that there has been no intimation of a surrender of our claim to control Behring Sea.[99]

There are obvious mis-statements in the remarks of both Mr. Dunn and Mr. Dingley. Russia had not enforced her contention that the Behring Sea was a closed sea, and Bayard had refrained from going on record in that respect. This was the very reason why he was so anxious to settle the Behring Sea dispute by means of a multilateral treaty that would control the actions of the citizens of the signatory powers.

It is apparent, however, that President Cleveland was in favor of the program sponsored by Mr. Dunn, and he was careful not to consult Secretary Bayard in this matter. On February 25, 1889, Senator Stockbridge introduced a bill to provide for the "better protection of the fur-seals and salmon fisheries of Alaska."[100] In the House of Representatives an important amendment was added to this bill (February 28). Under its terms, Section 1956 of the *Revised Statutes* was to be interpreted as applying to all the waters of Behring Sea which were included within the maritime boundaries of the treaty of March 30, 1867. This section of the *Revised Statutes* had expressly prohibited the killing of fur-bearing animals "within the limits of Alaskan territory, or the waters thereof."[101]

This House amendment was rejected by the Senate on March 1, 1889, and the bill was sent to conference. It emerged from conference with the provision that Section 1956 of the *Revised Statutes* included and applied to all "the dominion of the United States in the waters of the Behring Sea." The President was directed to issue at timely seasons in each year, a proclamation warning all persons against entering those waters for the purpose of violating the provisions of said section. He was also to send one or more vessels to cruise in these designated waters and arrest all persons, and seize all vessels, found to be, or to have been, engaged in any violations of the laws of the United States therein. On March 2, the President signed the bill and it became law.[102]

99. *Ibid.*, p. 2026. See also, *Senate Rept. No. 2687,* 50 Cong., *Senate Ex. Doc. No. 74,* 50 Cong., 2 sess., *Senate Ex. Doc. No. 90,* 50 Cong., 2 sess., and *House Rept. No. 3883,* 50 Cong., 2 sess.

100. *Congressional Record,* 50 Cong., 2 sess., XX, Pt. 3, 2282.

101. *Congressional Record,* 50 Cong., 2 sess., XX, Pt. 3, 2448–2449, 2502.

102. *Ibid.*, p. 2614. *United States Statutes at Large* (Washington, 1889), XXV, 1009–1010.

The person directly responsible for this legislation was Mr. Dunn, Chairman of the Committee on Merchant Marine and Fisheries of the House of Representatives. Needless to say, he must have worked in close co-operation with President Cleveland who had always been opposed to any surrender of the claim of American jurisdiction over Behring Sea. The President, it is true, has the control over the conduct of American foreign relations, but previous Presidents had usually formulated foreign policy in conjunction with their Secretaries of State. Cleveland had not hesitated to work behind Bayard's back in the matter of the Scott Act dealing with Chinese immigration into the United States,[103] and apparently he employed these same tactics in connection with the fur-seal legislation. This fact is made clear in the following excerpt from a conversation between Bayard and Baron Rosen on March 1, 1889:

Baron Rosen called bringing with him a report of Mr. Dunn, on the Alaska fur seal fisheries. He pointed out to me some of the conclusions reached by Mr. Dunn in regard to the title of the United States to the waters of Behring Sea being fixed and complete by the cession from Russia. I told him I had examined the book [*House Rept. No. 3883,* 50 Cong., 2 sess.]; found it had been reported to the House on the 29th of January, and had not been printed until within the last few days. I told him I had not seen it, and had had no consultation with Mr. Dunn, no knowledge of what he had reported, and I must distinctly decline being responsible for anything he did.[104]

For many months Bayard had held out against Presidential pressure in this matter of jurisdiction over Behring Sea. He had also been at odds with the Solicitor of the Department of State and with the Minister to Great Britain on this same point. Party leaders in Congress apparently knew of this defection, and felt free to disregard Bayard's viewpoint.[105] In the legislative rush that came in the last days of the 50th Congress, the State Department was neatly by-passed, and Bayard was left holding a position that the President had already con-

103. Tansill, *Bayard,* pp. 175–177.

104. *Memorandum* written by Bayard after a conversation with Baron Rosen, March 1, 1889, *Bayard MS.*

105. It is interesting to note that, due to the Sackville-West incident, Lord Salisbury was not at all friendly to Bayard or to the Cleveland Administration. In a letter to Mr. Samuel L. Barlow, January 18, 1889, Bayard gave expression to his feelings in this regard: "It passes my conception that a man like Lord Salisbury should place his government in the attitude of *apparently* being willing to hold diplomatic relations with but one of the political parties in the United States, and the one so selected should contain every Dynamiter and political assassin whose main purpose is to embroil this country in War with Great Britain." *Bayard Letter Book,* X, *Bayard MS.*

sented to surrender. By this surrender the President abandoned the principle of the freedom of the seas, and gave to the British Government the opportunity to stand as a leader in the fight for a free sea. Bayard was keenly aware of all the implications in the legislation sponsored by the President; he could have no doubt that he had been pushed aside in the matter of formulating American foreign policy. He could, however, console himself with the thought that he had closely adhered to the principles that had long been regarded as important articles in the American creed. Freedom of the Seas was a slogan that dated back to the American Revolution, and it had been a battle cry in the War of 1812. Successive Secretaries of State had regarded it as one of the great political labels that Americans had lived by—and had died by. But President Cleveland closed his ears to this old call to arms, and permitted Lord Salisbury to bring it out in a new edition with impressive English accents. The Foreign Office assumed the role of defender of a great American tradition, while the American Chief Executive strongly supported a barbarous principle that American blood, in heroic combat on the high seas, had forever removed from the law of nations. "Sturdy Americanism" was not always a Cleveland characteristic.

CHAPTER XI

LORD SALISBURY INSTRUCTS SECRETARY BLAINE IN THE PRINCIPLES OF INTERNATIONAL LAW

WHEN President Harrison came into office on March 4, 1889, he promptly installed James G. Blaine as Secretary of State. Blaine had held that office during the brief period of the Garfield Administration, and he had continued to serve for a short time under President Arthur. His long experience in public office had made him familiar with many of the problems he would face in the Department of State. His adaptability and mental agility would serve him well in preparing the diplomatic notes that were necessary in the conduct of foreign relations. The overtones that were so evident in his political speeches would not be appreciated by audiences that were foreign as well as domestic, and his gift of repartee was destined to win him few encomiums from diplomats who pressed him hard with facts and not mere phrases.

There is little doubt that Blaine was one of those likable persons who are able to put their genius into their living and their talents into political management. Baron Rosen has paid eloquent tribute to the "winning charm" of Blaine's magnetic personality,[1] and there is abundant evidence that other diplomats in Washington were strongly attracted by his ease of manner. But he was a brilliant debater rather than a cogent thinker, and he always had a quick eye for favorable publicity. In many ways he brings to mind Stevenson's penetrating comment upon James M. Barrie: "Genius is in him, but there's a journalist at his elbow."

In the matter of fur-seal diplomacy, Blaine consulted his emotions rather than his reason. He was ardently patriotic and therefore warmly opposed to any surrender of what he regarded as American rights. President Cleveland had refused to abandon the claim of American jurisdiction over a large portion of Behring Sea with reference to the

1. Baron Rosen, *Forty Years of Diplomacy* (New York, 1922), I, 77. In this same regard the following words of Samuel L. Barlow to Bayard, March 7, 1889, are pertinent: "After all that has been said and with a pretty good knowledge of the ways of Mr. Blaine, I am almost sorry that he is not at the head of the Government, *de jure* as he will be *de facto*. President Harrison's inaugural has not one sentence of manly straightforwardness, but it has . . . an air of hypocrisy and tricks, that annoys me. Blaine with all his failings has, as Vanderbilt said of his dead son-in-law, Clarke, 'some good pints.' He is bold and unscrupulous if you please, but he has friends and sticks to them, while if Harrison has any such appendages, he will cheat them in his own interests or in that of cant, and so long as his pent-up little conscience is satisfied, he will assume that he is doing God's work." *Bayard MS.*

prevention of pelagic sealing. Apparently, Blaine was loath to give up this position, and at times he supported pretensions that were in direct conflict with the stand that American statesmen had taken through many decades of our history. He labored hard to prove that he was mainly interested in protecting the fur-seal industry from ruin, and in the ardor of his arguments he forgot that the methods he devised in that regard were so far-reaching that they would make Behring Sea a closed area.[2]

Secretary Bayard had favored a policy of international co-operation in the matter of regulating the killing of fur-seals. During the early months of his service as Secretary of State, Blaine was willing to follow a similar pattern, but the lines of this design were to be prescribed by Russia and the United States. The first step in preparing this outline was taken by Baron Rosen, the Russian *chargé d'affaires* in Washington. Acting under instructions from the Russian Foreign Office, Rosen had several conferences with Secretary Blaine, and the whole question of Russian-American joint action was thoroughly canvassed. In one of Rosen's *aides mémoire* there were some interesting comments upon the best procedure to follow, and this matter was developed in detail. It was apparent, thought Baron Rosen, that the United States and Russia had a deep interest in the maintenance and protection of the seal fisheries, not only as "a matter of right but also as a matter of solicitude for the welfare of the native population of these islands whose only means of subsistence are entirely dependent on the continued existence of the fisheries." Scientific investigation had conclusively shown that, "unless the reckless and promiscuous killing of seals be carefully guarded against, seal life is certain to become extinct within a measurably short period of time."

The whole matter resolved itself simply into this question:

Is there anything in the principles of international law that could compel two Nations to witness in helpless inaction the wanton destruction of a most valuable property through the action, and for the sole and temporary benefit of a few illicit traders whose mode of operation besides is such as to ensure, if suffered to go on unchecked, the speedy destruction not only of the legitimate seal killing industry, but also of the very source of their own illicit gains, and this for the sole reason that these nefarious operations are carried

2. In the monograph entitled *American Diplomacy* (New York, 1919, p. 378), by Carl R. Fish, the statement is made that the Act of March 2, 1889 was pushed through the House of Representatives "largely through Blaine's influence." He cites no evidence to substantiate this statement. This Act was an Administration measure that reflected Cleveland's strongly held views, and if Blaine supported this legislation he was merely following Cleveland's lead.

on beyond the limits of their territorial waters. To this question, evidently, only one answer is possible, and that an emphatic NO. International Law recognizes not only the right but the solemn duty of a Nation to work for the perfection and security of its estate. . . . Then again, from the generally recognized principles that the high seas are open to all nations for all legitimate purposes, it does not by any means follow . . . that vessels of one nation may with impunity carry on on the high seas operations destructive of the lawful property of another nation and then, when interfered with in their nefarious pursuit, invoke the inviolability attaching to the flag of a friendly nation on the high seas.[3]

Baron Rosen's arguments are very similar to those employed by Francis Wharton and George A. Jenks, the Acting Attorney General of the United States. They struck a responsive chord in Blaine's breast, and it was not long before Blaine and Rosen completed the draft of a treaty dealing with the killing of fur-seals. This *projet* incorporated many of the points developed in Baron Rosen's *aides mémoire*, and it emphasized the contention that freedom of the seas could not confer upon the vessels of any nation the right to carry on "with impunity operations leading to the destruction of any other nation's lawful and incontestable property." Assuming this to be true, Russia and the United States were resolved to "apply to all vessels and all persons engaged in hunting fur seals in the seas surrounding the above named islands [the Commodore Islands, the Pribilof Islands, and Robben Island] the same laws and regulations governing the seal hunting industry in their own respective territories and Dominions applied to their own ships, and to their own subjects and citizens." In applying these regulations, the Governments of Russia and the United States disclaimed any intention to interfere with the "legitimate trade and commerce of other maritime powers," and they entertained the belief that all "friendly nations" would recognize the "necessity and justice" of the course of action that had been outlined. Such action would mean that instructions would be given to the commanders of Russian and American cruisers to "seize all vessels engaged in the pursuit or illicit

3. The *aides mémoire* of Baron Rosen in connection with the fur-seal question are contained in *Russian Embassy, Notes from,* XIII, MS. Dept. of State. These documents were first used by Tyler, *op. cit.,* pp. 373ff.

With reference to the financial returns from the fur-seal industry, John W. Foster, in his *Diplomatic Memoirs,* II, 22, makes the following statement: "For some years before the cession of Alaska the Russians were able to take approximately one hundred thousand skins annually from the Pribiloff Islands, and after the cession, up to the year 1890 under the American regime, the annual yield was about the same. For the same period the value of the skins taken by the American lessees was estimated to have been $31,000,000, and the receipts of the Government of the United States from the lease and duties $12,000,000."

killing of seals wherever found in the seas surrounding the above named islands."

The proclamation of this proposed Russo-American treaty would lead either to "acquiescence in the course adopted by the two Governments, or it would hasten the conclusion of the international agreement proposed by the United States in 1887." Under the threat of joint action by Russia and the United States, the other maritime powers would become conciliatory and the fur-seal controversy would be speedily settled.[4]

After this draft treaty had been accepted by Secretary Blaine, Baron Rosen sent it to the Minister of Foreign Affairs for approval. He was willing to give his support to this project, and so were the Ministers of Finance and of the Interior, but the Minister of the Navy opposed it on the ground that it might give serious offence to certain important maritime powers. Russia was having difficulties with Great Britain in the Near East and in Central Asia. Fearful of further troubles, the Minister of Foreign Affairs finally decided to put a stop to the negotiations between Blaine and Baron Rosen.[5] Blaine had suffered his first diplomatic defeat, but he had stocked his intellectual cupboard with the bones of contention that he and Lord Salisbury were to quarrel over during the remainder of his term as Secretary of State. Without Russian sauce they were not always appetizing.

Although deprived of Russian assistance in this matter of exerting pressure upon Great Britain with regard to the prevention of pelagic sealing, the Harrison Administration went right ahead with the policy that had been outlined in the Act of March 2, 1889. The President issued the proclamation warning sealing vessels against killing fur-seals within the maritime area that was claimed as a part of the dominion of the United States, and the British *chargé d'affaires* at Washington called it to the attention of Lord Salisbury as an irritant that might lead to serious difficulty.[6] In the summer of 1889 when American cruisers began seizing Canadian sealing schooners in Behring Sea, the British Foreign Office filed a prompt protest. It was indicated that these seizures had been made outside the three-mile limit. Needless to say, this action was in conflict with the principles of international law. Moreover, in 1888 Secretary Bayard had given "very clear assurances" that, "pending the discussion of the general questions at issue, no fur-

4. Draft treaty, and Baron Rosen's comments in his *aides mémoire, Russian Legation, Notes from,* XIII, MS. Dept. of State.
5. Rosen, *op. cit.,* II, 79–80.
6. H. G. Edwardes to Lord Salisbury, March 23, 1889, *F.S.A.,* V, 260.

ther interference should take place with British vessels in Behring Sea."[7]

Blaine readily admitted that he had heard rumors of these seizures, and he did not deny that they had a basis of truth. He gave assurances, however, that President Harrison was anxious to reach an understanding with the British Government in regard to the American claim of jurisdiction over Behring Sea. As soon as Sir Julian Pauncefote arrived in Washington, the Department of State would arrange for an early discussion of the points at issue, and he believed that an adjustment of the dispute could be quickly reached.[8]

The British *chargé d'affaires* tried to capitalize upon the friendly words of Blaine by drawing from the Secretary of State an explicit assurance that no further seizures would be made in Behring Sea.[9] But Blaine refused to give this assurance. The whole question would be exhaustively discussed when Sir Julian Pauncefote arrived in Washington. There was no necessity for any great haste in this matter. American cruisers had already left for Behring Sea, and no new instructions could reach them in time to prevent further seizures.[10] It was not long before news arrived in England of the seizures of Canadian vessels in the North Pacific, and Lord Salisbury instructed Mr. Edwardes to protest against them and to indicate to Secretary Blaine the readiness of Her Majesty's Government to discuss the regulation of the fur-seal industry by international agreement.[11]

7. H. G. Edwardes to Secretary Blaine, August 24, 1889, *Foreign Relations, 1890,* p. 358. Hereafter referred to as *F.R.* The instruction from Lord Salisbury to Mr. Edwardes, August 22, 1889, is given in the communication from Lord Knutsford to Lord Stanley, August 26, 1889, *Macdonald Papers, Behring Sea, 1889–1890,* III, 25, P.A.C.

8. Secretary Blaine to Edwardes, August 24, 1889, *F.R., 1890,* p. 359. In an instruction from Lord Knutsford to Lord Stanley, August 31, 1889, an assurance was given that Blaine had expressed to Mr. Edwardes the "very friendly feelings of Harrison's administration" with regard to the settlement of the fur-seal controversy. *Macdonald Papers, Behring Sea,* III, 28, P.A.C.

In a note to President Harrison, August 25, 1889, Blaine commented as follows upon Bayard's assurance concerning seizures of sealing vessels: "It seems very *Bayardish* for this Government to agree to take no further measures of protection in the Behring Sea 'pending the discussion of the general question' and then allow England to say when that discussion shall be reopened and for how long a time it shall be *drawled* along." Albert T. Volwiler, *The Correspondence between Benjamin Harrison and James G. Blaine, 1882–1893* (Philadelphia, 1940), p. 79.

9. Edwardes to Secretary Blaine, September 12, 1889, *F.R., 1890,* p. 360.

10. Secretary Blaine to Edwardes, September 14, 1889, *ibid.,* pp. 360–361.

11. Lord Salisbury to Edwardes, October 2, 1889, *ibid.,* pp. 361–362. In 1886 three British sealing vessels had been seized in Behring Sea; in 1887 six vessels were taken into custody. None were seized in 1888. The vessels that had been seized in 1886 were condemned in the United States District Court at Sitka, and the master and mates were fined or imprisoned. The vessels were stripped of everything saleable and then

Secretary Blaine was determined to take no decisive action with regard to the fur-seal industry until Pauncefote arrived in Washington. Pauncefote reached his destination in the latter part of October 1889, and on November 1 he reported back to Lord Salisbury the substance of a conversation with Blaine. The Secretary of State did not claim that Behring Sea was a *mare clausum;* he merely maintained the right of the American Government to prevent the wholesale destruction of the fur-seals. In May, 1888, at the request of the Canadian Government, Lord Salisbury had suspended the negotiations concerning the regulation of the fur-seal industry. Blaine felt that the British Foreign Office should now take the initiative in the matter of resuming the negotiations. If this action should be taken, Pauncefote thought that it was necessary once more to consult Canadian wishes in advance, and it was important to consider the question of securing compensation for the sealing vessels that had been seized by American cruisers.[12]

When this despatch was received at the Foreign Office it created something of a sensation. Lord Knutsford, at the Colonial Office, at once sent for Sir Charles Tupper, the High Commissioner for Canada, and disclosed the tenor of Secretary Blaine's comments to Pauncefote. He said it was apparent that Blaine had "frankly abandoned any claim to the contention that Behring Sea was a *mare clausum.*" The American Secretary of State had further stated that "if England would consent to appoint a commission, upon which England, Canada, the United States and Russia should be represented, to report upon the question of a close time for seals in Behring's Sea, the United States would admit the question of compensation." Assurances were given that "no further seizures would be made." At the close of the conference at the Department of State, Blaine had taken Sir Julian by the hand and had remarked: "I know that England and Canada consider me unfriendly, but I can assure you it is not so. I am most anxious that we should be on the best terms with both England and Canada."[13]

Lord Knutsford was deeply impressed with this conciliatory attitude assumed by Blaine, and he expressed to Lord Stanley the hope that the Canadian Government was "prepared to concur in any reasonable arrangement for the establishment of a close season in Behring Sea." He believed that the Governor-General and his advisers would agree

offered to their owners. Four of the vessels seized in 1887 were condemned and sold. In 1889 eight vessels were seized. These ships were ordered to go to United States ports, but they disobeyed orders and went to Victoria, and thus effected an escape. *C.S.P., 1892,* IX, lxxix–lxxxi.

12. Pauncefote to Lord Salisbury, November 1, 1889, *F.S.A.,* V, 386.

13. Sir Charles Tupper to Sir John Macdonald, November 21, 1889, *Macdonald Papers, Behring Sea,* III, 258–265, P.A.C.

that it was "expedient to commence the suggested negotiation at an early date."[14] On December 5 the Colonial Office pressed Lord Stanley for an early reply in connection with the fur-seal matter.[15]

The Governor-General sent an immediate and favorable response, and on December 7, 1889, Lord Salisbury forwarded to Pauncefote an outline of the conditions laid down by Canada with reference to any renewal of the negotiations concerning the seal fisheries. They were four in number: (1) The American Government would have to abandon all pretensions to regard Behring Sea as a closed sea, and would have to revise any legislation based upon that claim. (2) Canada should be represented upon any Joint High Commission intrusted with the settlement of the seal fisheries dispute. (3) The proceedings of the Commission should have the approval of Canada. (4) Great Britain and the United States should agree upon the amount of compensation to be paid to British subjects for the seizure of their sealing vessels by American revenue cutters in the North Pacific.[16]

Sir Julian realized that these conditions were so far-reaching that they had little chance of acceptance by the American Government. After a conference with Blaine, Pauncefote informed the Foreign Office that the American Government would not agree "to Canadian representative in negotiation as to close time." The proceedings would not be in the form of a commission, but would be more like a "diplomatic conference."[17] When this information was conveyed to Lord Stanley, he replied by stating that in his opinion the American Government had really asserted jurisdiction over Behring Sea "by instructing its officers to seize vessels in mid-ocean, by setting up that doctrine in the Courts, by obtaining condemnation of ships on that doctrine, and by selling the property of Canadians under such condemnation." Canada would expect the British Government "not to conclude arrangement" unless Behring Sea was declared to be an open sea. Moreover, Canada adhered "to opinion that agreement as to close season and preservation of seals should be subject to her approval as one of the parties chiefly interested."[18]

The Foreign Office was entirely willing to support any just Canadian demands, and Sir Charles Tupper informed Sir John Macdonald that the British Government was really pledged

14. Lord Knutsford to Lord Stanley, November 23, 1889, *ibid.*, pp. 48–49, P.A.C.
15. Colonial Office to Lord Stanley, December 5, 1889, *ibid.*, p. 55.
16. Lord Salisbury to Pauncefote, December 7, 1889, *F.S.A.*, V, 400.
17. Colonial Office to Lord Stanley, December 11, 1889, *Macdonald Papers, Behring Sea*, III, 63, P.A.C.
18. Lord Stanley to Colonial Office, December 13, 1889, *ibid.*, p. 65, P.A.C.

not to conclude *any* arrangement without securing an adequate public declaration by the United States that Behring Sea is open or free, and stands pledged to us that no agreement as to a close season shall be made without the approval of Canada. Lord Knutsford expects Blaine to abandon in the outset of the negotiations the pretension that Behring Sea is a *mare clausum,* if he does not formally do so before. . . . The British Minister will be assisted by a Canadian official, and even this discussion will be based upon the previous declaration that Behring Sea is open and the admission of compensation by the United States.[19]

On January 28, 1890 Lord Salisbury addressed to Sir Julian the terms which he thought should govern the proposed negotiations. The high contracting parties were limited to Great Britain, Russia and the United States, and the conversations should be conducted in Washington. The question of compensation to the owners of Canadian vessels that had been seized in the North Pacific should be the subject of separate negotiations. The American Government should give assurances that there would be no further seizures.[20]

Before receiving this note, Blaine had despatched to Pauncefote a long communication in which he strongly defended the right of the American Government to give adequate protection to the seal fisheries. Pelagic sealing would ruin an industry that had been "carefully developed for more than ninety years under the flags of Russia and the United States." This industry brought a considerable income into the Treasury Department. It was also an important economic asset to Great Britain. The skins were "regularly transported to London to be dressed and prepared for the markets of the world, and the business had grown so large that the earnings of English laborers, since Alaska was transferred to the United States, amount in the aggregate to more than twelve millions of dollars." This industry had been developed for the "use of mankind," and the profits derived from it had been of great benefit to the Indians in the North Pacific, and to many workers both in the United States and in England. Pelagic sealing, which would rapidly ruin this industry, was therefore against "good morals and good government the world over," and Blaine expressed "unfeigned surprise" that the British Government would defend the lawless course of these marauders. The law of the sea "is not lawlessness," nor can it be perverted to "justify acts which are immoral in themselves," and which "inevitably tend to results against the interests and against the welfare of mankind."

19. Sir Charles Tupper to Sir John Macdonald, December 16, 1889, London, *ibid.,* pp. 276–279.

20. Lord Salisbury to Pauncefote, January 28, 1890, *F.S.A.,* V, 435.

It would not be expedient for the British Government to insist too vigorously upon a strict observance of the three-mile limit, because this narrow restriction might prevent the continuance of the proper measures for the protection of the pearl fisheries of Ceylon. It should also be taken into account that a strict adherence to the three-mile limit might keep the British Government, if the occasion arose, from protecting the fisheries off the "Newfoundland banks." Suppose certain fishermen would start the practice of using dynamite along those banks? They would secure vast numbers of fish by such methods, but they would also ruin the fisheries. If these methods were used, would the British Government "think that so wicked an act could not be prevented and its perpetrators punished simply because it had been committed outside of the 3-mile line"?

It was significant that the sealing ships from Canada had not started on their destructive course until recent years. By what process of reasoning did Her Majesty's Government conclude that acts might be "committed with impunity against the rights" of the United States, when these same acts had never been attempted against the rights of Russia? The President was persuaded that "all friendly nations" would concede to the United States "the same rights and privileges on the lands and in the waters of Alaska which the same friendly nations always conceded to the Empire of Russia."[21]

These interesting legal points raised by Secretary Blaine did not receive any answer from Lord Salisbury until the latter part of May. In the meantime there were some interesting conversations between Blaine, Pauncefote and Mr. Charles H. Tupper. Tupper (the son of Sir Charles Tupper) held the office of Minister of Marine and Fisheries under Sir John Macdonald, and he had been sent to Washington to serve as a technical adviser to Pauncefote. On February 27, 1890, Tupper and Pauncefote called to see Secretary Blaine. Blaine began the discussion by reading from a statement made by Mr. Mowat, the Canadian Inspector of Fisheries in British Columbia. According to Mowat, sealing vessels in 1886 had killed some 40,000 seals, mostly cows. This large figure plainly indicated that some regulation was immediately necessary.

Using these statistics prepared by Mowat, Blaine declaimed with much heat against pelagic sealing, and expressed the opinion that unless action were promptly taken the sealing industry would be ruined. Tupper dissented from this view and challenged the figures presented by Mowat. After a long study of the best available evidence, Tupper

21. Secretary Blaine to Pauncefote, January 22, 1890, *F.R., 1890,* pp. 366–370.

was certain that the killing of the cow seals did not result in the death of the baby seals. Cow seals did not leave the rookeries "until the nurslings were able to look after themselves"; the cow seal "was a necessity to them for a very short period only." The most serious injury to the sealing industry did not arise from pelagic sealing but from the wasteful killings on the islands in Behring Sea.

At this point Pauncefote interjected the remark that the fur-seal question could be divided into three parts—1. Is a close season required outside of the three-mile limit? 2. If so, what territory and waters should it embrace? 3. What months should it cover?

Secretary Blaine quickly remarked that "the United States Government would not listen for a moment to any argument that no close season outside of the limit is required." When Tupper indicated that this point would have to be argued unless the American Government claimed control over Behring Sea, Blaine sought refuge in an ambiguity: "I have never claimed the Sea was a *mare clausum*," but "I have never abandoned that claim which my predecessor set up." After this veiled warning as to the course his policy might follow, Blaine stated that he was prepared to act on broad general principles, and was willing to give careful consideration to the matter of referring to arbitration the question of compensation to owners of seized Canadian sealing vessels. Before taking this action he would expect, however, that some arrangement as to a close season would be agreed upon.

Tupper questioned the need for a close season and requested Blaine to make a written statement proving that a cessation of pelagic sealing was necessary. Blaine was somewhat taken aback by Tupper's statement, and merely stammered: "I did not expect to meet a Canadian representative. I understood that the British Government and the United States . . . would agree upon a close season in the interests of this great and important industry, and then submit the agreement to Canada for approval." When Tupper remarked that he would not have joined in the discussion unless he had thought his opinion would be welcomed, Blaine "disclaimed any discourtesy" but repeated his statement that he had not expected to meet a Canadian representative. Blaine then asked Tupper what he would do if a Spanish vessel visited the Newfoundland banks and "began the use of the deadly dynamite." Would an English cruiser "stand by and wonder what the law of nations prescribed in such a case"? Tupper replied that the use of dynamite would unquestionably be "wanton destruction of the fish," but he thought that "hunting seals in mid-ocean was not yet shown to be destructive of the seal fishery."

After some further discussion, Blaine reminded Pauncefote and Mr. Tupper that "time pressed" and the matter would have to be quickly settled or the President would issue his proclamation and seizures of sealing vessels would follow. Tupper remarked that in 1888 the proclamation had been issued but seizures had been stopped. "Yes," said Blaine, "but that was in Mr. Bayard's time." In his opinion "the present Administration must carry out the law."[22]

Tupper was somewhat disturbed by the tone of Blaine's remarks, but Pauncefote was optimistic and expressed the view that Blaine talked "big words" but nevertheless everything would turn out all right. He was also convinced that Blaine knew that

> nothing can be done unless we all agree to a close season. . . . He further remarked that he and Mr. Blaine were to settle the *amount* of damages if possible before arranging definitely as to liability. He believes it well to humour Mr. Blaine in this respect, in view of the great party and political pressure upon him—considering as he does, that if we can agree to a close season all will come well, and that if not, the "fat will again be in the fire," as Sir Julian put it. I drew Sir Julian's attention to the embarrassment connected with the discussion of a close season caused by the negotiations in London between the United States Minister and the Russian Ambassador when Lord Salisbury expressed his readiness to agree to a close season from 15th April to 1st of November. Sir Julian agreed that this was very awkward, and he added "what is also odd, Lord Salisbury actually proposed to cover not only Behring Sea with the close season but all waters north of 47° of North Latitude."[23]

It was not long before Tupper discovered that the Russian Minister was supporting the contentions of Secretary Blaine, and he was surprised to find out that Pauncefote himself was "much impressed by the theory that females are killed in large numbers in the open sea, and their nurslings on islands consequently lost."[24] After much insistence, Tupper secured from Blaine a written statement in support of the contention for a close season in Behring Sea. While Tupper was pre-

22. Charles H. Tupper to Sir John Macdonald, February 27, 1890, *Macdonald Papers, Behring Sea, Correspondence of C. H. Tupper,* I, 23–60, P.A.C. In commenting upon the American demand for a close season from April 15 to November 1, Mr. C. H. Tupper, in his annual report as Minister of Marine and Fisheries, *C.S.P., 1892,* IX, lxxx, remarks: "Were any such dates entertained it would simply involve an entire abandonment of the industry. . . . The seals do not begin to enter Behring Sea until the middle or end of May, while they leave those waters by the end of October."

23. C. H. Tupper to Sir John Macdonald, February 28, 1890, *Macdonald Papers, Behring Sea, Correspondence of C. H. Tupper,* I, 62–69, P.A.C.

24. C. H. Tupper to Sir John Macdonald, March 3, 1890, *ibid.,* pp. 103–112.

paring an answer to this paper, Sir Julian paid a visit to the Department of State and had a confidential conversation with Blaine. Although it was supposed to remain confidential, Pauncefote gave the substance of it to Tupper. The gist of the conversation was that

> Sir Julian told Mr. Blaine it was utterly useless for the United States to think that England would, for one moment, agree to have the question of a close season treated in the way Mr. Blaine was now trying to deal with it. That the arrangement proposed by Mr. Blaine respecting a close season was another way of asserting the same control as under a *mare clausum,* and that unless we all pursued the subject, thoroughly recognizing that no one nation had the right to fix or determine the regulations, it would be impossible to come to any agreement. Mr. Blaine . . . then went into a fanciful theory regarding the right of the United States to preserve the seals breeding on Islands belonging to the United States, Mr. Blaine supporting this theory by the argument that Russia had in no way abandoned this right in favour of England or of the United States. Notwithstanding all this, Sir Julian still believes that Mr. Blaine is most anxious for a settlement of the question.[25]

In Ottawa, Lord Stanley, the Governor General, was following the course of the negotiations at Washington with deep concern, and after reading the Tupper correspondence he grew increasingly apprehensive. In a letter to Sir John Macdonald he expressed his fears: "If Blaine will not listen to reason we are in more danger than I have liked to think possible."[26] But Sir Julian continued to be optimistic, and he was inclined to agree with Blaine as to the necessity for a close season in connection with the killing of fur-seals. During a conversation with C. H. Tupper, Sir Julian "threw out a hint that he was making propositions on behalf of the British Government, and that he was not speaking for the Canadian Government in this Conference." Tupper promptly remarked that he was quite aware that Sir Julian was "acting directly for the British Government." However, when Sir Julian took the trouble to consult a Canadian representative or the Canadian Government, he "must expect the Canadian opinion." At this point Pauncefote said he had "understood that the Conference was to settle what the close season should be, taking as granted that some season should be agreed upon." Tupper replied that the Canadian Government had "never understood this nor did we at any time admit that a close season outside the three-mile limit was necessary."[27]

25. C. H. Tupper to Sir John Macdonald, March 10, 1890, *ibid.,* pp. 152–169.

26. Lord Stanley to Sir John Macdonald, March 18, 1890, *Macdonald Papers, Behring Sea,* II, 102–103.

27. C. H. Tupper to Sir John Macdonald, April 10, 1890, *Macdonald Papers, Behring Sea, Correspondence of C. H. Tupper,* II, 226–240.

In a letter to Sir John Macdonald on the following day (April 11), Tupper gave some further details of his difficulties with Sir Julian, who was inclined to be somewhat generous in his concessions to the United States. In the draft convention prepared by Sir Julian, provision was made that in the event of disagreement between the high contracting parties, the matter could be referred to "an independent Government" for settlement. The convention also provided that "pending the duration thereof (two years and a half), no sealing vessel shall be permitted within a radius of fifteen miles from any breeding island." Sir Julian had shown Tupper a letter he had written to Lord Salisbury in which the statement was made that unless this draft convention were submitted,

> the settlement of the question is impossible, and that in his opinion outside criticism will be adverse to our attitude throughout these negotiations. He [Sir Julian] claims that substantially no injury will be done our sealers by his last Convention, and that if it be not accepted by the United States, our position will then be commended by all disinterested parties.
>
> I need not discuss in this letter the provision regarding the radius. I have already told you we could safely concede 20 miles so far as our sealing operations are concerned. . . . I entertain strong objections to the clause which put us at the mercy of a foreign Government. If after scientific and thorough enquiry, we do not believe regulations for the seal hunting are required, it would be humiliating to find that by the ipse dixit of a foreign power we were practically excluded from sealing in Behring Sea. . . .
>
> It is in my opinion most unfortunate that he [Sir Julian Pauncefote] has conducted negotiations in such a way that Mr. Blaine has been able to learn all that he personally was willing to do. The consequence is that he fights now for his own reputation and standing, before Mr. Blaine. It seems clear from the above, that having informally told Mr. Blaine of his intended and very handsome concessions, he dare not retreat. It may be out of place for me to say it, but I cannot refrain from urging that in future negotiations with the United States, no British Minister at Washington should act for us. It is apparent that there is always present on his part a desire to make his future residence in Washington as pleasant as possible, and he is to some extent, therefore, unable to take and keep a firm and independent position.[28]

These letters of C. H. Tupper strongly influenced the attitude of Lord Stanley, at Ottawa, and he wrote to the Colonial Office that the Canadian Government was quite ready to "acquiesce in general principle of protection of seal life, but are most anxious that an enquiry by experts may precede permanent Treaty, as we believe facts to be

28. C. H. Tupper to Sir John Macdonald, April 11, 1890, *ibid.*, pp. 243–253.

incorrect on which United States proposals are based." There was no disposition to "raise difficulties," but he was certain that the "seal fishery will be seriously affected if we get no better terms than those proposed by United States."[29]

To Sir Julian Pauncefote, in Washington, Lord Stanley conveyed a distinct warning. He feared that if concessions to the United States were "carried too far," they would produce the "most serious consequences" in Canada.[30] Under this pressure from Canada and from the Foreign Office, the position of Pauncefote was at times distinctly uncomfortable. It is also true that Tupper's attitude was so aggressive and self-confident that Pauncefote must have resented the presence of this Canadian adviser. There is little doubt that Tupper was a thorn in the side of Blaine. On April 16 Tupper wrote to Sir John Macdonald and described the procedure at one of the conferences between Blaine, Pauncefote, and M. de Struve, the Russian Minister at Washington. His account clearly indicates Blaine's distaste for Tupper. It had been agreed that the American and British statements should be read and discussed in detail, but as soon as Tupper's paper was presented, Blaine "refused point blank" to discuss the questions raised in it, and requested the British Minister to state "the best offer he was authorized to make for a close season on behalf of his Government."[31]

Pauncefote was in favor of a close season, but Tupper was violently opposed to one, and the British Minister had to postpone his decision until he had talked the matter over with his Canadian adviser. After one of these conversations, Tupper wrote a note to Pauncefote and insisted that there should not be any admission of the necessity "for restrictions of pelagic sealing." In the event that a close season was finally agreed to, it should apply to the killing of seals on land as well as in the sea. He thought it was unreasonable to ask Canadian sealers to "abstain from killing seals in the open sea at times when United States lessees may kill and take seals on land."[32]

The draft convention that Pauncefote was trying to put in shape was a patch-work affair that contained suggestions from both the British Colonial Office and from the Canadian Government. As Blaine discussed these points with Pauncefote, he became discouraged as to the outcome of the negotiations. On April 25 Pauncefote reported to Tupper that he had just returned from a conference with Blaine, who was

29. Lord Stanley to Secretary of State for Colonies, April 11, 1890, *Macdonald Papers, Behring Sea,* III, 122.

30. Lord Stanley to Pauncefote, April 11, 1890, *ibid.,* p. 118.

31. C. H. Tupper to Sir John Macdonald, April 16, 1890, *Macdonald Papers, Behring Sea, Correspondence of C. H. Tupper,* II, 263–265.

32. C. H. Tupper to Sir Julian Pauncefote, April 26, 1890, *ibid.,* pp. 333–336.

"looking wretched," and who certainly was very "irritable and despondent." Blaine expressed the fear that "nothing was going to come from this Conference after all," but Sir Julian assured him that some settlement would be arrived at.[33]

On April 29 Sir Julian presented his draft convention to Blaine, and the "fat was in the fire." Provision was made for the appointment of a mixed commission of experts who were to study and report (within two years) upon the following questions: (1) Whether regulations properly enforced upon the breeding islands, and in the territorial waters surrounding those islands are sufficient for the preservation of the fur-seals? (2) If not, how far from the islands is it necessary that such regulations should be enforced in order to preserve them? (3) In either of the above cases, what should such regulations provide? (4) If a close season is required on the breeding islands and territorial waters, what months should it embrace? (5) If a close season is necessary outside of the breeding islands as well, what extent of waters and what period or periods should it embrace?

If the High Contracting Parties were not able to agree upon the regulations to be adopted, the questions of difference should be referred to the arbitration of an impartial government. Pending the report of the Commission, and for six months after the date of such report, the High Contracting Parties should put in force a series of proposed regulations. One of these regulations prohibited the taking of seals by *land*[34] or sea north of certain fixed lines, from May 1 to June 30, and from October 1 to December 30. A protective band of ten miles wide was suggested as a protection against poachers on the islands, and the masters of vessels who broke the provisional regulations should be turned over to the "authorities of the nation to which they respectively belong, who shall alone have jurisdiction to try the offence and impose the penalties for the same."[35]

Blaine did not give an immediate answer to the letter from Paunce-

33. C. H. Tupper to Sir John Macdonald, April 25, 1890, *ibid.*, p. 292. It is apparent that Blaine was often irritable and despondent during this period. His ill-temper and consequent remorse are well illustrated in the following note he wrote to John W. Foster, December 24, 1891: "Tired and hungry and sick to begin with, I spoke to you rather quickly at the Department. I beg pardon for so doing, and if you had not left so quickly, I would have spoken your pardon there. I have a very quick and very unfortunate temper, but it is over in a minute and hence I write you the first thing after getting home." *John W. Foster Papers,* Library of Congress.

34. This was a suggestion made by Mr. Tupper. Tupper's opposition to the submission of differences to the arbitration of an impartial government was unavailing.

35. Pauncefote to Secretary Blaine, April —, 1890, *House Ex. Doc. No. 450,* 51 Cong., 1 sess., pp. 52–57.

fote which enclosed the draft convention, but during the early days of May, 1890, he treated the British Minister with such friendly courtesy that optimism prevailed in the British Legation.[36] On May 10 Blaine informed Pauncefote that he would soon send him a letter concerning the proposed convention, and he expressed the belief that the "proposal was a satisfactory basis for a settlement." There would, of course, have to be some "important changes" made before the American Government "could accept it."[37]

On May 22 a statement appeared in the American press to the effect that a decision had been arrived at during a meeting of President Harrison's Cabinet to reject the draft treaty submitted by Pauncefote. It was also stated that instructions had been issued to the revenue cutter *Bear* to arrest pelagic sealers in Behring Sea. When Pauncefote called at the Department of State to make inquiries concerning this statement, Blaine made no attempt to deny its authenticity. He contented himself with the remark that in the United States the press was free from censorship. With regard to the draft treaty, he was strongly opposed to the regulation which would, within the close season, prohibit the killing of seals on *land* as well as in the sea.[38]

On May 23 Pauncefote sent a note of protest against the issuance of instructions to American revenue cutters authorizing them to seize Canadian vessels engaged in pelagic sealing.[39] He then made two visits to the Department and, after discussing the situation with Blaine, he wrote to Lord Stanley, in Ottawa, and expressed optimism as to the outcome of the negotiations.[40] But Stanley himself was somewhat apprehensive over the "bulldozing" tactics of Blaine, and he remained skeptical about the way things would turn out.[41]

His skepticism was confirmed when he received a copy of Blaine's note of May 29 to Pauncefote. This note was long and highly argumentative. Blaine protested against the course of the British Government "in authorizing, encouraging, and protecting vessels which are not only interfering with American rights in the Behring Sea, but which are doing violence as well to the rights of the civilized world." After this sharp indictment of British practices, Blaine asserted that Lord

36. C. H. Tupper to Sir John Macdonald, May 9, 1890, *Macdonald Papers, Behring Sea, Correspondence of C. H. Tupper,* II, 369–378, P.A.C.

37. C. H. Tupper to Sir John Macdonald, May 11, 1890, *ibid.,* pp. 386–388.

38. Moore, *History and Digest of International Arbitrations,* I, 789.

39. Pauncefote to Secretary Blaine, May 23, 1890, *F.R., 1890,* p. 424.

40. Pauncefote to Lord Stanley, May 29, 1890, *Macdonald Papers, Behring Sea,* III, 152, P.A.C.

41. Lord Stanley to Sir John Macdonald, May 23, 1890, *ibid.,* p. 149.

Salisbury, from November 11, 1887 to April 23, 1888, had "assented to the necessity of a close season for the protection of seals." During this period negotiations for a settlement of the Behring Sea dispute had been progressing satisfactorily, but suddenly on April 28 the British Government refused to take any further steps until "Canada is heard from." After a delay of several months the American Minister inquired about a resumption of negotiations, but he was again met with the reply that no convention could be agreed to until its terms had been approved by the Canadian Government. Lord Salisbury thus acknowledged that the negotiations into which he had "cordially entered" were "entirely subordinated to the judgment and desire of the Canadian Government." In view of this Foreign Office attitude, Blaine could not help but feel that "Lord Salisbury would have dealt more frankly if, in the beginning, he had informed Minister Phelps that no arrangement could be made unless Canada concurred in it, and that all negotiation with the British Government direct was but a loss of time."

When Pauncefote had arrived in the United States it had seemed for a while that the fur-seal dispute could be quickly settled. No obstacles were presented "on the American side of the question. No insistence was made upon the Behring Sea as *mare clausum;* no objection was interposed to the entrance of British ships at all times on commercial errands through all the waters of the Behring Sea." But these negotiations were suddenly broken off for many weeks "by the interposition of Canada." Under the terms of the proposed convention, British vessels would "be allowed to kill seals within 10 miles of the coast of the Pribylov Islands," whereas under Lord Salisbury's proposals of 1888 no British vessel hunting seals "should come nearer to the Pribylov Islands than the 47th parallel of north latitude, about 600 miles." Moreover, the open season provided for in the draft convention would include the months of July, August and September, the very months when the "areas around the breeding islands are most crowded with seals, and especially crowded with female seals going forth to secure food for the hundreds of thousands of their young."

The proposals made by Lord Salisbury in 1888 and the proposals made by Sir Julian Pauncefote in 1890 were in "significant contrast." The circumstances were the same, and the rights of the United States were the same, but the position of England had changed "because the wishes of Canada have demanded the change."

In view of these facts it was apparent that the draft convention submitted by Sir Julian could not be accepted by the American Government. Nevertheless, it was the wish of President Harrison to continue the negotiations in the hope "of reaching an agreement that may conduce to a good understanding and leave no cause for future dispute." Blaine thereupon proposed that the British Government "agree not to permit" sealing vessels "to enter the Behring Sea for this season, in order that time may be secured for negotiations that shall not be disturbed by untoward events."[42]

After waiting for a few days, Blaine sent another note to Pauncefote. He had talked the matter over with President Harrison, who was of the opinion that arbitration could not "be concluded in time for this season." The President, therefore, was anxious to know whether Lord Salisbury would, in order to promote a friendly solution of the question, make for a single season "the regulation which in 1888 he offered to make permanent."[43] This regulation would exclude, during the seal fishery season of 1890, all British sealing vessels from Behring Sea.

Pauncefote immediately replied that Lord Salisbury was now satisfied that "such an extreme measure as that proposed in 1888 goes far beyond the requirements of the case." Her Majesty's Government was quite willing to adopt all measures which shall be satisfactorily proved to be necessary for the preservation of fur-seals, but they were not prepared to agree to the regulation proposed by Secretary Blaine. And even if they were, there was no "legal power to enforce its observance on British subjects and British vessels."[44]

Blaine came back with a note that again endeavored to show that Lord Salisbury had receded from the stand he had taken in 1888, and he expressed the disappointment of the President that Her Majesty's Government was not "willing to suspend, for a single season, the practice which Lord Salisbury described in 1888 as 'the wanton destruction of a valuable industry.' "[45] When Pauncefote replied that it was "entirely beyond the power of Her Majesty's Government to exclude British or Canadian ships from any portion of the high seas, even for an hour, without legislative sanction,"[46] Blaine stated that it would satisfy the American Government if "Lord Salisbury would by public proclamation simply request that vessels sailing under the British flag should abstain from entering the Behring Sea for the present season."[47]

The British Government was willing to accede to this request if Sec-

42. Secretary Blaine to Pauncefote, May 29, 1890, *F.R., 1890,* pp. 425–429.

43. Secretary Blaine to Pauncefote, June 2, 1890, *ibid.,* p. 429.

44. Pauncefote to Secretary Blaine, June 3, 1890, *ibid.,* p. 430.

45. Secretary Blaine to Pauncefote, June 4, 1890, *ibid.,* pp. 430–432.

46. Pauncefote to Secretary Blaine, enclosing excerpt from telegram from Lord Salisbury, received June 9, 1890, *ibid.,* p. 433.

47. Secretary Blaine to Pauncefote, June 11, 1890, *ibid.,* pp. 433–434.

retary Blaine was ready to agree to a general scheme for the settlement of the Behring Sea controversy. The conditions that should serve as the basis for this settlement were then outlined by Pauncefote as follows: (1) The two Governments should agree forthwith to refer to arbitration the question of the legality of the action of the American Government in seizing or otherwise interfering with British vessels operating in Behring Sea, outside territorial waters, during the years 1886, 1887, and 1889. (2) Pending the arbitral award, all interference with British sealing vessels should absolutely cease. (3) The American Government, if the award should be adverse on the question of legal right, will compensate British subjects for the losses which they may sustain by reason of their compliance with the British proclamation.[48]

As matters drifted along without any settlement of the fur-seal dispute, the possibility of war came more and more to the front. On May 29, Lord Salisbury had informed Sir Julian Pauncefote that continued seizures of British sealing vessels in Behring Sea would produce "the most serious complications."[49] On June 28 Lord Knutsford had a conference in London with Sir Charles Tupper with reference to the measures that should be taken in connection with American seizures of British vessels in Behring Sea. Tupper was certain that the American Government did not wish war, and he told Knutsford that if "prompt action is not taken, Canada can only come to the conclusion that the British flag is not strong enough to protect her." The result was that "Sir Julian Pauncefote was instructed to say to Mr. Blaine that if the British flag was interfered with, the United States must be prepared for the consequences."[50]

This instruction referred to by Sir Charles Tupper was actually sent to Pauncefote by Lord Salisbury,[51] and it is apparent that the British Government was getting prepared to meet any emergency that might arise on the Pacific Coast. This fact is clearly established in the following note from the Collector of Customs at Victoria, British Columbia, to the Minister of Customs:

On Saturday afternoon Mr. Young and myself went down to Esquimault to see for ourselves what was doing and just how the work was being pressed . . . on the British ships of war there. As you are of course aware, we found in Harbor 5, five ships of the Royal Navy: the *Amphion, Champion, Espiè-*

48. Pauncefote to Secretary Blaine, June 27, 1890, *ibid.*, pp. 436–437.
49. Lord Salisbury to Pauncefote, May 29, 1890, *Macdonald Papers, Behring Sea,* III, 156–157, P.A.C.
50. Tupper, *Recollections of Sixty Years,* pp. 209–211.
51. Pauncefote to Secretary Blaine, June 14, 1890, *F.R., 1890,* pp. 435–436.

gle, Nymph, and *Daphne.* . . . We found that all these ships were being fitted for Sea with all speed, and that the carpenters and others were being kept working on Sunday; the vessels are coaled and ammunitioned to full capacity. They are being dry docked as fast as possible and their bottoms and all machinery being carefully looked after.

In addition to the abovementioned ships, the Flag Ship, known as the *Warspite,* is expected not later than the 15th instant, with the new Admiral on board. The *Warspite* . . . is one of the fastest and best of the latest additions to the Royal Navy. . . . Everything points to the fact that at last the Imperial Government have decided to at least make a demonstration of force, possibly much more in the event of our Sailors being seized in the Behring Sea outside of a certain defined limit.[52]

It is apparent that Lord Salisbury was in no mood to permit the Harrison Administration to seize with impunity the British sealing vessels in Behring Sea. Some compromise was imperatively necessary to stave off possible war.

With things in this unsettled state, Pauncefote turned over to Secretary Blaine a long note from Lord Salisbury. This communication was meant as an answer to Blaine's note of January 22. With regard to Blaine's contention that the killing of fur-seals in the waters around the Behring Sea islands was an offence *contra bonos mores,* Salisbury held that fur-seals "are indisputably animals *ferae naturae,* and these have universally been regarded by jurists as *res nullius* until they are caught." No person could have property in them "until he had actually reduced them into possession by capture." It would require more than a mere declaration "that the Government or citizens of the United States . . . are losers by a certain course of proceedings, to render that course an immoral one."

The action taken by the American Government in instructing the officers in charge of revenue cutters to seize British vessels on the high seas, in time of peace, because they were engaged in pelagic sealing, was a violation of international law. The American Government did not derive from Russia any special privileges or rights in the waters of the North Pacific outside the three-mile limit, and Her Majesty's Government wished to go on record as strongly opposed to all claims of that nature.[53]

In reply to this blast from Lord Salisbury, Blaine endeavored to show that the jurisdictional claim of Russia, as expressed in the ukase

52. A. R. Milne to M. Bowell, Minister of Customs, July 7, 1890, *Macdonald Papers, Behring Sea,* III, 319–322, P.A.C.

53. Lord Salisbury to Pauncefote, May 22, 1890, *F.R., 1890,* pp. 419–423.

of 1821, had been acquiesced in by both the United States and Great Britain as far as the area north of the sixtieth parallel was concerned. According to Blaine, there had been no attempt, in the treaties concluded by the United States and Great Britain with Russia, to regulate or control any "interest in the Russian possessions and the Behring Sea, which lie far to the north and west of the territory which formed the basis of the contention."[54] The protests of John Quincy Adams (as Secretary of State) had been aimed at the extension of Russian jurisdiction in the *Pacific Ocean* and not in Behring Sea, which was regarded as a separate body of water. The terms "Great Ocean," "Pacific Ocean," and "South Sea," which occur in the treaties and in the diplomatic correspondence of the early decades of the nineteenth century, did not include Behring Sea. With regard to the waters of that sea, the ukase of 1821 stood unchanged, and both the United States and Great Britain had recognized and obeyed it. This same recognition was still due from Great Britain, and it had not been altered by the cession of Alaska to the United States.[55]

Blaine followed this dubious note with another of July 19, in which

54. This historical argument presented by Blaine was quite weak. The Russian Government had been reluctant to support the sweeping terms of the ukase of 1821, which had probably been pushed through upon the suggestion of the Russian American Company. There had been very little official consideration given to it, and the American Minister flatly charged that it had been "surreptitiously obtained." *Proceedings of the Alaskan Boundary Tribunal,* II, 42. The Czar showed no desire to enforce it, and as early as July, 1822, an order was issued to Russian vessels of war, directing them to restrict their activities to the coast, and to exercise surveillance only over the prohibited commerce with actual Russian settlements. According to the Russian Chancellor, the true and only object of the ukase of 1821, was "to put a stop to enterprises which the laws of all nations recognize as unjust, and to protect interests, whose legality no one can contest." Dexter Perkins, *The Monroe Doctrine, 1823–1826* (Cambridge, 1927), pp. 28–29.

55. Secretary Blaine to Pauncefote, June 30, 1890, *House Ex. Doc. No. 450,* 51 Cong., 1 sess., pp. 78–89. It is more than likely that Blaine drew his inspiration for this argument from Henry W. Elliott, of the Smithsonian Institution. In a letter to Bayard, January 29, 1887, Elliott remarked: "I have been carefully reviewing the entire topic of Russian occupation and control of Behring Sea from the early time of Muscovitic discovery and possession in 1728, up to its transfer to us in 1867. I find it impossible to honestly construe the meaning of that phrase 'waters commonly known as the North Western Pacific Ocean,' and again, 'the great ocean commonly called the Pacific Ocean or South Sea,' which appear in the protests and treaty stipulations of 1824–1825, to strain these phrases so as to include the Sea of Kamchatka (Behring Sea), since it is beyond cavil or doubt that these 'waters' then 'commonly known as the North Western Pacific Ocean,' are precisely the same waters which we today commonly know as such: the charts, the records of hydrographic survey from 1799 up to date, prove the truth of my statement beyond all question.

"Therefore I venture to express the hope that while you carry out the determination which you promptly manifested, of protecting the interests of the Government now in danger on the Seal Islands of Alaska, that no release on our part will be made of our

he made an indirect attack upon Lord Salisbury's veracity. In discussing Salisbury's change of heart with reference to the Behring Sea negotiations, Blaine had charged (in his note of May 29, 1890) that the Foreign Office had been on the point of arriving at a settlement of this dispute when the Canadian Government interposed certain objections, and the whole matter was postponed. The basis for Blaine's attack had been a despatch from Phelps to Secretary Bayard, February 25, 1888.

On June 20 Salisbury had replied that Blaine was "under a misconception in imagining that I ever gave any verbal assurance, or any promise of any kind with respect to the terms of the projected convention."[56] Blaine returned to the attack by again referring to the text of Phelps's despatch of February 25, 1888. The issue lay between the veracity of Phelps and that of Lord Salisbury, and Blaine acridly announced that Phelps had long been known in the United States as "an able lawyer, accurate in the use of words and discriminating in the statement of facts." The Government of the United States reposed "im-

right and title to the full ownership of Behring Sea, east of the pelagic boundary laid down in it by Russia." *Bayard MS.*

Bayard turned this letter over to John Bassett Moore, who gave it a searching analysis and criticism in a note to Bayard, January 29, 1887. According to Moore, he had yet "to find a single geography, encyclopedia, chart, state paper, or writing of any kind, save a letter of Mr. Elliott, . . . that treats the Pacific Ocean or South Seas as not including all the waters on the coasts of Russia (Siberia) and America, clear up to Behring's Straits. The geographies so give it, and the *Encylopedia Britannica* so states it. In the same line are the protests to which Mr. Elliott refers. Mr. Poletica, in his note to Mr. Adams of the 28th of February, 1822, said: 'the Russian possessions in the *Pacific Ocean* extend, *on the northwest coast* of America, from Behring's Strait to the 51st degree of North Lat., etc.' He says further that 'the extent of sea *of which these possessions form the limits,' might be* treated as shut seas, but that Russia preferred to assert her *'essential rights, without taking advantage of localities.'* Consequently, Russia inhibited approach within *100 Italian miles of those coasts.*

"Nothing could be more conclusive against Mr. Elliott than the famous ukase of 1821, to which the above correspondence was due. It read as follows: 'Section 1. The transaction of *commerce,* and the pursuit of *whaling* and *fishing,* or any other industry on the *islands,* in the *harbors* and *inlets,* and in general all along the *northwestern coast* of America from *Behring Strait* to the 51st parallel of northern latitude, and likewise on the *Aleutian Islands,* and along the *eastern coast* of Siberia, and on the Kurile Islands, . . . are exclusively reserved to the subjects of the Russian Empire. Section 2. Accordingly, no foreign vessel shall be allowed either to put to shore 'at any of the *coasts and islands under Russian dominion as specified in the preceding section,'* or even to approach the *same to within* a distance of less than 100 Italian miles. . . .

"It appears, therefore, by the only papers upon which Mr. Elliott could rely for his doctrine of shut seas, that the Russian Government not only included in the terms Pacific Ocean and northwestern coast of America all waters and coasts up to Behring's Strait, but also expressly disclaimed an intention to enforce as to those waters the doctrine that they were *mers fermées.* This is so clear and explicit that argument is unnecessary." *Ibid.*

56. Lord Salisbury to Pauncefote, June 20, 1890, *F.R., 1890,* pp. 449–451.

plicit confidence in the literal correctness of the despatch above quoted."[57]

Blaine was pleased with the way that he had been able, through diplomatic circumlocution, to call Lord Salisbury a liar, and he wrote to President Harrison that he believed the British Foreign Secretary would be loath "to make a direct issue between Mr. Phelps & himself. . . . We bring him now direct to the explicit agreement of Feby 25—which is clean-cut, sharp edged, & gives us even more than we need for the protection of Seals."[58]

The President thought that the case had ended "very well for the public, and we can properly wait a response to your last despatch before opening any suggestion of our basis of an arbitration. . . . I am sure the publication of the correspondence will make a favorable impression and will do you great credit. The continued advantage is altogether with you."[59]

This Presidential praise for the way he had handled the Behring Sea dispute was very stimulating to Blaine, who thought that the case for the United States had been strengthened by the "coolness & lack of eagerness" he had displayed in handling the situation. Pauncefote was now "doing the walking," not only "metaphorically but actually. I have just telephoned him that I could not have a conference with him this morning. He had notified me that he would be here at 10."[60]

Pauncefote may have been perturbed by Blaine's diplomatic finesse, but this was not so with Lord Salisbury. In a long note of August 2 he sharply challenged Blaine's contention that Behring Sea had not been regarded in the early decades of the nineteenth century as an integral part of the Pacific Ocean. To prove his point he quoted long excerpts from the instructions of George Canning (British Secretary for Foreign Affairs) to Stratford Canning (British Minister to the United States) to show that England had refused to admit any part of the claim, asserted in the ukase of 1821, to an exclusive jurisdiction over a

57. Secretary Blaine to Pauncefote, July 19, 1890, *ibid.*, pp. 453–455.

58. Secretary Blaine to President Harrison, July 19, 1890, Volwiler, *op. cit.*, pp. 109–110. In commenting upon Lord Salisbury's note of June 20, E. J. Phelps remarks: "Lord Salisbury, in his allusion to my remark that a treaty could not be concluded by the late administration pending a presidential election . . ., has fallen into an error. I did say so, but it was at a different time, and in reference to a different subject—the fisheries." Phelps to Blaine, July 28, 1890, Gail Hamilton (Mary A. Dodge), *Biography of James G. Blaine* (Norwich, 1895), p. 670.

59. President Harrison to Secretary Blaine, July 23, 1890, Volwiler, *op. cit.*, pp. 111–112.

60. Secretary Blaine to President Harrison, July 25, 1890, *ibid.*, pp. 113–114.

belt of water one hundred miles from the coast, extending from Behring Straits to the fifty-first parallel of north latitude. Salisbury also argued that the treaty of 1825 had been regarded by both Russia and Great Britain as a renunciation of the claim advanced in the ukase of 1821. If the American Government continued to adhere to its viewpoint in this question of jurisdiction over Behring Sea, the whole matter could be amicably and effectively settled by a reference to impartial arbitration.[61]

Blaine waited many months before he attempted to answer this note from Lord Salisbury, and when he finally wrote his reply it was far from impressive.[62] He emphasized the fact that the Department of State was not claiming that Behring Sea was a *mare clausum*. On the contrary, "it expressly disavows it." The American Government was merely endeavoring to prevent the destruction of a valuable fur-seal industry, and it had expressly disclaimed any intention to interfere "with a single sail of commerce on any sea of the globe." With reference to the three-mile limit, the question was whether "there may not be exceptions whose enforcement does not interfere with those highways of commerce which the necessities and usage of the world have marked out."

The main question at issue between the two Governments was whether Behring Sea was included in the phrase "Pacific Ocean." The American Government had denied such inclusion, while the British Government had taken an affirmative stand in this regard. If Great Britain could "maintain her position that the Behring Sea at the time of the treaties of 1824 and 1825 was included in the Pacific Ocean, the Government of the United States has no well grounded complaint against her." If, however, the American Government could "prove beyond all doubt" that Behring Sea, at the date of the treaties of 1824 and 1825, was understood by the three signatory Powers to be a separate body of water and was "not included in the phrase 'Pacific Ocean,' then the American case against Great Britain is complete and undeniable." It would then be clear that under the terms of those treaties Russia had not renounced her exclusive jurisdiction over Behring Sea, and this

61. Lord Salisbury to Pauncefote, August 2, 1890, *F.R., 1890,* pp. 456–465.

62. Blaine had been worried over the possibility that Joseph Chamberlain might call upon President Harrison in an effort to settle the Behring Sea dispute, and he requested the President to refrain from seeing Chamberlain except when introduced by one of the officials of the Department of State. The President assured Blaine that he would not "be entrapped into any reference to foreign affairs except as they proceed through your department." Blaine to President Harrison, August 19, 1890; President Harrison to Blaine, August 29, 1890, Volwiler, *op. cit.,* pp. 117–120.

right of exclusive jurisdiction had passed on to the United States in the treaty of 1867.[63]

Blaine also proposed five questions on which an arbitration might be had. The first four related to the jurisdictional rights of Russia and their transfer to the United States. The fifth had to do with the rights of the United States in the fur-seal fisheries in Behring Sea outside of the ordinary territorial limits.[64]

It was plain to Lord Salisbury that Blaine was in full retreat from a position he had once so boldly held, and in a note to Sir Julian Pauncefote he described this flight in graphic terms:

It is now quite clear that the advisers of the President do not claim Behring's Sea as a *mare clausum,* and indeed that they repudiate that contention

63. In commenting upon the diplomatic correspondence between Lord Salisbury and Blaine, John W. Foster remarked: "In no part of that statesman's career did his devotion to his country more conspicuously rise above partisanship than in that correspondence. It is doubtful if any other living American could have made a more brilliant or effective defense of the action of his government." "Results of the Bering Sea Arbitration," *North American Review* (December, 1895), p. 696.

There is no doubt that Blaine was a brilliant orator, but mere oratory was out of place in diplomatic correspondence. While Blaine openly disclaimed any thought that he was contending that Behring Sea was a closed sea, yet his argument inevitably led to that very point. He claimed that the United States and Great Britain had recognized the exclusive jurisdiction of Russia over Behring Sea, and that all these Russian rights had passed to the United States as a result of the cession of Alaska in 1867. It was only because of the alleged right of exclusive jurisdiction that the United States could seize British ships on the high seas, and this was equivalent to holding that Behring Sea was a *mare clausum.* Blaine closed his eyes to the implications of his stand. If the British Government had conceded the right to seize British ships on the high seas for pelagic sealing, the American Government could have used this concession as a means of forcing other concessions.

64. Secretary Blaine to Pauncefote, December 17, 1890, *F.R., 1890,* pp. 477–501. The five questions that Blaine proposed to Lord Salisbury were as follows: "(1) What exclusive jurisdiction in the sea now known as the Behring Sea, and what exclusive rights in the seal fisheries therein, did Russia assert and exercise prior and up to the time of the cession of Alaska to the United States? (2) How far were these claims of jurisdiction as to the seal fisheries recognized and conceded by Great Britain? (3) Was the body of water now known as the Behring Sea included in the phrase 'Pacific Ocean,' as used in the Treaty of 1825 between Great Britain and Russia; and what rights, if any, in the Behring Sea were given or conceded to Great Britain by the said treaty? (4) Did not all the rights of Russia as to jurisdiction, and as to the seal fisheries in Behring Sea east of the water boundary in the treaty between the United States and Russia of March 30, 1867, pass unimpaired to the United States under that treaty? (5) What are now the rights of the United States as to the fur seal fisheries in the waters of the Behring Sea outside of the ordinary territorial limits, whether such rights grow out of the cession by Russia of any special rights or jurisdiction held by her in such fisheries or in the waters of Behring Sea, or out of the ownership of the breeding islands and the habits of the seals in resorting thither and rearing their young thereon and going out from the islands for food, or out of any other fact or incident connected with the relation of those Seal Fisheries to the territorial possessions of the United States?" *Ibid.,* p. 500.

in expressed terms. Nor do they rely, as a justification for the seizure of British ships in the open sea, upon the contention that the interests of the seal fisheries give to the United States Government any right for that purpose which, according to international law, it would not otherwise possess. Whatever importance they attach to the preservation of the fur-seal species, . . . they do not conceive that it confers upon any maritime power rights over the open ocean which that power could not assert on other grounds.

The claim of the United States to prevent the exercise of the seal fishery by other nations in Behring's Sea rests now exclusively upon the interest which by purchase they possess in a ukase issued by the Emperor Alexander I in the year 1821, which prohibits foreign vessels from approaching within 100 Italian miles of the coasts and islands then belonging to Russia in Behring's Sea. . . . It is said that this prohibition, worthless in itself, acquired validity and force against the British Government because that Government can be shown to have accepted its provisions. . . . Our contention is that not only can it not be shown that the Government of Great Britain, at any time since 1821, has admitted the soundness of the pretension put forward by that ukase, but it can be shown that it has categorically denied it on more than one occasion.[65]

Blaine had pelted Lord Salisbury with sonorous Latin phrases that condemned British practices as being in violation of good morals. This verbal barrage had given so little disturbance to the British Foreign Secretary that Blaine hastily changed his ammunition. In his broadside of December 17 he no longer castigated the British morals, but he shifted his attack from ethical principles to geographical definitions. If the Foreign Office could not be breached by moral imperatives, it might be brought to terms by phrases from a gazetteer. But the main difficulty that faced Blaine was the fact that even in the matter of gazetteers the British seemed to have the heavier artillery, and Salisbury won an easy victory.

With Blaine in full flight as a result of this diplomatic duel, Pauncefote was finally able to catch up with him and urge an agreement upon a *modus vivendi* for the approaching sealing-season in Behring Sea. Under its terms there should be no slaughter of seals on the islands under American jurisdiction, and British subjects should be forbidden to engage in pelagic sealing. Blaine replied by suggesting the establishment of a twenty-five-mile zone around the seal islands in which pelagic sealing would be prohibited, but Pauncefote believed that such

65. Lord Salisbury to Pauncefote, February 21, 1891, *ibid., 1891,* pp. 542–546. With reference to the matter of answering Lord Salisbury's notes, Blaine remarked as follows in a letter to President Harrison, March 6, 1891: "If we get up a war-cry and send vessels to Behring Sea it will re-elect Lord Salisbury. England always sustains an administration with the prospect of war pending." Hamilton, *op. cit.,* p. 671.

a zone would be impracticable. On April 7 Pauncefote urged Blaine to accept a plan whereby, for the season of 1891, there would be a suspension of all killing of seals upon the islands in Behring Sea and in the waters of the sea itself. Blaine accepted this suggestion, and Pauncefote immediately advised Lord Salisbury of this agreement.[66] It would

66. On November 19, 1890, Henry W. Elliott, accompanied by Secretary Windom, had called upon Blaine with reference to the seal fisheries. Elliott had just returned from an investigation of these fisheries in Behring Sea, and he pointed out to Blaine that a serious destruction of the herds of seal would take place unless the American Government soon "came to an agreement with Great Britain. I showed him how absolutely necessary it was to close all of Behring Sea to the pelagic hunter: and, too, how absolutely necessary it was that we reform the work of excessive driving and killing as done on the islands by the lessees."

In an earlier letter to Secretary Gresham, April 2, 1893, Elliott had given a similar account of his relations with Secretary Blaine in 1890–1891: "In April, 1890, Congress passed after full debate in both Houses, a Special Act for the sole purpose of enabling me to go up to the Seal Islands and make another careful investigation of the condition of the fur-seal herds, just as I had done under authority of a similar Act passed in April, 1874. . . . I finished my work on the islands and returned and had my report with maps and illustrations ready for the printer, November 19, 1890, gave it to Mr. Windom, who at once sent me over to Mr. Blaine with it.

"I found that the seal herds had been as badly injured by abuses on the islands since 1882 as they had been by the shameful waste of killing in the water to which they had been subjected since 1886, that the killing on land must stop for at least seven years, and the killing in the waters of Behring Sea and portions of the North Pacific Ocean must be forever prohibited if we ever expect to restore the Pribylov herds to the fine form and number which I recorded of them in 1872–1874.

"I stopped the killing on the islands, July 20, 1890, in co-operation with Charles J. Goff, an honest Treasury Agent. . . . At once Mr. Steve Elkins took up his residence in Mr. Blaine's house, bitterly denounced me behind my back, and drew from Mr. Blaine a promise that my order saving the remnant on the Pribylov Islands in 1890, should be repealed in 1891. He actually got the permit before I knew it, on April 14, 1891. I learned of it on the 20th of that month in spite of Charlie Foster's secrecy and trickery, published the shameful truth, and Harrison finding that the job could not be covered, vetoed the license on the 3rd. of May. . . .

"In short, I may truly say, the whole business, since that day, November 19, 1890, when Mr. Blaine tried to make me supress the truth as to the abuse on the islands and lay all the blame on the poachers, the whole business has been one of systematic duplicity, pettifogging, and secrecy in the State and Treasury Depts., under Blaine and C. Foster, dominated by Steve Elkins, a silent partner in this present Seal Company—all done with the full understanding and permit of Benj. Harrison." *Walter Q. Gresham Papers,* Library of Congress.

On May 4, 1891, the Cleveland *Leader and Morning Herald* published a copy of the letter of Henry W. Elliott to the Secretary of the Treasury which transmitted his report on the fur-seal fisheries. On February 10, 1893, the British Agent in the Fur-Seal Arbitration, called upon the Agent of the United States for a full copy of this report. Both Phelps and Carter, Counsel for the United States, opposed the granting of this request, but after some discussion finally stated that they were ready to produce Elliott's report. Their opposition was based upon the fact that this report clearly indicated the destructive effect of the seal killings on the islands as well as in the waters of Behring Sea. See Moore, *History and Digest of International Arbitrations,* I, 904–907.

In a letter to Secretary Gresham, April 13, 1893, Elliott makes the following per-then appear that Blaine violated this agreement of April 7 by secretly arranging with Charles Foster, Secretary of the Treasury, to issue a permit to the lessees of the seal islands, authorizing them to kill 60,000 seals on the islands, "if they can be found." When news of this permit leaked out, Henry W. Elliott and William McKinley, then a member of the House of Representatives, called upon Secretary Foster, who explained that he had issued this order "because Blaine authorizes it, and has told me that Salisbury is ugly and will not stop his people from killing."[67] Elliott then called upon Sir Julian Pauncefote, who denied that the British Government was "ugly" about the matter of prohibiting, for a season, all pelagic sealing. Enraged at what he called Blaine's "venality and duplicity," Elliott published the whole story in the New York *Evening Post*, April 24, 1891, and the Harrison Administration was placed on the defensive.[68]

tinent comments: "On the 3rd instant I mailed to your address a letter which I deemed my duty to write touching the Behring Sea Commission. Since then the Paris Court has ordered out my report of 1890 touching upon the status of the fur-seal herds of the Government on the Pribylov Islands. No living man possesses the knowledge or the ability to set aside the findings of my investigation, and before the Court adjourns, I shall be honored for doing my duty and telling the truth. I have one request to make of you in order that the business at Paris shall be the more certainly expedited—I respectfully ask that I may be permitted to read the proof of this copy of my report, and be free in my mind as to mutilation or garbling of it. If it is done, I can and will detect it, but that only creates delay and fresh scandal if it should so turn out. I have abundant reason to suspect the present conduct of affairs, of which you are entirely irresponsible and wholly uninformed except it be filtered through State Department clerks.

"One word in conclusion: I enclose a sample newspaper dispatch. There is not a word of truth in it in so far as my meeting Sir Julian is concerned or as to my 'printed copy' of my report. The story of my meeting Sir Julian is a very different one, and one that I have never given to the press, tho, it reflects the highest credit on the British Minister and covers Mr. Blaine with disgrace." *Gresham MS.*

67. After Blaine had made the agreement with Sir Julian, April 7, 1891, he violated it under pressure from Mr. S. B. Elkins, and on April 11 he had Mr. Foster, Secretary of the Treasury, give to the lessees of the Seal Islands, D. O. Mills, Isaac and Herman Liebes, Lloyd Teavis, and S. B. Elkins, a secret permit to kill 60,000 seals on the island "if they can be found." On April 13 Foster admitted this secret order when questioned by Elliott and William B. McKinley. See sworn statement by Henry W. Elliott, May 2, 1912 in *ibid.*

On July 31, 1890, Charles J. Goff, the Treasury Agent in charge of the seal fisheries, made a report on the situation on the Pribilof Islands. It was his opinion that the "killing of the seals in the Pacific Ocean along the Aleutian Islands, . . . and the indiscriminate slaughter upon the islands, . . . have at last . . . reduced these rookeries to their present impoverished condition. . . . The time has come when . . . the truth be told. . . . I suggest that there be no killing of fur seals for their skins on these islands . . . for an indefinite number of years." *F.S.A.*, V, 703–706. Goff [as indicated above] worked with Henry W. Elliott in a joint attempt to stop the fur-seal slaughter on the Pribilof Islands, and for his honest endeavors he was dismissed from the Treasury Department.

68. This was an unsigned letter in the New York *Evening Post,* April 24, 1891, and

On April 20 Pauncefote had informed Secretary Blaine that Lord Salisbury was ready to approve a *modus vivendi* which pending arbitration would stop "all sealing both at sea and on land."[69] Blaine inquired of President Harrison as to what action should be taken with reference to this *modus vivendi*,[70] and Harrison replied that the lessees of the islands were bound to feed and care for the natives, and therefore, "some seals must be killed for food." He thought it might be practicable for the Secretary of the Treasury to "fix a moderate number under the lease as an independent act of our Government." He also expressed the opinion that "the value of the fisheries would be enhanced by taking none for one season, but as our right to take on the Islands is not in dispute, would prefer to make the prohibition our own act and let E[nglish] action follow on notice of our wishes."[71]

Blaine replied on April 28 that "British Minister does not agree to the essential points. If sealing is to be prohibited for season many obstacles are thrown in the way."[72] On the following day Blaine sent a telegram that clearly showed his prompt response to the pressure of public opinion that had developed after the revelations of Mr. Elliott. Blaine now thought that it would be a "serious political mistake to allow contractors full liberty with seals and refuse co-operation with England in rigidly preserving all seals for this year."[73] The question of the seal fishery was a pressing one. The Secretary of the Treasury had

fixed maximum number for season at sixty thousand. Revenue Cutter *Rush* is to leave on fourteenth with seal agents for Islands. You do not return here

it was entitled, "Some Seal History." It began with a severe indictment of Secretary Blaine: "I know of some strange and devious performances over the seal question in Bering Sea that have taken place here [Washington] within the last ten days—some of Blaine's sharp trickery that will soon rise to confuse him." The New York *Evening Post* led the fight against Blaine's policy in Behring Sea, but the Elliott letter was seized upon by the opposition press and widely exploited. See Boston *Herald,* April 27, and New York *Herald,* April 28, 1891.

On April 28, 1891, the New York *Evening Post* remarked as follows concerning the suspension of seal killing: "The company of which Elkins is a leading member and Mr. D. O. Mills is President, would lose heavily this year if the catch were suspended, . . . so Elkins naturally enough damns *bonos mores* and the *modus vivendi.* It is a curious and extremely interesting fact that whenever Mr. Blaine gets up an international shindy of any kind, there is sure to be a commercial enterprise somewhere in the background."

69. Pauncefote to Secretary Blaine, April 20, 1891, *F.R., 1891,* p. 552.
70. Secretary Blaine to President Harrison, April 23, 1891, Volwiler, *op. cit.,* p. 144.
71. President Harrison to Secretary Blaine, April 24, 1891, *ibid.,* pp. 144–145.
72. Secretary Blaine to President Harrison, April 28, 1891, Volwiler, *op. cit.,* p. 145.
73. Secretary Blaine to President Harrison, April 29, 1891, *ibid.,* p. 146.

until 15th. Meanwhile British Minister presses agreement to your suggestion that both sides abstain from taking seals this year. British Minister declines to consider the necessity of some seals being taken to support natives and repay company for trouble and expense. They wish entire business to be suspended. It is embarrassing to resist British Minister's position in view of the fact that abstaining from sealing this year was first suggested by yourself.[74]

President Harrison was alive to the situation, and on April 30 he informed Blaine that after a careful consideration of the whole question he had come to the conclusion that it was "best to stop killing this season, on proper guarantees."[75] Three days later (May 3) he ordered the cancellation of the permit that would have permitted the lessees of the islands to kill 60,000 seals for the season of 1891.[76]

By these successive steps, President Harrison was preparing the way for a reference to arbitration of the fur-seal fisheries dispute. Blaine was entirely willing to have the controversy settled in this manner, and his notes to Sir Julian Pauncefote were distinctly conciliatory. In a communication of April 14, 1891, he took the occasion to state the American case:

The Government of the United States . . . holds that the ownership of the islands upon which the seals breed, that the habit of the seals in regularly resorting thither and rearing their young thereon, that their going out from the islands in search of food and regularly returning thereto, and all the facts and incidents of their relation to the islands, give to the United States a property interest therein; that this property interest was claimed and exercised by Russia during the whole period of its sovereignty over the land and waters of Alaska; that England recognized this property interest so far as recognition is implied by abstaining from all interference with it during the whole period of Russia's ownership of Alaska, and during the first nineteen years of the sovereignty of the United States. It is yet to be determined whether the lawless intrusion of Canadian vessels in 1886 and subsequent years has changed the law and equity of the case theretofore prevailing.[77]

With special reference to the approaching sealing season, Blaine wished to control the situation by a *modus vivendi* under whose terms the killing of seals, for commercial purposes, would be prohibited both on land and in the sea. But this would not prevent the slaughter of 7500 seals in order to provide food for the natives of the islands.

74. Secretary Blaine to President Harrison, April 29, 1891, *ibid.*, pp. 146–147.
75. President Harrison to Secretary Blaine, April 30, 1891, *ibid.*, p. 147.
76. See sworn statement of Henry W. Elliott, May 2, 1912, *Gresham MS.*
77. Secretary Blaine to Pauncefote, April 14, 1891, *F.R., 1891*, p. 552.

Pauncefote was anxious to accept this settlement, and he sent a telegram to Ottawa expressing the hope that the Canadian Government would favor Blaine's proposal. A rejection of these terms would give Blaine "a signal triumph and alienate our supporters, who are already irritated by the knowledge that the sealing fleet is mainly equipped by American crews and capital. The Canadian government were prepared for legislation at this season last year. We cannot consistently reply that it is too late now."[78]

President Harrison was of the opinion that the Canadian Government was "interposing objections and delays,"[79] but even if such a policy were pursued it could not long check the strong drift towards arbitration. On June 15, 1891, a *modus vivendi* was signed in Washington,[80] and it was promptly proclaimed by President Harrison.[81] The British Government had already secured the passage of legislation permitting it to execute the terms of the anticipated *modus vivendi*, and an Order in Council was issued putting it into effect.[82] In order that the Foreign Office could collect further data concerning the fur-seal fisheries, the Queen appointed Sir George Baden-Powell and Professor George M. Dawson as commissioners to proceed to the Pribilof Islands and study conditions there.[83]

After several months of diplomatic fencing about questions of liability for acts committed by British citizens on the high seas, the agreement to arbitrate was finally signed on December 18, 1891.[84] On the same day an agreement was also signed providing for the appointment

78. Pauncefote to Lord Stanley, May 16, 1891, *Macdonald Papers, Behring Sea,* III, 223, P.A.C. Pauncefote went out of his way to try to conciliate Blaine in the matter of arranging for a *modus vivendi.* Blaine's note to Pauncefote, May 4, 1891 is distinctly disingenuous in its attempt to fasten upon the British Government the responsibility for delaying the conclusion of some working agreement for the season of 1891. Pauncefote's reply, May 5, 1891 puts the situation in the proper light, and absolves Lord Salisbury from any blame in the matter of delay. *F.S.A.*, V, 695–697.

79. President Harrison to Secretary Blaine, May 25, 27, 1891, Volwiler, *op. cit.,* pp. 152–155.

80. According to Article 2 of this *modus vivendi* the American Government would prohibit during the approaching season the killing of seals in Behring Sea and on the seal islands in excess of 7500, which were to be used only for the "subsistence and care of the natives." The British Government undertook to prevent pelagic sealing for the same period. See *F.R., 1891,* pp. 570–571. This prevention of pelagic sealing was carried out in good faith by the British Government. By June 15, 1891 most of the sealing vessels had already cleared from Victoria, British Columbia, for Behring Sea. Forty-nine vessels had actually cleared from Victoria. They were valued at $425,150, and were of a tonnage of 3203. Forty-one of these ships were expelled from Behring Sea during the summer of 1891, by British or American cruisers.

81. *Ibid.,* pp. 570–571.

82. *Ibid.,* pp. 577–583.

83. Pauncefote to Mr. Wharton, June 21, 1891, *ibid.,* p. 573.

84. *Ibid.,* pp. 605–606.

of a Behring Sea Joint Commission. Each of the high contracting parties was to appoint two commissioners who were to "investigate all the facts having relation to seal life in Behring's Sea, and the measures necessary for its proper protection and preservation."[85]

The British Government had appointed Baden-Powell and Dawson as commissioners, and President Harrison selected Professor Thomas C. Mendenhall and Dr. Clinton H. Merriman. After receiving formal notice from Pauncefote as to the appointment of the British commissioners, Blaine filed a protest against the caliber of the men selected as British commissioners. The American Government had selected "gentlemen who were especially fitted by their scientific attainments, and who were in no wise disqualified for an impartial investigation . . . by a public declaration of opinion previous or subsequent to their selection."[86]

Pauncefote, in reply, expressed his great surprise that Blaine should question the appointment of men like Sir George Baden-Powell and Dr. Dawson. Both of them were widely known for their scientific attainments, and they had special qualifications for the positions to which they were appointed. Moreover, the American commissioners had already published opinions that were known to be adverse to the British contention. But Pauncefote did not hold this fact against them, and he was certain that the four commissioners were "equally entitled to the confidence of both Governments."[87]

It was apparent that these commissioners were likely to disagree in their reports to their respective governments. This is exactly what happened. The American representatives claimed that the seal herds were diminishing in size because of pelagic sealing, while the British commissioners blamed the decrease of the seal herds upon the widespread killing upon the islands in Behring Sea.[88] The reports were a perfect example of patriotic science.

But despite this battle of the books on the part of the scientists, and the petty squabbling on the part of the statesmen, the long-sought-for arbitration treaty was at length concluded on February 29, 1892. The first article provided that the questions that arise between the United States and Great Britain "concerning the jurisdictional rights of the United States in the waters of Behring's Sea, and concerning also the preservation of the fur-seal in, or habitually resorting to the said sea,

85. *Ibid.*, p. 606.
86. Secretary Blaine to Pauncefote, February 6, 1902, *ibid.*, pp. 609–610.
87. Pauncefote to Secretary Blaine, February 8, 1892, *ibid.*, pp. 610–611.
88. Moore, *Digest of International Arbitrations,* I, 808. See also, *F.S.A.*, V, 865ff., and *ibid.*, VI, 13–150.

and the rights of the citizens and subjects of either country as regards the taking of fur-seal in, or habitually resorting to the said waters," should be submitted to a tribunal of seven arbitrators, two to be named by the President of the United States, two by Her Britannic Majesty, and one each by the King of Italy, the King of Sweden and Norway, and the President of France.[89]

The treaty was approved by the Senate of the United States on March 29, 1892, and President Harrison named John M. Harlan, a justice of the Supreme Court of the United States, and Senator John T. Morgan, of Alabama, as the American arbitrators. John W. Foster was appointed as agent for the United States, and Edward J. Phelps, James C. Carter, Henry W. Blodgett, and Frederic R. Coudert were retained as counsel. In the first week of September, 1892, the Case of the United States was turned over to the arbitrators.[90] On February 3,

89. *F.R., 1891,* pp. 615–619. The five points submitted to arbitration were included in Article VI of the treaty. They read as follows: "(1) What exclusive jurisdiction in the sea now known as the Behring's Sea, and what exclusive rights in the seal fisheries therein, did Russia assert and exercise prior and up to the time of the cession of Alaska to the United States? (2) How far were these claims of jurisdiction as to the seal fisheries recognized and conceded by Great Britain? (3) Was the body of water now known as the Behring's Sea included in the phrase 'Pacific Ocean' as used in the treaty of 1825 between Great Britain and Russia; and what rights, if any, in the Behring's Sea were held and exclusively exercised by Russia after said treaty? (4) Did not all the rights of Russia as to jurisdiction, and as to the seal fisheries in Behring's Sea east of the water boundary in the treaty between the United States and Russia of the 30th March, 1867, pass unimpaired to the United States under that treaty? (5) Has the United States any right, and if so, what right of protection or property in the fur seals frequenting the islands of the United States in Behring Sea when such seals are found outside the ordinary three-mile limit?"

90. When the printed Case of Great Britain was delivered by the agent of that government, it was discovered that it contained no evidence concerning the nature and habits of seals, the consideration of which was regarded by the United States as necessary to the settlement by the tribunal of questions of right as well as of regulation. On September 27, 1892, John W. Foster wrote to Sir Michael Herbert, the *chargé d'affaires* of the British Legation, to complain of this omission of everything pertaining to the American contention of property interest in seals. The President had observed "with surprise and extreme regret" this dubious action on the part of the British agent. The American Government had furnished in its printed Case all the evidence it planned to offer in defense of its contention, in this way giving the British Government ample time to prepare its rebuttal. It expected the British Government to do the same, and was surprised to discover that it had not done so. *Great Britain, Notes to,* XXII, MS. Dept. of State. See also, Foster to Robert T. Lincoln, September 29, 1892, *Great Britain Instructions,* Vol. XXX, MS. Dept. of State, and Foster to Secretary Gresham, April 17, 1893, *Gresham MS.*

In a personal letter to Henry White, September 29, 1892, John W. Foster remarked: "I infer from what you said to me and from what I see in the papers, that Mr. Lincoln will have left London before this letter and the instruction and letter to Mr. Lincoln about the Seal Arbitration reaches the Legation. That being the case, you will, of course, open and act upon the letter to him. It affords you a capital opportunity to

1893, the Counter-Case of the United States was submitted, and on February 23, the first session of the arbitral tribunal was held in Paris.

do a good piece of work for the Government as well as yourself credit, and I have no doubt you will be fully alive to the importance of the question. Mr. Phelps is, if anything, more positive than any of us . . . that we should give notice to Great Britain that the Arbitration will not go forward till this wrong is righted, but we have thought best to give Great Britain the opportunity . . . to do right. The function of diplomacy is to promote peace and good understanding, and I hope you can help to bring about a satisfactory settlement of this question." *Henry White MS.*

In his reply, October 12, 1892, White assured Foster that he fully realized the "grave importance of the question at issue, and shall do everything in my power . . . to assist you in its solution. I wrote you yesterday a despatch containing an official account of my interview with Lord Rosebery. As you saw fit to keep out of your instruction Number 893, all intimation of your wish which is conveyed in the letter to Mr. Lincoln, 'that Lord Rosebery should be clearly informed that a persistence in the course adopted may lead to a complete abandonment of the arbitration,' I have also said nothing on that subject in my despatch. I told him this, however, and he replied that he was quite aware of the fact from Herbert. I added that in my opinion such persistence would certainly lead to our abandonment of the arbitration, and he seemed to be of the same opinion. His manner was eminently conciliatory. . . . I am of course too familiar with the ways of the Foreign Office to suppose that the proposals Lord Rosebery intends making will be entirely satisfactory at first; but I cannot believe that having once got Canada to submit to an arbitration, the British Government will not make every effort to avoid having the whole matter thrown back upon their hands. . . . I repeated to him that we feel very strongly that the United States should be afforded a fair and full opportunity to reply to the British case, from which he did not dissent. . . . I gathered the impression that the result of Lord Rosebery's interview with the Law Officers had been a conviction that there is much to be said for your view of the case." *Ibid.*

CHAPTER XII

SECRETARY KNOX CONCLUDES A LONG CHAPTER IN FUR-SEAL HISTORY

On March 23, the arbitral tribunal held its first formal session, and after the credentials of the members had been verified, Lord Hannen proposed that Baron de Courcel assume the office of President.[1] When this proposal was agreed to, De Courcel made an appropriate address and the formal proceedings began.[2] The questions before the Tribunal were five in number:

(1) What exclusive jurisdiction in the sea now known as the Behring's Sea, and what exclusive rights in the seal fisheries therein, did Russia assert and exercise prior and up to the time of the cession of Alaska to the United States?

(2) How far were these claims of jurisdiction as to the seal fisheries recognized and conceded by Great Britain?

(3) Was the body of water now known as the Behring's Sea included in the phrase "Pacific Ocean" as used in the Treaty of 1825 between Great Britain and Russia; and what rights, if any, in the Behring's Sea were held and exclusively exercised by Russia after said Treaty?

(4) Did not all the rights of Russia as to jurisdiction, and as to the seal fisheries in Behring's Sea east of the water boundary in the Treaty between the United States and Russia of the 30th March, 1867, pass unimpaired to the United States under that Treaty?

(5) Has the United States any right, and if so, what right of protection or property in the fur-seals frequenting the islands of the United States in

1. The members of the arbitral tribunal were: for Great Britain Lord Hannen, of the English High Court of Appeal, and Sir John Thompson, Minister of Justice for Canada; for the United States, Mr. Justice John M. Harlan of the Supreme Court, and Senator John T. Morgan. As neutral arbitrators the President of France named Baron Alphonse de Courcel a Senator and Ambassador of France; the King of Italy, the Marquis Emilio Visconti Venosta, a Senator of the Kingdom and formerly Minister of Foreign Affairs; and the King of Sweden and Norway, Mr. Gregers Gram, a Minister of State.

2. Sessions were held each week from Tuesday through Friday. From March 23 to April 7 they were occupied with hearing motions and arguments concerning the admission of evidence. The oral arguments of counsel began on April 12, and continued until July 8. On July 10 the Tribunal began its secret sessions, and the award was finally reached on August 15, 1893.

The opening and closing of the oral arguments were conceded to the United States. Mr. Carter spoke for eight days; Mr. Phelps for eleven days; Sir Richard Webster for ten days; and Sir Charles Russell for fifteen days.

Behring Sea when such seals are found outside the ordinary three-mile limit?[3]

After the Tribunal had formally convened, Phelps began to have some worries about the outcome. In a letter to Bayard, in London, he expressed his misgivings:

The arbitration begins its hearings on the 4th, under many embarrassments growing out of the crudeness and imperfections of the treaty, and the previous mistakes in the conduct of the proceedings under it, against which I have remonstrated in vain. I fear the case will be much protracted and with arbitrators holding the balance who understand neither the English language nor English law, the result cannot be predicted. We have a powerful case, which may or may not have anything to do with the decision. Of course we have the American press against us, as we should equally have if we were contending for precisely the opposite of what we now claim. If there is anything meaner than the average American newspaper, I hope I shall never find it.[4]

In the United States there were many distinguished lawyers who did not share the view of Phelps that the American case was a "powerful" one, and this was particularly true with reference to the contention that this country had a right of property in the seals in Behring Sea.

3. Malloy, *op. cit.*, I, 748–749.

4. E. J. Phelps to Ambassador Bayard, April 2, 1893, *Bayard MS.* As early as May 9, 1892, Phelps had begun his list of complaints against the attitude of the newspapers. In a letter to Secretary Blaine, of that date, he remarks: "I have had . . . an interview with Mr. Reid, late Minister at Paris, who speaks in terms of despair as to our success. The new Minister to Paris is an entire stranger there, and will not arrive, I fear, till this question is decided. . . . Some judicious measures should . . . be taken abroad to counteract the impression which has been created there in respect to the case, and which cannot fail to influence the arbitrators. Mr. Reid tells me that the Paris edition of the New York *Herald* has labored persistently against us, as has the *Evening Post* and other newspapers, and they have succeeded in inducing a universal belief that our claim is not regarded in America, nor by American lawyers, as having any foundation, and is only an effort on the part of President Harrison and yourself, to create some political capital to affect the presidential election, and that we do not expect a decision in our favor. This ought to be met, but should be dealt with very judiciously." *Foster MS.*

There were many criticisms in the American press in the spring of 1893 concerning the extravagant way that the American agent in the Behring Sea arbitration, John W. Foster, was spending the public funds. In this regard see letter from Blanton Duncan to Secretary Gresham, March 31, 1893, *Gresham MS.*

Mr. Foster bitterly resented these charges, and he defended his course in a letter to Secretary Gresham, April 4, 1893. He was certain that the charges could be traced back to Mr. Henry L. Bryan, the private secretary of Secretary Gresham. It was Foster's belief that Bryan entertained towards him an "unaccountable malignity." In a second letter to Secretary Gresham, April 17, 1893, Foster recalled these accusations. *Ibid.*

In a letter to Secretary Gresham,[5] B. H. Bristow expressed his great interest in the arguments that were being presented by the American counsel before the Tribunal, but he was not convinced that the United States had a "property right to unidentified seals in the Pacific Ocean as entitles us to damages for their destruction."[6]

But John W. Foster was pleased with the way the fur-seal arbitration was progressing. The American Counsel had shown themselves "quite able to cope with their adversaries. It is too early to make any prediction as to the result, but nothing has yet occurred to shake our confidence in securing a decision which will give substantial protection to the seals."[7]

On May 1, 1893, ex-President Harrison expressed to Foster his pleasure upon hearing that the Behring Sea arbitration was "progressing satisfactorily,"[8] but John Bassett Moore, after reading about the

5. Gresham had assumed the duties of Secretary of State on March 6, 1893.

6. B. H. Bristow to Secretary Gresham, April 8, 1893, *ibid.* In the April issue of *Harper's Magazine,* 1891, pp. 766–774, Mr. Phelps published an article entitled "The Behring Sea Controversy." He strongly defended the contention that the United States had a property right in the seals in Behring Sea: "This colony of seals, making their home on American soil and unable to exist without a home on some soil, belong to the proprietors of the soil and are part of their property; and do not lose this quality by passing from one part of the territory to another, in a regular and periodic migration necessary to their life even though in making it they pass temporarily through water that is more than three miles from land." In commenting upon this statement the New York *Evening Post,* March 23, 1891, remarked: "It is difficult to decide whether this should be treated as law or natural history. In either view it is as novel as erroneous."

7. On January 24, 1891, Bayard wrote to Howard Pyle and declined an invitation to write an article for *Harper's Magazine* on the Behring Sea situation. He still adhered to his position that the United States had no control over seals outside the three-mile limit. *Bayard MS.* In a letter to President Cleveland, March 27, 1891, Bayard discussed in detail his attitude towards the theory of Mr. Phelps: "Since Blaine began his maladroit treatment of the Behring Sea matter, I have been importuned to contribute papers on the subject, and have steadily declined from obvious propriety. . . . When Mr. Phelps and I met lately in New York, we seemed to be in general accord on the subject. . . . When his article appeared I knew not what to say, but I began to recall that in his correspondence from London, Mr. Phelps had intimated that the case should be considered and settled on *other grounds* than that of maritime jurisdiction, although he did not define his theory. . . . I remember too, Mr. Phelps explained in private letters his regret at the discharge of the sealing vessels in 1887, and I did not find him *heartily* in accord with my methods . . . in settling British matters. . . . He always exhibited a disposition for *small* aggressiveness against Great Britain, which I did not consider politic, wise or self-respecting in the United States." *Cleveland Papers,* Library of Congress.

8. Benjamin Harrison to John W. Foster, May 1, 1893, *Foster MS.* In this same letter to Mr. Foster, Harrison makes the following dubious statement: "I have already expressed in a letter to Mr. Halford my disgust at the treatment Judge Gresham gave you. . . . I never knew a man so given to aspersing the motives of other people as he." In a letter to Gresham himself, May 5, 1893, Foster wrote as follows: "I had

way that Phelps was conducting himself before the Tribunal, was filled with apprehensions about the final outcome.[9] In his oral argument, Phelps had not only claimed that the United States had a property right in the fur-seals swimming in Behring Sea, but he had also rehearsed the old Blaine contention that the destruction of these seals was contrary to good morals. He had no doubt that the fur-seal controversy involved the

question of the freedom of the seas, . . . but it is not whether the sea at this day is free in the general acceptation of that term. That question has been settled for more than a century. . . . Not all the seals in the world would compensate the United States for having the freedom of navigation, of commerce, of passage and of use of all the open seas of the globe fail to be maintained intact. But . . . what are the limits of the freedom of the sea? How far does it go? . . . It has limits; there are things we cannot do upon the sea; there are bounds we cannot overstep. . . .

Our general proposition . . . is this:—that this slaughter of the seals . . . is barbarous and inhuman, and wrong in itself. . . . It is contrary to those rules of law which are established by the municipal government of every civilized country on earth for the protection of all wild animals that are of any value. . . . In the third place, it is the destruction of an important and valuable industry, . . . and finally, this extermination of a race of animals that . . . are a valuable race to mankind, is conduct that the freedom of the sea does not embrace.[10]

As the oral arguments of the counsel were dragging their slow length

already written you that it did not require any statement from you to satisfy me that the newspaper criticism of the Arbitration allowances did not appear with your knowledge or approval. I highly appreciate the kindly way in which you refer to my connection with the work of the Arbitration, and the assurance given by you and for the President of your support in my mission." *Gresham MS.*

9. In a letter to Bayard, May 12, 1893, Mr. Moore remarks: "If Mr. Phelps has his way, you may be called on to take up the Behring Sea question. He seems to be trying to break up the arbitration. His contradiction of Sir Charles Russell yesterday, when the latter said you had never justified the seizure of the British sealers in 1886 on the grounds now alleged by counsel for the United States, . . . was extraordinary. . . . This declaration by Messrs. Phelps and Morgan that the United States may refuse to pay damages if the decision of the arbitrators on the question of exclusive right is against us, was not in good taste and was scarcely defensible. . . . I have always felt that it was most unfortunate that our Government should have assumed positions against which some of the most glorious parts of our history have been a direct protest. We have stood as the special champion before the world of the freedom of the seas. And shall it be said that for the sake of a few seal skins the United States at the close of the nineteenth century was willing to dishonor its own history and enforce the barbarous doctrine that Great Britain was compelled by us to abandon at the beginning of the century?" *Bayard MS.*

10. *F.S.A.*, XV, 9–10.

along, John W. Foster retained his optimism as to the result. The British arguments had proved to be

> unexpectedly prolonged. They are now on their twenty-first day of four-hour sessions and may continue two or three days longer. When we first assembled the British talked of getting through in a month. . . . They evidently anticipated a "small job," but after examining the Case and hearing Mr. Carter's oral argument, they became satisfied we were making a strong impression on the Tribunal, and hence their prolonged and earnest efforts. They have been hammering away to break the force of our Case, and have displayed great ingenuity and acumen in their attacks, but after these many days of argument we feel as strong as ever in our position—not a single one of our essential claims has been overthrown.
>
> I believe we have the best of the argument on our property-claim to the seals, but it may be the Tribunal will not have the courage to announce a decision which may seem to its members a new declaration of legal principles. But I feel very confident that if we do not secure a recognition of property, we shall obtain regulations which will be an effective protection to the seals and save to our Government the large revenues from them.[11]

Mr. Foster's optimism was soon shaken by the news that the British and Russian Governments had concluded an agreement whereby sealing operations would be permitted anywhere in Behring Sea outside of a zone of thirty miles around the Russian seal-islands. As early as March, 1893, Foster cabled Secretary Gresham and expressed his apprehension that the Russian Government was ready to make this concession to England. Such an agreement would seriously prejudice the position of the United States before the Tribunal![12]

The Russian Minister at Washington disclaimed any knowledge of a proposed agreement between Russia and Great Britain concerning fur-seals, but he frankly stated that his government was not in support of the stand that had been taken by the American counsel in their argu-

11. John W. Foster to Secretary Gresham, June 20, 1893, *Gresham MS.* In discussing the arguments advanced by the American counsel before the Paris Tribunal, Professor P. E. Corbett, in his monograph, *The Settlement of Canadian-American Disputes,* p. 103, remarks: "The American case for exclusive control of the sealing industry in the Behring Sea oscillated from prescription, through estoppel by acquiescence, to the appropriation by *occupatio* of animals *ferae naturae.* For prescription or estoppel the historical evidence was fatal, since it demonstrated, on the part of Great Britain, active opposition to, rather than acquiescence in, the Russian claims upon which the United States based their argument. . . . As for *occupatio,* nothing approaching effective possession of the seal herds could be established; and we have already seen how the tribunal rejected the analogy between the annual breeding visit to the Pribilof Islands and the *animus revertendi* which the Roman law recognized as an element in the title to doves and tamed deer."

12. John W. Foster to Secretary Gresham, March 20, 1893, *Despatches from John W. Foster, Bering Sea Fur Seal Arbitration,* MS. Dept. of State.

ments before the arbitral tribunal.[13] On May 30, despite pressure from the United States, the Russian Government concluded a convention with Great Britain which provided for a zone of thirty miles around the Commander Islands in Behring Sea. Within this zone, and within ten miles of the Russian continental coasts, sealing operations were forbidden. On the islands the number of seals to be killed should not exceed 30,000.

Mr. Foster had been "especially anxious" that Russia should take no action of this type while the fur-seal arbitration was in progress.[14] Secretary Gresham had tried in every way to exert pressure upon the Russian Government in this regard, but he received scant encouragement from the Russian Minister who complained that the United States had declined

to allow Russia to become a party to that arbitration, and his Government was therefore obliged to treat independently with Great Britain. He also stated that notwithstanding what had been said from time to time, his Government did not believe the right of property which we had asserted in the fur seals in the open sea, was well-founded; and that his Government could not afford to assert the right. He said that while his Government entertained the most friendly feelings towards the United States, it could not be blamed for taking such action as its own safety seemed to demand; and that when the treaty between Great Britain and Russia was entered into, his Government had given to Great Britain a confidential note admitting that the Behring Sea was an open, free sea, and disclaimed jurisdiction over it for any purpose. . . . I am convinced that for some reason, Russia desires that we shall fail in our contention before the Arbitration Tribunal.[15]

With reference to the remark of Prince Cantacuzene to the effect that the United States had declined to permit Russia to become a party to the fur-seal arbitration, Mr. Foster made the following comment:

I do not know the foundation he has for that statement. I was in communication with Secretary Blaine and the President when the treaty with Great Britain for Arbitration was put into form, and I have sought to become fully acquainted with the diplomatic events leading up to that treaty, and I am not aware that Russia ever asked or that the Government of the United States declined to allow her to become a party to the Arbitration. . . . I am satisfied that if Russia at that time had heartily co-operated with the United States in the manner proposed by Mr. Blaine, the necessity for the present arbitration never would have arisen.[16]

13. Secretary Gresham to John W. Foster, March 23, 1893, *ibid.*
14. John W. Foster to Secretary Gresham, July 18, 1893, *ibid.*
15. Secretary Gresham to John W. Foster, July 14, 1893, *Foster MS.*
16. John W. Foster to Secretary Gresham, July 27, 1893, *Despatches from John W. Foster, Bering Sea Fur Seal Arbitration,* MS. Dept. of State.

In another letter to Secretary Gresham, Foster made some very pertinent and interesting observations concerning the recent Russian-British convention relative to fur-seals:

I desire to bring to your attention a suggestion made to me from a responsible source that if, as stated to you by the Russian Minister, his Government at the time the *modus vivendi* of May last was entered into with Great Britain, gave to the latter a confidential note of the character indicated by the Minister, there must have been some reciprocal assurance given by Great Britain. What the nature of that assurance was can only be conjectured by us, but it is not unreasonable to suppose that it had reference to the character of the protection or immunity which Great Britain would allow to the Russian seal herd after the Tribunal of Arbitration had fixed the regulations which were to be applied to the Alaskan seal herd. If the Canadian sealers were left free to attack the latter in the seas adjoining the American continent, there would be less inducement for them to resort to the distant waters of the Asiatic coast. . . .

I am told by our Ambassador, Mr. Eustis, that the Russian Ambassador in Paris, is on very confidential terms with Baron de Courcel, the President and French member of the Tribunal. If the latter is made aware of the confidential note and of the views of the Russian Government as expressed to you by Prince Cantacuzene, I should abandon all hope of securing the Baron's vote in favor of our contention as to the right of property or protection in the seals. In this connection it may be stated that the Russian Ambassador has so far as I have been able to learn, shown no interest in our cause since the Tribunal met.[17]

On July 10, after the action of the Russian Government concerning fur-seals had become widely known, the Arbitration Tribunal began to hold secret sessions, and on August 15, 1893 the award was announced. The result should not have been surprising to the forewarned Mr. Foster. A majority of the arbitrators decided every one of the five questions against the contentions of the United States.[18] The decision on

17. John W. Foster to Secretary Gresham, August 2, 1893, *ibid.*

18. The text of the award of the Tribunal reads as follows: "As to the first of the five points, We . . . do decide and determine as follows: By the Ukase of 1821, Russia claimed jurisdiction in the sea now known as the Behring's Sea, to the extent of 100 Italian miles from the coast and islands belonging to her, but in the course of the negotiations which led to the conclusion of the Treaties of 1824 with the United States and of 1825 with Great Britain, Russia admitted that her jurisdiction in the said sea should be restricted to the reach of cannon shot from shore, and it appears that, from that time up to the time of the cession of Alaska to the United States, Russia never asserted in fact or exercised any exclusive jurisdiction in Behring's Sea or any exclusive rights in the seal fisheries therein beyond the ordinary limit of territorial waters.

"As to the second of the said five points, We . . . do decide and determine that Great Britain did not recognize or concede any claim, upon the part of Russia, to

the fourth question was unanimous, and on the first three questions, Justice Harlan voted with the majority. The fifth question dealt with the right of property in the seals in Behring Sea, and in this regard both Harlan[19] and Morgan supported the American contention. The Tribunal also enacted certain regulations which were believed to be necessary for the preservation of the fur-seal fisheries in Behring Sea.[20]

In the United States public opinion was much divided over the award of the Tribunal. In a letter to Bayard, H. L. Bryan expressed his criticism of the arguments advanced in the American Case:

> What a "glorious victory" the decision of the Paris Tribunal! How the "property right" in the seals, that pet discovery of Mr. Phelps, has faded away before the breath of the award! And yet the ultra-Republican newspapers are claiming "another triumph of Harrison's and Blaine's Diplomacy." Now we haven't even an undefined right that might have been useful in sustaining some sort of surveillance. All is gone.[21]

exclusive jurisdiction as to the seal fisheries in Behring Sea, outside of ordinary territorial waters.

"As to the third of said five points, . . . We . . . do unanimously decide and determine that the body of water now known as the Behring Sea was included in the phrase 'Pacific Ocean' as used in the said Treaty. . . . We [also] do decide and determine that no exclusive rights of jurisdiction in Behring Sea and no exclusive rights as to the seal fisheries therein, were held or exercised by Russia outside of ordinary territorial waters after the Treaty of 1825.

"As to the fourth of the said five points, We . . . do unanimously decide and determine that all rights of Russia as to jurisdiction and as to the seal fisheries in Behring Sea, east of the water boundary in the Treaty between the United States and Russia of the 30th March, 1867, did pass unimpaired to the United States under the said Treaty.

"As to the fifth of the said five points, We . . . do decide and determine that the United States has not any right of protection or property in the fur-seals frequenting the islands of the United States in Behring Sea, when such seals are found outside the ordinary three-mile limit." Malloy, *op. cit.*, I, 751–754.

19. Justice Harlan was strongly of the opinion that the United States had a definite right of property in the seals in Behring Sea outside the three-mile limit. In his opinion, Mr. Harlan observed: "I am of the opinion that these fur seals, conceived, born and reared on the islands of St. Paul and St. George, belonging to the United States, are, when found in the high seas on their way back to their land home and feeding grounds on those islands, the property of the United States, and that this right of property is qualified only in the sense that it will cease when, but not before, they cease to have the habit of returning to the Pribilof Islands after their customary migration into the open waters of Behring Sea and the North Pacific Ocean.

"If the claim of the United States to own these fur seals rests, in law, upon a sound foundation, the next inquiry is whether it may protect its property? There can be but one answer to this question. Manifestly it would have the same authority to protect its property that an individual has for the protection of his property. . . . No one questions its right to afford protection . . . while the seals are on its islands, and while they are within territorial waters. That right . . . is not lost while they are temporarily absent in the high seas." *F.S.A.*, I, 186.

20. Malloy, *op. cit.*, I, 754–759.

21. H. L. Bryan to Bayard, August 17, 1893, *Bayard MS.*

Lambert Tree was glad that the decision had gone against the United States, for victory "would have been worse for us than defeat. We were contending for an utterly unsound principle . . . which as a great maritime nation we could never afford to have established as a rule of International Law."[22]

Secretary Gresham accepted the award of the Tribunal with as much grace as he could muster, but he had definite suspicions that the British Government would "find excuses and pretexts for delay" in carrying out the regulations that had been suggested.[23] In order to ascertain the attitude of the British Foreign Office with reference to these regulations, Gresham cabled to Bayard and instructed him to take the matter up with the Foreign Secretary.[24] The following day he wrote to Bayard and indicated that he entertained some suspicions of British good faith in the matter of agreeing to regulations that would effectively protect the fur-seals. Concurrent legislation should be obtained

> and supplemental rules or orders agreed upon and published before the next sealing season begins. Owners of sealing vessels should know in advance the restrictions under which they will have to act. Will Great Britain unite with us in an honest effort to enforce the regulations in spirit as well as letter? If not, they will be of no avail. The Canadians will doubtless endeavor to induce the British Government to consent to nothing which will make pelagic sealing more hazardous or difficult than heretofore. I fear that whatever is done, Canadians, and perhaps Americans, will transfer the ownership of their sealing vessels to citizens or subjects of other Powers, thus avoiding the effect of the regulations. It remains to be seen whether other Powers will now give their adhesion.[25]

Bayard hastened to carry out Gresham's instructions, and he found that Lord Rosebery concurred in the view that the British and American Governments should act with expedition in the matter of adopting regulations concerning the fur-seals. Rosebery inclined to the view that the negotiations could best be conducted in Washington,[26] but Gresham sent a formal instruction directing Bayard to continue his efforts to arrange matters in London.[27] When Lord Rosebery again suggested

22. Lambert Tree to Bayard, August 20, 1893, *ibid.*

23. Secretary Gresham to John W. Foster, September 11, 1893, *Gresham MS.*

24. Secretary Gresham to Bayard, September 12, 1893, *F.R., 1894,* App. I, p. 107.

25. Secretary Gresham to Bayard, September 13, 1893, *Gresham MS.* See also Gresham to J. W. Foster, September 13, 1893, *ibid.*

26. Bayard to Secretary Gresham, September 13, 1893, *F.R., 1894,* App. I, pp. 107–108.

27. Secretary Gresham to Bayard, September 16, 1893, *ibid.*, p. 109.

that Washington was the place where the negotiations should be carried on,[28] Gresham held firm and repeated his instruction of September 16.[29]

The reason for Gresham's insistence upon London as the place where the fur-seal discussions should be held, is explained in a letter to Bayard from H. L. Bryan. Gresham had informed Bryan that both the President and himself were aware of Bayard's complete knowledge "of all the questions involved in the Behring Sea matters," and they were of the opinion that "useless correspondence and delay" would be avoided if Bayard would handle the matter through conversations with Lord Rosebery.[30]

Bayard was glad to carry out this instruction, but he wrote to President Cleveland and indicated the fact that there would be a delay in the negotiations because of Lord Rosebery's temporary absence from London. He then made some comments upon the role played by Phelps during the sessions of the fur-seal tribunal. The only result of his arguments was the fact that the Blaine-Harrison-Foster management had been able to

> tie the hands of the United States and Great Britain in seal-protection and advertise to every other nation an opportunity for them to kill seal freely anywhere and at any time three miles from shore. In short, a "spirited policy" has wholly miscarried, and brought humiliation to its proponents. It only makes our duty more difficult, but does not make it less *our duty*.[31]

Gresham did not share Bayard's adverse view with reference to the arguments of Phelps before the Tribunal. In a letter to John W. Foster, Gresham expressed the opinion that

> our right of property in the fur-seals and our right to protect them were the most important questions submitted to the Tribunal, and . . . if the award had been in our favor on those questions there would have been little necessity for regulations. . . . If Great Britain is willing to co-operate cordially with us, the seal industry may be preserved, but I must say I can not get rid of the impression that various pretexts may be resorted to for delay on the part of that Government. Mr. Bayard is perfectly familiar with the questions

28. Bayard to Secretary Gresham, September 20, 1893, *ibid.*, p. 118.

29. Secretary Gresham to Bayard, October 3, 1893, *ibid.*, pp. 119–120. In a letter to Bayard, October 29, 1893, Gresham observed: "Mr. White informed me he saw Lord Rosebery just before he sailed, and after he parted from you, and that Rosebery said he should strenuously object to the final settlement of the Behring Sea regulations at London, adding that Sir Julian had the Canadians somewhat in hand, and he (Rosebery) could not get along with them." *Gresham Letter Book, Gresham MS.*

30. H. L. Bryan to Bayard, October 3, 1893, *Bayard MS.*

31. Bayard to President Cleveland, October 3, 1893, *Bayard Press Copy Book,* I, *Bayard MS.*

submitted to the Tribunal and its action, and the President and I are satisfied that he will be zealous in upholding our interests.[32]

This right of property in the fur-seals, and the right to protect these far-ranging animals, had implications of a most serious nature. If the Tribunal had decided in favor of the American contention, it would have meant that the United States had the power, outside the three-mile limit, to enforce regulations designed to prevent pelagic sealing. The exercise of such a power would have constituted a crushing American attack upon the doctrine of the freedom of the seas. In a letter to Bayard, John Bassett Moore made reference to this fact:

The other day, President Low [of Columbia University] remarked that, while he was not familiar with the subject, it seemed to him that the tribunal at Paris "had given Great Britain the past and the United States the future." I replied that I scarcely understood how that could be; that on every question of law submitted to arbitration, we had lost; that Great Britain had already consented to joint regulations, and that the United States, instead of getting a close season for seals in the whole of the North Pacific from May till October, which was conceded to you, had got a close season for three months, till July 31, and after that a sixty-mile zone about the Pribyloff Islands, which was practically worthless. . . . I . . . readily concur in the opinion that the tribunal *saved* the United States the future, by confirming to it and to all other nations the freedom of the seas.[33]

When the Tribunal made its award it also decided that certain regulations were necessary for the preservation of seal life in Behring Sea.[34]

32. Secretary Gresham to J. W. Foster, October 9, 1893, *Gresham Letter Book, Gresham MS.* In this same letter Gresham commented as follows upon the difficulties of coming to an agreement with Great Britain on the matter of the regulations: "Being satisfied that I could not come to a speedy understanding with Sir Julian upon the subject of concurrent legislation and regulations for giving practical force to the award and recommendations of the Paris Tribunal, it was deemed advisable to entrust the entire matter to Mr. Bayard at London. I do not wish to be understood as saying that Sir Julian was not willing to act with the promptness which the situation demands, but it was very plain that, inasmuch as he did not expect to return to Washington until after September, (he is not here yet), there was danger that the next sealing season would begin before joint action could be had. Some three weeks ago, after Mr. Bayard had received his instructions, he telegraphed me that Lord Rosebery had assured him of his willingness to proceed without delay in negotiations for needed action by the two Governments, and that he believed the British Government was sincere in its professions of a desire to co-operate promptly with our Government in all necessary ways for the protection of the fur-seal. Mr. Bayard was instructed to urge the matter with all possible despatch. . . . I fully realize that the seals will be speedily exterminated unless Great Britain and the United States take prompt concurrent action for their preservation."

33. John Bassett Moore to Bayard, October 14, 1893, *Bayard MS.*

34. There were nine of these regulations, and they read as follows: "(1) The Governments of the United States and of Great Britain shall forbid their citizens and

Secretary Gresham was anxious to have both countries pass the concurrent legislation that would authorize the execution of these regulations. Finding that Lord Rosebery continued to delay negotiations,[35] Gresham sent Bayard a cablegram telling of the President's desire for speedy action.[36] Bayard replied that negotiations had been prevented by the absence of the British Foreign Secretary, but he had "good reason to expect efficient co-operation."[37] Five days later, Bayard cabled that Lord Rosebery had presented "impressive reasons for not withdrawing seal fishery negotiations from British ambassador at Washington."[38]

In a personal letter to Secretary Gresham, Bayard stated that he was certain that the Behring Sea negotiations would be "continually interrupted and delayed" if carried on in London. If they were transferred to Washington he could pay a flying visit to the Department of State, and through the medium of diplomatic conversations the whole

subjects respectively to kill, capture or pursue at any time and in any manner whatever, the animals commonly called fur seals, within a zone of sixty miles around the Pribilov Islands, inclusive of the territorial waters. . . . (2) The two Governments shall forbid their citizens and subjects respectively to kill, capture or pursue, in any manner whatever, during the season extending, each year, from the 1st of May to the 31st of July, both inclusive, the fur seals on the high sea, in the part of the Pacific Ocean, inclusive of the Behring Sea, which is situated to the North of the 35th degree of North latitude, and eastward of the 180th degree of longitude from Greenwich till it strikes the water boundary described in Article 1 of the Treaty of 1867 between the United States and Russia, and following that line up to Behring straits. (3) During the period of time and in the waters in which the fur seal fishing is allowed, only sailing vessels shall be permitted to carry on or take part in fur-seal fishing operations . . . (4) Each sailing vessel authorised to fish for fur seals must be provided with a special license issued for that purpose by its Government and shall be required to carry a distinguishing flag to be prescribed by its Government. (5) The masters of the vessels engaged in fur seal fishing shall enter accurately in their official log book the date and place of each fur seal fishing operation, and also the number and sex of the seals captured upon each day. . . . (6) The use of nets, fire arms and explosives shall be forbidden in the fur seal fishing. . . . (7) The two Governments shall take measures to control the fitness of the men authorized to engage in fur seal fishing . . . (8) The regulations contained in the preceding articles shall not apply to Indians dwelling on the coast of the territory of the United States or of Great Britain. . . . (9) The concurrent regulations hereby determined with a view to the protection and conservation of the fur seals, shall remain in force until they have been . . . abolished or modified by common agreement between the Governments of the United States and of Great Britain. The said concurrent regulations shall be submitted every five years to a new examination, so as to enable both interested Governments to consider whether . . . there is occasion for any modification thereof." Malloy, *op. cit.*, I, 754–756.

35. In a letter to Bayard, October 30, 1893, H. L. Bryan remarks: "Mr. White has been here and had an interview with the Secretary, during which he stated that before leaving London he had been told by Lord Rosebery that the British Government was very much averse to having the Bering sea negotiations conducted in England." *Bayard MS.*

36. Secretary Gresham to Bayard, November 17, 1893, *F.R., 1894,* App. I, p. 131.

37. Bayard to Secretary Gresham, November 18, 1893, *ibid.,* p. 131.

38. Bayard to Secrctary Gresham, November 23, 1893, *ibid.,* p. 133.

matter could be speedily adjusted.[39] Under this steady pressure from Lord Rosebery, Gresham finally gave way and consented to the transfer of the negotiations to Washington. Apparently he was a little piqued at this outcome of his efforts to avoid taking personal charge of the fur-seal negotiations, and he informed Bayard that, while his offer to visit Washington and be of assistance was appreciated by the President, it was thought that the situation of affairs in London would require his presence there.[40]

Bayard believed that it would not be difficult for the Department of State to secure the adherence of Japan and Russia to any regulations that might be adopted, but he had his suspicions about the Canadian Government. The Canadians were "small and sharp—very." He was still at a loss to understand the actions of Phelps, and he had met many others who were equally in doubt.[41]

Phelps was not aware that his conduct had been questionable, and he continued to regard himself as an expert on everything connected with the fur-seals. In a note to Bayard he complained that the

> regulations of the Paris tribunal in respect to the killing of the seals are most flagrantly disregarded. If observed they would be quite sufficient to preserve the seals, and one wiser than you and I would have been glad to obtain [them] in the outset. So there are materials enough for trouble if any one desires to make it. And with ten months of Congress before us, what may happen can not be foretold.[42]

Secretary Gresham shared these fears that there were "materials enough for trouble" in Behring Sea, and he was very anxious to have the controversy settled as quickly as possible. But the British Government seemed in no hurry to arrive at an agreement even after the negotiations had been transferred to Washington.[43] On January 6, Gresham

39. Bayard to Secretary Gresham, November 25, 1893, *Gresham MS.*

40. Secretary Gresham to Bayard, December 4, 1893, *F.R., 1894,* App. I, p. 136. In a personal letter to President Cleveland, Dec. 1, 1893, Bayard expressed the opinion that Washington was the "proper place" to conduct the fur-seal negotiations. He believed a "conclusive result" would be reached sooner in the atmosphere of Washington. *Cleveland MS.*

41. Bayard to John Bassett Moore, December 1, 1893, *Bayard MS.*

42. Phelps to Bayard, December 3, 1893, *ibid.*

43. In a personal letter to Bayard, December 17, 1893, Gresham stated that he had made "no headway in negotiations with the British Ambassador for an agreement which will make the award of the Paris Tribunal practically effective. The first of the three declarations made by the Tribunal will likely embarrass this government not a little. The arbitrators had no jurisdiction to bind the powers within the limits of their respective sovereignties, and yet the first declaration solemnly declares that the reported regulations should be supplemented by others 'applicable within the limits of the sovereignty of the two powers interested, and to be settled by their common agreement.'

"Sir Julian has not said in terms that Great Britain would expect the United States

informed Bayard, by telegram, that the British Ambassador was still urging the American Government to agree that a Canadian be admitted as a "negotiator for concurrent action to make regulations reported by Paris Tribunal effective." But Gresham instructed Bayard to inform Lord Rosebery that the Department of State would "treat with the Imperial Government only."[44] Bayard replied that Lord Rosebery was entirely willing that the British Ambassador at Washington should conduct the negotiations without a "Canadian colleague."[45]

Lord Rosebery was conciliatory, but it was soon evident that he was not able to speed the negotiations because of certain objections raised by the Canadian Government.[46] Weary of waiting for some action on

to come to an agreement regulating the taking of seals within our own jurisdiction, but he has intimated as much. I can imagine that later on he will say: 'Why should Great Britain be required to protect the zone around the Pribylof Islands at joint expense with the United States unless the latter government agrees to some reasonable restriction as to the number of seals which shall be taken on the islands. . . .

"Sir Julian . . . was instructed by Lord Rosebery to say Great Britain desired that a Canadian should be admitted as a negotiator, but he was informed that while this government would not object to one or more Canadians being present at the negotiations, it was unwilling to treat with any one except a representative of the British Government." *Ibid.*

In his reply to Secretary Gresham, December 28, 1893, Bayard expressed the view that he did not think that "the *extent* of the interests of either party in the fur-sealing on land, or the preservation of the seal species should control their clear duty and obligation to assist in policing the seas. . . . If the Canadians shall honestly accept the decisions of the Tribunal, and the United States will actively patrol the interdicted waters for one year, or for two at the most, the business of pelagic sealing will cease." *Gresham MSS.*

44. Secretary Gresham to Bayard, January 6, 1894, *F.R., 1894,* App. I, p. 140.

45. Bayard to Secretary Gresham, January 8, 1894, *ibid.,* p. 141.

46. On January 21, 1894, Secretary Gresham wrote to Bayard and expressed his displeasure at the way things were going. He had spoken to Sir Julian and after making a reference to the time that had already elapsed with reference to the negotiations, he "reminded him that the sealing season had commenced and informed him we thought this not a little strange, in view of the earnest desire of his Government that the negotiations should be transferred from London to Washington. He again informed me that he hoped to receive instructions very soon which would enable him to speak more definitely. My confidence in his candor remains unshaken. I think he and Lord Rosebery are embarrassed by the Canadians. While the regulations are not self-executing, I agree with you that the award, including the regulations, is obligatory upon the contracting parties. The three declarations are not part of the award and do not bind the Powers. I shall send you tomorrow or the next day copies of a draft of the proposed convention and my note transmitting it to Sir Julian. Until recently he steadily insisted that a convention was unnecessary, asserting that legislation would fully accomplish the end desired. I think, however, he has now changed his mind and sees the necessity of a mutual agreement which will enable us to prevent pelagic sealing during this season. If the Canadians are permitted to have their way, no agreement of any kind will be reached, and the seal herds will speedily disappear.

"It was to oblige Sir Julian that you were instructed to inform Lord Rosebery the negotiations must be between the United States and the Imperial Government, and that Great Britain can empower a Canadian to represent her as a Minister Plenipotentiary,

the part of the British Foreign Office, Gresham finally sent to Pauncefote a draft of a convention between the United States and Great Britain which would provide for the execution of the regulations adopted by the Tribunal. The President was desirous to have some action taken at once, and it was ardently hoped that the British Ambassador would respond to this overture. But Pauncefote paid little attention to this plea to expedite negotiations, and John Bassett Moore concluded that the reason for this procrastination was that pressure was being exerted by the Canadian Government in favor of a policy of inaction. It seemed to Moore that "colonies, like small children, sometimes think it pays to be bad, but their parents ought not to encourage them in such conduct."[47]

At length, on February 22, 1894, Gresham cabled to Bayard that the President was unable to understand the do-nothing attitude on the part of the British Government, and he wished to have the situation stated "impressively to Her Majesty's Government."[48] Bayard immediately sent a strong note to Rosebery expressing President Cleveland's disappointment at the "unexpected and regretted delay in coming to an agreement for the efficient execution of the regulations for the conduct of fur-sealing fishing in Behring Sea."[49] After waiting several days, Bayard had an interview with Rosebery, who "did not seem aware of the proposition for a convention, and asked why the co-operative legislation would not be sufficient."[50] In a note to Bayard, March 2, 1894, Rosebery repeated his belief that a convention was not necessary to carry out the regulations adopted by the Paris Tribunal. This matter could be handled efficiently by a mere legislative enactment.[51]

In his note of March 2, Rosebery had frankly admitted that one of the chief reasons why negotiations had been delayed was on account of the necessity of referring all questions of sealing regulations to the Canadian Government for approval. The British Foreign Office did not seem to realize that the fast-rising tide of resentment in the United States against this policy of delay, might cause an abrupt break in the negotiations at Washington. Some Republican Senators, aided by

but the matter had already been entrusted to Sir Julian, and we were not willing that a Canadian should act with him with authority to vote. . . . Sir Julian feared our refusal to treat with a Canadian would be attributed to his influence and he desired a record showing the contrary." *Bayard MS.*

47. John Bassett Moore to Bayard, February 3, 1894, *ibid.*
48. Secretary Gresham to Bayard, February 22, 1894, *F.R., 1894,* App. I, p. 147.
49. Bayard to Lord Rosebery, February 23, 1894, *ibid.,* pp. 149–150.
50. Bayard to Secretary Gresham, February 28, 1894, *ibid.,* pp. 148–149.
51. Lord Rosebery to Bayard, March 2, 1894, *ibid.,* pp. 151–152.

Senator Morgan, were losing patience with British inaction, and were ready to take matters into their own hands.[52] But before they could carry out any program of anti-British legislation, Lord Rosebery was suddenly advanced to the position of Prime Minister (through the resignation of Gladstone), and Lord Kimberley became the new Foreign Secretary. Bayard believed that Kimberley was a "straight-forward man of ability and experience," who would not "permit the Canadians to be tricky in relation to Behring Sea."[53]

Kimberley lived up to these expectations, and on April 18 Bayard was able to cable to Secretary Gresham that the British Parliament had just passed an act to carry out the regulations adopted by the Paris Tribunal.[54] Almost two weeks earlier, Gresham had informed Bayard that Congress had enacted similar legislation.[55]

It was a great relief to Bayard to have this difficult matter of the execution of the fur-seal regulations finally settled by concurrent legislation,[56] but there was another item that demanded immediate attention. This had to do with the matter of the payment of British claims arising out of American seizures of sealing vessels in Behring Sea. On October 28, 1893, Bayard had expressed the opinion that there would be a "smart Behring Sea bill to be paid by the United States,"[57] and John

52. Secretary Gresham was strongly opposed to any Senatorial action in this matter of fur-seal regulations, and on February 23, 1894 he wrote to Senator Morgan and attempted to explain the situation: "I have just read your letter of yesterday. I drafted the bill, a copy of which was sent to you and to Governor McCreary. My idea was that, for the present, we had better not assume Great Britain was not going to meet us in a proper spirit and agree, as the treaty obliges her, to make the reported regulations effective. Of course, I expected you to exercise your own judgment as to the kind of a bill to be introduced. I think you saw the copy of my note to Sir Julian, enclosing the draft of a treaty strictly within the terms of the convention and the award. It seems to me that we should do nothing of record just now indicating the belief on our part that Great Britain is not going to be fair. I had another interview with Sir Julian yesterday, and he told me he expected to receive instructions from Lord Rosebery in three or four days. I agree with you that I should see Senator Sherman, and I shall ask him to come to the Department tomorrow with you, if you can find time to accompany him. I have an impression I ought to go before your full committee on this question. I am perfectly willing to disclose all that has been done." *Gresham MS.*

53. Bayard to Secretary Gresham, March 7, 1894, *Bayard Press Copy Book,* I, *Bayard MS.*

54. Bayard to Secretary Gresham, April 18, 1894, *F.R., 1894,* App. I, pp. 178–179.

55. Secretary Gresham to Bayard, April 5, 1894, *ibid.,* p. 165.

56. It appeared to Mr. Phelps, May 2, 1894, that Bayard had "adjusted the Behring Sea matter most satisfactorily. The regulations given in the award are ample for the protection of the seals if they are honestly enforced. I thought and still think it was the intention of Great Britain to escape their enforcement for this year at least." *Bayard MS.*

57. Bayard to Frederick Emory, October 28, 1893, *Bayard Press Copy Book,* I, *Bayard MS.*

Bassett Moore was afraid that the American Government would "have a fine sum to pay" with reference to these claims.[58]

But there were some members of Congress who were strongly opposed to the payment of claims to Great Britain on account of these seizures. As early as February 22, 1894, Secretary Gresham wrote to Bayard that Senator Morgan was openly working against such a settlement.[59] John Bassett Moore wrote in a similar vein concerning the actions and views of Morgan:

Remembering the course of Mr. Morgan with respect to the fisheries in 1886, you may not be astonished to learn that he now maintains that the Paris Tribunal did not decide against our claim of property in the seals, and that he also maintains that nothing is due Great Britain for our previous seizures. He argues that the vessels that were seized (sixty miles and more from land) were *hovering* with intent to depredate on our property, and that we therefore had a right to seize them! In matters generally, Mr. Morgan is ranged with the Republicans against the Administration, and he is bent on mischief.[60]

Despite this Congressional opposition, Secretary Gresham went ahead, and on August 21, 1894, offered the sum of $425,000 in final settlement of all claims as to American seizures of British sealing vessels. This offer was subject to "the action of Congress on the question of appropriating the money."[61] Pauncefote replied that the British Government would accept this sum, although the amount offered was "much below their estimate of the compensation" that was fairly due.[62]

Thanks to the opposition of Senator Morgan and others of like mind, this appropriation was not passed by Congress, and the matter of unpaid British claims remained unsettled.[63] To Bayard, this action by Congress was most "humiliating and painful." He had strongly complained to Lord Rosebery about Canadian breaches of "the practice of arbitration," and now the American Congress had refused to carry out a plain obligation! Lord Kimberley had expressed his "surprise and disappointment" at this American failure to live up to its

58. John Bassett Moore to Bayard, November 14, 1893, *Bayard MS.*

59. Secretary Gresham to Bayard, February 22, 1894, *ibid.*

60. John Bassett Moore to Bayard, February 28, 1894, *ibid.*

61. Secretary Gresham to Pauncefote, August 21, 1894, *F.R., 1894,* App. I, pp. 224–225.

62. Pauncefote to Secretary Gresham, August 21, 1894, *ibid.*, pp. 225–226.

63. In a letter to Secretary Gresham, May 25, 1895, Bayard made the following comment upon the attitude of Senator Morgan: "It is greatly to be regretted that your sensible and honorable proposition to settle the Sealing vessels claims was defeated by the mischievous Morgan, who seems to delight in striking splinters into public questions." *Bayard Press Copy Book,* II, *Bayard MS.*

promises, but he realized that there had been no bad faith on the part of the President and the Secretary of State.[64]

This matter of claims was finally settled by the conclusion of a convention, February 8, 1896, which provided for the appointment of a mixed commission. William L. Putnam, now justice of the U. S. Circuit Court, was chosen as the American commissioner, and the Honorable George E. King, of the Supreme Court of Canada, was selected to represent Canada. On December 17, 1897, the commissioners made a detailed award, and on June 16, 1898, the Secretary of State delivered to the British Ambassador at Washington a draft for the sum of $473,151.26.[65]

But the payment of these claims did not put an end to the fur-seal controversy. The problem of saving the fur-seal herds from destruction still plagued the Department of State. In Congress there was a growing feeling of irritation against Great Britain, and Henry W. Elliott, taking note of this rancor, sent a letter to Representative Nelson Dingley, of Maine, in which he reviewed the fur-seal situation and indicated the importance of securing amendments to the regulations that were enacted by the Paris Tribunal.[66] On December 11, 1894, Mr. Dingley introduced a resolution in the House of Representatives calling upon the Secretary of the Treasury to furnish information as to the effectiveness of these regulations in preserving the fur-seal herds from possible extermination. This resolution was promptly adopted,[67] and Mr. Dingley then introduced a bill (H.R. 8633) which would save the seals from pelagic butchery by authorizing wholesale mercy killings on the Pribilof Islands. In this way the United States would anticipate the eventual slaughter of the seals in the waters of Behring Sea, and would also secure the entire profit from the sale of these skins. Section 3 of this bill authorized the President to suspend the execution of this

64. Bayard to Secretary Gresham, March 9, 1895, *ibid.*

65. Malloy, *op. cit.*, I, 766–770; Moore, *History and Digest of International Arbitrations*, II, 2123–2131; *F.R., 1898*, pp. 371–373.

In a letter to John W. Foster, December 27, 1897, John Hay makes the following comments with reference to this award: "Now comes the Putnam-King award. Of course it is monstrous. But we must pay something for the luxury of having such a President as Grover Cleveland. Putnam's procedure was evidently merely to take the Gresham argument and add interest. I can understand the irritation it must cause in Congress; but I cannot see how we are to avoid paying up without infinitely greater damage. It seems to me now a debt of honor. The luck is against us and to kick would be discreditable. But that being done, I hope no further attempt will be made at negotiation with Canada for the present." *Foster MS.*

66. *Congressional Record*, 53 Cong., 3 sess., p. 217.

67. *Ibid.*, p. 217.

law in the event that the British Government would agree to amendments that would really make the regulations effective.[68]

On February 18, 1895, a substitute measure was introduced by William L. Wilson (H.R. 8909). This made provision for the appointment of a joint commission to investigate the fur-seal situation and report upon the best means of saving the seal herds. Pending the filing of this report, the President was authorized to conclude a *modus vivendi* which would temporarily put into force regulations that would prohibit pelagic sealing, and would conserve seal life. If Great Britain would not agree to a *modus vivendi*, then a program of mercy killings of seals could be adopted.[69]

This bill was passed by the House on February 28,[70] but it was too late in the session to push it through the Senate. In the meantime, Secretary Gresham hoped that this threat of Congressional legislation providing for mercy killings might influence the British Government in favor of immediate amendment of the fur-seal regulations. On January 23, 1895, he addressed a note to Pauncefote in which he called attention to the apparent fact that the regulations enacted by the Paris Tribunal were inadequate to afford sufficient protection against the dangers of pelagic sealing. During the 1894 season the total "pelagic catch" of seals amounted to about 142,000. In Behring Sea, in the short space of five weeks, 31,585 seals had been killed, which number was 8,000 more than were killed during the entire season of 1891. This "startling increase" in the pelagic slaughter of both the American and the Asiatic herds had convinced President Cleveland that the regulations of the Tribunal had "not operated to protect the seal herd from . . . destruction." Unless a speedy change in the regulations was effected, the "extermination of the herd must follow." Any new system of regulations should "embrace the whole North Pacific Ocean from the Asiatic side to the American side," and Japan and Russia should be invited to adhere to this protective device. In order that these regulations be carefully designed, a new commission should be appointed, "consisting of one or more men from each country, eminent for scientific knowledge and practical acquaintance with the fur trade."[71]

After waiting for some months for an answer from the Foreign Office, Mr. Uhl, the Acting Secretary of State, called Pauncefote's attention to Secretary Gresham's note of January 23. Early action by the Brit-

68. *Ibid.*, p. 1258. This bill was introduced on January 23, 1895.

69. *Ibid.*, p. 2361.

70. *Congressional Record*, 53 Cong., 2 sess., pp. 3010–3011.

71. Secretary Gresham to Pauncefote, January 23, 1895, *F.R., 1894*, App. I, pp. 228–229.

ish Government upon the proposals of Secretary Gresham would have done much to check "the appalling diminution" of the Alaskan seal herd within the area of the "award and avert the imminent destruction of the important industries to which the seal fisheries give rise." Recent statistics relative to the effect of pelagic sealing had "not only confirmed the grave apprehensions" expressed by Gresham, but had forced upon the Department of State the conviction that further suggestions to expand by mutual agreement the scope of the Paris award were most necessary. The fatal defect in the regulations was "in opening Bering Sea during August and September to pelagic sealing and prohibiting only the use of firearms." It had been demonstrated that the spear was as destructive as the shotgun. In Behring Sea the seals could be found asleep in large numbers, and could easily be killed by "silent and skillful spearsmen." It was important, therefore, to change the existing regulations by adopting four new suggestions: (1) close Behring Sea to pelagic sealers pending consideration of the proposition for extending the protective area of the North Pacific Ocean along the thirty-fifth parallel to the Asiatic coast; (2) arrange through a *modus vivendi* for the effective concurrence of Great Britain, Russia, Japan and the United States in a program for the protection of the fur-seal herds; (3) appoint a joint commission to study the fur-seal question; (4) amend the concurrent legislation of the two countries so as to permit a more precise definition of the scope of the Paris award and the duty of the two Governments thereunder.[72]

In reply to Mr. Uhl, the British Foreign Office instructed Pauncefote to point out that Secretary Gresham's use of statistics had led him to "erroneous conclusions." There was nothing alarming in the pelagic catch for 1894, and after a careful consideration of all the facts in the case, Her Majesty's Government could not agree that "any sufficient evidence as yet exists to show that the regulations have failed in their effect or that there is such urgent danger of total extinction of the seals as to call for a departure from the arbitral award." With regard to a *modus vivendi* for the current season, it was felt that there was no necessity for such an arrangement. Moreover, to put a sudden stop to sealing operations would be an act of "great injustice, and would involve Her Majesty's Government in the payment of heavy compensation." Finally, it was the firm conviction of the Foreign Office that the appointment of a joint commission to study the fur-seal question would not "lead to any useful result."[73]

72. Edwin F. Uhl to Pauncefote, May 10, 1895, *ibid., 1895,* Pt. 1, pp. 611–615.

73. Instructions to Sir Julian Pauncefote, May 17, 1895, handed to Mr. Uhl, May 27, 1895, *ibid.,* pp. 618–623.

This note from the Foreign Office was delivered to the Department of State on the day previous to the death of Secretary Gresham. Gresham had become thoroughly convinced that the regulations enacted by the Paris Tribunal were entirely inadequate to the preservation of the seal herds in Behring Sea, and in January, 1895, as said, he had employed Elliott as a confidential adviser to the Department of State. Elliott had "opened" Gresham's eyes "to a hundred things that he had not dreamed of." On the basis of these revelations, he had decided to take "prompt steps to better the wretched state of affairs on the Seal Islands and to place the responsibility of their ruin on the right men." From Elliott, Gresham had learned of the "shameful dishonesty" of Blaine, Elkins and Foster in April-May, 1891, in the matter of fur-seal killings on the Pribilof Islands, and he was anxious to have the whole fur-seal matter placed in its proper light.[74]

Gresham's death on May 28, 1895, put an end to any far-reaching plans concerning the fur-seals, and the Venezuela boundary controversy, which came to a head on July 20, 1895, diverted the attention of the State Department to another and more pressing issue. But on June 18 Secretary Olney sent a note to the Foreign Office in which he complained that British naval officers were not carrying out the terms of the Paris award. Certain British sealing vessels had been seized by American cruisers and turned over to British cruisers for alleged infractions of the sealing regulations. Instead of turning these vessels over to a British court of admiralty for trial, the British naval officers had released the offending vessels. Such action was obviously an infraction of the terms of the fur-seal regulations.[75]

On June 24 Secretary Olney replied to the British note of May 17 with reference to the protection of the fur-seals. He tried to make it clear that Secretary Gresham's note of January 23, 1895 had been based upon a strong desire to preserve the fur-seal herds because they constituted an economic asset not only to the United States but to other countries like England, Russia and Japan. The note, therefore, had been based upon "broad humanitarian principles," and no "peculiar benefit or gain" had been sought by the United States. With reference to the fur-seals, it was evident that the "slaughter of the so-called 'American' or 'Alaskan' herd during the past season has been greater than in any season in the history of pelagic sealing." After disputing the figures advanced by the Foreign Office with regard to pelagic sealing in Behring Sea, Olney then stated that there was a

74. Henry W. Elliott to J. Sterling Morton, December 5, 1895, *Olney MS.*
75. Secretary Olney to Mr. Roosevelt, June 18, 1895, *F.R., 1895,* Pt. 1, pp. 647–649.

"startling decrease" in the number of seals on the Pribilof Islands. This was undoubtedly due to the methods of conducting sealing operations. After the sealing fleet of 1894 had left Behring Sea, some 20,000 dead pups were found on the Islands. They had starved to death because their mothers had been killed in pelagic sealing. Because of this type of sealing, the extermination of the fur-seal herds was "imminent." In order to prevent such a catastrophe, Olney suggested that the Governments of Great Britain, Russia, Japan and the United States appoint agents who should examine "carefully into the fur seal fishery" and recommend needful changes in the existing regulations.[76]

After the usual long delay in answering communications from the Department of State, Lord Gough, then British *chargé* in Washington, finally replied in a note that challenged the view that there had been an alarming increase in the pelagic catch of seals in Behring Sea. But Her Majesty's Government was ready to appoint an agent who would act with an American representative in studying the condition of affairs on the Pribilof Islands. It should be clearly understood, however, that the Foreign Office was of the opinion that neither Japan nor Russia had any "interest in the seal fishery on the American side of the North Pacific." For that reason, no agents from those powers should be permitted to take part in the study of conditions on the seal islands.[77]

Secretary Olney could extract little comfort from this latest note of Lord Gough, and the fur-seal question was allowed to slumber quietly while the more important controversy over the Venezuelan boundary engaged most of the attention of the Department of State. But there were certain members of Congress who were resolved to force the hand of the British Government with reference to amending the fur-seal regulations. On January 3, 1896, Mr. Dingley introduced a bill that was equivalent to the measure that had been sponsored by Mr. Wilson in the last session of Congress.[78] It provided for the appointment of a joint commission to study and report upon the fur-seal situation. Pending the completion of this report, the President was authorized to conclude a *modus vivendi* that would conserve seal life in Behring Sea and in the North Pacific. If the British Government would not agree to some working agreement in this regard, the President was then authorized to proceed upon a wholesale program of mercy killings of the seals upon the Pribilof Islands.

This bill easily passed the House on February 25, 1896,[79] and was

76. Secretary Olney to Lord Gough, June 24, 1895, *ibid.*, pp. 649–653.
77. Lord Gough to Secretary Olney, August 19, 1895, *ibid.*, pp. 665–666.
78. *Congressional Record,* 54 Cong., 1 sess., p. 476.
79. *Ibid.*, p. 2125.

favorably reported by the Senate Committee on Foreign Relations.[80] It would have passed the Senate by a large majority, but Secretary Olney believed that this mere display of sentiment on the part of the House of Representatives was sufficient to accelerate the slow processes of the British Foreign Office. He intimated to Senator Frye that any further action on the bill would "greatly embarrass" the conduct of negotiations which he expected soon to initiate. Frye immediately suspended all further efforts, and the matter was left in Olney's hands.[81]

Olney soon discovered that the Foreign Office was not influenced by the threat of mercy killings on the Pribilof Islands, and he was not able to arrange for the appointment of a joint commission to study the fur-seal situation. He was equally unsuccessful with reference to the conclusion of a *modus vivendi* that would temporarily solve his problem. He had failed in his negotiations with Lord Salisbury, and during the last months of his tenure as Secretary of State he handled a few odds and ends of the difficulties that had eluded settlement. In December, 1896 he brought to the attention of the Foreign Office the matter of permitting seal skins landed at British ports to be examined by American inspectors for the purpose of determining their sex. He also referred to the proposal to amend the regulations with reference to the use of firearms by pelagic sealers.[82] Pauncefote replied that permission to American inspectors to examine the seal skins at British ports could be extended only after legislation to that end had been passed by the Canadian Parliament.[83]

On March 4 the McKinley Administration assumed office, and Senator John Sherman was appointed Secretary of State. When Sherman made an inquiry as to the fur-seal situation,[84] he was promptly informed that, on the basis of reports that had been submitted to the British Government, there was "no reason to fear that the seal herd is threatened with early extermination." The Foreign Office, however, favored the appointment of special agents who could carry on "inquiries and observations in the Pribilof Islands," and their reports could be the basis for further action.[85]

There was a striking disparity between the views of the British and American experts on conditions in the fur-seal industry, and on April 8, 1897, Secretary Sherman cabled to the American Embassy in London

80. *Ibid.,* March 4, 1896, pp. 2418–2419.
81. Washington *Evening Star,* February 3, 1905.
82. Secretary Olney to Pauncefote, December 15, 1896, *F.R., 1897,* pp. 258–260.
83. Pauncefote to Secretary Olney, January 16, 1897, *ibid.,* pp. 260–261.
84. Secretary Sherman to Pauncefote, March 12, 1897, *ibid.,* p. 261.
85. Pauncefote to Secretary Sherman, March 23, 1897, *ibid.,* pp. 261–262.

and stressed the President's great concern over the "depleted condition and the prospective early extinction of the Alaskan seal herd." He was convinced that it was "indispensable that immediate steps be taken to stop indiscriminate slaughter through pelagic sealing."[86] On the following day, Secretary Sherman sent a long note to Pauncefote in which he repeated the phrase about the President's deep concern over the depletion of the seal herds in Behring Sea. A report by the distinguished American expert, David Starr Jordan, showed conclusively that there had been a "distinct and steady decrease both in the total number of breeding seals and in the number of breeding cows in the season of 1896 as compared with that of 1895. It further appears from said report conclusively that this diminution has been caused by pelagic sealing." In view of this fact the President urgently requested that a *modus vivendi* be agreed upon, with "equitable provision for the interests involved, suspending all killing for the season of 1897, and that this should be accompanied by an arrangement for a joint conference at an early day, of the powers concerned, to agree upon measures necessary to preserve the seals of the North Pacific Ocean from extermination."[87]

Henry White carried out this instruction in a note to Lord Salisbury, April 10, 1897.[88] Salisbury, then British Foreign Secretary, lost no time in making his reply. It was distinctly argumentative. Lord Salisbury was unable to see how the President could have been alarmed at the statistics given in the report by Dr. Jordan. These data appeared clearly to indicate that there was no "measurable diminution" of the seal herd of 1896 as compared with that of the previous year. The American Government had made many statements in recent years about the dangers to be apprehended from pelagic sealing, but experience had shown that "the fears then expressed were groundless." It should be obvious, therefore, that "further investigation" would be required "before the question of revising the regulations can be considered."[89]

The tone of Lord Salisbury's instruction was unfortunate. He had a way of "talking down" to American statesmen that was distinctly irritating. England was in strong need of American good will, and it was important to calm American feelings that had been so sharply ruffled in the Venezuela boundary controversy during the previous two years. "Hands across the sea" could be a phrase of potent meaning if

86. Secretary Sherman to Henry White, April 8, 1897, *ibid.*, pp. 263–264.

87. Secretary Sherman to Pauncefote, April 9, 1897, *ibid.*, pp. 264–266. See also, *House Rept. No. 295,* 62 Cong., 2 sess.; David Starr Jordan, *The Days of a Man* (Yonkers, 1922), I, 547 ff.

88. Mr. White to Lord Salisbury, April 10, 1897, *F.R., 1897,* pp. 267–268.

89. Lord Salisbury to Pauncefote, April 21, 1897, *ibid.*, pp. 270–272.

the British Foreign Office would make the proper gestures. At a time when Lord Salisbury should have been glad to make concessions to the American Government, he spent his time quibbling over the statistics concerning fur-seal killings in Behring Sea. The financial item was a small one as compared with the intangible assets of American friendship. The failure of Salisbury to see this fact clearly is a measure of the quality of his statesmanship.

On April 27 John Hay, the recently arrived American Ambassador at London, called at the Foreign Office and expressed the "earnest desire of the President" for an immediate, and if possible, a favorable reply to Secretary Sherman's suggestion concerning the cessation of pelagic sealing for the coming season. He was blandly informed that Her Majesty's Government would not be "inclined to make any change in the present regulations."[90]

Secretary Sherman was an old man who was none too vigorous in the spring of 1897, but the attitude of the British Government angered him and he commissioned John W. Foster, special agent in charge of fur-seal negotiations, to write a stinging reply to the notes of the Foreign Office. Foster had no trouble in carrying out the prescription. First of all he adverted to the fact that the report of the British special agent on the fur-seal situation had not been promptly published like the report of the American representative. It seemed, therefore, to suit the

> purpose of Her Majesty's Government to withhold Professor Thompson's report until an opportunity was afforded to examine that of Dr. Jordan, and thus enable the former to pass the latter in review, criticise its statements, and as far as possible minimize its conclusions. It is not pleasant to have to state that the impartial character which it has been the custom to attribute to the reports of naturalists of high standing has been greatly impaired by the apparent subjection of this report to the political exigencies of the situation.

After this sharp shaft at dubious British practices, the American note stated that Dr. Jordan's report clearly revealed that the fur-seal herd was steadily diminishing in size. Even Professor Thompson's report had stated that the "margin of safety is a narrow one," and that with reference to the fur-seals it might already have been "overstepped." In view of such explicit language it was not easy to understand how Lord Salisbury could reconcile "his refusal to entertain the proposals of the President with the interests of his own countrymen."

The American note then showed how Secretaries Gresham and Olney

90. Mr. Hay to Secretary Sherman, April 27, 1897, *ibid.*, pp. 272–273.

had repeatedly asked for some revision of the sealing regulations, but the British Government had "firmly resisted all overtures for even a conference of the Governments concerned for the purpose of considering whether further regulations were required to protect the seals." The indifference with which the Foreign Office treated the numerous appeals of the American Government for prompt action, "illustrates the measure of respect entertained for that august Tribunal." Moreover, the manner in which the British Government had discharged its "police duties under the award is in marked contrast with its appeal for a strict observance of the five years' period of the regulations."

Under Article 6 of the regulations the use of firearms in Behring Sea was prohibited, and to enforce that prohibition it was agreed between the British and American Governments for the year 1894 that sealing vessels might have their arms and ammunition placed under seal. But on May 11, 1895 the British Government gave notice that it would not renew this arrangement. This action had led to "much trouble and inconvenience in connection with the patrol of Bering Sea."

In no respect had the American Government failed to observe the exact terms of the award or

> to accept its recommendations in their true spirit and full effect, even though they have entailed heavy expense and caused great damage to long-established interests of this nation. On the other hand, . . . the British Government has from the beginning and continuously failed to respect the real intent and spirit of the Tribunal or the obligations imposed by it. This is shown by the refusal to extend the regulations to the Asiatic waters; by the failure to put in operation the recommendation for a suspension of the killing of the seals for three, for two, or even for one years; by the neglect to put the regulations in force until long after the first sealing season had been entered on; by the almost total evasion of the patrol duty; by the opposition to suitable measures for the enforcement of the prohibition against firearms; by the omission to enact legislation necessary to secure conviction of the guilty; and by the refusal to allow or provide for an inspection of skins in the interest of an honest observance of the regulations.[91]

Hay had some misgivings about presenting this sharp instruction to Lord Salisbury. Before taking any action in this regard, he had an informal conversation with Joseph Chamberlain, who suggested that the fur-seal difficulty might be adjusted through the payment of a reasonable compensation to Canadian sealers for abandoning pelagic sealing. Hay was impressed with the reasonableness of this suggestion, and

91. Secretary Sherman to Mr. Hay, May 10, 1897, *ibid.*, pp. 280–290.

he cabled to Secretary Sherman to inquire if the instruction of May 10 might be withheld until the arrival in London of John W. Foster, who had been commissioned to take care of everything pertaining to fur-seals.[92]

Foster did not wish to have the instruction delayed in this manner, so he persuaded Secretary Sherman to direct Hay to present it at once.[93] Hay presented the instruction to the Foreign Office "without comment," and awaited the results with some trepidation. On July 1, Secretary Sherman sent another instruction which dealt with the fur-seal question. The British Government was asked whether it would agree "to a Conference of the Powers interested in the protection and preservation of the seals, to be held in Washington in October next."[94]

During his audience with Lord Salisbury, Hay was asked about the agenda of this conference in which Secretary Sherman seemed so interested. Hay replied that he believed the conference "would be merely for consultation as to the best means of preserving seal life in Behring Sea." This seemed a little indefinite, and Lord Salisbury said that before he could give a "definite answer" with reference to participation in this proposed conference, he would have to consult "his Colleagues of the Colonial Office." The matter was "essentially a Colonial one," and that in such circumstances England was "rather the trustee for Canada than the Principal."[95]

On July 15, 1897, the New York *Tribune* published the explosive instruction of May 10. The reaction in the British press was immediate and sharp. To the London *Times* it seemed apparent that the instruction was

> a manifest attempt to fasten upon this country a charge of bad faith, and this attempt is made in offensive language. Whether this was or was not Mr. Sherman's intention when he wrote it is a subjective problem with which we need not concern ourselves. If it was not, he has shown himself singularly unfitted for the delicate and responsible duties of his high office.[96]

In a private letter to President McKinley, Hay gave a brief account of the situation in London. He appeared to have been making real

92. John Hay to Secretary Sherman, May 28, 1897, *Great Britain, Despatches,* CLXXXVIII, MS. Dept of State.

93. Secretary Sherman to John Hay, May 21, 1897, *Great Britain, Instructions,* XXXII, MS. Dept. of State.

94. Secretary Sherman to John Hay, July 1, 1897, *ibid.*

95. John Hay to Secretary Sherman, July 7, 1897, *Great Britain, Despatches,* CLXXXVIII, MS. Dept. of State.

96. July 16, 1897.

headway in the fur-seal matter when this bombshell burst on the diplomatic stage. Immediately, the British Lion began

> standing on his head and lashing his tail all around the lot. . . . I forsaw all this rumpus from the moment I read the despatch. It was an admirable paper in its facts and arguments, but the tone was very unusual. I therefore wired the Department of State asking permission to hold it over a week until Foster arrived. I felt sure I could convince him that a very slight change of phraseology would not weaken but rather strengthen it. I received in reply a peremptory order to present it at once. When Foster arrived he told me that *you* had thought the tone of it rather severe, and that he had said he had meant to have it so. It is certainly not your style—you have the rare gift of being strong and courteous at the same time. . . .
>
> It is not a little curious that neither Lord Salisbury nor Chamberlain have ever mentioned the despatch to me in any of our talks. We have discussed the general subject in as friendly a tone since, as before it was received. Chamberlain did say to Foster that American diplomacy was peculiar: "You will carry it too far some day and get hurt," he added.[97]

Anglo-American relations had become somewhat strained as a result of the publication of the instruction of May 10, but Secretary Sherman did not expect any real trouble with England. In an interview with a correspondent of the New York *World*, he remarked: "I do not expect that any trouble will cloud our relations with Great Britain. . . . England is a great country, but it is not always safe to assume she is ready to follow up every quarrel with blows. She quarrels oftener than she fights, and it would be exceedingly difficult for her to fight us alone about our seal-catching."[98]

It was soon evident that Lord Salisbury had no wish for a serious quarrel with the United States. On July 28 he sent a note to Ambassador Hay in which he expressed his acceptance of the American proposal for a meeting of fur-seal experts at Washington some time in the autumn.[99] This meeting, however, should be confined to representatives of the United States and Great Britain. Neither Japan nor Russia had "experts" who had made special studies of seal life.[100] After a further exchange of notes, the British Government announced the appointment of Professor D'Arcy W. Thompson and Mr. James M. Macoun, of Canada, to serve as the British representatives at the coming confer-

97. John Hay to President McKinley, July 16, 1897, *Confidential, McKinley Papers,* Library of Congress.

98. New York *World,* August 7, 1897.

99. Lord Salisbury to Ambassador Hay, July 28, 1897, *F.R., 1897,* pp. 300–301.

100. Mr. Adams to Secretary Sherman, September 22, 1897, *ibid.,* p. 303.

ence.[101] After receiving this news, Secretary Sherman hastened to appoint David Starr Jordan and Charles S. Hamlin as the American experts on seal life.[102] The conference was to convene in Washington in November.

Ambassador Hay was glad to have the "Bering Sea business" disposed of "for the time being." He had been "amazed" at the solid way in which the press of England had "stood together around Lord Salisbury and steadily refused to print the truth."[103] In a similar key, Hay wrote to John W. Foster concerning the fur-seal situation. He had received the great surprise of his life when the British Government objected to entering a conference of seal experts if any Russian or Japanese representatives were present. He had always thought of British diplomacy as overbearing and pig-headed, but he had never imagined it "was tricky and tortuous."[104]

After the British and American fur-seal experts had assembled in Washington and had discussed the problem of the fur-seals, they finally signed a joint statement in which it was frankly admitted that the seal herds had declined since 1884 "at a rate varying from year to year." The methods of driving and killing that were practiced on the Pribilof Islands were free from criticism, and it should also be noted that the "pelagic industry" was being conducted in "an orderly manner and in a spirit of acquiescence in the limitations imposed by the law." But pelagic sealing did involve the slaughter of males and females alike, and it was manifest that the "take of females in recent years has been so far in excess of the natural increment as to lead to a reduction of the herd." It should be kept in mind, however, that the diminution of the seal herd was still "far from a stage which involves or threatens the actual extermination of the species so long as it is protected in its haunts on land." It was not possible, during the "continuance of the conservative methods at present in force upon the islands, with the further safeguard of the protected zone at sea, that any pelagic killings should accomplish this final end."[105]

From the accounts that appeared in the American press it appeared to Mr. Hay that the conference of seal experts in Washington was a "most successful meeting." He doubted if "anything" could save the

101. Mr. Adams to Secretary Sherman, October 15, 1897, *ibid.,* pp. 310–311.

102. Secretary Sherman to Mr. Adams, October 20, 1897, *ibid.,* pp. 311.

103. John Hay to Henry White, October 16, 1897, *White MS.*

104. John Hay to John W. Foster, October 18, 1897, *Foster MS.*

105. "Joint Statement respecting the fur-seal herd frequenting the Pribilof Islands in Bering Sea," *F.R., 1897,* pp. 314–318.

seals, but the joint statement fixed the responsibility for the diminution of the seals "so plainly that a fool ought to see it."[106]

Secretary Sherman was certain that the conclusions of the seal experts substantially confirmed "the facts contended for by the Government of the United States since the regulations of the Paris Tribunal went into operation," and he became increasingly anxious to protect the seal herds through some form of international agreement.[107] Through the efforts of John W. Foster, the Department of State was able to arrange for a conference in Washington between the representatives of Japan, Russia and the United States. The conference held meetings from October 23 to November 6. After a "careful and detailed examination" of all the facts concerning seal life in the North Pacific, the delegates reached the unanimous conclusion that under existing regulations the fur-seal and sea-otter were "threatened with extinction," and that "an international agreement of all the interested powers is necessary for their adequate protection." On November 6, 1897 a convention was signed which prohibited the citizens of the high contracting parties from killing seals in all the waters of the North Pacific Ocean, outside of territorial limits, for the period of one year. But this treaty was to take effect only in the event that the British Government became a party to it.[108]

Secretary Sherman sent this convention to London with instructions that the British Government be urged to adhere to it with all convenient speed. Lord Salisbury invoked the usual formula that he would have to consult "his Colleagues and especially the Colonial Department."[109] Some weeks later he informed Mr. Hay that the Foreign Office was of the opinion that "no useful purpose could be served" by British adhesion to the fur-seal treaty.[110] The controversy concerning seals was essentially a matter between Great Britain and the United States; too many international cooks might spoil the diplomatic broth that had long been brewing.

Hay was not surprised at the result of these diplomatic overtures. He was certain that the Canadians were at the root of the trouble. The Foreign Office had frankly avowed its "slavery to Canada," and al-

106. John Hay to John W. Foster, November 20, 1897, *Foster MS.*

107. Secretary Sherman to Hay, *F.R., 1897,* pp. 319–320.

108. Secretary Sherman to John Hay, November 29, 1897, *Great Britain, Instructions,* XXXII, MS. Dept. of State.

109. John Hay to Secretary Sherman, December 10, 1897, *Great Britain, Despatches,* CXC, MS. Dept. of State.

110. Lord Salisbury to John Hay, December 23, 1897, *Pamphlets Relating to the Canadian-American Joint High Commission, 1898, Fur Seals,* State Dept., pp. 13 ff.

though this dependence was resented, nothing was ever done to change the situation. In a private conversation with Hay, Lord Salisbury had openly complained of Canadian coquetry. But even though Canada would not listen to reason, England would not dare "to cross her."[111]

Despite further pressure from the Department of State with reference to British adhesion to the treaty of November 6, 1897, the Foreign Office refused to accede to American desires. To John Hay it was apparent that British statesmen could not act "independently of Canada, and Canada will do nothing unless she is bought off." The American Government was "on the right track in acting on our own responsibility, inside our own rights." There would be some "squealing on the part of the ladies, but there is some friction in all legal processes."[112]

On January 12, 1898, Lord Salisbury had written a note to John Hay in which he based his refusal to sign the treaty of November 6, 1897, upon the grounds that certain negotiations were then being carried on between Canadian and American representatives concerning the fur-seals, and that the convention of November 6 made no provision for the restriction of the killing of seals on the Pribilof Islands. In reply, Hay definitely stated that there were "no negotiations whatever . . . in progress between the Government of the United States and that of Canada." With reference to the restriction of the killing of seals on the Pribilof Islands, the President would "be glad to consider the matter from that point of view."[113] In response to this overture, Lord Salisbury merely indicated that "the offer to suspend the killing of seals on the Pribiloff Islands . . . would not suffice to remove the grounds upon which Her Majesty's Government have declined to accede to the Convention."[114]

Senator Lodge regarded this British attitude concerning the fur-seals as "utterly indefensible." England should make Canada "behave herself." If she did not wish to take such action, she should then "decline responsibility and leave us to settle the matter with Canada."[115]

The Department of State was not unduly discouraged by this re-

111. John Hay to John W. Foster, December 27, 1897, *Foster MS.*

112. John Hay to John W. Foster, January 17, 1898, *ibid.* In this letter Hay had particular reference to the fact that on December 29, 1897, the President had approved a law that prohibited American citizens from engaging in pelagic sealing and prohibiting the importation of fur-seal skins taken in the waters of the North Pacific or Behring Sea.

113. John Hay to Lord Salisbury, January 17, 1898, enclosed in Hay to Secretary Sherman, January 17, 1898, *Great Britain, Despatches,* CXC, MS. Dept. of State.

114. Lord Salisbury to Henry White, February 11, 1898, enclosed in White to Secretary Sherman, February 15, 1898, *ibid.*

115. Senator Lodge to Henry White, January 31, 1898, *White MS.*

fusal on the part of the British Government to become a party to the convention of November 6, 1897. On March 1, 1898, Sir Julian Pauncefote was asked about the attitude of the Foreign Office towards agreeing to a revision of the fur-seal regulations prescribed under the award of the Behring Sea Arbitration Tribunal. On March 26 he informed Secretary Sherman that he had just received a cablegram from Lord Salisbury "to the effect that Her Majesty's Government agree to a discussion for the revision of the Behring Sea regulations, and that the Canadian Minister of Marine will be associated with me for the purpose."[116]

On May 25, 1898, Sir Julian Pauncefote and Sir Louis H. Davies presented themselves at the Department of State, where they were met by John W. Foster and John A. Kasson. After a series of conferences on the more outstanding questions in Canadian-American relations including that of the fur-seals, an agreement was signed which outlined the agenda for a Joint High Commission which was to meet in Quebec on August 23, 1898. The first article in this agenda dealt with "the questions in respect to the fur seals in Bering Sea and the waters of the North Pacific Ocean."[117]

The Joint High Commission convened in Quebec on August 23, 1898, and further meetings were held in that city until October 10 when an adjournment was called. The meetings were resumed in Washington on November 9, and one of the outstanding questions that came up for discussion was the old one concerning the preservation of the fur-seals.

The American commissioners were supplied with a memorandum that embodied the views of the Department of State. Attention was directed to the long-continued efforts of the American Government to devise measures for the protection of the fur-seals, and reference was made to the enactment of the law of December 29, 1897 which prohibited American citizens from engaging in pelagic sealing, and which also prohibited the importation of fur-seal skins taken in the waters of Behring Sea or in the North Pacific. It was evident that pelagic sealing was seriously destructive of seal life, and should be stopped.[118]

The British commissioners were willing to consider the matter of prohibiting pelagic sealing under two conditions. There must be "fair and equitable compensation to the owners of sealing vessels and to

116. Sir Julian Pauncefote to Secretary Sherman, March 26, 1898, *Kasson Papers,* MS. Dept. of State.

117. Malloy, *Treaties and Conventions, etc.,* I, 770–773.

118. *Pamphlets Relating to the Canadian-American Joint High Commission, Fur Seals, 1898,* State Dept., pp. 1–5.

others engaged in the industry," and there must be "some adequate concession in consideration of Great Britain giving up her national right and undertaking to enforce the prohibition." The American point of view was that the sealing industry, under the regulations prescribed by the Paris Tribunal, could not continue operations upon a profitable basis. The British viewpoint was decidedly different. The seal herds were not diminishing at the rate the Americans claimed, and the industry could be carried on indefinitely at a reasonable profit. Compensation for the prohibition of pelagic sealing would have to be based, at least partly, upon this contention.

In a letter to Senator Fairbanks, Lord Herschell strongly voiced the Canadian arguments. The British commissioners had been constantly reminded that they would have to make concessions in order to arrive at any agreement that would be accepted by the American Senate. It should be brought to the notice of the American commissioners that Canadian public opinion was much averse to giving up pelagic sealing, and concessions should be made on both sides. The chief obstacle to an agreement was the proposal that the sealers should retain their vessels. But this would mean that Canadian sealers would have a large number of boats on hand which they could not profitably use or sell. Compensation should be allowed for these vessels which could be disposed of only at a mere fraction of their cost.

With reference to the compensation that should be awarded to Great Britain for the surrender of a national right, Lord Herschell thought that some arrangement might be agreed upon whereby the United States would pay to Canada "a certain proportion of the receipts derived from the seals taken on land."[119]

In his reply to this overture from Lord Herschell, Senator Fairbanks admitted that Great Britain had a national right to take fur-seals in Behring Sea. Some compensation should be given for the relinquishment of this right, but this sum should be merely nominal because of the doubtful future of the sealing industry. With reference to awarding compensation to those persons engaged in sealing operations, Fairbanks proposed that they should be

> paid for the fair present value of their vessels in commission and those out of commission because of the unprofitable nature of the industry—in short we not only propose to purchase the entire fleet at its present value, pay one year's profits to the owners, one year's wages to the captains, etc., but leave the fleet in the hands of the owners. As you are aware, fully forty per cent.

119. Lord Herschell to Senator Fairbanks, December 21, 1898, *Confidential, Alaska Boundary Papers,* MS. Dept. of State.

of the fleet has been out of commission during several years past. Why? Obviously because there was and is no reasonable or profitable demand for it. With the continued diminution of the seal herd, is it not fair to presume, not only that the vessels not in commission will continue inactive, but that the number commissioned will diminish?

With reference to granting to Great Britain a certain percentage of the receipts derived from the seals killed on the islands, Fairbanks was happy to say that this proposal seemed to offer "a solution compatible with the mutual interests of the two countries."[120]

But any such arrangements as contemplated by Lord Herschell and Senator Fairbanks were dependent upon Canadian consent. This would not be easy to secure. On January 25, 1899, David Mills, the Canadian Minister of Justice, wrote to Prime Minister Laurier and warned him that the "view generally prevailing among our best-informed people" is that "we ought not to abandon a sovereign right" like pelagic sealing.[121]

Laurier was not greatly disturbed by this warning, and the British commissioners indicated their willingness to discuss the question of compensation for the abandonment of pelagic sealing. Senator Fairbanks, thereupon, made an offer of $500,000 for the sealing fleet, and in addition, to pay seven and one-half per cent of the "gross annual receipts derived by the United States from the sealing industry as compensation for the national interest." After some further discussion, agreement was reached on the basis of a payment of $600,000 for the sealing fleet, and for the surrender of the British national right to pelagic sealing there would be an allocation to the British Government of twenty-five per cent of the gross receipts on all skins taken in excess of 20,000 annually.[122]

With agreement practically in sight with reference to the fur-seal question, the Joint High Commission reached a deadlock in connection with the Alaska boundary controversy. Further discussion proved useless, so the commission adjourned on February 20, 1899, with no real accomplishment to its credit. With regard to the consequences of this adjournment, John W. Foster remarks: "We were so near an agreement on the fur-seal question, it seems too bad that such a useful herd of animals should be gradually destroyed because of a failure to agree about the ownership of some glaciers."[123]

120. Senator Fairbanks to Lord Herschell, December 24, 1898, *Alaska Boundary Papers,* MS. Dept. of State.

121. David Mills to Sir Wilfrid Laurier, January 25, 1899, *Laurier Papers,* P.A.C.

122. Senator Fairbanks to Secretary Hay, March 25, 1899, *Alaska Boundary Papers,* MS. Dept of State.

123. Foster, *Diplomatic Memoirs,* II, 189.

The Alaskan boundary controversy occupied a good deal of the attention of Secretary Hay during the years from 1900 to 1903, but he still found time to give some consideration to the question of fur-seal preservation. On April 28, 1900, Henry W. Elliott wrote to Hay and requested authorization to visit the seal islands again and investigate conditions thereon. Hay was willing to have Elliott make this investigation if Congress would appropriate the necessary funds. Secretary Gage seemed to favor this appropriation, and Senator Foraker (May 7, 1900) introduced an amendment to the Sundry Civil Bill providing $15,000 for the expenses of a "new examination into the condition of affairs on the Seal Islands of Alaska."[124] But suddenly, pressure was exerted upon the Senate to defeat this amendment, and Elliott, realizing that the lessees of the Pribilof Islands had strong Congressional backing, ceased for a while to carry on the fight in favor of new fur-seal regulations.[125]

In 1903 the matter of fur-seal conservation once more came before Congress, and on February 2 a bill (H.R. 13,387) with far-reaching provisions was passed by the House of Representatives.[126] In the Senate, strong opposition developed against this proposed legislation, and Senator Fairbanks requested the Committee on Foreign Relations to postpone any action upon it.[127] The bill was buried in a Senate Committee pigeonhole, and the fur-seal situation remained as confused as ever.

But there were certain members of the Senate who were determined to get some accurate information with regard to the condition of affairs on the Pribilof Islands. In the summer of 1903 they paid a visit to these islands and discovered the shameful conditions to which Mr. Elliott had referred. According to Mr. Elliott himself, the Senators discovered the "lessees killing female seals and yearlings in violation of the law: indeed they found that the work of the lessees was more injurious to the life of the fur seal rookeries than was that of the pelagic hunters."[128]

124. *Congressional Record,* 56 Cong., 1 sess., p. 5209.

125. See letter from Henry W. Elliott to Representative J. A. Beidler, December 3, 1901, *Congressional Record,* 57 Cong., 2 sess., pp. 1597–1606. In a memorandum prepared for Senator Spooner, January 19, 1904, Elliott discussed the actions of Secretary Gage and Senator Fairbanks relative to this appropriation. In explaining their stand, he remarked: "There is only one reply that can be made. . . . They did so because the lessees did not want the Truth as to the desperate and unlawful character of their work to be made known." *Spooner MS.*

126. *Congressional Record,* 57 Cong., 2 sess., p. 1616.

127. Elliott *Memorandum,* January 19, 1904, *Spooner MS.*

128. Henry W. Elliott to Senator Spooner, January 19, 1904, *ibid.*

It would appear that Secretary Hay was entirely in sympathy with the attitude taken by Mr. Elliott,[129] and on July 28 he wrote to Ambassador Choate and instructed him to act in concert with Sir Michael Herbert in an effort to arrive at some agreement in the matter of prohibiting pelagic sealing.[130] Sir Michael's death intervened before these negotiations could be commenced, but Choate talked the matter over with Lord Lansdowne, who thought it was necessary to consult Canada before any action could be taken. Lansdowne agreed, however, that pelagic sealing had been at least partly responsible for the starvation of some 16,000 seal pups on the Pribilof Islands.[131]

Hay was glad that Lansdowne was friendly to the idea of resuming negotiations about the fur-seals, and he stressed the importance of early action. The "matter of the extermination of the seals" was "becoming a serious one, and if the species is to be saved, there ought to be no time lost."[132] But the British would not be pushed into any premature action. The Canadians were still angry over the adverse decision in the Alaskan boundary controversy, and the time was not opportune to discuss fur-seal conservation. In a personal letter to Secretary Hay, November 18, 1903, Choate reported that no further action had been taken with reference to the fur-seals. In the "present state of irritation in the Canadian mind, Lord Lansdowne evidently shrinks from acting just now." Choate himself could not see how the seals could be preserved from extinction "unless with the co-operation of all the nations whose subjects engage in seal fishing. Their numbers are now so reduced that the fishermen of a single nation could exhaust what remain."[133]

On November 25, Choate paid a visit to the Foreign Office and inquired about the possibility of initiating negotiations concerning the fur-seals. Lord Lansdowne frankly informed him that the Foreign Office thought "it wise to give Canada a little more time" to get over the resentment that still nestled in Canadian minds with regard to the Alaska decision. It was apparent, thought Choate, that it would be some time before he could report any progress in the fur-seal matter.[134]

In January, 1904, new pressure developed in favor of legislation to protect the fur-seals from pelagic sealing and from wasteful slaughter

129. See sworn statement made by Mr. Elliott on May 2, 1912, and deposited in the *Gresham Papers* in the Library of Congress.

130. Secretary Hay to Choate, July 28, 1903, *Great Britain, Instructions,* XXXIV, MS. Dept. of State.

131. Choate to Secretary Hay, October 9, 1903, *Choate MS.*

132. Secretary Hay to Choate, October 19, 1903, *ibid.*

133. Choate to Secretary Hay, November 18, 1903, *Choate Letter Book,* II, *Choate MS.*

134. Choate to Secretary Hay, November 25, 1903, *Personal and Confidential, ibid.*

on the Pribilof Islands. On January 13, the indefatigable Henry W. Elliott wrote to Senator Spooner with reference to the bill (S. 3355) that had just been introduced by Senator Dillingham.[135] He warmly urged the speedy passage of this "imperative measure which alone can save the fur seal species of Alaska from swift, impending extermination." The season for pelagic sealing would begin in February, and this meant that something would have to be done at once.[136]

On February 2, Mr. Elliott renewed his pressure upon Senator Spooner in favor of the Dillingham bill,[137] and on February 11 he emphasized the importance of the section in that bill which provided that if pelagic sealing were not prohibited through international agreement, the seals on the Pribilof Islands should be wiped out through mercy killings under American control. In the graphic phraseology of Mr. Elliott,

> if the Canadian hunter insists upon our supplying him, year after year, with this highly organized life to indecently and cruelly kill at sea, supplemented with the unspeakable shame of starving tens and tens of thousands of hapless young . . . on the islands annually—if he insists on this, then in the name of mercy . . . let us . . . put these animals *at once* out of pain, . . . while we save enough of them to preserve the species.[138]

This threat contained in the Dillingham bill had an immediate effect upon Sir Mortimer Durand, the British Ambassador, who had some long conferences with Elliott.[139] He was ready to meet Mr. Elliott's

135. The Dillingham bill was introduced on January 12, 1904, *Congressional Record,* 58 Cong., 2 sess., p. 613. This bill would prevent the excessive slaughter of male seals on the Pribilof Islands, and it laid the basis for the settlement of the fur-seal dispute through international adjustment. It also provided for mercy killings of seals on the islands if the British Government refused to agree to amendments to the existing regulations.

136. Henry W. Elliott to Senator Spooner, January 13, 1904, *Spooner MS.*

137. Henry W. Elliott to Senator Spooner, February 2, 1904, *ibid.* See also the data compiled by Elliott in his letter to Spooner, January 26, 1904.

138. Henry W. Elliott to Senator Spooner, February 11, 1904, *ibid.*

139. In a long letter to Secretary Hay, February 16, 1904, Elliott discussed his conferences with Sir Mortimer Durand, and recorded his impressions of his attitude: "Yesterday and today I have had extended and free conferences with the British Ambassador. I have laid the whole situation . . . of the fur seal question before him, honestly, frankly, and in detail. I have showed him how he could so act in the premises as to be able to transfer the Canadian hunters from Bering Sea into the North Pacific, where at any season of the year they cannot do violence to decency by killing 'seals in milk,' with the added indecency of starving thousands and tens of thousands of helpless young animals to death on the islands of their birth. . . . All that he has got to do in the premises is to insist that the months of *August* and *September,* now open to pelagic sealing, shall be closed, and, in lieu therefore, that the months of *May* and *June,* now closed, *shall be open.* This brings the entire year's work of the pelagic hunter into the North Pacific. . . .

"I explained the pending fur seal bill to him, killing clause and all: That if the

suggestions "more than half-way."[140] On February 24, at a hearing before the Senate Committee on Foreign Relations, Senators Dillingham and Nelson spoke in favor of the pending Dillingham bill, and there seemed little doubt that this measure would compel the British Government to take effective action to protect the seals.[141] But President Roosevelt thought that such tactics were not necessary, and the situation of 1896 was repeated. On March 16, 1904, action on the Dillingham bill was indefinitely postponed, and Senator Foraker introduced Senate Joint Resolution 61 as a substitute.[142] This made provision for the opening of negotiations between England and the United States for the revision of the fur-seal regulations. When this revision was completed, an attempt would then be made to conclude a four power pact that would bind Japan, Russia, Great Britain and the United States to carry out a realistic program of seal conservation.

The Senate promptly passed this joint resolution (March 16). The House took similar action on April 2,[143] and the resolution was signed by the President on April 8, 1904. But Secretary Hay soon discovered that without the threat of mercy killings on the Pribilof Islands, the British Government could not be induced to take any real interest in the amendment of the fur-seal regulations. Angered by British procrastination, Dillingham had Senator Redfield Proctor introduce in the Senate, on January 14, 1905, a new resolution (S.R. 90) that once more revived the question of the slaughter of the seals on the Pribilof Islands if the Foreign Office would not agree to amend the regulations.[144]

As soon as this resolution came before the Senate Committee on For-

Canadians insisted on our breeding mother seals for them to cruelly kill at sea, . . . then it became our duty and act of mercy . . . to these hapless creatures, for us to put them out of pain *at once*. . . . Sir Mortimer assented to the plain sense of this. I told him that we were going to set aside our butchers 'at once and indefinitely': That the removal of his butchers from Bering Sea was only the first step to their ultimate removal from the entire field. That his government would come to see the need and fitness of it, and would unite with us in no distant future to prevent all sea-killing of fur seals, but I knew that this could not be done at once. . . .

"Sir Mortimer understands that action on his part must be prompt, and I believe that he is ready to take it. He has met me more than halfway: I am impressed by the determination he has expressed to have that wretched shambles in Bering Sea abolished before the season of 1904 opens." *Ibid.*

140. In a letter to Senator Spooner, February 19, 1904, Elliott tells of his conferences with Sir Mortimer Durand (with the approval of Secretary Hay), and speaks of the Ambassador's "hearty sympathy" with the viewpoint that pelagic sealing should be prohibited. *Ibid.*

141. Elliott to Senator Spooner, February 26, 1904, *ibid.*

142. *Congressional Record,* 58 Cong., 2 sess., p. 3337.

143. *Ibid.*, p. 4202. See also, *House Rept. No. 2076,* 58 Cong., 2 sess., and *Senate Doc. No. 149,* 58 Cong., 3 sess.

144. *Congressional Record,* 58 Cong., 3 sess., p. 828.

eign Relations, Elliott re-opened his correspondence with Senator Spooner, the chairman of this committee. He pressed for immediate action, and he informed Spooner that the "Canadian butchers are now assuring Sir Wilfrid Laurier that no legislation by the United States Congress will be passed which interferes with them: that they control it through friends in Washington. I have the proof of this statement."[145]

But despite all the efforts of Mr. Elliott, the resolution failed to pass the Senate, and the President was no longer disturbed by these legislative attempts to influence the conduct of American foreign relations. In April, 1906, Secretary Root submitted to Sir Mortimer Durand the *projet* of a treaty which would prohibit pelagic sealing,[146] but nothing came of this overture. There were many factors, however, that were preparing the way for a final settlement of this fur-seal controversy. After 1900, Japanese pelagic sealers began to make their appearance in the North Pacific. They were not bound by the regulations of the Paris Tribunal, and therefore, could ignore the close season and the sixty-mile zone of protection around the seal islands. By using firearms in the open sea outside the three-mile limit, they were able to kill large numbers of seals in Behring Sea, and once more the seal herds were threatened with destruction.[147]

As Japanese sealers began to crowd the Canadians out of the picture in Behring Sea, our relations with Japan were seriously disturbed by certain incidents that arose. Not content to observe the three-mile limit, Japanese poachers pursued the seals close to the shores of the Pribilof Islands. Emboldened by their success in these maneuvers, they next landed on the islands (July 16 and 17, 1906) and began to butcher the seals on the rookeries. They were promptly fired upon by American officials, several of the poachers were killed, and twelve of them were taken prisoner.[148]

President Roosevelt was so stirred up by this poaching exploit that he went all the way back to the Dingley Bill of 1895, and suggested to Congress in his annual message (Dec. 3, 1906) the possibility of exterminating the seals on the Pribilof Islands through mercy killings

145. Henry W. Elliott to Senator Spooner, January 17, 1905, *Spooner MS.*

146. Secretary Root to Sir Mortimer Durand, April 18, 1906, *Great Britain, Notes to,* XXVII, MS. Dept. of State.

147. *House Doc. No. 93,* 62 Cong., 1 sess., pp. 276, 503, 605, 783, 858, 1083; *Report of the Secretary of Commerce and Labor,* 1905, p. 43; *ibid.,* 1908, p. 78; *ibid.,* 1909, p. 742.

148. Thomas A. Bailey, "The North Pacific Sealing Convention of 1911," *Pacific Historical Review,* IV, 5. See also, *Report of the Secretary of Commerce and Labor,* 1906, p. 34.

rather than have them butchered by Japanese sealers in the open sea.[149] The situation was a dangerous one that might easily lead to open conflict with Japan. Fortunately, however, the Japanese Government had secured, as one of the fruits of the Russo-Japanese War, control over the seal herd on Robben Island.[150] This might be increased to large numbers through careful conservation, and this possibility led the Japanese Government to become more interested in an international agreement that would preserve the seal herds from extermination. In August, 1908, word came to the Department of State that a Russian proposal to abolish pelagic sealing along the Asiatic coast was being seriously considered by the Japanese Government.[151] The spirit of concession was in the air.

In November, 1908, Secretary Root made a proposal to the British Foreign Office which looked towards the abolition of pelagic sealing by Canadian vessels. As compensation for the relinquishment of this right, Canada would share in the revenues derived from the slaughter of seals on the Pribilof Islands.[152] James Bryce, the British Ambassador at Washington, informed Earl Grey, the Governor-General of Canada, that this offer was the most generous that could be expected.[153] When this American overture brought no results, Secretary Root addressed on January 21, 1909, an identic note to the ambassadors of Japan, Russia and Great Britain proposing a conference or joint commission to consider some course of action for the preservation of the fur-seals.[154]

Russia and Japan acceded to this proposal, but Great Britain, still deferring to certain Canadian interests, held aloof. On July 27, 1909, Earl Grey pointed out to Sir Wilfrid Laurier the fact that for three years the American Government had been making overtures that had received no Canadian response. The time had arrived for some action by the Ottawa Government.[155] On September 9, and on November 13, Grey again attempted to exert pressure upon Laurier with reference to making some effort to work with the American Government in an attempt to settle the fur-seal controversy.[156]

149. *Congressional Record,* 59 Cong., 2 sess., p. 34.

150. *Japan Mail,* August 18, 1908. 151. Bailey, *op. cit.,* p. 8.

152. Callahan, *American Foreign Policy in Canadian Relations,* p. 525.

153. James Bryce to Earl Grey, December 31, 1908, *Laurier Papers, Governor-General's Correspondence,* pp. 5–7, P.A.C.

154. Bailey, *op. cit.,* p. 8.

155. Earl Grey to Sir Wilfrid Laurier, July 27, 1909, *Laurier Papers, Governor-General's Correspondence,* pp. 444–448, P.A.C.

156. Earl Grey to Sir Wilfrid Laurier, September 9, and November 13, 1909, *ibid.,* pp. 487–509, 654–656.

In London, Ambassador Reid took the matter up with Sir Edward Grey, the British Foreign Secretary, and indicated that Canada's interest in the fur-seal industry was merely that "of ownership by people at Victoria of a fleet of worn out and unprofitable sealers engaged in the wasteful business of pelagic sealing." It was distinctly unwise, thought Mr. Reid, for the British Government to permit this "trivial Canadian interest" to prolong a state of affairs that meant for the United States, Japan and Russia the destruction of the seal herds.[157]

On April 7, 1910, James Bryce, British Ambassador in Washington, wrote to Lord Grey and stressed the importance of early action with regard to the fur-seal question.[158] Grey passed this word on to Laurier with the following remark: "I know how pressed you are, but I do not think it would take much time in Council to decide the answer which should be sent to Washington."[159]

Canada was in no hurry to send a favorable answer to Washington in the matter of the fur-seals, and it was not until February 7, 1911, that the long-sought-for treaty was signed between the United States and Great Britain. Under its terms pelagic sealing in Behring Sea and in the North Pacific Ocean north of the thirty-fifth degree of north latitude and east of the one hundred and eightieth meridian was prohibited. In return for this concession, the United States agreed to deliver to an authorized agent of the Canadian Government one fifth "in number and in value of the total number of sealskins taken annually upon the Pribilof Islands, or any other islands . . . subject to the jurisdiction of the United States." It was further agreed that the United States should pay to Great Britain the sum of $200,000 as an advance payment in lieu of such "number of fur-seal skins, to which Great Britain would be entitled under the provisions of this treaty, as would be equivalent to that amount reckoned at their market value at London at the date of delivery."[160]

But this treaty was not to go into effect until an international agreement was concluded and ratified by the Governments of the United States, Great Britain, Japan and Russia. In order to prepare the way for the signature of this convention, Secretary Knox called a conference at Washington on May 5, 1911, with delegates present from the four powers interested in seal protection. After the sessions had lasted

157. Bailey, *op. cit.*, p. 9.

158. James Bryce to Earl Grey, April 7, 1910, *Laurier Papers, Governor-General's Correspondence*, pp. 186–189, P.A.C.

159. Earl Grey to Sir Wilfrid Laurier, April 18, 1910, *ibid.*, pp. 214–215.

160. Malloy, *Treaties, Conventions, etc., between the United States of America and Other Powers, 1910–1923*, III, 2629–2632.

some five weeks, a deadlock was reached with regard to the amount of compensation that should be paid to Japan for giving up pelagic sealing. President Taft took the extraordinary step of cabling an appeal to the Emperor of Japan to accept an arrangement that would give his government 15 per cent of the sealskins obtained each year on the Pribilof Islands. The Emperor gave his approval to this proposal, and on July 7, 1911, a convention was signed by the representatives of the four powers. Pelagic sealing was prohibited, and each nation was given the right to deal independently with the matter of killings on land. To compensate the pelagic sealing interests that were destroyed by the terms of this convention, the United States agreed to give Great Britain 15 per cent of the sealskins secured annually on the Pribilof Islands. A similar share was given to Japan. In order to give some immediate compensation to the pelagic sealers, the United States agreed to pay to Great Britain and to Japan alike the sum of $200,000, these cash disbursements to be credited in lieu of the sealskins that were due. The treaty was to remain in force for fifteen years, and as long thereafter as it should remain undenounced by any one or more of the signatory powers.[161]

It is apparent that Canada had been able to drive a hard bargain in the matter of the fur-seals, and in Russia it was suspected that President Taft was willing to make these concessions in order to prepare the basis for reciprocity negotiations. There is little doubt that Canada secured a nice diplomatic plum in the settlement of July 7, 1911, but it does not appear that this confection made Canadians forget their resentment over the decision of the Alaska Boundary Tribunal. In later years the rich returns from their astute arrangement of 1911 have sweetened Canadian tempers and have justified their statesmen,[162] but this happy situation was not anticipated by Canadians who voted on the issue of reciprocity. The factors that determined the outcome of that issue will be given extended consideration in the next two chapters.

161. *Ibid.*, pp. 2966–2972. Under the terms of this convention, Russia agreed to surrender to Canada annually 15 per cent of all the skins obtained from the Commander Islands, and 15 per cent to Japan. Japan, in turn, assigned 10 per cent of the skins taken from her herds to each of the other three powers.

162. After the abolition of pelagic sealing, as was prophesied by American scientists and statesmen, the seal herds grew rapidly in numbers. In 1911 the herd on the Pribilof Islands was estimated at 100,000; in 1932 it had increased to 1,219,000. In 1934 Canada and Japan each received $1,085,971.01 as their share of the receipts derived from the killings of seals on the Pribilof Islands. See Bailey, *op. cit.*, p. 13.

CHAPTER XIII

THE MOVEMENT FOR COMMERCIAL UNION

American interest in the establishment of a system of commercial reciprocity with the British North American colonies may be traced back to the early years of the American Republic. According to Henry Clay, the American founding fathers had always shown a readiness to apply to these British possessions the principles of a "fair reciprocity and equal competition."[1] But as Secretary of State, Clay had not been able to discover any inclination on the part of Canadians to seek closer commercial contacts with the United States. They had been quite content with the ample markets open to their produce in the Mother Country, and through tariff preferences given to colonial goods, they were insured against sharp competition from the outside world. In 1840 there were more than eighty articles in the British tariff schedules upon which differential duties were levied in favor of the produce of the colonies. Although the Peel tariff of 1842 increased in a significant manner this system of preferences, it reduced the differential duties on colonial lumber, and in 1845 a further reduction went into effect.[2] But these were small holes in a high tariff wall; colonial preference was still securely established and Canadian business men faced the future with confidence.

In the middle decades of the nineteenth century there were several factors that began to upset this imperial equilibrium. England was becoming the workshop of the world. Her commerce was expanding on all the seven seas, and she had a surplus of capital that sought investment in lands outside the British Empire.[3] British statesmen began to think in world terms rather than in terms of empire. Interest in colonies rapidly waned, and anti-imperialism became one of the chief articles in the political creed of a large number of British leaders.[4]

1. Secretary Clay to Mr. Vaughan, October 11, 1826, *Senate Ex. Doc. No. 23,* 31 Cong., 2 sess., p. 6.

2. A. R. M. Lower, *The North American Assault on the Canadian Forest* (New Haven, 1938), pp. 103–105; Bernard Holland, *The Fall of Protection* (London, 1913), pp. 104 ff.; Robert L. Schuyler, "British Imperial Preference and Sir Robert Peel," *Political Science Quarterly,* XXXII (1917), 429–449.

3. Leland H. Jenks, *The Migration of British Capital to 1875* (New York, 1927), chaps. vi–xi.

4. C. A. Bodelson, *Studies in Mid-Victorian Imperialism* (London, 1924); R. L. Schuyler, "The Recall of the Legions," *American Historical Review,* XXVI (1920–1921), 18–36; Albert C. Cooke, "Empire Unity and Colonial Nationalism, 1884–1911," *Rept. of Canadian Historical Association, 1939,* pp. 77–79.

As English industrial evolution progressed, there was a constantly increasing need for cheaper food and cheaper raw materials: the old imperial economy with its system of colonial preferences was hopelessly out of date. This fact was dramatized by the bad harvest of 1845–1846, and Sir Robert Peel was compelled to lead his famous attack upon the ancient Corn Laws. The repeal of these laws had serious implications for Canada. Thanks to the differential duties levied in favor of colonial produce, Canadian grain had been assured of a good English market; and Canadian timber had been sold for high prices in English ports. To Canadian exporters, the success of the Peel program meant economic ruin unless an equivalent market in the United States could be secured. Commercial reciprocity with their southern neighbor appeared to many Canadians as the only means of escaping impending ruin.[5]

There were additional factors that helped to accelerate this Canadian drive towards the goal of reciprocity. Since the early decades of the nineteenth century, Canadian *entrepreneurs* had been engaged in the tremendous task of making the St. Lawrence River a great commercial highway that would afford cheap transportation facilities for the farmers who shipped their surplus crops to England. A chain of canals had been built at great expense, and it was ardently hoped that the "mighty trade of the West" would pass along these waterways and quickly repay the cost of construction.[6] But the repeal of colonial preferences in the English tariff would cause a sharp decline in the export trade, and tolls on the canals would shrink to an insignificant figure. How could the huge canal debt be paid?

This question was asked with increasing emphasis when the American Government in 1845–1846 enacted drawback legislation which remitted duties on goods imported or exported by Canada through American ports and across American transportation facilities. There was grave danger that because of these serious handicaps the St. Lawrence would never become the great highway on which Canadians had so confidently counted.[7] Canada had been caught in a vise that was being tightened by British and American statesmen in a manner that threatened to crush Canadian economy.

5. Robert L. Schuyler, "The Climax of Anti-Imperialism in England," *Political Science Quarterly,* XXXVI (1921), 537–560; Charles S. Parker, *Sir Robert Peel* (London, 1899), pp. 583–609; D. L. Burn, "Canada and the Repeal of the Corn Laws," *Cambridge Historical Journal,* II (1928), 252–272.

6. Thomas C. Keefer, *Eighty Years' Progress of British North America* (Toronto, 1863), pp. 166–174; R. H. Bonnycastle, *Canada and the Canadians in 1846* (London, 1846), pp. 289–292.

7. D. G. Creighton, *The Commercial Empire of the St. Lawrence, 1760–1850* (New Haven, 1937), pp. 349–350; H. A. Innis and A. R. M. Lower, *Select Documents in Canadian Economic History, 1784–1885* (Toronto, 1933), pp. 315 ff.

Because of these severe economic pressures, Canada was eager to secure some form of commercial reciprocity with the United States.[8] But the treaty of 1854 was not a panacea for all the economic ills that plagued the British North American provinces. Canal construction had caused a large indebtedness that brought serious concern to Canadian leaders, and the building of railroads ushered in a new period of frenzied finance. In 1853 the project of the Grand Trunk Railway of Canada was launched with a fanfare that impressed the Canadian public. Thomas Baring and George C. Glyn headed the board of directors, and many Canadian officials were connected with the enterprise. But in 1855, despite its brilliant background, the Grand Trunk Railway encountered financial difficulties, and these troubles soon proved to be legion. In 1859, when the dedication of the costly Victoria bridge at Montreal brought the railroad to completion, "the finances of the Canadian government were hopelessly compromised, together with those of the company."[9]

The Grand Trunk Railway débâcle was only one aspect of the widespread financial depression that settled upon Canada in the late fifties. Faced with this situation, Alexander T. Galt, the Canadian Minister of Finance, introduced in Parliament in 1859–1860, a series of measures which he hoped would bring speedy relief. First he converted tariff duties from a specific to an *ad valorem* basis, and had them levied according to the valuation of imports at the last port of shipment. This would operate to reduce the business of American jobbing and commission firms engaged in handling foreign goods in transit to Canada. His second and most important move was to increase the revenue by raising the tariff rates on manufactured goods.[10] The reciprocity treaty with the United States had made no mention of manufactures, but the British Minister at Washington had intimated that the Canadian Government would always hold to a "most liberal commercial policy."[11] In the tariff law of 1859, Galt, with little fear of American reaction, made provision for a significant increase in the duties on manufactured goods, and thereby aroused bitter hostility in American business circles.[12] The way was being prepared for the abrogation of the reciprocity treaty of 1854.

8. Tansill, *The Canadian Reciprocity Treaty of 1854,* pp. 9–16.

9. Jenks, *op. cit.,* p. 203; Oscar D. Skelton, *The Railway Builders* (Toronto, 1916), chaps. iv–v.

10. Porritt, *Sixty Years of Protection in Canada, 1846–1907,* chaps. vii–viii.

11. *Senate Ex. Doc. No. 1,* 32 Cong., 1 sess., p. 89.

12. United States Tariff Commission, *Reciprocity and Commercial Treaties* (Washington, 1919), p. 79. In the tariffs of 1856 and 1858 the duties on certain types of manufactured goods were already as high as twenty per cent.

In Canada, during the early years of the treaty, there were many evidences that reciprocity had strong popular support. In 1855 a committee of the Legislative Assembly submitted a report that called for an extension of reciprocity along the lines of the interstate commerce between the states of the American Union.[13] In this same year, the Legislative Council of New Brunswick and the Council of the Quebec Board of Trade expressed themselves in the same general manner, and suggested the advisability of having some sort of Provincial representative in the United States to promote the interests of the British North American colonies.[14]

It is very apparent that before the Galt tariffs went into operation,[15] there had been a large export of American products to Canada, and American dissatisfaction with the treaty had been largely confined to the South which felt that it received no benefits from the operation of reciprocity. In 1860, the Minnesota legislature passed a resolution asking for a more comprehensive reciprocal arrangement with Canada,[16] and the official report of Israel T. Hatch condemned the Galt tariffs but advocated the establishment of a Zollverein or a commercial union with British North America.[17]

This proposal of a commercial union between Canada and the United States was exceedingly distasteful to Galt, who regarded it as "wholly inconsistent" with the maintenance of a connection with England. It required no great foresight to perceive that a customs union meant

> the imposition of duties by the confederacy, on articles produced outside the confederation, coupled with free trade among its members. In other words, Canada would be required to tax British goods, while she admitted those of the United States free, a state of things that could only accompany a sever-

13. Shippee, *Canadian-American Relations, 1849–1874,* pp. 99–100.

14. *Ibid.,* pp. 100–101. In Canada, one of the most earnest advocates of commercial union with the United States was Isaach Buchanan. In 1859, in an address to his constituents in Hamilton, he urged the extension of reciprocity to manufactures, and openly declared himself to be in favor of a customs union or Zollverein between the United States and Canada. In 1863 he elaborated his suggestions concerning a customs union: "The natural policy of Canada is clearly seen . . . to be the establishment of an American Zollverein such as exists in the German States. Under this the United States and Canada would neither of them levy any customs taxes on their frontiers, but only at the seaports from Labrador to Mexico, the same duties being levied, and each country getting its share in proportion to its population." Porritt, *op. cit.,* pp. 130–134.

15. In the report of the United States Tariff Commission, *Reciprocity and Commercial Treaties,* pp. 84–85, it is stated that "the most important part of the United States exports to Canada consisted of manufactures, and the trade in these was checked during this period by the increase in duties established thereon by the Galt ministry."

16. Shippee, *op. cit.,* p. 109.

17. *House Misc. Doc. No. 96,* 36 Cong., 1 sess.

ance of all the ties of affection, nationality and interest that now unite Canada and the Mother Country.[18]

With Galt helping to block any movement towards commercial union, and with his fiscal program checking the export of American manufactured goods into Canada, it was inevitable that hostility towards the treaty of 1854 should rapidly gather strength in the United States. The fish, lumber and coal interests combined with the manufacturers to form a pressure group that demanded the abrogation of reciprocity, and Anglo-American friction during the Civil War helped to confirm their arguments. In January 1865, the Senate agreed to the House resolution calling for the termination of the reciprocity treaty, and on March 17, President Lincoln conveyed to the British Government the required year's notice of abrogation. An experiment that had promised commercial expansion and political understanding had come to an inglorious close.[19]

The abrogation of the reciprocity treaty was a severe blow to the economic structure of Canada that was still suffering from the blows of 1846. In the Maritime Provinces the situation became acute. In the sixties these provinces were "one of the world's great commercial maritime powers, holding fourth place in registered tonnage of shipping." Their vessels plied the seven seas. Coal was carried from England to the Orient, guano from the Chincha Islands to England and France, petroleum from the Gulf ports to Europe and South America and wool from Australia to Europe.[20]

Nova Scotia was the most diversified of the Maritime Provinces. Although its exports were of a greater variety than those of the other provinces, in 1866 fish accounted for more than 40 per cent of the value of her total exports. The two principal markets for these fish were the West Indies and the United States. The reciprocity treaty of 1854 had greatly stimulated the fishing industry: between 1860 and 1866 the value of exports of fish rose nearly 50 per cent, and a large part of this increase went to the United States.[21]

During the period of the American Civil War the shipbuilding industry had a great boom in Nova Scotia. For the period 1863–1866, the

18. Skelton, *Galt,* p. 298.

19. Masters, *The Reciprocity Treaty of 1854* (London, 1937), pp. 132–226.

20. *Report of the Royal Commission on Dominion-Provincial Relations, Canada: 1867–1939* (Ottawa, 1940), I, 22–24 (hereafter referred to as *R.R.C.D.P.R.*); S. A. Saunders, "The Reciprocity Treaty of 1854: A Regional Study," *Canadian Journal of Economics and Political Science,* II (1936), 41–53; *ibid.,* "The Maritime Provinces and the Reciprocity Treaty," *Dalhousie Review,* XIV (1934–1935), 355–371.

21. *R.R.C.D.P.R.,* I, 23.

annual value of ships built averaged one-third of the total value of all exports. In New Brunswick there was a similar expansion in shipbuilding during the early sixties, and during certain years the value of ships built reached as high as three-quarters of the value of all other exports.

The prosperity of these provinces rested chiefly upon their fish and lumber exports, wooden shipbuilding, and their carrying trade. Northern needs during the Civil War had expanded these exports which had no adequate outlet after the termination of the reciprocity treaty. But the decline of this export trade to the United States was not the sole reason for depression in Nova Scotia. The development of steam navigation struck a mortal blow at the carrying trade and the shipbuilding industries of Nova Scotia and New Brunswick. The wood-wind-water techniques that had been so successful in former years were now becoming obsolete, and hard times were about to descend upon communities that had no adequate answer to this new challenge.

In Upper and Lower Canada the prospect was almost as dark. Wasteful expenditures and flagrant misuse of government funds helped to plunge the provinces into a slough of economic despond.[22] By 1866 the Government of Canada had invested $33,000,000 in railway development, and the municipalities had advanced some $7,000,000 more. If canal expenditures were included, government investments in transportation facilities amounted to nearly 60 per cent of the provincial and municipal debt. The attempt at "commercial integration with the interior of the continent had irretrievably failed and left behind it a burden of debt which weighed oppressively on the economy." In each of the British North American colonies the basis of prosperity "threatened to disappear as the 1860's drew to a close." The Province of Canada had a transportation system designed for a continental commerce that had not materialized. The limits of agricultural expansion had been reached, and the exploitation of marginal land awaited upon the opening of new markets. The termination of the reciprocity treaty with the United States had shut the door upon an export trade that had been rapidly expanding. Soon it swelled into a great flood that had no adequate outlet.[23]

These were the economic forces that compelled Canadian statesmen to seek, again and again, some form of reciprocity with the United States. Confederation[24] and a bold program to build a transcontinental

22. Gustavus Myers, *History of Canadian Wealth* (Chicago, 1914), chaps. x–xv.

23. *R.R.C.D.P.R.*, I, 25–29.

24. For data on the interest of English financial groups in Canadian Confederation, see Reginald G. Trotter, "British Finance and Confederation," *Rept. of Canadian Historical Association, 1927*, 89–96. See also, Chester Martin, "British Policy in Canadian Confederation," *Canadian Historical Review*, XIII (1932), 3–19.

economy helped to divert attention from the financial ills that beset the new Dominion, but these were only palliatives and not cures. Before Confederation could be realized, Galt led (January, 1866) a delegation from Canada, and the Maritime Provinces, to Washington to discuss with members of Congress the question of reciprocity;[25] and in 1869 Sir John Rose talked with Secretary Fish unofficially on the same subject.[26] These attempts failed to interest the American Government in any return to reciprocity, and a short period of comparative prosperity led the Canadian officials to refrain for a while from further visits.

Between 1868 and 1874 Canadian exports to Great Britain were doubled. Lumber was in strong demand, fish were sent abroad in large quantities, agricultural products found good markets, and shipbuilding in the Maritime Provinces approached the high peak attained during the American Civil War.[27] Dominion revenues increased nearly 100 per cent, most of the increase coming from customs duties. This rapid rise in revenues led the Government to push the construction of transportation facilities. The canal system of the St. Lawrence was deepened, expenditures on public buildings, harbors and wharves were greatly increased, and generous assistance was pledged to Sir Hugh Allan and his associates in the building of a railway to the Pacific over an all-Canadian route. This buoyant financial condition had enabled the new Federal Government to "consolidate the union and assume the dominant and aggressive role which the Fathers of Confederation had assigned to it."[28]

But this period of prosperity came to an end in the last months of 1873. Canadian economy was closely linked to that of England, and in 1873 the price index in the British Isles began a decline from its high point of 111. As this recession continued, "there began the greatest depression trend of modern times, which was to reach its limit in 1896 with a price index of 61. Export values fell off dramatically, while quantities could with difficulty be increased." England was at the end of an era. From 1815 to 1875 English investors had exported a capital surplus of half a billion pounds, a great part of this sum coming between the years 1850–1873 when prices were surging upward during years of mounting prosperity. This golden flood suddenly ceased in

25. Shippee, *op. cit.*, pp. 294–296.

26. A. H. U. Colquhoun, "The Reciprocity Negotiation with the United States in 1869," *Canadian Historical Review*, VIII (1927), 233–242.

27. *R.R.C.D.P.R.*, I, 47–53.

28. *Ibid.*, pp. 47–49.

1873. England found it difficult to balance her requirements of food and raw materials with the manufactured goods she was able to export and the freights her merchant marine could earn. There was no longer any capital surplus to send abroad for investment.[29]

This financial revolution in England had an immediate effect upon Canada. The lumber industry suffered a sharp decline. Between 1873 and 1879 the exports of forest products fell off some fifty per cent. Other industries were equally hard hit, and by 1876 "the country was generally enveloped in a depression which grew slowly worse until 1879."[30] For twenty years this pall of economic gloom shrouded the hopes of Canadian statesmen.[31] As the men, money, and markets necessary for the successful operation of the national machinery failed to materialize, certain Canadian leaders turned towards the United States with the hope that some form of commercial reciprocity could be arranged. As a desperate chance, the Mackenzie Government sent George Brown to Washington in the spring of 1874 to negotiate a reciprocity treaty along the general lines of the convention of 1854. A draft treaty, with a long schedule devoted to manufactured goods, was agreed to by Secretary Fish, and sent by the President to the Senate on June 18, with a request for advice as to its final negotiation.[32] On February 3, 1875, the Senate refused to recommend it, and the Brown mission ended in failure.[33]

But despite the failure of the Brown mission, there was strong sentiment in many American business circles in favor of some sort of commercial reciprocity with Canada. Many manufacturers were anxious to secure access to the Canadian market, and they would have welcomed the free entry of Canadian raw materials including foodstuffs. During the summer of 1874 while the draft reciprocity treaty was before the Senate for consideration, letters poured into the British Legation in Washington from numerous American manufacturing concerns with reference to the establishment of closer trade relations with Canada.

29. Jenks, *op. cit.,* pp. 330–333. See also, Sir Robert Giffen, *Economic Inquiries and Studies* (London, 1904); Stephen Bourne, *Trade, Population and Food* (London, 1880).

30. *R.R.C.D.P.R.,* I, 49–50.

31. With reference to the economic situation in Canada after 1873, Marcus Lee Hansen and John B. Brebner, *The Mingling of the Canadian and American Peoples* (New Haven, 1940), p. 164, remarked: "The financial crash of 1873, . . . and the depression which followed it ushered in for Canada as a whole a profoundly discouraging twenty-three years of falling prices and shattered hopes."

32. Richardson, *Messages and Papers of the Presidents,* VII, 266–267.

33. Secretary Fish to Mr. Thornton, February 11, 1875, *F.R., 1875–1876,* p. 653. See also, Nevins, *Hamilton Fish,* pp. 919–920; Alexander Mackenzie, *The Life and Speeches of the Hon. George Brown* (Toronto, 1882), 212 ff.; Shippee, *op. cit.,* pp. 460–471.

A large number of these communications were in favor of a treaty similar to the one before the Senate.[34]

American opinion favorable to reciprocity with Canada was further reflected in recommendations to Congress from chambers of commerce in various parts of the country. As a result of this pressure, the House Committee on Commerce made a report (January 18, 1876) which dealt with the feasibility of a limited customs union with Canada. The subject was of such obvious importance that the committee suggested the appointment of a Joint High Commission to study the various aspects of Canadian-American fiscal relations.[35]

When no action was taken on this recommendation, Sir John Macdonald delivered a speech in the Dominion Parliament in which he advised the Mackenzie Government to change its policy towards the United States. There was nothing to be gained from further missions to the United States with regard to commercial reciprocity. Canada should cease making such overtures. American statesmen could not be induced to "alter their plans." The best course for Canada to pursue was one that aimed at providing adequate tariff protection for the infant industries of the Dominion. When the door of commercial opportunity was suddenly closed in American faces, the Government at Washington would probably awaken to the need of conciliating Canada.[36]

In these remarks Macdonald was acting as the herald of a new economic order in the Dominion. He was sounding the first notes in an ambitious symphony that he called his National Policy; a symphony of several movements that would win wide popular acclaim and keep him in the office of Prime Minister for more than a decade.

In the face of increasing hard times, Canada adopted three basic national economic policies: the settlement of the Northwest, transcontinental transportation through all-Canadian territory, and the promotion of Canadian industries through adequate tariff protection.[37]

34. Dr. Charles E. Cayley, in his MS. dissertation entitled "The North Atlantic Fisheries in United States–Canadian Relations" was the first scholar to direct attention to these letters in the *Macdonald Papers.*

35. *House Rept. No. 9,* 44 Cong., 1 sess.; *House Rept. No. 389,* 44 Cong., 1 sess.

36. *Canada: House of Commons, Debates, 1878,* March 7, 1878, p. 862.

37. With reference to the Macdonald program, Professor D. G. Creighton, "Conservatism and National Unity," in *Essays in Canadian History,* pp. 165–170, remarks: "The lands of the Hudson's Bay Company offered a territorial empire not unequal to that lost commercial dominion in the United States. The free-trade area of a united British North America would provide at least a partial substitute for the protected markets which had been lost in Great Britain and were soon to be lost in the United States. . . . In place of the international commercial empire of the St. Lawrence, which had been lost irretrievably to the United States, the Conservatives proposed to establish a na-

For a few years after this bold program had been embarked upon, the Macdonald Government was favored by a brief trade revival (1879–1883), but hard times returned in 1884 and continued until 1896.[38] This lingering and far-reaching depression once more turned Canadian minds to thoughts of reciprocity with the United States.

There were some Americans who would welcome such overtures. In certain commercial circles the belief had persisted that reciprocity with Canada would open markets for American manufactures and provide a convenient source of supply for much-needed raw materials. An unrestricted exchange of goods across the frontier would help to lift the United States out of the depression that had settled upon the country since 1873. To Elijah Ward it was evident that a customs union like the German Zollverein would solve many of the difficulties that beset Canada and the United States. In a speech in the House of Representatives, May 18, 1876, he strongly urged the adoption of some plan for commercial union which would bestow upon both countries ample commercial benefits and yet commit neither of them to political alliance. This could easily be worked out by studying the operation of the Zollverein in Germany.[39]

These sentiments were an inspiration to Goldwin Smith, who had left his chair in history in Cornell University to live in Toronto, Canada, in an atmosphere of independent thought and action made possible by his wife's ample means. In 1877, Smith wrote an interesting article in which he told his Canadian readers that annexation to the United States was the ultimate destiny of Canada. Commercial union was a step in that direction, and it should be taken at once.[40] Two years later, Smith preached this same theme to the American public.[41]

tional transcontinental system in British North America. . . . The advent of the depression in 1873 and the failure to secure a new reciprocity agreement with the United States provoked a growing interest in protection; and the Tory party, as if inspired, seized upon this novel and somewhat questionable doctrine and glorified it by the resounding title of the 'National Policy.' 'The word *protection* itself,' Macdonald had written as early as 1872, 'must be taboo, but we can ring the changes on National Policy, paying U. S. in their own coin.' "

38. *R.R.C.D.P.R.*, I, 52–53.

39. *Congressional Record*, 44 Cong., 1 sess., pp. 3158–3164.

40. Callahan, *op. cit.*, p. 360.

41. Goldwin Smith, "Canada and the United States," *North American Review*, CXXXI (July, 1880), 14–25. In discussing the question of commercial union between Canada and the United States, Smith observed: "Herculean efforts have been made . . . by Canadian statesmen . . . to reverse the order of nature, to sever Canada commercially from her continent, and to bind her economically to England, . . . and to every portion of the world except the dreaded republic. . . . During the last five or six years, . . . all engines, social and political, have been plied to stimulate imperialist, aristocratic, and anti-continental feeling. . . . But there will be an end of making Can-

Many Canadians refused to accept this counsel because they feared that commercial union with the United States would be a mere prelude to eventual annexation. But they could not disregard the relentless pressure of hard times, and they often looked wistfully across the line to the vast American market that beckoned to Canadian raw materials. If commercial union was too dangerous an experiment to try, perhaps some form of reciprocity might relieve Canada's economic ills! Wishful thinking about reciprocity became a habitude of thought in Canada during the Macdonald regime. As Professor Underhill remarks: "It is only on reading the newspapers and periodicals and party pamphlets of the 1870's and 1880's that one gets an adequate conception of this importance of the American market in Canadian thinking and of the persistent vitality of the idea of reciprocity."[42]

In Liberal circles, despite the growing coolness of Edward Blake to the idea of unrestricted reciprocity, there was a strong sentiment in favor of commercial union. In the correspondence of Blake there are many letters from men like L. S. Huntingdon, who felt that the issue should be pushed. They were restrained by their leader's lack of interest in the project, but they were not converted to the idea that commercial union was not feasible.[43]

In the Conservative Party there were certain important members who were targets for a barrage of letters from American business men in favor of a wide measure of reciprocity between Canada and the United States. Sir John Macdonald was the recipient of many of these communications, and one of his chief correspondents was S. J. Ritchie, of Akron, Ohio. Ritchie owned certain nickel and copper deposits in the Sudbury region of Ontario Province. As President of the Central Ontario Railway he had a wide acquaintance in Canada. In May 1884, he wrote to Sir John Macdonald to invite him to attend the opening of one of his mines at Coe Hill. He had persuaded Senator Henry B. Payne, of Ohio, to attend this ceremony, as well as William Chisholm and other American representatives of "big business." He assured Sir John that Senator Payne was a "staunch advocate of the widest reciprocal trade

ada the engine of hostility to the American Republic. . . . With Lord Beaconsfield, who was everywhere a conspirator, conspiracy has passed away. . . . It may be safely predicted that Canadian and American statesmen will soon be in conference on the subject of commercial relations. . . . Two plans will present themselves for consideration—commercial union and a partial reciprocity treaty. . . . A commercial union would . . . give perfectly free circulation to capital and commercial life. It is to be hoped that commercial union will receive the first consideration."

42. Frank H. Underhill, "Edward Blake, the Liberal Party, and Unrestricted Reciprocity," *Rept. of Canadian Historical Association, 1939,* p. 133.

43. Underhill, *op. cit.,* p. 134.

relations between Canada and the United States," and Senator John Sherman was a "recent convert to these views." It would be an excellent thing for Canadian and American business men to get together on the question of reciprocity.[44]

Sir John Macdonald did not find it convenient to join this party sponsored by Mr. Ritchie, but he did not discourage correspondence on the subject of reciprocity, and the *Macdonald Papers* contain a large number of letters from Ritchie.[45] It was not the business men, however, who were responsible for Canadian overtures with regard to reciprocity. It was the pressure of the fisheries question that forced the Macdonald Government to make an effort to balance concessions to American fishermen with tariff reductions on Canadian products.

On February 26, 1883, Congress adopted a resolution which directed the President to give notice to the British Government of the termination of Articles XVIII to XXV, inclusive, and also of Article XXX of the Treaty of May 8, 1871.[46] The President carried out this direction, and on July 1, 1885 the liberty granted to American fishermen to use the Canadian inshore fisheries would come to an end.

It was apparent to Sir John Macdonald that the termination of this liberty would probably lead to serious friction with the United States. With this thought in mind he wrote to Sir Charles Tupper, in London, and expressed the opinion that it would be best not to make an attempt to open negotiations with the American Government until a new Administration was installed in Washington. If Cleveland were elected, there would be some chance of success in the matter of reciprocity. The door

would be ajar, but I fear we could not open it wide. The United States won't agree to an Agricultural Reciprocity Treaty like that of 1854, and we can't agree to a Zollverein. We must have our customs for Revenue and our manufactures are too young and weak yet. Ten years hence they might agree that they would gain by the opening of the market of 60 millions to them on even terms, . . . but they would be crushed out just now.[47]

44. S. J. Ritchie to Sir John Macdonald, May 29, 1884, *Macdonald Papers, S. J. Ritchie Correspondence,* pp. 1–2, P.A.C.

45. Macdonald was always eager to encourage capitalists to invest their money in Canadian enterprises. According to Professor Underhill, "Edward Blake and Canadian Liberal Nationalism," in *Essays in Canadian History,* p. 140, Macdonald "believed that the future of the country depended upon the Government's energy in attracting adventurous and ambitious business capitalists to the work of developing its natural resources and in giving them the widest possible opportunities."

46. *Congressional Record,* 47 Cong., 2 sess., pp. 3055–3056.

47. Sir John Macdonald to Sir Charles Tupper, July 28, 1884, *Macdonald Papers, Correspondence with Sir Charles Tupper,* p. 212, P.A.C.

As soon as the Cleveland Administration came into power, Macdonald wrote to Lord Lansdowne and suggested that the time might be ripe to discuss with Secretary Bayard the troublesome fishery question.[48] Sir Lionel West was instructed to open negotiations for a *modus vivendi* that would cover the approaching fishing season. He was also to discuss the possibility of effecting some arrangement that would admit Canadian fish in American markets.[49] When he opened negotiations with the Department of State, Bayard remarked that he "was by no means unfavourable to a wider measure of reciprocity," but the British Government should not make "any formal proposal" until Bayard was in a position to say that the President approved such a measure.[50]

Lord Lansdowne was entirely willing to postpone the matter of reciprocity until after the *modus vivendi* had been agreed upon, but he held the view that some announcement with regard to later reciprocity negotiations would help to quiet Canadian discontent over temporary concessions to the United States in connection with the inshore fisheries.[51]

In the *modus vivendi* that was finally agreed to, the inshore fishing liberties were extended during the current fishing season, and it was specifically provided that President Cleveland would recommend to Congress an authorization for the appointment of a joint commission which would deal not only with the fisheries question but with the whole subject of "good neighborhood and intercourse."[52]

Lord Lansdowne was thoroughly in favor of negotiating a *modus vivendi*, but he realized that in Canada there would be open dissatisfaction with any agreement that did not deal with the subject of reciprocity. On March 9, he wrote to Sir Lionel West and suggested the inclusion of some measure of reciprocity in the terms of the proposed *modus vivendi*. West broached this matter to Secretary Bayard, who frankly admitted that in the United States there was a "strong feeling in favour of reciprocity with Canada in all commercial matters; in fact that the commercial relations between the two countries ought to partake of the character of the interstate commerce of the Union." Bayard believed, however, that it would be best to postpone any further discus-

48. Sir John Macdonald to Lord Lansdowne, March 9, 1885, *Macdonald Letter Books*, XXIII, 132, P.A.C.

49. See *ante*, p. 15.

50. Sir Lionel West to Lord Lansdowne, May 22, 1885, *Macdonald Papers, Governor-General's Correspondence*, XII, 429–430, P.A.C. With reference to President Cleveland's liberal attitude with regard to the tariff, see Allan Nevins, *Grover Cleveland* (New York, 1934), chaps. xvii, xxi–xxii.

51. Lord Lansdowne to Sir John Macdonald, May 25, 1885, *ibid.*, XII, 428.

52. Secretary Bayard to Sir Lionel West, June 19, 20, 22, 1885, *British Legation, Notes to*, XX; West to Secretary Bayard, June 20, 22, 1885, *British Legation, Notes from*, CXII, MS. Dept. of State.

sions of reciprocity until he had been able to sound out the other members of the Cabinet with regard to it.[53]

Upon receipt of this communication from West, Lord Lansdowne wrote a second letter in which he again stressed the importance of pushing the matter of reciprocity.[54] When West resumed his conversations with Bayard, he was once more informed that the time was not ripe to discuss the question of reciprocity. As Secretary of State, Bayard was not averse to negotiating for a "wider measure of reciprocity in which the settlement of the fisheries question might be included," but the way would have to be carefully prepared before any steps in that direction were taken. The subject was under the "serious consideration of the United States Government," and at the proper moment, negotiations would be started.[55]

Lansdowne made no further objection to Bayard's policy of postponement with reference to reciprocity, but he wrote to Sir John Macdonald and inquired as to the objectives that Canada should aim at in the proposed settlement with the United States.[56] The Prime Minister's answer showed careful thought on the subject. It would be advisable to ask for a renewal of the abrogated articles of the Treaty of Washington. In addition, it was important to secure the free admission of "whale and seal-oil" as well as "free fish and fish-oil." An effort should be made to secure the inclusion of the marine products of the Northwest Coast. With reference to general commercial relations, Canada should be "satisfied with the terms of the Reciprocity Treaty of 1854," but a treaty affecting "manufactures would not be entertained by the United States nor . . . by England."[57]

In the United States there was continued interest in the subject of reciprocity with Canada. In August, 1885, Mr. Ritchie wrote to Sir Charles Tupper and strongly urged him to pay a visit to New York, where a meeting could be arranged with several important Senators. Through these unofficial conferences, Ritchie was certain that a program could be agreed upon with reference to reciprocity, and the main items in this program could be pushed through Congress without any great difficulty.[58]

53. Sir Lionel West to Lord Lansdowne, May 12, 1885, *Macdonald Papers, Governor-General's Correspondence,* XII, 411–412, P.A.C.

54. Lansdowne to Sir Lionel West, May 18, 1885, *ibid.,* pp. 431–432.

55. Sir Lionel West to Lansdowne, May 22, 1885, *ibid.,* pp. 429–430.

56. Lord Lansdowne to Sir John Macdonald, August 24, 1885, quoted in Tansill, *Bayard,* pp. 200–201.

57. Sir John Macdonald to Lord Lansdowne, September 5, 1885, *Macdonald Papers, Macdonald Letter Books,* XXIII, 277–278, P.A.C.

58. S. J. Ritchie to Sir Charles Tupper, August 18, 1885, Tansill, *Bayard,* p. 527.

In the early part of October, Sir Lionel West directed Bayard's attention to a circular issued by the Boston Fish Bureau, in which a plea was made for the remission of duties on Canadian fish. The circular also referred to the general topic of reciprocity, and it urged the people of Boston to vote on such a question in accordance with their interests and "with the interests of a large majority of the people of the country."[59]

On October 17, Representative R. W. Townshend wrote to Bayard to advocate the establishment of a "Commercial Union or Zollverein among the nations on the American Continent,"[60] and some weeks later, Goldwin Smith assured Bayard that the "people on this side of the Line are about ready for the question of Commercial Union, if it can be brought before them in a definite and authoritative form."[61]

During this same period, Sir John Macdonald was receiving letters from prominent Canadians with regard to commercial reciprocity with the United States. On December 24, Joseph W. Trutch, former Lieutenant-Governor of British Columbia, expressed the opinion that the large forests and rich mineral deposits of that province would provide the basis for infant industries if they were given adequate tariff protection. It was probably true that "any measure of Reciprocity with the United States, acceptable to the Eastern Provinces of the Dominion," would be beneficial to the interests of British Columbia. The principal items that his section wished on the free list were coal, lumber, fish and fish oils.[62]

From Fredericton, New Brunswick, S. L. Tilley, former Minister of Finance, informed Macdonald that Ontario would favor a reciprocity treaty that would secure a free market for their cattle and agricultural produce. Quebec was not particularly interested in free entry for fish, but was anxious to get access to the American markets for "their lumber, hay, oats, and potatoes." The Maritime Provinces wished to have free entry for their "fish, lumber and agricultural products." In 1880 and 1881, Mr. Tilley had talked in Washington with Blaine and William M. Evarts. They had been in favor of "large reciprocal arrangements, covering a large list of manufactures, but at the same time imposing a duty on British productions." This proposition "could not be entertained for a moment. The free admission of manufactures from the

59. Sir Lionel West to Secretary Bayard, October 5, 1885, enclosing the circular from the Boston Fish Bureau, *Bayard MS.*

60. R. W. Townshend to Secretary Bayard, October 17, 1885, *ibid.*

61. Goldwin Smith to Secretary Bayard, January 29, 1886, *ibid.*

62. Joseph W. Trutch to Sir John Macdonald, December 24, 1885, *Macdonald Papers, Washington Treaty, 1888,* I, 135 ff., P.A.C.

United States and a duty on British manufactures, would be practical independence in the worst form."[63]

These Canadian hopes for a reciprocity treaty rested largely upon President Cleveland's recommendation to Congress to authorize the appointment of a joint commission to study the fisheries question.[64] It was expected that the commission would make a joint proposal that would deal not only with the fisheries controversy but also with the important topic of reciprocity. The President shared these Canadian expectations, and there was no doubt in his mind that Canada and the United States would derive mutual advantage from the establishment of closer commercial relations. These relations should be in accordance with a plan "based on the free interstate commerce of the [American] Union."[65]

But the temper of the American Congress soon made it clear that no co-operation could be expected from that body. Representatives from Maine, Vermont and Massachusetts played a prominent role in the 49th Congress, and they were bitterly opposed to any arrangement that would permit the admission of Canadian fish and fish oil into the United States free of duty. On January 18, 1886, Senator William P. Frye, of Maine, introduced a resolution which expressed the view that there was no necessity for the appointment of a joint commission to study the fisheries question, and many of his colleagues promptly supported him.[66]

Sir Lionel West followed this Senate debate with great care. In a letter to Lord Salisbury he reported that the majority in the Senate was opposed to Secretary Bayard's policy in general, and a large number of Representatives were on record against any settlement of the question of reciprocity with Canada by means of a treaty.[67]

To Lord Lansdowne, West gave a detailed picture of the situation in Washington. It was apparent that there was not "much chance of either reciprocity or the appointment of a Commission." The feeling among Republican Senators towards reciprocity was clearly illustrated by some remarks of Senator Allison. Allison admitted that "if the commercial relations with Canada were placed upon the footing of the interstate commerce of the Union, great benefit would accrue to the Northwestern States." But he thought "the opinion was general that

63. S. L. Tilley to Sir John Macdonald, January 12, 1886, *ibid.*, pp. 146 ff.

64. Message to Congress, December 8, 1885, Richardson, *op. cit.*, VIII, 332.

65. Sir Lionel West to Lord Salisbury, December 11, 1885, Tansill, *op. cit.*, p. 204.

66. *Congressional Record*, 49 Cong., 1 sess., p. 702.

67. Sir Lionel West to Lord Salisbury, February 2, 1886, *Macdonald Papers, Governor-General's Correspondence*, XIII, 24–25, P.A.C.

this would sooner or later be obtained by the incorporation of Canada with the United States."[68]

A few days later, Secretary Bayard spoke to West in bitter terms with regard to the obstructionist spirit in Congress, and he gave assurances that he still cherished a strong "desire for more intimate commercial relations with Canada, but Congress seemed opposed to reciprocity."[69] This spirit of opposition in Congress was clearly exemplified on April 13 when the Senate adopted by an overwhelming vote (35 yeas to 10 nays) the Frye resolution which was directed against the appointment of a joint commission to settle Canadian-American disputes.[70]

It was apparent to Bayard that the protectionist group in the Senate was in the saddle, and there was no chance for any reciprocity arrangement to get a fair hearing. The New England fishing industry would consistently oppose all attempts to lower the duties on fish, even though the mill operatives of that section needed cheap food.[71]

With things in this unsettled state, S. J. Ritchie called upon Secretary Bayard with a letter of introduction from Senator H. B. Payne, of Ohio.[72] According to Ritchie, Bayard was quite "free and liberal" in his attitude towards reciprocity with Canada. He was opposed to "the United States taxing anything which was produced by Canada, and was opposed to Canada taxing anything which was produced by the United States." Because of these liberal convictions, Bayard would be entirely willing to negotiate a reciprocity treaty with Canada "if he thought the Senate would ratify it." In this regard, Ritchie believed that a "large portion" of the Senate was in favor of reciprocity with Canada, but they did not "want the Democratic President to have the credit of accomplishing it."[73]

68. Sir Lionel West to Lord Lansdowne, February 4, 7, 1886, *ibid.*, pp. 16g–16i, 22.

69. Sir Lionel West to Lord Rosebery, February 19, 1886, *ibid.*, pp. 54–55.

70. *Congressional Record*, 49 Cong., 1 sess., p. 3440.

71. Secretary Bayard to Phelps, November 15, 1886, *Bayard MS.* In a letter to Bayard, November 20, 1886, President Cleveland discussed the different topics that should be included in the annual message to Congress. He was anxious to avoid any "squint" at "another reciprocity treaty with Canada." *Ibid.*

72. Senator H. B. Payne to Secretary Bayard, December 8, 1886, *ibid.*

73. S. J. Ritchie to Sir John Macdonald, December 8, 1886, *Macdonald Papers, Commercial Union, 1886–1887*, pp. 7–10, P.A.C.

At this point it is pertinent to refer to the following table in the Bayard manuscripts giving the trade between the United States and Canada for the fiscal year 1886:

Imports into the United States from:

(a)	Nova Scotia, New Brunswick, Prince Edward Island	$ 4,556,980
(b)	Quebec, Ontario, Manitoba and Northwest Territory	31,263,469
(c)	British Columbia	1,483,587
(d)	Newfoundland and Labrador	192,302
	Total	$ 37,496,338

After further conversations with some "prominent Senators," Ritchie wrote to Macdonald and expressed the belief that many of the members of that body were willing to vote for a treaty which would "embrace not only the fishery question but the whole question of reciprocity between the two countries." Senator Sherman was emphatic in his opinion that "the only proper way to deal with the question" was for the British Minister to "negotiate a treaty with the State Department and . . . he would support it when it reached the Senate." Several important members of the House of Representatives, hitherto unfriendly to the idea of a reciprocity treaty with Canada, pledged their support to any new movement in that direction. Indeed, it seemed apparent to Ritchie that it only required "some one on the ground, thoroughly well-informed, to keep the members of both Houses stirred-up and alive to the question."[74]

Exports from the United States to:

(a)	Nova Scotia, New Brunswick, Prince Edward Island . .	$ 2,502,011
(b)	Quebec, Ontario, Manitoba and Northwest Territory . .	26,301,962
(c)	British Columbia	1,840,312
(d)	Newfoundland	1,308,839
	Total	$ 31,953,124

Amount of the above dutiable and the amount free:

Imports into the United States from the above provinces:

	Free of duty	Dutiable
(a)	$ 2,130,649	$ 2,426,331
(b)	9,361,506	21,901,963
(c)	513,378	970,209
(d)	37,094	155,208
	$ 12,042,627	$ 25,453,711

Imports into Canada from the United States:

	Free of duty	Dutiable
(a)	$ 1,845,586	$ 3,530,362
	12,911,559	24,317,090
	441,018	1,812,424
	(not included)	– –
	$ 15,198,163	$ 29,659,876

In the fiscal year of 1885, the amount of free fish imported into the United States was valued at $3,378,896. In the fiscal year 1886, free fish now included fresh fish of all kinds, lobsters canned and preserved otherwise than in oil, shrimps, shellfish and turtles. The imports of free fish in 1886 were estimated at $985,573. In this same year (1886) the value of imported dried, smoked, preserved, pickled and salted fish reached a total of $1,297,589, with duties of $251,871.

74. S. J. Ritchie to Sir John Macdonald, December 12, 1886, *ibid.*, pp. 20–24. According to Ritchie, Senator Frye had asked him to go to the Committee on Foreign Affairs of the House of Representatives and have his Bill "proposing a Congress of the representatives of the countries of Central and South America . . . so amended as to extend an invitation to Canada to participate in the deliberations of this Congress." On

It was high time for some representative of "big business" to have talks with members of Congress concerning relations with Canada. On January 19, 1887, Senator Edmunds introduced a bill which authorized the President, whenever he was satisfied that American rights were being violated in Canadian waters, to exclude from United States ports all vessels from the British Dominions of North America.[75] This bill was approved by President Cleveland on March 3, 1887.[76]

To make matters worse, Senator Hoar introduced on February 24, 1887, a resolution which opposed any negotiations with Great Britain "in regard to existing difficulties with her province of Canada which has for its object the reduction, change, or abolition of any of our existing duties on imports."[77] This action was designed to block any attempt of the Department of State to negotiate a treaty providing for commercial reciprocity with Canada.

American business men like S. J. Ritchie strongly deprecated the attitude of Senator Hoar and some of his colleagues. On December 7, 1885, in an address delivered in Washington, he made a plea for unrestricted reciprocity with Canada. To his audience he presented a very important question: "Shall we remove the custom houses, or shall we support them by two lines of fortifications, each nearly 4,000 miles long, the one to be built by ourselves and the other by our neighbors?"[78]

After setting the stage in Washington for the drama of commercial union, Ritchie then wrote to Senator John Sherman with reference to a bill which Representative Butterworth would soon introduce in the House of Representatives. It would provide for unrestricted reciprocity between the United States and Canada, and Butterworth would talk matters over with Sherman, who had shown a friendly attitude towards such a measure.[79]

Butterworth began to take a very active role in this matter of commercial union. On February 11, he sent to Secretary Bayard a letter introducing C. W. Bunting, the editor of the Toronto *Mail.*[80] Bunting

May 6, 1886, Senator Frye had submitted a report (*Senate Rept. No. 941,* 49 Cong., 1 sess.), accompanying Senate Bill 2362. This bill authorized the President to invite on behalf of the Government and the people of the United States, delegates from the South and Central American republics to meet in Washington on the formation of an American customs union, *et al.*

75. *Congressional Record,* 49 Cong., 2 sess., p. 793.

76. *F.R., 1887,* pp. 466–467.

77. *Congressional Record,* 49 Cong., 2 sess., p. 2191.

78. S. J. Ritchie, *Commercial Union between the United States and Canada* (Toronto, 1887), p. 35.

79. S. J. Ritchie to Senator John Sherman, January 31, 1887, *John Sherman Papers,* Library of Congress.

80. Representative Benjamin Butterworth to Secretary Bayard, February 11, 1887, *Bayard MS.*

had a conference with Bayard, who was not backward in avowing his interest in the establishment of commercial reciprocity with Canada. A few days later, the *Mail* came out with an editorial that favored reciprocity. Ritchie was so impressed with this reversal of opinion on the part of a leading Canadian newspaper that he sent a copy of the *Mail* to Bayard for perusal.[81]

In the meantime, on February 14, Butterworth introduced a bill in the House of Representatives providing for commercial union between the United States and Canada.[82] In commenting upon the Butterworth bill, the Halifax *Morning Chronicle* remarked that there was no doubt that "the people of this Dominion, and more especially of the lower provinces have long been warmly in favor of a measure of unrestricted reciprocal trade with the United States." One important difficulty about commercial union, however, was the matter of securing sufficient revenue to run the Canadian Government. Two fifths of Canadian imports were from the United States. If these imports paid no duties, the customs revenue would be reduced from $20,000,000 to $12,000,000 per annum. How could the Canadian Government get along on such a "pittance"?[83]

For this question Mr. Erastus Wiman had a ready answer. Wiman was a native of Canada who had prospered in business in the United States. He was President of the Great Northwest Telegraph Company which controlled many telegraph lines in Canada, and he was deeply

81. S. J. Ritchie to Secretary Bayard, February 16, 1887, *ibid.* With reference to the origins of the movement for commercial union, J. S. Willison, *Reminiscences, Political and Personal* (Toronto, 1919), pp. 166–167, remarks: "It was said that Sir Richard Cartwright imposed Commercial Union . . . upon the Liberal Party. But probably Commercial Union was conceived in *The Mail* office. Although Mr. Erastus Wiman was the reputed father, one suspects that Mr. Edward Farrer instructed Wiman." In a letter to John A. Kasson, June 9, 1898, Mr. Wiman observed: "In order that you may apprehend some of the work that has been previously done in this direction, I venture to send you three little pamphlets which were printed during the discussion of the movement for commercial union between the two countries, which, with Goldwin Smith, I had the honor of originating." *Kasson Papers,* MS. Dept. of State.

82. *Congressional Record,* 49 Cong., 2 sess., p. 1735. This bill provided that "whenever . . . the Government of the . . . Dominion of Canada shall, by act of her Parliament, permit all articles of trade and commerce of whatever name or nature . . . of the United States . . . to enter the ports of the said Dominion of Canada free of duty, then all articles manufactured in Canada, and all products of the soil and waters, and all minerals and coal products of the mines of the said Dominion of Canada, . . . shall be permitted to enter the ports of the United States free of duty; it being the intention of this act to provide for absolute reciprocity in trade between the two countries as to all articles of whatever name or nature produced in the said countries respectively."

83. Halifax *Morning Chronicle,* March 15, 1887. The *Chronicle* was an organ of the Liberal Party.

interested in every project to establish closer commercial relations between Canada and the United States. In his many pamphlets and articles Wiman cogently argued that the prosperity of the United States was largely due to the absence of tariff barriers between the different states. If these barriers could be removed between Canada and the United States, both countries would be immensely benefited by such action.[84] In an open letter to Valancey E. Fuller, President of the Farmers' Institute Convention, Toronto, Canada, April 26, 1887, Wiman emphasized the importance of the American market to the Canadian farmer: "A market such as the world has never equalled."[85]

Wiman's arguments awakened a responsive chord in Nova Scotia. Edward Young, the American Consul at Windsor, sent a long, confidential despatch to Secretary Bayard in which he recounted the results of a careful canvass of the situation. He was confident that it was the "earnest desire of both parties, and of almost every individual in this Province, to have more intimate trade relations with the United States."[86]

There was much truth in these observations of Mr. Young. On March 28, 1887, J. W. Longley, the Attorney-General of Nova Scotia, wrote

84. Wiman's many pamphlets include: *The Canadian Farmer's Future* (1887); *Is Reciprocity Possible?* (1887); *Commercial Union with Canada from a United States Point of View* (1887); *What is the Destiny of Canada?* (1889); *Commercial Union in North America* (1888).

85. Ritchie, *op. cit.*, pp. 21–24. With regard to Mr. Wiman, J. S. Willison, *Sir Wilfrid Laurier and the Liberal Party* (Toronto, 1903), II, 122–123, remarks: "He had . . . never renounced his British citizenship; and there is fair evidence that he laboured, whether wisely or unwisely, not to change the political relations, but to better the commercial relations between Canada and the United States. With much vigour of pen and tongue and some originality of method, he pressed Mr. Butterworth's bill upon Congress. . . . Mr. Wiman was a fluent and persuasive speaker, he had thoroughly mastered the economic relationships of the two countries, and rarely revealed the economist's contempt for popular sympathies."

One of Wiman's arguments in favor of commercial union made a strong appeal to Canadian mothers. Wiman set forth again and again the fact that the migration from Canada to the United States was very large, and the cream of Canadian youth was thus being drained off to American advantage. Commercial union would restore Canadian prosperity and stop this migration: "If commercial union could accomplish nothing else than keep our young men at home, it would be a boon of the greatest magnitude. For there is not a mother . . . but dreads the day when her boy, her precious boy, will look with longing eyes across the border." Ritchie, *op. cit.*

In the elections of February, 1887, the Macdonald Government was victorious. In a letter to Macdonald, February 24, 1887, Sir Donald Smith remarks: "I heartily congratulate you on your personal victory. . . . I was not aware that Blake and Wiman had joined hands in the effort to carry constituencies by the weight of American dollars—a most unrighteous compact, which ought to make their defeat all the more welcome to every one having a spark of patriotism or manly feeling in him." Joseph Pope, *Correspondence of Sir John Macdonald* (Toronto, 1922), p. 394.

86. Edward Young to Secretary Bayard, March 19, 1887, *Confidential, Bayard MS.*

a long letter to Wiman with regard to commercial union. To him it was apparent that this was the "most wide-reaching and important political matter now demanding the consideration of the great English-speaking communities of North America." From the Canadian standpoint, commercial union was "the complement necessary to the commercial existence and prosperity of the Dominion." If the people of the United States were "Turks or Chinese" there might be a "reason for wishing to discourage intimate intercourse." But when it was remembered that the people of the two countries were "identical in race, language, laws and institutions, then these [tariff] barriers indeed seem absurd and unaccountable."[87]

In order to accelerate the development of this sentiment throughout Canada, Goldwin Smith,[88] Valancey E. Fuller, Henry W. Darling, President of the Toronto Board of Trade, and G. Mercer Adam organized Commercial Union Leagues at Toronto and in other parts of Ontario. They worked in close co-operation with the different Farmers' Institutes of the province, and supplied speakers and literature on the subject of unrestricted reciprocity with the United States. On April 28, 1887, a convention of these institutes met at Toronto and adopted a resolution in favor of the "removal of all trade restrictions between Canada and the United States, either by reciprocity or otherwise." Many of the other Farmers' Institutes passed similar resolutions favoring commercial union.[89]

The Toronto *Mail* was eager to take a prominent part in this movement. On March 1 it expressed the opinion that commercial union would be of great benefit to Canada. The chief objection raised in Canada to unrestricted reciprocity with the United States was that it might endanger the "British connection." The *Mail* then asked the question as to whether Canadians could "afford to be swayed by sentiment."[90] Some weeks later, the *Mail* returned to this same topic: "Should it be found necessary, in order to reach a settlement with the Americans, still further to alter our relations with the Mother Country, . . . we must face the question like men."[91]

87. J. W. Longley to Erastus Wiman, March 28, 1887, Ritchie, *op. cit.*, pp. 12–13.

88. For a comprehensive and scholarly treatment of the economic and political views of Goldwin Smith, see Ronald A. McEachern, "Goldwin Smith." This is a MS. Ph.D. dissertation at the University of Toronto, 1934.

89. Willison, *op. cit.*, II, 123–124.

90. Toronto *Mail*, March 1, 1887.

91. *Ibid.*, April 26, 1887. See also, the Toronto *Globe*, April 20, 1887, and the Montreal *Herald*, April 18, 1887. On April 28, 1887, the Toronto *Globe* editorially remarked: "If commercial union between Canada and the United States is, as we believe, consistent with either the political connection of Canada and Great Britain, or

In Western Canada there was a widespread feeling in favor of commercial union. To the Manitoba *Free Press* it was apparent that "commercial union would give us a free market of 62,000,000 people in the United States, . . . and while our exports to Great Britain would probably remain the same, those to the United States, the duty being removed, would so exceed those to Great Britain that Diogenes would not require his lantern to find out the natural trend of our trade."[92]

These Canadian sentiments concerning commercial union were very pleasing to certain American business men who hoped to profit by the situation. Wharton Barker, a Philadelphia banker, had long been interested in closer commercial relations between Canada and the United States. In January, 1886, he expressed the view that "commercial union of the two countries would furnish the best possible solution of the fisheries question," and would prepare the way for a close fellowship "in the administration of our common heritage of resources and capacities."[93] When the movement for commercial union gained headway in Canada, Barker wrote to Sir John Macdonald and stressed the importance of early action. In the United States there was a general feeling that "we must not trifle with these questions, and there is a fixed purpose to come to an understanding at once. Our people will reject any and all reciprocity treaties, yet they are ready . . . for Commercial Union."[94]

Sir John did not believe that commercial union would be the best panacea for the economic ills that still plagued Canada, and he was distinctly suspicious of the political implications of any type of unrestricted reciprocity. Many of his Canadian correspondents entertained similar suspicions. Samuel Hughes was certain that Bunting, Farrer[95] and the Toronto *Mail* were "body and bones" for annexation to the United States. Commercial union was merely a "sugar-coated name. That I know for *certain.*" Erastus Wiman and his associates were laying plans to "hold the *Grits,* . . . and by the *Mail's* assistance, allies sufficient will be gained over to bounce you."[96]

the political independence of Canada, then there can be no sentimental argument against it. On the contrary, all sound sentiment is for it. A great service would be rendered to Great Britain by a trade arrangement that would remove all causes of dispute between Canada and the States."

92. Manitoba *Free Press,* July 13, 1887.

93. Wharton Barker to William M. Evarts, January 5, 1886, quoted in Ritchie, *op. cit.,* pp. 14–15.

94. Wharton Barker to Sir John Macdonald, April 17, 1887, *Macdonald Papers, Commercial Union, 1886–1887,* pp. 31–32, P.A.C.

95. Edward Farrer was the chief editorial writer on the Toronto *Mail.*

96. Samuel Hughes to Sir John Macdonald, May 25, 1887, *Macdonald Papers, Commercial Union, 1886–1887,* pp. 37–40, P.A.C.

With Canadian manufacturers strongly behind Sir John, there was small chance for the Liberals to "bounce" him. In the *Canadian Manufacturer and Industrial World*, April 15, 1887, the manufacturers published a manifesto of their aims and principles. Reciprocity would affect adversely the infant industries of Canada that were still struggling to maintain themselves during a period of depression. American factory owners saw in Canada a rich and "inviting field in which they desire to market their products," but Canadian business men would not be willing to play a subordinate part in the exploitation of these commercial opportunities. The Canadian "national policy" of tariff protection would not be abandoned at a time when it was most badly needed.[97]

This hostile sentiment of Canadian manufacturers towards the idea of commercial union was quite apparent to Benjamin Butterworth, who made a tour of certain parts of Canada in the summer of 1887 for the purpose of studying the reaction to the bill he had introduced in the American Congress. He found the "feeling among the manufacturers of Canada not especially friendly to full reciprocity with the United States. Some of the merchants thought it not to be a thing desirable, but taking the population as a whole, I have not a doubt that three out of every four desire free and unrestricted trade with the United States."[98]

In his enthusiasm for commercial union, Butterworth was voicing the sentiments of many prominent Republicans in the United States. On April 11, 1887, Robert R. Hitt, an important member of the House of Representatives, wrote a letter to Wiman in which he expressed the opinion that American troubles with Canada would never be "permanently and satisfactorily settled by any measure short of commercial union, and the removal of all restrictions upon trade and intercourse between the two countries."[99]

Bayard was interested in these activities on the part of Republican politicians, and he tried to fathom their meaning. In a letter to Phelps he refers to them as follows:

A proposition for unlimited reciprocity . . . has been introduced into the House of Representatives by Mr. Butterworth, and he has since been frequently to this department, accompanied by persons interested in the Canadian trade, and it is their purpose to have a great meeting called very shortly in the city of New York which is intended to give voice to a desire for reci-

97. VI, 229.
98. Montreal *Star,* July 15, 1887.
99. Robert R. Hitt to Erastus Wiman, April 11, 1887, quoted in Ritchie, *op. cit.,* pp. 6–7.

procity and free trade with Canada. The support of this plan is very marked from high protective sources, . . . and Blaine's fugleman Hitt, of Illinois, has been very prominent in favoring a Commercial Union with Canada.[100]

This meeting to which Bayard referred was held in New York City on May 19, with Mr. Wiman as presiding officer. The principal event of the evening was a speech by Mr. Butterworth on the subject of commercial union. It was a long and detailed effort in which the modern note of hemispheric solidarity was clearly sounded. As against the old world, "both Americans and Canadians may invoke the protective system; but as between Canadians and Americans it has no proper place." The existing tariffs between the two countries should be immediately abolished. The

present system which compels our Canadian neighbors to pay a high duty on fifty millions of dollars worth of goods a year for the privilege of supplying to the citizens of the United States articles indispensable to their comfort and prosperity, and which compels the citizens of the United States to pay a like sum into the public treasury of Canada for the privilege of doing like service for Canadians, . . . is absolutely defenceless and wholly without excuse.

After this sharp indictment of the protective system as applied to Canada, Butterworth endeavored to banish the fears of Canadian manufacturers with regard to American competition, and he warmly assured his audience that commercial union would not be a prelude to annexation. After having glibly dismissed all the objections to unrestricted reciprocity between the United States and Canada, Butterworth called upon "every chamber of commerce, every agricultural association, every society composed of manufacturers and producers" to echo his arguments.[101]

This heated oratory from Butterworth must have been read by Sir Charles Tupper with keen interest. Tupper had been encouraged by Erastus Wiman to visit the United States and talk over matters with Secretary Bayard. After some hesitation he adopted the suggestion.[102]

100. Secretary Bayard to Phelps, April 23, 1887, *Bayard Letter Book,* IV, *Bayard MS.* J. S. Moore wrote a letter of protest to Bayard, April 25, 1887, with reference to establishing a system of commercial union with Canada. He thought a "Zollverein with Canada, as long as we groan under the present outrageous tariff, would be a misfortune, because we would be asked to carry some 6,000,000 Canadian infants and their infant industries on our backs until they grew up." *Bayard MS.*

101. Benjamin Butterworth, *Commercial Union between Canada and the United States* (New York, 1887), pp. 5–39.

102. See letters from Erastus Wiman to Secretary Bayard, April 18, 22, 30, 1887, *Bayard MS.*

On May 21 he paid a visit to the Department of State and had a long conversation with Bayard. He referred to the "strong movement" in favor of commercial reciprocity between Canada and the United States, but he discounted any possibility that commercial union between the two countries could be established. In this regard Mr. Wiman's efforts were in vain. Even with reference to reciprocity, there would be objections from Canadian owners of coal mines and from Canadian farmers.

At this point Bayard remarked that he and President Cleveland were "strongly in favor of reciprocity," and it was evident that the "disposition to a freer trade between the United States and Canada" had gained ground "with the present Administration." He agreed with Sir Charles Tupper that there was not "the slightest necessity for proceeding in a commercial union to the extent advocated by Messrs. Butterworth and Wiman." In the matter of reciprocity negotiations, the best procedure would be to place everything in the hands of a joint commission that "could sift the statistics of production and the present course of trade."[103]

Bayard next discussed the situation with President Cleveland, and on May 31, he wrote to Tupper and expressed the conviction that the only way to secure a permanent settlement of the questions at issue between Canada and the United States was through the adoption of a "liberal and statesmanlike plan" that would deal with the "entire commercial relations of the two countries." The gravity of the situation demanded a mutual attitude of "entire frankness." The "roundabout manner," so characteristic of previous negotiations, should be discarded in favor of direct and friendly conversations. In order that these could begin at the "earliest possible day," Bayard was ready to welcome representatives of the British Government whenever they could find it convenient to visit Washington.[104]

103. *Memorandum* dictated by Bayard after a conversation with Sir Charles Tupper, May 21, 1888, *ibid.* In a personal letter to Phelps, May 30, 1887, Bayard spoke of Tupper's visit and observed: "He came to propose negotiations, and was, of course, very friendly. He was opposed to a Commercial Union, but willing for reciprocity in certain staple productions. I agreed with him as to the Commercial Union, for it necessarily involves a blending of the systems of taxation, and is 'entangling' in the strongest sense. But he proposed to treat *here,* and after conversation with the President, I have determined to agree to it." *Bayard Letter Book,* V, *Bayard MS.*

In the summer of 1888, Bayard had a long conversation with Lawrence Oliphant who expressed the opinion that if the Marcy-Elgin Treaty of 1854 had not been abrogated in 1866, "Canada would have been under the same government as the United States." Bayard to S. L. Barlow, December 28, 1888, *Bayard MS.*

104. Secretary Bayard to Sir Charles Tupper, May 31, 1887, Tupper, *op. cit.,* pp. 177–180. In a personal letter to Phelps, May 31, 1887, Bayard remarked: "If the *principle* of a settlement on the basis of reciprocity is agreed upon in the treaty, the schedule of articles can be (must be) regulated by Legislation. If there is anything

Bayard had also referred to the advisability of sending a Canadian statesman to conduct these negotiations which should aim to settle not only existing disputes but should lay the basis for a plan to adjust all future controversies. In his reply to Bayard's letter, Sir Charles Tupper mentioned with approval these important suggestions. It was also clear that he was willing to admit that the British Government would show great wisdom in selecting him as the Canadian representative.[105]

While the British Government was giving careful consideration to the question of the appointment of a joint commission to deal with the questions that disturbed Canadian-American relations, in Canada the feeling in favor of commercial union became more pronounced. To Goldwin Smith it seemed apparent that victory for commercial union was inevitable. In a letter to Francis Wharton he commented upon the opposition of the protectionist element in Canada, but when the great "natural industries of the country, agriculture, lumbering, mining and shipping" were heard from, the result could "hardly be doubtful."[106]

From W. L. Putnam, Bayard received word that the idea of commercial union had made "amazing progress" in Canada, not only in the Lower Provinces, but also in Ontario. It was expected that Sir John Macdonald would have to start a crusade against it with "fire and sword."[107] But Sir John would have some doughty foes to meet in this struggle, for some of the leaders of the Liberal Party were breaking through the restraints imposed by Edward Blake, and were openly advocating unrestricted reciprocity with the United States.[108] This was particularly true of Sir Richard Cartwright, former Dominion Minister of Finance, and now one of the most forceful speakers in the Liberal Party. On October 12, at Ingersoll, Cartwright threw out the following challenge:

I have no hesitation in saying frankly that if the United States are willing to deal with us on equitable terms the advantages of commercial union to both countries, and especially to us, are so great that scarcely any sacrifice is too severe to secure them. . . . I say deliberately that the refusal or failure

in John Sherman's profession of a desire for 'Commercial Union' with Canada, there will be no difficulty in procuring a majority in the Senate for a bill that will include a settlement of the present difficulty." *Bayard Letter Book,* V, *Bayard MS.*

105. Sir Charles Tupper to Secretary Bayard, June 6, 1887, Tupper, *op. cit.,* pp. 181–182.

106. Goldwin Smith to Francis Wharton, June 11, 1887, *Bayard MS.*

107. W. L. Putnam to Secretary Bayard, June 21, 1887, *ibid.*

108. It is interesting to note that in 1887, Wilfrid Laurier was opposed to the idea of commercial union. At Somerset, Quebec, in August 1887, Laurier frankly stated that he was "not ready to declare that commercial union is an acceptable idea. . . . A great deal of study and reflection are needed to solve this question, for and against which there is much to be said." Willison, *Laurier,* II, 141.

to secure free trade with the United States is much more likely to bring about just such a political crisis as these parties affect to dread than even the very closest commercial connection that can be conceived.[109]

This speech caused widespread comment in the Canadian press because it was regarded not only as a manifesto on the part of an outstanding Liberal leader, but also as an attempt to color the thought of the British representatives on the Joint Commission that was soon to sit in Washington.[110] Erastus Wiman followed the lead of Cartwright, and on October 14, in an interview with a reporter of the Toronto *Globe,* he discussed some of the implications of commercial union. He admitted that in the United States there was "no public sentiment of any weight as yet in regard to the matter," but the Butterworth bill had awakened in Congress a very real interest in unrestricted reciprocity with Canada. There was, he believed, a "very good chance" that the bill would pass the House of Representatives. In the Senate there would be "greater difficulty," but it was to be hoped that many Senators would regard commercial union "as the best settlement possible of the Fishery question." It was almost certain that Secretary Bayard favored such a solution.[111]

Some of the Canadian newspapers were aroused by the report that in a speech in Belfast, Joseph Chamberlain, one of the British representatives on the Joint Commission, that was soon to sit in Washington, had exploded that if Canada desired commercial union "she must be made to know that it means political separation from Great Britain." In commenting upon this statement, the Toronto *Mail* expressed the opinion that this threat would "not disturb the friends of Commercial Union, nor diminish the enthusiasm which the movement is evoking in every part of the country."[112] The Montreal *Witness* believed that the only conclusion that could be drawn from Chamberlain's alleged remarks was that he had either allowed himself flippantly "to prejudge

109. New York *Times,* October 14, 1887. On April 2, 1887, the Toronto *Globe* had published a series of letters from farmers who were desirous of unrestricted reciprocity with the United States. For other comments in the *Globe* on commercial union, see September 20, October 26, 30, 1887. See also, Ottawa *Free Press,* July 13, 19, 1887, the Montreal *Herald,* July 15, 1887.

110. In his Ingersoll speech, Cartwright had pungently stated with reference to the attitude of the Canadian representative on the Joint Commission: "The present is precisely one of those cases in which it is absolutely indispensable that the parties who conduct the negotiation on our side shall be thoroughly in earnest. There is any amount of room for trickery and evasion if the negotiator so desires, and therein lies your danger." Toronto *Globe,* October 15, 1887.

111. Toronto *Globe,* October 15, 1887.

112. October 17, 1887.

the most important matter ever placed before him without weighing his words," or his solution of Canadian difficulties "is to hand Canada over as a contemptible mischief-maker to the United States."[113] To the Toronto *World*, however, the remarks of Chamberlain meant that commercial union "is a very dead duck."[114]

This estimate of the situation was apparently far from correct. Word came from Ottawa that Lord Lansdowne was strongly in sympathy "with the movement towards closer commercial relations with the United States,"[115] and at St. Johns, New Brunswick, the President of the Board of Trade came out in favor of commercial union because of "mutual benefits enjoyed during the previous treaty."[116] In commenting upon the spread of the idea of commercial union in Canada, Erastus Wiman observed: "The progress of the movement in favor of commercial union in Canada is one of the most remarkable events that has ever occurred in any community."[117]

In confirmation of this view, the Interprovincial Conference met in Quebec in November, 1887, and unanimously adopted a resolution in favor of "unrestricted reciprocity" with the United States.[118] The Toronto *Mail* was certain that this resolution must have fallen like a "bombshell in the opposite camp." Sir Charles Tupper might "pooh-pooh this important declaration," but neither Mr. Chamberlain nor Lord Salisbury was likely to do so.[119]

In the United States, the indifference, about which Wiman had complained, had evaporated, and so stalwart a Republican newspaper as the Chicago *Tribune* came out in favor of commercial union.[120] In Maine there was open approval of the movement. A. J. Fuller, President of the Bath Board of Trade, came out with a declaration for commercial union, and J. E. Blabon, President of the Portland Board of Trade, was a little confused, but generally favorable: "I have always believed in reciprocity. . . . I have not studied into the matter of commercial union; but, if it is reciprocity, I believe in it."[121]

113. October 17, 1887. 114. October 17, 1887.

115. Boston *Herald,* October 28, 1887.

116. New York *Herald,* October 30, 1887.

117. New York *Sun,* October 23, 1887. On August 27 and 30, 1887, Wiman had made long speeches in favor of commercial union before the "commercial bodies" of Detroit and Buffalo. See Wiman, *Commercial Union with Canada from a United States Point of View.*

118. Toronto *Globe,* November 10, 1887. The Interprovincial Conference was made up of representatives of the Liberal Governments of Ontario, Quebec, Nova Scotia, and Prince Edward Island, of the Coalition Government of New Brunswick, and of the Conservative Government of Manitoba.

119. November 12, 1887. 120. October 24, 1887.

121. Portland *Argus,* November 4, 1887.

Interest in commercial union suddenly became manifest in New York City when the Chamber of Commerce adopted a resolution which provided for the appointment of a committee to study the question.[122] To the New York *Evening Post*, this action was a clear indication of the rapidity with which the idea of commercial union was penetrating the business world. It was also a sign of ultimate success.[123]

The movement spread to Boston where the advocates of commercial union held a large meeting on December 28, which was attended by many prominent Canadians including J. W. Longley, Attorney-General of Nova Scotia, and James Perrault, Vice-President of the Montreal Chamber of Commerce. Members of Congress like Robert Hitt and J. J. Rogers were present, and they promised their continued support of the Butterworth bill. Mr. Longley, in one of the more important addresses before the meeting, announced that he was "both a commercial unionist and an annexationist."[124] Mr. Wiman made his usual remarks about the blessings that would attend the consummation of such a union.

There is little doubt that in the autumn of 1887, belief in commercial union was widespread in Canada, and Goldwin Smith inclined towards the view that nearly seven-eighths of the people were in favor of such a system.[125] It is impossible to test the verity of this estimate, but it is certain that the movement was spreading fast. It had been apparent that even Lord Lansdowne was not unaffected by the contagion, and in a despatch to the Colonial Office he had no hesitation in declaring that commercial union would be of distinct advantage to many Canadian farmers.[126]

Through the agency of Joseph Chamberlain, a copy of Lansdowne's despatch was sent to Sir John Macdonald. He read it with "some regret, but without surprise." He had long known that Lansdowne was a "free trader to the bone, and all such men are deaf and blind to any other considerations but the blind teachings of abstract political economy." But there was nothing to be worried about in this movement

122. New York *Herald,* November 4, 1887.

123. November 4, 1887.

124. Boston *Post,* December 29, 1887. On October 18, 1887, M. H. Phelan, U. S. Consul at Halifax, wrote to Bayard with reference to J. W. Longley: "Longley is one of the leaders of *Commercial Union,* and I believe the father of the movement. He is an *annexationist,* bold and indiscreet in his utterances, and if an opportunity presents itself, you will learn some of the absurdities of Canadian politics." *Bayard MS.*

125. Goldwin Smith to Francis Wharton, October 18, 1887, *ibid.*

126. Lord Lansdowne to the Colonial Office, October 31, 1887, *Macdonald Papers, Commercial Union, 1886–1887,* pp. 189–205, P.A.C.

towards commercial union. He was certain that it was a "dead duck," and that all fears concerning it were groundless.[127]

In the Liberal Party there was a sharp split over the question of commercial union. Laurier, who had succeeded Blake as the party leader was cautious about taking any decided stand in the matter, but many of his colleagues were not so wary. J. D. Edgar believed that it would be found "that Unrestricted Reciprocity, as distinguished from Commercial Union with uniform tariffs, will be as far as we can go as a party unless events march very fast."[128]

Louis H. Davies saw the dangers of commercial union, but was willing to brave them for the benefits that might follow the adoption of such a far-reaching system. The strength of the movement in Canada rested upon the popular belief that the American Government was not interested in any form of restricted reciprocity. If this belief were true, Davies thought that the Liberals should be ready to "jump at" commercial union, notwithstanding the "loss our revenue would sustain and the apparent unfairness of discrimination against Great Britain."[129]

While Canadians were disputing over the implications contained in the movement for commercial union, the members of the Joint Commission began to assemble in Washington for the purpose of preliminary discussions on the topic of the fisheries. Joseph Chamberlain had landed in New York City on November 7, and it was not long before he made the acquaintance of Mr. Wiman. Chamberlain was familiar with Wiman's viewpoint, and he took occasion bluntly to inform him that the British Government "would not listen to the proposal for Commercial Union between the United States and Canada while Canada remained in the British Empire."[130]

When the Joint Commission formally met on November 22, 1887, it was soon discovered that Secretary Bayard was determined to restrict discussions to the fisheries question;[131] there would be no opportunity

127. Sir John Macdonald to Sir Charles Tupper, January 15, 1888, *ibid.*, pp. 187–188.

128. J. D. Edgar to Laurier, November 30, 1887, *Laurier MS.*, P.A.C.

129. Louis H. Davies to Laurier, November 26, 1887, *ibid.*

130. John S. D. Thompson to Sir John Macdonald, November 18, 1887, *Macdonald Papers, Washington Treaty, 1888,* III, 2–5, P.A.C.

131. In a personal letter to Phelps, December 6, 1887, Bayard commented upon the discussions at the meetings of the Joint Commission and remarked: "It may well be that by legislation an expanded *free list* may procure for Canada access to our markets, which she has apparently been using a harsh and vexatious administration of her Fishery laws, and an extreme interpretation of the treaty of 1818 to obtain. But to establish reform of the tariff to suit her local interests by means of a Commercial Treaty at this time, would be impossible." *Bayard Letter Book,* VI, *Bayard MS.*

to go into the merits or demerits of commercial union. But this decision on the part of Bayard did not mean there would be no informal conversations on this important topic. In a letter to Sir John Macdonald, Sir Charles Tupper gave the gist of some of these conversations: "I have discussed the unrestricted Commercial Union question with Mr. Carlisle and Mr. Bayard, . . . and they both agree that it is utterly impracticable."[132]

On December 10, the Joint Commission reached a deadlock, and Chamberlain decided to visit Canada in order to get a first-hand acquaintance with the opinions of Sir John Macdonald and Lord Lansdowne. While in Canada he made a speech before the Toronto Board of Trade in which he sounded a warning against commercial union with the United States. He was in favor of one type of commercial union—union with "all the world." That would be the "true Unrestricted Reciprocity." Less than this idea would be a restricted reciprocity that would make Canadians dependent for their financial freedom "upon the Government of another state, and perhaps pave the way for the surrender of something which is still more important—I mean political independence."[133]

In his biography of Joseph Chamberlain, James L. Garvin gives a

132. Sir Charles Tupper to Sir John Macdonald, November 25, 1887, *Macdonald Papers, Washington Treaty, 1888,* III, 116–124, P.A.C. On November 24, Tupper had a long conversation with Mr. Carlisle, Speaker of the House of Representatives, concerning reciprocity and the framing of American tariff schedules: "After mailing my letter to you yesterday, I returned the visit of Mr. Carlisle at Riggs Hotel where he received me with the utmost cordiality. . . . He said he was arranging with the President and Cabinet the Tariff policy of the coming session and that they had decided to put coal, lumber, fish, iron and copper ores, salt and wool on the free list, and that he expected that it would be carried as the democratic party had a large majority in the House of Representatives and there was only a majority of one opposed to them in the Senate, and they would not be united in opposition to such a policy. We discussed the fish and lumber and coal questions fully. He took the ground that the admission of raw products free was not in antagonism with the protective policy and would assist in reducing the surplus which has become so embarrassing. He said the President told him that he had no intention of sacrificing the whole country to the clamor of a few fishermen and said the duty on lumber was an injury to the whole country. . . . I found him disposed to talk freely and thought it better to listen than ask questions and therefore did not enquire how they proposed to deal with the products of the farm. I have however asked Mr. S. J. Ritchie who is here and who has gone to see Mr. Carlisle, to ascertain that confidentially for me."

In a personal letter to Phelps, November 21, 1887, Bayard discussed the matter of tariff concessions to Canadian products and stated: "All the proposed free lists I have seen contain: coal, fish, cereals and lumber. Thus it is plain that a market for their fish may await the Canadians as a consequence of our own domestic arrangements if they do not thwart it by their own folly and stupidity." *Bayard Letter Book,* VI, *Bayard MS.*

133. Toronto *Globe,* December 31, 1887.

graphic picture of the effect of Chamberlain's speech upon his audience. The enthusiasm he evoked appeared to indicate that in Toronto the idea of commercial union was dead, and that in other parts of Canada it was moribund.[134] But Goldwin Smith would not have agreed with such a judgment. In November, 1887, he had assured one of his correspondents that the movement for commercial union was spreading fast, and that only in the province of Quebec had it failed to make substantial progress. There the "dominant priesthood opposes everything that is likely to bring the people more into contact with the liberalizing influences of the Republic."[135] To Secretary Bayard, Smith gave similar assurances even after the Chamberlain speech. In February, 1888, he was certain that the idea of commercial union was gaining an increasing hold "on the popular mind." Forty-three of the Farmers' Institutes in Ontario Province had declared in its favor, while "only two or three have demurred."[136]

During this period of discussion in Canada concerning the subject of unrestricted reciprocity with the United States, a Joint High Commission in Washington was dealing with the same topic. As the chief spokesman for the American delegation, Bayard declared that the failure to frame a reciprocity treaty or even to agree to certain tariff adjustments should not be considered by the British Commissioners as a just grievance. He had noticed with regret that they had been constantly pushing for certain tariff concessions with a pertinacity that was, at times, disturbing. The chief item they clamored for was the one concerning the entry of all Canadian fish free of duty. From the first meeting this item had been with them a *sine qua non*, and every proposal they submitted had contained "this feature and made to depend upon its acceptance." In various forms on different days, and "at some part of every proposal, this has been put forward by the British Plenipotentiaries." In substance they have said: "You can procure no re-

134. Garvin, *Chamberlain,* II, 333–335.

135. Goldwin Smith to Lord Farrer, August 21, 1887, *Goldwin Smith's Correspondence* (London, 1913), p. 204.

136. Goldwin Smith to Secretary Bayard, February 20, 1888, *Bayard MS.* In order to influence Bayard's mind with reference to Canadian opinion regarding closer commercial connections with the United States, Erastus Wiman sent to the Department of State, December 13, 1887, a letter introducing William MacDougall. MacDougall was visiting Washington "in the interest of the Great Party in Canada who are desirous of closer commercial relations with the United States, and his views and information, will, I am sure, be of great value to you. He is not in sympathy with the existing Government, but I am certain that he more correctly represents the state of public sentiment in Canada than any man you have met." *Bayard MS.*

dress, no satisfaction unless you do so by an alleviation of your tariff."[137]

At the meeting on January 14, Bayard, in an endeavor to find some solution for the threatened deadlock of the commission, encouraged a discussion of the topic of closer commercial relations between Canada and the United States. In conclusion he presented the American viewpoint in concise form:

> Commercial Union—We may agree that it is impracticable, yet we will agree that a liberal system of reciprocity may be obtained by free exchanges and through voluntary concerted Legislation. That a strong disposition exists in the public mind on this subject, has been variously exhibited, and happily in the United States no party expression has accompanied it. Is it not obvious that if this current of sentiment is not arrested, that much *freer trade* must soon take place between Canada, Newfoundland and the United States? . . . In other words, we earnestly desire to seek an opportunity for Canada and Newfoundland to have access to their best and most necessary market, and at the same time to save their government all cost of policing their shores at cost greater than the duties they at present pay on their fish, for more than half . . . come in free already.[138]

Bayard realized that it would be impossible to get the Senate to agree to a reciprocity treaty. His plan, therefore, was to secure a form of reciprocity through tariff concessions inserted into the legislation of both countries. With the Democrats in control of the House of Representatives, and with the Republican majority in the Senate reduced to a very slight margin, reciprocity with Canada in many items seemed to be well within the range of possibility.

In the treaty that the Joint Commission signed on February 15, 1888, there was one item that dealt with tariff concessions. In the event that Congress should remove the duties on fish oil, whale oil, seal oil and fish of all kinds coming from Canada and Newfoundland, the governments of those countries would issue licenses free of charge which would enable American fishing vessels to purchase provisions and fishing supplies in any ports they might enter. It would be a very slight tariff concession, but it might lead to a more liberal attitude on the part of American legislators. This fact seemed obvious to Bayard, who wrote with satisfaction to Putnam concerning the recent action of Congress:

> Do you see the proof of what we told the British Plenipotentiaries about

137. Undated *memorandum* written by Bayard, *ibid.*
138. *Memorandum* written by Bayard, January 14, 1888, *ibid.*

Canada's interests in our tariff, which is shown in the proposed bill of the Committee on Ways and Means? Free wool, free lumber, free vegetables, are worth ten times over free fish to Canada. She fought for the last and did not get it, and the first three will probably come without application. No more severe commentary upon the miserably unwise policy which dictated the treatment of our Fishermen in 1886–87 could be found than in this very tariff bill. Who can doubt that Fish would have been put in the free list but for Canadian action?[139]

Many leaders in the movement for commercial union agreed with Bayard that it would be good policy to support the treaty of February 15, 1888. S. J. Ritchie hoped to exploit the situation so as to bring large financial rewards to him and his intimate friends. He had long been trying to get the Canadian Government to build a railroad close to some of his mines in Ontario Province, but he had not been able to secure any favorable action on the part of Canadian officials. In order to compel them to take an interest in his project he would have to gain the support of Sir John Macdonald. It might be possible to do this by means of a deal whereby he would promise to go to Washington and lobby for the ratification of the fisheries treaty if Sir John would pledge assistance in the matter of building the railroad connection to the mines near Sudbury. On March 23, he wrote to Sir John and outlined his plan: "If you will see that this railways bill of mine goes through when the Committee meets next Tuesday, I will go to Washington tomorrow and do what I can to have the treaty matter arranged as we talked this afternoon. I feel quite sure it can be done."[140]

Without waiting for the details of a definite arrangement to be worked out, Ritchie repaired to Washington and talked the situation over with Senator Sherman, the chairman of the Senate Committee on Foreign Relations. Sherman was evasive in his answers, but he did promise that the treaty would be considered "outside and separate from any party standpoint or bias." Senator Payne was more co-operative, and apparently was glad to make strenuous efforts to "create a favorable opinion in behalf of the measure." If it became apparent that the treaty could not be ratified, the vote would be postponed until a more favorable moment.[141]

139. Secretary Bayard to W. L. Putnam, March 3, 1888, *Bayard Letter Book,* VII, *Bayard MS.* Bayard's reference is to the Mills Bill, whose schedules were made public on March 1. The bill was passed by the House of Representatives on July 21, 1888. See Ida M. Tarbell, *The Tariff in Our Times* (New York, 1911), chap. vii.

140. S. J. Ritchie to Sir John Macdonald, March 23, 1888, *Macdonald Papers, S. J. Ritchie Correspondence, 1884–1891,* pp. 1–2, P.A.C.

141. S. J. Ritchie to Sir John Macdonald, March 27, 1888, *ibid.,* pp. 18–21.

Ritchie found that Speaker Carlisle was "very favorable to liberal trade arrangements with Canada," and he had high hopes that a sentiment in favor of the fisheries treaty could be developed in a short time. He was deeply disappointed, however, at Macdonald's failure to secure favorable consideration of the railroad to the mines: "I understood when I left that you would see my Railroad Bill did not miscarry for lack of a formal compliance with regulations, and of course was not a little surprised to get a telegram from Ferguson that the Committee had thrown it out. I fully understand the potency of any word that you may say to this Committee. . . . In the meantime I am doing all I can for you."[142]

Macdonald was too wily a politician to give any formal assurances to Ritchie with reference to his railroad connection, but Ritchie continued to nurse his hopes and he did not relax his efforts on behalf of the fisheries treaty. While he was lobbying in Washington, some of his friends renewed their activities in favor of commercial union. On January 23, 1888, Butterworth introduced a resolution which declared that the American Government should "in the interest of peace and amity between nations, and in response to the demands of our manufacturers," remove all "obstacles and hindrances to complete and unrestricted trade and commerce between the United States and the Dominion of Canada."[143] On February 6, he followed this resolution with a bill (H.R. 6668) which made provision for "full reciprocity" with Canada.[144]

Mr. Hitt was equally active in the cause of commercial union. On March 5, 1888, he introduced a joint resolution (H. Res. 129) intended to "promote commercial union with Canada."[145] Some ten days later (March 16) he reported his resolution back from the House Committee on Foreign Affairs, with a favorable recommendation,[146] and it finally passed the House of Representatives on March 1, 1889, without a record vote.[147]

In response to these American overtures, Sir Richard Cartwright introduced in the Canadian House of Commons (March 14, 1888) a resolution which called for the establishment of "full and unrestricted reciprocity" with the United States.[148] On March 26, he wrote to Bayard

142. S. J. Ritchie to Sir John Macdonald, March 31, 1888, *ibid.*, pp. 23–24.

143. *Congressional Record,* 50 Cong., 1 sess., p. 635. See also, *House Misc. Doc. No. 133,* 50 Cong., 1 sess.

144. *Congressional Record,* 50 Cong., 1 sess., p. 984.

145. *Ibid.*, p. 1746.

146. *Congressional Record,* 50 Cong., 1 sess., p. 2157. See also, *House Rept. No. 1183,* 50 Cong., 1 sess.

147. *Congressional Record,* 50 Cong., 2 sess., p. 2539.

148. *Canada: House of Commons, Debates, 1888,* March 14, 1888, p. 144.

and enclosed a copy of the speech he had delivered in support of his resolution.[149] He was firmly of the opinion that his resolution represented the "real wishes of the *people* of Canada very much more than the division thereon in our present House of Commons is likely to do."[150]

In reply to this friendly letter, Bayard assured Cartwright that "all reciprocal commerce and convenience that can be induced and fostered between the people of Canada and those of the United States meets my approval."[151]

When Cartwright's resolution was defeated in the Canadian House of Commons (April 6, 1888), Goldwin Smith was anxious that Bayard should not get the wrong impression of the situation in Canada. The vote in the House was not a "decision of the Canadian people, but simply that of a Parliament elected before Commercial Union had come into the field." The next election would tell "a very different tale."[152]

Cartwright himself was a little fearful that President Cleveland might misinterpret the action of the Canadian Parliament and be inclined to take some retaliatory action under the terms of the Act of March 3, 1887. He wrote to Wiman about his apprehensions, and they were promptly placed before Secretary Bayard.[153] In his reply to Wiman's letter, Bayard was somewhat noncommittal, but it was not hard to read between the lines and see that no harsh policy would be put in force by the President.[154]

149. In his speech of March 14, 1888, Cartwright gave a careful review of the economic relations between Canada and the United States. He believed it was hardly necessary for him to indicate "the enormous advantage which unrestricted trade with the United States would be to us. Who does not know that for an immense number of the products of the people of this country, the United States is not merely the best market, but substantially the only market? . . . With the absurdity of two hostile tariffs stretching for three thousand miles between these two countries, let hon. gentlemen consider what we do already in the way of mutual trade. Of the $202,000,-000 which represents our total volume of trade, over $80,000,000, . . . or nearly one-half . . . is with the United States. . . . I will venture to say that . . . with unrestricted intercourse with the United States, that $80,000,000 might within a very few years swell to $300,000,000." *Ibid.,* pp. 144ff.

150. Sir Richard Cartwright to Secretary Bayard, March 26, 1888, *Bayard MS.*

151. Secretary Bayard to Sir Richard Cartwright, March 31, 1888, *Bayard Letter Book,* VII, *Bayard MS.*

152. Goldwin Smith to Secretary Bayard, April 11, 1888, *ibid.* The Cartwright resolution was defeated by a vote of 124 nays to 67 yeas. The opposition then adopted a resolution that expressed a desire for an extension of Canada's trade relations with the United States, but this extension should not "conflict with the policy of fostering the various industries and interests of the Dominion." *Canada: House of Commons, Debates, 1888,* April 6, 1888, p. 646.

153. Erastus Wiman to Secretary Bayard, May 29, 1888, *Bayard MS.*

154. Secretary Bayard to Erastus Wiman, May 31, 1888, *Bayard Letter Book,* VI, *Bayard MS.*

Goldwin Smith was greatly encouraged by the friendly attitude of the Cleveland Administration, and he continued to cherish hopes for the success of commercial union and eventual annexation. In the last week in May, 1888, he wrote to Bayard to record the fact that five by-elections had gone in favor of the candidates who were known to be friendly to unrestricted reciprocity.[155] Some weeks later he informed Bayard that the Liberal Party in Manitoba, which was "identified with Commercial Union," had carried "thirty-five elections out of thirty-eight." There was no doubt about the success of this party "in a general election."[156]

In the meantime, the debate in the Senate on the fisheries treaty had opened on May 29, with a bitter attack by Senator Frye. It was soon apparent that some Republican Senators were in opposition to the treaty because they feared it might put an end to the difficulties that had long existed between Canada and the United States. If this dissatisfaction would continue and conditions in Canada remain unsettled, there was a strong possibility that the Canadian Government might turn to annexation as the only way of saving the situation.

This was the viewpoint of Senator Sherman, who showed no hesitancy in avowing it in a speech he made on August 7, 1888. He took pains to emphasize the economic ties that had been established between Canada and the State of Ohio. The citizens of his state had invested large sums of money in Canadian mines and other properties. Their commercial intercourse was of the "closest character." Therefore, anything that would

> tend to promote free commercial intercourse between these countries, yes, anything that will tend to produce a union of Canada with the United States of America, will meet with my most hearty support. . . . I would favor . . . something in the nature of a Zollverein to relieve us from establishing a line of customs-houses . . . along the border. . . . I want Canada to be part of the United States.

He was opposed to the pending fisheries treaty because it would "erect a barrier and prevent the very objects that are sought to be accomplished."[157]

155. Goldwin Smith to Secretary Bayard, May 31, 1888, *Bayard MS.*

156. Goldwin Smith to Secretary Bayard, July 20, 1888, *ibid.*

157. *Congressional Record,* 50 Cong., 1 sess., p. 7286. See also, Sherman's speech on September 18, 1888, *Congressional Record,* 50 Cong., 1 sess., pp. 8666–8667, and his *Recollections of Forty Years* (New York, 1895), II, 1017–1021. On August 9, 1888, Jonathan A. Lane, President of the Boston Merchants Association, wrote to Sherman and praised the speech of August 7. It seemed apparent to Mr. Lane that "the mani-

Mr. Ritchie was delighted with Senator Sherman's speech. He believed that in Canada there was a rapidly developing sentiment in favor of annexation to the United States. This political union would not be opposed by Great Britain, and it would help American investors like himself. His mines at Sudbury had been opened. They would soon be producing copper and nickel, and these ores should be immediately placed on the free list. He expected Sherman to take care of these details.[158]

Ritchie also wrote to Sir John Macdonald and recounted all he had done in favor of the fisheries treaty. Under this condition of affairs, he had expected that he and his associates would "receive the same treatment and recognition from your Government that all others engaged in like enterprises had and still continue to receive." But these expectations had not been fulfilled, and he could hardly "escape the conclusion that every interest with which I am identified has, when coming under the operations of the different portfolios of your Government, been singled out for unfortunate action." He hoped that such discrimination would be terminated at once, and that he would get some return for the services he had rendered.[159]

But it was soon evident to Sir John Macdonald that the services of S. J. Ritchie in connection with the fisheries treaty were not of any

fest destiny of the people of this continent is to become one. At present they [the Canadians] are possessed largely by a sentimental devotion to the English throne and Crown, but in time, a proper regard for their true interests will compel them to seek that representation in our Congress which they have not in the Parliament of Great Britain. They are having mighty hard times just now, and may have it worse and more of it before the present government of the Dominion is overthrown." *Sherman MS.*

From J. J. Mott, August 12, 1888, there came a letter which indicated the annexation sentiment in certain quarters; annexation even at the cost of war with England. It was Mr. Mott's belief that "England should have no footing on the North American continent. She is too powerful to neighbor with except across the seas. We should inculcate in Canada the idea of annexation, and ultimately encroach on this line. Sensible opposing opinion there would be found yielding in view of the possible occupation of the country by armies. . . . Our country is interested against any permanent settlement of a Fisheries treaty with England. It should be left as the means to obtain all British possessions north of us. . . . A war with England is 'logically deducible' for our safety. . . . Outside wars, following family wars, heal old sores." *Ibid.*

158. S. J. Ritchie to Senator John Sherman, August 8, 1888, *ibid.* On August 11, 1888, W. M. Day, editor of the *Iron Trade Review,* wrote to Senator Sherman and expressed his strong objections to any lowering of duties on Canadian ores. *Sherman MS.* From Montreal A. W. Ogilvie warned Sherman that there was little annexationist sentiment in Canada: "You would hardly get a corporal's guard of educated men in the Dominion of Canada today, who would be willing to exchange our good old flag for even yours." *Ibid.*

159. S. J. Ritchie to Sir John Macdonald, August 8, 1888, *Macdonald Papers, S. J. Ritchie Correspondence,* pp. 44–51, P.A.C.

great value. On August 21, 1888, the treaty was defeated in the Senate by a vote of Yeas—27, Nays—30. Senator Sherman, despite the lobbying activities of Ritchie, had led the opposition to the Bayard-Chamberlain convention partly because of partisan hostility towards anything that was the handiwork of a Democratic Administration, but more because he believed that it would be politically unwise to approve a treaty that would silence the dissatisfaction voiced in Canada with reference to the hard times that were still stalking the Government of Sir John Macdonald. Let these hard times continue, and it would not be long before the Canadian people would call out in stentorian tones for annexation to the United States. The voice of the people might well be the voice of God, but there was no particular reason why it should not take on an economic accent.

This exercise in political subtlety did not work out as Sherman had planned. Before the winter of Canadian discontent had grown so rigorous that it inclined all eyes towards the United States, the returning sun of prosperity made the old connection with England seem glorious once more, and ushered in a new day of British imperialism. The story of this transition from economic despair to comparative affluence is the subject of the next chapter.

CHAPTER XIV

RECIPROCITY, 1888–1911

In June, 1887, Edward Blake retired as the leader of the Liberal Party in Canada. He had indicated his desire that Wilfrid Laurier be chosen as his successor, and his party associates gratified this wish.[1] Because of his loyalty to Blake, Laurier followed for a while the political path that had been blazed by his predecessor. It was only by slow degrees that he shifted his position and became an advocate for intimate commercial relations with the United States. Not wishing to go as far as frank acceptance of the idea of commercial union, he halted at an intermediate station and announced his decision to Blake: "We have adopted Unrestricted Reciprocity. . . . We have narrowed the issue to the mere commercial aspect of the question and we intend to keep it strictly on that line. There are political aspects which will spring up, but for the present it is better to leave them out."[2]

There was little real difference between unrestricted reciprocity and commercial union; one merged into the other as inevitably as day into night. In Germany, commercial union in the form of a Zollverein had prepared the way for eventual political union. Goldwin Smith and Edward Farrer recognized the political implications in the movement for commercial union, and this fact merely increased their ardor. But Laurier, and some of his intimate friends, refused to admit the realities of the situation, and they talked glibly of establishing the closest kind of commercial contacts with the United States without compromising the political independence of Canada. In pursuance of this line of thought, they made numerous speeches and printed many pamphlets setting forth the advantages of unrestricted reciprocity with their southern neighbor. Some Liberals went further and advocated commercial union. They were not chided for these advanced views.[3]

In the spring and summer of 1888, there was increased activity on

1. For an interesting analysis of the character of Edward Blake and of his position in the Liberal Party, see Sir Richard Cartwright, *Reminiscences* (Toronto, 1912), pp. 147–152, 272–275.

2. Wilfrid Laurier to Edward Blake, March 29, 1888, quoted in Underhill, *op. cit.*, p. 135.

3. With reference to the program that the Liberal Party adopted in 1888, Willison, *Laurier,* II, 150, remarks: "The policy of unrestricted reciprocity was now . . . irrevocably adopted, and for the next three years all the energies of the Liberal press and the Liberal leaders were devoted to educating the country to acceptance of the proposition."

behalf of the idea of commercial union. Thomas Shaw, Secretary of the Permanent Farmers' Institute, of Hamilton, used both pen and voice to indicate to Canadian farmers the great advantages they would gain from an abolition of the tariff barriers between Canada and the United States. The commercial union he advocated would involve "(1) an assimilation of tariff rates against all other countries; (2) of internal revenue taxes; and (3) very probably an arrangement for pooling receipts and customs, and distributing the same." This system would save the cost of customs administration, and would benefit every farmer by lowering the cost of living and by giving him "access to the markets of the United States, thus enlarging his present market *twelve-fold*."[4]

T. D. Ledyard waxed enthusiastic over the many benefits that would accrue to Canadian mining interests from the adoption of commercial union.[5] Alfred F. Jury showed how the lot of the common laborer would be improved by commercial union;[6] John Dryden, Jr., described the advantages that such a system would bring to manufacturers;[7] and J. W. Longley attempted to answer all the objections that had been raised against such an intimate commercial relationship.[8] Commercial union was pictured as the perfect panacea for all Canadian economic ills; delay in its adoption meant prolonging the depression that still hung over Canada. John Charlton, David Mills and Goldwin Smith joined in this chorus of praise. Smith was optimistic as usual, and he assured the New York Chamber of Commerce that the prospect for commercial union was very promising. He could say with confidence that the idea was "taking a strong hold on the minds of the Canadian people."[9]

In Canada, the followers of Wilfrid Laurier were still divided over the merits of unrestricted reciprocity and commercial union. John A. Barron was in favor of unrestricted reciprocity, but he was opposed to its adoption on "any such terms as annexation. If we could put a resolution before the Country repudiating Mr. Butterworth's annexation resolutions, yet holding to Free Trade, I think we would be improving our position immensely."[10] Other correspondents called attention to the demand for free trade with the United States despite annexationist implications. H. H. Cook spoke of the "undercurrent of feeling in favor of annexation with the United States. There is a strong out-

4. *Handbook of Commercial Union*, pp. 54–72.
5. *Ibid.*, pp. 73–85.
6. *Ibid.*, pp. 142–146.
7. *Ibid.*, pp 175–189.
8. *Ibid.*, pp. 111–121.
9. New York *Evening Post*, November 21, 1888.
10. John A. Barron to Wilfrid Laurier, December 29, 1888, *Laurier MS.*, P.A.C.

spoken sentiment on this question such as I never heard expressed before."[11] George E. Casey urged Laurier to preach reciprocity "more and more as the chief and *almost the only* doctrine of our gospel."[12] There should be no turning back in this movement for intimate commercial relations with the United States!

On February 18, 1889, this question of unrestricted reciprocity with the United States came before the Canadian House of Commons in connection with a resolution introduced by Sir Richard Cartwright relative to securing for Canada "the power of negotiating commercial treaties with foreign States."[13] In discussing his resolution, Sir Richard made a sharp attack on the conduct of foreign relations concerning Canada. He was of the opinion that "in North American affairs more particularly, in all that relates to the affairs of Canada on this continent, with all due respect, I say that no English statesman will do." After this acid introduction, he passed on to a survey of the economic ties that bound Canada to the United States:

It is clear that, with the exception of England and her Colonies, our commerce with the United States is of incalculably more value to the people of Canada than our commerce with all the rest of the world—ten times over. . . . We find that, last year, the total volume of our trade was $193,000,000. Of that the United States alone took $91,000,000 export and import. Our trade with nearly every country in the world, not excepting Great Britain, declined considerably. . . . Out of our five principal articles of export, the United States were beyond comparison our best customer. . . . They were the best customers we had, and the only customers we had in whose case there was a large and manifest increase.[14]

11. H. H. Cook to Wilfrid Laurier, December 29, 1888, *ibid.* On December 1, 1888, Sir Charles Tupper wrote to Sir John Macdonald and significantly remarked: "I cannot conceal from myself that the question of annexation to the United States threatens to become an issue at no distant day, and I should not be greatly surprised to see the Opposition making common cause with the United States who are practically a unit on that question." Pope, *op. cit.*, p. 432. On March 9, 1889, Lord Lansdowne wrote to Sir John Macdonald with reference to commercial union: "I confess that even now I am not without misgivings as to the effects which a revival of the movement might, under altered circumstances, produce. While you are there, we have not much to fear from a crusade led by Laurier, Wiman or Goldwin Smith, and the aggressive conduct of the U. S. during the last two or three years has, no doubt, done something to discourage a *rapprochement.*" Pope, *op. cit.*, pp. 438–439.

12. George E. Casey to Laurier, December 31, 1888, *Laurier MS.*, P.A.C.

13. *Canada: House of Commons, Debates, 1889,* February 18, 1889, p. 172. In an editorial in the Toronto *Globe,* February 20, 1889, the following significant statement was made: "The strongest reason for demanding the commercial treaty-making right is that it would enable Ottawa at any time to negotiate for Unrestricted or other Reciprocity with the States."

14. *Canada: House of Commons, Debates, 1889,* February 18, 1889, pp. 172–176.

If Canada had the authority to negotiate commercial treaties with foreign nations, Cartwright believed that it would be a simple matter to make an arrangement with the United States that would be mutually beneficial. He emphasized this point many times in his speech, and his statistics were as impressive as his logic was sound. But his resolution was defeated by a vote of 94 nays to 66 yeas.[15]

This defeat did not unduly discourage Cartwright, who introduced on March 5, 1889 a new resolution in favor of unrestricted reciprocity with the United States.[16] It was a second attack upon the position of the Conservative Party, and it was skillfully led and strongly pushed. The Conservatives, however, had the situation well in hand. When the resolution was brought to a vote the majority against it was decisive—121 nays to 77 yeas.[17]

To some members of the Liberal Party, this large adverse vote appeared to sound the death knell of the movement for commercial union. James Young considered the "Commercial Union agitation one of the stupidest mistakes ever made by any section of our Party,"[18] but some Liberals like Sidney A. Fisher had a very different viewpoint. He wrote to Laurier that he had heard that the people in Arthabaskaville were "solid for Commercial Union," and the same was true of British Columbia.[19]

But Laurier was not greatly influenced by communications that stressed the spread of the idea of commercial union, and he continued to cling to the view that unrestricted reciprocity with the United States was as far as a majority of the Liberal Party wished to go. In order to sound out the Harrison Administration that came into office in March, 1889, he directed Louis H. Davies to write to Secretary Blaine and make certain discreet inquiries. Davies assured Blaine that Laurier and "his immediate confidential advisers" were "desirous that the commercial relations of the United States and Canada, embracing the Fishery question, should be confidentially discussed with you by one of their own party in the hope that the policy they have adopted, popularly called Unrestricted Reciprocity, might commend itself to your judgment." The Liberal Party was anxious "to cultivate the most friendly and cordial relations with the people of the United States," and it was hoped that the visit of Davies would lay the basis for some far-reaching understanding.[20]

15. *Ibid.,* pp. 193–194.
16. *Ibid.,* p. 468.
17. *Ibid.,* March 19, 1889, p. 739.
18. James Young to Wilfrid Laurier, November 19, 1889, *Laurier MS.,* P.A.C.
19. Sidney A. Fisher to Wilfrid Laurier, August 28, 1890, *ibid.*
20. Louis H. Davies to James G. Blaine, May 4, 1889, *Laurier MS.,* P.A.C.

While the Liberals were making these overtures to Secretary Blaine, S. J. Ritchie was trying to effect a *rapprochement* between the Conservatives and the Harrison Administration. In a letter to Sir John Macdonald, November 3, 1888, he expressed the opinion that the result of the elections would be to place all branches of the American Government in the hands of the Republican Party. After March, 1889, Sir John could "depend upon it that measures as broad and as liberal as Canada can wish, will be passed."[21] In his reply, Macdonald remarked that he was glad to learn that "things are likely to look pleasantly between the United States and Canada under the reign of Mr. Harrison. I don't see why in the world it should not be so."[22]

Ritchie was pleased with this note of conciliation that was sounded by Sir John, and in order to bind him closer to the United States, he extended a cordial invitation to visit the United States. Sir John could include in his entourage a "large number" of Canadian officials, and Ritchie would provide free transportation.[23] Macdonald was not interested in receiving this Christmas present, and Ritchie had to adopt other devices in order to curry favor with the Prime Minister. He next inspired E. A. C. Pew, President of the Toronto, Hamilton and Buffalo Railway Company, to write to Macdonald with reference to reciprocity. Pew believed that in Congress the feeling was "strong against reciprocal trade in natural products unless as a means to an end." Commercial union was the goal at which many influential Republicans were aiming, and they would not be satisfied with anything less comprehensive. Pew then went into a little-known chapter of history in order to show Sir John how much he knew of the real situation:

I am aware you gave G. W. Brega $5,000 in gold in 1867 . . . to obtain a renewal of the trade relations which existed between 1854 to 1864, but I told Brega at the time that all such efforts would be futile and useless, but the times are now ripe for renewal of such efforts, and while maintaining the principle of the National Policy inaugurated by your Government in 1878, you can secure the most desirable result of obtaining a free market with 60,000,000 people for our fish, lumber, ores and farm products. Five years have been proposed for the assimilation of the respective tariffs of the two countries.[24]

21. S. J. Ritchie to Sir John Macdonald, November 3, 1888, *Macdonald Papers, S. J. Ritchie Correspondence, 1884–1891,* pp. 57–58, P.A.C.

22. Sir John Macdonald to S. J. Ritchie, November 24, 1888, *Macdonald Letter Book,* XXXV, 243, P.A.C.

23. S. J. Ritchie to Sir John Macdonald, December 25, 1888, *Macdonald Papers, S. J. Ritchie Correspondence,* pp. 59–60, P.A.C.

24. E. A. C. Pew to Sir John Macdonald, October 28, 1889, *Macdonald Papers, Commercial Relations with the United States,* pp. 50–51, P.A.C. On September 6, 1884,

Sir John was not likely to be impressed by any arguments that Mr. Pew could advance, but he was ready to give careful consideration to any statements that came from trusted members of the Conservative Party. Ritchie, therefore, turned to Sir Charles Tupper, who wrote to Macdonald about the importance of erecting steel mills in Canada. In order to manufacture a high grade of steel, it would be possible, thought Tupper, to use nickel from the mines owned by Mr. Ritchie.[25]

After securing the co-operation of Sir Charles Tupper, Ritchie wrote to Senator Sherman. A perusal of some of the statements Sherman had made in recent speeches in the Senate had made it apparent that he was in favor of "the broadest and most liberal policy" with reference to commercial relations between Canada and the United States. Would he not, therefore, be in favor of "admitting coal, coke, lumber and iron ore from Canada free on condition that Canada shall admit like articles of our product free of duty"? Inasmuch as Canada purchased ten times as much coal from the United States as we purchased from her, it was only fair that we should make certain concessions to our northern neighbor. Canada had the "principal nickel mines of the world," and nickel was a very important alloy that was needed to make the best grade of steel. Was it not obvious that nickel ore should be admitted free of duty?[26]

Ritchie did more than merely write letters to Senator Sherman. He visited Washington and appeared before the Ways and Means Committee of the House of Representatives with reference to tariff concessions to Canada. Needless to say, he was especially anxious to secure

Erastus Wiman described to Sir John some advances of Mr. Pew looking towards securing for the United States the Northwestern territories of Canada. Pew thought that the three newspapers in Manitoba could be bought for $100,000, and they could then be used to further his project which had already secured the support of S. J. Ritchie, Senator H. B. Payne, and other prominent Americans. Pope, *op. cit.*, pp. 322–324.

25. Sir Charles Tupper to Sir John Macdonald, November 5, 1889, *Macdonald Papers, Commercial Relations*, pp. 121–129, P.A.C. On December 23, 1889, Lord Stanley, the Governor-General, wrote to Sir John Macdonald with regard to Ritchie and his projects: "I return, with many thanks, the very interesting letters from Sir C. Tupper, which you were good enough to send to me. Mr. Ritchie knows what he is about, and is not likely to be misled by oversanguine projects. Much depends on details, both with regard to the distances over which traffic has to be hauled, and as to the conditions of chemical treatment of the ores—but if there is likely to be such a future as is predicted for the use of nickel, and if there are actually so few known deposits, it looks as if a great industry might be built up near Sudbury. I shall look out eagerly for any further developments and shall be glad if you hear more from Sir Charles." Pope, *op. cit.*, p. 464.

26. S. J. Ritchie to Senator John Sherman, November 22, 1889, *Macdonald Papers, Commercial Relations*, pp. 144–145, P.A.C.

the admission of nickel ore free of duty, but he wrote to Sir John Macdonald and promised to extend his efforts to other articles of trade if Sir John would make a deal with him. He was confident that he could "paddle his own canoe" without any great trouble, but he would like to secure Sir John's support of a "very large enterprise" in Canada. If this were promised, he and his friends would give their prompt assistance to any projects in which Sir John was deeply interested.[27]

While Macdonald was reading letters from Ritchie and his friends urging the establishment of a system of commercial union or its equivalent, he was also receiving correspondence which struck a very different note. In Conservative circles there was strong opposition to any inclination towards unrestricted reciprocity. To E. W. Rathbun it seemed clear that intimate commercial relations with the United States meant eventual annexation. Free trade between Canada and the United States was "out of the question for it would mean a discrimination against other Nations, including the Mother Land." Canada could not afford to abandon its "hard-earned privileges of trading with the Nations of the World, comprising hundreds of millions of purchasers," and confine itself "to a quarter of the number even though they be the most lavish and generous buyers."[28]

Macdonald did not need letters from Conservatives to confirm his faith in the National Policy he had inaugurated in 1878. He had no intention of veering towards unrestricted reciprocity, but he was quite willing to negotiate for tariff concessions. In this regard he could make good use of S. J. Ritchie as an unofficial agent, and letters and telegrams from this American representative of big business fill several volumes of the *Macdonald Papers.* On March 12, Ritchie wrote to Macdonald from Washington, and informed him that a tariff bill would soon be reported from the Ways and Means Committee of the House of Representatives. The House was not favorable to concessions to Canada, but the Senate was disposed to take "broader views." When the House bill reached the Senate there was "no doubt" that "some provision for Canadian trade would be added." With regard to items favoring Canadian products, Ritchie would bend every effort to induce Congress to adopt a liberal attitude.[29]

As a result of his lobbying activities, Ritchie believed that he could arrange for a "reduction of one-half the present duty on Canadian lumber" if Sir John would authorize him to say that Canada would

27. S. J. Ritchie to Sir John Macdonald, January 19, 1890, *ibid.,* p. 147.
28. E. W. Rathbun to Sir John Macdonald, February 4, 1890, *ibid.,* pp. 41–46.
29. S. J. Ritchie to Sir John Macdonald, March 12, 1890, *ibid.,* pp. 15–16.

remove the export duty on logs. If, along with this authorization, Macdonald would add some expression of "national good will," the members of Congress would be induced by this friendly gesture to make further concessions.[30]

It was soon apparent that Ritchie's efforts were effecting certain results. On April 15, he had a long talk with Charles H. Tupper, who was assisting Sir Julian Pauncefote in the fur-seal negotiations. During the course of the conversation he informed Tupper that he had "not only succeeded in getting the nickel ore put on the United States free list but he had got the duty on the manufactured article cut down to a nominal rate." When the tariff bill reached the Senate, Ritchie expected further favors. He was confident that Senator Sherman was in a position to grant sweeping concessions that were beyond the power of Blaine to affect.[31]

On April 16, William McKinley reported from the Committee on Ways and Means the new tariff bill.[32] Before the debates in the House of Representatives began with reference to this measure, Ritchie paid a hurried visit to Ottawa to confer with Macdonald and other leading members of the Conservative Party. After concluding these conferences, he went to Cleveland to talk with certain business men in that city. From Cleveland he wrote to Macdonald in order to clarify matters. He wished to give assurances that he had not been sent to Canada by any "parties in Washington." No one in that city knew of his trip to Canada. It was important also to keep clearly in mind the fact that there was nothing in the nature of an "understanding between either Mr. Hitt and Mr. Butterworth and Mr. McKinley, who is the head of the Tariff committee." There was "absolutely nothing in this conclusion." Hitt might reflect some of the views of Secretary Blaine, but there was no certainty in this regard. In the case of Butterworth, there was no doubt that he did not "in any way represent the Secretary, nor is he likely under any circumstances to do so." Butterworth was willing to accept "either a partial or a complete reciprocity between Canada and the United States."[33]

Ritchie now tried to persuade Butterworth to visit Ottawa, but he refused to leave Washington at that time. Ritchie was not dismayed at this stubbornness because he thought there was a good chance for But-

30. S. J. Ritchie to Sir John Macdonald, March 15, 1890, *ibid.*, pp. 17ff.

31. Charles H. Tupper to Sir John Macdonald, April 16, 1890, *Macdonald Papers, Behring Sea, C. H. Tupper Correspondence,* II, 270–273, P.A.C.

32. H. R. 9416. *Congressional Record,* 51 Cong., 1 sess., p. 3443.

33. S. J. Ritchie to Sir John Macdonald, April 21, 1890, *Macdonald Papers, Commercial Relations,* pp. 19–20, P.A.C.

terworth to "force concessions on a number of articles in the tariff bill which would be very important to Canada." As matters stood, it seemed evident that Butterworth was "the most important figure in the House in Canadian interests."[34]

In the first week in May, before the debate opened in the House on the tariff bill, Ritchie went to see Mr. McKinley and requested him to offer an amendment which would provide for some measure of reciprocity with Canada. McKinley refused to take this step, but he promised that when his bill had passed the House of Representatives, he would then "agree upon a bill for the free exchange of all or a certain number of articles between the two countries." Ritchie regarded this pledge as a most significant concession, and he advised Macdonald to cable to Sir Charles Tupper and instruct him to proceed at once to Washington in order to assist in conducting an intensive lobby on behalf of restricted reciprocity. There was "not a moment to be lost."[35]

But Macdonald was not to be hurried into any decisions that were premature. He had to walk with wary step in this matter of tariff adjustment. On May 14 he telegraphed to C. H. Tupper, in Washington, to inform Mr. McKinley that his Government was willing to remove the export duty on logs if Congress would reduce the import duty "to one dollar per thousand." Tupper carried out this instruction at once, and found McKinley to be a most agreeable person who expressed his "personal readiness to agree to a fair trade arrangement between the two countries." He regarded commercial union as "utterly chimerical." It was difficult to see how such a scheme could be put into operation between Canada and the United States since any "discrimination against England would necessarily lead to a very bitter feeling on the part of English taxpayers and manufacturers." With reference to the duty on logs, McKinley had been

led to believe by Mr. Charlton that we would remove the export duty on logs in consideration of the reduction of the import duty on sawn timber by the United States to $1.50 per thousand feet. I explained to him that Mr. Charlton spoke without any authority on the subject and that in my judgment the present decision was as liberal on the part of Canada as could with fairness be expected by the United States. He agreed with me and intimated that while it was improbable that he would amend his Bill in the House of Representatives, . . . it was not unlikely that the question would receive consideration in the Senate. . . . In referring again to trade relations, Mr. Mackinley said that trade arrangements with foreign countries must be with the State

34. S. J. Ritchie to Sir John Macdonald, April 28, 1890, *ibid.*, pp. 21–22.
35. S. J. Ritchie to Sir John Macdonald, May 4, 1890, *ibid.*, pp. 23–26.

Department, and he again mentioned that his Bill was a domestic bill and not a foreign bill, and that the duties made no bar to reciprocity, on the contrary he contended that in some respects they promoted it.[36]

With McKinley opposed to any immediate amendment of his tariff bill, there was nothing to do but wait until it reached the Senate. The bill was passed by the House of Representatives on May 21, 1890,[37] and debate upon it began in the Senate on July 7. Before this debate opened, President Harrison sent to the Senate (June 19, 1890) a message which pointed out the difficulties which the pending McKinley bill would place in the way of reciprocal agreements with the countries of Latin America.[38] With his message he enclosed a report by Secretary Blaine on this matter of reciprocity with Latin America. In the McKinley bill, hides were taken from the free list, and duties were raised on wool. Such action was deprecated by Blaine because it would defeat any possibility of establishing commercial reciprocity with the states south of the Rio Grande. In order to save the situation, he suggested a comprehensive amendment to the pending bill.[39]

In response to Secretary Blaine's suggestion, Senator Hale introduced a sweeping amendment to the pending tariff bill. If this amendment had been adopted, it would have prepared the way for a wide measure of reciprocity not only with Latin America but also with Canada.[40] Needless to say, it met with immediate opposition from the protected interests, and was shelved. But this action did not discourage S. J. Ritchie, who continued his lobbying activities in Washington. On July 30, he telegraphed to Sir John Macdonald and expressed the belief that it would be possible to amend the McKinley bill "so as to make coal,

36. C. H. Tupper to Sir John Macdonald, May 14, 1890, *Macdonald Papers, Behring Sea, C. H. Tupper Correspondence,* II, 407–413, P.A.C.

37. *Congressional Record,* 51 Cong., 1 sess., pp. 5112–5113. The vote was yeas 164, nays 142.

38. *Ibid.,* pp. 6256–6257.

39. Secretary Blaine to President Harrison, June 4, 1890, *ibid.,* pp. 6257–6258. See also Secretary Blaine to William McKinley, April 10, 1890, Hamilton, *op. cit.,* p. 683.

40. The text of the Hale amendment reads as follows: "And the President of the United States is hereby authorized, without further legislation, to declare the ports of the United States free and open to all the products of any nation of the American hemisphere upon which no export duties are imposed, whenever and as long as such nation shall admit to its ports, free of all national, provincial (state), municipal and other taxes, flour, corn-meal and other breadstuffs, preserved meats, fish, vegetables, and fruits, cottonseed oil, rice and other provisions, including all articles of food, lumber, furniture and all other articles of wood, agricultural implements and machinery, mining and mechanical machinery, structural steel and iron, steel rails, locomotives, railway cars and supplies, street cars, refined petroleum, or such products of the United States as may be agreed upon." *Congressional Record,* 51 Cong., 1 sess., p. 6259.

lumber and ores from Canada, free, on the basis of coal and lumber being admitted free from the United States." A communication from the Canadian Government showing a "disposition to reciprocate this offer," would "greatly facilitate" efforts to secure tariff concessions.[41] Macdonald's reply was immediate and affirmative. The Dominion Parliament was ready to

> take off all customs duty on coal, ores and lumber imported from the United States whenever Congress makes those articles free of duty. The Canadian Government has already authorized Sir Julian Pauncefote to state to the American Government that they will be prepared to take off the export duty on logs whenever Canadian lumber is admitted into the United States market at a reduced rate of $1.50 per thousand board measure. You are at liberty to show this to such members of Congress or the Government as you please.[42]

As soon as Ritchie received this telegram, he wrote to Senator Aldrich and stressed the importance of giving some tariff concessions to Canada. He knew that Aldrich had great influence with the members of the Senate Finance Committee, and he hoped that he could persuade him to favor restricted reciprocity with Canada.[43] After making fur-

41. S. J. Ritchie to Sir John Macdonald, July 30, 1890, *Macdonald Papers, Commercial Relations,* p. 27, P.A.C.

42. Sir John Macdonald to S. J. Ritchie, July 30, 1890, *Macdonald Letter Book,* XXVII, 99–100, P.A.C.

43. In his letter to Senator Nelson W. Aldrich, August 1, 1890, Ritchie says: "It seems very important while the Senate is discussing the tariff bill that such articles as we could make a free exchange with our neighbors, and which would increase a profitable trade, should receive special consideration. We have a large trade in coal with Canada, and if the Canadian duty were removed it would be much increased, but in order to have the Canadian duty removed we must remove ours. I do not need to point out to you how much this would be to the interest of California, nor how much your own New England States would be benefited by free coal from Nova Scotia; nor how much Ohio and Pennsylvania would be benefited by having a free market for their coal of the whole of Ontario and nearly all of Quebec. I believe every man who ships coal to Canada is in favor of having coal put upon the free list, and I do not know of a single exception to this opinion. There is no reason why lumber should be taxed. Fully seventy-five per cent. of the lumber interests in Canada belongs to American citizens, and the present duty is substantially a tax upon home production. . . . More than seventy-five per cent. of all the known mines and minerals in Canada belong to American citizens. This is even true of Canadian coal. . . . Last week I went to Canada and had quite a lengthy interview with the premier, Sir John A. Macdonald, and I am happy to say that he manifested the most friendly and liberal spirit upon the entire trade relations between the two countries." Mr. Ritchie then informed Senator Aldrich that he had received a letter from Macdonald with reference to tariff concessions that Canada was willing to make. This letter, which Ritchie enclosed, was open to the inspection of the other members of the Senate Finance Committee. It was so generous that Ritchie had hopes that the Committee would respond in kind. S. J. Ritchie to Senator Nelson W. Aldrich, August 1, 1890, *Macdonald Papers, Commercial Relations,* pp. 162–165, P.A.C.

ther efforts to convince dubious Senators with regard to the advantages of letting down tariff bars along the Canadian frontier, he wrote to Sir John Macdonald and described the situation to him:

We shall now probably have substantial progress and the Senate may even go over the whole tariff bill during the next week. . . . I hope to fasten the articles agreed upon between you and myself upon the tariff bill in the Senate but the real struggle, I fear, will come with the House afterwards. . . . I went to Bar Harbor, Maine, this week to see Mr. Blaine and spent Wednesday evening with him, very fully discussing the whole Canadian question, and it is quite probable that during the coming week he may make a speech at Augusta, in which he will announce his opinion on the commercial relations between Canada and the United States. I must say that he talked both fairly and friendly upon all the questions involved, and I believe it is quite possible for you and he to arrive at a satisfactory conclusion.[44]

As a result of his persistent lobbying, Ritchie finally persuaded Senator Sherman (September 1, 1890), to offer an amendment to the McKinley bill with regard to reciprocity with Canada. The amendment provided for the mutual free admission of coal, and it authorized the President to appoint American representatives on a joint commission that would be empowered to consider the best method of extending the trade relations between the two countries.[45]

Ritchie was not certain that this amendment would pass the Senate, but he assured Sir John Macdonald that he was doing "everything" in his power to push it through. If it was adopted by the Senate, he would pay a hurried visit to Ottawa to discuss the situation in detail. The amendment would suit the purposes of Sir John, and would permit him to choose "between complete or partial reciprocity." Although Secretary Blaine had not said a word about reciprocity with Canada in his latest speeches, Ritchie was confident that "a fair arrangement can be made with him if the tariff measure fails."[46]

The Sherman amendment was not given serious consideration by the Senate, and the McKinley bill passed on September 10, without any

44. S. J. Ritchie to Sir John Macdonald, August 23, 1890, *ibid.*, pp. 151–152.

45. *Congressional Record,* 51 Cong., 1 sess., p. 9454.

46. S. J. Ritchie to Sir John Macdonald, September 2, 1890, *Macdonald Papers, Commercial Relations,* pp. 153–154, P.A.C. In the Baltimore *Sun,* September 2, 1890, there is the following comment, dated September 1: "Senator Sherman created a mild sensation in the Senate this morning by giving notice of an amendment to the tariff bill providing for free coal from Canada on condition that the latter shall admit American coal free. In the same connection he proposed that the President be empowered to appoint a commission to confer with Canadian authorities on the general subject of reciprocity whenever the latter indicate a disposition to take steps in a similar direction."

provision for reciprocity with Canada. But Ritchie refused to be downcast by this turn of events. He reported to Sir John Macdonald that the situation was "not nearly as bad as it looks." There had been a strong movement in Congress to "put a measure upon the tariff bill providing for Canadian reciprocity, but its friends at the last moment feared that with the South American measure already fastened on, they might endanger the passage of the measure and finally agreed that it had better go over to the sessions meeting again in December, when it would be taken up as a separate measure." There was no doubt in his mind that there was a majority in both Houses of Congress in favor of reciprocity with Canada. Sir John should not feel "in the least disturbed" by the recent vote upon the McKinley bill.[47]

Macdonald had little time for thought upon the McKinley tariff bill. Other important measures soon demanded his full attention. One of his chief items of interest was the attempt of the Government of Newfoundland to secure a reciprocity treaty with the United States. On February 28, 1890, Sir Terence O'Brien, Governor of Newfoundland, wrote to Lord Knutsford with regard to negotiations with the United States: "My Ministers are strongly of opinion that, as our interests are not identical, and we have no burning questions with the United States such as those existing between that country and the Dominion, we would be more likely to obtain better reciprocal advantages for our fisheries by negotiating direct with the former."[48] The Colonial Office realized the implications that lay behind this request, and they gave the matter lengthy consideration. Finally, in September, 1890, it was decided to accede to the request of Sir Terence O'Brien, and the Foreign Office was advised accordingly. Lord Salisbury then sent a note to Sir Julian Pauncefote, at Washington, introducing Robert Bond, the Colonial Secretary of Newfoundland.[49]

In October, 1890, Bond and Pauncefote held several conferences with Secretary Blaine. The outlines of a treaty were quickly agreed upon, and Pauncefote was asked to draft a convention that would cover the main points that had been discussed. His project provided that American vessels should be allowed to purchase bait, to touch and trade, sell their fish and oil, and procure supplies on condition that they pay the same dues as Newfoundland vessels, and conform to the harbor regu-

47. S. J. Ritchie to Sir John Macdonald, September 29, 1890, *ibid.*, pp. 173–174.

48. Sir Terence O'Brien to Lord Knutsford, February 28, 1890, *C.S.P., 1891,* No. 38, pp. 21–22.

49. Sir W. V. Whiteway, Premier and Attorney-General of Newfoundland, to the Colonial Office, September 9, 1890, *ibid.*, p. 25; Lord Salisbury to Sir J. Pauncefote, September 10, 1890, *ibid.*, p. 26.

lations.[50] On its part, the United States would admit, free of duty, the produce of the "fisheries of Newfoundland, including cod and seal oil, and also the produce of mines." This convention was to remain in force for ten years, and after the expiration of that period it would be subject to abrogation upon one year's notice.[51]

When Sir Julian Pauncefote was asked to draft the treaty between Newfoundland and the United States, he sent a telegram to the Foreign Office suggesting that the Government of Canada be informed of the negotiations.[52] But before this notice could be sent, Sir John Macdonald learned of the situation through articles in the New York *Herald* (October 13), and the Boston *Herald* (October 18).[53] Alarmed by this news, he cabled a protest to Sir Charles Tupper, the Canadian High Commissioner in London: "Please represent strongly how the fishery and commercial interests of Canada will be injured by such an arrangement as Bond is currently reported as making, and how disastrous, from a national point of view, it would be for a separate colony to effect an arrangement with the United States more favourable than would be given to the Confederated Provinces."[54]

When the Canadian Government ascertained the terms of the proposed convention between Newfoundland and the United States, the Governor-General informed the Colonial Office that some of the provi-

50. Sir Julian Pauncefote to Lord Salisbury, November 5, 1890, *C.S.P., 1891,* No. 38, pp. 30–31.

51. There is a copy of this draft convention in the note from Sir Julian Pauncefote to Secretary Blaine, October 18, 1890, *Great Britain, Notes from,* CXVIII, MS. Dept. of State.

52. Sir Julian Pauncefote to Lord Salisbury, received, October 17, 1890, *C.S.P., 1891,* No. 38, pp. 27, 73.

53. In the Boston *Herald,* October 18, 1890, there is a long statement by Robert Bond with reference to the purpose of his mission to the United States. On October 10, 1890, Robert Bond gave a talk to the businessmen of Boston with reference to reciprocity with the United States. After listening to this talk, Edward T. Russell, a prominent commission merchant of Boston, wrote to Bond and remarked: "We listened with much interest this morning to your statement of the proposal from the Government of Newfoundland for a reciprocal tariff arrangement with the United States. . . . The proposition is one that we believe a body of Merchants and Fishermen familiar with the subject would agree to at once, and we hope you may be able to bring about such a result. It is not generally known but it is a fact that the great bulk of codfish imported into the United States do not suit our domestic trade, but . . . are used for export. The importation of Salmon and Salmon Trout interferes with no fishery in the States. We do not produce Salmon enough on the Atlantic seaboard to supply demand for them fresh—none are salted. It may be said also of Labrador Herring. . . . We shall be very glad indeed to see Reciprocity with Newfoundland." Enclosed in letter from Bond to Secretary Blaine, December 18, 1890, *Great Britain, Notes from,* CXVIII, MS. Dept. of State.

54. Sir John Macdonald to Sir Charles Tupper, October 21, 25, 1890, quoted in Tupper to Lord Knutsford, October 27, 1890, *C.S.P., 1891,* No. 38, pp. 4–5.

sions were viewed with the "utmost alarm."[55] The Colonial Office responded at once to this pressure, and assurances were given to Lord Stanley that the negotiations initiated by Newfoundland would be delayed until they could proceed, *pari passu*, with those of Canada.[56]

The Government of Newfoundland was indignant over this enforced delay in the negotiations with the United States. On December 10, Sir Terence O'Brien sent a heated protest to the Colonial Office: "We decline being involved in Canadian disputes, and . . . we repudiate the interference of Canada."[57]

This spirit of independence so manifest in the communications of the Governor of Newfoundland, was reflected in the conduct of Robert Bond in Washington. In December, 1890, he had several conferences with Secretary Blaine to which Sir Julian Pauncefote was not invited. He emerged from these talks with Blaine with a new draft treaty which he submitted to Pauncefote on December 16.[58] This new *projet* contained a very important article which admitted into Newfoundland, duty free, some American manufactures. Other American manufactures were admitted subject to a small specific duty.[59]

Sir Julian Pauncefote regarded Bond's separate negotiations with Blaine as "entirely irregular," and he did not relish being left out of the diplomatic picture. The British Foreign Office was equally displeased with Bond's conduct in this regard. The new *projet* did not meet with Imperial approval, and Blaine, sensing the situation and also responding to pressure from American mining interests, submitted to Pauncefote a draft treaty which omitted all mention of Newfoundland mineral ores being admitted into the United States free of duty.[60] The Newfoundland Government was deeply disappointed at this turn of events, and Sir Terence O'Brien placed the responsibility for Blaine's action squarely upon the shoulders of Lord Knutsford.[61] Although Knutsford promptly denied such a responsibility, it was clear that the intervention of the British Government had defeated a project which, in the beginning, had met with its approval. Canadian protests had been more potent than the supplications of Newfoundland.[62]

55. Lord Stanley to Lord Knutsford, received, November 19, 1890, *ibid.*, p. 35.
56. Lord Knutsford to Lord Stanley, November 25, 1890, *ibid.*, p. 35.
57. Sir Terence O'Brien to Lord Knutsford, December 12, 1890, *ibid.*, pp. 36–37.
58. Sir Julian Pauncefote to Lord Salisbury, December 26, 1890, *ibid.*, pp. 49–51.
59. *Ibid.*, pp. 51–53.
60. There is a copy of the draft in *Great Britain, Notes from,* CXVIII, MS. Dept. of State.
61. Sir Terence O'Brien to Lord Knutsford, January 13, 1891, *C.S.P., 1891,* No. 38, pp. 48–49.
62. Lord Knutsford to Sir Terence O'Brien, February 12, 1891, *ibid.*, pp. 56–57. As

Secretary Blaine was displeased with the way in which his negotiations with Newfoundland had been checked, and he was in no cordial mood to listen to any proposals for a reciprocity treaty that would include both Newfoundland and Canada. Sir Julian Pauncefote was well aware of Blaine's displeasure with the way matters had been handled, and he sought to find some general formula that would settle not only the question of reciprocity but some of the other important issues between Canada and the United States. After some conversations with Blaine, Pauncefote wrote to the Governor-General of Canada and inquired as to the position of the Canadian Government.[63] In reply, Lord Stanley suggested the following bases for negotiations: the renewal of the reciprocity treaty of 1854 with certain modifications; admission of Canadian fishery products into American markets free of duty in return for permission to American fishermen to buy bait and supplies and transship cargoes from Canada; protection of the mackerel and other fisheries on the Atlantic Ocean and in inland waters; relaxation of the coasting laws of the two countries on the inland waters; mutual salvage of wrecked vessels; and some arrangement for the settlement of the Alaskan boundary dispute.[64]

When Pauncefote placed these proposals before Secretary Blaine, he remarked:

> I am satisfied that it would be utterly idle to attempt to secure the appointment of a formal Commission to consider any arrangements for reciprocal trade between the United States and the Dominion. At the same time the United States stand ready to have a full but private conference with the British Minister and one or more agents from Canada, and will go over any points of difference and consider any subject upon which a mutual interest could be founded. If an agreement is reached all [is] well. If not, no official mention is to be made of the effort. Above all things it is important to avoid all public reference to the matter. This the President insists upon.[65]

The initiative in this matter had been taken by Sir Julian Pauncefote, and Blaine had reluctantly agreed to an informal conference on

late as January 23, 1891, the Colonial Office cabled to the Governor-General of Canada and observed: "Newfoundland's interests should not be indefinitely postponed." Her Majesty's Government expressed the hope that Canada would "withdraw opposition to ratification of convention between Newfoundland and the United States." *Ibid.*, pp. 16–17.

63. Sir Julian Pauncefote to Lord Stanley, Dec. 7, 1890, *ibid.*, p. 77.

64. Lord Stanley to Lord Knutsford, December 13, 1890, *C.S.P., 1891,* No. 38, p. 78.

65. "Copy given to the British Minister by the Secretary of State for information of British Government, December 22, 1890." *Great Britain, Notes from,* CXVIII, MS. Dept. of State. Also, Lord Knutsford to Lord Stanley, Jan. 2, 1891, *C.S.P., 1891,* No. 38, p. 78.

the questions at issue between Canada and the United States. Moreover, Blaine had laid down one condition that should be observed in the negotiations: "Above all things it is important to avoid all public reference to the matter." It would not be difficult, therefore, to estimate the extent of Blaine's displeasure when he discovered that on January 16, 1891, *The Empire*, the chief organ of the Conservative Party in Canada, had published a despatch from its Ottawa correspondent to the effect that the Canadian Government had "recently been approached by the United States Government with a view to the development of trade relations between the two countries."[66]

On January 27, Sir Julian Pauncefote wrote a "private and confidential" note to Secretary Blaine in which he stated that the Canadian Government was willing to agree to an unofficial conference on the subject of reciprocity. It wished, however, to make public the proposals that Lord Stanley had sent to Lord Knutsford on December 13, 1890. It also desired to make a public announcement that the United States had agreed to an informal discussion of the whole topic of reciprocity. Would the American Government have any objection to this announcement?[67] On January 31, Sir Julian requested a reply to his note of January 27,[68] but before Blaine could send an answer, Sir John Macdonald, on the same day, delivered a speech in Toronto in which he expanded the statement that had already appeared in *The Empire* on January 16.[69]

Blaine regarded Macdonald's action as a breach of faith. In a note to Sir Julian Pauncefote he gave the situation its proper setting, and showed that the initiative had come from the British Minister: "I deem it important . . . to have it settled that the conference was not 'initiated' by me, but on the contrary that the private arrangement of which I spoke was but a modification of your proposal, and in no sense an original suggestion from the Government of the United States."[70]

It was readily recognized in Canada that Blaine's statement was entirely correct. The initiative had come from Pauncefote, and he had been embarrassed by the tactics employed by Macdonald. The Prime Minister was getting ready to dissolve Parliament and go before the country in a general election. He had not hesitated, therefore, to resort

66. Willison, *Laurier,* II, 151–152.

67. Sir Julian Pauncefote to Secretary Blaine, January 27, 1891, *Private and Confidential, Great Britain, Notes from,* CXIX, MS. Dept. of State.

68. Sir Julian Pauncefote to Secretary Blaine, January 31, 1891, *ibid.*

69. Toronto *Empire,* January 28, 1891.

70. Secretary Blaine to Sir Julian Pauncefote, April 1, 1891, *C.S.P., 1891,* No. 38, pp. 82–83.

to "misrepresentation in order to baffle and checkmate the leaders of the Opposition."[71]

Several factors had influenced this decision. The rising tide of reciprocity sentiment might carry the Liberals to victory if the elections were postponed.[72] Moreover, the story of the gross mismanagement of the Department of Public Works would soon be given to the press, and it would seriously damage Conservative prospects. Macdonald himself was growing infirm; his death would be an irreparable blow to the party he had so long led to victory. An early election was required by every precept of Canadian politics, so Sir John dissolved Parliament on February 3 and set the elections for March 5, 1891.[73]

It was an essential part of Conservative strategy to stigmatize the Liberals as traitors who would detach Canada from the Empire and merge its destinies with those of the United States. Patriotism became the rallying cry of the Conservatives, whose voices became more strident as their fears of defeat increased. For some months before the election, Macdonald had been stressing the dangers of annexation in the event of a Liberal victory. There was grave danger that Canadian voters would be corrupted by American money. In a letter to Sir George Stephen, Macdonald expressed his fears that "a large amount of Yankee money will be expended to corrupt our people. I have no doubt that that rascal Wiman is already raising a fund for the purpose. Sir C. Tupper will tell you that every American statesman . . . covets Canada."[74] These suspicions of Americans suddenly extended to persons with whom he had long been acquainted. In November, 1890, he warned Sir Charles Tupper about having any further relations with S. J. Ritchie,[75] and Tupper gave assurances that he would be sufficiently cautious when dealing with this enterprising American.[76]

71. Willison, *op. cit.,* II, 151–152. Skelton, in his *Life and Letters of Sir Wilfrid Laurier,* I, 412, refers to this action of Sir John Macdonald as "an audacious move, and as disreputable as it was audacious."

72. The large amount of free goods entering Canada from the United States is clearly indicated in the following table in the *Kasson Papers,* Dept. of State.

Imports into Canada from Great Britain, the United States and from other countries for the year ending June 30, 1891.

	Dutiable Goods	Free Goods	Total
Great Britain	$31,447,660	$10,509,866	$42,047,526
United States	29,790,404	23,895,255	53,685,657
Other Countries	13,297,974	4,403,967	17,611,941

73. Skelton, *op. cit.,* I, 404–411.

74. Sir John Macdonald to Sir George Stephen, November 10, 1890, Pope, *op. cit.,* pp. 477–478.

75. Sir John Macdonald to Sir Charles Tupper, November 22, 1890, *ibid.,* p. 481.

76. Sir Charles Tupper to Sir John Macdonald, January 12, 1891, *ibid.,* p. 483. On

In his search for ammunition for his patriotism drive, Macdonald was delighted to get possession of the manuscript of a pamphlet written by Edward Farrer, which dealt primarily with the fisheries question. The proof sheets of this pamphlet were stolen from a Toronto printing office and carried to Macdonald, who affected to see in Farrer's statements conclusive proof of treasonable designs on the part of Liberal leaders. Farrer was a firm believer in political union between Canada and the United States, and his brochure had declared that Sir John's disappearance from the political stage would be the "signal for a movement in Canada towards annexation." To Sir John it appeared evident that any thought of his early demise was equivalent to constructive treason. Like Louis XIV he had long identified himself with the State; any forecast of his death was a prophecy of doom for Canada.[77]

But Farrer was not the spokesman for the Liberal Party, and his views were not accepted by Laurier and other prominent Liberals.[78] It is true that the Liberal Party sent Louis H. Davies to Washington to assure Secretary Blaine that his political associates were anxious to "cultivate the most friendly and cordial relations with the people of the United States,"[79] and it is well known that Farrer made many trips to the United States to talk with American statesmen, but these contacts did not lead to any agreement "affecting the political status of Canada."[80] Laurier issued a strong refutation of the statements of Sir John Macdonald, and he bitterly condemned the charge of treason as a "direct and unworthy appeal to passion and prejudice." But the Conservative Party made good use of these potent appeals to prejudice. In the West, the Canadian Pacific Railway exerted great pressure in favor

October 21, 1890, William Van Horne, President of the Canadian Pacific Railway, wrote to Sir John Macdonald with regard to Ritchie's projects at Sudbury: "I have your note of yesterday with Ritchie's letter to you of the 19th. That is all very fine talk of Ritchie's, but there is nothing in it. Quite a number of years ago he induced a number of his Ohio friends to put money into the Central Ontario Railway and into a lot of iron deposits along its projected route. The railway proved to be worthless because all the iron deposits turned out to carry a large percentage of titanium. . . . He tried for a number of years to get us to take hold of his Central Ontario road and used to come to us every week or two with a new batch of lies about it. These same lies are now being served up with nickel sauce to induce the Government to give him a subsidy for extending his Central Ontario Railroad to Sudbury." *Macdonald Papers, S. J. Ritchie Correspondence,* pp. 107–109, P.A.C. Van Horne was a good prophet. On January 24, 1891, Ritchie wrote to Macdonald and requested "a bonus of six thousand dollars per mile for the extension of this line from Coe Hill to Sudbury, a distance of about 206 miles." *Ibid.,* p. 157.

77. Willison, *op. cit.,* II, 164–169.

78. For an interesting account of the background and activities of Edward Farrer, see Willison, *Reminiscences,* pp. 210–215.

79. Louis H. Davies to Secretary Blaine, May 4, 1889, *Laurier MS.,* P.A.C.

80. Willison, *Reminiscences,* pp. 226–227.

of the Conservatives, and in the Maritime Provinces the "coarse and blatant prodigality" of Sir Charles Tupper carried the day.[81] The Liberal Party went down to defeat, and "the old man, the old flag, and the old policy," were partially vindicated.[82] But it was a Pyrrhic victory, for Macdonald, worn out with the burdens of the elections, was taken seriously ill in May, 1891, and died on June 6. His death prepared the way for a new political order in Canada.

But this new order did not take shape immediately after the passing of Macdonald. The Liberals were badly split in the summer of 1891, and Edward Blake, a former leader of the party, was chiefly responsible for this division. When he gave way in favor of Laurier in 1887, he still cherished a faint hope that when his health improved he could resume the reins of authority. But Laurier was too big a personality to be pushed aside after he had taken over the leadership of the Liberals, and Blake should have realized, as Henry Adams did in later years, that "a friend in power is a friend lost." In the early months of 1891, Laurier issued a call for the leaders of the Liberal Party to meet in Toronto on February 17 and 18. Blake was not consulted about this call, and feeling humiliated because of this oversight, he sent to J. S. Willison, the editor of the Toronto *Globe*, a letter which contained a "sweeping attack upon the Liberal trade policy as unwise, elusive and misleading, feeble in conception and impossible of execution." Willison was able to prevent the publication of this letter, but Blake merely bided his time until after the elections, and then on March 6 he prevailed upon Mr. Willison to publish another letter equally critical of Liberal policy.[83]

This letter was an indication of the overwrought nerves of Mr. Blake. It was a pattern of confusion, and no one seemed to know its exact meaning. The policy of the Conservative Party was sharply condemned, but the Liberal Party did not go unscathed. With regard to commercial relations with the United States, Blake was as indecisive as the Delphic oracle. Unrestricted reciprocity would greatly advance the material interests of Canada by creating an influx of population and capital, and it would promote a rapid development of forces and materials

81. Skelton, *Laurier,* I, 417.

82. In a letter to Sir George Stephen, March 31, 1891, Sir John Macdonald indicated the line of political strategy the Conservative Party had followed: "I have of course pointed out that U. R. meant annexation, and the movements of Cartwright, Farrer and Wiman enabled us to raise the loyalty cry, which had considerable effect." Pope, *op. cit.,* p. 485.

83. The best account of the Blake letter and its effects upon the fortunes of the Liberal Party is given in Willison, *Reminiscences,* pp. 224-244.

hitherto unused.[84] It would provide a golden alliteration of men, money and markets. But there would be the handicap of lost revenue from the omission of duties on imports from the United States. This decrease in revenue was a fatal objection to any scheme of unrestricted reciprocity.[85] Commercial union would not be open to the same criticism, but it would probably be a mere prelude to political union. Such a union would involve a fundamental constitutional question which Canadians were not prepared to answer. It was obvious, therefore, that the time was not ripe either for unrestricted reciprocity or for commercial union with the United States.[86]

This Blake letter was variously interpreted by Conservative and Liberal newspapers. There was a great deal of uncertainty as to the exact meaning of the missive, but there was no doubt in most minds that Blake's position in the Liberal Party was hopelessly compromised. He continued to exchange letters with Laurier, and he kept up relations with Charlton and Mills. It was clear, however, that he no longer retained the confidence of a large number of Liberal leaders, and Sir Richard Cartwright was so deeply incensed over the letter that he never spoke to Blake again.[87]

This rift in the ranks of the Liberal Party prevented it from capitalizing upon the weakness of the Conservatives under the new leadership of Sir John Abbott.[88] Abbott had none of the political genius of

84. It is interesting to note that the manufacturing interests in Canada strongly disagreed with Blake's viewpoint that unrestricted reciprocity would bring prosperity to Canada. At the annual meeting of the Canadian Manufacturers' Association in Toronto, April 16, 1891, the following resolution was adopted: "The Canadian Manufacturers' Association is most decidedly opposed to any change in the policy of the Dominion Government which would subject Canadian manufacturers to the unequal competition of any foreign manufacturers, . . . and therefore, this Association now places itself upon record as opposed to unrestricted reciprocity with the United States in manufactured products." This resolution was enclosed in a letter from J. J. Cassidy to Sir John Macdonald, April 18, 1891, *Macdonald Papers, Commercial Relations*, pp. 56–57, P.A.C.

85. For a penetrating criticism of Blake's argument, see Cartwright, *op. cit.*, pp. 278–282.

86. Toronto, *Globe,* March 6, 1891. See also, Underhill, *op. cit.*, pp. 137–141.

87. Cartwright, *op. cit.*, pp. 297–299.

88. Sir Charles Tupper would have made a much more virile leader than Sir John Abbott, but Tupper had many characteristics that were distasteful even to the Conservatives. Moreover, there were suspicions as to his integrity. The view that belligerent Liberals took of Tupper is illustrated in an editorial written by Goldwin Smith in the Toronto *Mail,* June 9, 1891. Smith was sharp in his condemnation of the widespread system of corruption of which, he claimed, Tupper was the agent: "All that is worst in it and has tended most to debase the national character is familiarly connected with his name, which may be said to be a household word for corruption. . . . He will protest his innocence, . . . but his word unhappily is that of a man whose veracity is much impugned. . . . He is the prince of political cracksmen."

Sir John Macdonald, and his health was so seriously undermined that he did not have the strength to carry out the vigorous program that was needed to keep Canadian economy functioning successfully during the depression of 1891–1892. The census reports for the decade ending in 1891 were particularly discouraging. Railway expansion had not brought the expected prosperity, and poor crops and bank failures seemed the chief items in Canadian annals.[89] Exports of Canadian produce for 1891 fell considerably below the shipments for 1882. Farmers had grown weary of working long hours for meagre returns, and were emigrating in large numbers to the United States.[90] Canadian manufacturing industries had not developed as had been hoped. Exports in 1891 showed only a slight increase over the exports of a decade previous, and hard times were closing some of the Canadian mills.[91] The McKinley Tariff, with its increased duties on Canadian wheat, barley, Indian corn, potatoes and eggs, had sharply curtailed exports to the American market.[92] The future of Canada seemed darkly clouded, and the new Abbott Government sought some silver lining in negotiations for commercial reciprocity with the United States.

Even before the death of Sir John Macdonald there had been an effort to conciliate the Harrison Administration and lay the basis for a commercial accord. In April, Sir Charles Tupper paid a visit to Washington as a guest of Sir Julian Pauncefote. On April 2, Tupper and Pauncefote made a formal call upon Secretary Blaine and were received with "great cordiality." Tupper, responding to this courtesy, gave assurances of his knowledge that the American Government had not taken the initiative in the reciprocity negotiations that had been alluded to in the recent Canadian elections. In other words he admitted that Sir John Macdonald and Sir John Thompson[93] had made deliberate misstate-

89. *R.R.C.D.P.R., 1867–1939,* pp. 52–53.

90. Hansen and Brebner, *op. cit.,* chap. ix. In each of the three decades, 1871 to 1901, the increase in Canadian population was less than the estimated natural increase. While slightly more than one-and-a-half million immigrants intending to settle, entered Canada, almost two million people left the country. In the Maritime Provinces the rates of increase in population showed a significant reduction: 1851–61, 24.6 per cent; 1871–81, 13.5 per cent; 1881–91, 1.1 per cent; 1891–1901, 1.5 per cent. See also, Cartwright, *Reminiscences,* pp. 99–101.

91. *C.S.P., 1891,* No. 4, 646 ff.; W. A. Mackintosh, in *The Economic Background of Dominion-Provincial Relations* (Ottawa, 1939), p. 22, remarks: "In the early 1890's neither the value nor the volume of exports per capita was higher than it had been twenty years earlier. . . . The record was disappointing and belied the fair prophecies with which the national policies had been launched."

92. *Province of Quebec: Sessional Papers, 1891,* XXV, No. 2, 156 ff.

93. In a speech in a public meeting in Toronto, February 6, 1891, Sir John Thompson had stated that "the answer made by Mr. Blaine . . . on behalf of his Government, was an overture to reciprocity." Toronto *Globe,* February 7, 1891.

ments in that regard. After this frank declaration, Tupper informed Blaine that the Macdonald Government was strongly desirous of effecting some sort of reciprocal arrangement with the United States. Their hopes in this connection had been raised by Blaine's admitted interest in negotiating reciprocity agreements with the countries of Latin America.

When Tupper inquired if Blaine would discuss this question of reciprocity with a small delegation of Canadian statesmen including Sir John Thompson, George Foster, and Tupper himself, Blaine suggested April fifth as the best date for this proposed conference.[94] But President Harrison, who was absent from Washington on a trip through the West, wished to take an active part in these negotiations, so they were postponed until October. Foster and Thompson had arrived in Washington before they heard of this decision. They returned to Ottawa, and Tupper went back to England.[95]

In September, 1891, Blaine suggested another postponement of negotiations until February, 1892,[96] and this change was accepted by the British Government. It is apparent that Blaine was not deeply interested in reciprocity with Canada. In a letter to President Harrison, September 23, 1891, he observed:

> It is of the highest possible importance in my view that there be no treaty of reciprocity (with Canada). They will aim at natural products, to get all the products of the farm on us in exchange for Heaven knows what. They certainly will not give us manufactured articles, as that will interfere with their own and break down their tariff. This might be pushed by our friends against the natural products, but I would not put the subject to risk by saying we will take the tariff if you will throw in the manufactures, because when the Liberals come into power they will agree to that. I would cut the whole thing up by the roots. . . . The fact is we do not want any intercourse with Canada except through the medium of a tariff, and she will find that she has a hard row to hoe and will ultimately, I believe, seek admission to the Union.[97]

Like other prominent Republicans, Blaine believed that the ultimate destiny of Canada was political union with the United States.[98] Partial

94. Sir Charles Tupper to Sir John Macdonald, April 21, 25, 1891, *C.S.P., 1891,* No. 38, pp. 67–72.

95. Sir Julian Pauncefote to Lord Stanley, April 5, 6, 1891, *ibid.,* p. 84.

96. Sir Julian Pauncefote to the Governor-General of Canada, September 29, 1891, *C.S.P., 1892,* No. 37, p. 1.

97. Hamilton, *Blaine,* pp. 693–694.

98. Alice F. Tyler, in her monograph, *The Foreign Policy of James G. Blaine,* p. 20, expresses the opinion that Blaine's attitude towards England and Canada was "always suspicious, sometimes hostile, never entirely friendly." If annexation to the

reciprocity might help to relieve the economic distress that was seriously hampering Canadian development, and it would certainly postpone the movement towards annexation. As an expansionist Blaine was in favor of the absorption of Canada. Unrestricted reciprocity would serve as a means to this end, and Blaine adhered resolutely to this formula.

On February 10, 1892, the Canadian delegates met Blaine in an informal conference that was scheduled to deal with the most important questions at issue between the United States and Canada. Canada was represented by Sir John Thompson, the Minister of Justice, George E. Foster, the Minister of Finance, and MacKenzie Bowell, the Minister of Customs. England was represented by Sir Julian Pauncefote. Blaine was assisted by John W. Foster, who became Secretary of State in June, 1892, after Blaine's retirement from office.

With reference to reciprocity, the Canadian delegation asked for a renewal of the Treaty of 1854 with certain modifications. As Blaine had anticipated, they wished for reciprocity in natural products but not in manufactures. In order to place the situation in the clearest light possible, Blaine frankly stated that "American manufactures must be included in order to give the United States any benefit from the treaty." When the Canadian commissioners inquired if the American Government would insist upon preferential tariff rates with regard to the exports of manufactures, Blaine indicated that he stood for the free entry of both the natural and manufactured products of the United States into Canada, "coupled with discrimination against all other countries." There was only one satisfactory solution to the question of commercial relations between Canada and the United States—free and unrestricted reciprocity along the lines of the interstate commerce that existed within the American Union. When Blaine spoke about "equalizing the Canadian tariff with that of the United States," George E. Foster made the objection that Canadian industries would greatly suffer from competition with the more securely established American manufacturing industries. Foster then asked if Blaine could suggest any modified plan which would "tend to diminish the revenue difficulties and avoid the disturbance of Canada's present relations with the mother country." Blaine was opposed to any modified plan, and he merely repeated his formula of unrestricted reciprocity.[99]

United States was inevitable, Blaine "would assuredly not desire to take any action which would make the Canadians fully content with any condition short of that destiny." *Ibid.*, p. 351.

99. *C.S.P., 1893,* No. 52, pp. 2–8; John W. Foster, *Diplomatic Memoirs,* II, 179–181; Tyler, *op. cit.*, pp. 356–359. See also, *Senate Ex. Doc. No. 114,* 52 Cong., 1 sess.

After listening to Blaine's remarks, the Canadian commissioners stated that the only return England received from the colonies, as a recompense for services granted, was the right to enter their ports on the same trade basis as other countries. Therefore, they did not consider "it competent for the Dominion government to enter into any commercial arrangement with the United States, from the benefits of which Great Britain and its colonies should be excluded." Moreover, from the viewpoint of Dominion revenues, the question of unrestricted reciprocity or commercial union was a very serious one. Such a system would deprive the Dominion Government of at least $8,000,000 now derived from duties on American manufactures. With the advantage of a protected market in Canada, American manufactures would supplant the manufactured goods of other nations and thus cut off further revenues from duties on those imports.

Blaine did not deny the truth of these statements. There would doubtless be some dislocations of trade and other difficulties, but he would not modify his viewpoint. Unrestricted reciprocity was the only true solution for the commercial problems that had long vexed Canadian-American relations.[100] The Canadian commissioners refused to accept the proposals of Secretary Blaine, and the conversations turned to other topics.[101] A general agreement was reached with reference to the Alaskan boundary, the protection of the fisheries and the boundary line in Passamaquoddy Bay, but no compromise seemed possible with regard to reciprocity, and the conference adjourned without arriving at any settlement of the most important question before it.

Instead of pointing the way to some solution of the reciprocity difficulties, this conference at Washington aggravated differences between Canada and the United States. Members of the Conservative Party were now confident that nothing could be gained from further negotiations with the United States, and George E. Foster, who had been one of the Canadian commissioners, in his budget speech in the Dominion Parliament expressed the view that the Canadian farmer should cease looking southward to an American market that would never be opened. He should "prepare himself to find a market for his wares in other countries where they get more favourable entrance, and he can especially prepare himself to enter fully upon that almost inexhaustible market which awaits him for all his products in Great Britain, our mother land."[102]

100. *C.S.P., 1893,* No. 52, pp. 1–8. For the protocols of these conferences see *Kasson Papers, Reciprocity Treaties, 1898–1907,* MS. Dept. of State.

101. Foster, *op. cit.,* p. 180.

102. *Canada: House of Commons, Debates, 1892,* March 22, 1892, p. 334. On March

Foster's speech which frankly reported Blaine's unbending stand for unrestricted reciprocity, made a profound impression upon Edward Blake, who promptly communicated his views to Wilfrid Laurier. Laurier felt downcast because of the intransigent attitude of the Canadian commissioners towards the Blaine program,[103] but Blake thought the time had come for the Liberal Party to disavow unrestricted reciprocity, and he urged Laurier to announce this change of policy at the earliest possible moment:

I am absolutely convinced that it will be a fatal mistake for the party to let slip the present occasion. You can never expect so good a chance for re-consideration; and I think you ought to hail Blaine's declaration as a Godsend. . . . I am . . . strongly of opinion . . . that you should . . . make this the occasion for revision. In my view, the Liberal party will be repeating, and that, without a shadow of excuse, what was its former serious error, if (as you tell me is its present consensus of opinion) it first decides to adhere to Unrestricted Reciprocity, and thereafter proceeds to enquire what that decision involves. . . . By a reference to my letter to Mills you will see that I express my willingness to adopt as a good thing, though not sanguine of its success in our present political condition, the policy of Limited Reciprocity.[104]

In a second letter to Laurier, Blake returns to this theme. He strongly felt that the

Policy of the party . . . must be revised. . . . If the party policy had been or could fairly be interpreted as one for a large measure of Reciprocity, embracing agricultural and raw products, and also a liberal list of manufactured goods, then, however strongly I might have felt the risk of staking all upon the success of such a policy, and the importance of coming to some private understanding amongst the leaders as to the extent of the operation, the application of discrimination, and the method of meeting the revenue difficulty and the subject of assimilation of duties, I should still have felt that, after all that has passed, it would be impossible for you . . . to make any change.

You cannot, however, in my opinion, creditably avow this to have been always the meaning of your policy. If you think differently, I would advise you to avow the meaning. If not, I would advise you to take advantage of the

23, 1892, J. D. Edgar wrote to John W. Foster with reference to the speech of George E. Foster: "You can see the glee with which it is stated that reciprocity is dead, and the Tory cheers were deafening." *Kasson Papers.*

103. In March, 1892, Goldwin Smith paid a visit to Washington, and on March 21 he wrote to John W. Foster and remarked: "I shall tell Mr. Laurier that, though I am sure he would be cordially received, there is little practically to be done here till the Presidential election is over." *Kasson Papers, Reciprocity Treaties, 1898–1907,* MS. Dept. of State.

104. Edward Blake to Wilfrid Laurier, April 12, 1892, *Laurier MS.*, P.A.C.

recent negotiations . . . as the best opportunity you are ever likely to have to make a revision; and I would advise you to make that revision in the above sense. . . . It may be that the course of the Liberal Party, in presenting Unrestricted Reciprocity as the one thing needful, for the past five years, has brought a section of the people to such a point that they are prepared to give anything for it. It may be that it is prudent for a political party which recognizes Political Union as the inevitable destiny of Canada, to advance in that direction. . . . But my conjectures are against that view, and my feelings are in favor of an effort to secure Canadian independence in preference to an agreement for Political Union.[105]

While Laurier was pondering what course to adopt, in the United States the Democrats won the elections of 1892 with President Cleveland once more as their standard-bearer. Leaders of the Liberal Party drew new encouragement from this change of political leadership in the United States, and John Charlton paid a visit to Washington to look over the situation. He reported to Laurier that the attitude of prominent Democrats was "most satisfactory and the policy of the Liberal Party on Reciprocity will be endorsed." Unlike the Republicans, the Democrats did not emphasize the political implications of reciprocity.[106] Their program of reciprocity was a comprehensive one that would stress commerce with Canada and the Latin American countries, and they would not use these trade connections to strengthen political bonds. Representative Springer assured Mr. Charlton that the Democratic Party would pass a law that would offer to

Canada, Mexico and the Central American States reciprocity on the following lines, viz., All productions of the soil, the mine and the forest to be free. All wares produced from raw materials supplied by either country to be free. All wares produced in whole or in part from raw materials admitted into both countries free of duty, to be free. I asked him if he could not get Mr. Cleveland to embody this in his message. He said he was to see him in about two weeks, and he would try to do so. . . . I consider the position of matters

105. Edward Blake to Wilfrid Laurier, April 23, 1892, *ibid.*

106. In this regard it is interesting to note that Secretary Gresham was something of an expansionist who viewed American absorption of Canada as inevitable. Gresham wrote to Bluford Wilson in 1893 and expressed the opinion that with regard to Canada there was an "inevitable drift" towards the United States that would end in political union. Wilson was not content to wait for this "inevitable drift" to work. He believed that "in peace it should be the highest aim of American statesmanship to aid and not obstruct the natural drift of Canada towards the Union. The 'inevitable drift,' as you justly remark, is doubtless towards us, but we should help it by every honorable means known to statecraft. 'Drift' alone is fitful and uncertain. We should try to create a Gulf Stream of National Continental sentiment and to aid it by all the appliances of statesmanship to bring the derelict to a safe anchorage under the protection of the National Flag and the National Constitution." Bluford Wilson to Secretary Gresham, July 24, 1893, *Gresham MS.*

most satisfactory. We can go ahead upon the line of policy we have adopted with no uncertain or faltering step.[107]

These fair words from leading Democrats were not as potent as they would have been some years earlier. Laurier was responding to the impact of letters like those he had received from Edward Blake, and he was ready to recede from his former stand in favor of unrestricted reciprocity. In June, 1893, the Liberal National Convention met in Ottawa. The plank the convention adopted with regard to reciprocity was a cautious one:

Having regard to the prosperity of Canada and the United States as adjoining countries with many mutual interests, it is desirable that there should be the most friendly relations and broad and liberal trade intercourse between them. . . . A fair and liberal reciprocity treaty would develop the great natural resources of Canada, would enormously increase the trade and commerce between the two countries, . . . and would promote those kindly relations between the Empire and the Republic which afford the best guarantee for peace and prosperity.[108]

This statement of policy was very pleasing to Edward Blake and other Liberals who believed that the program for unrestricted reciprocity was no longer suited to a Canada that could achieve its destiny without too much dependence upon its southern neighbor. The Liberals had turned an economic corner that would lead them along new paths, and returning prosperity in 1896 would speed their footsteps.

Among Conservative leaders there was still a hope that some measure of reciprocity with the United States could be achieved. In 1893, Sir John Thompson, the new Prime Minister of Canada, instructed Sir Charles Tupper to consult Ambassador Bayard, in London, with reference to the attitude of the Democratic Party towards reciprocity. After an opening inquiry by Tupper, Bayard stated that he believed the Cleveland Administration would proceed to a revision of existing tariff laws. This drew from Tupper the admission that he was authorized to say that the Government of Canada "stood ready to meet halfway any movement on the part of the United States to create freer trade relations with Canada of a reciprocally-beneficial nature, and that any steps in that direction would be promptly and efficiently met by Canadian co-operation." Bayard thought that reciprocity should be effected by legislation rather than diplomatic negotiations, and he suggested that it would be expedient for representatives of Canadian manufacturing interests to intimate to the chairmen of the finance commit-

107. John Charlton to Wilfrid Laurier, January 18, 1893, *Laurier MS.*, P.A.C.
108. Willison, *Laurier*, II, 181–183.

tees in both Houses of Congress that the Canadian Government was ready to go halfway in any program of reducing duties on imports. In order that this matter should be handled in the most appropriate manner, Bayard finally suggested that the Canadian Government should send to Washington "a discreet person" with well-considered instructions.[109]

In reply to this despatch from Bayard, Secretary Gresham sent the following terse note: "I have to inform you that the President concurs in your suggestion that legislation is preferable to an international agreement in reference to the matter."[110]

In the 53d Congress the Democratic Party had a majority in both Houses of Congress. In view of this fact, President Cleveland had strong hopes that some measure of tariff reform could be accomplished. On December 19, 1893, a new tariff bill was reported from the Committee on Ways and Means, and with its able chairman, James L. Wilson, to pilot it through the House of Representatives, there seemed to be an excellent chance for the enactment of a law that would include some reciprocity provisions.[111] In its early stages the Wilson bill contained a reciprocity clause providing for the free entry of Canadian agricultural products in return for similar concessions to American products. In discussing this aspect of the bill, Senator Gallinger stated:

> A comparison between the Wilson bill as it comes from the House and the new Canadian tariff shows how close an understanding must have existed between the framers of the two measures. In each bill, lumber, buckwheat, rye and rye-flour, and corn are put on the free list when imported from any country which admits these articles free of duty. Canada offers to place apples, beans, peas, potatoes, hay, vegetables, and barley on her free list wherever any other countries do the same; and the Wilson bill places apples and peas on the free list absolutely. Eggs and salt are made free in both countries, and the United States offers Canada free oats, oatmeal, wheat and wheat-flour in exchange for like favors. Ores of metals are on both free lists, and so is wool. . . . The Wilson bill is a virtual attempt to obtain by co-ordinate legislation in the two countries, the revival of the provisions of the reciprocity treaty of 1854.[112]

This attempt to arrange for partial reciprocity between Canada and the United States by means of concurrent legislation was defeated by

109. Bayard to Secretary Gresham, September 19, 1893, *Great Britain, Despatches,* CLXXV, MS. Dept. of State.

110. Secretary Gresham to Bayard, November 2, 1893, *Great Britain, Instructions,* XXX, MS. Dept. of State.

111. Tarbell, *op. cit.,* pp. 200–221; F. W. Taussig, *The Tariff History of the United States,* pp. 284–299.

112. *Congressional Record,* 53 Cong., 2 sess., pp. 3900–3901.

an adverse Senate which so amended the House bill that few of its original provisions were left unaltered.[113] Certain pressure groups in the United States were insistent upon protection for the industries in which they were chiefly interested, and they did not look with favor upon any program of reciprocity with Canada. But despite this rebuff, some Canadians still hoped for a change of heart in the American Congress. Until 1897, the Dominion tariff included an offer of reciprocity in natural products, but this was merely a gesture with little meaning. In the previous year, Canada began to feel the first effects of the tide of prosperity that was to sweep over the continent and bring abundant life to areas that had long been barren. Canadian economy soon took on an international aspect in which the United States appeared increasingly less important.

But before this transformation came to Canada, the Government of Newfoundland made another attempt to prepare the basis for a reciprocity negotiation with the United States. The interference of Canada in 1890 had ruined an arrangement which seemed to promise many benefits to Newfoundland, and Robert Bond continued to cherish a hope that some economic accord could be reached with the United States. In a letter to Carl Schurz, John Fretwell, an ardent apostle of commercial union, discussed the matter of an intimate connection with Newfoundland through concurrent legislation. He had been in communication with Mr. Bond, who thought that

> a Tariff Arrangement might be made . . . without danger of being vetoed by the Imperial Government, and that such an arrangement might . . . be preferable to a Treaty or Convention. . . . During my visit last Autumn to the Maritime Provinces, Newfoundland and Labrador, I was convinced that the people look rather to the United States than to Canada for their natural Commercial connections, and if our Government would pursue a generous policy towards our weaker neighbors to the North, they would promote an irresistible movement towards coalition, first commercial, and in due course, . . . political. The Newfoundlanders would welcome annexation to the United States. . . . Do you not think that our present Secretary of State . . . would do well to use the opportunity afforded by the distress in Newfoundland, by offering to make some mutually advantageous tariff arrangement?[114]

A few days later, Mr. Fretwell wrote another letter to Schurz. He had already met Robert Bond in Boston, and they would soon visit New York and Washington. Bond was very anxious to raise a loan in the

113. Edward Stanwood, *American Tariff Controversies in the Nineteenth Century* (Boston, 1903), II, 320–359.

114. John Fretwell to Carl Schurz, May 17, 1895, *Schurz Papers,* Library of Congress.

United States and to make some reciprocity agreement with the American Government. The admission of salt fish from Newfoundland into the American market would

> be sufficient to relieve the Island from most disadvantages of the French bounties. The admission of the New England fishermen to the right of taking bait on the Newfoundland Coast would be regarded by them as an equivalent, and might pave the way to a Zollverein or Customs Union which would be most beneficial to the two Countries and serve as an example for Canada to follow. . . . If Mr. Bond succeeds in his mission, the way is open for still more liberal arrangements between the two countries; but if he fails, then his people may be forced either to relapse into their former condition as a Crown Colony, or to enter into confederation with Canada, and then the interests of the highly protected Canadian manufacturers will postpone every chance of a Customs Union for a long time.[115]

Robert Bond's visit to Washington came at a most inopportune time. Secretary Gresham was gravely ill in the latter part of May, 1895, and finally died on the twenty-eighth of that month. Richard Olney succeeded him on June 8, but he was soon occupied with the Venezuelan boundary dispute and had no time for reciprocity negotiations. Bond had to wait until after the turn of the century when he concluded a convention with Secretary Hay. The outcome of his efforts in that regard is told in another chapter.[116] Meanwhile, in Canada, far-reaching economic changes were preparing the way for a reversal of policy concerning reciprocity. Returning prosperity made Canadian leaders less anxious to arrange an intimate economic accord with the United States; the role of suppliant no longer suited a Canada that found ample European markets for the surplus products that America did not want.[117]

In 1896 the Great Depression in Canada began to lift. There were many factors responsible for this change. In the late nineties the large-

115. John Fretwell to Carl Schurz, May 22, 1895, *ibid.*

116. See *ante*, pp. 92–97.

117. In commenting upon the movement for unrestricted reciprocity with the United States, Sir Richard Cartwright observes: "Looking back and bearing in mind the assurances I received from many leading men in the United States, I have very little doubt that if there had been a Liberal Government in Canada in 1887 and, indeed, at any time up to 1892, such a treaty could have been brought about." With reference to the attitude of American statesmen concerning unrestricted reciprocity, he further remarks: "For a considerable period, say from 1887 to 1893, they were all well affected. I had interviews with many of them, among others with Mr. Carlisle, Mr. Sherman, Mr. Cleveland, Mr. Blaine, Mr. Dingley, and others, and I found them all, not excepting Mr. Dingley, more than courteous. They were at that time anxious to discuss the question, and they had, I think, in the majority of cases made up their minds that it was desirable to modify their protective system, and that a series of

scale development of the steel industry in the United States, Germany, Great Britain and France, ushered in a new industrial revolution. This led to increased urbanization with larger demands for foodstuffs, particularly cereals. The United States could not meet all these new demands, and Canada became one of the important granaries for the Old World. On the Canadian prairies the handicaps of rainfall deficiency and a short growing season were overcome by improved dry-farming techniques and the planting of superior strains of wheat. In the middle nineties the Liverpool price for wheat began a steady ascent while transportation costs gradually declined. These factors provided a "wheat boom" for Western Canada which resulted in a flood of settlers and the development of two new and flourishing provinces. Immigration from the Maritimes and Central Canada helped to break down regional differences; economic unity and a new spiritual accord went hand in hand. Canada was on the march towards a goal that was still beyond the horizon, but with Laurier as leader, Liberals had little fear of the future.[118]

Their confidence was confirmed by the fact that wheat was not the only element in this new situation that promised so much for Canada. Minerals would make more than a modest contribution to Canadian wealth. Deposits of nickel, silver, lead and copper were developed and these exports helped to bring a favorable balance of trade to Canada. But it was the discovery of gold in the Klondyke that awakened the world to the riches that lay beneath Canadian soil and led to the famous gold rush of the last years of the nineties. The whole Dominion was astir with new energy; confidence replaced the pessimism that the Great Depression had planted in Canadian hearts.[119]

In 1896, at the very beginning of this age of prosperity, general elections were held in Canada and the Liberals were successful. As the

reciprocity treaties would afford the easiest way out of it. This was more especially the view of Mr. Blaine, whom I had rather expected to find pretty much of an Anglophobist. If he had been he had outgrown it. . . . No doubt after 1894 the political situation changed entirely, but all through the period I have named, from 1887 to 1894, any really serious effort on the part of the Canadian Government to obtain reciprocity would in all likelihood have been successful." *Reminiscences,* pp. 276, 286.

118. Mackintosh, *op. cit.,* pp. 22–25; *R.R.C.D.P.R., Canada, 1867–1939,* pp. 66–80; A. S. Morton, "History of Prairie Settlement," *Canadian Frontiers of Settlement* (Toronto, 1938), II, 96–139.

119. Innis, "Settlement and the Mining Frontier," *Canadian Frontiers of Settlement,* IX, 178–389. It should be kept in mind that this significant economic advance was limited to Central and Western Canada. The Maritimes did not "share equally in the buoyant prosperity of the period. . . . During 1896–1913, the population of the three Provinces increased a mere 9 per cent compared with an increase of nearly 60 per cent in the rest of Canada." *R.R.C.D.P.R., op. cit.,* pp. 77–78.

Prime Minister, Laurier would bear the burden of responsibility at a time when economic changes would alter the emphasis that his party leaders had placed upon certain political labels. The old pressures that had compelled Dominion statesmen to seek access to American markets were no longer in existence. Canadian statesmen began to assume a more independent attitude towards the United States, and they did not hesitate to criticize the tone of Secretary Olney's note to Great Britain (July 20, 1895) with reference to the Venezuela boundary dispute.[120] They regarded as both impudent and untrue the statement that "distance and three thousand miles of intervening ocean make any permanent political union between a European and an American state unnatural and inexpedient."[121] Old antagonisms, long dormant, began to stir with new life. With their economic interests shifting more and more to Europe, Canadians felt free to indulge their criticisms of the way of life south of the border.[122]

But Laurier had no desire to foment friction between Canada and the United States. At one of the first meetings with his Cabinet he announced that a "cardinal feature" of his policy would be the establishment of close and friendly relations with his great southern neighbor. In January, 1897, both John Charlton and Edward Farrer visited Washington in order to study the situation. Charlton found that John Sherman, who was slated to be the new Secretary of State, was quite vague about the policy of the McKinley Administration which would come into office on March 4, 1897. It was clear, however, that the possibilities of negotiating a reciprocity treaty were very slim.[123]

In order to acquire an accurate understanding of the program of the Republican Party in the United States, Laurier made a trip to Cleveland early in 1897 to talk things over with the President-elect. During a conversation at the home of Myron T. Herrick, Laurier suggested the establishment of a system of commercial union which would "wipe out all the custom houses on the boundary." McKinley held out no hope that such a program could be adopted. At the most, it might be possible for Canada to secure from the United States some "material

120. On December 19, 1895, Goldwin Smith wrote to Bayard as follows: "The President's message has produced in Canada some talk, but I think no real apprehension of war. You are the man to keep the peace. However, I trust to commercial interests and connections. I am myself heartily in favour of the Monroe doctrine . . . as a Charter of the freedom of the New World and its destinies from Old World interference." *Bayard MS.*

121. For a trenchant criticism of Secretary Olney's note of July 20, 1895, see Tansill, *Bayard,* pp. 704–708.

122. Skelton, *Laurier,* II, 121–123.

123. *Ibid.,* pp. 124–125.

concessions" in the tariff that would soon be placed before Congress for consideration.[124]

But the Dingley tariff of July, 1897, raised the walls of protection higher than ever before in American history, and it contained no items that represented "material concessions" to Canada.[125] Rebuffed by the United States, Canada enacted in this same year a tariff law that clearly indicated the end of the movement towards reform that had been in evidence since 1890.[126] The new tariff law was so definitely protectionist in spirit that George E. Foster declared that in both the Liberal and Conservative parties there was "practically no difference upon the expediency of the principle of protection as the guiding principle of our fiscal system."[127]

The most significant innovation in the Canadian tariff of 1897 was the introduction of the principle of a maximum and a minimum schedule of duties. As a substitute for the usual section which invited a reciprocal trade agreement with the United States, a new reciprocal tariff clause was inserted which offered an immediate reduction in duties of one-eighth (after July 1, 1898, one-fourth) to all countries that accorded equally favorable treatment to Canadian products. This "equally favourable treatment" would be indicated by the "lowness of duties and not by the differential treatment of Canadian products."[128] The benefits of this minimum schedule were immediately extended to Great Britain. In the following year (1898) this reciprocal section was replaced by a British preferential schedule with duties one-fourth lower than the ordinary duties. In 1900 this differential was increased to one-third. Canada was moving perceptibly closer to the Mother Country.

In response to the first of these Canadian overtures, the British Government announced on July 30, 1897, that it had taken steps to denounce the commercial treaties that had been concluded with Belgium in 1862 and with the German *Zollverein* in 1865. Under the terms of those treaties the minimum schedule of the tariff of 1897 would have to be applied to imports into Canada from Belgium and the *Zollverein*.

124. Charles M. Pepper, memorandum entitled: "The Open Door to Canada," *Knox Papers,* Library of Congress. In this memorandum, drawn up in July, 1909, Laurier's visit to Major McKinley is placed in the year 1907. This is evidently a mistake.

125. Taussig, *op. cit.,* pp. 328–360.

126. S. J. McLean, *The Tariff History of Canada,* Toronto University Studies in Political Science (Toronto, 1895), IV, 34 ff.

127. Skelton, *Laurier,* II, 53. Thanks to this bulwark of protection, Canadian industries grew with remarkable speed. Between 1890 and 1910, "the net value of manufacturing production increased by nearly three times." *R.R.C.D.P.R., Canada, 1867–1939,* p. 73.

128. Mackintosh, *op. cit.,* p. 35.

After a year, Canada would be free to impose such duties as she pleased, and tariff preferences would be given only to wares from the United Kingdom and from certain of the low-tariff British colonies.[129]

In keeping with this growing spirit of Imperial unity, English capitalists began to send to Canada large sums for investment. Loans were made at the lowest interest rates in modern history. Between 1900 and 1913, nearly $1,400 million were invested in railways, canals and harbors. These were the

> main instruments of development and the necessary means for the promotion of internal trade. . . . During the fourteen years prior to the War, between $4,500 and $5,000 million was invested in capital goods. The expenditure of this vast sum was the chief basis of the rising prosperity of the time. . . . Between 1900 and 1913, well over a million immigrants came and remained in the country; these, together with the large inflow of capital, built a greater, more prosperous, and more economically interdependent Canada.[130]

It is against this background of prosperity and consequent Canadian optimism that we have to view the negotiations carried on by the Joint High Commission of 1898–1899. In order to prepare the way for these negotiations, Sir Wilfrid Laurier and Louis H. Davies, the Canadian Minister of Marine and Fisheries, made a visit to Washington in November, 1897. They were accompanied by certain Canadian advisers, and were assisted in Washington by an official of the British Embassy. During the course of his conversations with Secretary Sherman and John W. Foster, Laurier expressed the warm desire to arrange for a settlement of the more important questions at issue between Canada and the United States. This conciliatory disposition was deeply appreciated by President McKinley, who was anxious to remove all causes of friction between the two countries.[131]

These discussions were nothing more than a diplomatic reconnaissance, and in the spring of 1898 another attempt was made to reach some basis of agreement. In March, 1898, Sir Julian Pauncefote informed Secretary Sherman that Lord Salisbury was willing to consent to the appointment of a Joint High Commission that would deal with Canadian-American problems. The British Foreign Secretary was also of the opinion that "it might be desirable to hold a preliminary discussion of those questions."[132] William R. Day, the Assistant Secretary of

129. Skelton, *op. cit.*, II, 76–77. 130. *R.R.C.D.P.R.*, *op. cit.*, pp. 75–76.

131. Secretary Sherman to John Hay, November 29, December 17, 1897, *Great Britain, Instructions*, XXX, MS. Dept. of State; *F.R.*, *1897*, pp. 258–324; Foster, *op. cit.*, II, 20–50, 183–186.

132. Sir Julian Pauncefote to Secretary Sherman, March 26, 1898, *Kasson Papers, Reciprocity Treaties, 1898–1907*, MS. Dept. of State.

State, expressed agreement with the idea of preliminary conferences that would prepare the agenda for the proposed Joint High Commission, and he assured Sir Julian that it was the President's wish to consider Canadian-American problems "in the spirit tendered in the hope of reaching some more definite understanding."[133]

The preliminary conferences alluded to by Sir Julian Pauncefote and Mr. Day were held in Washington from May 25 to May 30, 1898. Great Britain was represented by Sir Julian Pauncefote and Sir Louis H. Davies; the American representatives were John W. Foster and John A. Kasson, who had been appointed by President McKinley to negotiate a series of reciprocity treaties. The delegates promptly agreed that it was expedient to refer the more important questions between Canada and the United States to a Joint High Commission for settlement. These questions were then listed, the methods of procedure were agreed upon, and the opening date for the meeting of the Joint High Commission was fixed (August 23, 1898, at Quebec). The eighth article on the agenda dealt with the question of commercial reciprocity: "Such readjustment and concessions as may be deemed mutually advantageous, of customs duties applicable in each country to the products of the soil or industry of the other, upon the basis of reciprocal equivalents."[134]

In July and August, 1898, the British and American Governments exchanged notes with reference to the instructions that would be given to the members of the Joint High Commission. The instructions given to the American Commissioners with regard to commercial reciprocity were as follows:

The Government of the United States is heartily committed to the policy of commercial reciprocity, and trusts that the labors of the Commission will result in some such arrangement with Canada on the basis indicated in this paragraph of the Protocol. The United States has found no inconvenience in seeking broad reciprocity, for the reason that it has always claimed that the most favored nation clause does not apply to reciprocal concessions granted for a specific consideration, and has inserted this principle in many of its treaties with foreign governments.[135]

Lord Salisbury's instructions to the British Commissioners, with reference to reciprocity, pointed out the fact that the geographical location of the United States and Canada made it desirable for the two countries to adopt some measure of free trade. But this was rendered difficult by the protective system that each country had been operating

133. William R. Day to John A. Kasson, March 29, 1898, *ibid.*
134. Malloy, *op. cit.*, I, 770–773.
135. *Kasson Papers, Reciprocity Treaties, 1898–1907,* MS. Dept. of State.

under for many years. Nevertheless, it might be possible to arrange for the free "interchange of a wide list of natural products, and for a mutual reduction of duties on a carefully selected list of manufactured products." But the Canadian Government should not grant to the United States tariff concessions that would not apply equally to other countries that were entitled by treaty to the most-favored-nation treatment. It was also essential that "the Dominion should maintain unimpaired its right to grant preferential treatment to the mother country and other parts of the Empire of which it is a member." In this regard it should be remembered that Canada, in recent years, by granting subsidies to a merchant marine and by the introduction of a cold storage system, had "succeeded in finding a profitable market for a large portion of her surplus natural products in Great Britain." This market was capable of "indefinite expansion, and . . . in consequence, the desirability of obtaining access to the markets of the United States has been appreciably diminished."[136]

The first meeting of the Joint High Commission was held in Quebec on August 23. The American members were Senators Charles W. Fairbanks and George Gray, John W. Foster, John A. Kasson, Nelson A. Dingley and T. Jefferson Coolidge. The British members were Lord Herschell, Sir Wilfrid Laurier, Sir Richard Cartwright, Sir Louis H. Davies, Sir James Winter, and John Charlton. Neither Sir James Winter nor Mr. Dingley was present at the first meeting of the Commission. Sir Wilfrid Laurier and the other three Canadians on the Joint High Commission had long been connected with the Liberal agitation for commercial reciprocity with the United States. The change in the economic situation in Canada caused them to shift from their fervent advocacy of previous years to a cautious policy of partial reciprocity. Since 1895, Canadian exports to the United States had fallen steadily while imports from that country had been rising in a significant manner.[137] This adverse trade balance had been compensated for by a

136. Lord Salisbury to the High Commissioners, July 19, 1898, enclosed in note from Sir Julian Pauncefote to Secretary W. R. Day, August 1, 1898, *Great Britain, Notes from,* CXXX, MS. Dept. of State.

137. The trade between Canada and the United States may be briefly summarized in the following table:

Year	Exports from Canada to U.S.	Exports from U.S. to Canada
1895	$40,748,940	$58,398,009
1896	37,355,805	62,335,303
1897	38,899,873	72,627,690
1898	30,450,208	90,454,866

See *United States Commercial Relations, 1895–1896,* I, 99–104; *ibid., 1896–1897,* I, 109–112; *ibid., 1898,* I, 100–298, 302, 311, 324.

larger volume of exports to the Mother Country, but such a maladjustment of the trade between the United States and Canada could not continue indefinitely. The instructions from Lord Salisbury had definitely indicated the advantages of the British market. Perhaps it might be better to develop the trade within the Empire and pay less and less attention to the possibility of reciprocity with the United States!

The Canadian newspapers were sounding a strong note of conservatism in their comments upon reciprocity with the United States. This was true even of Liberal papers that had formerly been enthusiastic for a more intimate economic accord between the two countries. The Toronto *Globe* frankly stated that "the Canadian market today is a better one for American produce and manufactures than the American market for Canada."[138] This was the view held by most Canadian editors. If Sir Wilfrid Laurier were able to secure a workable reciprocity treaty with the United States, such an achievement would be welcome. If he were asked to make far-reaching concessions in order to win American consent, such sacrifices were not worth while and would be unacceptable to the majority of Canadians.[139]

In the correspondence that poured into the office of Sir Wilfrid Laurier in Ottawa, and that followed him to Quebec and to Washington, there was a wealth of conflicting data that must have mystified him at times. But through all the din that beset his ears, there came a definite note of caution from the manufacturing interests. Robert Meighen, President of the Lake of the Woods Milling Company, assured Laurier that reciprocity in grain and grain products would "affect the farmer very injuriously and it would practically annihilate the milling industry of the Northwest, and not only in the Northwest, but in fact throughout the Dominion of Canada."[140] But Archibald Campbell, owner of the Queen City Mills, of Toronto, strongly disputed this view. He believed that Canadian millers could successfully compete with American millers in the world market, and it was this market that set the price of wheat. He was strongly of the opinion that

> if the American Government would take the duty off wheat and flour it would be of enormous advantage to the Canadian milling industries, and that our Government would be perfectly justified in removing our duty also. . . . There are hundreds of cars of feed going into the New England States

138. August 19, 1898.

139. See in this regard the Toronto *Globe,* August 23, 25; Toronto *Mail and Empire,* August 19, 20, 24, 26, 31; Manitoba *Free Press,* August 23, 1898; Halifax *Chronicle,* August 17, 24, 25; Halifax *Herald,* August 23, 26, 1898; Montreal *Herald,* August 22, 26, 1898; Montreal *Gazette,* August 11, 30, 1898.

140. Robert Meighen to Sir Wilfrid Laurier, December 9, 1898, *Laurier MS.,* P.A.C.

especially from the millers of Canada. If we had reciprocity we would then have an open market for mill feed and I believe a large market for flour.[141]

The Canadian manufacturing interests were concerned with tariff changes, and they sent a large number of communications to Laurier with reference to their particular industry. Owners of factories producing sewing-machines, typewriters, bicycles, furniture, shoes, cotton goods and agricultural implements, constituted a pressure group that pushed hard for continued protection. Producers of mineral ores wished to have admission to the American market, and so did farmers who raised barley and corn.[142]

In Ontario there was a strong demand for the admission of American coal, but this evoked prompt opposition from the mine operators of Nova Scotia. To Laurier, the coal question seemed "full of difficulties on all sides," and he admitted his "deep anxiety" over the matter. The same was true of pig iron which W. S. Fielding wished to have placed on the free list. This could be accomplished, but Laurier reminded Fielding that such action might have disastrous effects upon "the furnace at Hamilton in which our friend A. T. Wood is especially interested."[143]

While these letters were being exchanged between Laurier and his friends, and while the flood of communications from interested parties continued to pour into the office of the Prime Minister, a similar situation existed in Washington with regard to the activities of American manufacturers. Resolutions from Boards of Trade, Chambers of Commerce and other commercial organizations began to inundate the Department of State. The following resolution indicates the type of these communications:

Whereas, after thirty years of anxious hope for a revival of reciprocal relations with the Dominion of Canada and the Crown Colony of Newfoundland, and believing most thoroughly that reciprocal relations are decidedly for the best interest of New England and the entire United States, . . . *Resolved,* that we, . . . earnestly petition that such a treaty be negotiated as soon as possible.[144]

141. Archibald Campbell to Sir Wilfrid Laurier, October 1, 1898, *ibid.*

142. In the *Laurier Papers* in the Public Archives of Canada, there is a very large amount of this type of correspondence preserved. I was not able to secure access to the additional Laurier collection in the possession of the family of the late O. D. Skelton. For a convenient listing of letters in the *Laurier Papers* concerning reciprocity, see Joan M. V. Foster, "Reciprocity and the Joint High Commission of 1898–1899," *Rept. of the Canadian Historical Association, 1939,* pp. 91–93.

143. Sir Wilfrid Laurier to W. S. Fielding, January 10, 28, 1899, *Laurier MS.,* P.A.C.

144. Resolution of the Boston Chamber of Commerce, enclosed in letter from

American manufacturers pressed strongly upon the Secretary of State for innumerable favors. The American Nickel Works wished to have nickel ore from Canada retained on the free list; the Armour Fertilizer Works was anxious to have the Canadian tariff lowered with reference to glue and curled hair; while the National Millers' Association desired admission to Canadian markets. The New England Shoe and Leather Association requested lower duties on hides, and it emphasized the importance of "cordial, friendly and free intercourse" with Canada.[145]

The lumber interests were vehemently opposed to reciprocity with Canada, and almost a score of letters came to the Department of State in favor of the retention of the duty of two dollars per thousand feet on sawn white pine. E. M. Herrick, President of the Pacific Pine Lumber Company informed Mr. Kasson that the entire lumber interests of the United States were a "unit upon the question of the maintenance of the present duty as an absolute salvation to the preservation of the business."[146] Mr. W. H. Day had a similar viewpoint: "It would seem unfortunate if the first glimmer of prosperity for the lumber interests should be snuffed out through a losing deal, ycleped reciprocity, with our over-sharp neighbors."[147]

The close relationship between the lumber interests and those of wood pulp and paper was clearly indicated by the attitude of the International Paper Company. In January, 1899, the company informed the American members of the Joint High Commission that any serious re-

Elwyn G. Preston to President McKinley, January 25, 1898, *Kasson Papers, Reciprocity Treaties, 1898–1907,* MS. Dept. of State.

145. For typical letters from these manufacturers, see Joseph Wharton to Mr. Hobart, December 17, 1898, George C. Houghton to John A. Kasson, December 27, 1897, *Kasson Papers.* Beverly K. Moore, Secretary of the Boston Merchants Association, wrote to Secretary Lyman Gage, November 13, 1897, and remarked: "We are unalterably convinced that the magnificent resources of the entire North American Continent can, by a wise reciprocity between the United States and Canada, be made available for the unity, prosperity and the progress of the entire North American people." *Kasson Papers.*

146. E. M. Herrick to John A. Kasson, December 21, 1897, *ibid.*

147. W. H. Day to Senator William B. Allison, January 20, 1898, *ibid.* The usual American lumber dealer failed to appreciate the danger of the depletion of the American supply of white pine and the consequent Canadian advantage in the near future. Some more careful observers noted this contingency. In a letter to Sir Wilfrid Laurier, November 15, 1898, L. P. Graves remarked: "I am impressed with the fact that the good people of Canada underestimate the value and importance of their White Pine timber. White Pine will always be a dominant wood. . . . The forests of Michigan, Wisconsin and Minnesota will be practically denuded in five years time at the present rate of manufacture. Without logs from Canada the extensive mills along the Huron shore of Michigan . . . will practically go out of commission." *Laurier MS.,* P.A.C.

duction of the existing duties on wood pulp and paper would mean the removal of the industry to Canada.[148] Other paper companies were equally fearful.

American farmers were distinctly apprehensive over competition with the rich agricultural belt of Canada. G. G. Benedict, of the Burlington *Free Press* (Vermont), warned Mr. Kasson that "no arrangement with Canada which should permit agricultural products to come in free, would now be approved by the Vermonters."[149] Representative coal miners on the Pacific Coast complained to Senator Perkins that any substantial reduction of the duty on Canadian coal would be "a heavy blow to the coal-business of the Pacific Coast."[150]

Out of this confusion of counsel and expressions of selfish interest, the Joint High Commission had the onerous task of formulating a reciprocity treaty along with providing a settlement for several other thorny problems in Canadian-American relations. When the first meeting of the Commission was held in Quebec on August 23, 1898, Lord Herschell, on the motion of Senator Fairbanks, was chosen as the presiding officer. The Commission then deliberated upon the methods of procedure to be followed. The Canadian Commissioners objected to "a full daily protocol of proceedings." Furthermore, they did not "desire the names inserted of the members appointed on the sub-commissions, nor the insertion in the Protocol of their reports, nor a statement of the positions taken by the individual commissioners, nor the propositions for settlement agreed on in Committee."[151] The discussions were chiefly in the sub-committees. No records of these were preserved, and it is very difficult, therefore, to follow with accuracy the work of the Joint High Commission. There were thirteen committees appointed to deal with the more important questions before the Commission. Senator Fairbanks, Mr. Dingley, Mr. Kasson, Sir Richard Cartwright, Sir Louis Davies and Mr. Charlton were selected as the members of the reciprocity committee.[152]

It was soon apparent that there were many serious obstacles in the way of a satisfactory settlement of the more important questions that had long bedeviled Canadian-American relations. After several weeks of conferences in Quebec, the Joint High Commission adjourned (Octo-

148. Warner Mills to the Joint High Commission, January 7, 1899, *Kasson Papers.*

149. G. G. Benedict to John A. Kasson, *ibid.*

150. Representative coal miners, Seattle, Washington, to Senator George C. Perkins, January 15, 1899, *ibid.*

151. *Ibid.*

152. Mr. Dingley died on January 16, and Senator Sereno E. Payne was appointed to fill the vacancy.

ber 10),[153] and the meetings were resumed in Washington on November 9, 1898. Sir Wilfrid Laurier thought that in Washington a new spirit of "general good-will" was discernible, but he noticed that the Commission was "bounded on the east by Gloucester cod and on the west by Indiana lambs, no, sometimes on the west by Seattle lions."[154]

Secretary Hay complained that the minds of the Canadian Commissioners were "completely occupied with their own party and factional disputes," and were not able to take a long range and objective view of the situation.[155] He also paid his respects to Lord Herschell, who was "more cantankerous than any of the Canadians, raises more petty points, and is harder than any of the Canadians to get along with."[156]

In such a troubled atmosphere it was difficult to arrive at a peaceful settlement of Canadian-American problems. Early in December the Washington *Post* announced that the Canadian Commissioners had at last become convinced that it would be impossible to place lumber on the free list. They had been flatly informed of this fact by the American members of the Commission. Later, they were invited "to the Capitol, and while there met several prominent members of the House and Senate, who impressed the fact still more firmly upon them."[157]

On December 24, 1898, Senator Fairbanks wrote to Lord Herschell with reference to the question of commercial reciprocity. Although it had not been possible for the Commission to arrange for the free admission of lumber and certain staple agricultural products into the United States,[158] a considerable list of articles had

153. The Protocols of the Joint High Commission are contained in the *Kasson Papers,* but they "are empty records of the progress made," and were "useless to enlighten" the respective governments with regard to the negotiations.

154. Skelton, *op. cit., Laurier,* II, 127–129.

155. Secretary Hay to Henry White, January 3, 1899, Thayer, *Hay,* II, 204–205.

156. Secretary Hay to Henry White, December 3, 1898, *White MS.*

157. Washington *Post,* December 12, 1898.

158. In a letter to Ambassador Sir H. M. Durand, May 3, 1906, Secretary Root made the following observations concerning the work of the Joint High Commission: "As to the eighth question, tariff reciprocity. This subject was very fully discussed by the Joint High Commission. My understanding is that at the outset the American Commissioners proposed complete free trade between Canada and the United States, if Canada would adopt the same tariff as that of the United States against all outstanding countries, including Great Britain. This was declined. It is difficult to see how such an arrangement could be practically carried out except upon the condition stated. . . . The British Commissioners in turn offered to accord free trade between Canada and the United States in all natural products of the sea, the forest, the farm and the mine, and also in certain unimportant manufactured products, a small list of which they proposed to submit to be agreed upon.

"As the principal articles for which Canada sought a market in the United States consisted of natural products, while the principal articles for which the United States sought a market in Canada consisted of manufactured products, this proposal was practically to take off the American duties on what Canada had to sell, and to leave the Canadian duties upon what the United States had to sell." *Root MS.*

been agreed upon by the sub-committee charged with considering the subject of Reciprocity. The difficulties with which we have had to deal are not new to the present negotiations. For some fifty years the statesmen of the two countries, except during the treaty of 1854, have been engaged in the consideration of the subject of improving the commercial relations between them. It will be observed that the chief articles which are desired to be admitted free now, have been frequently urged for free admission hitherto. Like articles are produced in abundance in this country, and the difficulty in placing them in a reciprocal schedule has been so frequently emphasized that nothing further need be said with reference thereto. The pending negotiation has, it seems to me, established the fact that we can safely agree upon a larger measure of reciprocity than has been possible at any time except in 1854.[159]

In the second week in January, 1899, Sir Wilfrid Laurier's hopes for a successful conclusion of a reciprocity treaty with the United States began to rise. In a letter to W. S. Fielding he stated:

I have had an important conference last night with Fairbanks, and I have now more reason to expect some substantial concessions than I have had since the beginning of the negotiations. I must say, however, that up to the present time, I see no hope of the removal of the duties on lumber, but we do not intend to give up the fight. . . . In mining ores, we are . . . where we stood at the time of our last adjournment, with perhaps the possibility of some improvement. Coal is a subject of deep anxiety.[160]

At this time, Laurier was striving hard to secure for Canadian farmers access to the American market for certain products. He was strongly of the opinion that such articles as "hay, potatoes and vegetables generally," should find an increasing demand in the United States. It was possible that Canadian farmers "would do better to consume their hay on their own farms; but as to that I must leave them the judges. My intention, at the present time, is to get them, if possible, one more market, leaving them afterwards to use their own judgment as to how best to use their opportunities."[161]

On February 3, 1899, Senator Fairbanks made a report to President McKinley on the progress of the work of the Joint High Commission. With reference to commercial reciprocity, the following results had been obtained:

We have agreed substantially to put minerals, stone, marble, slate etc., upon

159. Senator C. W. Fairbanks to Lord Herschell, December 24, 1898, *Alaska Boundary Papers,* MS. Dept. of State.

160. Sir Wilfrid Laurier to W. S. Fielding, January 10, 1899, *Laurier MS.,* P.A.C.

161. Sir Wilfrid Laurier to John Mather, January 10, 1899, *ibid.*

the free list, and to make a reduction in the duty upon, or put upon the free list, articles manufactured of iron, steel etc.

We have also agreed to reduce the duty on bituminous coal from sixty cents to forty cents per ton for the first year, to twenty-five cents the second, and to put it upon the free list the third year. This proposition was once accepted. They now seem somewhat indifferent because of their Nova Scotia coal.

They demand free lumber. We have been unable thus far to agree to more than a reduction of 20 per cent (present duty is $2) upon all lumber except first class lumber, which we agree to put upon the free list. We might agree to a reduction of 25 per cent. as an ultimatum. We may be unable to do this with safety.

We have agreed to put upon the free list a large number of articles of wood, such as posts, ties, telegraph poles, etc.

They are very earnest in their desire that we should admit free hay, potatoes, lambs, eggs, and poultry. We have substantially agreed to put lambs upon the free lists, and may add poultry. Whether we can prudently do more is yet undetermined.[162]

This report by Senator Fairbanks was distinctly encouraging, and it appeared as though the labors of the Joint High Commission would be crowned with success. But suddenly the British Commissioners announced that their proposals with reference to the Alaskan boundary would have to be accepted or they would withdraw from the conferences. The effect of this ultimatum is recorded in a memorandum prepared by John A. Kasson:

Their conduct at this time impressed us as in some way influenced by the conditions of party politics in the Dominion, and not by a conviction that an adjustment was impracticable. We were the more surprised by this sudden termination of negotiations because they had previously indicated to us that the question of reciprocity in trade relations was the hinge upon which success or failure of negotiations would turn.[163]

On February 20, 1899, after the presentation of this ultimatum from the British Commissioners, the meetings of the Joint High Commission came to an abrupt close. Inasmuch as no compromise seemed possible with reference to the Alaskan boundary dispute, there was nothing to do but call for an adjournment of the meetings of the Commission. The next meeting was scheduled for August 2.[164]

In a letter to his friend, Principal Grant, Laurier gave a brief report

162. Senator C. W. Fairbanks to President McKinley, February 3, 1899, *Kasson Papers,* MS. Dept. of State.

163. *Kasson Papers, Reciprocity Treaties, 1898–1907,* MS. Dept. of State. See also, Foster, *op. cit.,* II, 188–189.

164. Protocol of the meeting of February 20, 1899, *Kasson Papers,* MS. Dept. of State.

upon the situation. The impression had gone abroad that the main struggle at Washington had been in connection with commercial reciprocity. The reverse was the truth. The Canadian Commissioners had struggled to obtain "reciprocity in lumber, because the condition of things in so far as lumber is concerned is acute and may become worse." But no progress had been made in this regard. An effort had then been made to secure a

> fair measure of reciprocity in minerals; in which we were altogether successful; in quarry products . . . we were also quite successful; and in a few agricultural products . . . we have some partial success. On the whole, with reference to the reciprocity question, I am quite satisfied with the progress which we made, . . . and we can at any moment make a very fair treaty. . . . The stumbling block was the Alaska boundary.[165]

In a letter to Secretary Hay, Senator Fairbanks confirmed the statements made by Sir Wilfrid Laurier in the above-quoted communication. During the sessions of the Joint High Commission, a "fairly liberal" reciprocal arrangement had been agreed upon. The mineral schedule had "in the main, been placed upon the free list." The duty on coal had been reduced from 60 cents to 40 cents for the first year, 25 cents the next, and free the following year. The American Commissioners had offered "free lambs and free poultry." They had also placed upon the free list a "large number of the products of wood," and had reduced the duty on lumber from "$2.00 to $1.50 per thousand feet." While they had not been able "to grant all that the British Commissioners desired," nevertheless, they had "granted much which we regard as very substantial concessions."[166]

The adjournment of the meetings of the Joint High Commission came as a shock to Secretary Hay, who sharply blamed the Canadian

165. Sir Wilfrid Laurier to Principal Grant, February 27, 1899, Skelton, *Laurier,* II, 131–132.

166. Senator C. W. Fairbanks to Secretary Hay, March 25, 1899, *Alaska Boundary Papers,* MS. Dept. of State. See also, Senator Fairbanks to Sir Wilfrid Laurier, July 18, 1901, Skelton, *op. cit.,* II, 133–134.

In the *Kasson Papers,* in the Department of State, there is the draft of a proposed reciprocity treaty with some lists of articles that might be placed on the free list of both countries. The treaty proposed that articles, the produce of either country, when imported into the other, should be "admitted at rates of duty no higher than the lowest rates imposed upon the like articles imported from any other country." No export duty should be levied in either country upon articles which should be admitted at reduced rates, and others that would be on the free list. All goods "of whatever origin," imported into either country by way of the other, should be admitted at the lowest rates of duty charged upon like imports from, or by way of, any other country.

One article suggested by Mr. Kasson was to the effect that woolen cloth made in Canada and imported into the United States for further manufacture, should be

Commissioners for their refusal to accept the American proposals.[167] T. J. Coolidge, one of the American Commissioners, was strongly opposed to any renewal of the meetings of the Joint High Commission as it was then organized. It was impossible to make any real headway in the face of the captious criticism of English lawyers like Lord Herschell and of his rumored successor Lord Russell. If the American Government remained firm, the Canadian Government would "soon suggest another commission. This might be smaller, and diplomats instead of lawyers might be chosen. I feel so strongly about it that I wish you would suggest leaving me off the present commission."[168]

In Canada, Prime Minister Laurier did not immediately abandon all thought of resuming the meetings of the Joint High Commission. In March, 1900, he spoke of the possibility of further meetings,[169] and as late as May 29, 1903, he expressed to the secretary of the Canadian Manufacturers' Association his expectation that the Joint High Commission would re-assemble in the near future.[170] But the adverse decision of the Alaskan Boundary Tribunal aroused such indignation in Canada that any thought of reviving the Commission was immediately abandoned.

It should not be thought, however, that Canadian resentment over this decision of the Tribunal was a major factor in preventing any further efforts to secure reciprocity with the United States. The Great Depression no longer hovered over Canada. European markets clamored for Canadian goods, and there was no necessity to seek for American concessions. On March 21, 1899, Laurier himself clearly voiced this change in the situation. In his defence of the action of the Cana-

admitted free into the United States. If re-imported into Canada it should be placed on the free list.

Another proposed article of importance dealt with imports of fish from Canada. These fish should be admitted free into bonded warehouses in the United States, where they could be sorted and cured. They could then be exported, without any special charge, to any "dependency of the United States on the same terms as the products of American fisheries." If any of these fish should be removed from the warehouses for sale in the United States, they would be subject to the same duty that was levied on Canadian fish ordinarily entering American ports.

In the large free list included in this draft treaty were such articles as coal; ores of all kinds in their natural condition; products of the forest, cut, rough, squared or sided but not further manufactured; corn and corn meal; butter and cheese; mining tools and machinery; marble and stone in block or squared; garden seeds; eggs; trees; and salt.

167. Secretary Hay to Henry White, February 21, 1899, *White MS.*

168. T. J. Coolidge to John A. Kasson, March 21, 1899, *Kasson Papers,* MS. Dept. of State.

169. *Canada: House of Commons, Debates, 1900,* March 19, 1900, pp. 2147–2148.

170. Joan M. V. Foster, *op. cit.,* p. 95.

dian members of the Joint High Commission in refusing the American proposals and thus forcing a stalemate on February 20, 1898, Laurier remarked: "There was a time when Canadians . . . would have given many things to obtain the American market; there was a time not long ago when the market of the great cities of the union was the only market we had for any of our products. But, thank Heaven! those days are past and over now."[171]

Canada could now afford to be more independent in her attitude towards the United States, even though her best market continued to be with her great neighbor to the south. On March 26, 1901, John L. Bittinger, the American Consul General at Montreal, sent an interesting report to Mr. Kasson. The failure of the Canadian preferential tariff seriously to affect trade movements was clearly illustrated by the very moderate increase in imports from Great Britain. The following table will indicate this fact:

Year	Imports into Canada from United Kingdom	From the U.S.
1896	$32,979,742	$ 58,574,024
1898	32,500,917	78,705,590
1899	37,060,123	93,007,166
1900	44,789,730	109,844,578

Analysis of these figures shows that the United States enjoyed more "of Canadian custom than the rest of the world put together. . . . And yet Great Britain is by far a better customer to Canada than is the United States. . . . Canada pays to the United States in business the money she gets from Great Britain. . . . If we would continue to hold and increase our trade with Canada, a Reciprocity Treaty should be negotiated without delay."[172]

In a speech in Boston before the New England Free Trade League (March 16, 1901), John Charlton repeated many of these figures given by Mr. Bittinger, and he warned Americans that they must offer Canada substantial concessions or this situation would rapidly change.[173]

171. *Canada: House of Commons, Debates, 1899,* p. 102.

172. John L. Bittinger to John A. Kasson, March 26, 1901, *Kasson Papers,* MS. Dept. of State.

173. In this speech Mr. Charlton remarked: "While Canada was an enormous purchaser of American wares and products, her farmers were practically excluded from the American market by prohibitory duties, and every branch of her export trade was hampered by a policy that reduced it to insignificant proportions. . . . In 1900 . . . the export of farm products to the United States amounted to but $7,367,000, while the purchase by Canada of American farm products for consumption amounted

But there was no possibility that the American Government would offer any important commercial concessions to Canada along the lines suggested by Mr. Charlton. On November 8, 1902, Secretary Hay concluded with Sir Robert Bond, of Newfoundland, a partial reciprocity treaty. The bitter opposition that such action evoked in New England convinced the Department of State that it would be futile to initiate negotiations with Canada with reference to an extensive reciprocity treaty.[174]

In Canada there was equal indifference to the idea of reciprocity. In 1906, Edward Porritt reported that "the reciprocity movement is dead beyond all possibility of early resurrection."[175] Although this statement was probably exaggerated,[176] it was certainly true that the boom times Canada enjoyed in the decade before the outbreak of the World War were not conducive to thoughts of reciprocity with the United States.

On May 3, 1906, Secretary Root wrote a long letter to the British Ambassador in which he recounted the important questions that were disturbing the course of Canadian-American relations. He referred to the topic of reciprocity, and commented upon the efforts of the Joint High Commission of 1898–1899 to reach an agreement in that regard. It was his opinion, after studying the protocols, that

> the negotiations made it apparent that Canada might have obtained a large part of the relief or reductions which she desired upon her natural products. The principal product in which Canada was interested was lumber, and upon

the same year to $17,862,000. . . . In 1900 Canada imported from the United States $62,000,000 of manufactures; the same year her importation from Great Britain was $37,895,000. . . . In 1900 the balance of trade in favor of Canada from Great Britain was $62,263,000, and the balance of trade against her with the United States was $48,353,000. . . . She took the enormous balance of trade in her favor with Great Britain and paid nearly every dollar of it to the United States." Toronto *Globe*, March 18, 1901.

174. The attitude of President Roosevelt towards reciprocity is indicated in his letter to Senator Lodge, October 31, 1905: "I said to Mr. Whitney and those with him that I was entirely in accord with you and Crane on the question of Canadian reciprocity; that we all three wished it, but that in my judgment the Canadians did not wish it, and that this was the only interpretation I could put upon the official acts of their government; and that, furthermore, while I personally would be delighted to favor any measure of Canadian reciprocity, no measure had yet been presented which it seemed to me there was any hope of having both our government as a whole and the Canadian government approve; that while I should do anything I could in support of the Massachusetts Senators in favor of Canadian reciprocity, yet I did not believe there was, as a matter of fact, justification for going further at that time in a movement which . . . offered no chance of success." *Selections, etc.*, II, 207–208.

175. "Canada's Tariff Mood towards the United States," *North American Review*, CLXXXII (April, 1906), 577.

176. H. S. Patton, "Reciprocity with Canada: The Canadian Viewpoint," *Quarterly Journal of Economics*, XXXV (August, 1921), 574–596.

this the American Commissioners appear to have been ready to remove a large amount of duties, and as to some classes, all the duties. This could be done, however, only in case Canada was willing to admit a substantial part of American manufactured products free or under reduced duties. This Canada does not seem to have been willing to do. I have an impression that if the Canadian attitude upon this subject has changed at all, it has been in the direction rather of protecting her manufacturing industries by tariff than of facilitating the introduction of American manufactures. If I am mistaken in this, and Canada is now ready to make substantial tariff concessions in favor of American manufactures in exchange for American concessions as to Canadian products, I shall be glad to be advised of it, and I will take up the subject where the American Commissioners left it and ascertain what concessions we are now able to make.[177]

Although Root failed to receive from Ambassador Durand any data that indicated Canadian interest in a renewal of reciprocity negotiations, he continued to study the problem in the hope that something could be done. In a letter to Charles M. Hays, of Montreal, he stated that he had been "talking with various members of the Senate and House . . . for the purpose of ascertaining what the prospects are of getting a treaty through. If it is possible I should like to do it."[178] Some weeks later he wrote to General James H. Wilson with reference to reciprocity: "Unfortunately, a policy which I must think mistaken, has carried the Canadian situation far beyond any possibility of general reciprocity. Canada has definitely entered upon a career of protection and of building up her infant industries. . . . She does not wish reciprocity with us."[179]

In the United States there were several pressure groups that exerted all their influence to keep Secretary Root and the Roosevelt Administration interested in reciprocity with Canada. Among the more important of these were the National Association of Manufacturers, the National Reciprocity League, and the New England Reciprocity League.[180] Allied with these groups in a common objective was that towering personality, James J. Hill, whose advocacy had been so sustained that Senator Borah referred to him as the "real author of reciprocity in this country of late years."[181]

In the United States the efforts of these advocates of reciprocity began to make real headway in 1909 when resentment over the high

177. Secretary Root to Sir H. M. Durand, May 3, 1906, *Root MS.*

178. Secretary Root to Charles M. Hays, February 18, 1907, *ibid.*

179. Secretary Root to General James H. Wilson, April 3, 1907, *ibid.*

180. L. Ethan Ellis, *Reciprocity, 1911* (New Haven, 1939), p. 9.

181. J. G. Pyle, *The Life of James J. Hill* (Garden City, New York, 1917), II, 287–288.

rates in the Payne-Aldrich tariff rapidly assumed ominous proportions. To President Taft it seemed possible to quiet this alarming situation by negotiating a reciprocity treaty with Canada. This action would meet, in part, the demands of the advocates for tariff reform. It would ease pressure from the newspaper editors who were deeply interested in reduced duties on Canadian newsprint, and it might increase the volume of Canadian-American trade. In Canada, Prime Minister Laurier discovered that the farmers of Western Canada were belligerent in their demands for some arrangement that would give them access to the American market. He also realized that the Liberal Party lacked a real issue that would set it clearly aside from political opponents and would give it the vitality needed to assure continuance in power. Perhaps reciprocity with the United States would provide the issue so badly needed![182]

The initiative in the negotiations came from the United States, with Canada a little coy because of the anticipated opposition from the manufacturing interests. On February 23, 1910, Ambassador Bryce sent a telegram to Lord Grey, in Canada, informing him of President Taft's "urgent desire to begin at the earliest possible moment negotiations with Canada."[183] The Dominion Government responded favorably to this overture, and Professor Henry C. Emery, Charles M. Pepper, and John G. Foster were sent to Ottawa in March, 1910, to discuss the situation. When certain difficulties developed, President Taft made a trip to Albany, New York, where on March 19 he met W. S. Fielding, the Canadian Minister of Finance. As a result of his conversations with the American Chief Executive, Fielding returned to Ottawa to talk matters over with Laurier. On March 25 he appeared in Washington for further conversations with American officials.[184]

After these preliminary conversations had terminated, Secretary Knox indicated to Ambassador Bryce his desire to commence negotiations for a reciprocity treaty with Canada.[185] It was Bryce's belief that this overture was dictated by the President's desire to have "some substantial progress made before the Congressional elections, which come early in November."[186]

But these efforts to expedite negotiations were doomed to failure. Lord Grey informed Ambassador Bryce that the Canadian Minister

182. Ellis, *op. cit.*, pp. 10–17.

183. Ambassador Bryce to Lord Grey, February 23, 1910, *Laurier MS.*, P.A.C.

184. The story of these negotiations is given in full in the pamphlet entitled *Canadian Tariff Negotiations*, in the *Knox Papers*, Library of Congress.

185. Secretary Knox to Ambassador Bryce, May 12, 1910, *Governor-General's Correspondence, Grey, 1910*, p. 353, P.A.C.

186. Ambassador Bryce to Lord Grey, May 12, 1910, *ibid.*, p. 352.

had not expected any early action on the part of Secretary Knox, and Mr. Fielding, who had charge of the negotiations, was ready to leave on a trip to England.[187] Fielding returned to Canada in the latter part of September, and the negotiations were resumed. In November, 1910, Secretary Knox sent Henry M. Hoyt, Counselor of the Department of State, and Charles M. Pepper, of the Bureau of Trade Relations of the same Department, to Ottawa for a series of conferences with W. S. Fielding. They soon discovered that the manufacturing interests, the large banks, and the United Empire Loyalist Society were a unit in their opposition to reciprocity. In some Canadian circles there was a good deal of talk about reciprocity being merely a prelude to annexation to the United States. Such a contingency, however remote, was regarded with open apprehension by many Canadians who took pride in the bonds that bound Canada to the Empire.[188]

On November 10, Hoyt and Pepper decided to return to Washington to report on the progress of the negotiations. They had been definitely disappointed in the attitude of the Canadian officials with regard to American proposals. In January, 1911, W. S. Fielding and William Paterson, the Canadian Minister of Customs, visited Washington and on January 21 an agreement was finally reached.

These negotiations and the text of the agreement have been treated in sufficient detail in another volume in this series,[189] so it is not necessary to give more than an outline of the situation. President Taft submitted the agreement to Congress on January 26, along with a message that indicated the many advantages that the United States would derive from the establishment of reciprocity with Canada. In conclusion he significantly remarked that the Canadians had come to the parting of the ways: "They must soon decide whether they are to regard themselves as isolated permanently from our markets by a perpetual wall or whether we are to be commercial friends."[190]

187. Lord Grey to Ambassador Bryce, May 16, 1910, *ibid.*, p. 354. In a letter to Secretary Knox, June 4, 1910, Mr. Fielding remarked that he would try to find an opportunity to make it clear to all concerned that the Canadian Government would adhere "to the position taken by me at Washington and that the negotiations are only postponed." *Canadian Tariff Negotiations, Knox MS.*

188. *Canadian Tariff Negotiations, Knox MS.*

189. Ellis, *op. cit.* In summarizing the terms of the agreement, Professor Ellis remarks: "Many agricultural products were allowed to enter the United States duty free; in return American agricultural implements entered Canada at reduced rates, and identical rates were levied upon the exchange of a list of manufactures numerically imposing but economically unimportant." "Canada's Rejection of Reciprocity in 1911," *Rept. of Canadian Historical Association, 1939,* p. 100.

190. *Congressional Record,* 61 Cong., 3 sess., pp. 1515–1519. It should be kept in mind that Taft was thinking primarily of American interests in this whole reciprocity question, and he foresaw the shift of business from Canada to the United States. In a

The agreement was approved by the House of Representatives on February 14,[191] but the Senate failed to act before the end of the session of Congress. The President then called a special session of Congress, and the bill which incorporated the agreement finally passed both Houses of Congress and was signed by the President on July 26, 1911.[192]

During the debate in the House of Representatives, Champ Clark made a speech that rang through all Canada. He openly declared that he favored reciprocity because he hoped to see the day "when the American flag will float over every square foot of the British North American possessions clear to the North Pole."[193] Needless to say, this utterance deeply stirred all Canadians who prized the Imperial connection, and it helped to mobilize Canadian sentiment against the reciprocity agreement.

It was the opinion of W. S. Fielding that the reciprocity agreement with the United States was so advantageous to Canada that American voters might oppose it on that very ground, but many Canadians sharply dissented from this view. The Liberal Party was soon in the midst of one of the most bitter fights in Dominion history, and Sir Wilfrid Laurier realized that he had opened a Pandora's box of political hatreds that threatened to destroy him. On March 18, he remarked to George W. Mitchell that the Liberals would have to fight a "powerful combination of capitalists whose policy is to take up and apply in Canada the American policy of exclusion which the American people are now forced to reject." He had, however, "no reason to fear the result."[194] Two days later he expressed the view that the Liberals would have "a big fight" with reference to reciprocity, but he had no doubt of ultimate success.[195]

In the Canadian Parliament Laurier faced a rising tide of opposition. During twenty-five legislative days of attack, the Opposition laid

letter to Theodore Roosevelt, January 10, 1911, he remarked: "The amount of Canadian products we would take would produce a current of business between western Canada and the United States that would make Canada only an adjunct of the United States. It would transfer all their important business to Chicago and New York, with their bank credits and everything else, and it would increase greatly the demand of Canada for our manufactures. I see this is an argument made against reciprocity in Canada, and I think it is a good one." Henry F. Pringle, *The Life and Times of William Howard Taft* (New York, 1939), II, 588.

191. *Congressional Record,* 61 Cong., 3 sess., p. 2564.

192. *Senate Doc. No. 80,* 62 Cong., 1 sess., Pt. 3, pp. 4663–4665.

193. *Congressional Record,* 61 Cong., 3 sess., February 14, 1911, p. 2520.

194. Sir Wilfrid Laurier to George W. Mitchell, March 18, 1911, *Laurier MS.,* P.A.C.

195. Sir Wilfrid Laurier to Theophilus Moor, March 20, 1911, *ibid.*

down a barrage of arguments that caused increasing concern to Liberal leaders. The manufacturing interests were devoted to protection and viewed with hostility the agreement of January, 1911. Their attitude was confirmed by the large banks that had intimate fiscal relations with them. The transcontinental railroads were fearful of the effects of reciprocity upon the volume of freight from the West, and some representatives of agriculture were alarmed at the threat of competition from American farmers.[196] The Montreal *Star* played upon the fears of Canadian farmers by printing pictures of deserted farms in New England as an indication of what Canadians could expect if reciprocity were approved.[197]

Liberals were embarrassed by the desertion of such a stalwart member as Clifford Sifton, who spared no effort to defeat reciprocity. As one of the organizers of the Canadian National League, Sifton helped to inspire literature that appealed to British immigrants to defeat reciprocity and thus preserve the old Imperial ties.[198] Other pamphlets indicated different aspects of the evils of reciprocity, and attempted to portray the destruction that would be visited upon the agricultural and manufacturing interests by any closer economic accord with the United States.[199]

It was evident as early as mid-April, 1911, that the Liberals were distinctly on the defensive, and they strove desperately to prove to the Canadian public that reciprocity was economically good and politically safe. This was difficult to do in the face of the good times that had been so evident in Canada during the first decade of the twentieth century. This period of prosperity had evoked a spirit of Canadian nationalism that took pride in Canada's independent course and which resented any admission that Canadian welfare would be increased by close association with the United States. The "conviction that the nation could work out its own destiny, imperialist sentiment, resentment at the United States and the pressure of special interests combined to turn down Reciprocity when it was at last offered."[200]

196. L. Ethan Ellis, "Canada's Rejection of Reciprocity in 1911," *Rept. of the Canadian Historical Association, 1939,* pp. 102–108; G. E. Foster, "The Reciprocity Agreement from a Canadian Standpoint," *North American Review,* CXCIII (1911), 663–671; O. D. Skelton, "Canada's Rejection of Reciprocity," *Journal of Political Economy,* XIX (1911), 726–731; F. W. Taussig, "Reciprocity with Canada," *ibid.,* pp. 542–549; W. G. Swartz, "The Proposed Canadian-American Reciprocity Agreement of 1911," *Journal of Economic and Business History,* III (1930), 118–147.

197. Montreal *Star,* March 14, 22, 25, 1911.

198. Dafoe, *Sifton,* p. 371.

199. Arthur Hawkes, Manitoba *Free Press,* September 21, 1929.

200. *R.R.C.D.P.R., op. cit.,* p. 80.

On July 29 Laurier dissolved Parliament and took the issue of reciprocity to the country. In the general elections of September 21, 1911, the Conservatives won by a popular vote of 669,000 to 625,000. In the new House of Commons they controlled 133 seats; the Liberals were a bad second with only 85 seats. It was significant that the province of Ontario, with its large industrial establishments, gave the Conservatives a large majority.[201]

Contrary to some old suppositions in the United States, the English Conservative Party was not so deeply concerned over the fate of reciprocity that it took measures to encompass its defeat. The correct picture in this regard is given by Whitelaw Reid in a letter to Secretary Knox:

> The opposition to reciprocity . . . has recently become noisy, but it is chiefly noisy in a few and rather uninfluential quarters. "The Morning Post" has always been hard to satisfy on any question where Newfoundland or Canada was concerned. It and the "Standard," which has also been somewhat hostile to us of late, are both vehement "Tariff Reformers," and the most devoted supporters Mr. Chamberlain has had. But the Liberals, who are carrying everything before them, are nearly free traders, and "Tariff Reform" seems at present a lost cause.[202]

W. S. Fielding thought that President Taft had contributed to the defeat of reciprocity by some utterances that were unfortunately ambiguous. The expression, "We have come to the parting of the ways," had been distorted in Canada to "mean that we had come to the point when we must choose between annexation and British institutions." Fielding also believed that the Conservatives had made good use of an enormous campaign fund: "Our opponents undoubtedly had the greatest campaign fund ever held by a political party in Canada. . . . Most of the manufacturers and powerful financial interests identified with them took the view that the reciprocity agreement was only the beginning of a tariff movement, and that if this was allowed to succeed, further assaults would be made on the wall of protection."[203]

It is evident that there were many reasons for the defeat of reciprocity in Canada in 1911. Not the least of these was the resentment caused by the adverse attitude of the United States towards repeated Canadian overtures in the period from 1865 to 1895. The decision of the Alaskan Boundary Tribunal deepened this feeling of hostility which

201. Skelton, *Laurier,* II, 365–383; H. S. Patton, *op. cit.*
202. Whitelaw Reid to Secretary Knox, May 11, 1911, *Knox MS.*
203. W. S. Fielding to Secretary Knox, September 29, 1911, *ibid.*

found vehement expression in the elections of 1911. But this storm of anti-Americanism blew itself out in the excesses of that year, and prepared the way for a new climate of opinion that was increasingly friendly. Joint efforts in the first World War on behalf of a new design for living that incorporated many of the ideals that lay closest to Canadian hearts, gave indisputable evidence that Americans shared Canadian dreams of a new world order, and were willing to die to preserve a common heritage. Speaking a common language, devoted to the same traditions, knit by ties of blood and economic circumstance into a close relationship, and separated by a boundary line whose lack of frowning forts indicates a common trust, it was inevitable that Canadian-American discord would disappear when the two nations were challenged by forces that threatened their way of life. The formula of hemispheric solidarity may be invoked by some glib statesmen to explain the links that bind together the nations of the New World. It would take a more subtle definition to describe the essence of the Canadian-American connection. This is a thing of the spirit, and few living historians can move with assurance in that field.

APPENDIX

MANUSCRIPT MATERIALS

The more important manuscript materials consulted in the preparation of this monograph are located in the Public Archives of Canada, and in the National Archives and the Library of Congress in Washington, D.C.

In the Public Archives of Canada (Ottawa) the following series in the John A. Macdonald Papers are of primary importance:

Governor-General's Correspondence, 1880–1891.
Macdonald Letter Books, 1880–1891.
Washington Treaty, 1888.
Commercial Union, 1886–1887.
Commercial Relations with the United States, 1890–1891.
Sir Charles Tupper Correspondence, 1885–1891.
Alaska Boundary, 1886–1888.
Behring Sea Correspondence, 1888–1891.
Behring Sea, Correspondence of Charles H. Tupper, 1890.
S. J. Ritchie Correspondence, 1884–1891.

The Laurier Papers in the Public Archives of Canada are of great value to all students of Canadian-American relations. It is to be hoped that they will soon be carefully catalogued and arranged in some satisfactory sequence. In this collection the following series were used: Miscellaneous Correspondence; Governor-General's Correspondence, 1900–1911.

In the National Archives in Washington the following series of State Department papers were examined:

Great Britain: Instructions; Despatches; Notes to; Notes from; 1880–1906.
Miscellaneous Letters, 1885–1906.
Domestic Letters, 1885–1906.
Bering Sea Arbitration: John W. Foster Correspondence.
Alaska Boundary Papers.
Special Agents, 1893–1897.
John A. Kasson Papers.
Montreal: Consular Despatches, 1885–1906.
Halifax: Consular Despatches, 1885–1906.
Correspondence Relating to the Joint High Commission, 1898–1899.

The Library of Congress has many collections of official and private papers that are of particular importance to students interested in the later period of Canadian-American relations. The papers of the following representative Americans are of special significance:

Thomas F. Bayard	Theodore Roosevelt
Joseph H. Choate	Elihu Root
Grover Cleveland	Carl Schurz
John W. Foster	John Sherman
Walter Q. Gresham	George W. Smalley
Philander C. Knox	John C. Spooner
William McKinley	David A. Wells
Richard Olney	Henry White

The extensive bibliographies given in Samuel F. Bemis and Grace G. Griffin, *Guide to the Diplomatic History of the United States* (Washington, 1935), and in R. A. MacKay and E. B. Rogers, *Canada Looks Abroad* (New York, 1938), have made it unnecessary to append a lengthy list of references to secondary materials. The footnotes in the present monograph will fill in any gaps in the above-mentioned guides.

INDEX

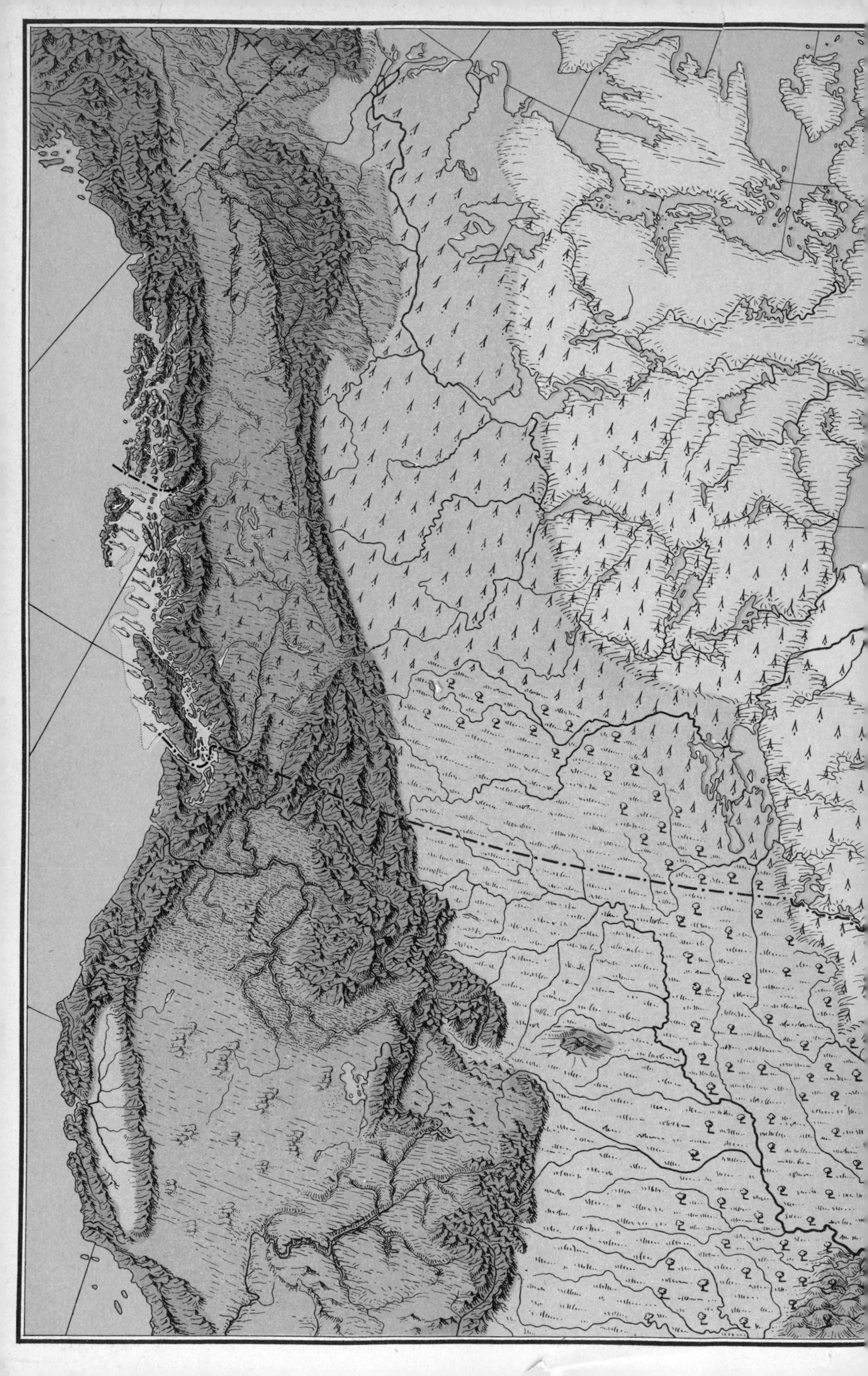